BLADE OF HEAVEN

VOLUME 10

STORY BY
YONG-SU HWANG

ART BY
KYUNG-IL YANG

HAMBURG // LONDON // LOS ANGELES // TOKYO

Blade Of Heaven Vol. 10
written by Yong-Su Hwang
illustrated by Kyung-Il Yang

Translation - Sora Han
English Adaptation - Troy Lewter
Retouch and Lettering - Star Print Brokers
Production Artist - Michael Paolilli
Graphic Designer - Al-Insan Lashley

Editor - Bryce P. Coleman
Digital Imaging Manager - Chris Buford
Pre-Production Supervisor - Erika Terriquez
Art Director - Anne Marie Horne
Production Manager - Elisabeth Brizzi
Managing Editor - Vy Nguyen
VP of Production - Ron Klamert
Editor-in-Chief - Rob Tokar
Publisher - Mike Kiley
President and C.O.O. - John Parker
C.E.O. and Chief Creative Officer - Stuart Levy

A **TOKYOPOP** Manga

TOKYOPOP and are trademarks or registered trademarks of TOKYOPOP Inc.

TOKYOPOP Inc.
5900 Wilshire Blvd. Suite 2000
Los Angeles, CA 90036

E-mail: info@TOKYOPOP.com
Come visit us online at www.TOKYOPOP.com

© 2004 YONG-SU HWANG & KYUNG-IL YANG, DAIWON C.I. Inc. All Rights Reserved. First published in Korea in 2004 by DAIWON C.I. Inc. English translation rights in North America, UK, NZ, and Australia arranged by DAIWON C.I. Inc.

English text copyright © 2007 TOKYOPOP Inc.

All rights reserved. No portion of this book may be reproduced or transmitted in any form or by any means without written permission from the copyright holders. This manga is a work of fiction. Any resemblance to actual events or locales or persons, living or dead, is entirely coincidental.

ISBN: 978-1-59532-336-1

First TOKYOPOP printing: August 2007

10 9 8 7 6 5 4 3 2 1

Printed in the USA

PREVIOUSLY IN

BLADE of HEAVEN

UPON RETURNING WITH THE HEART OF THE HUMAN FACE FIRE DRAGON, SACHUNSA WAS STUNNED TO LEARN THAT HIS DEATH-DEFYING EFFORTS MAY HAVE BEEN FOR NAUGHT. THE DRAGON S HEART WAS TO BE THE CURE FOR A GRAVELY ILL YOUNG GIRL, BUT THE THIEF KING FORBADE IT AND HIS WORD IS LAW. THIS TRIGGERED A ONE-AGAINST-ALL BATTLE WHEN SACHUNSA VOWED TO FIGHT THIS INJUSTICE! SOON, SACHUNSA LEAVES THE SNAIL PROVINCE AND FINDS HIMSELF ENTERED INTO THE FABLED HERO COMPETION. AS THE COMPETITION BEGINS, SACHUNSA DRAWS EVER CLOSER TO DISCOVERING THE SECRET OF HIS TRUE SELF, AND TO BEING REUNITED WITH THE MYSTICAL BLADE...

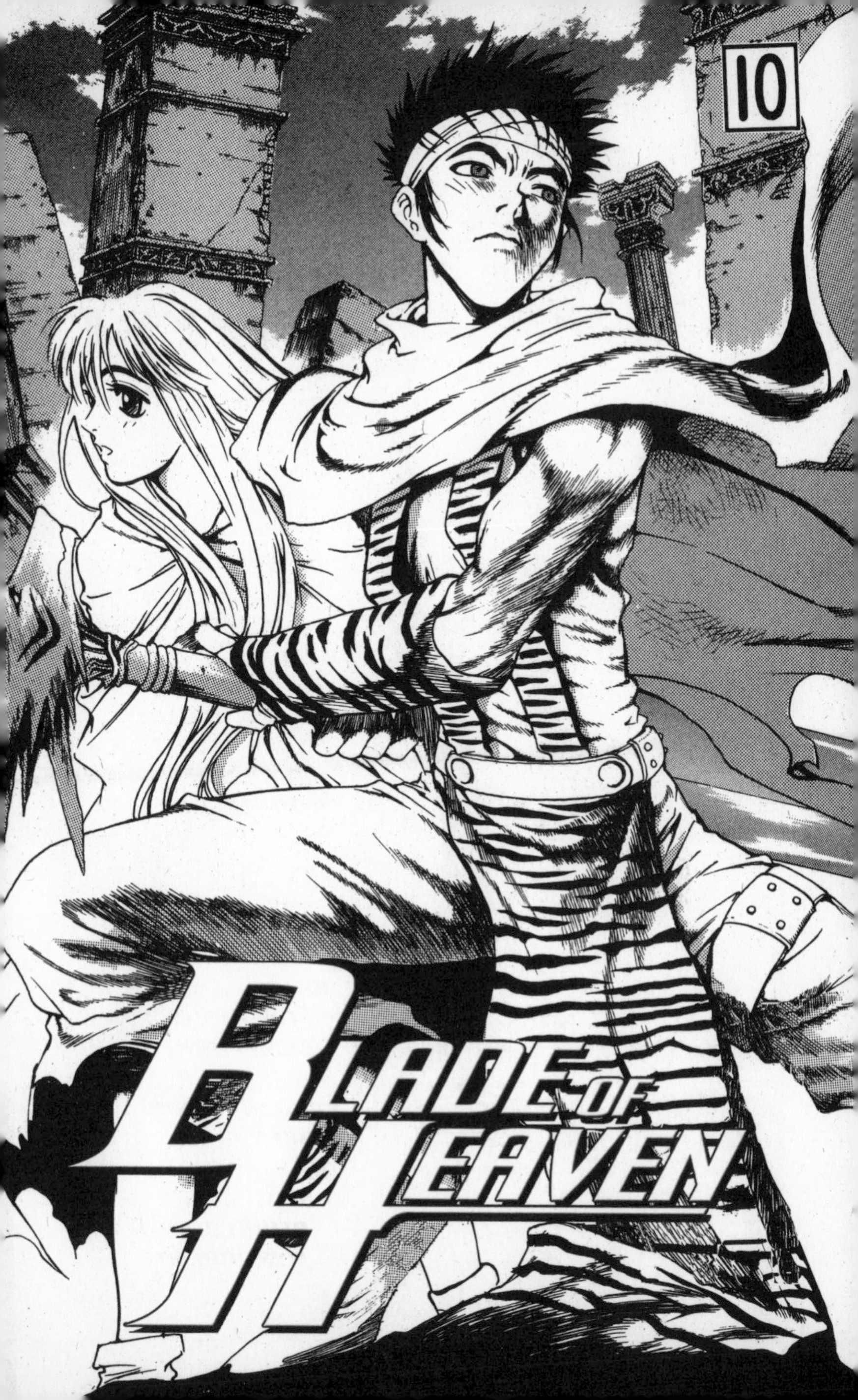
10
BLADE OF HEAVEN

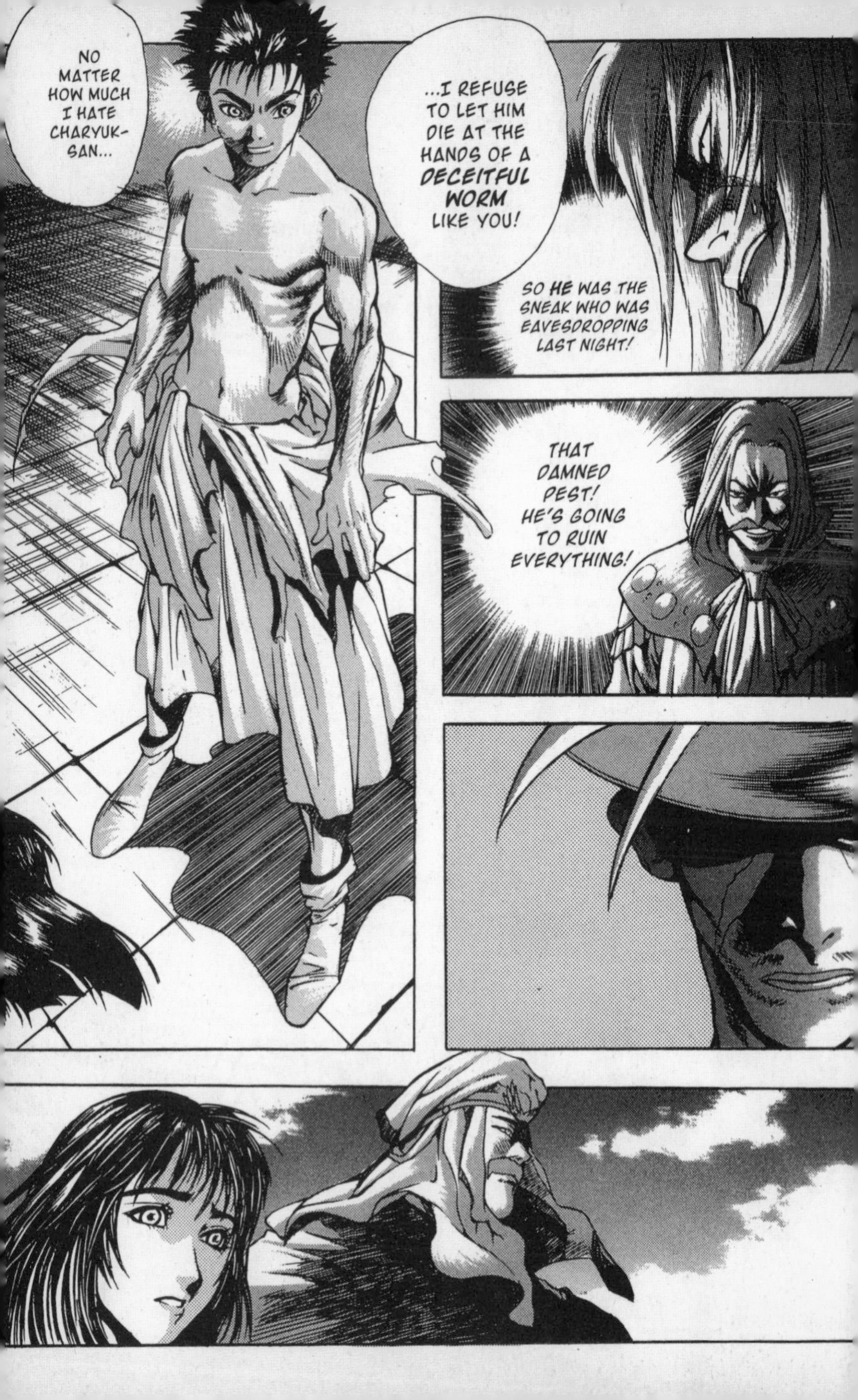

...I REFUSE TO LET HIM DIE AT THE HANDS OF A DECEITFUL WORM LIKE YOU!
NO MATTER HOW MUCH I HATE CHARYUK-SAN...
SO HE WAS THE SNEAK WHO WAS EAVESDROPPING LAST NIGHT!
THAT DAMNED PEST! HE'S GOING TO RUIN EVERYTHING!

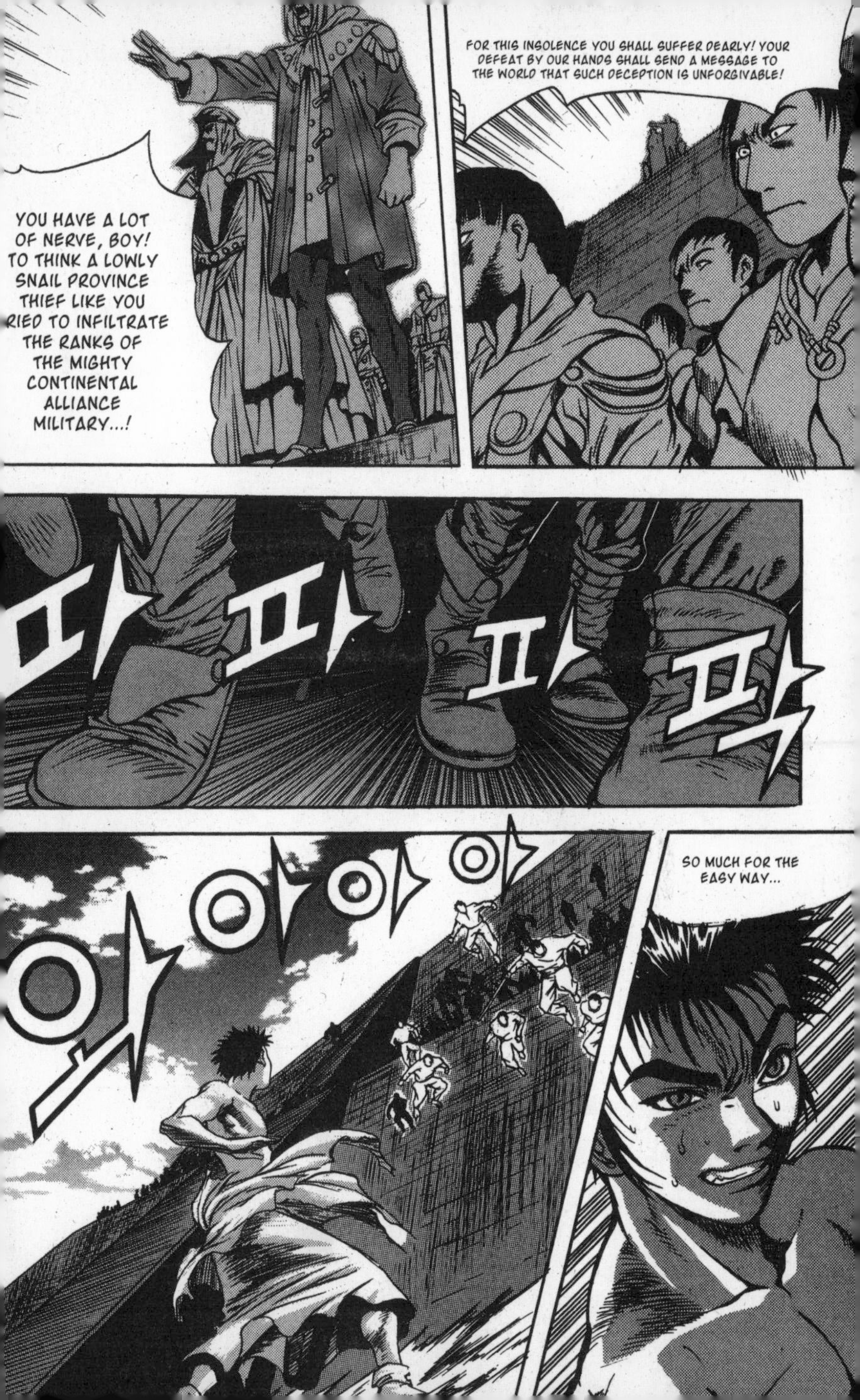
YOU HAVE A LOT OF NERVE, BOY! TO THINK A LOWLY SNAIL PROVINCE THIEF LIKE YOU RIED TO INFILTRATE THE RANKS OF THE MIGHTY CONTINENTAL ALLIANCE MILITARY...!
FOR THIS INSOLENCE YOU SHALL SUFFER DEARLY! YOUR DEFEAT BY OUR HANDS SHALL SEND A MESSAGE TO THE WORLD THAT SUCH DECEPTION IS UNFORGIVABLE!
SO MUCH FOR THE EASY WAY...

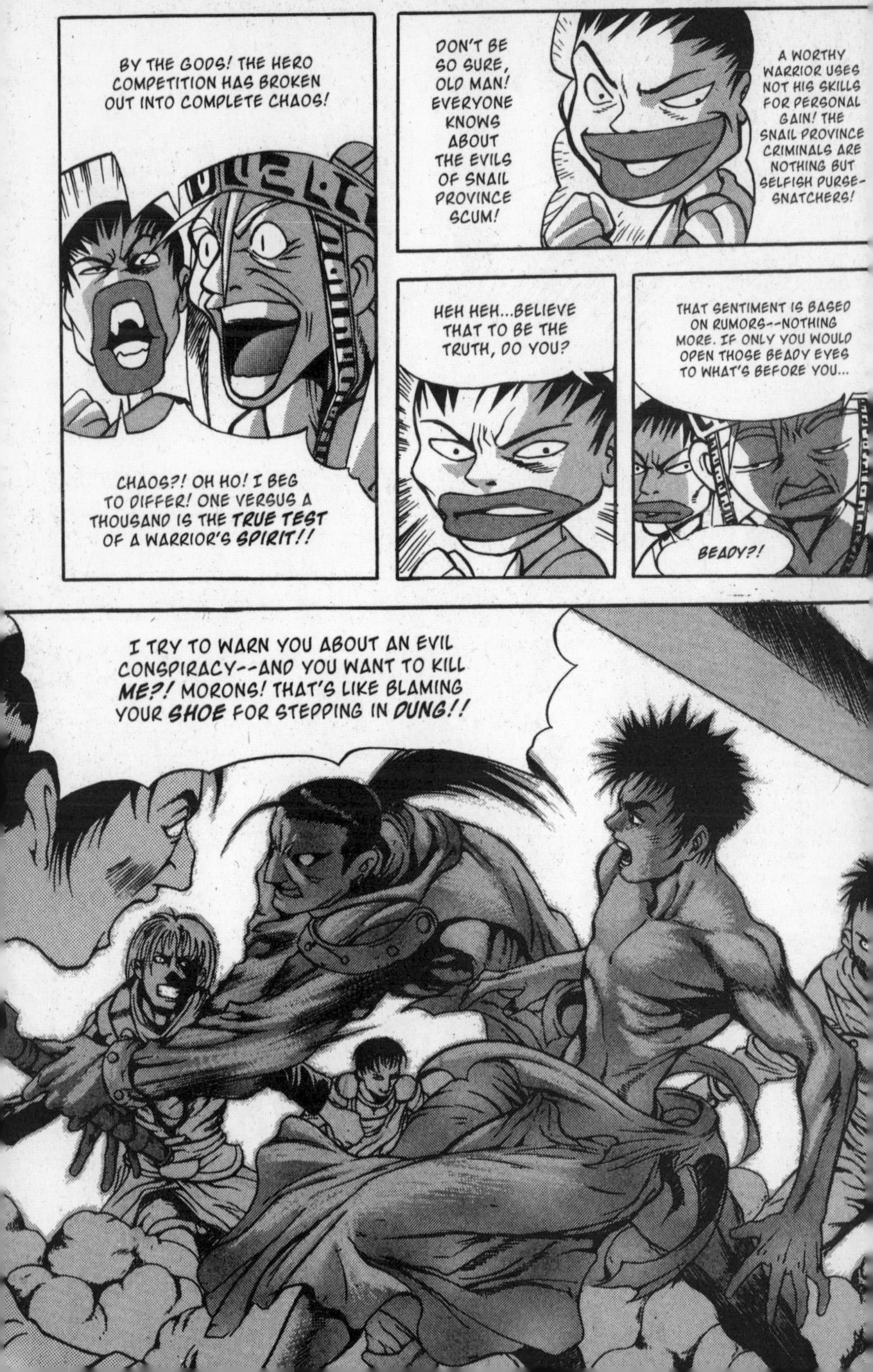
BY THE GODS! THE HERO COMPETITION HAS BROKEN OUT INTO COMPLETE CHAOS!
CHAOS?! OH HO! I BEG TO DIFFER! ONE VERSUS A THOUSAND IS THE TRUE TEST OF A WARRIOR'S SPIRIT!!
DON'T BE SO SURE, OLD MAN! EVERYONE KNOWS ABOUT THE EVILS OF SNAIL PROVINCE SCUM!
A WORTHY WARRIOR USES NOT HIS SKILLS FOR PERSONAL GAIN! THE SNAIL PROVINCE CRIMINALS ARE NOTHING BUT SELFISH PURSE-SNATCHERS!
HEH HEH...BELIEVE THAT TO BE THE TRUTH, DO YOU?
THAT SENTIMENT IS BASED ON RUMORS--NOTHING MORE. IF ONLY YOU WOULD OPEN THOSE BEADY EYES TO WHAT'S BEFORE YOU...
BEADY?!
I TRY TO WARN YOU ABOUT AN EVIL CONSPIRACY--AND YOU WANT TO KILL ME?! MORONS! THAT'S LIKE BLAMING YOUR SHOE FOR STEPPING IN DUNG!!

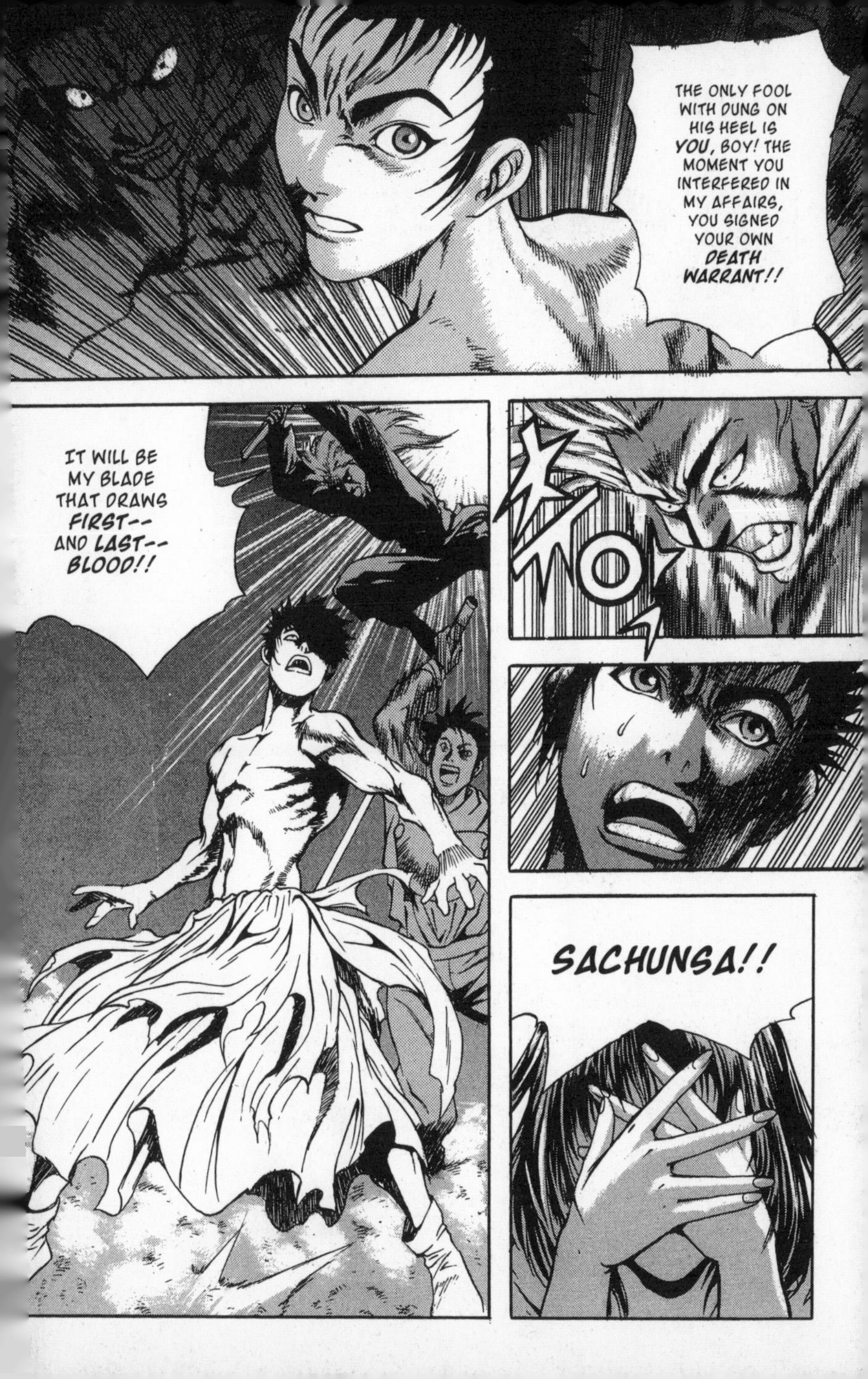
THE ONLY FOOL WITH DUNG ON HIS HEEL IS YOU, BOY! THE MOMENT YOU INTERFERED IN MY AFFAIRS, YOU SIGNED YOUR OWN DEATH WARRANT!!
IT WILL BE MY BLADE THAT DRAWS FIRST-- AND LAST-- BLOOD!!
WO
SACHUNSA!!

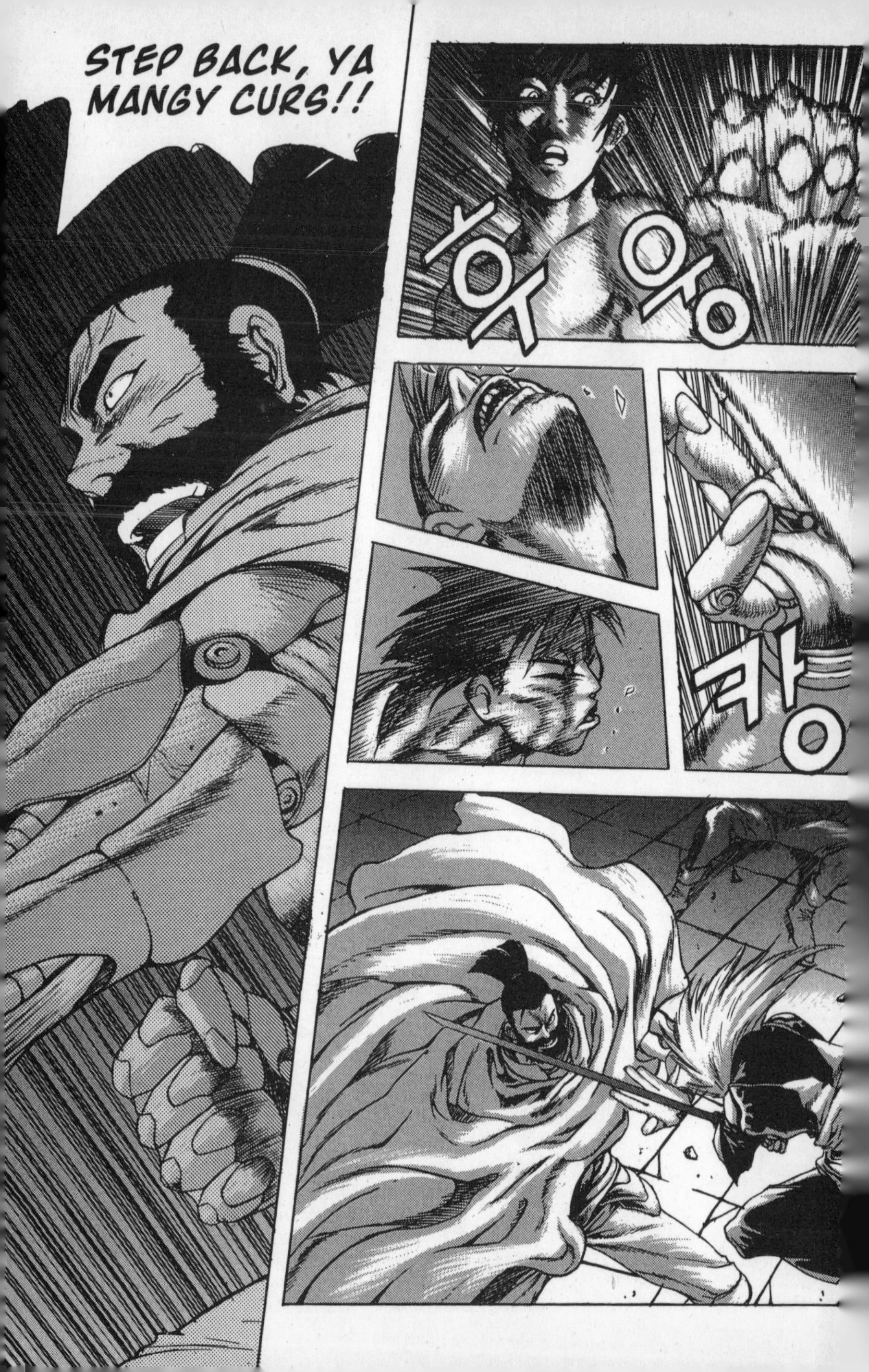
STEP BACK, YA MANGY CURS!!

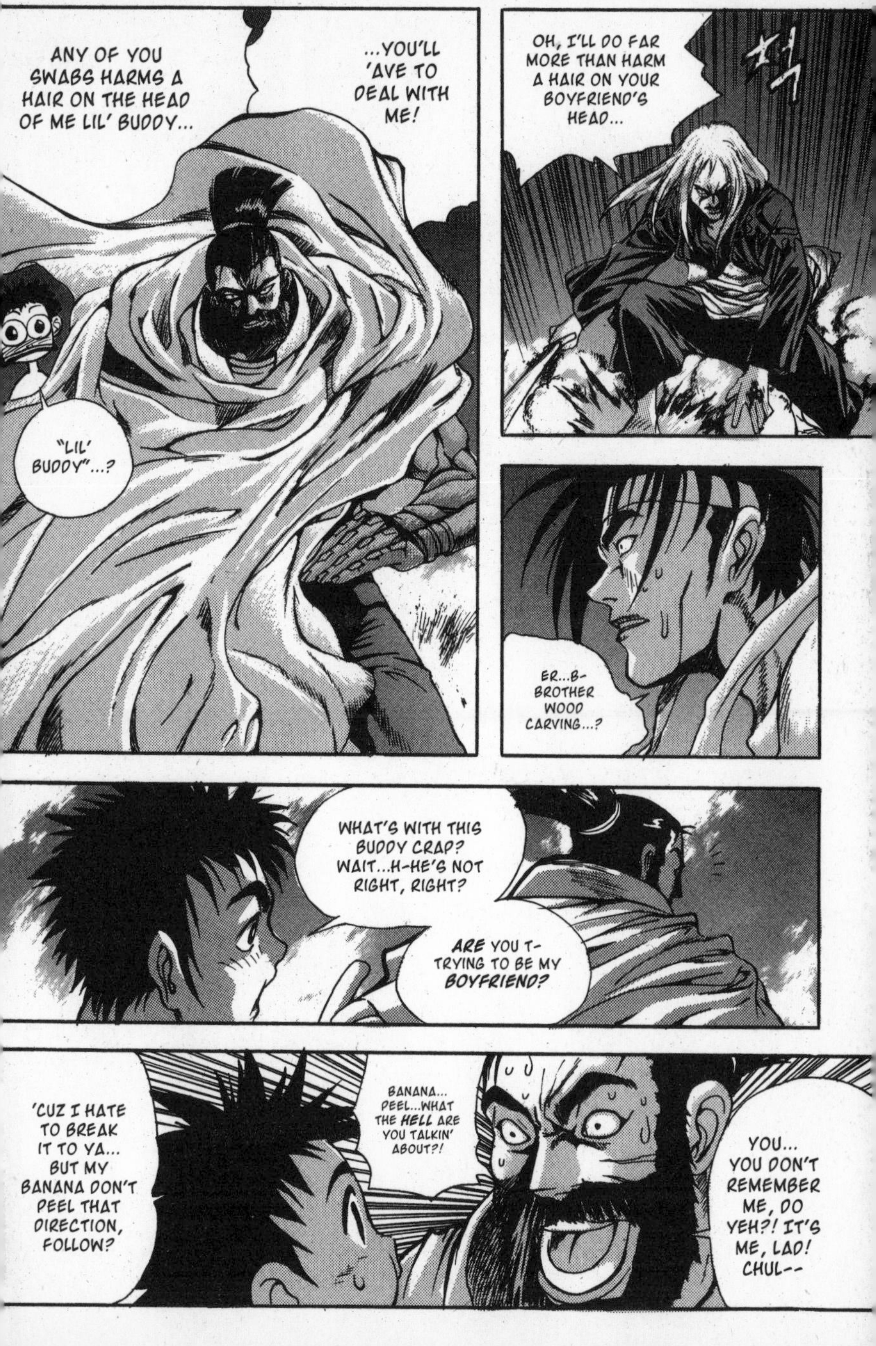
ANY OF YOU SWABS HARMS A HAIR ON THE HEAD OF ME LIL' BUDDY...
...YOU'LL 'AVE TO DEAL WITH ME!
"LIL' BUDDY"...?
OH, I'LL DO FAR MORE THAN HARM A HAIR ON YOUR BOYFRIEND'S HEAD...
ER...B-BROTHER WOOD CARVING...?
WHAT'S WITH THIS BUDDY CRAP? WAIT...H-HE'S NOT RIGHT, RIGHT?
ARE YOU T-TRYING TO BE MY BOYFRIEND?
'CUZ I HATE TO BREAK IT TO YA... BUT MY BANANA DON'T PEEL THAT DIRECTION, FOLLOW?
BANANA... PEEL...WHAT THE HELL ARE YOU TALKIN' ABOUT?!
YOU... YOU DON'T REMEMBER ME, DO YEH?! IT'S ME, LAD! CHUL--

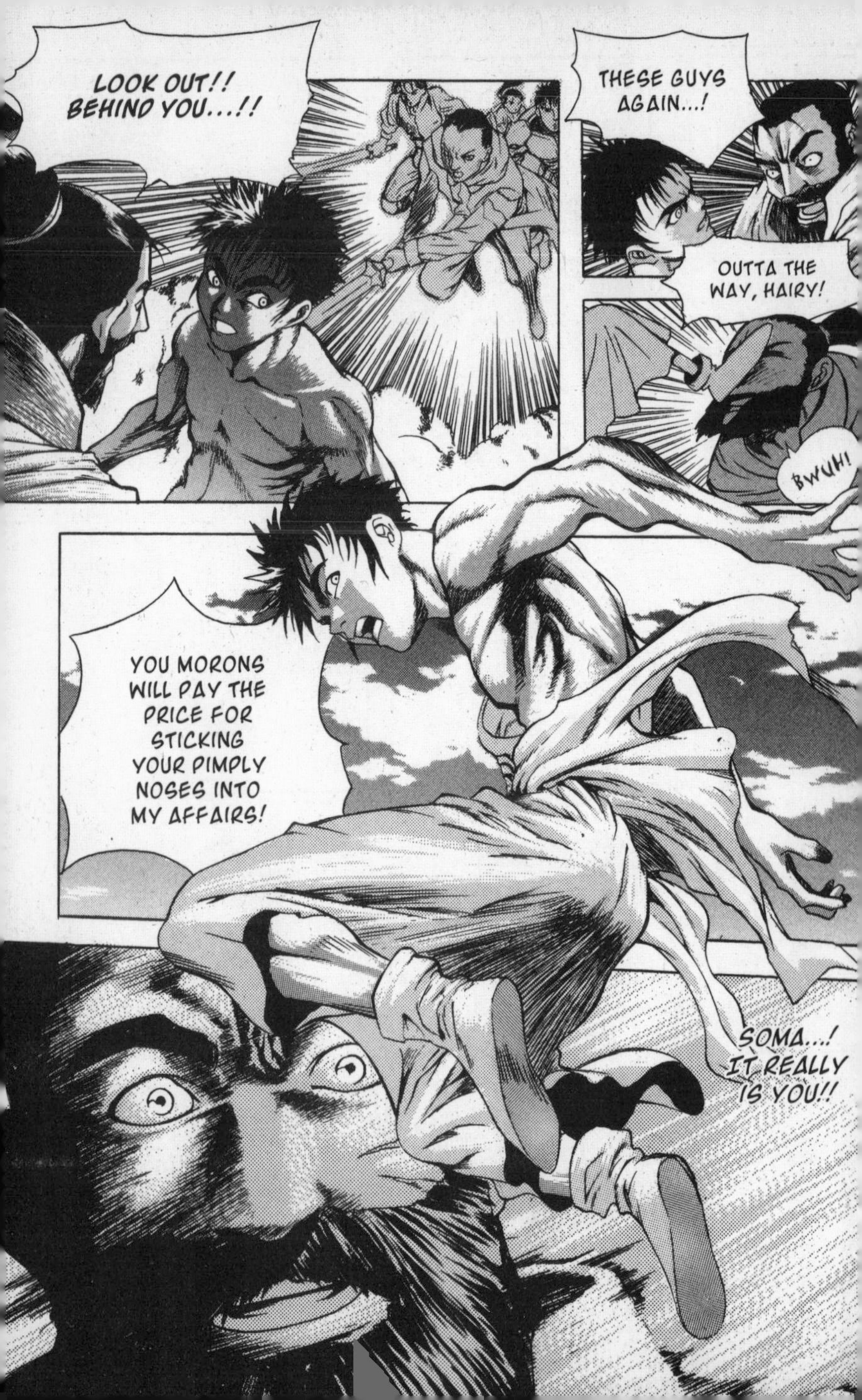
LOOK OUT!! BEHIND YOU...!!
THESE GUYS AGAIN...!
OUTTA THE WAY, HAIRY!
BWUH!
YOU MORONS WILL PAY THE PRICE FOR STICKING YOUR PIMPLY NOSES INTO MY AFFAIRS!
SOMA...! IT REALLY IS YOU!!

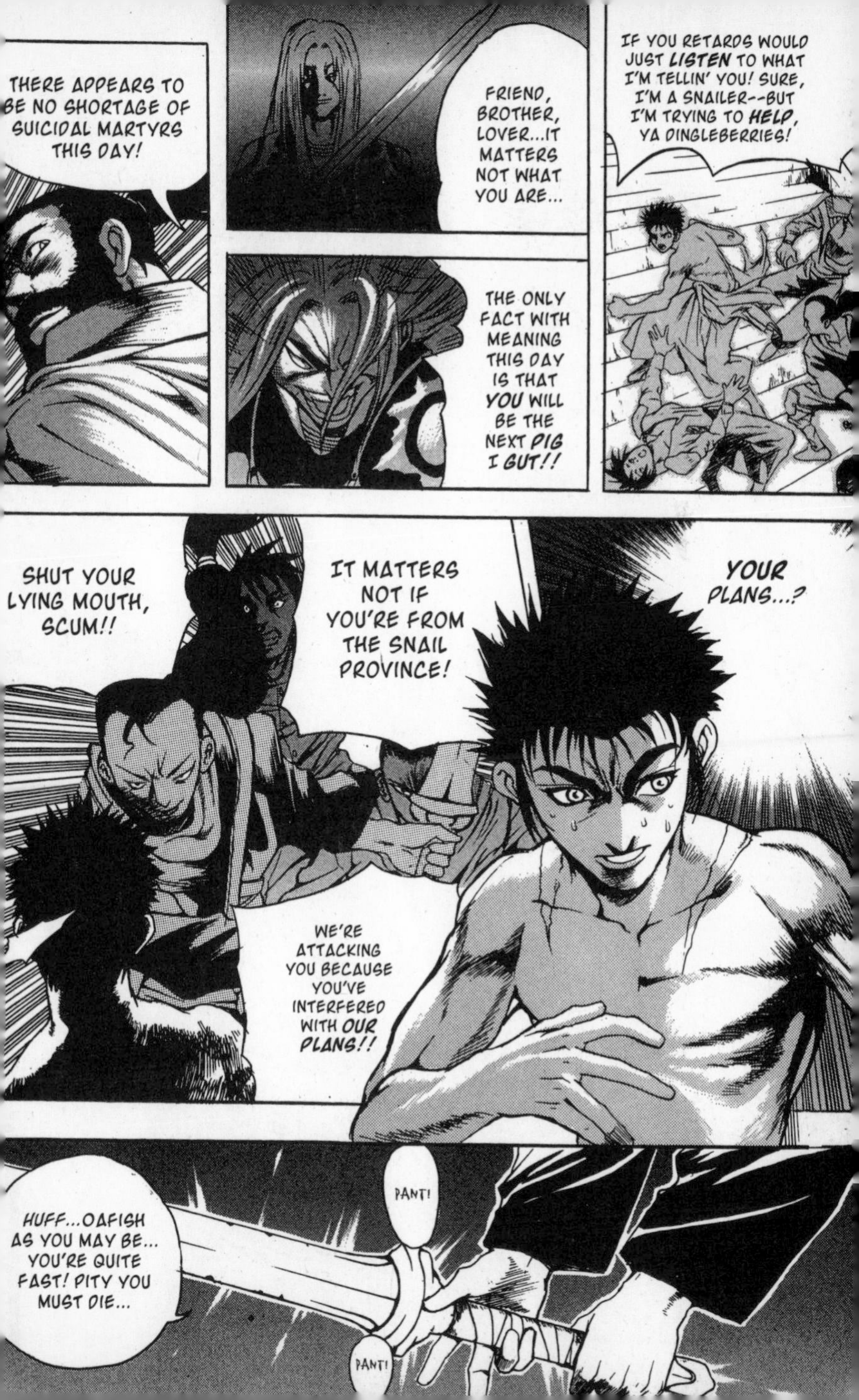

THERE APPEARS TO BE NO SHORTAGE OF SUICIDAL MARTYRS THIS DAY!
FRIEND, BROTHER, LOVER...IT MATTERS NOT WHAT YOU ARE...
THE ONLY FACT WITH MEANING THIS DAY IS THAT YOU WILL BE THE NEXT PIG I GUT!!
IF YOU RETARDS WOULD JUST LISTEN TO WHAT I'M TELLIN' YOU! SURE, I'M A SNAILER--BUT I'M TRYING TO HELP, YA DINGLEBERRIES!
SHUT YOUR LYING MOUTH, SCUM!!
IT MATTERS NOT IF YOU'RE FROM THE SNAIL PROVINCE!
WE'RE ATTACKING YOU BECAUSE YOU'VE INTERFERED WITH OUR PLANS!!
YOUR PLANS...?
HUFF...OAFISH AS YOU MAY BE... YOU'RE QUITE FAST! PITY YOU MUST DIE...
PANT!
PANT!

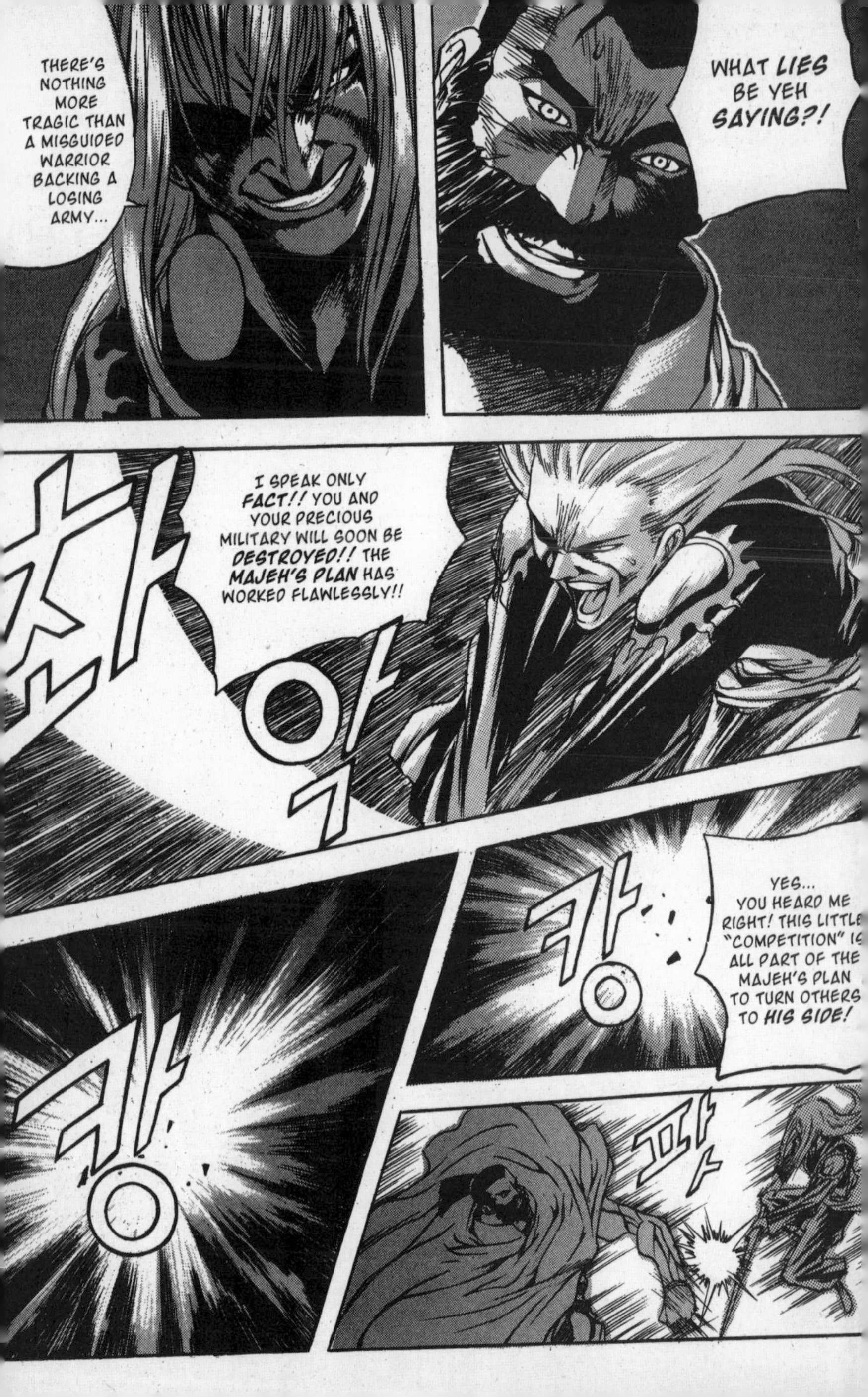

THERE'S NOTHING MORE TRAGIC THAN A MISGUIDED WARRIOR BACKING A LOSING ARMY...
WHAT LIES BE YEH SAYING?!
I SPEAK ONLY FACT!! YOU AND YOUR PRECIOUS MILITARY WILL SOON BE DESTROYED!! THE MAJEH'S PLAN HAS WORKED FLAWLESSLY!!
YES... YOU HEARD ME RIGHT! THIS LITTLE "COMPETITION" IS ALL PART OF THE MAJEH'S PLAN TO TURN OTHERS TO HIS SIDE!

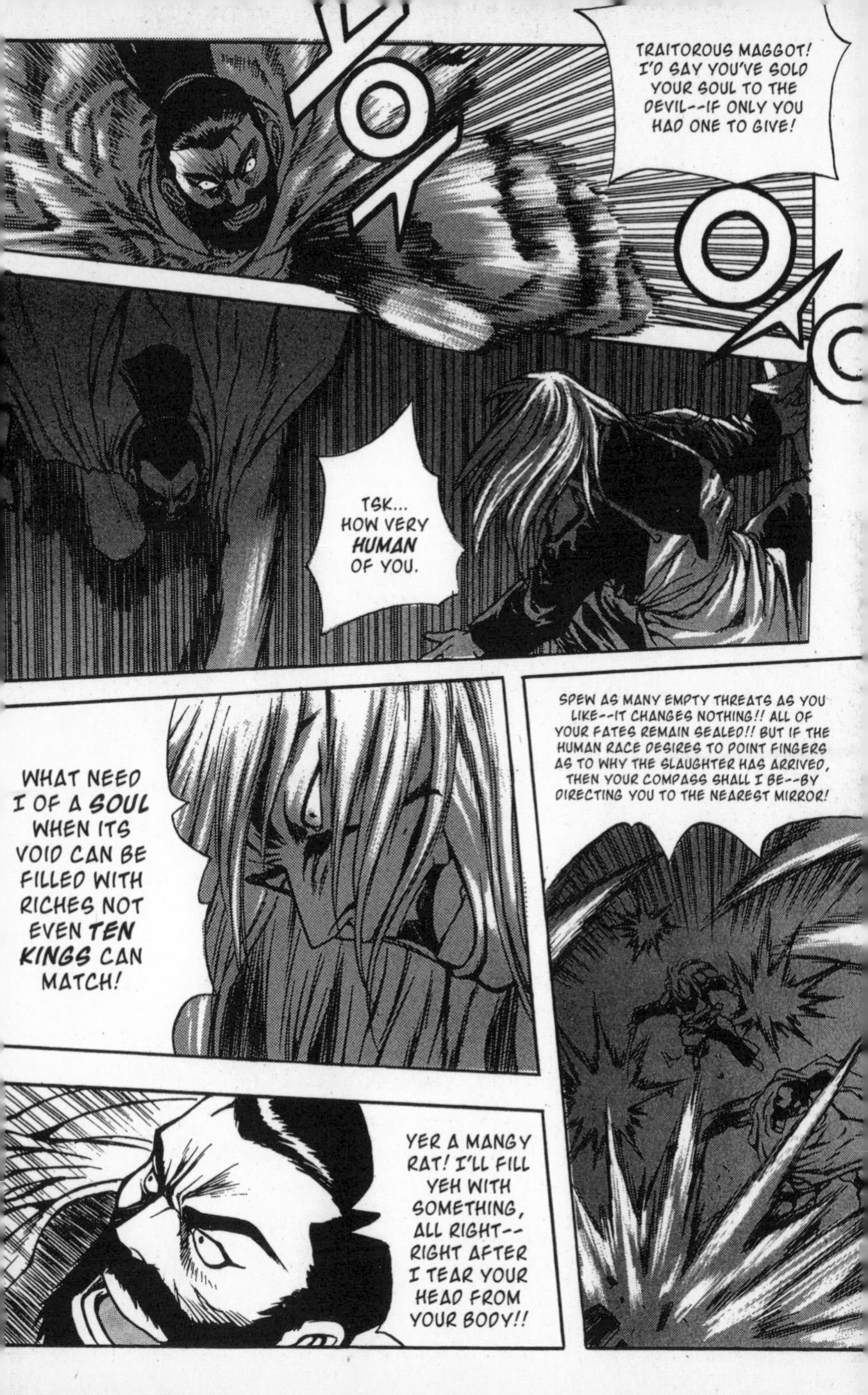
TRAITOROUS MAGGOT! I'D SAY YOU'VE SOLD YOUR SOUL TO THE DEVIL--IF ONLY YOU HAD ONE TO GIVE!
TSK... HOW VERY HUMAN OF YOU.
WHAT NEED I OF A SOUL WHEN ITS VOID CAN BE FILLED WITH RICHES NOT EVEN TEN KINGS CAN MATCH!
YER A MANGY RAT! I'LL FILL YEH WITH SOMETHING, ALL RIGHT--RIGHT AFTER I TEAR YOUR HEAD FROM YOUR BODY!!
SPEW AS MANY EMPTY THREATS AS YOU LIKE--IT CHANGES NOTHING!! ALL OF YOUR FATES REMAIN SEALED!! BUT IF THE HUMAN RACE DESIRES TO POINT FINGERS AS TO WHY THE SLAUGHTER HAS ARRIVED, THEN YOUR COMPASS SHALL I BE--BY DIRECTING YOU TO THE NEAREST MIRROR!

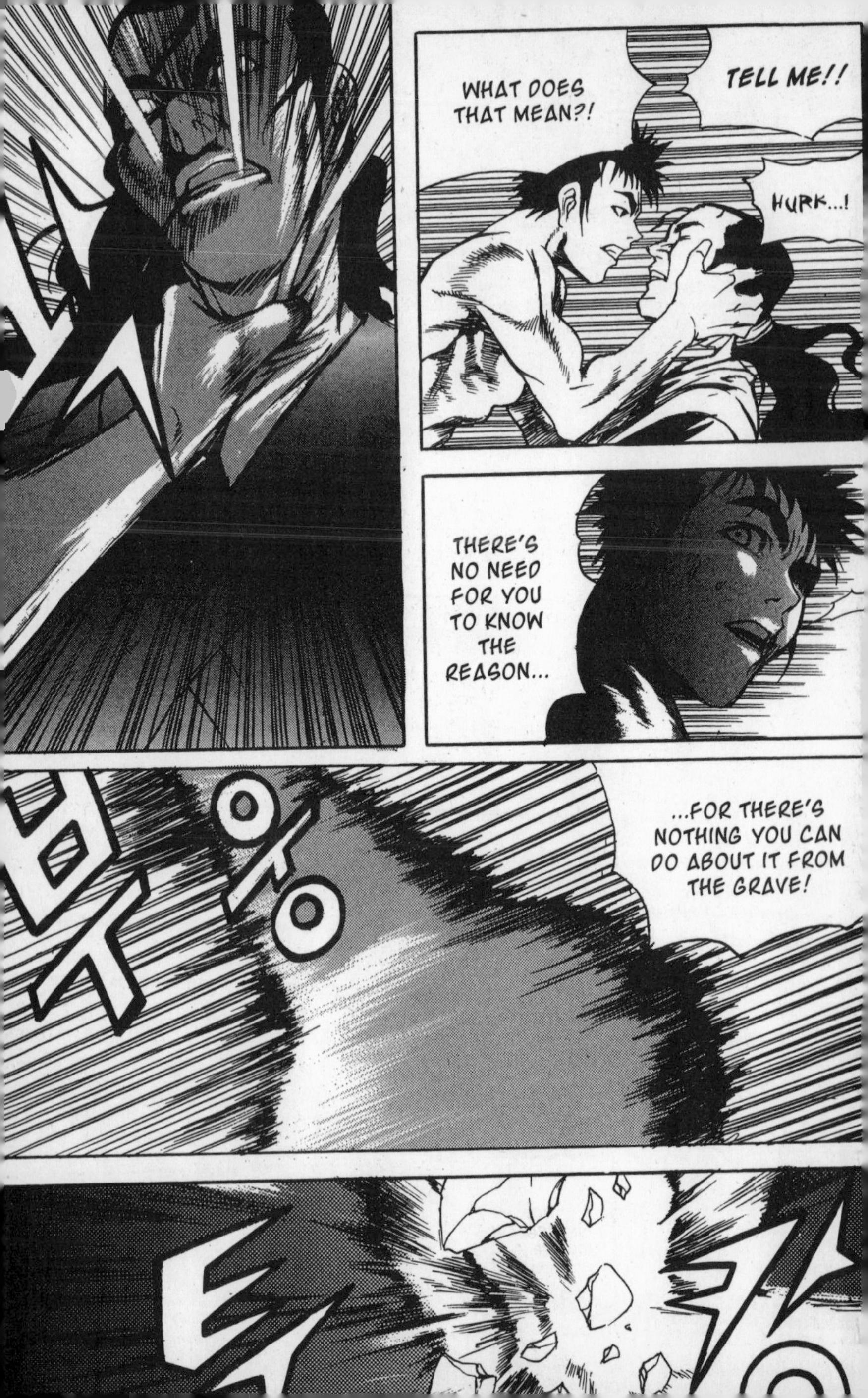
TELL ME!!
WHAT DOES THAT MEAN?!
HURK...!
THERE'S NO NEED FOR YOU TO KNOW THE REASON...
...FOR THERE'S NOTHING YOU CAN DO ABOUT IT FROM THE GRAVE!

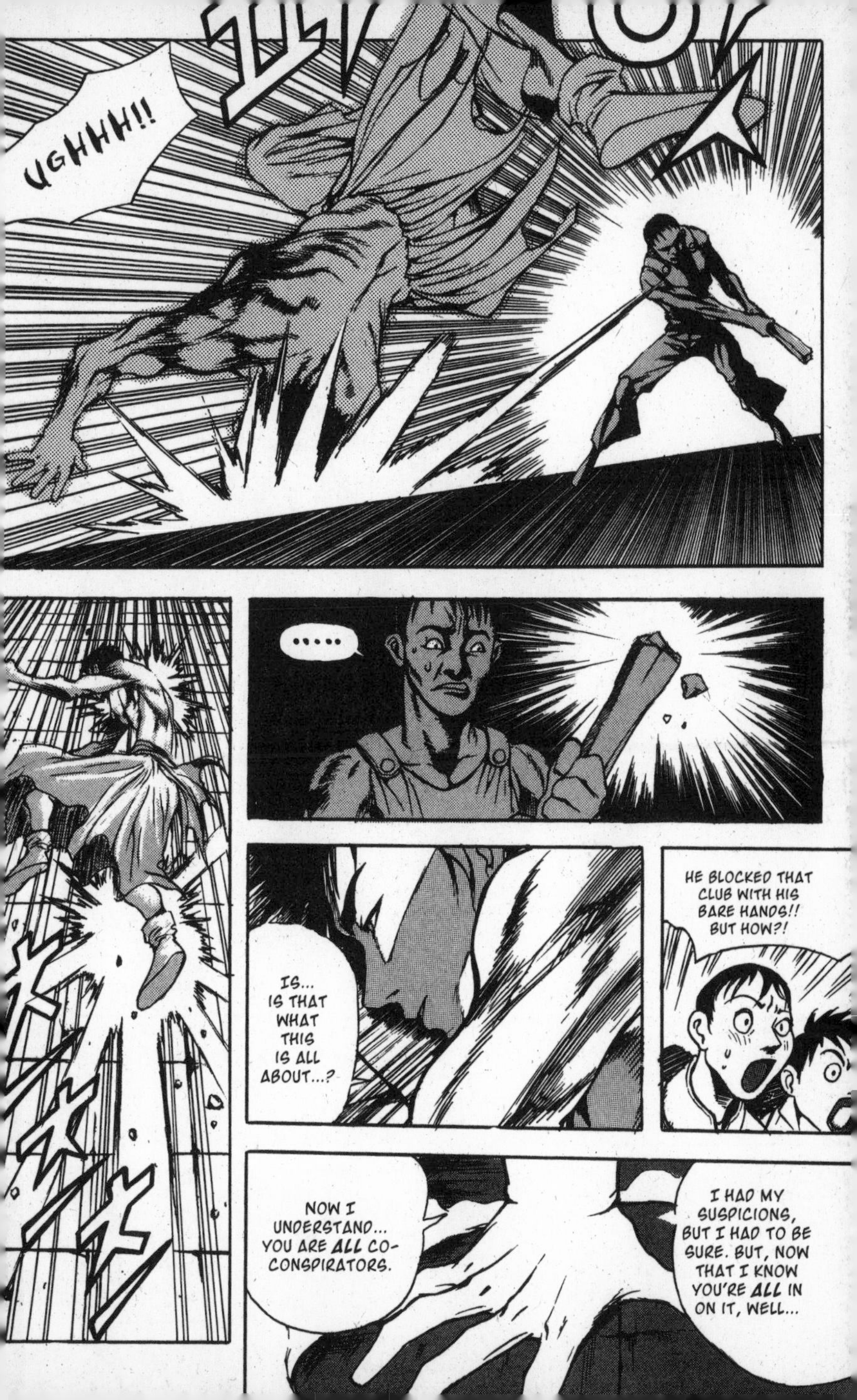
UGHHH!!
.....
IS... IS THAT WHAT THIS IS ALL ABOUT...?
HE BLOCKED THAT CLUB WITH HIS BARE HANDS!! BUT HOW?!
NOW I UNDERSTAND... YOU ARE ALL CO-CONSPIRATORS.
I HAD MY SUSPICIONS, BUT I HAD TO BE SURE. BUT, NOW THAT I KNOW YOU'RE ALL IN ON IT, WELL...

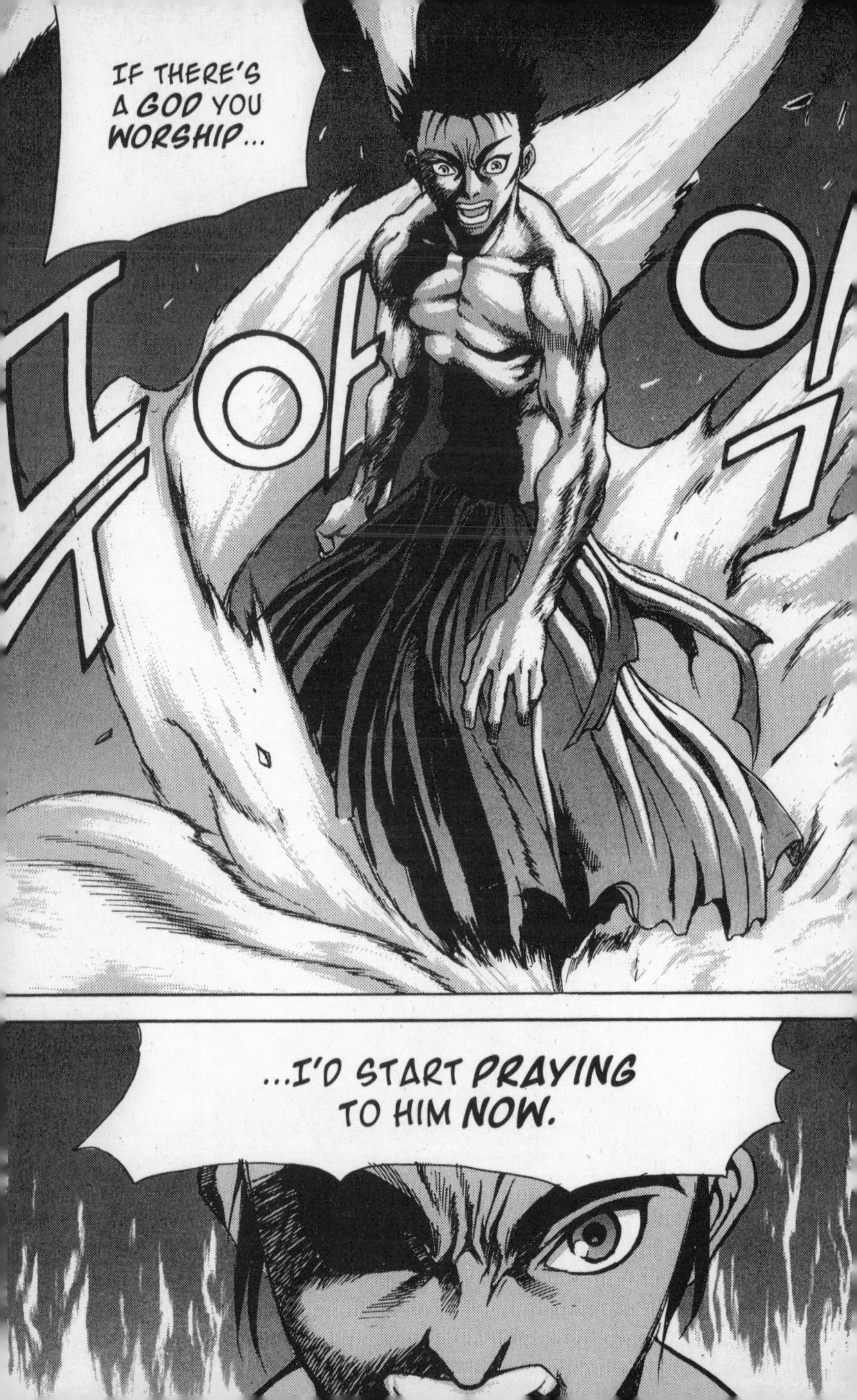
IF THERE'S A GOD YOU WORSHIP...
...I'D START PRAYING TO HIM NOW.

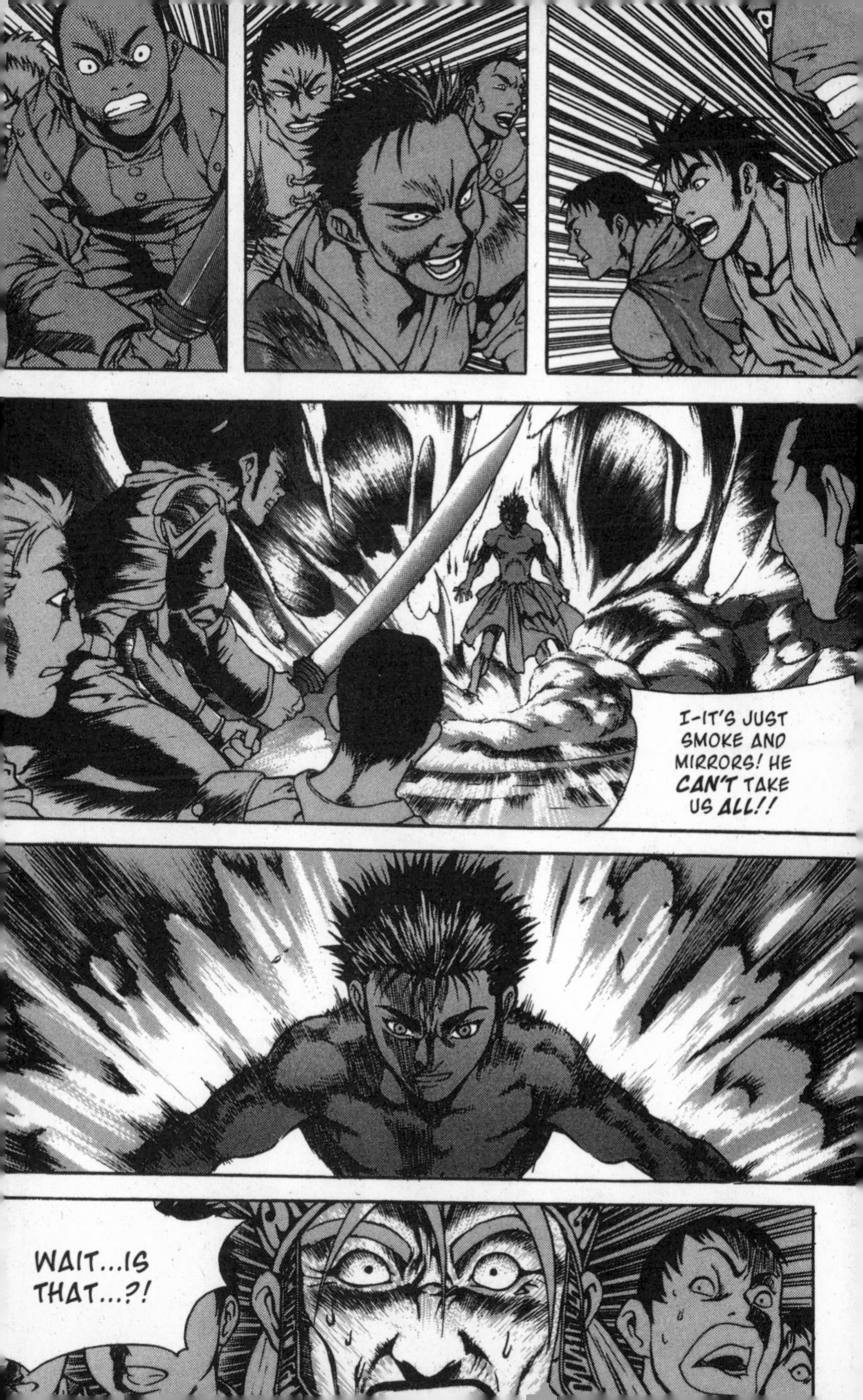
I-IT'S JUST SMOKE AND MIRRORS! HE CAN'T TAKE US ALL!!
WAIT...IS THAT...?!

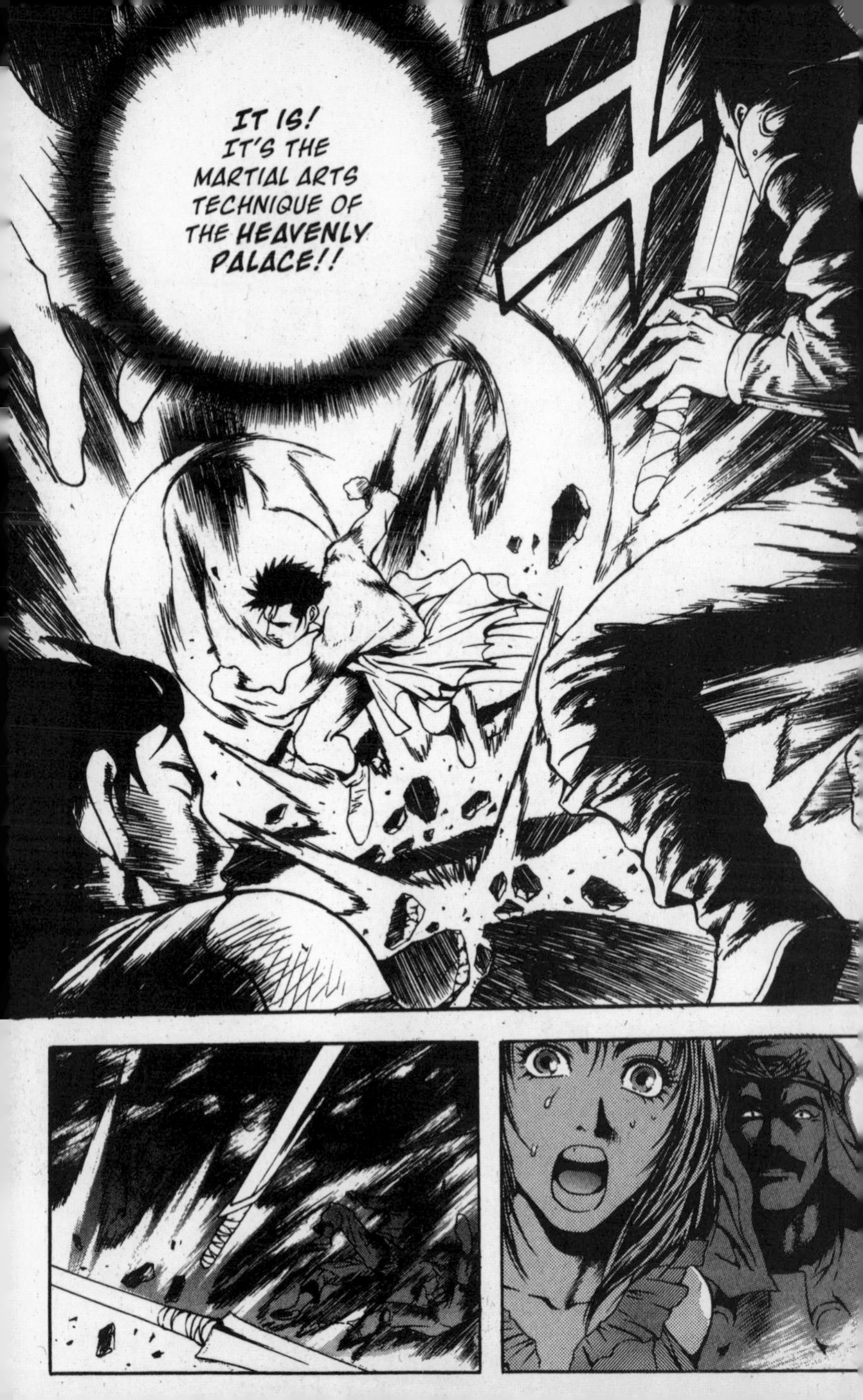
IT IS!
IT'S THE MARTIAL ARTS TECHNIQUE OF THE HEAVENLY PALACE!!

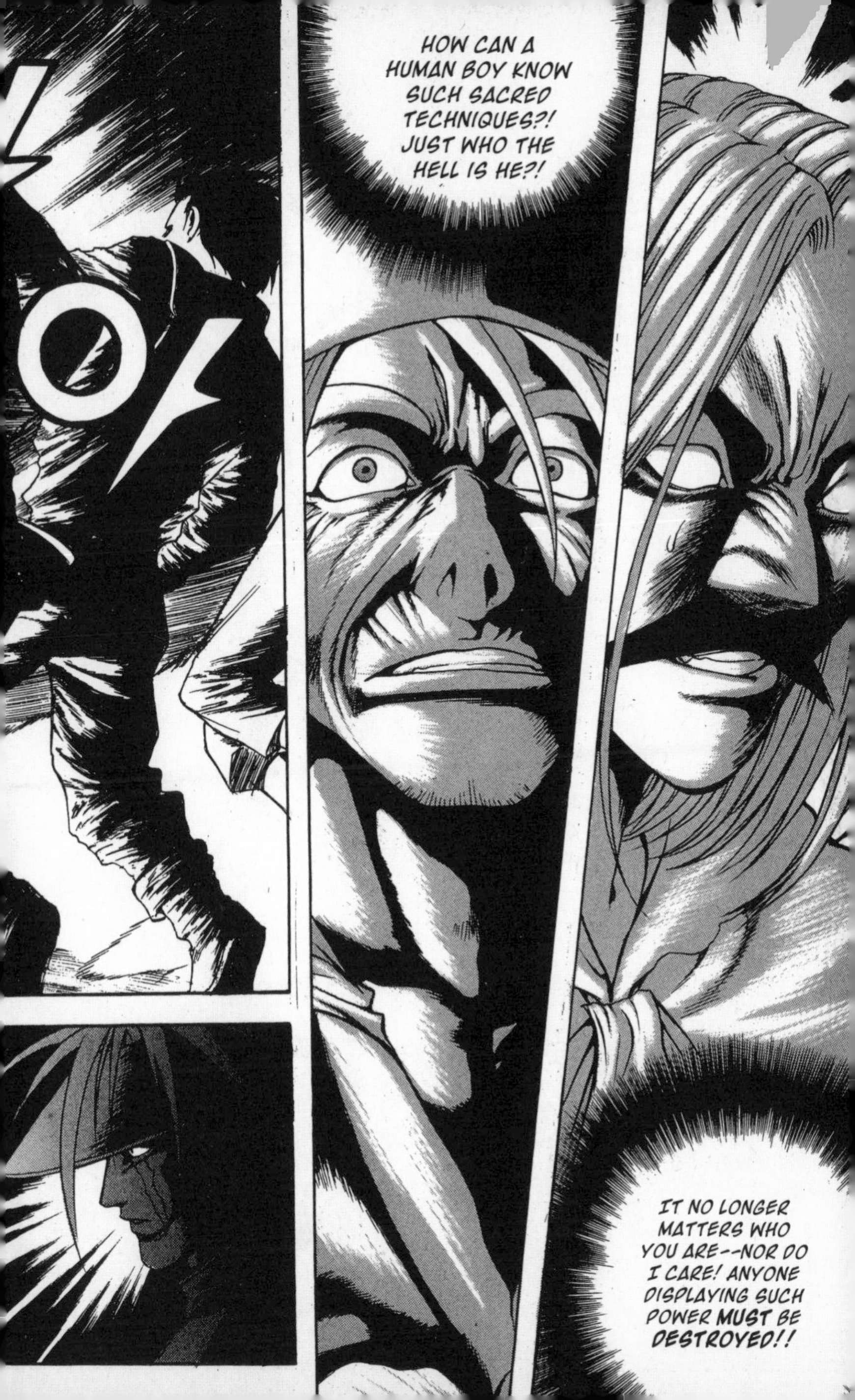
HOW CAN A HUMAN BOY KNOW SUCH SACRED TECHNIQUES?! JUST WHO THE HELL IS HE?!
IT NO LONGER MATTERS WHO YOU ARE--NOR DO I CARE! ANYONE DISPLAYING SUCH POWER **MUST** BE DESTROYED!!

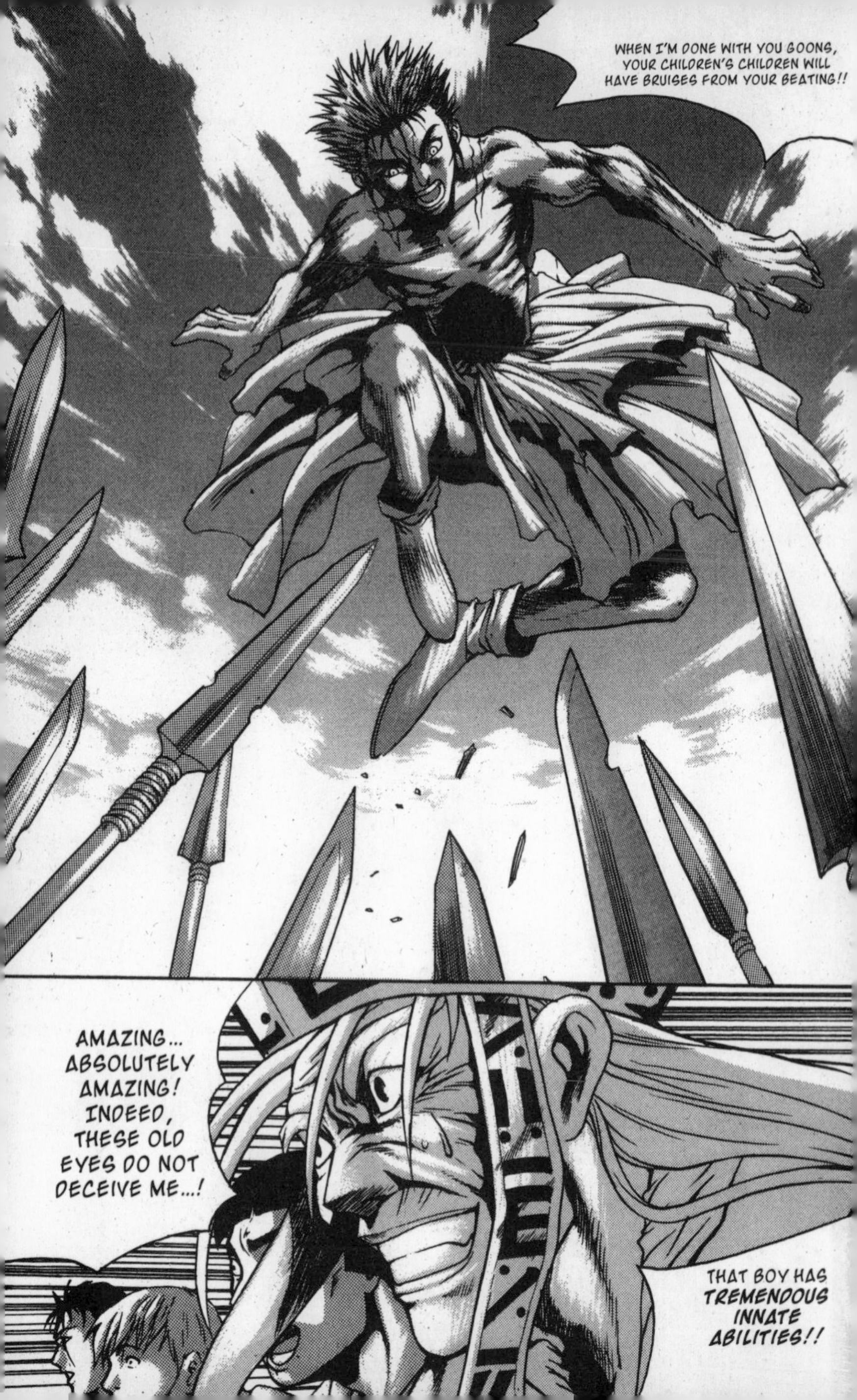
WHEN I'M DONE WITH YOU GOONS, YOUR CHILDREN'S CHILDREN WILL HAVE BRUISES FROM YOUR BEATING!!
AMAZING... ABSOLUTELY AMAZING! INDEED, THESE OLD EYES DO NOT DECEIVE ME...!
THAT BOY HAS TREMENDOUS INNATE ABILITIES!!

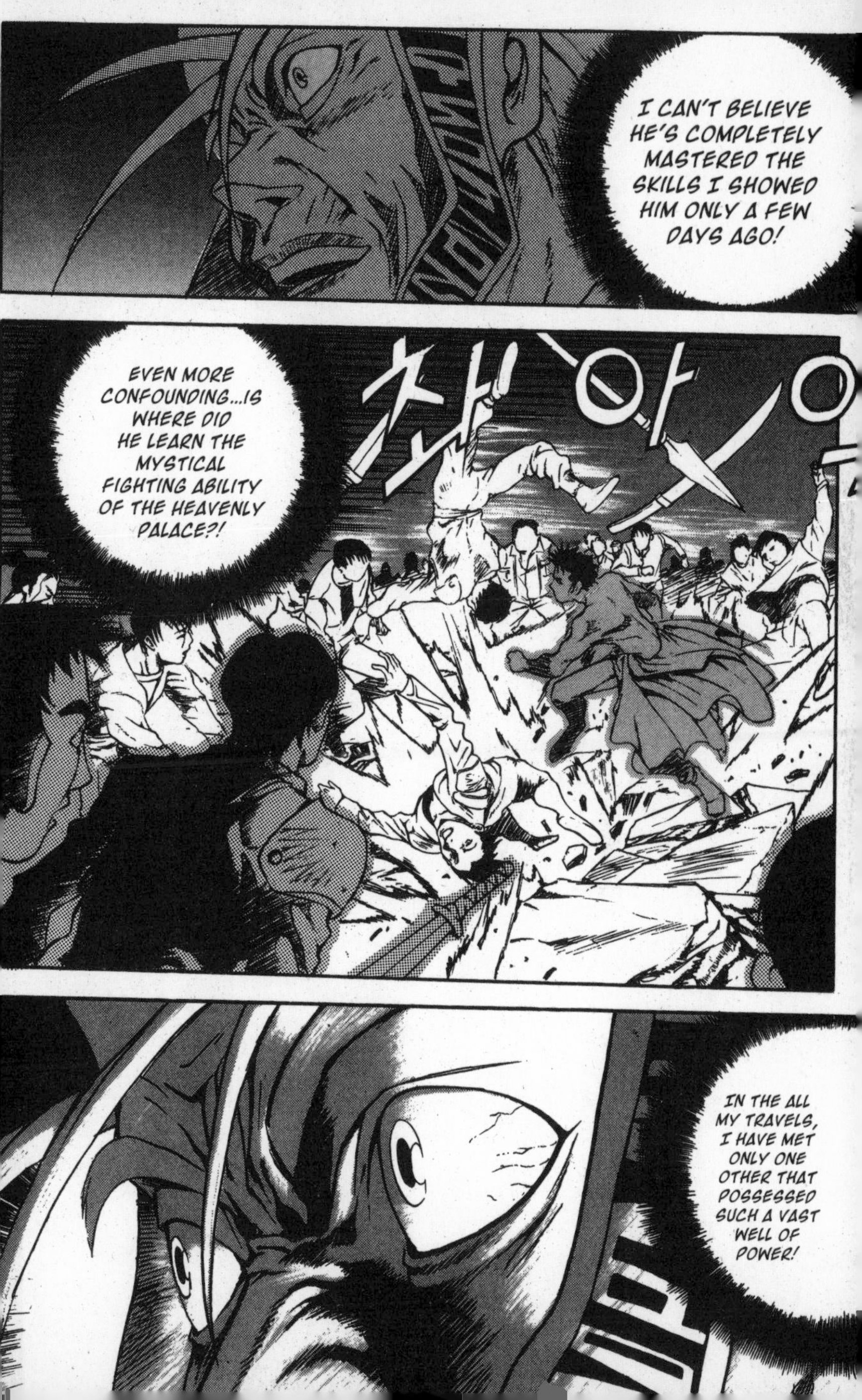
I CAN'T BELIEVE HE'S COMPLETELY MASTERED THE SKILLS I SHOWED HIM ONLY A FEW DAYS AGO!
EVEN MORE CONFOUNDING...IS WHERE DID HE LEARN THE MYSTICAL FIGHTING ABILITY OF THE HEAVENLY PALACE?!
IN THE ALL MY TRAVELS, I HAVE MET ONLY ONE OTHER THAT POSSESSED SUCH A VAST WELL OF POWER!

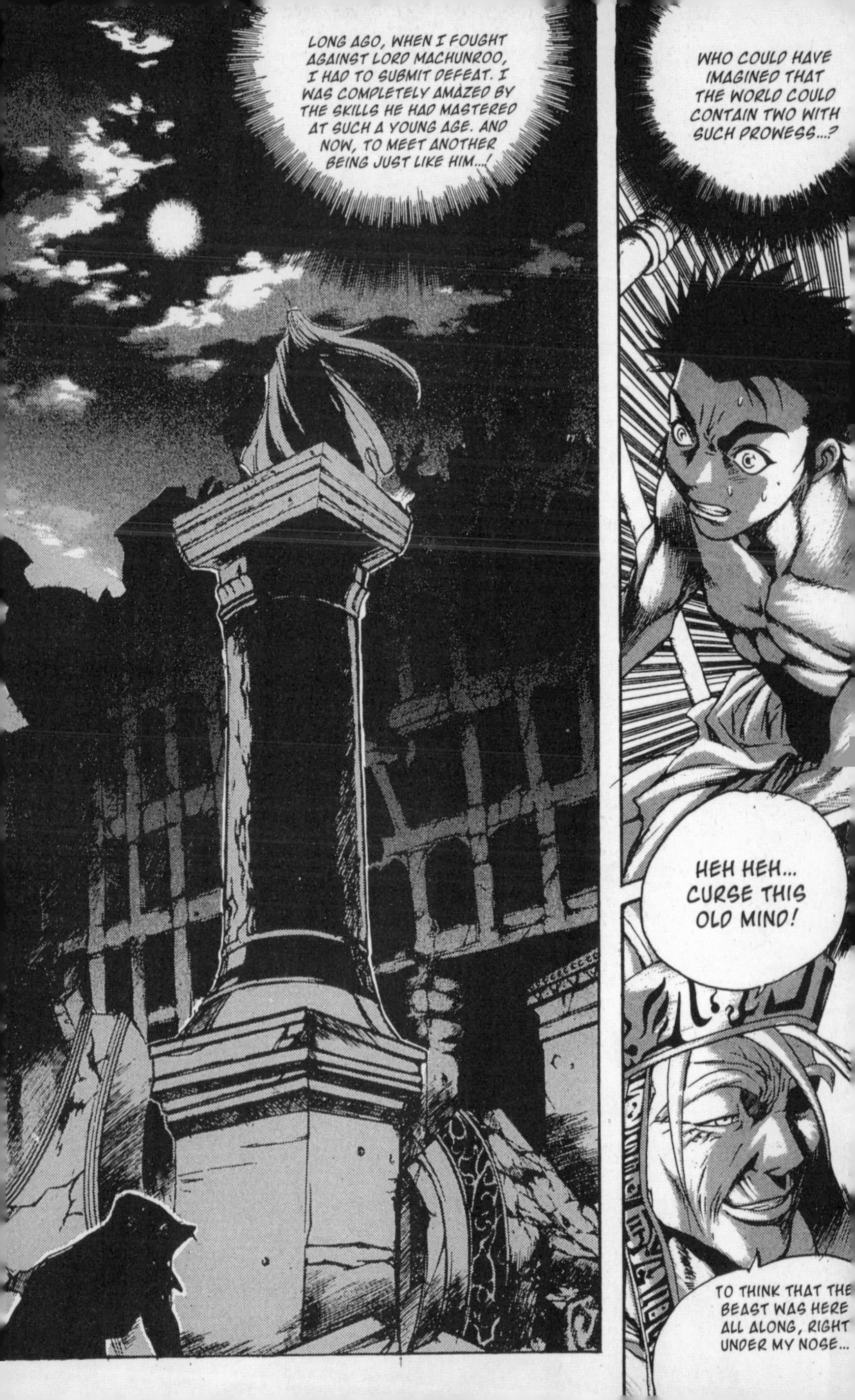
LONG AGO, WHEN I FOUGHT AGAINST LORD MACHUNROO, I HAD TO SUBMIT DEFEAT. I WAS COMPLETELY AMAZED BY THE SKILLS HE HAD MASTERED AT SUCH A YOUNG AGE. AND NOW, TO MEET ANOTHER BEING JUST LIKE HIM...!
WHO COULD HAVE IMAGINED THAT THE WORLD COULD CONTAIN TWO WITH SUCH PROWESS...?
HEH HEH... CURSE THIS OLD MIND!
TO THINK THAT THE BEAST WAS HERE ALL ALONG, RIGHT UNDER MY NOSE...

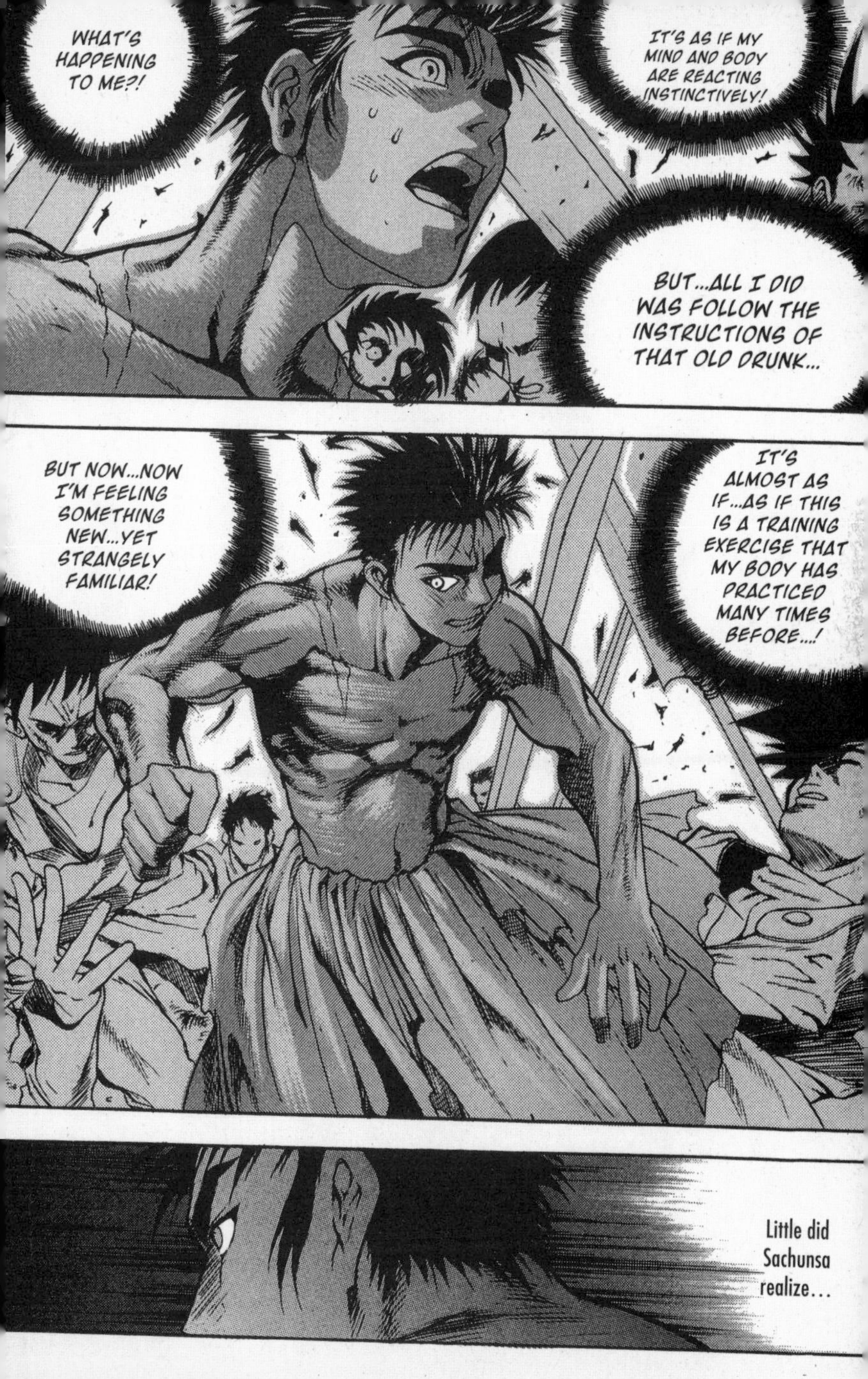
IT'S AS IF MY MIND AND BODY ARE REACTING INSTINCTIVELY!
WHAT'S HAPPENING TO ME?!
BUT...ALL I DID WAS FOLLOW THE INSTRUCTIONS OF THAT OLD DRUNK...
IT'S ALMOST AS IF...AS IF THIS IS A TRAINING EXERCISE THAT MY BODY HAS PRACTICED MANY TIMES BEFORE...!
BUT NOW...NOW I'M FEELING SOMETHING NEW...YET STRANGELY FAMILIAR!
Little did Sachunsa realize...

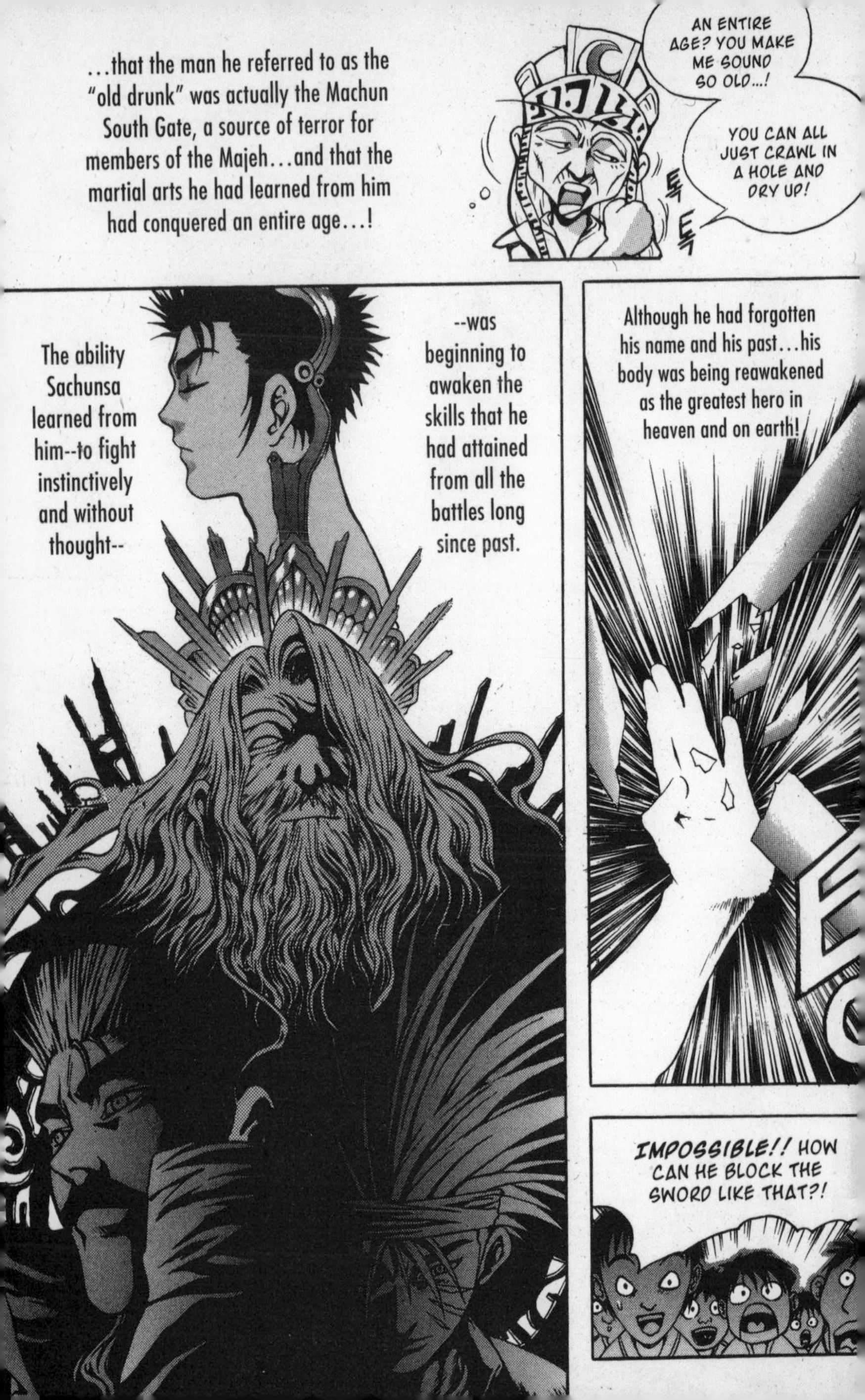

...that the man he referred to as the "old drunk" was actually the Machun South Gate, a source of terror for members of the Majeh...and that the martial arts he had learned from him had conquered an entire age...!
AN ENTIRE AGE? YOU MAKE ME SOUND SO OLD...!
YOU CAN ALL JUST CRAWL IN A HOLE AND DRY UP!
The ability Sachunsa learned from him--to fight instinctively and without thought--
--was beginning to awaken the skills that he had attained from all the battles long since past.
Although he had forgotten his name and his past...his body was being reawakened as the greatest hero in heaven and on earth!
IMPOSSIBLE!! HOW CAN HE BLOCK THE SWORD LIKE THAT?!

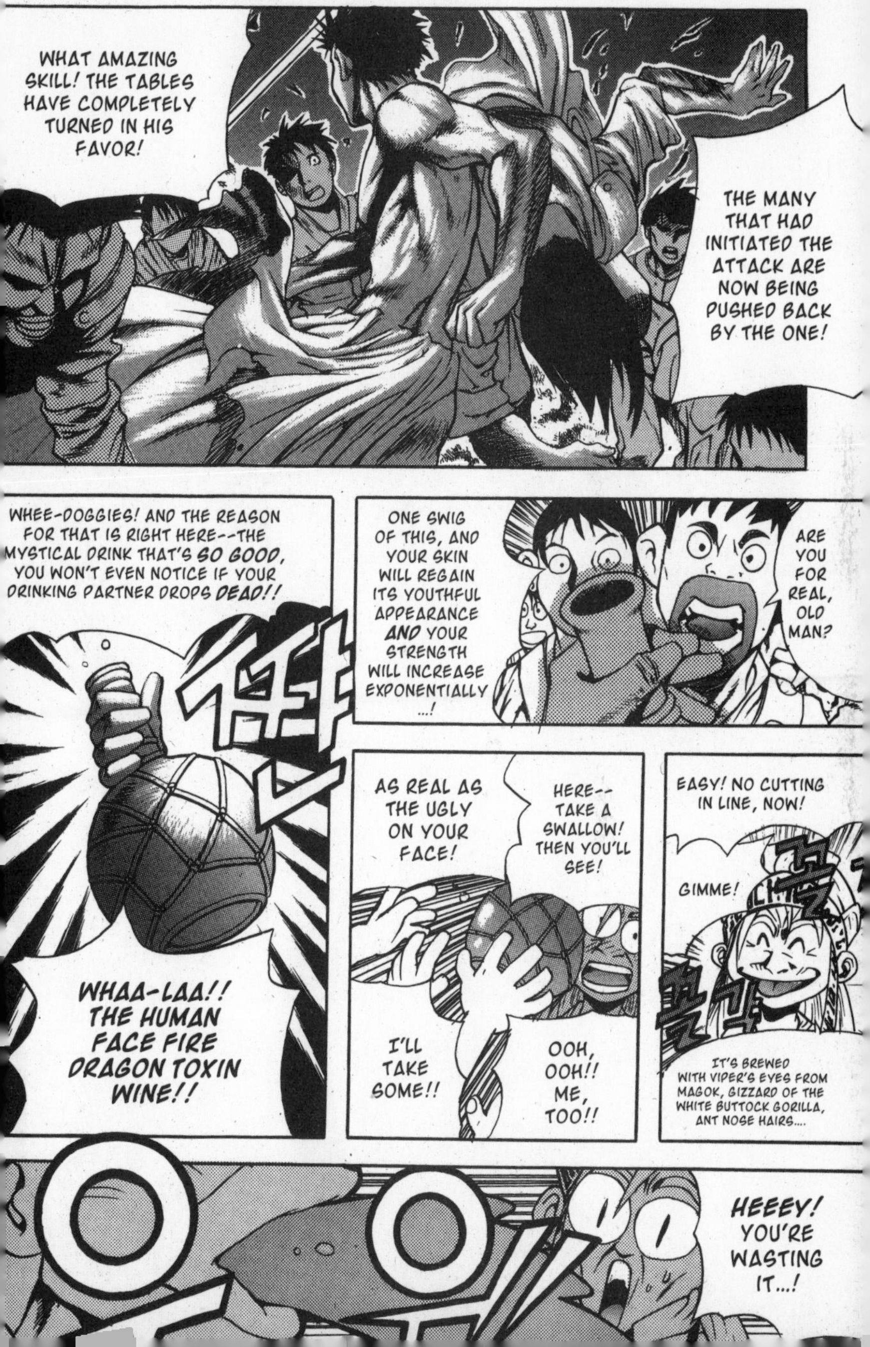
WHAT AMAZING SKILL! THE TABLES HAVE COMPLETELY TURNED IN HIS FAVOR!
THE MANY THAT HAD INITIATED THE ATTACK ARE NOW BEING PUSHED BACK BY THE ONE!
WHEE-DOGGIES! AND THE REASON FOR THAT IS RIGHT HERE--THE MYSTICAL DRINK THAT'S SO GOOD, YOU WON'T EVEN NOTICE IF YOUR DRINKING PARTNER DROPS DEAD!!
WHAA-LAA!! THE HUMAN FACE FIRE DRAGON TOXIN WINE!!
ARE YOU FOR REAL, OLD MAN?
ONE SWIG OF THIS, AND YOUR SKIN WILL REGAIN ITS YOUTHFUL APPEARANCE AND YOUR STRENGTH WILL INCREASE EXPONENTIALLY ...!
HERE--TAKE A SWALLOW! THEN YOU'LL SEE!
AS REAL AS THE UGLY ON YOUR FACE!
OOH, OOH!! ME, TOO!!
I'LL TAKE SOME!!
EASY! NO CUTTING IN LINE, NOW!
GIMME!
IT'S BREWED WITH VIPER'S EYES FROM MAGOK, GIZZARD OF THE WHITE BUTTOCK GORILLA, ANT NOSE HAIRS....
HEEEY! YOU'RE WASTING IT...!

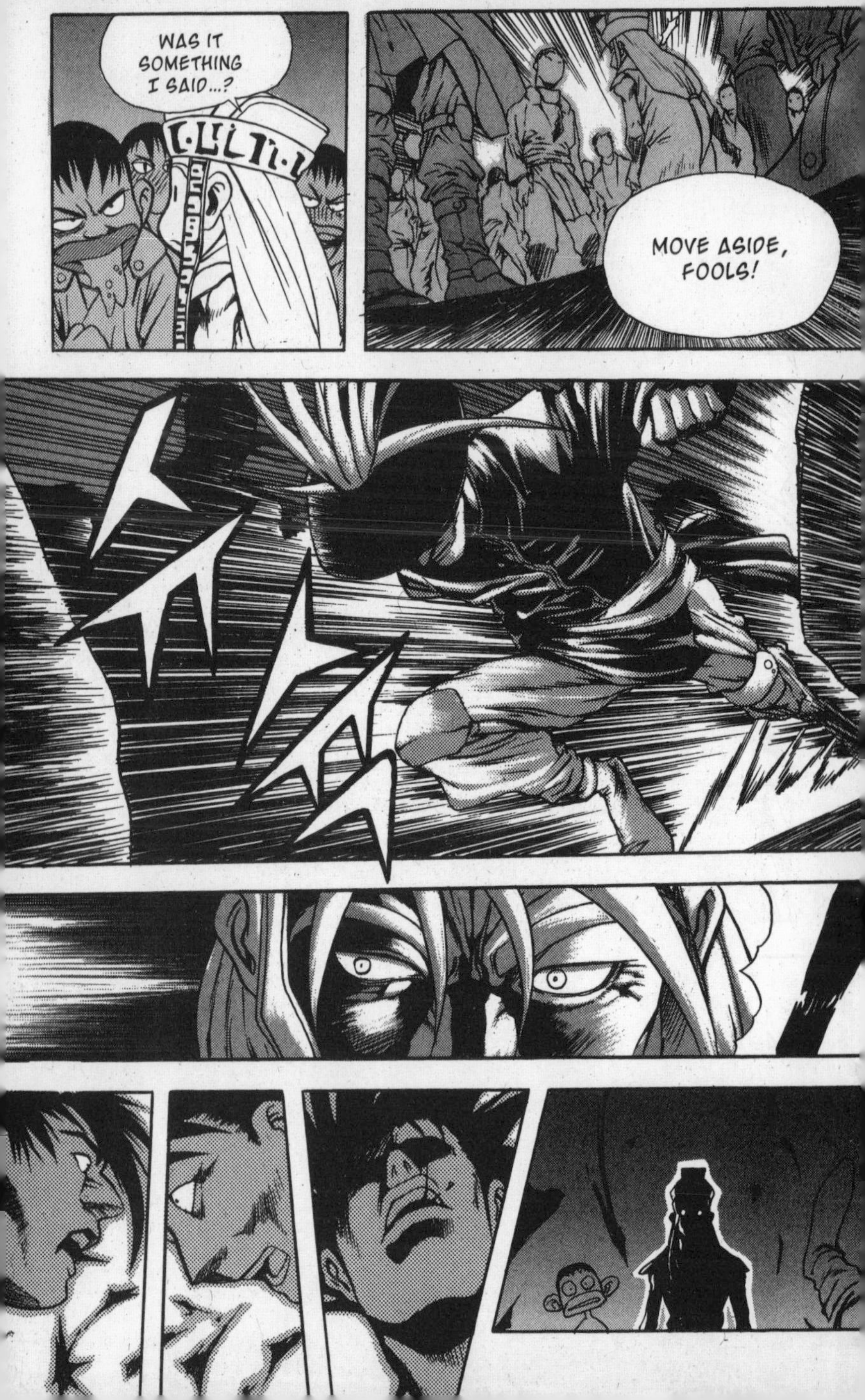
WAS IT SOMETHING I SAID...?
MOVE ASIDE, FOOLS!

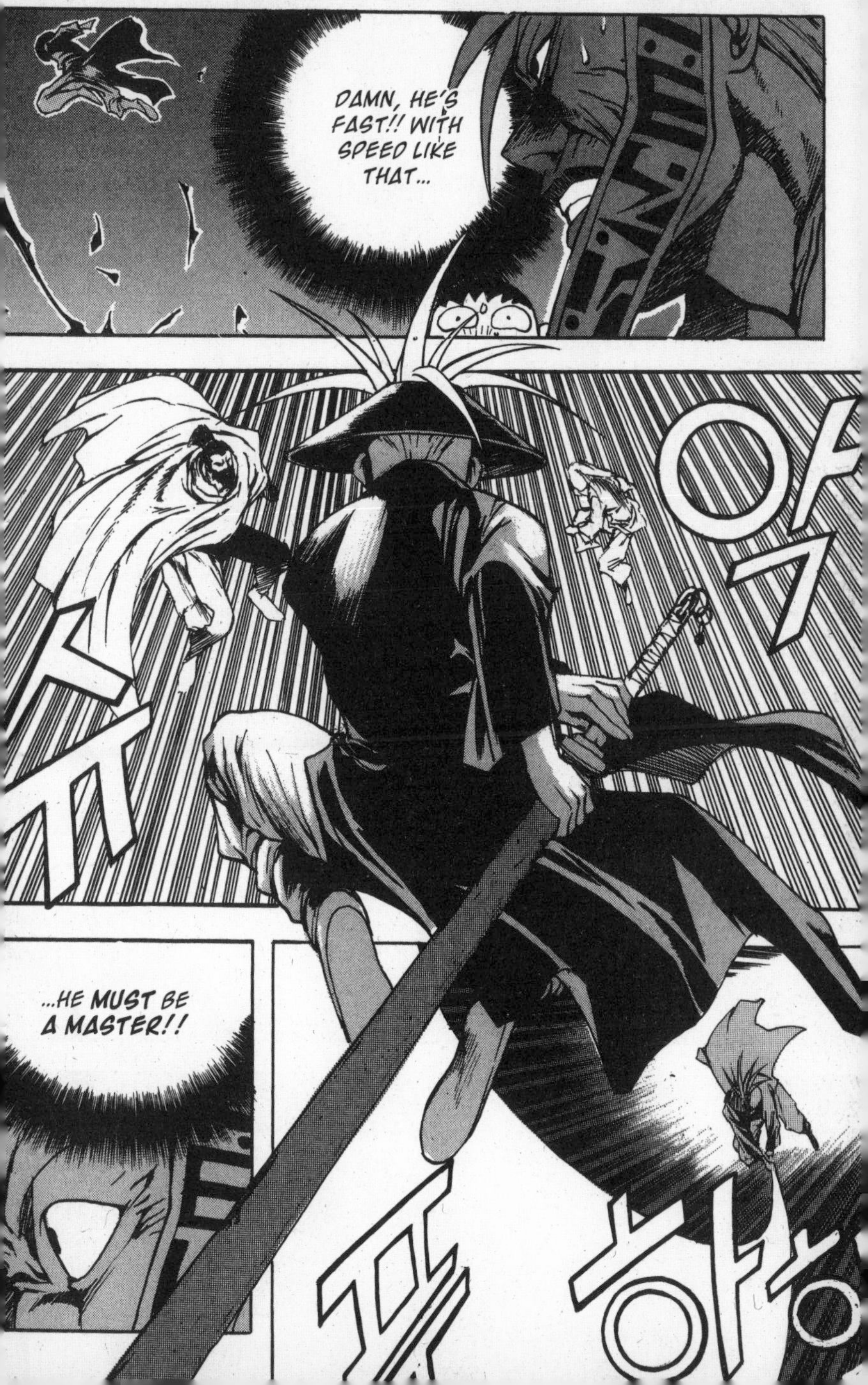
DAMN, HE'S FAST!! WITH SPEED LIKE THAT...
...HE MUST BE A MASTER!!

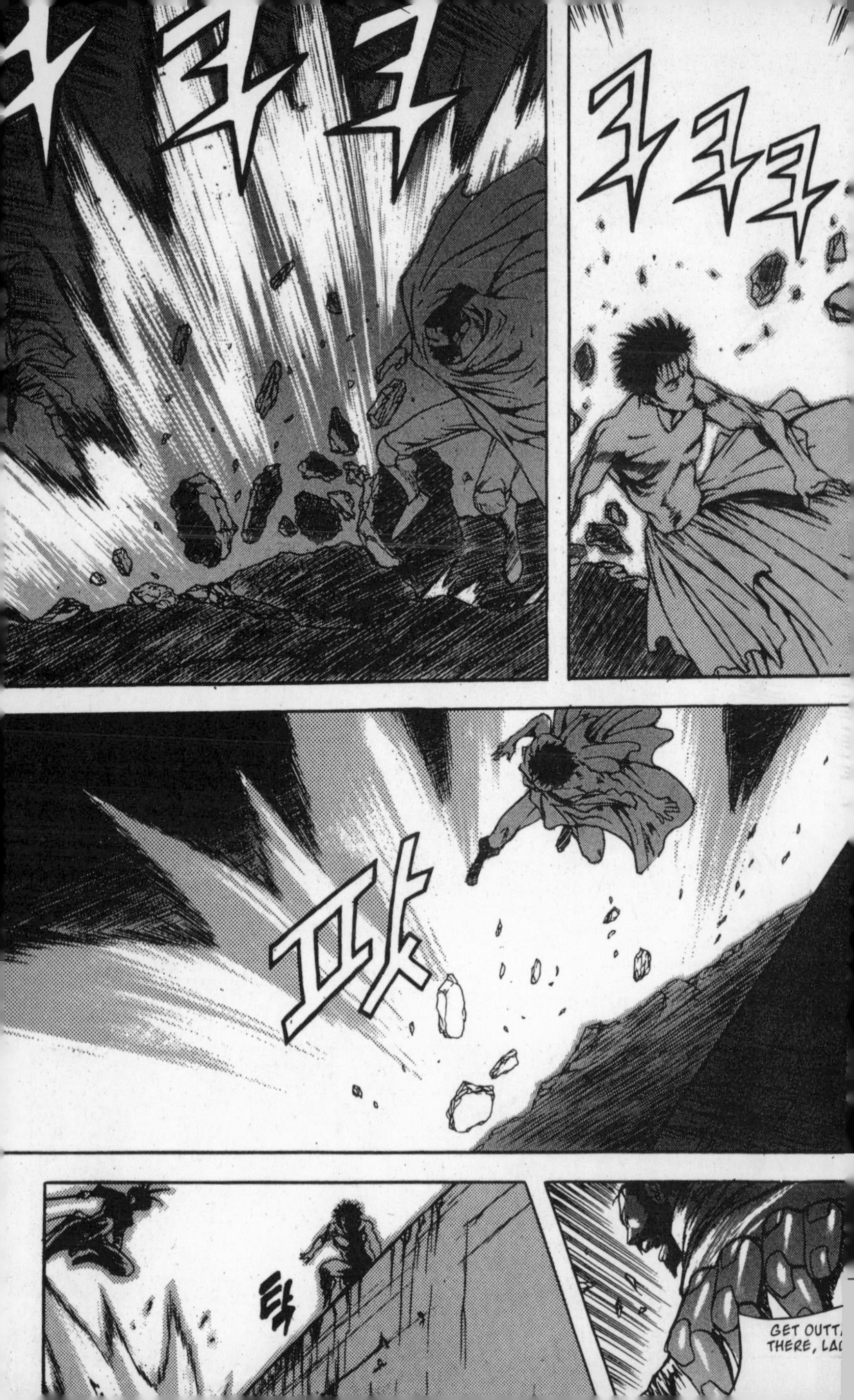
GET OUTTA
THERE, LA

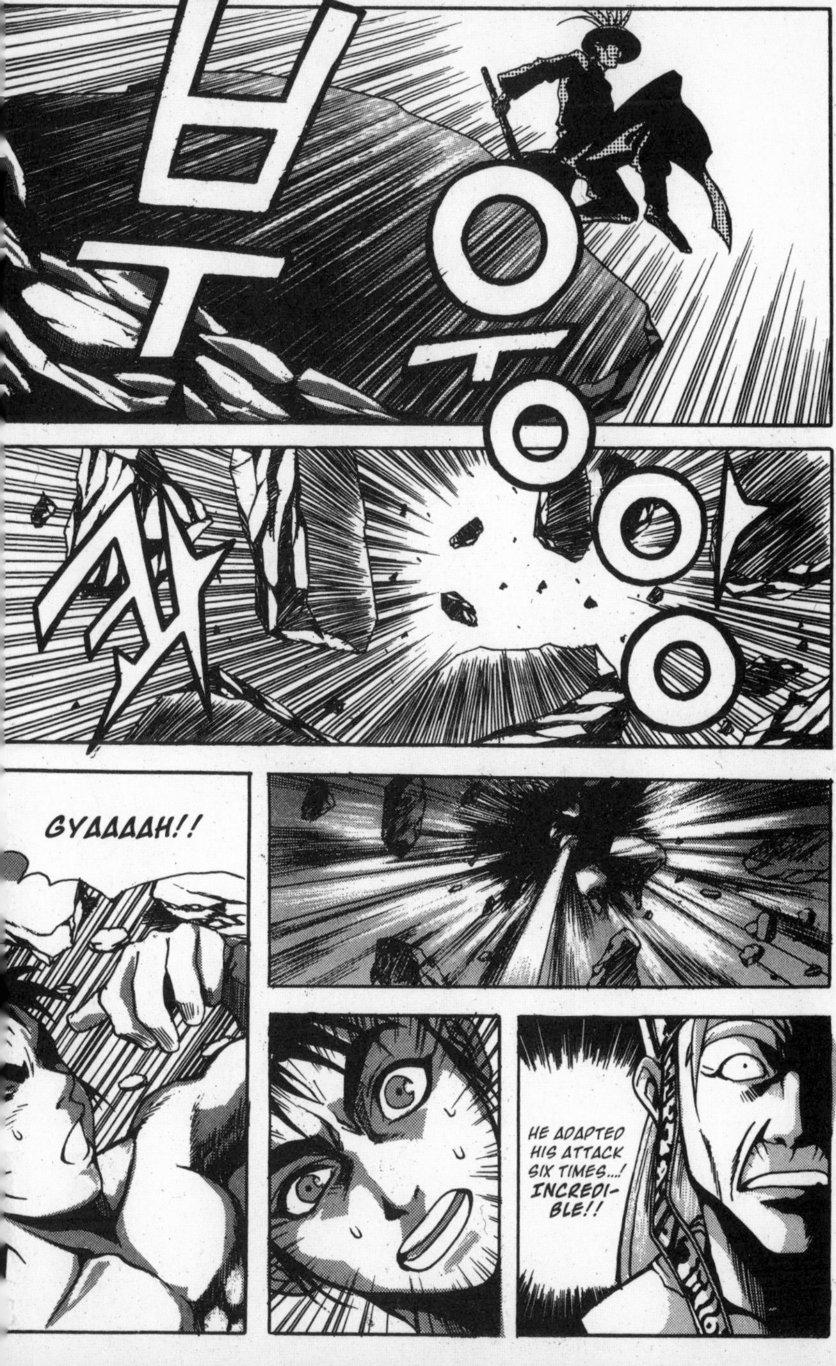
HE ADAPTED HIS ATTACK SIX TIMES...! INCREDIBLE!!
GYAAAAH!!

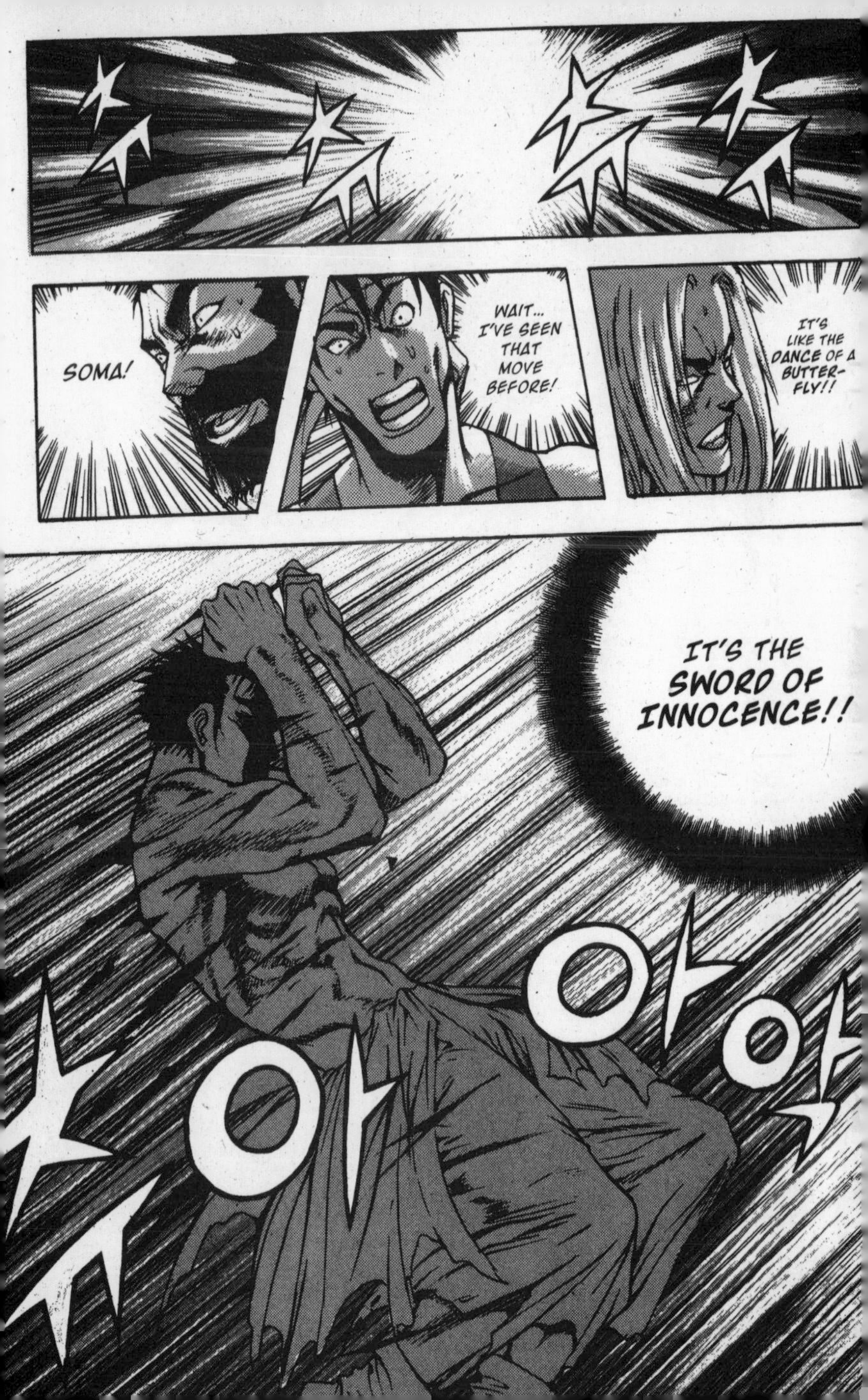

SOMA!
WAIT... I'VE SEEN THAT MOVE BEFORE!
IT'S LIKE THE DANCE OF A BUTTER-FLY!!
IT'S THE SWORD OF INNOCENCE!!

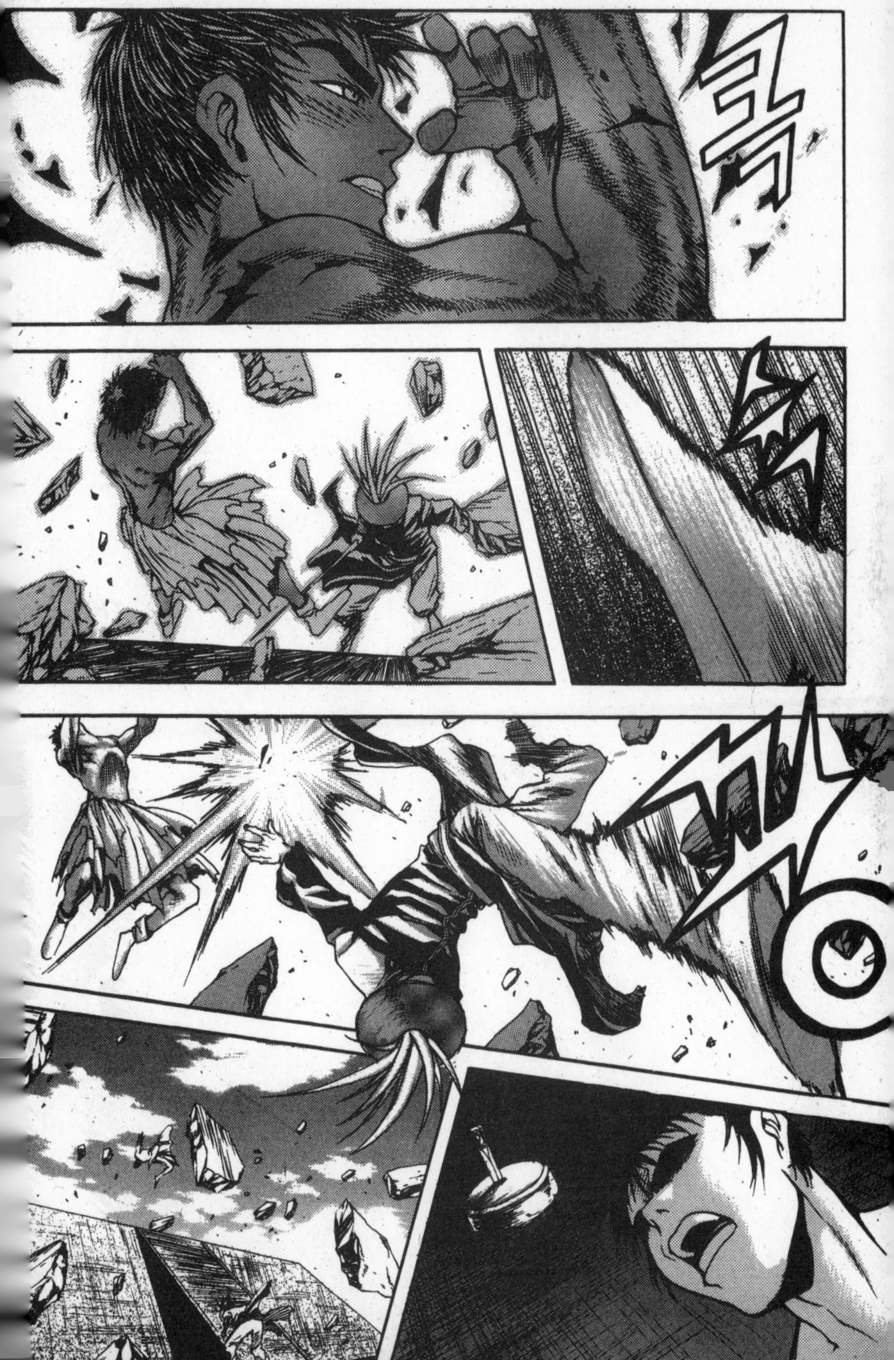

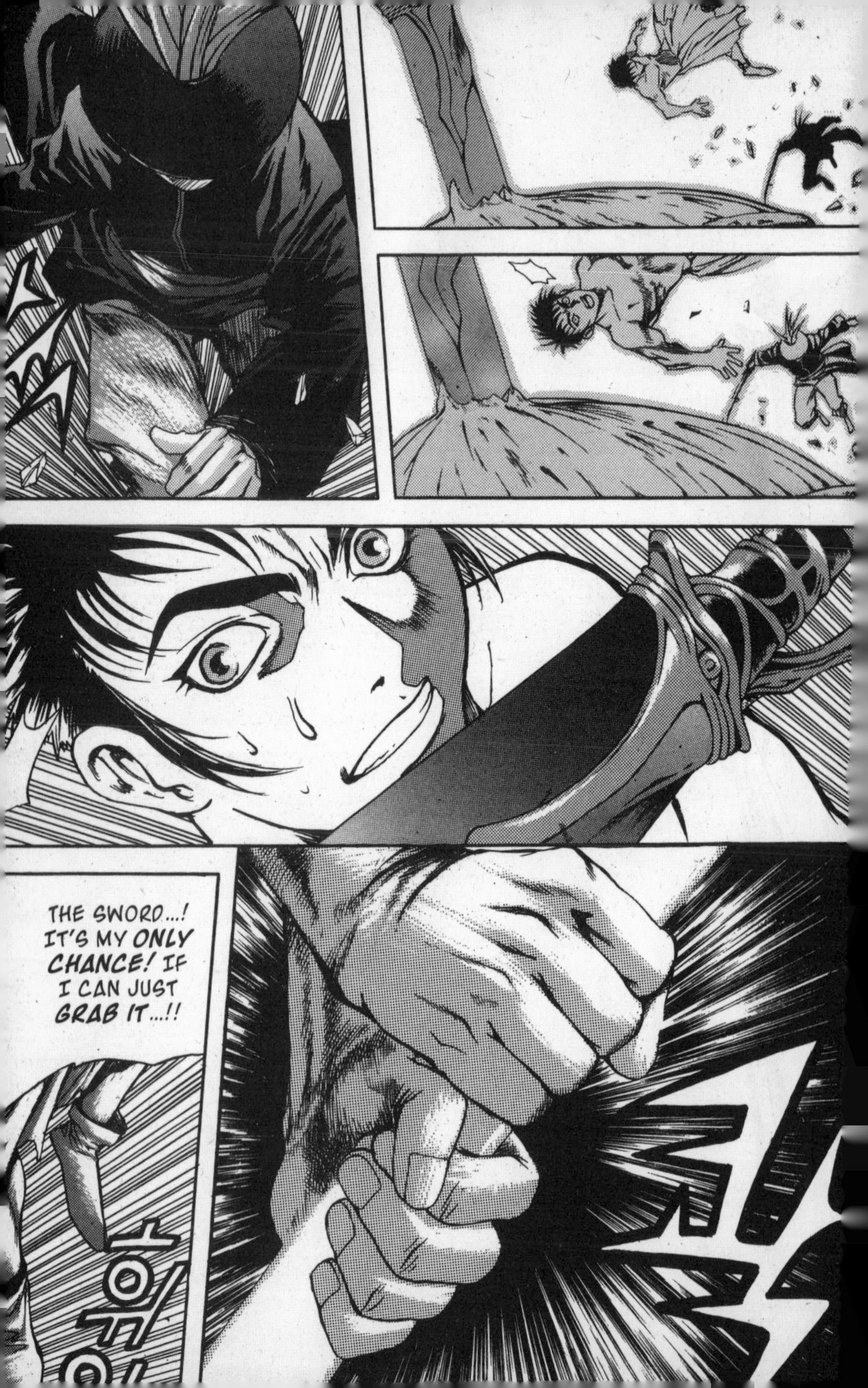
THE SWORD...! IT'S MY ONLY CHANCE! IF I CAN JUST GRAB IT...!!

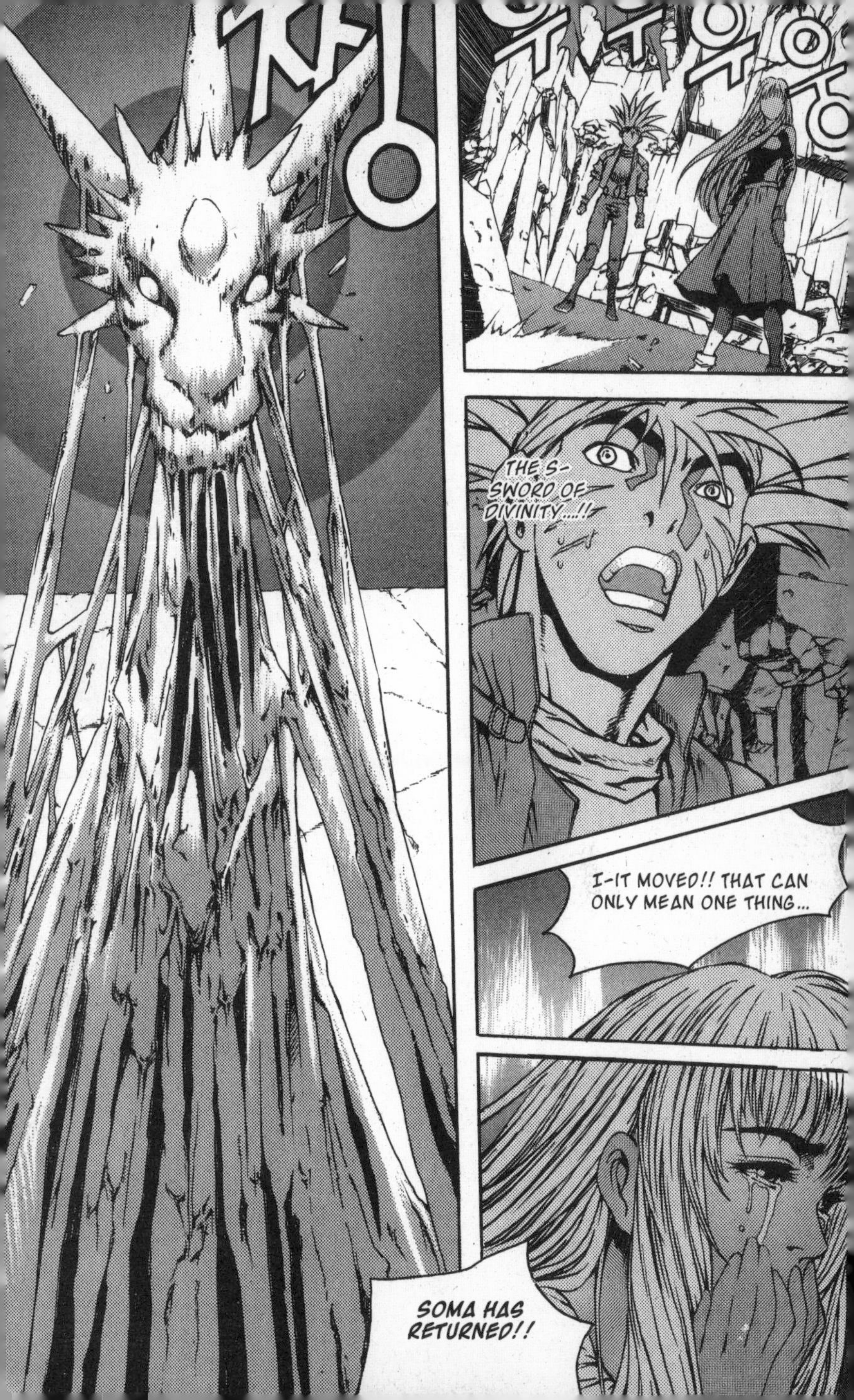
THE S-SWORD OF DIVINITY...!!
I-IT MOVED!! THAT CAN ONLY MEAN ONE THING...
SOMA HAS RETURNED!!

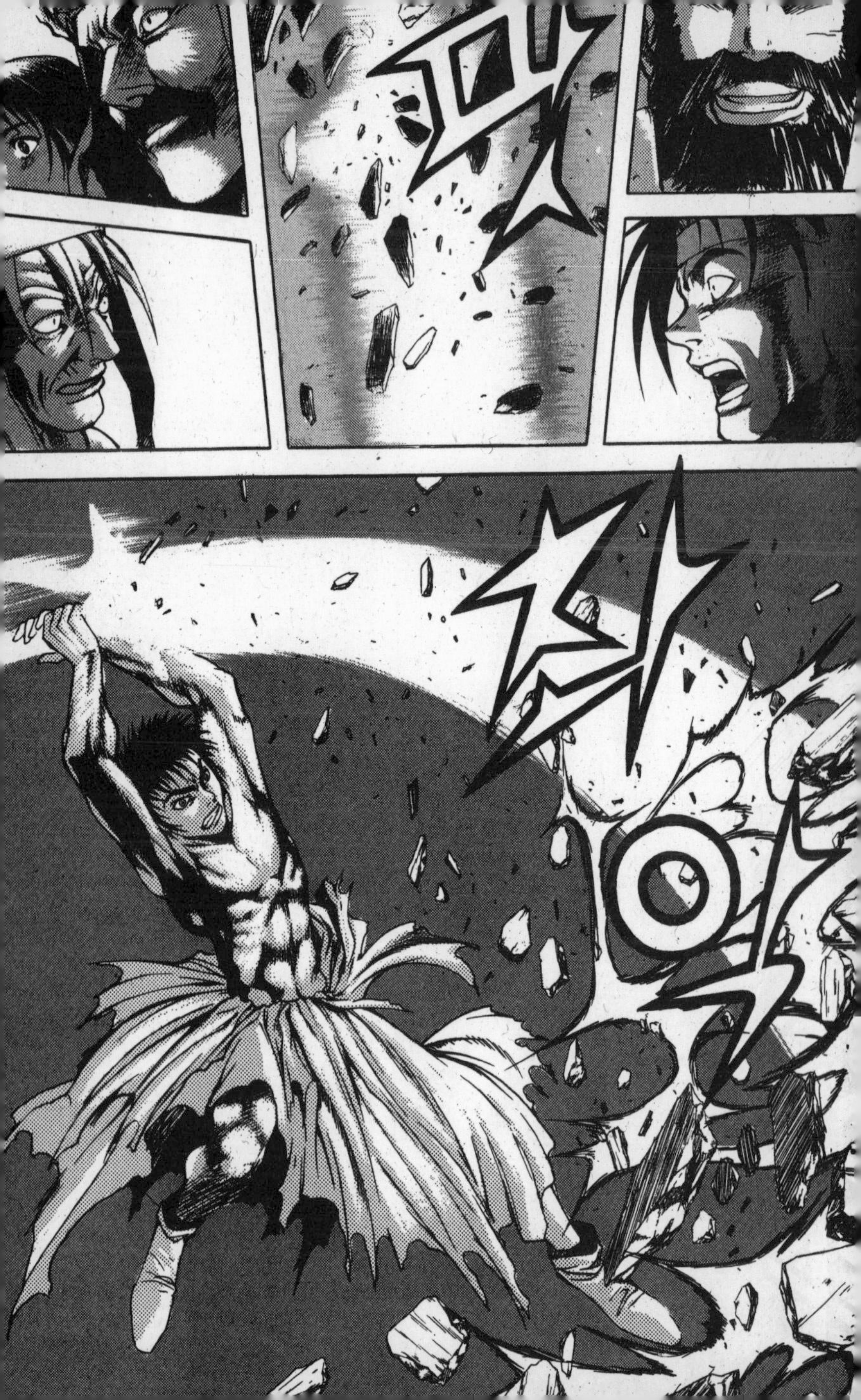

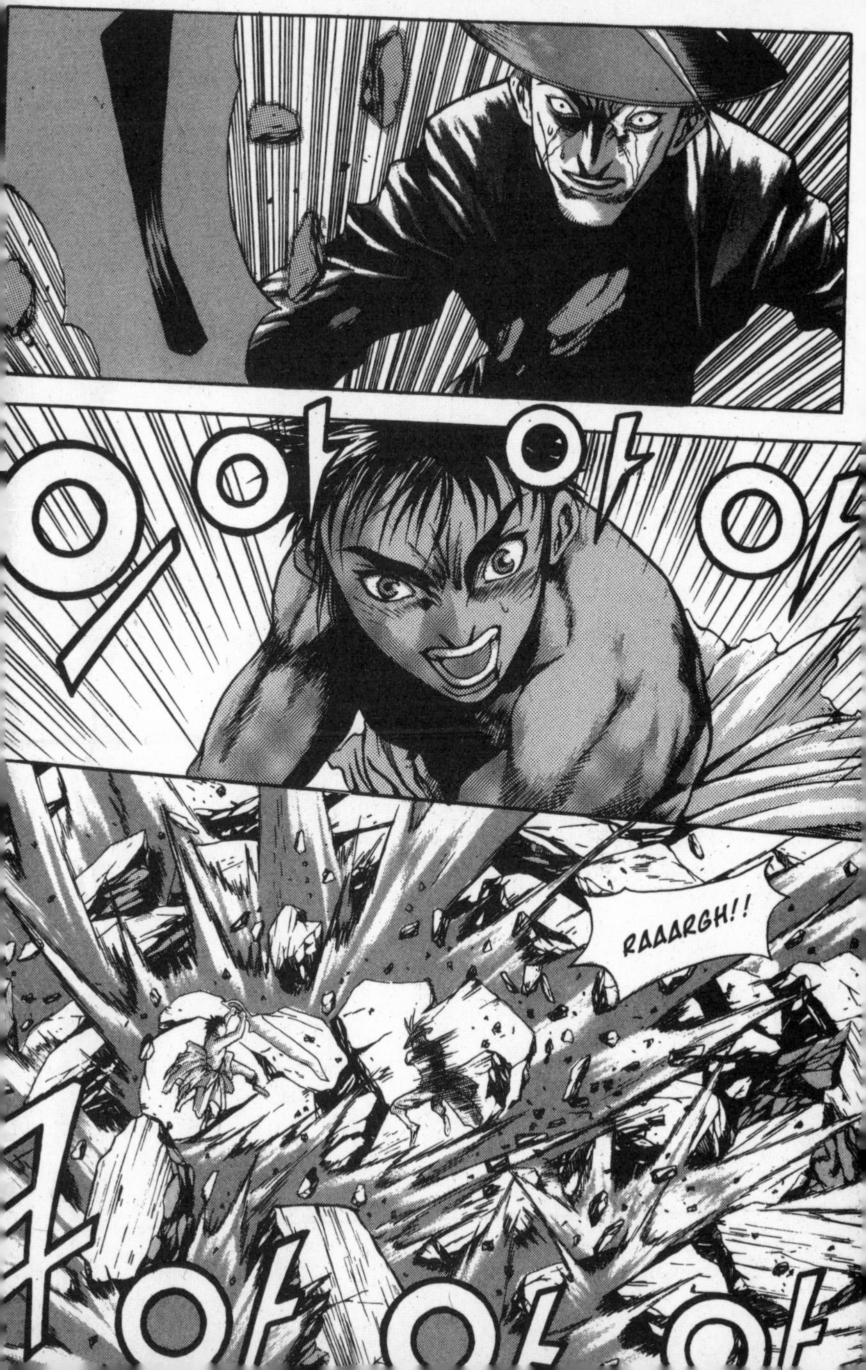
RAAARGH!!

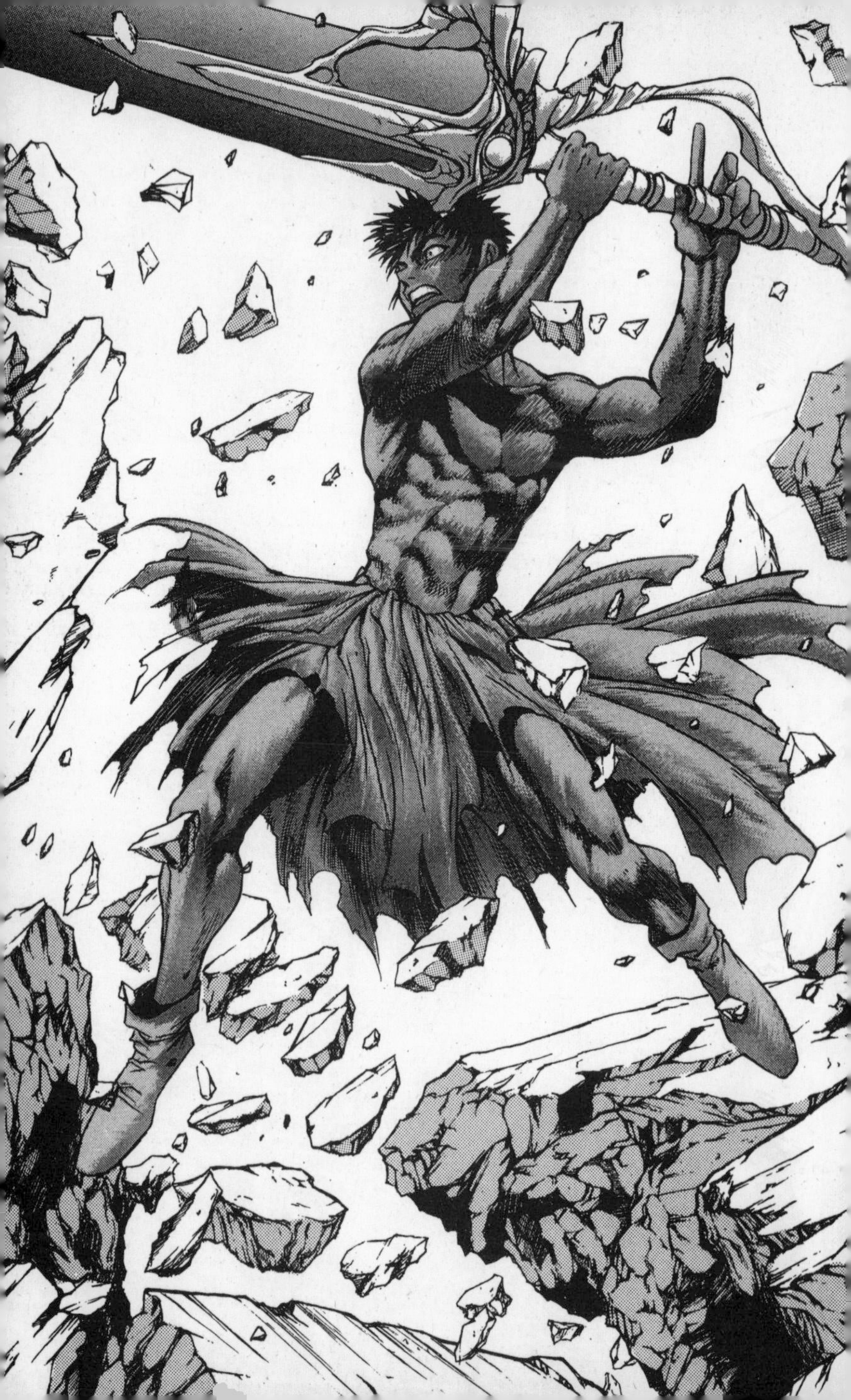

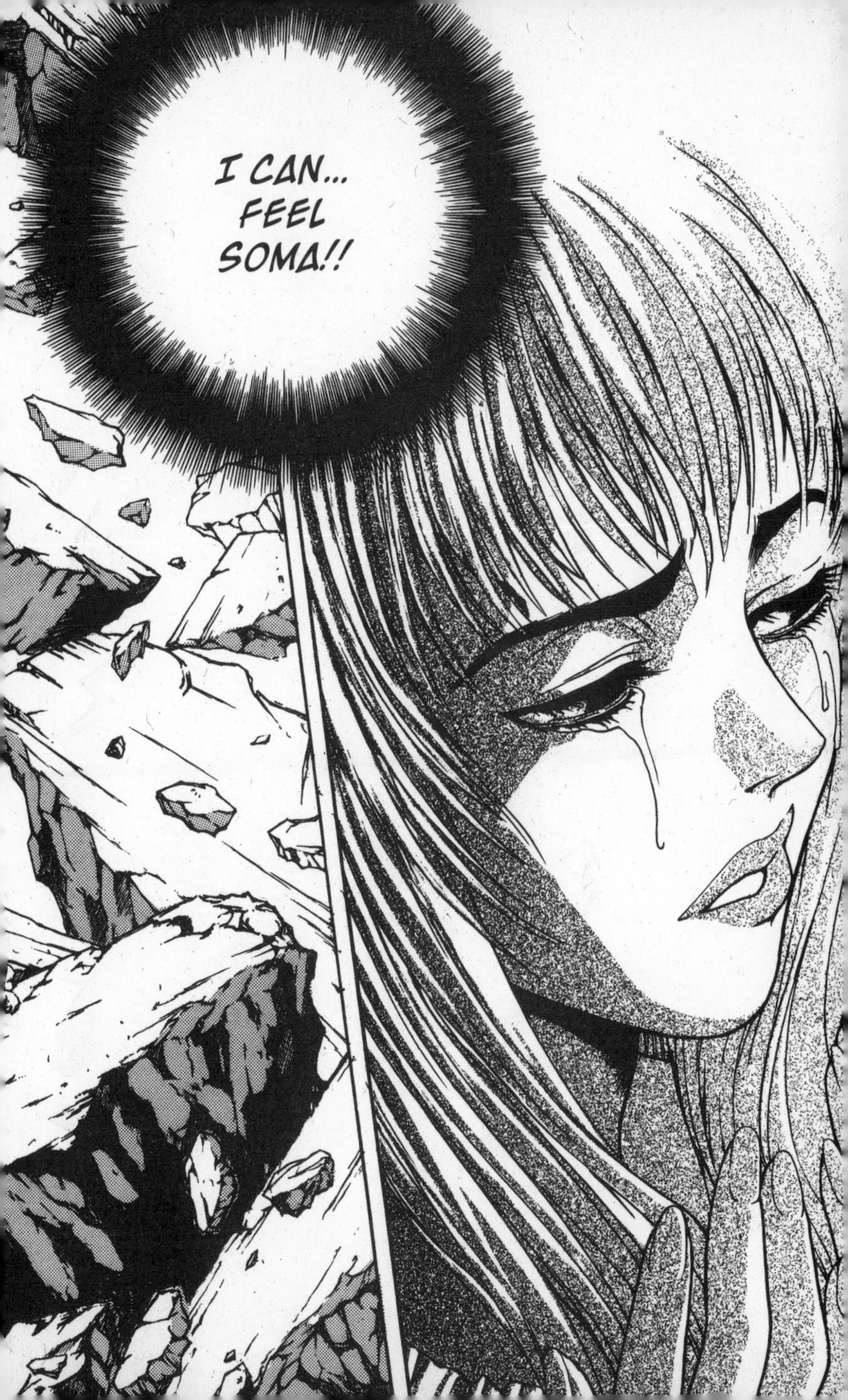
I CAN... FEEL SOMA!!

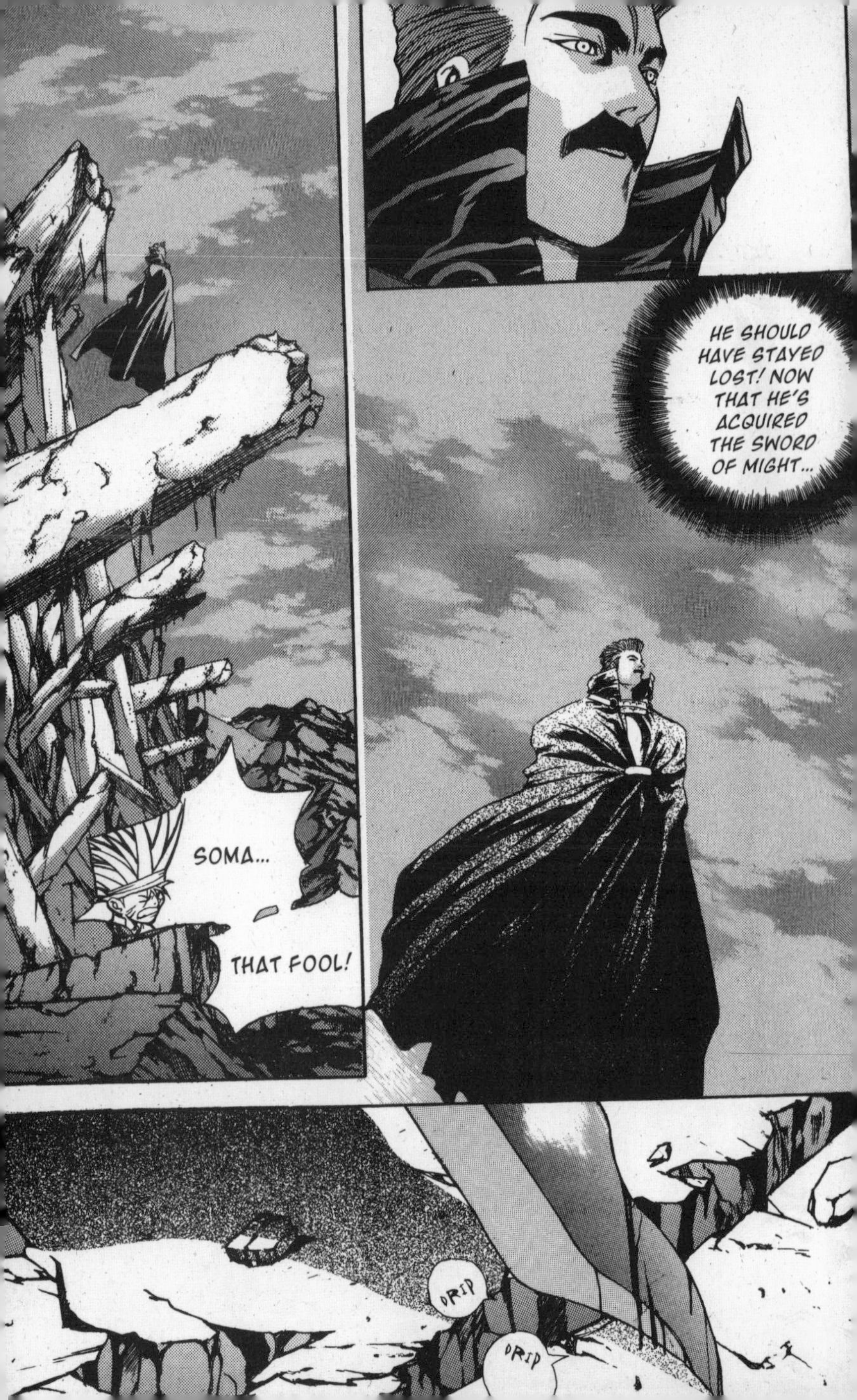
SOMA...
THAT FOOL!
HE SHOULD HAVE STAYED LOST! NOW THAT HE'S ACQUIRED THE SWORD OF MIGHT...
DRIP
DRIP

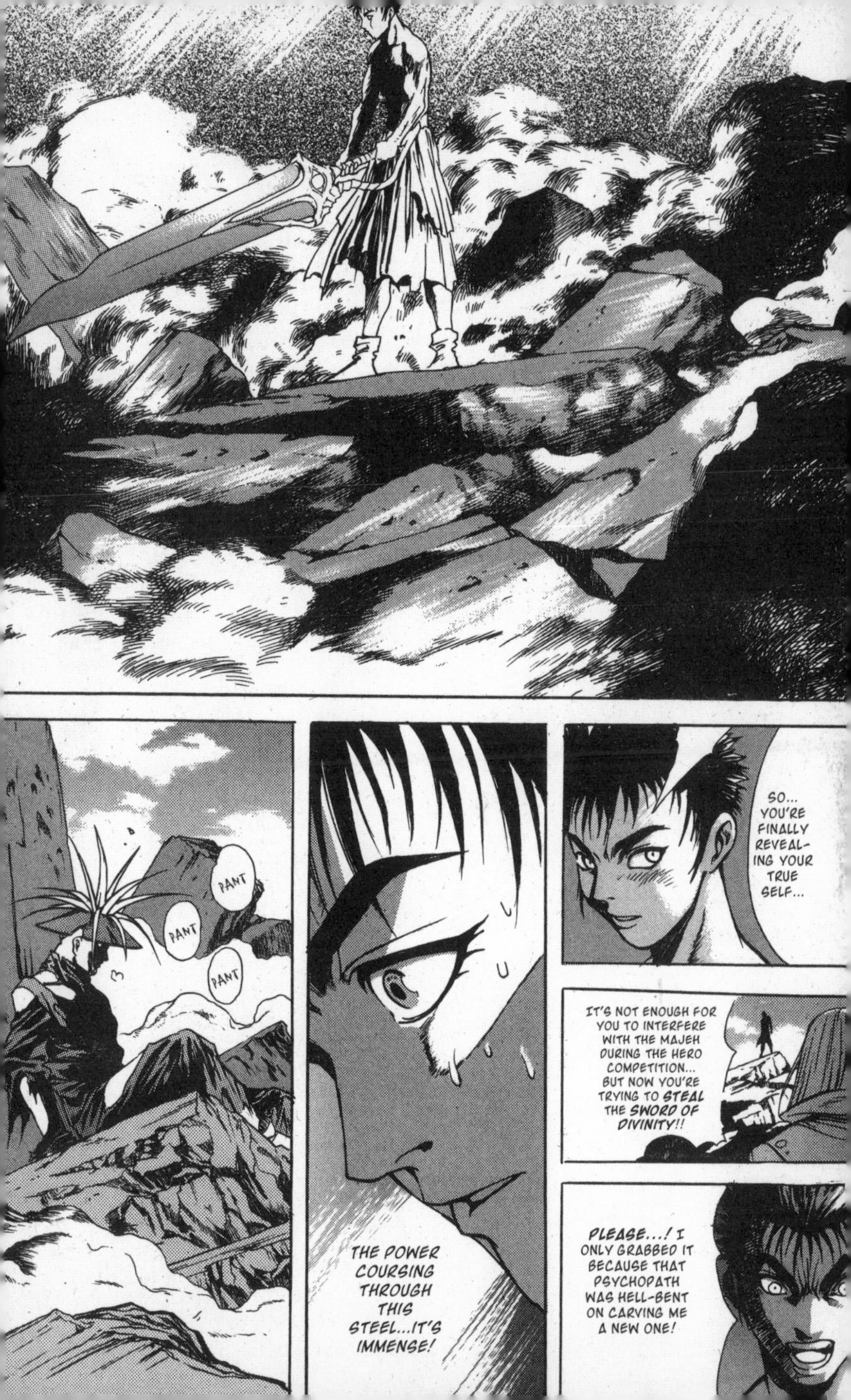
PANT
PANT
PANT
THE POWER COURSING THROUGH THIS STEEL...IT'S IMMENSE!
SO... YOU'RE FINALLY REVEALING YOUR TRUE SELF...
IT'S NOT ENOUGH FOR YOU TO INTERFERE WITH THE MAJEH DURING THE HERO COMPETITION... BUT NOW YOU'RE TRYING TO STEAL THE SWORD OF DIVINITY!!
PLEASE...! I ONLY GRABBED IT BECAUSE THAT PSYCHOPATH WAS HELL-BENT ON CARVING ME A NEW ONE!

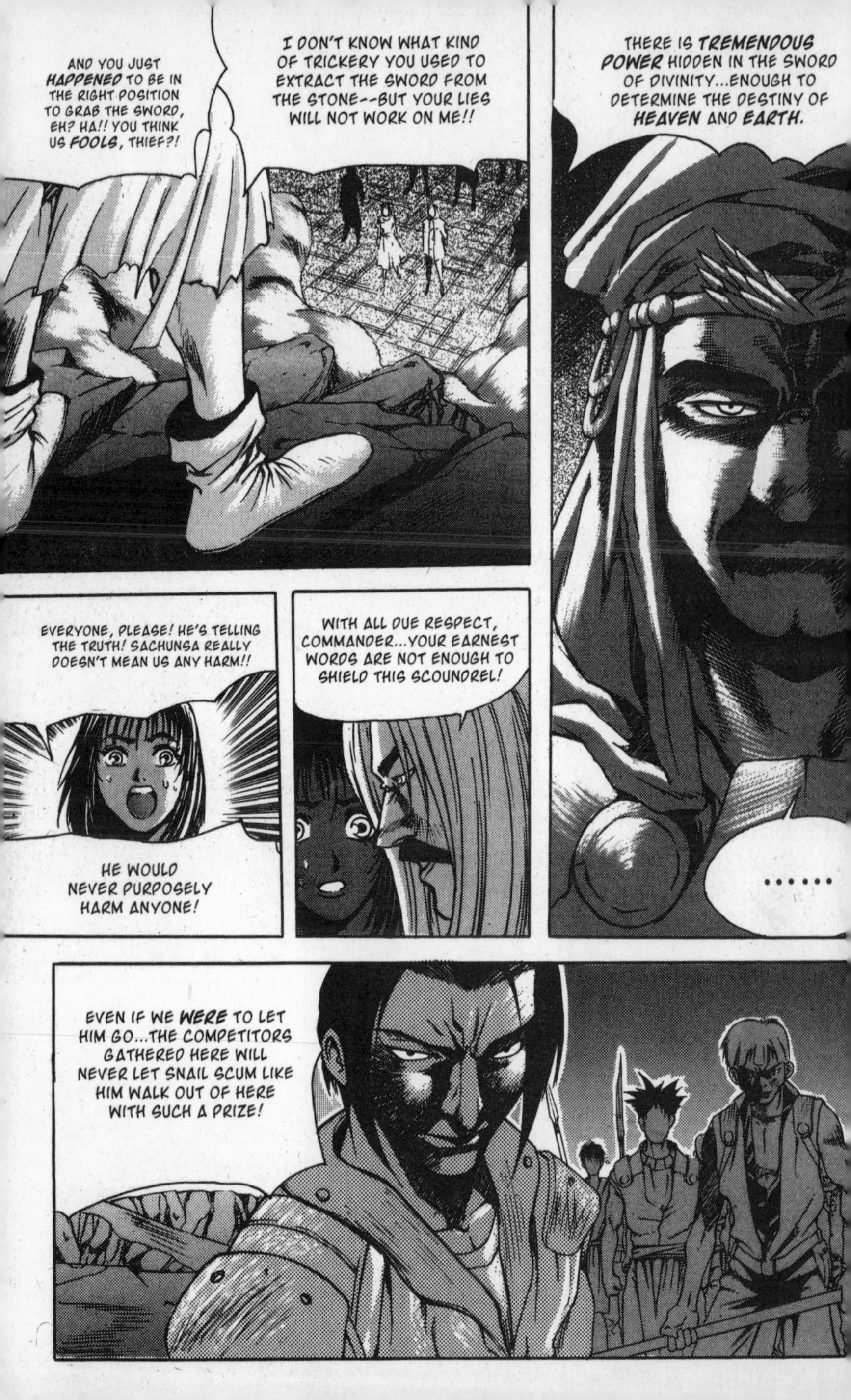
AND YOU JUST HAPPENED TO BE IN THE RIGHT POSITION TO GRAB THE SWORD, EH? HA!! YOU THINK US FOOLS, THIEF?!
I DON'T KNOW WHAT KIND OF TRICKERY YOU USED TO EXTRACT THE SWORD FROM THE STONE--BUT YOUR LIES WILL NOT WORK ON ME!!
THERE IS TREMENDOUS POWER HIDDEN IN THE SWORD OF DIVINITY...ENOUGH TO DETERMINE THE DESTINY OF HEAVEN AND EARTH.
EVERYONE, PLEASE! HE'S TELLING THE TRUTH! SACHUNSA REALLY DOESN'T MEAN US ANY HARM!!
HE WOULD NEVER PURPOSELY HARM ANYONE!
WITH ALL DUE RESPECT, COMMANDER...YOUR EARNEST WORDS ARE NOT ENOUGH TO SHIELD THIS SCOUNDREL!
......
EVEN IF WE WERE TO LET HIM GO...THE COMPETITORS GATHERED HERE WILL NEVER LET SNAIL SCUM LIKE HIM WALK OUT OF HERE WITH SUCH A PRIZE!

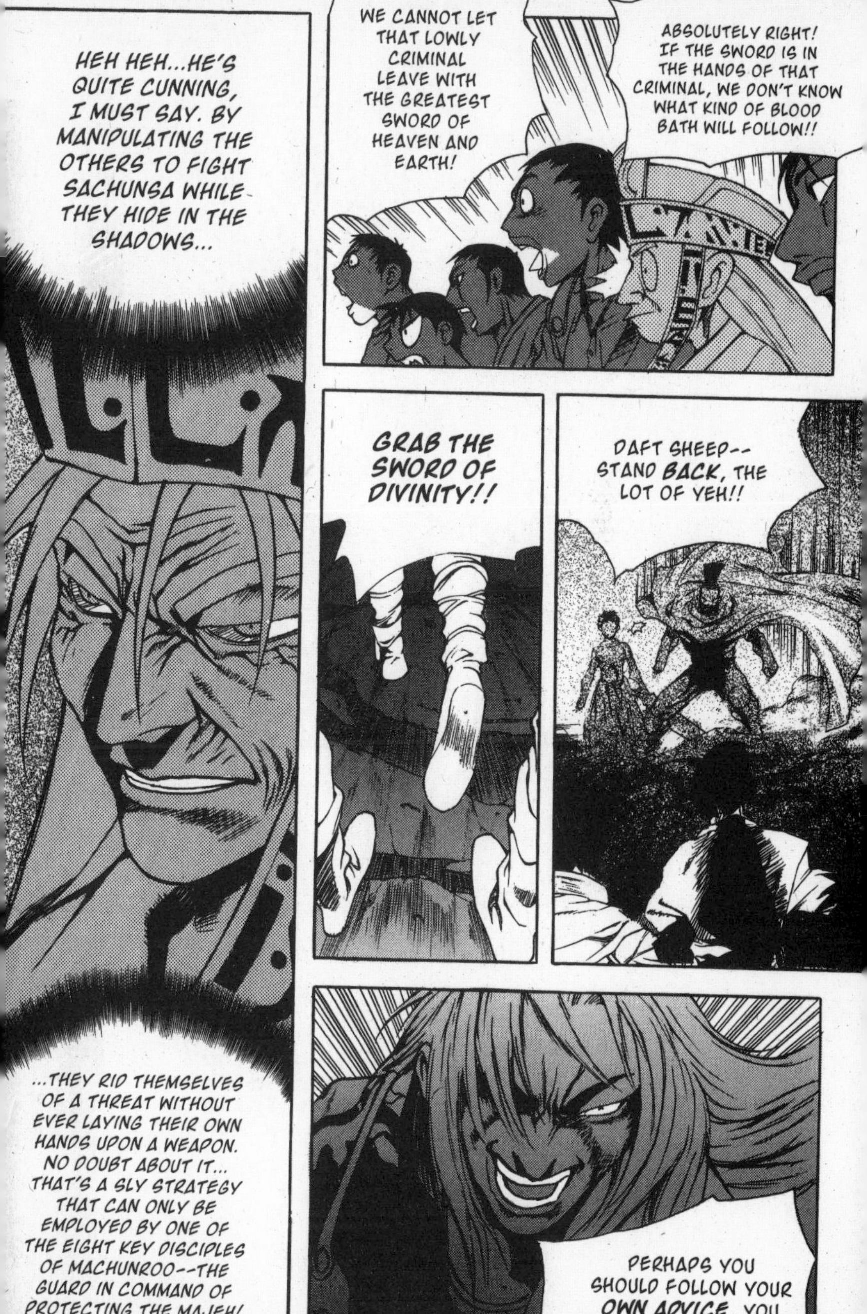
HEH HEH...HE'S QUITE CUNNING, I MUST SAY. BY MANIPULATING THE OTHERS TO FIGHT SACHUNSA WHILE THEY HIDE IN THE SHADOWS...
...THEY RID THEMSELVES OF A THREAT WITHOUT EVER LAYING THEIR OWN HANDS UPON A WEAPON. NO DOUBT ABOUT IT... THAT'S A SLY STRATEGY THAT CAN ONLY BE EMPLOYED BY ONE OF THE EIGHT KEY DISCIPLES OF MACHUNROO--THE GUARD IN COMMAND OF PROTECTING THE MAJEH!
WE CANNOT LET THAT LOWLY CRIMINAL LEAVE WITH THE GREATEST SWORD OF HEAVEN AND EARTH!
ABSOLUTELY RIGHT! IF THE SWORD IS IN THE HANDS OF THAT CRIMINAL, WE DON'T KNOW WHAT KIND OF BLOOD BATH WILL FOLLOW!!
GRAB THE SWORD OF DIVINITY!!
DAFT SHEEP--STAND BACK, THE LOT OF YEH!!
PERHAPS YOU SHOULD FOLLOW YOUR OWN ADVICE, YOU MEDDLESOME FOOL!!

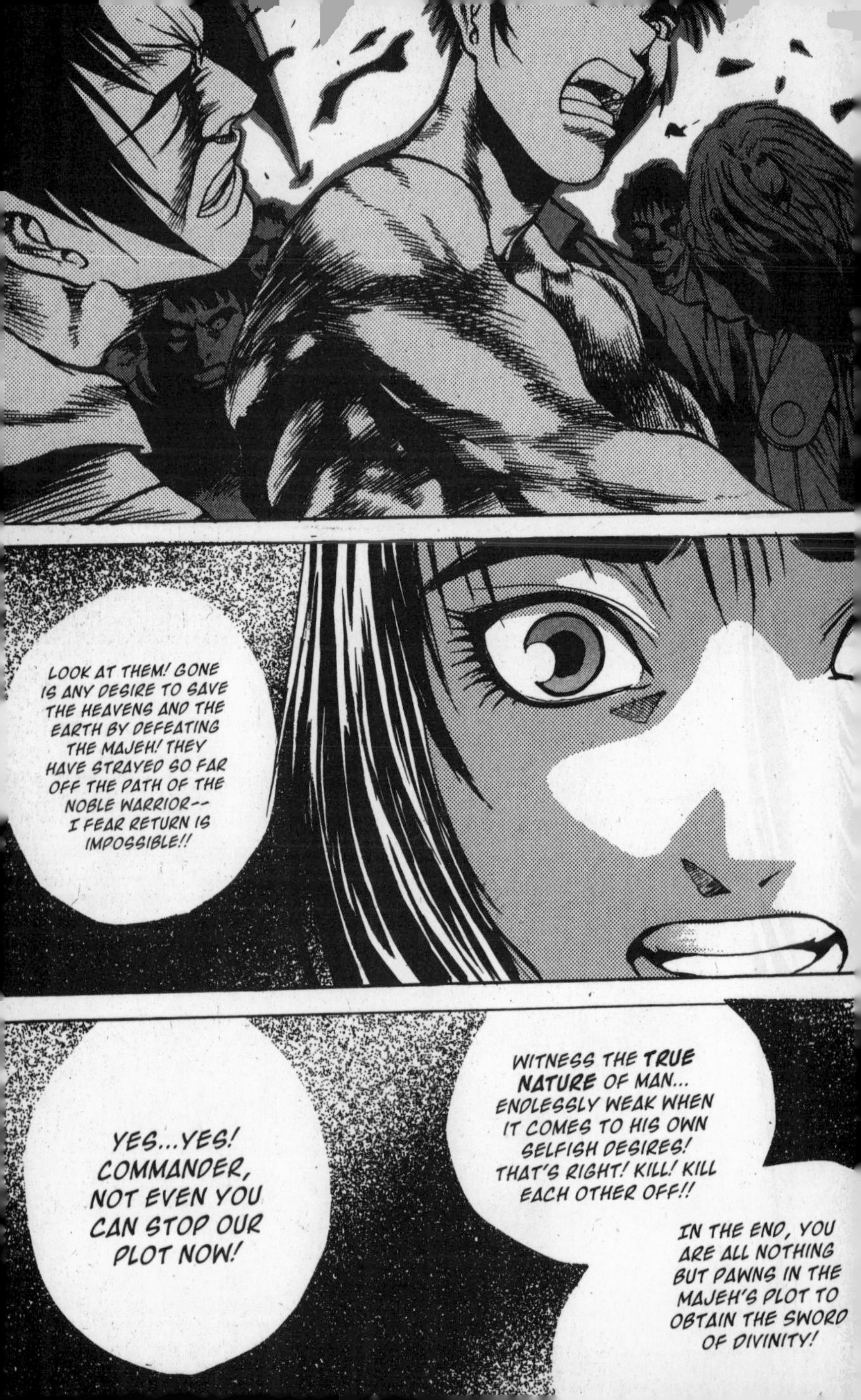
LOOK AT THEM! GONE IS ANY DESIRE TO SAVE THE HEAVENS AND THE EARTH BY DEFEATING THE MAJEH! THEY HAVE STRAYED SO FAR OFF THE PATH OF THE NOBLE WARRIOR-- I FEAR RETURN IS IMPOSSIBLE!!
WITNESS THE TRUE NATURE OF MAN... ENDLESSLY WEAK WHEN IT COMES TO HIS OWN SELFISH DESIRES! THAT'S RIGHT! KILL! KILL EACH OTHER OFF!!
IN THE END, YOU ARE ALL NOTHING BUT PAWNS IN THE MAJEH'S PLOT TO OBTAIN THE SWORD OF DIVINITY!
YES...YES! COMMANDER, NOT EVEN YOU CAN STOP OUR PLOT NOW!

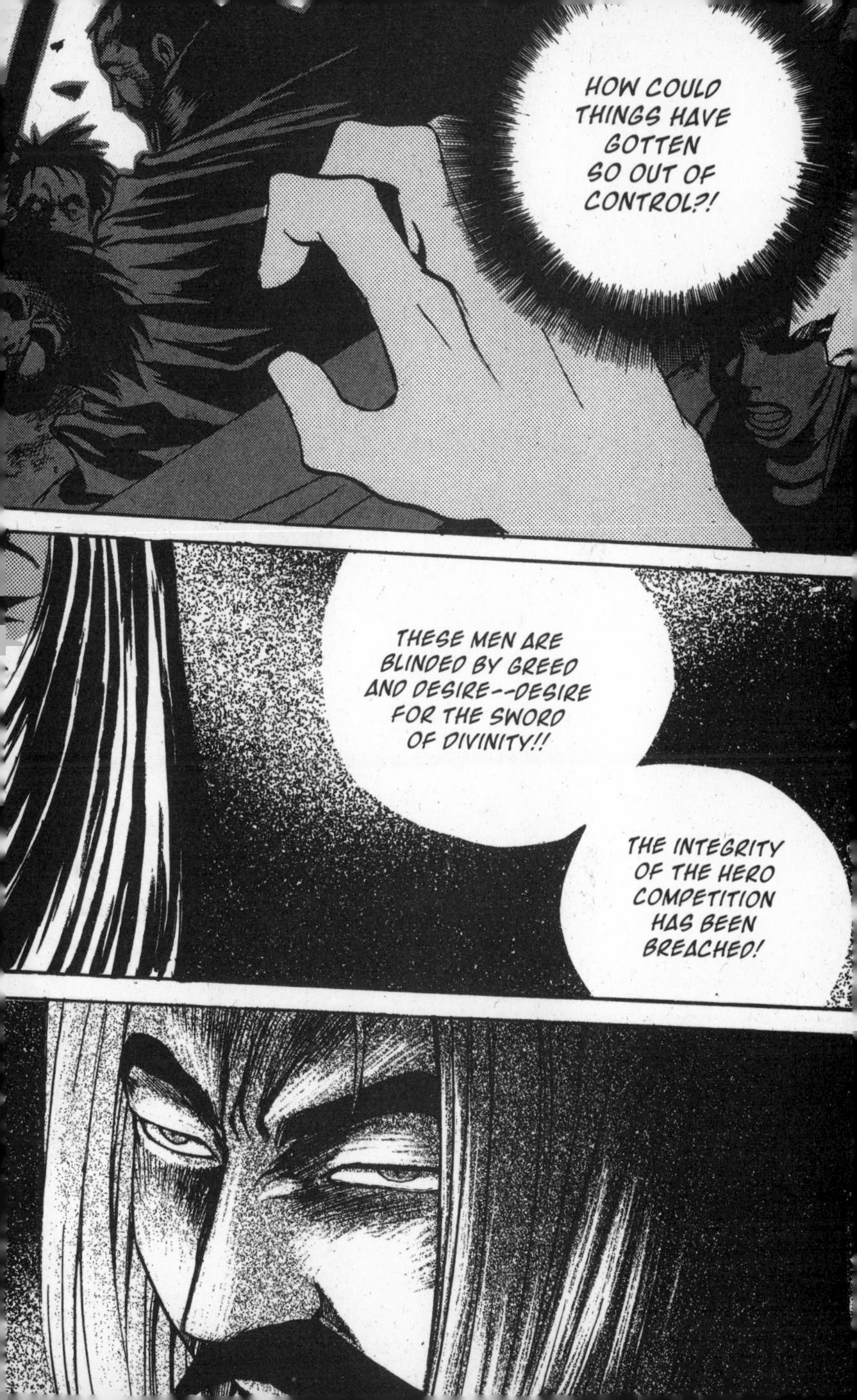
HOW COULD THINGS HAVE GOTTEN SO OUT OF CONTROL?!
THESE MEN ARE BLINDED BY GREED AND DESIRE--DESIRE FOR THE SWORD OF DIVINITY!!
THE INTEGRITY OF THE HERO COMPETITION HAS BEEN BREACHED!

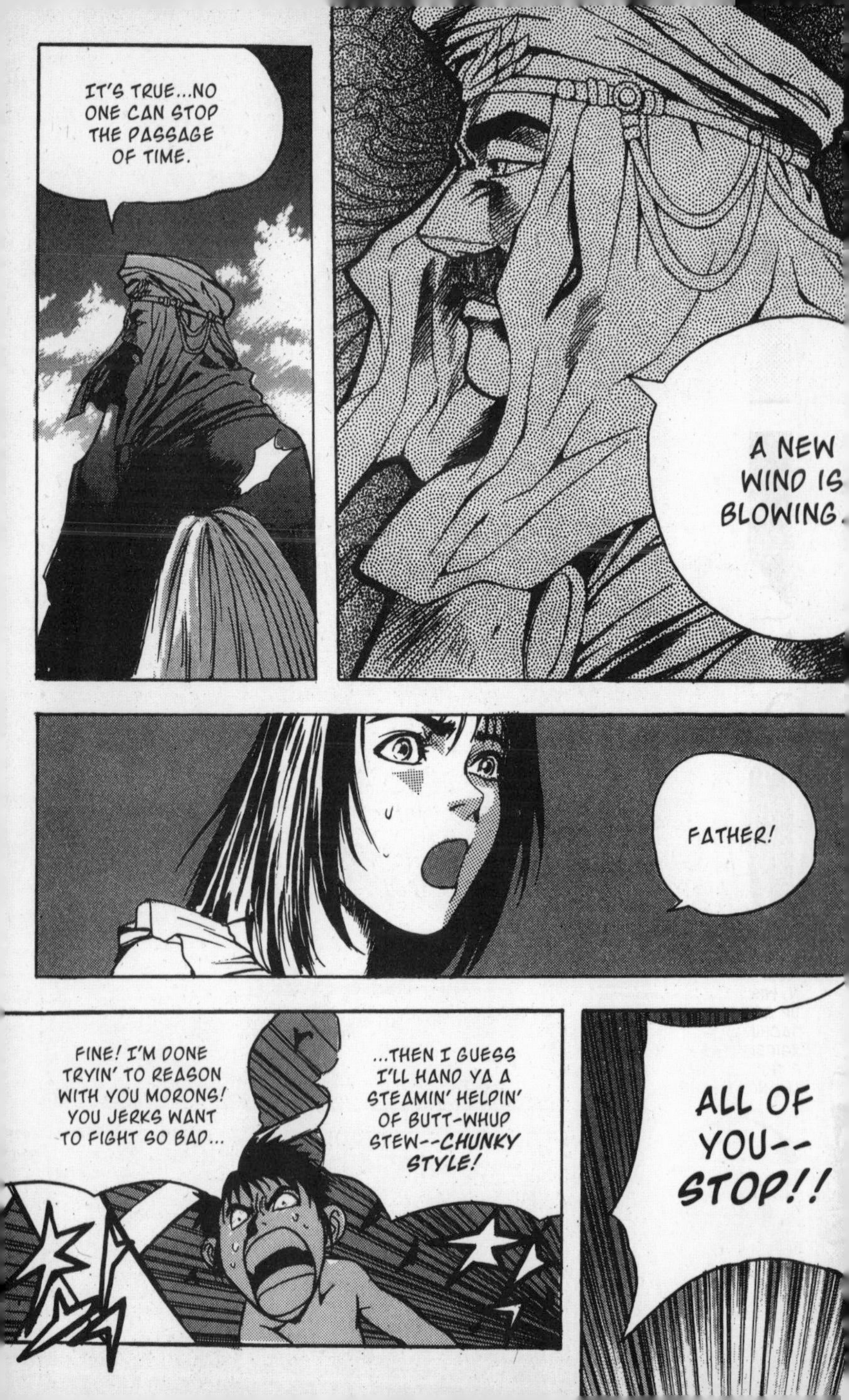
IT'S TRUE...NO ONE CAN STOP THE PASSAGE OF TIME.
A NEW WIND IS BLOWING.
FATHER!
FINE! I'M DONE TRYIN' TO REASON WITH YOU MORONS! YOU JERKS WANT TO FIGHT SO BAD...
...THEN I GUESS I'LL HAND YA A STEAMIN' HELPIN' OF BUTT-WHUP STEW--CHUNKY STYLE!
ALL OF YOU--STOP!!

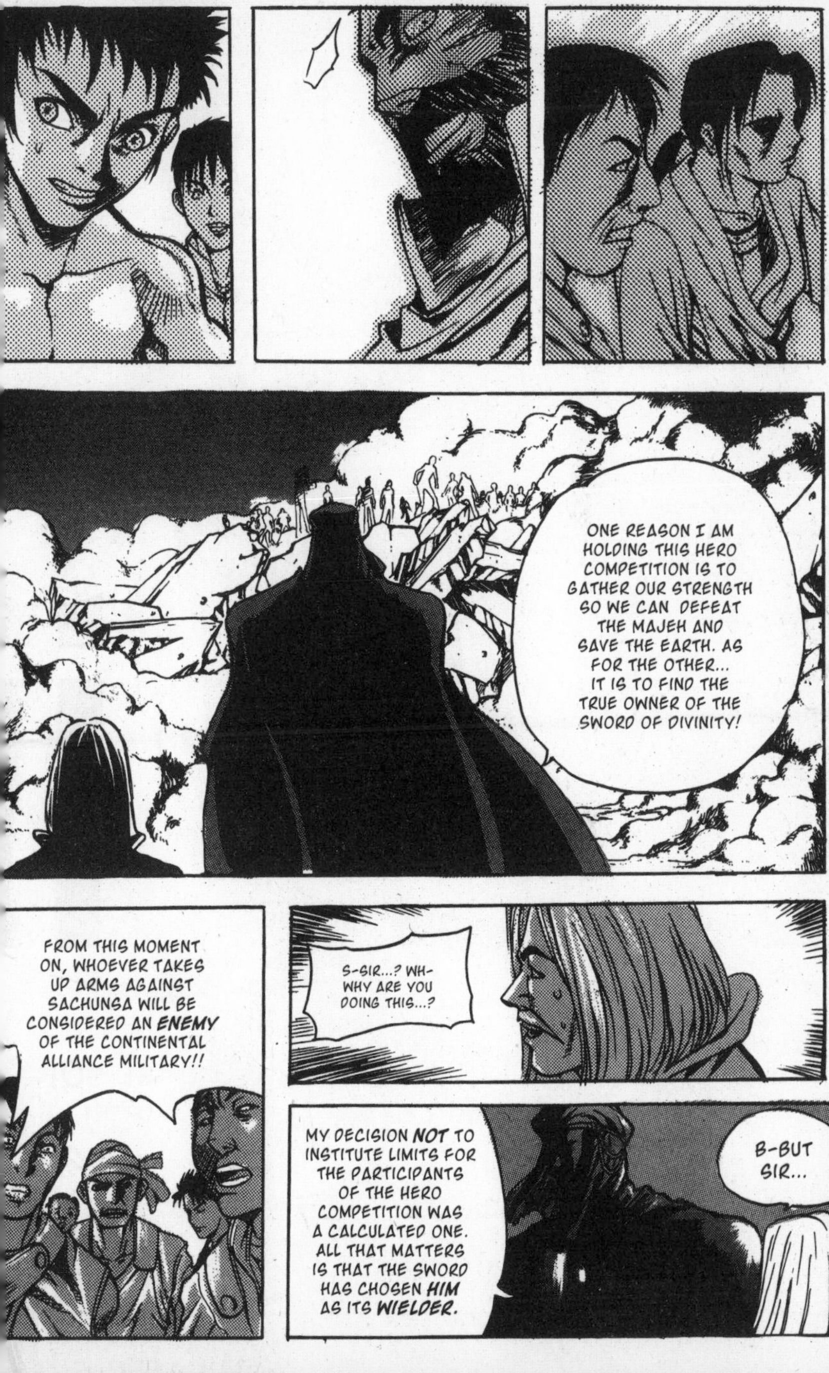
ONE REASON I AM HOLDING THIS HERO COMPETITION IS TO GATHER OUR STRENGTH SO WE CAN DEFEAT THE MAJEH AND SAVE THE EARTH. AS FOR THE OTHER... IT IS TO FIND THE TRUE OWNER OF THE SWORD OF DIVINITY!
FROM THIS MOMENT ON, WHOEVER TAKES UP ARMS AGAINST SACHUNSA WILL BE CONSIDERED AN ENEMY OF THE CONTINENTAL ALLIANCE MILITARY!!
S-SIR...? WH-WHY ARE YOU DOING THIS...?
MY DECISION NOT TO INSTITUTE LIMITS FOR THE PARTICIPANTS OF THE HERO COMPETITION WAS A CALCULATED ONE. ALL THAT MATTERS IS THAT THE SWORD HAS CHOSEN HIM AS ITS WIELDER.
B-BUT SIR...

...THE BOY'S IDENTITY HASN'T EVEN BEEN VERIFIED! IF THE SWORD WERE TO END UP IN THE HANDS OF THE MAJEH...!

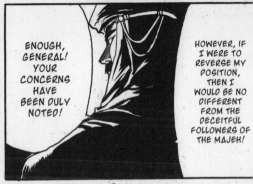

ENOUGH, GENERAL! YOUR CONCERNS HAVE BEEN DULY NOTED!

HOWEVER, IF I WERE TO REVERSE MY POSITION, THEN I WOULD BE NO DIFFERENT FROM THE DECEITFUL FOLLOWERS OF THE MAJEH!

DID YOU SAY YOUR NAME WAS... SACHUNSA?

......

BLADE OF HEAVEN

I drew this for no apparent reason...

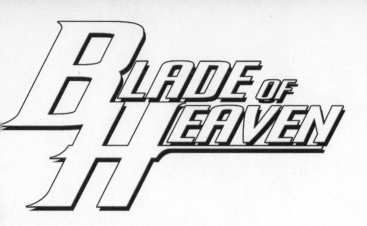

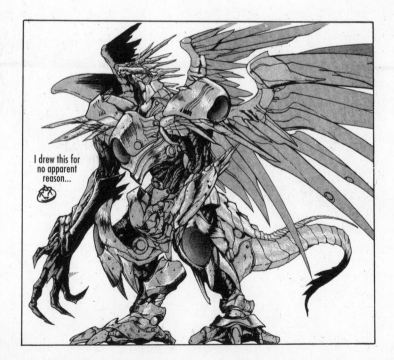

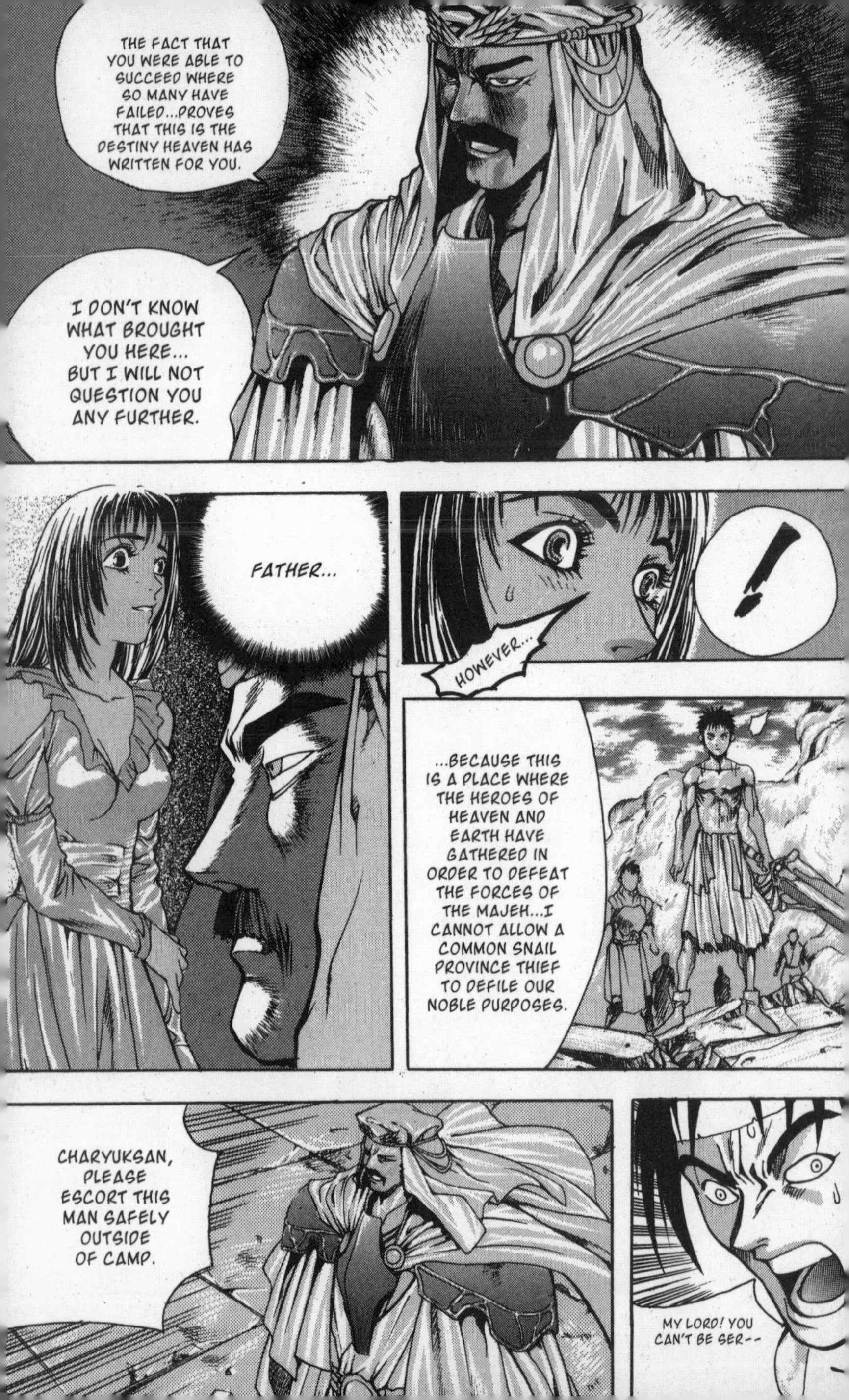
THE FACT THAT YOU WERE ABLE TO SUCCEED WHERE SO MANY HAVE FAILED...PROVES THAT THIS IS THE DESTINY HEAVEN HAS WRITTEN FOR YOU.
I DON'T KNOW WHAT BROUGHT YOU HERE... BUT I WILL NOT QUESTION YOU ANY FURTHER.
FATHER...
!
HOWEVER...
...BECAUSE THIS IS A PLACE WHERE THE HEROES OF HEAVEN AND EARTH HAVE GATHERED IN ORDER TO DEFEAT THE FORCES OF THE MAJEH...I CANNOT ALLOW A COMMON SNAIL PROVINCE THIEF TO DEFILE OUR NOBLE PURPOSES.
CHARYUKSAN, PLEASE ESCORT THIS MAN SAFELY OUTSIDE OF CAMP.
MY LORD! YOU CAN'T BE SER--

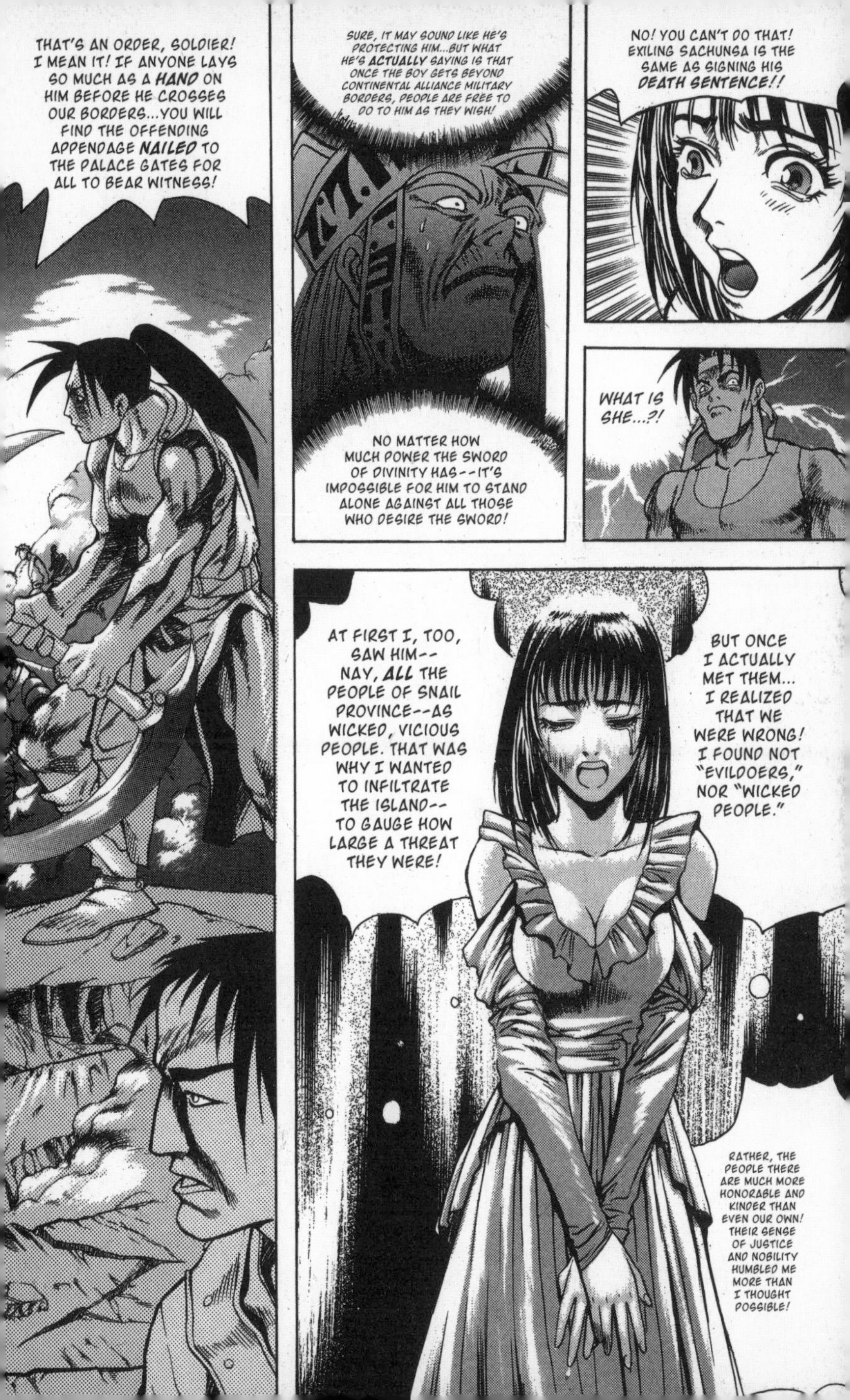
THAT'S AN ORDER, SOLDIER! I MEAN IT! IF ANYONE LAYS SO MUCH AS A HAND ON HIM BEFORE HE CROSSES OUR BORDERS...YOU WILL FIND THE OFFENDING APPENDAGE NAILED TO THE PALACE GATES FOR ALL TO BEAR WITNESS!
SURE, IT MAY SOUND LIKE HE'S PROTECTING HIM...BUT WHAT HE'S ACTUALLY SAYING IS THAT ONCE THE BOY GETS BEYOND CONTINENTAL ALLIANCE MILITARY BORDERS, PEOPLE ARE FREE TO DO TO HIM AS THEY WISH!
NO MATTER HOW MUCH POWER THE SWORD OF DIVINITY HAS--IT'S IMPOSSIBLE FOR HIM TO STAND ALONE AGAINST ALL THOSE WHO DESIRE THE SWORD!
NO! YOU CAN'T DO THAT! EXILING SACHUNSA IS THE SAME AS SIGNING HIS DEATH SENTENCE!!
WHAT IS SHE...?!
AT FIRST I, TOO, SAW HIM--NAY, ALL THE PEOPLE OF SNAIL PROVINCE--AS WICKED, VICIOUS PEOPLE. THAT WAS WHY I WANTED TO INFILTRATE THE ISLAND--TO GAUGE HOW LARGE A THREAT THEY WERE!
BUT ONCE I ACTUALLY MET THEM... I REALIZED THAT WE WERE WRONG! I FOUND NOT "EVILDOERS," NOR "WICKED PEOPLE."
RATHER, THE PEOPLE THERE ARE MUCH MORE HONORABLE AND KINDER THAN EVEN OUR OWN! THEIR SENSE OF JUSTICE AND NOBILITY HUMBLED ME MORE THAN I THOUGHT POSSIBLE!

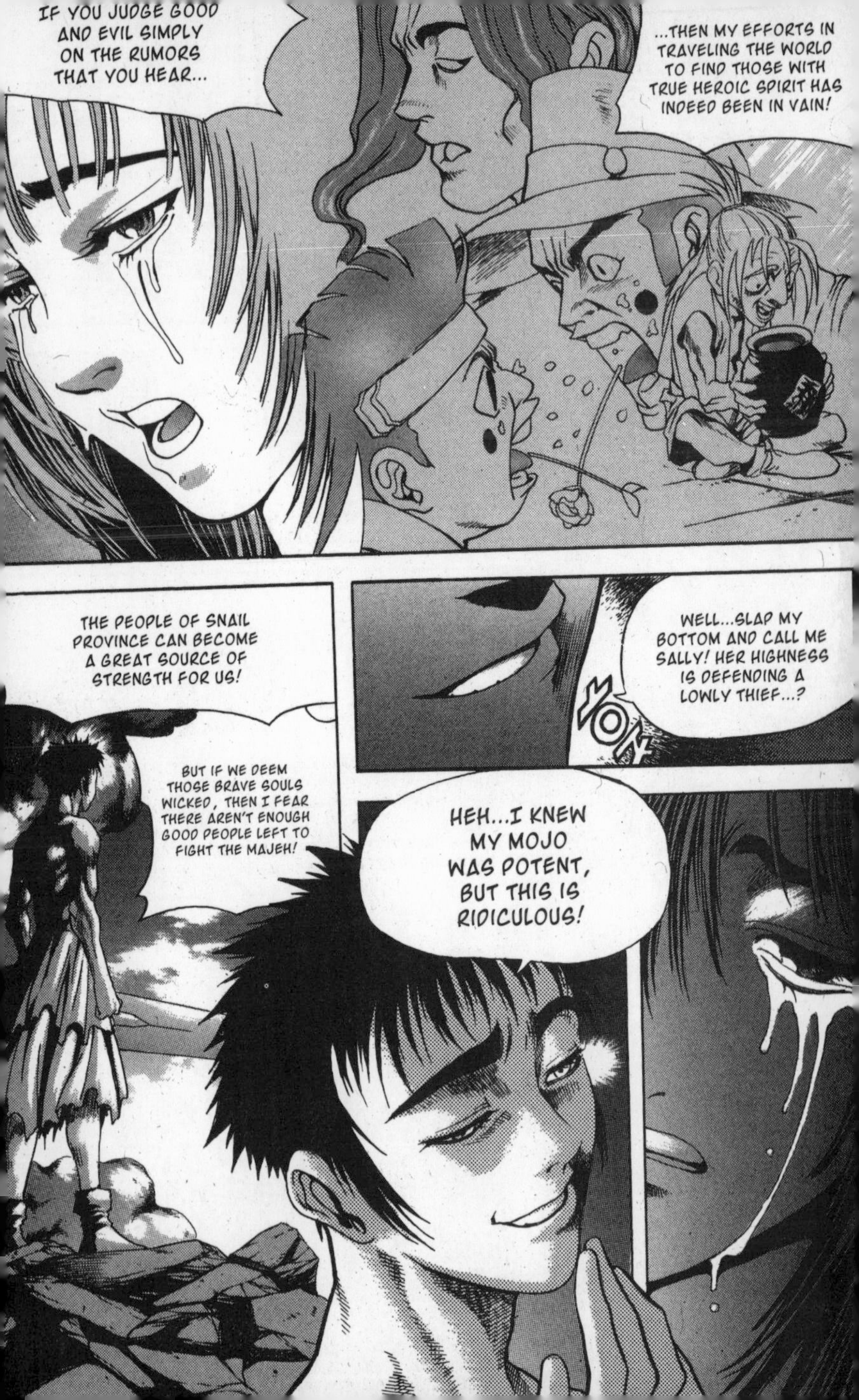
IF YOU JUDGE GOOD AND EVIL SIMPLY ON THE RUMORS THAT YOU HEAR...
...THEN MY EFFORTS IN TRAVELING THE WORLD TO FIND THOSE WITH TRUE HEROIC SPIRIT HAS INDEED BEEN IN VAIN!
THE PEOPLE OF SNAIL PROVINCE CAN BECOME A GREAT SOURCE OF STRENGTH FOR US!
BUT IF WE DEEM THOSE BRAVE SOULS WICKED, THEN I FEAR THERE AREN'T ENOUGH GOOD PEOPLE LEFT TO FIGHT THE MAJEH!
WELL...SLAP MY BOTTOM AND CALL ME SALLY! HER HIGHNESS IS DEFENDING A LOWLY THIEF...?
YOK
HEH...I KNEW MY MOJO WAS POTENT, BUT THIS IS RIDICULOUS!

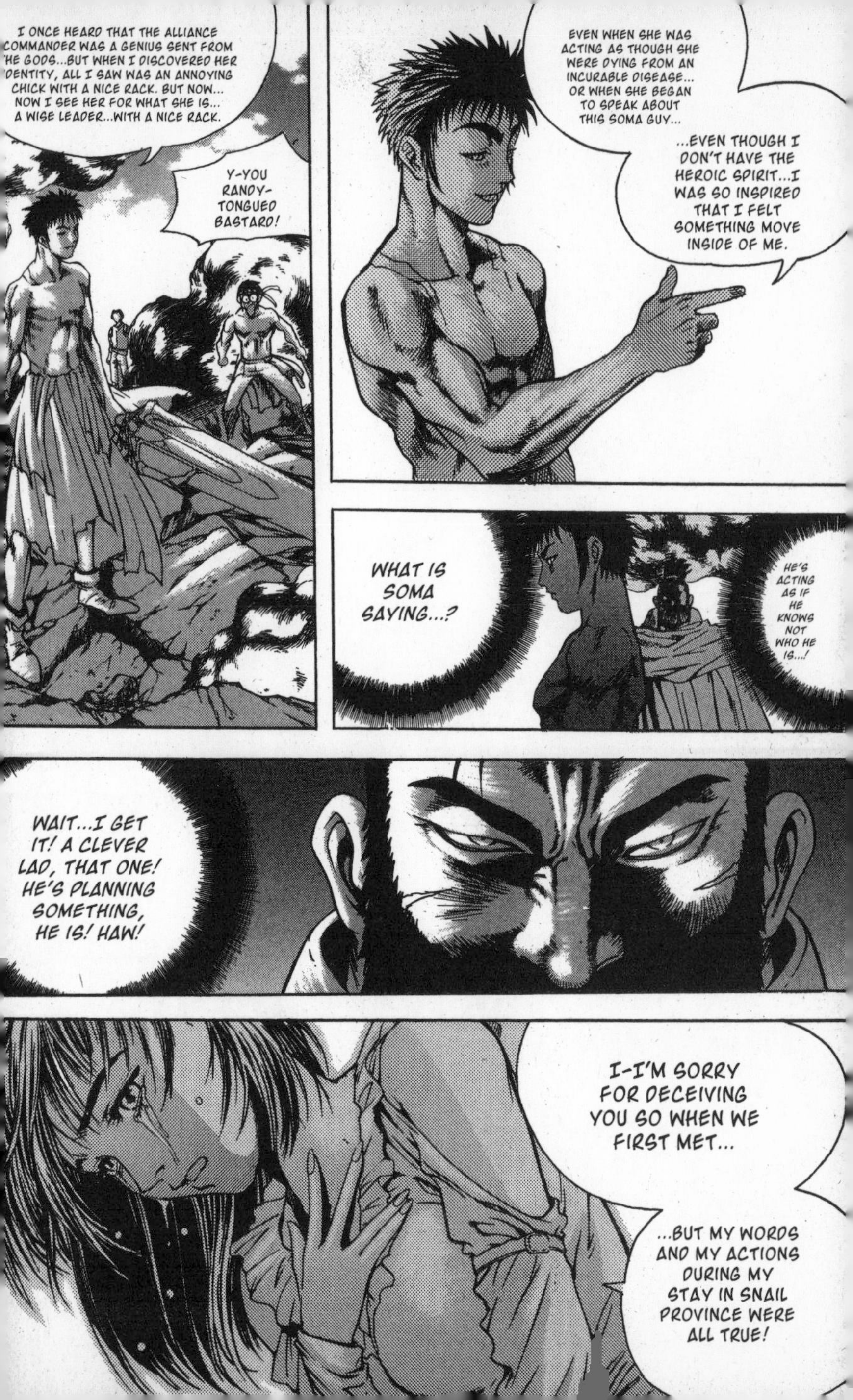
I ONCE HEARD THAT THE ALLIANCE COMMANDER WAS A GENIUS SENT FROM THE GODS...BUT WHEN I DISCOVERED HER IDENTITY, ALL I SAW WAS AN ANNOYING CHICK WITH A NICE RACK. BUT NOW... NOW I SEE HER FOR WHAT SHE IS... A WISE LEADER...WITH A NICE RACK.
Y-YOU RANDY-TONGUED BASTARD!
EVEN WHEN SHE WAS ACTING AS THOUGH SHE WERE DYING FROM AN INCURABLE DISEASE... OR WHEN SHE BEGAN TO SPEAK ABOUT THIS SOMA GUY...
...EVEN THOUGH I DON'T HAVE THE HEROIC SPIRIT...I WAS SO INSPIRED THAT I FELT SOMETHING MOVE INSIDE OF ME.
WHAT IS SOMA SAYING...?
HE'S ACTING AS IF HE KNOWS NOT WHO HE IS...!
WAIT...I GET IT! A CLEVER LAD, THAT ONE! HE'S PLANNING SOMETHING, HE IS! HAW!
I-I'M SORRY FOR DECEIVING YOU SO WHEN WE FIRST MET...
...BUT MY WORDS AND MY ACTIONS DURING MY STAY IN SNAIL PROVINCE WERE ALL TRUE!

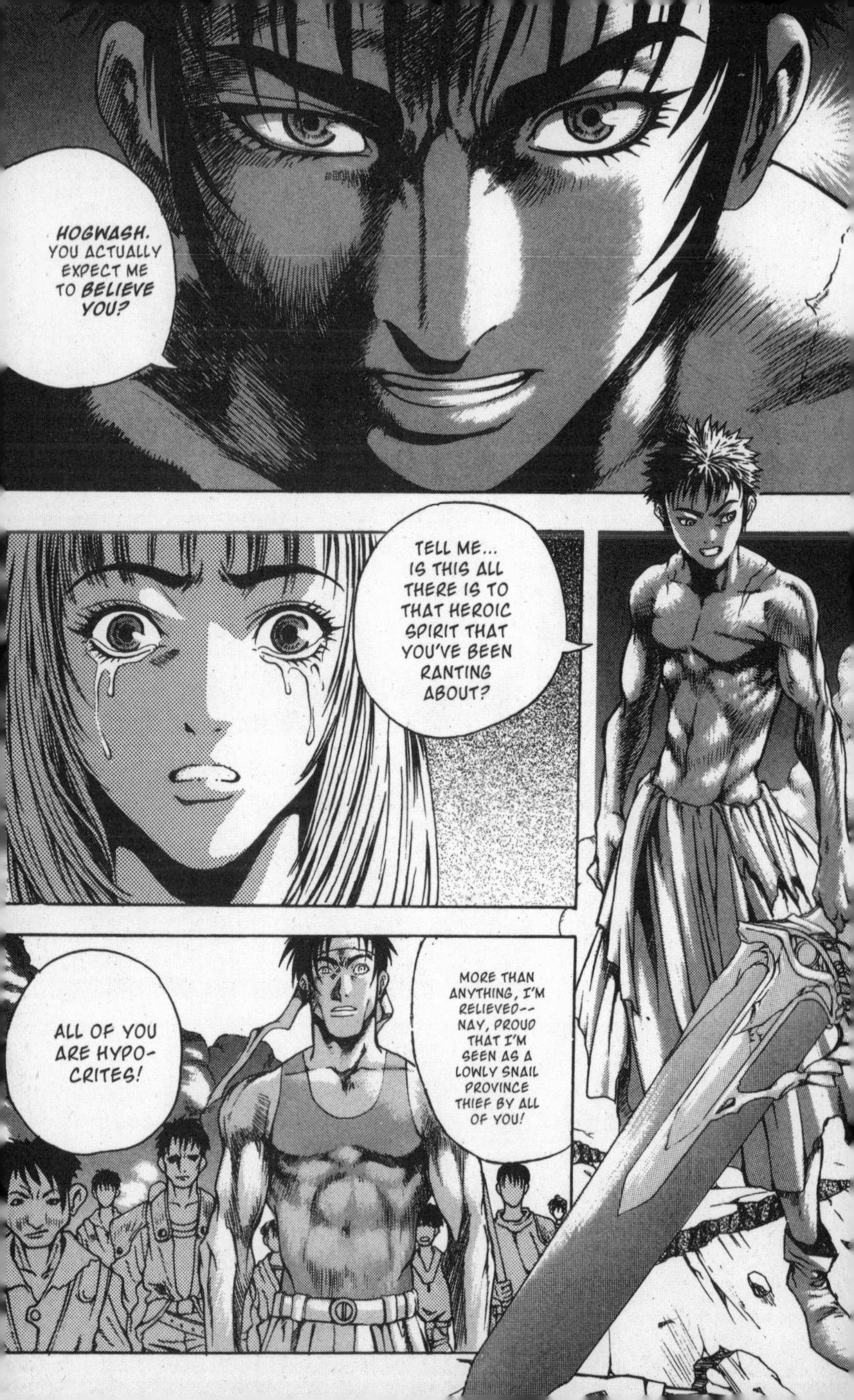
HOGWASH. YOU ACTUALLY EXPECT ME TO BELIEVE YOU?
TELL ME... IS THIS ALL THERE IS TO THAT HEROIC SPIRIT THAT YOU'VE BEEN RANTING ABOUT?
MORE THAN ANYTHING, I'M RELIEVED-- NAY, PROUD THAT I'M SEEN AS A LOWLY SNAIL PROVINCE THIEF BY ALL OF YOU!
ALL OF YOU ARE HYPO-CRITES!

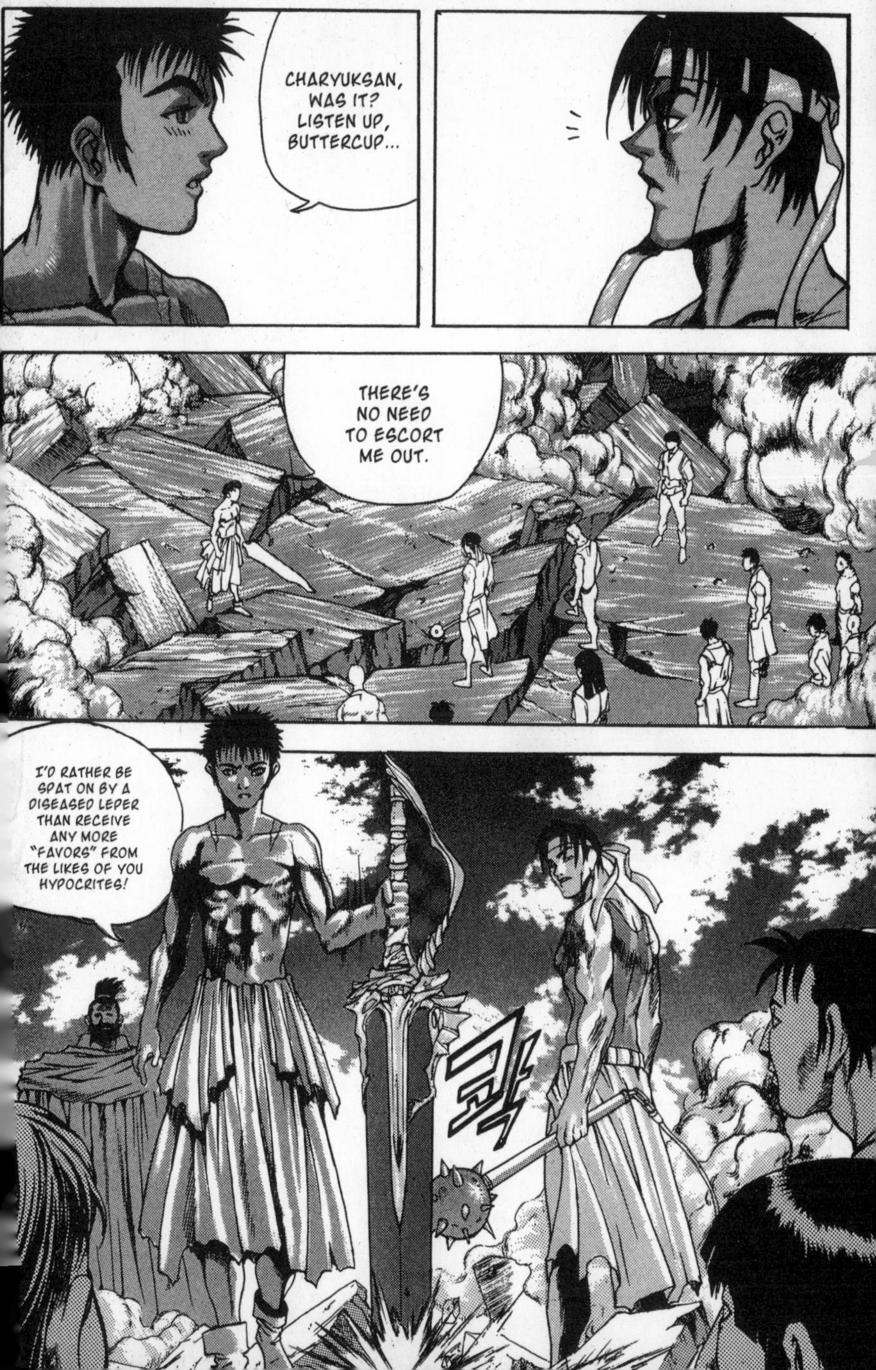
CHARYUKSAN, WAS IT? LISTEN UP, BUTTERCUP...
THERE'S NO NEED TO ESCORT ME OUT.
I'D RATHER BE SPAT ON BY A DISEASED LEPER THAN RECEIVE ANY MORE "FAVORS" FROM THE LIKES OF YOU HYPOCRITES!

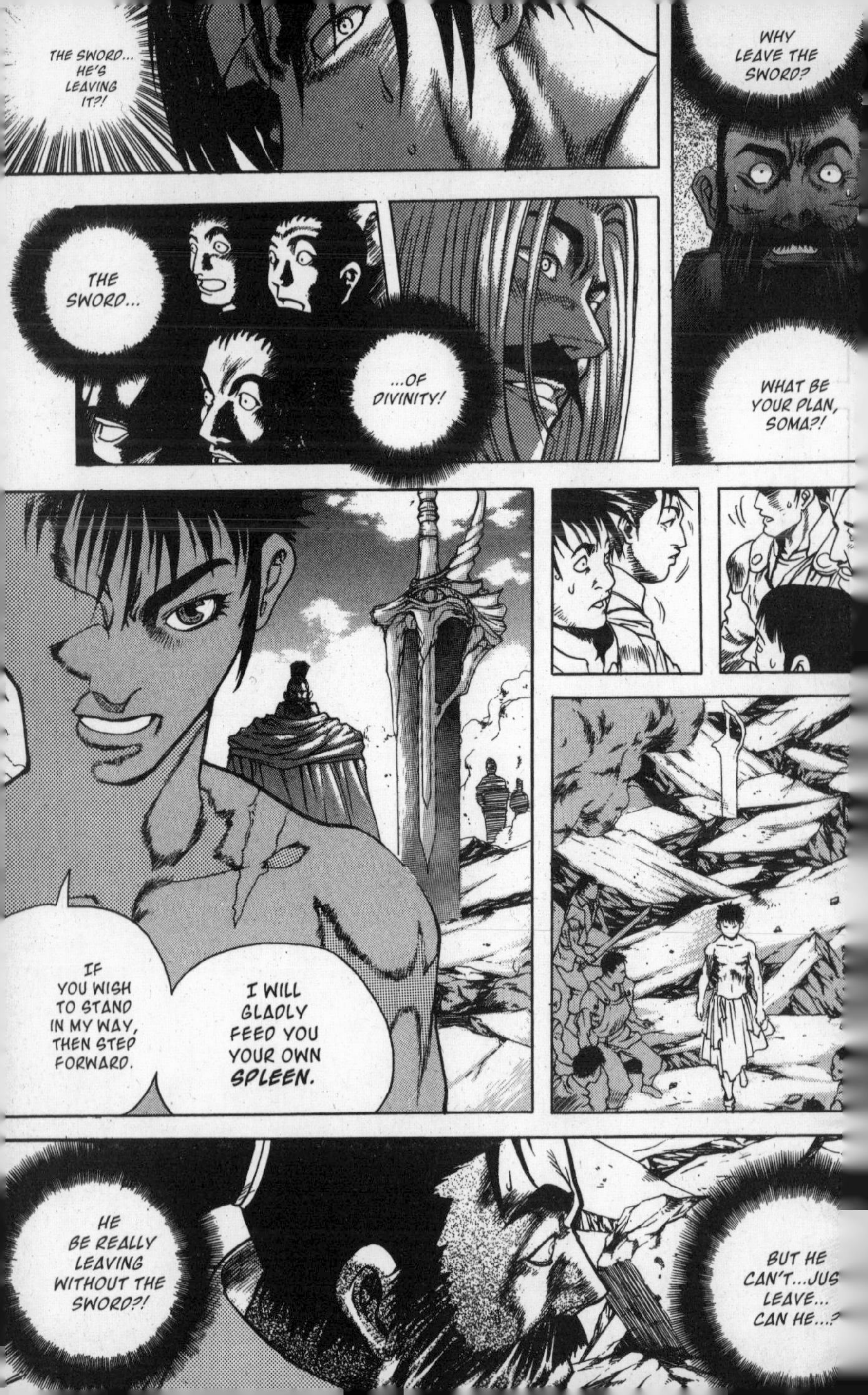
THE SWORD... HE'S LEAVING IT?!
WHY LEAVE THE SWORD?
THE SWORD...
...OF DIVINITY!
WHAT BE YOUR PLAN, SOMA?!
IF YOU WISH TO STAND IN MY WAY, THEN STEP FORWARD.
I WILL GLADLY FEED YOU YOUR OWN SPLEEN.
HE BE REALLY LEAVING WITHOUT THE SWORD?!
BUT HE CAN'T...JUS LEAVE... CAN HE...?

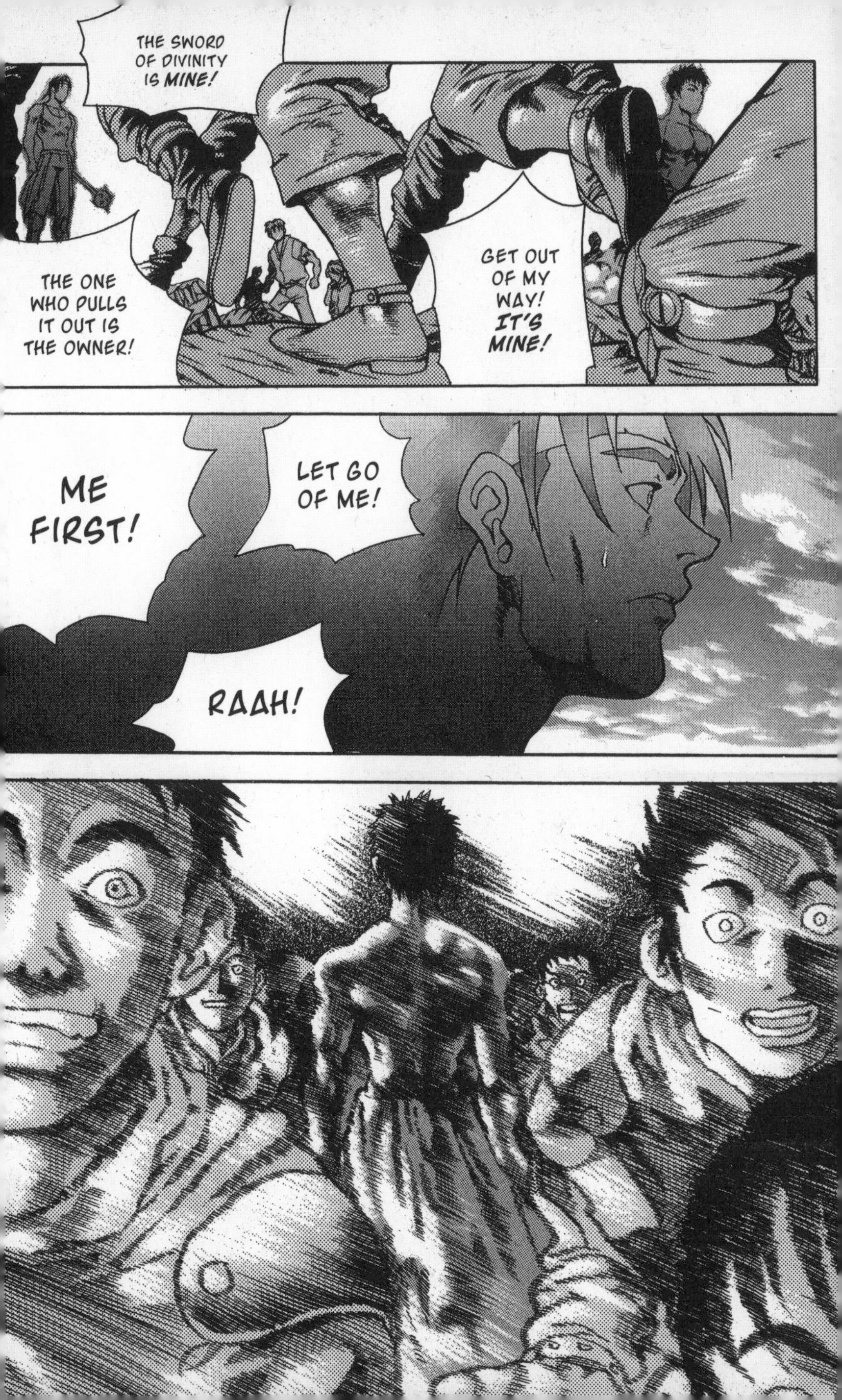
THE SWORD OF DIVINITY IS MINE!
THE ONE WHO PULLS IT OUT IS THE OWNER!
GET OUT OF MY WAY! IT'S MINE!
ME FIRST!
LET GO OF ME!
RAAH!

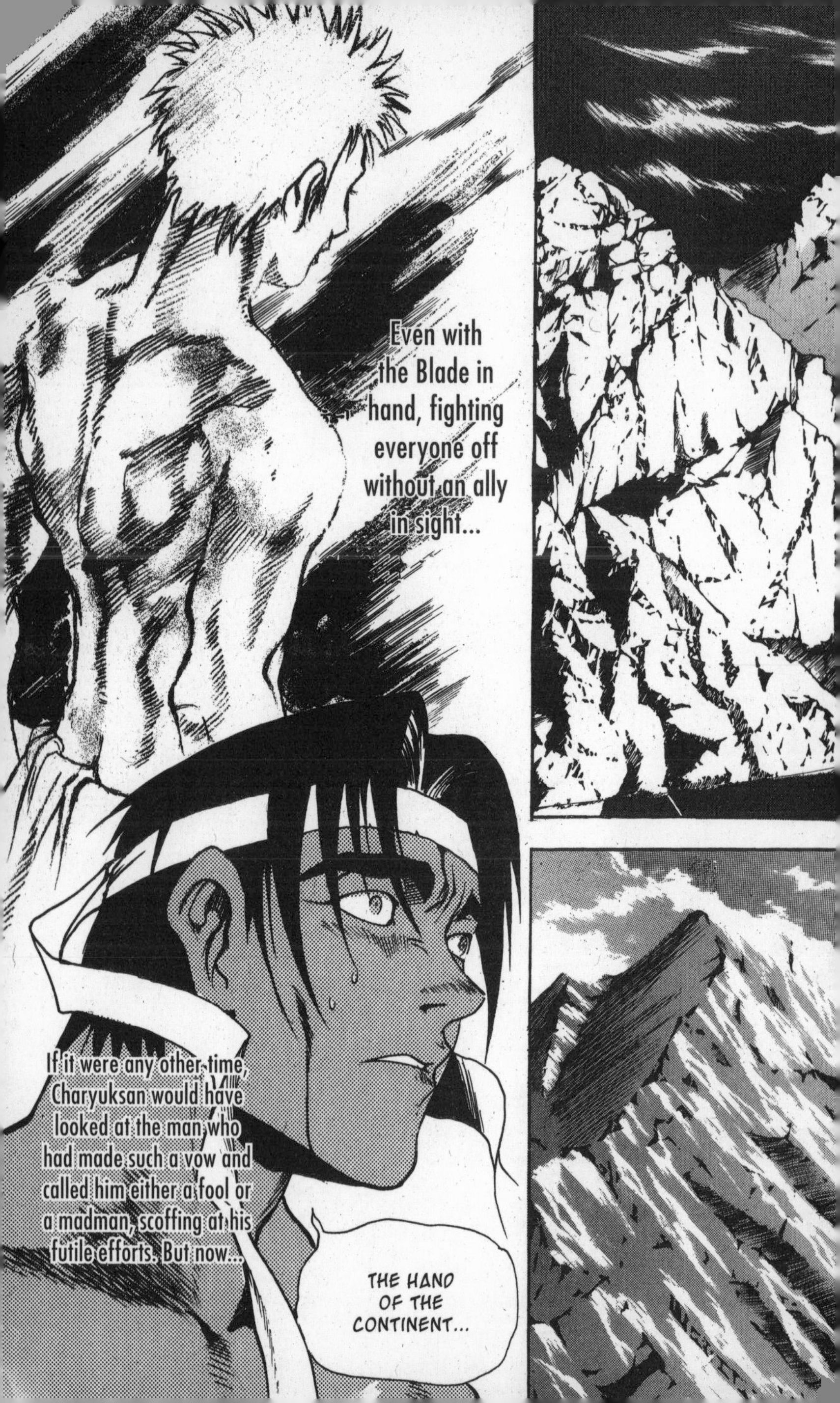
Even with the Blade in hand, fighting everyone off without an ally in sight...
If it were any other time, Charyuksan would have looked at the man who had made such a vow and called him either a fool or a madman, scoffing at his futile efforts. But now...
THE HAND OF THE CONTINENT...

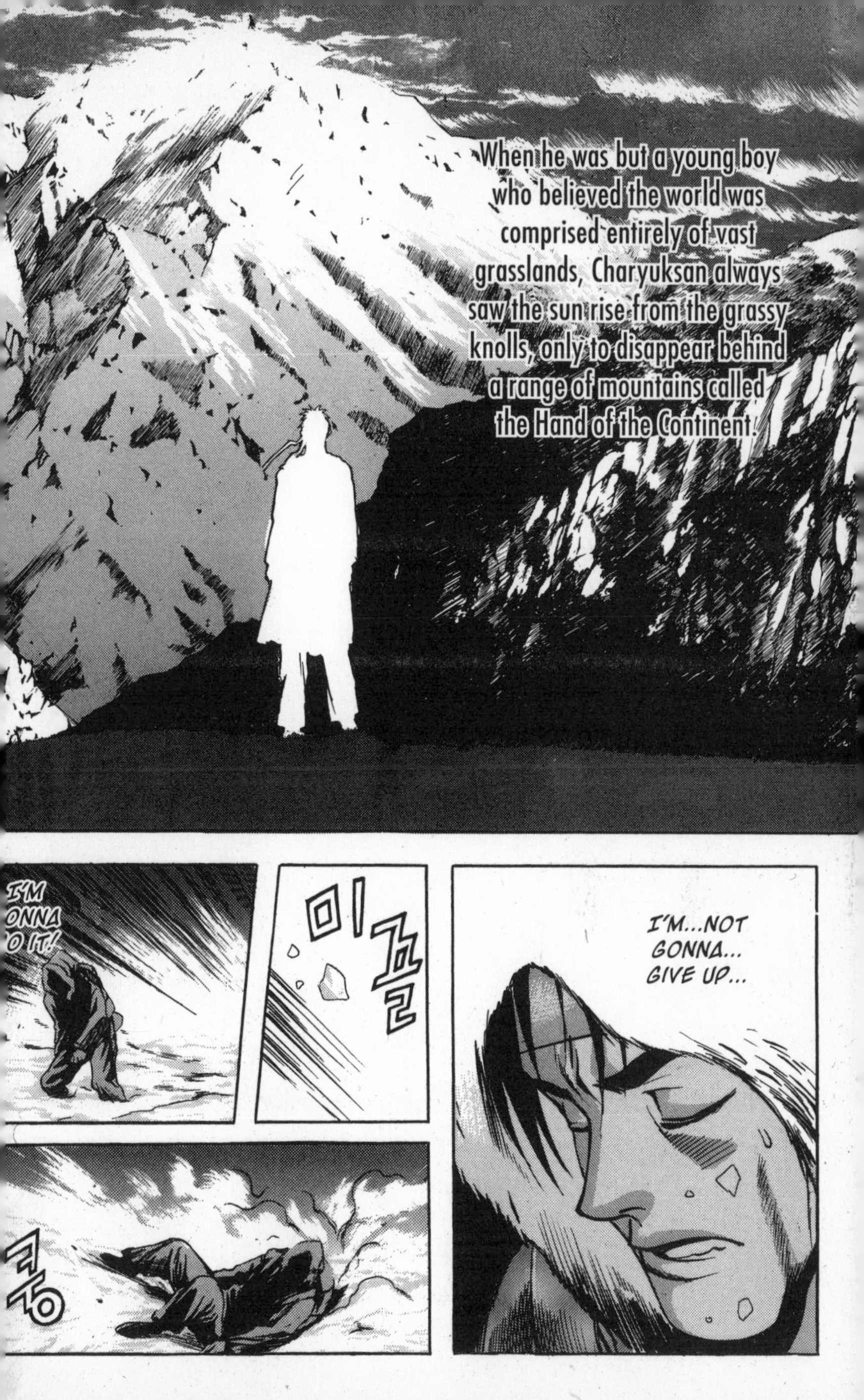
When he was but a young boy who believed the world was comprised entirely of vast grasslands, Charyuksan always saw the sun rise from the grassy knolls, only to disappear behind a range of mountains called the Hand of the Continent.
I'M
ONNA
O IT!
미끌
I'M...NOT GONNA... GIVE UP...

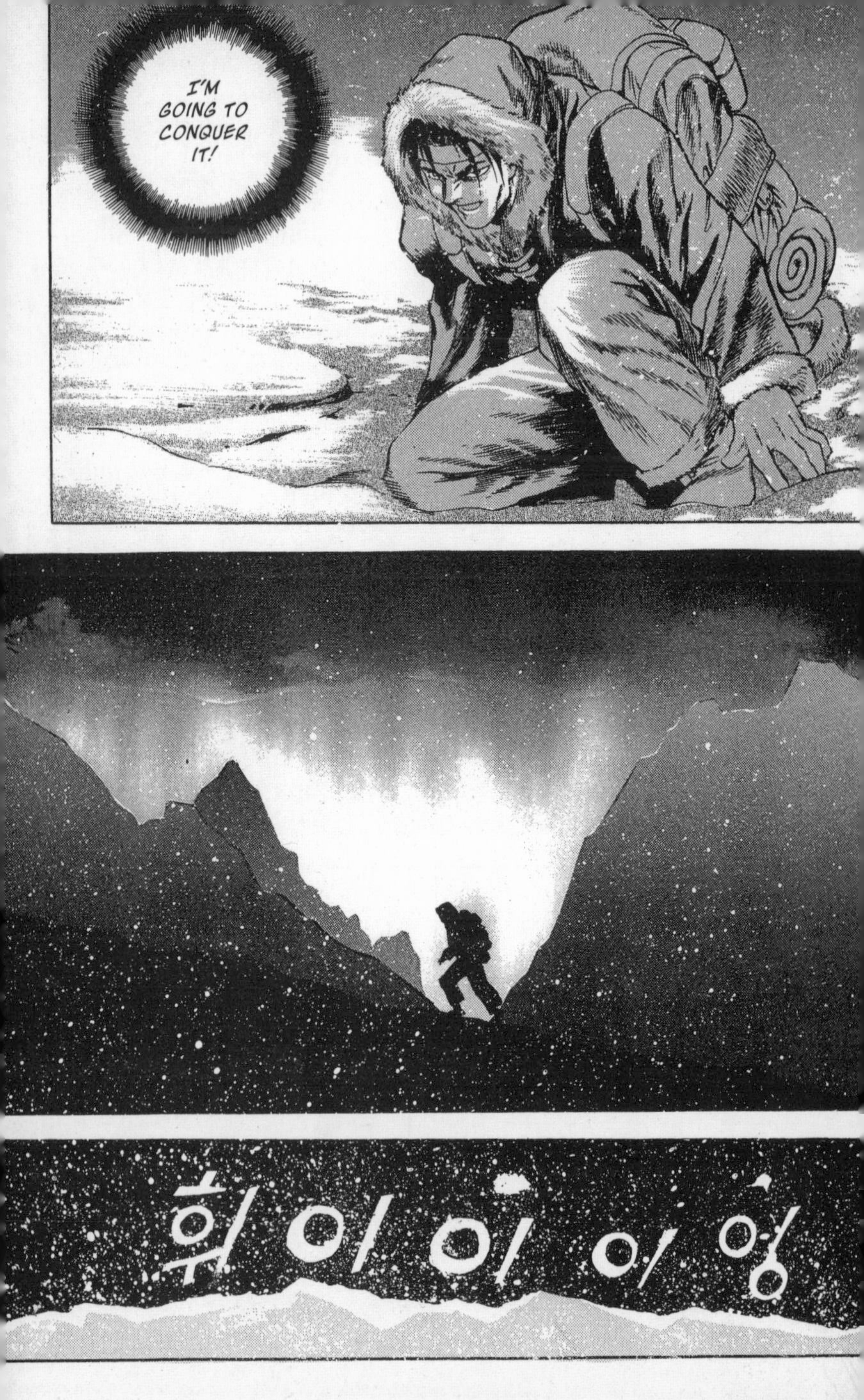
I'M GOING TO CONQUER IT!
휘이이이잉

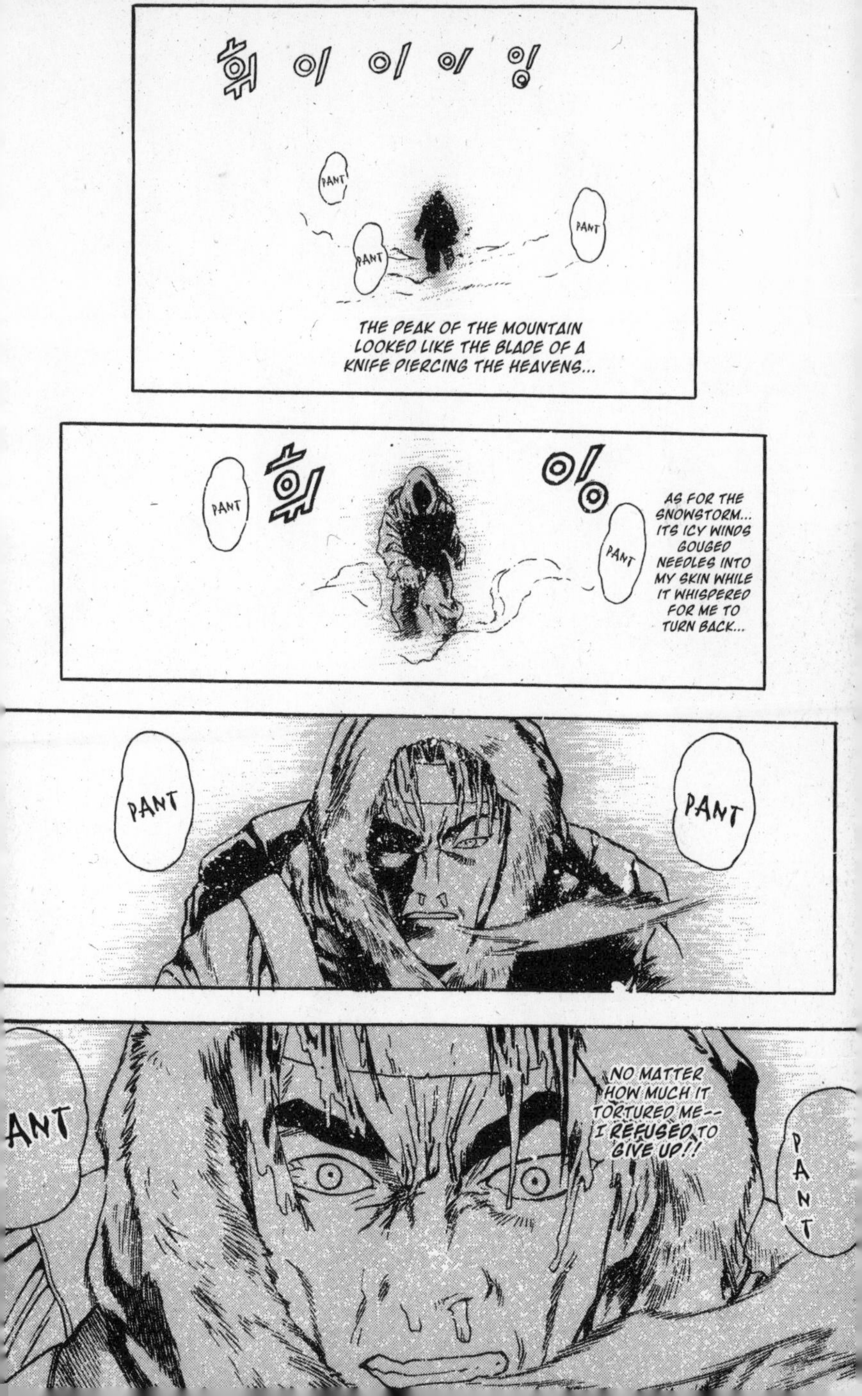

휘 이 이 이 잉
PANT
PANT
PANT
THE PEAK OF THE MOUNTAIN LOOKED LIKE THE BLADE OF A KNIFE PIERCING THE HEAVENS...
PANT
휘 잉
PANT
AS FOR THE SNOWSTORM... ITS ICY WINDS GOUGED NEEDLES INTO MY SKIN WHILE IT WHISPERED FOR ME TO TURN BACK...
PANT
PANT
ANT
NO MATTER HOW MUCH IT TORTURED ME-- I REFUSED TO GIVE UP!!
PANT

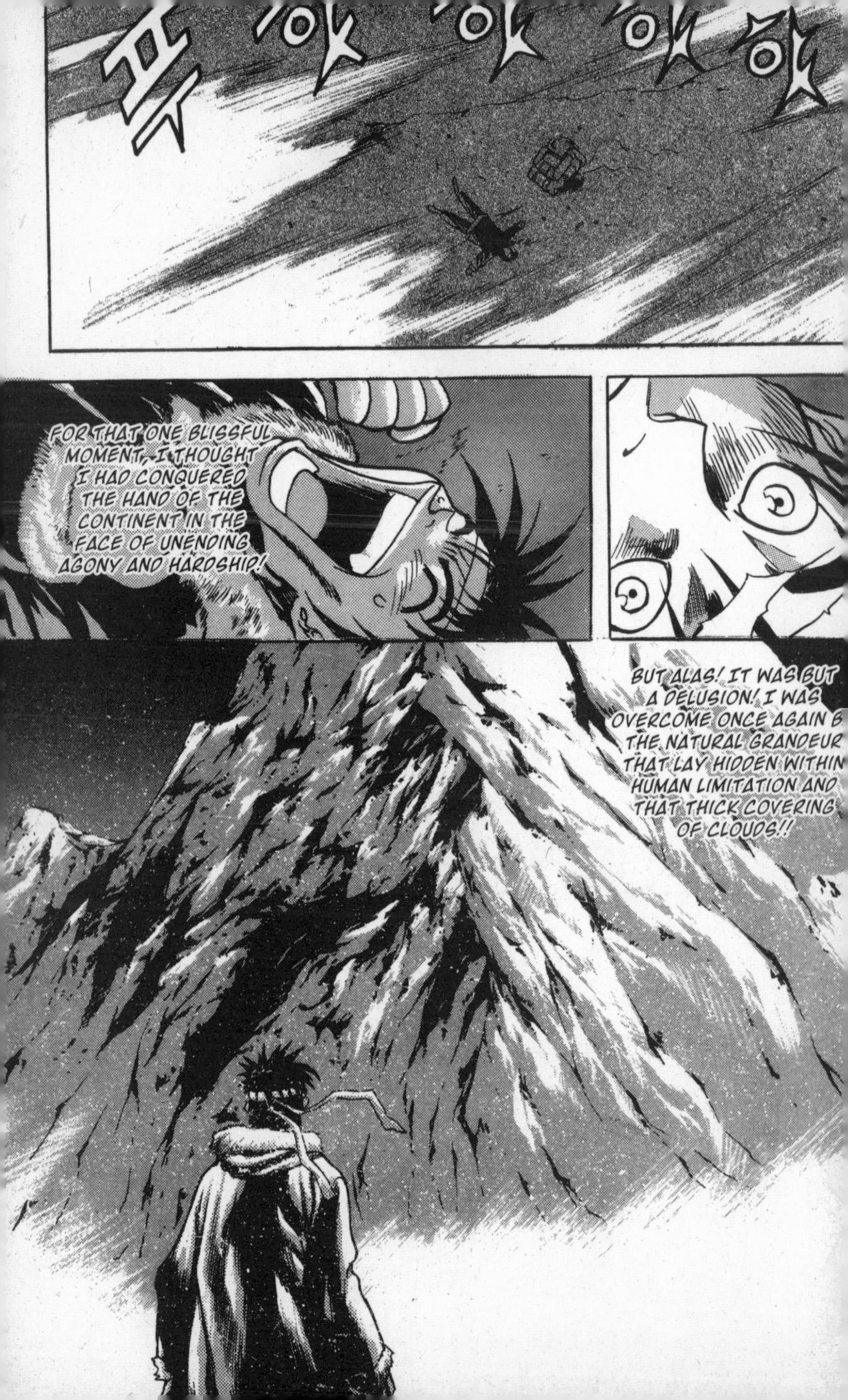
FOR THAT ONE BLISSFUL MOMENT, I THOUGHT I HAD CONQUERED THE HAND OF THE CONTINENT IN THE FACE OF UNENDING AGONY AND HARDSHIP!
BUT ALAS! IT WAS BUT A DELUSION! I WAS OVERCOME ONCE AGAIN B THE NATURAL GRANDEUR THAT LAY HIDDEN WITHIN HUMAN LIMITATION AND THAT THICK COVERING OF CLOUDS!!

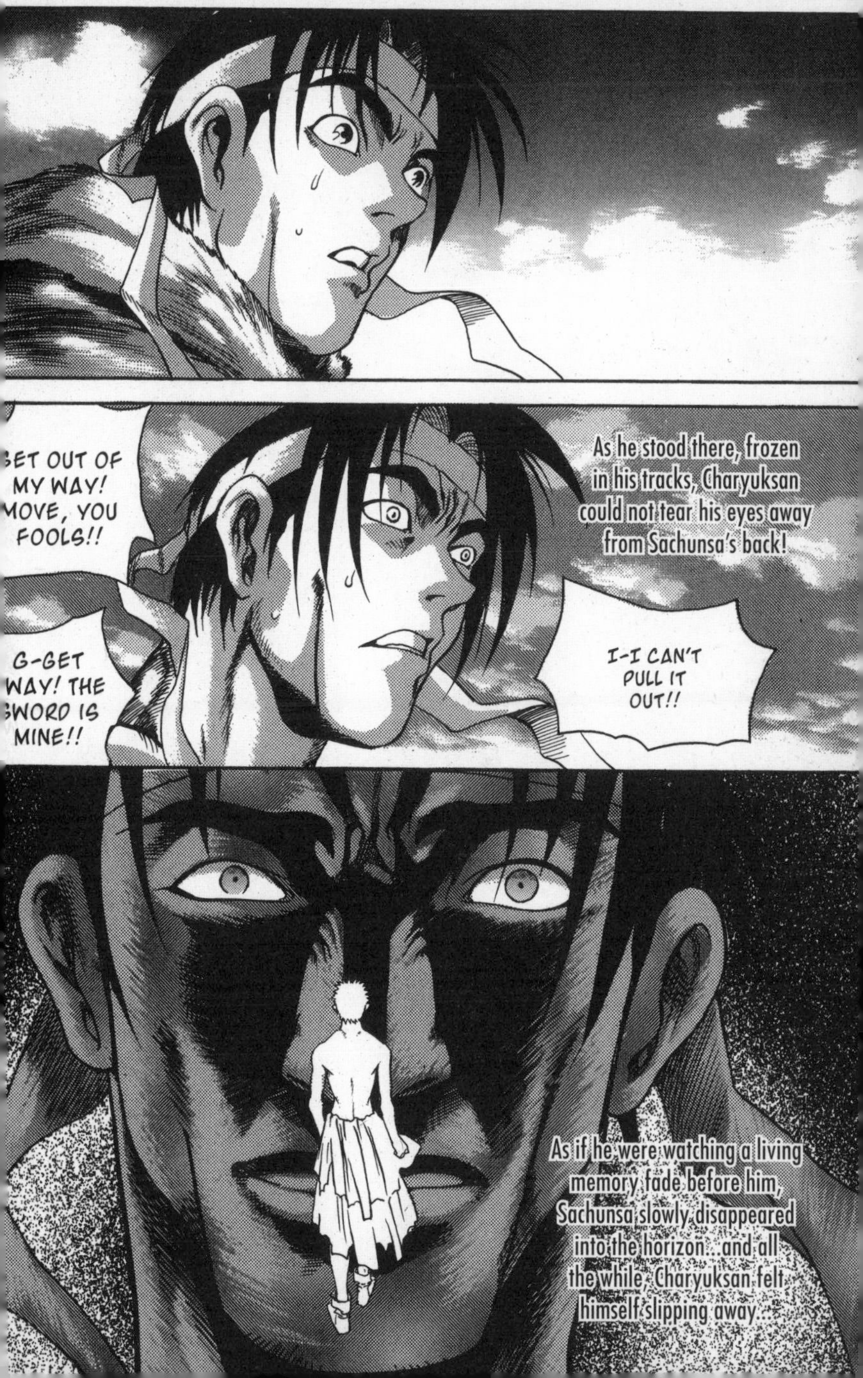
As he stood there, frozen in his tracks, Charyuksan could not tear his eyes away from Sachunsa's back!
I-I CAN'T PULL IT OUT!!
GET OUT OF MY WAY! MOVE, YOU FOOLS!!
G-GET WAY! THE SWORD IS MINE!!
As if he were watching a living memory fade before him, Sachunsa slowly disappeared into the horizon...and all the while, Charyuksan felt himself slipping away...

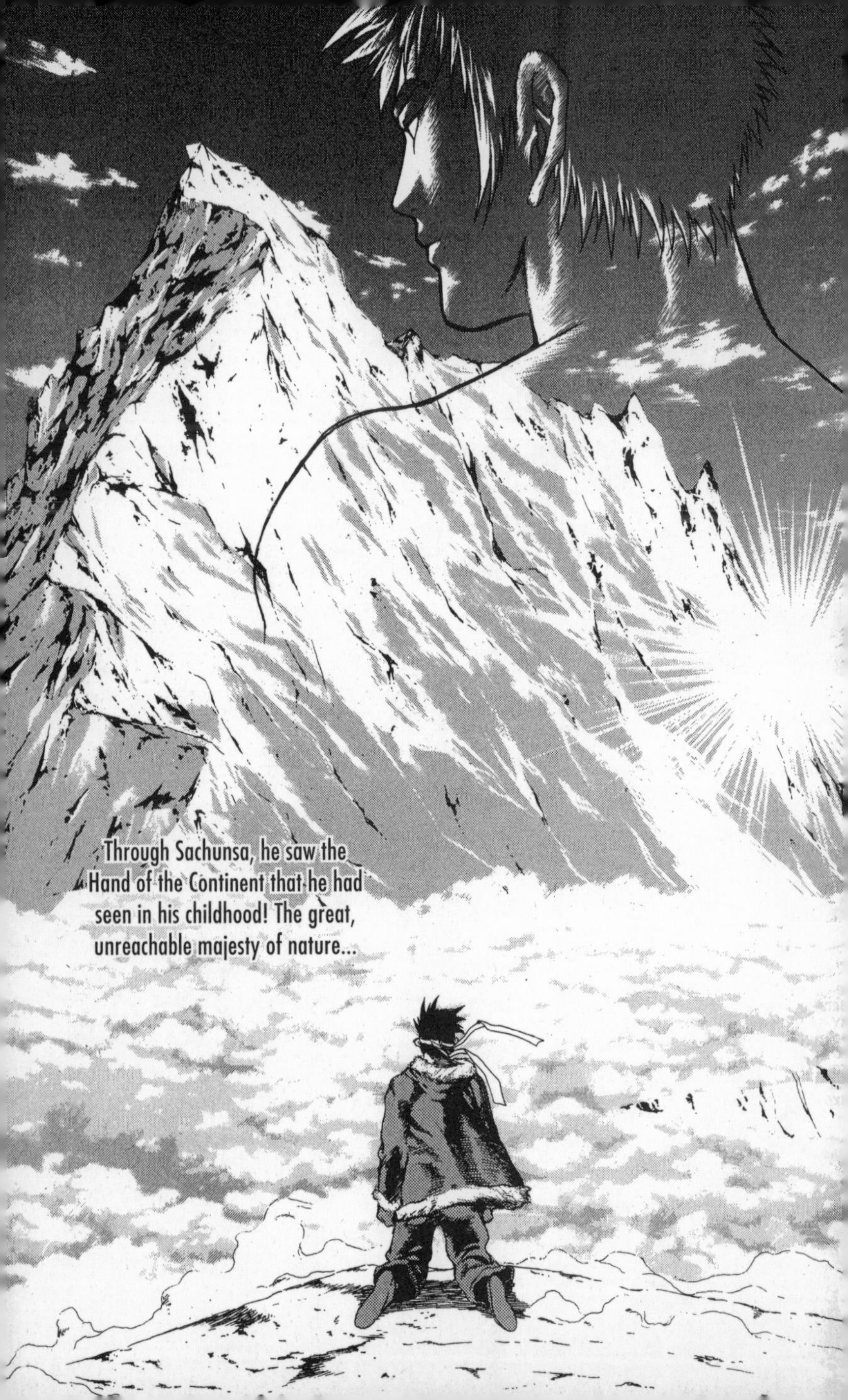
Through Sachunsa, he saw the Hand of the Continent that he had seen in his childhood! The great, unreachable majesty of nature...

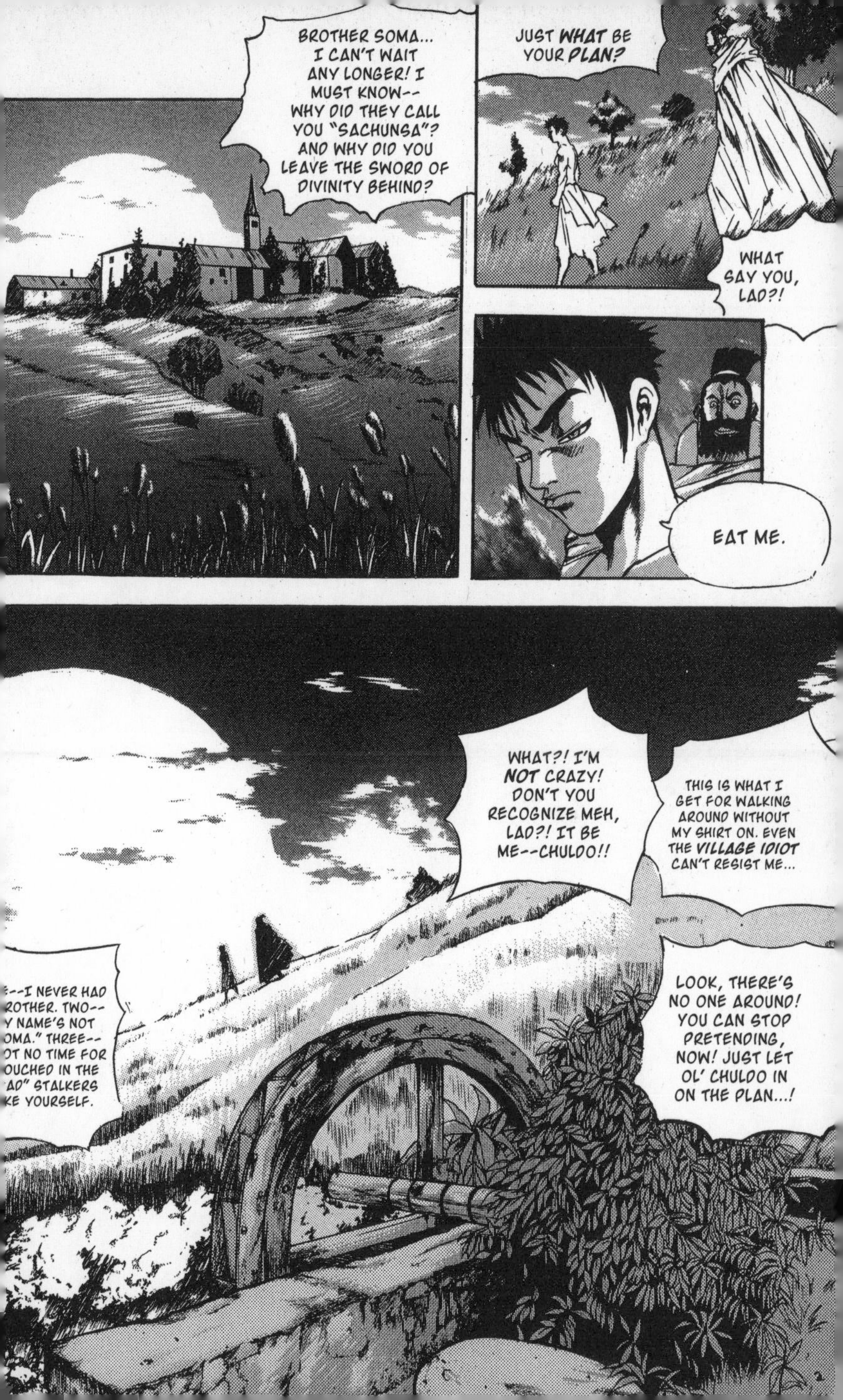

BROTHER SOMA... I CAN'T WAIT ANY LONGER! I MUST KNOW-- WHY DID THEY CALL YOU "SACHUNSA"? AND WHY DID YOU LEAVE THE SWORD OF DIVINITY BEHIND?
JUST **WHAT** BE YOUR **PLAN?**
WHAT SAY YOU, LAO?!
EAT ME.
WHAT?! I'M **NOT** CRAZY! DON'T YOU RECOGNIZE MEH, LAO?! IT BE ME--CHULDO!!
THIS IS WHAT I GET FOR WALKING AROUND WITHOUT MY SHIRT ON. EVEN THE **VILLAGE IDIOT** CAN'T RESIST ME...
LOOK, THERE'S NO ONE AROUND! YOU CAN STOP PRETENDING, NOW! JUST LET OL' CHULDO IN ON THE PLAN...!
--I NEVER HAD
ROTHER. TWO--
Y NAME'S NOT
OMA." THREE--
OT NO TIME FOR
OUCHED IN THE
AO" STALKERS
KE YOURSELF.

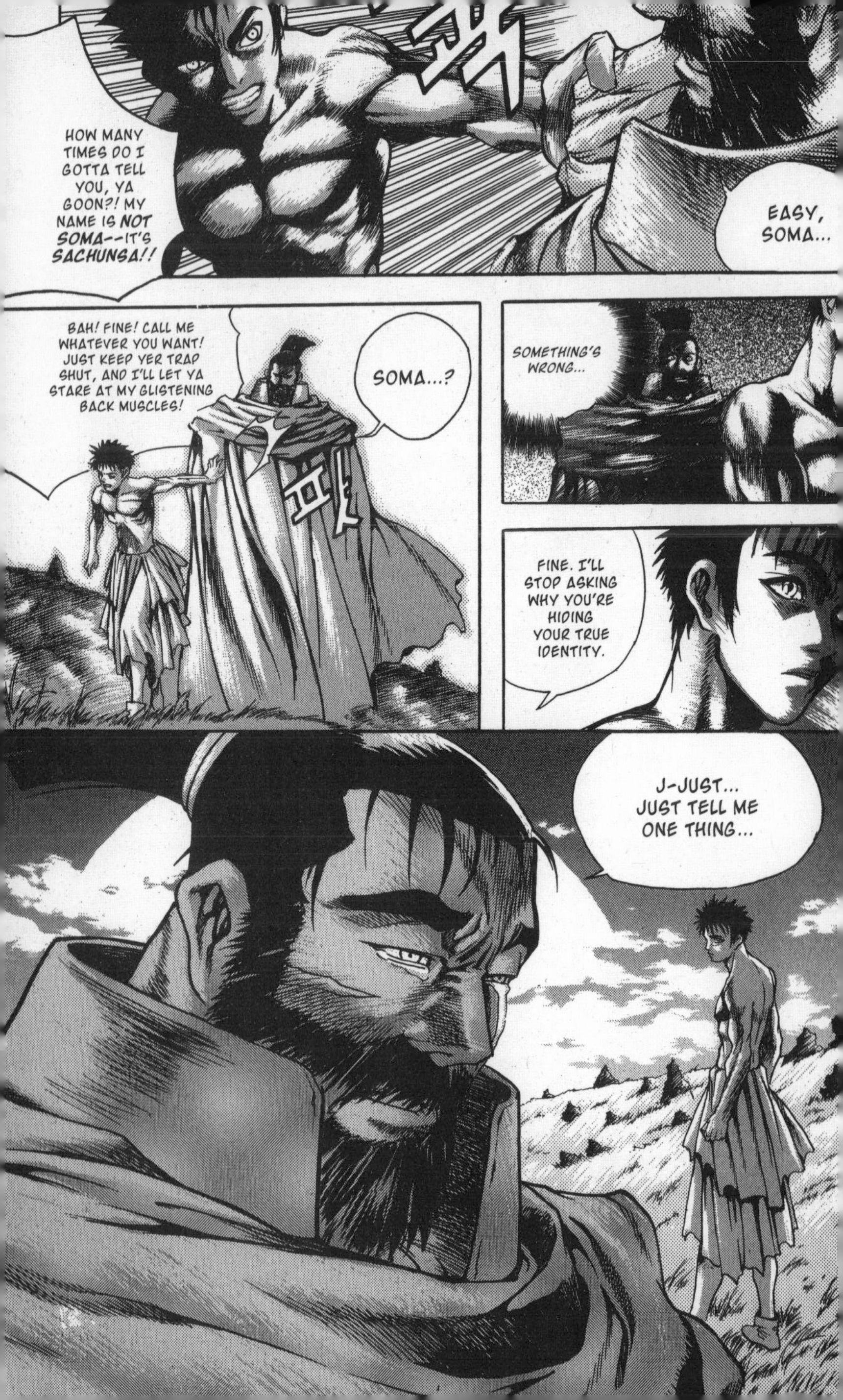
HOW MANY TIMES DO I GOTTA TELL YOU, YA GOON?! MY NAME IS NOT SOMA--IT'S SACHUNSA!!
EASY, SOMA...
BAH! FINE! CALL ME WHATEVER YOU WANT! JUST KEEP YER TRAP SHUT, AND I'LL LET YA STARE AT MY GLISTENING BACK MUSCLES!
SOMA...?
SOMETHING'S WRONG...
FINE. I'LL STOP ASKING WHY YOU'RE HIDING YOUR TRUE IDENTITY.
J-JUST... JUST TELL ME ONE THING...

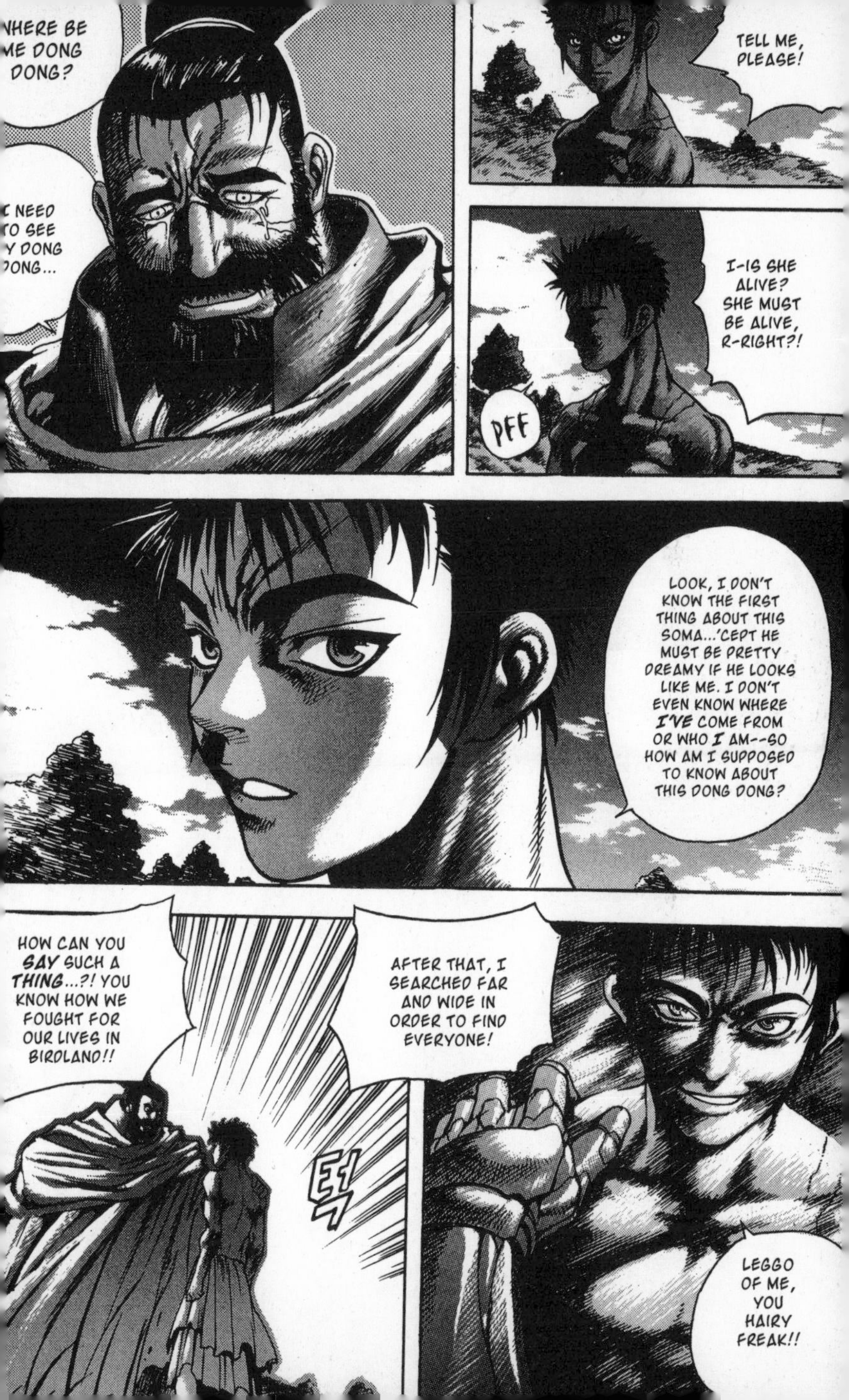

WHERE BE ME DONG DONG?
I NEED TO SEE MY DONG DONG...
TELL ME, PLEASE!
I-IS SHE ALIVE? SHE MUST BE ALIVE, R-RIGHT?!
PFF
LOOK, I DON'T KNOW THE FIRST THING ABOUT THIS SOMA...'CEPT HE MUST BE PRETTY DREAMY IF HE LOOKS LIKE ME. I DON'T EVEN KNOW WHERE I'VE COME FROM OR WHO I AM--SO HOW AM I SUPPOSED TO KNOW ABOUT THIS DONG DONG?
HOW CAN YOU SAY SUCH A THING...?! YOU KNOW HOW WE FOUGHT FOR OUR LIVES IN BIRDLAND!!
AFTER THAT, I SEARCHED FAR AND WIDE IN ORDER TO FIND EVERYONE!
LEGGO OF ME, YOU HAIRY FREAK!!

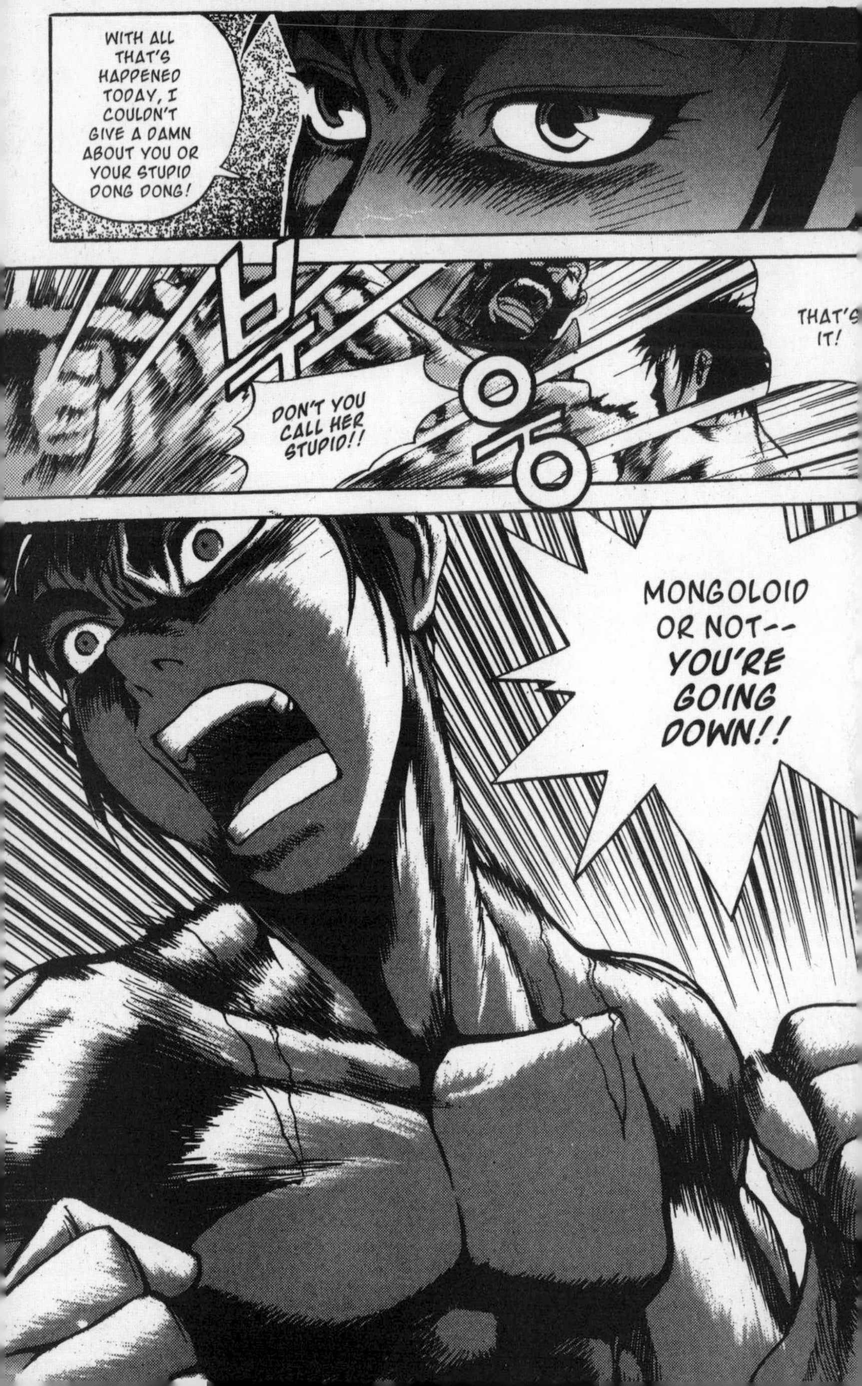
WITH ALL THAT'S HAPPENED TODAY, I COULDN'T GIVE A DAMN ABOUT YOU OR YOUR STUPID DONG DONG!
DON'T YOU CALL HER STUPID!!
THAT'S IT!
MONGOLOID OR NOT-- YOU'RE GOING DOWN!!

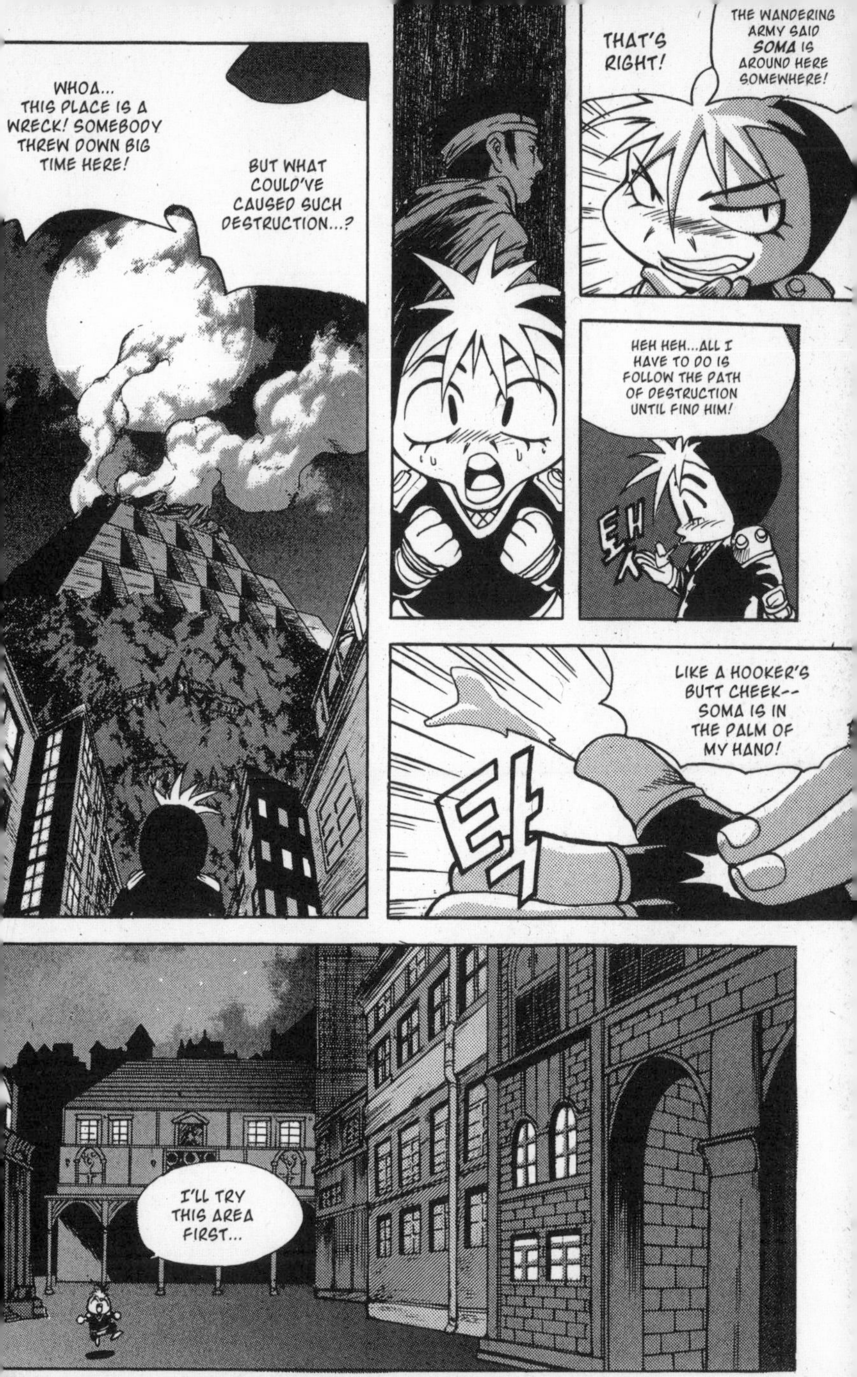
WHOA... THIS PLACE IS A WRECK! SOMEBODY THREW DOWN BIG TIME HERE!
BUT WHAT COULD'VE CAUSED SUCH DESTRUCTION...?
THAT'S RIGHT!
THE WANDERING ARMY SAID SOMA IS AROUND HERE SOMEWHERE!
HEH HEH...ALL I HAVE TO DO IS FOLLOW THE PATH OF DESTRUCTION UNTIL FIND HIM!
LIKE A HOOKER'S BUTT CHEEK-- SOMA IS IN THE PALM OF MY HAND!
I'LL TRY THIS AREA FIRST...

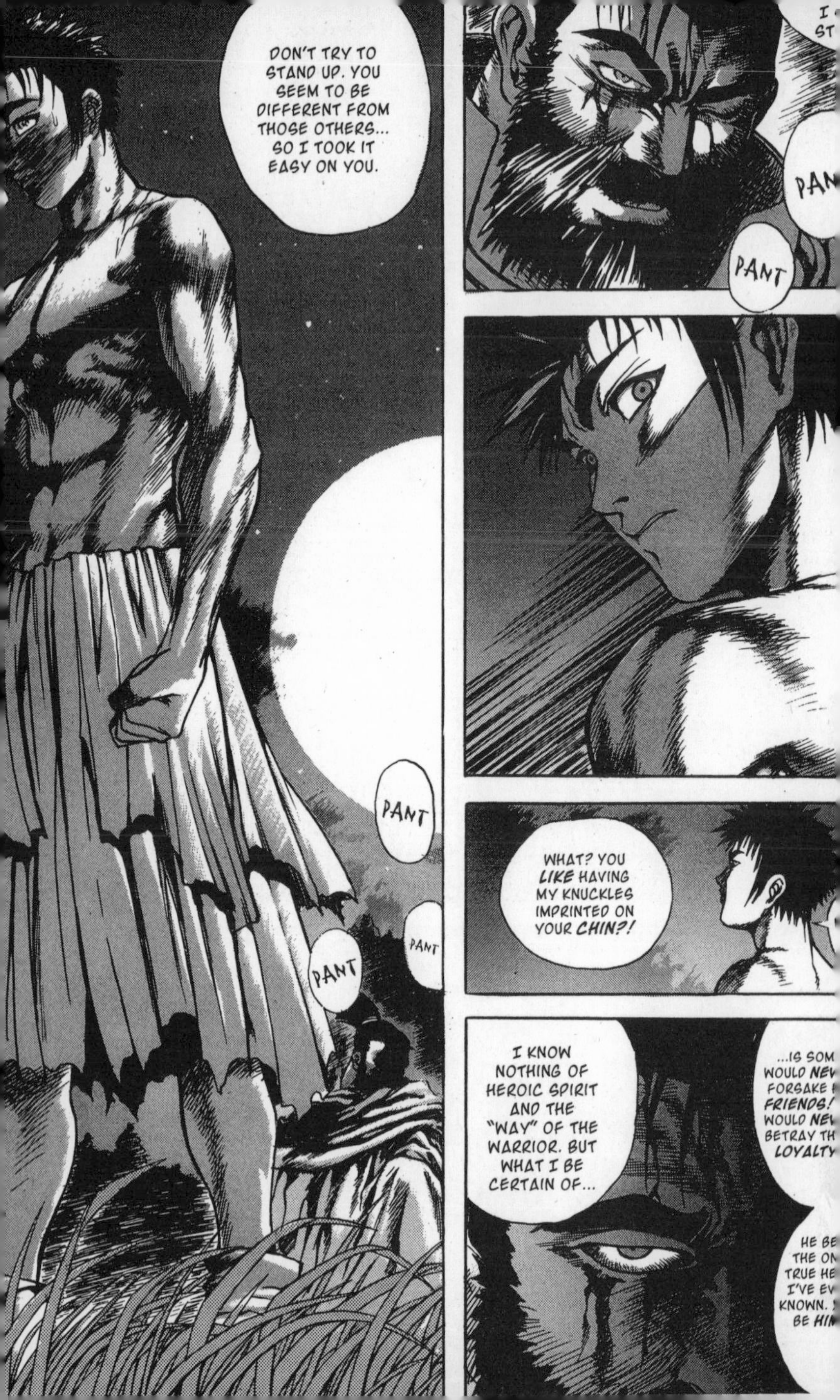
DON'T TRY TO STAND UP. YOU SEEM TO BE DIFFERENT FROM THOSE OTHERS... SO I TOOK IT EASY ON YOU.
PANT
PANT
PANT
PANT
WHAT? YOU *LIKE* HAVING MY KNUCKLES IMPRINTED ON YOUR *CHIN?!*
I KNOW NOTHING OF HEROIC SPIRIT AND THE "WAY" OF THE WARRIOR. BUT WHAT I BE CERTAIN OF...

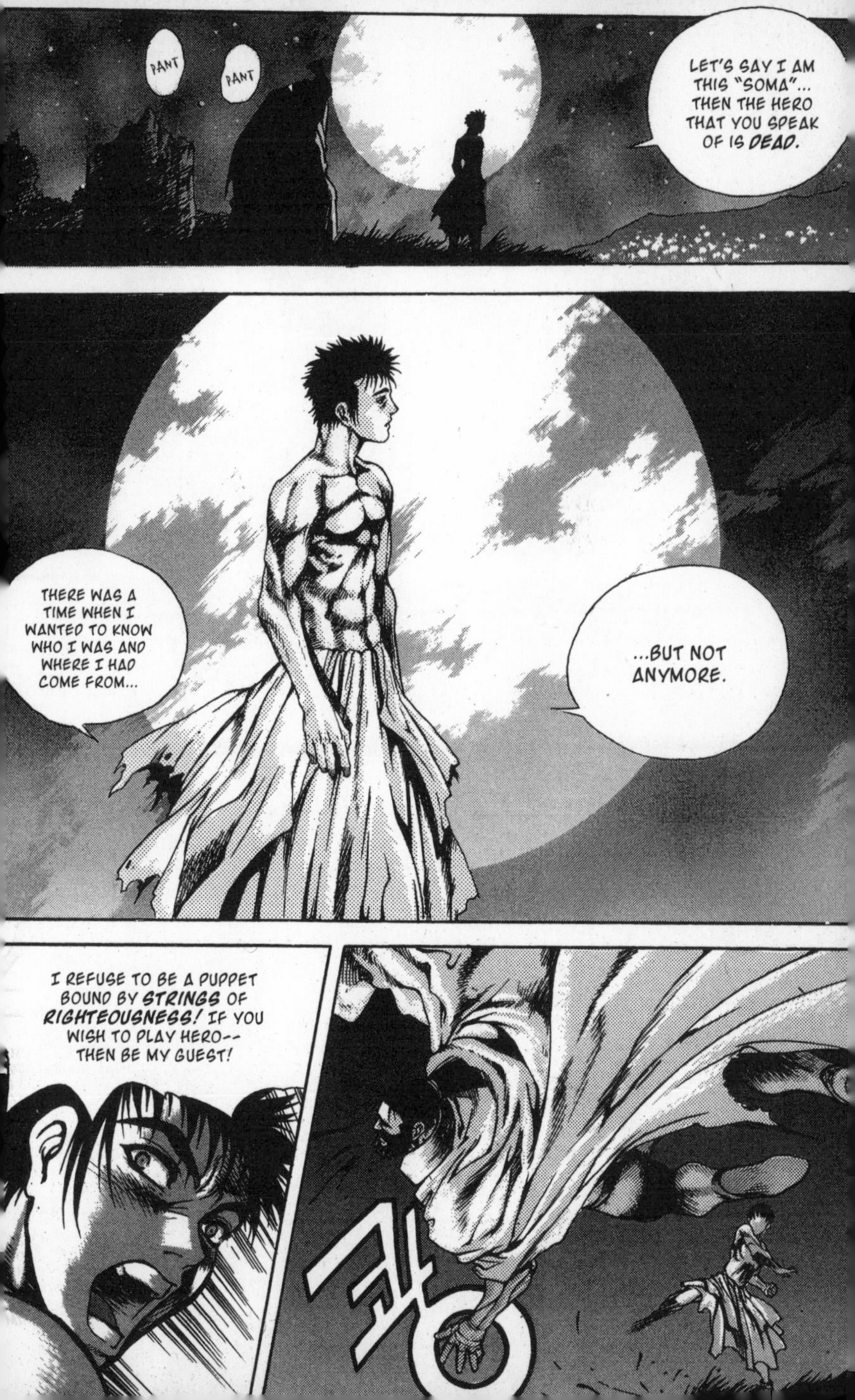
PANT
PANT
LET'S SAY I AM THIS "SOMA"... THEN THE HERO THAT YOU SPEAK OF IS DEAD.
THERE WAS A TIME WHEN I WANTED TO KNOW WHO I WAS AND WHERE I HAD COME FROM...
...BUT NOT ANYMORE.
I REFUSE TO BE A PUPPET BOUND BY STRINGS OF RIGHTEOUSNESS! IF YOU WISH TO PLAY HERO-- THEN BE MY GUEST!

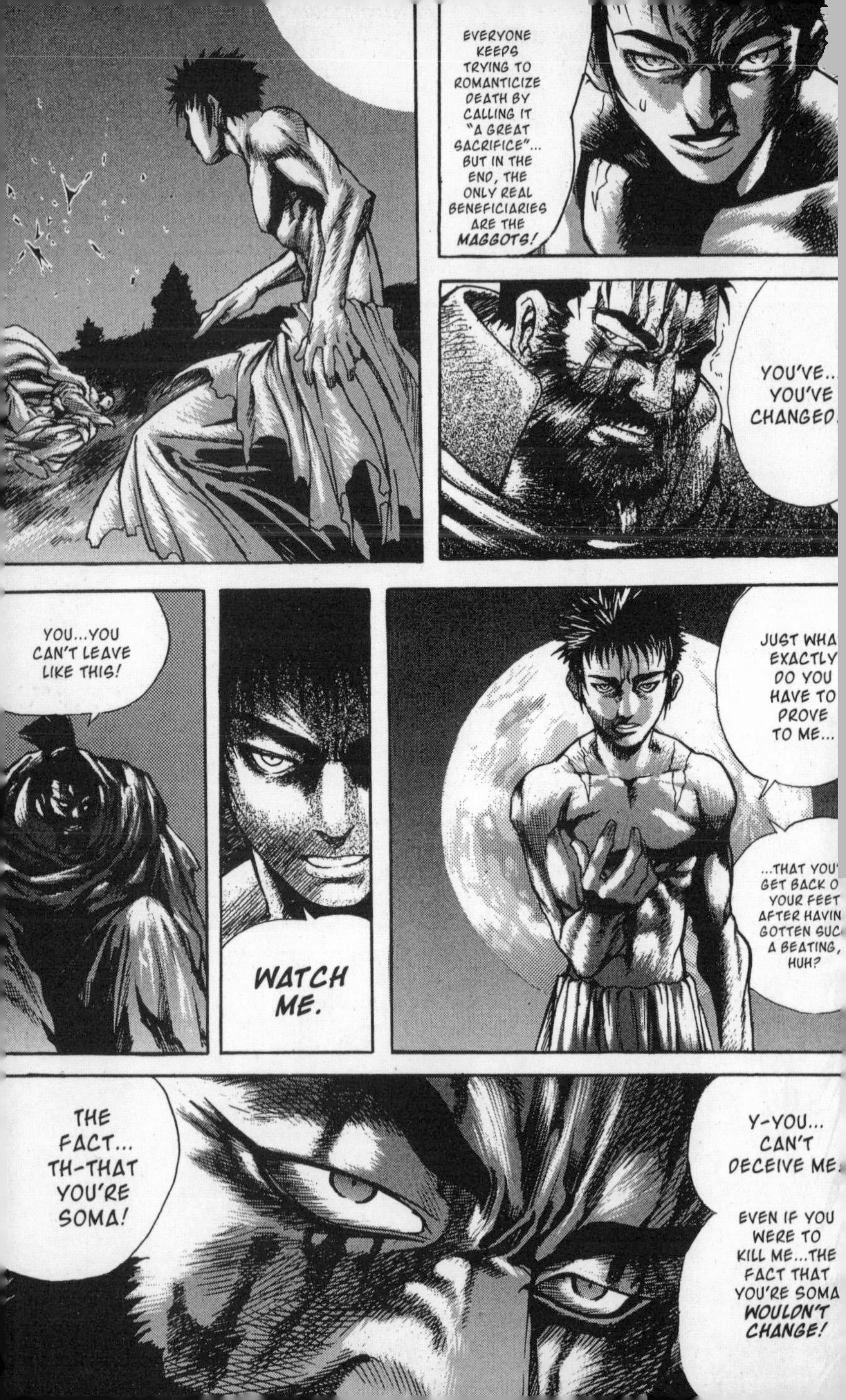

EVERYONE KEEPS TRYING TO ROMANTICIZE DEATH BY CALLING IT "A GREAT SACRIFICE"... BUT IN THE END, THE ONLY REAL BENEFICIARIES ARE THE *MAGGOTS!*
YOU'VE... YOU'VE CHANGED.
YOU...YOU CAN'T LEAVE LIKE THIS!
WATCH ME.
JUST WHA EXACTLY DO YOU HAVE TO PROVE TO ME...
...THAT YOU GET BACK O YOUR FEET AFTER HAVIN GOTTEN SUC A BEATING, HUH?
THE FACT... TH-THAT YOU'RE SOMA!
Y-YOU... CAN'T DECEIVE ME.
EVEN IF YOU WERE TO KILL ME...THE FACT THAT YOU'RE SOMA *WOULDN'T CHANGE!*

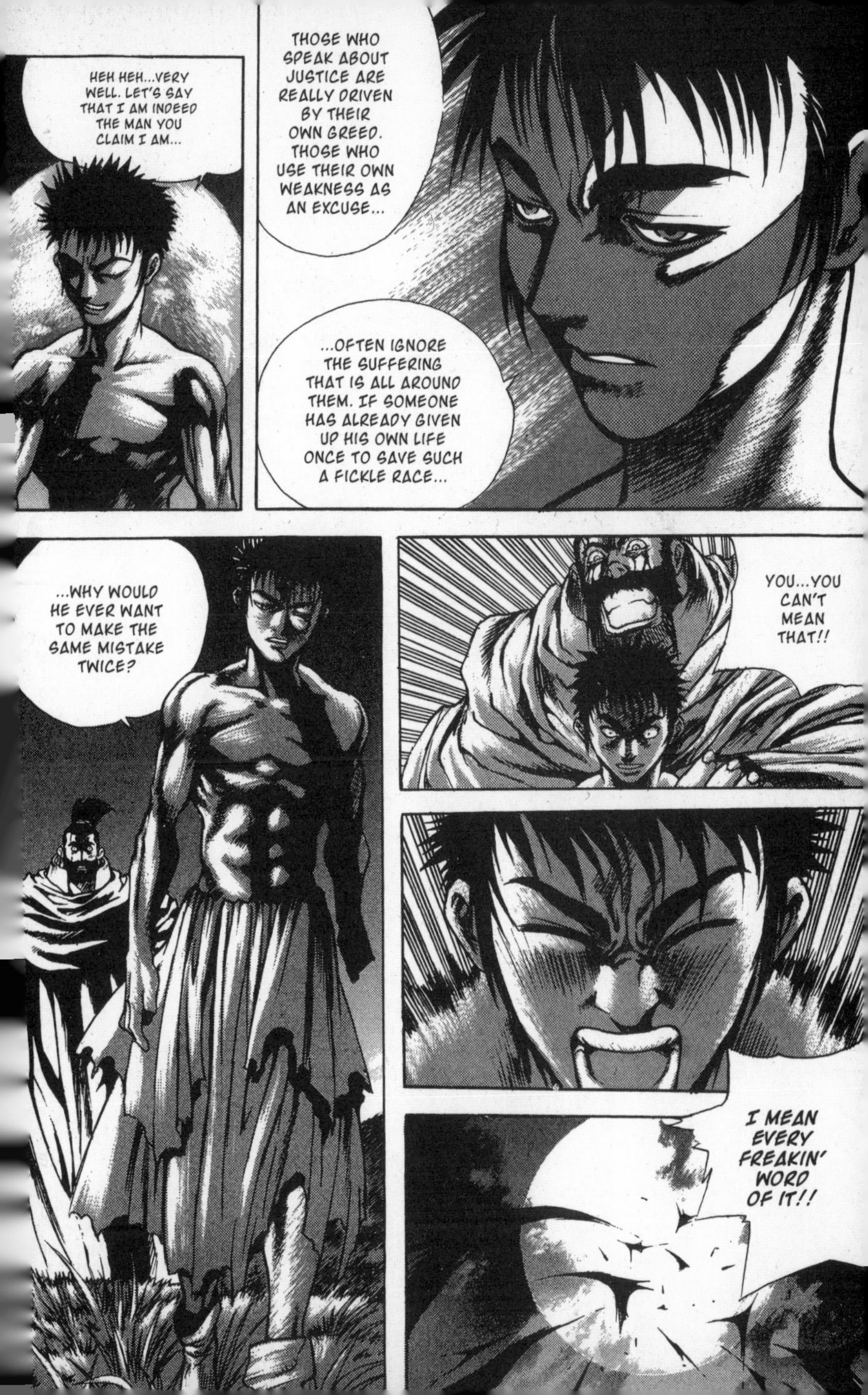
HEH HEH...VERY WELL. LET'S SAY THAT I AM INDEED THE MAN YOU CLAIM I AM...
THOSE WHO SPEAK ABOUT JUSTICE ARE REALLY DRIVEN BY THEIR OWN GREED. THOSE WHO USE THEIR OWN WEAKNESS AS AN EXCUSE...
...OFTEN IGNORE THE SUFFERING THAT IS ALL AROUND THEM. IF SOMEONE HAS ALREADY GIVEN UP HIS OWN LIFE ONCE TO SAVE SUCH A FICKLE RACE...
...WHY WOULD HE EVER WANT TO MAKE THE SAME MISTAKE TWICE?
YOU...YOU CAN'T MEAN THAT!!
I MEAN EVERY FREAKIN' WORD OF IT!!

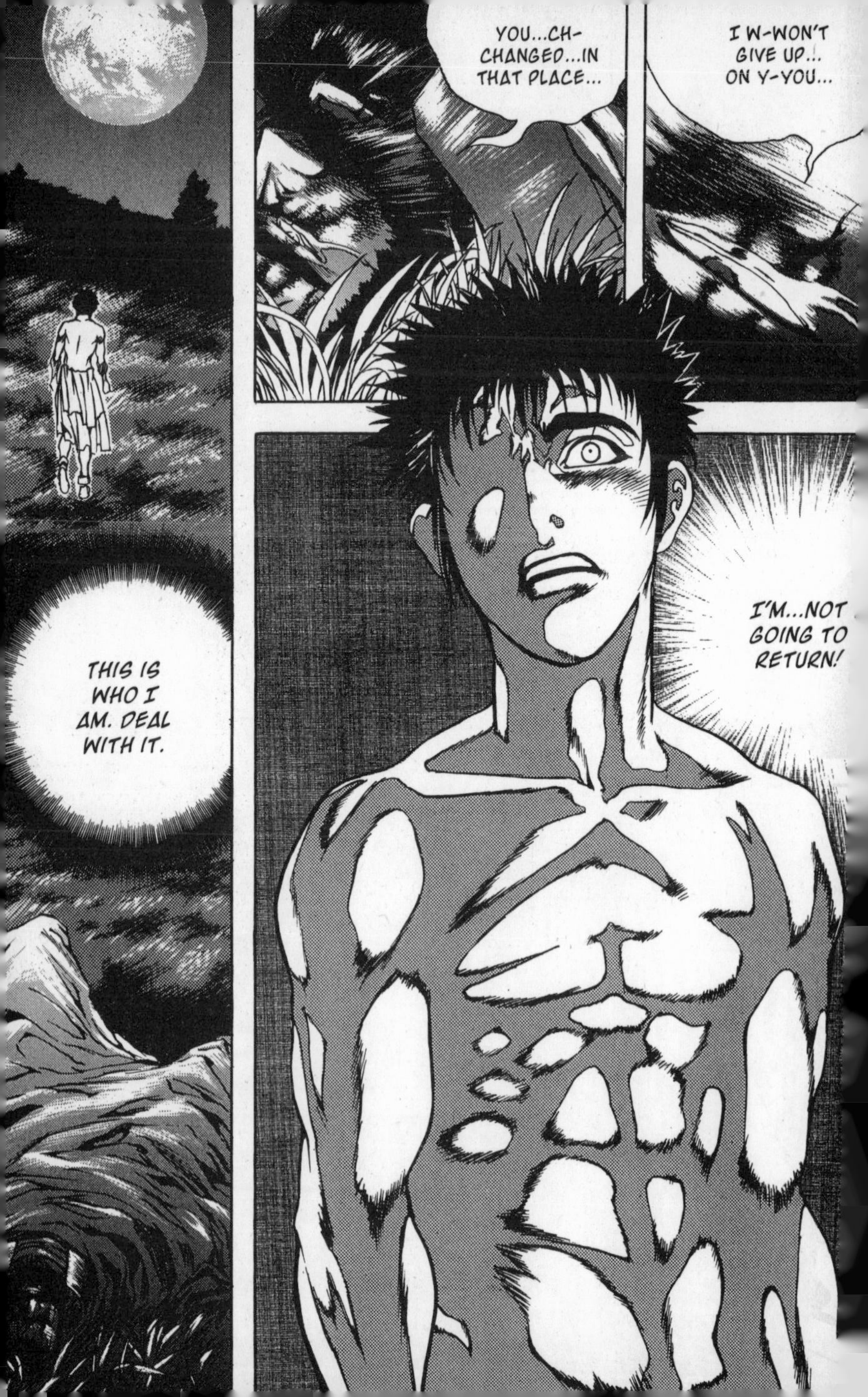
I W-WON'T GIVE UP... ON Y-YOU...
YOU...CH-CHANGED...IN THAT PLACE...
I'M...NOT GOING TO RETURN!
THIS IS WHO I AM. DEAL WITH IT.

HEY, BARKEEP! HAVE YOU ENCOUNTERED A GUY NAMED SOMA?

WHAT ARE YOU TALKING ABOUT, LITTLE BABY? SOMA IS DEAD! EVERYONE KNOWS THIS! NOW, WHERE'S YOUR MOMMY?

IDIOT! I'M A MAN, NOT A BABY! LISTEN...

THEN WHY ARE YOU WEARING A DIAPER...?

HE'S NOT GOING BY THAT NAME ANYMORE. EVER HEARD OF A SACHUNGA...?

WHISKEY. LEAVE THE BOTTLE.

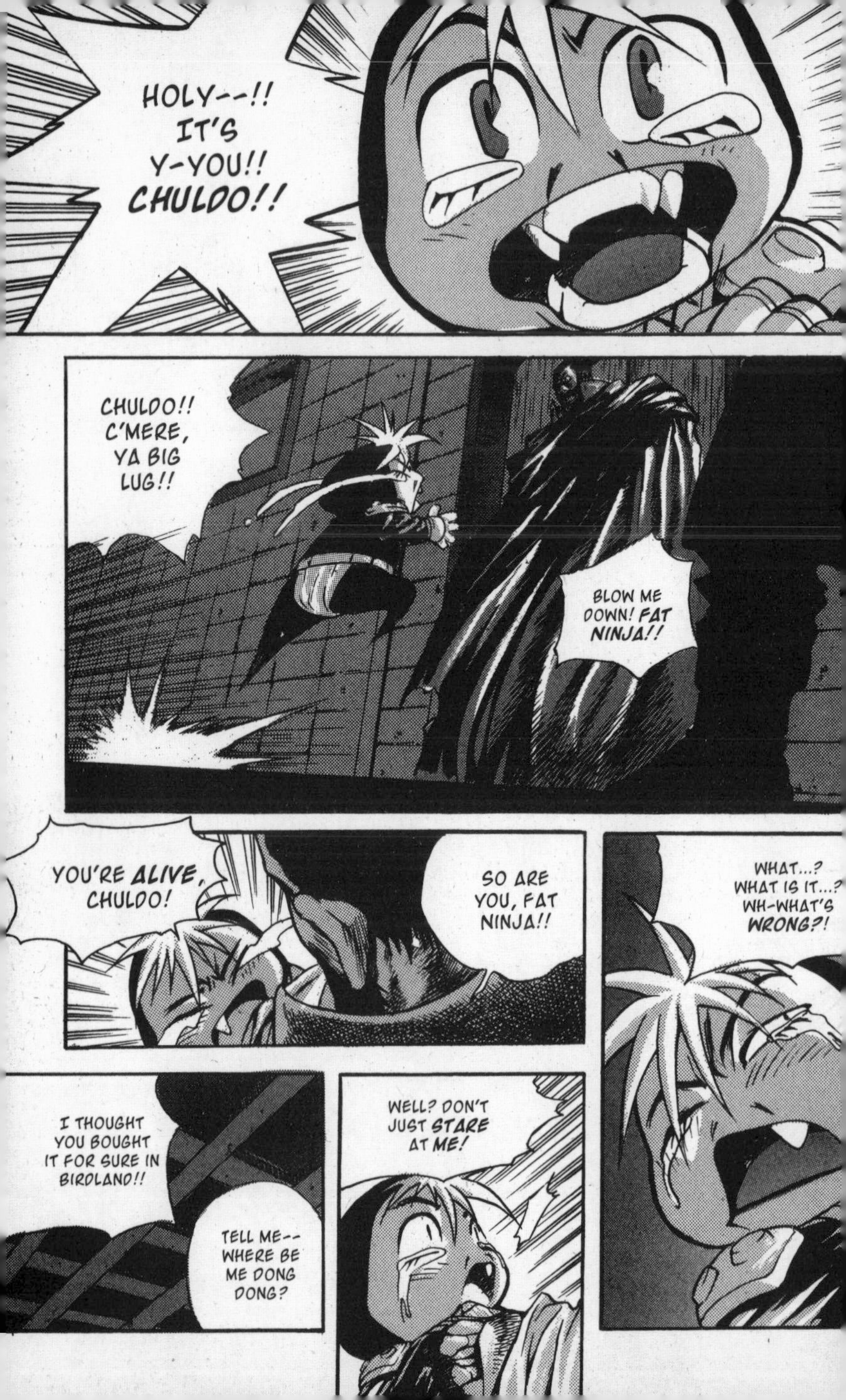
HOLY--!! IT'S Y-YOU!! CHULDO!!
CHULDO!! C'MERE, YA BIG LUG!!
BLOW ME DOWN! FAT NINJA!!
YOU'RE ALIVE, CHULDO!
SO ARE YOU, FAT NINJA!!
WHAT...? WHAT IS IT...? WH-WHAT'S WRONG?!
I THOUGHT YOU BOUGHT IT FOR SURE IN BIRDLAND!!
TELL ME-- WHERE BE ME DONG DONG?
WELL? DON'T JUST STARE AT ME!

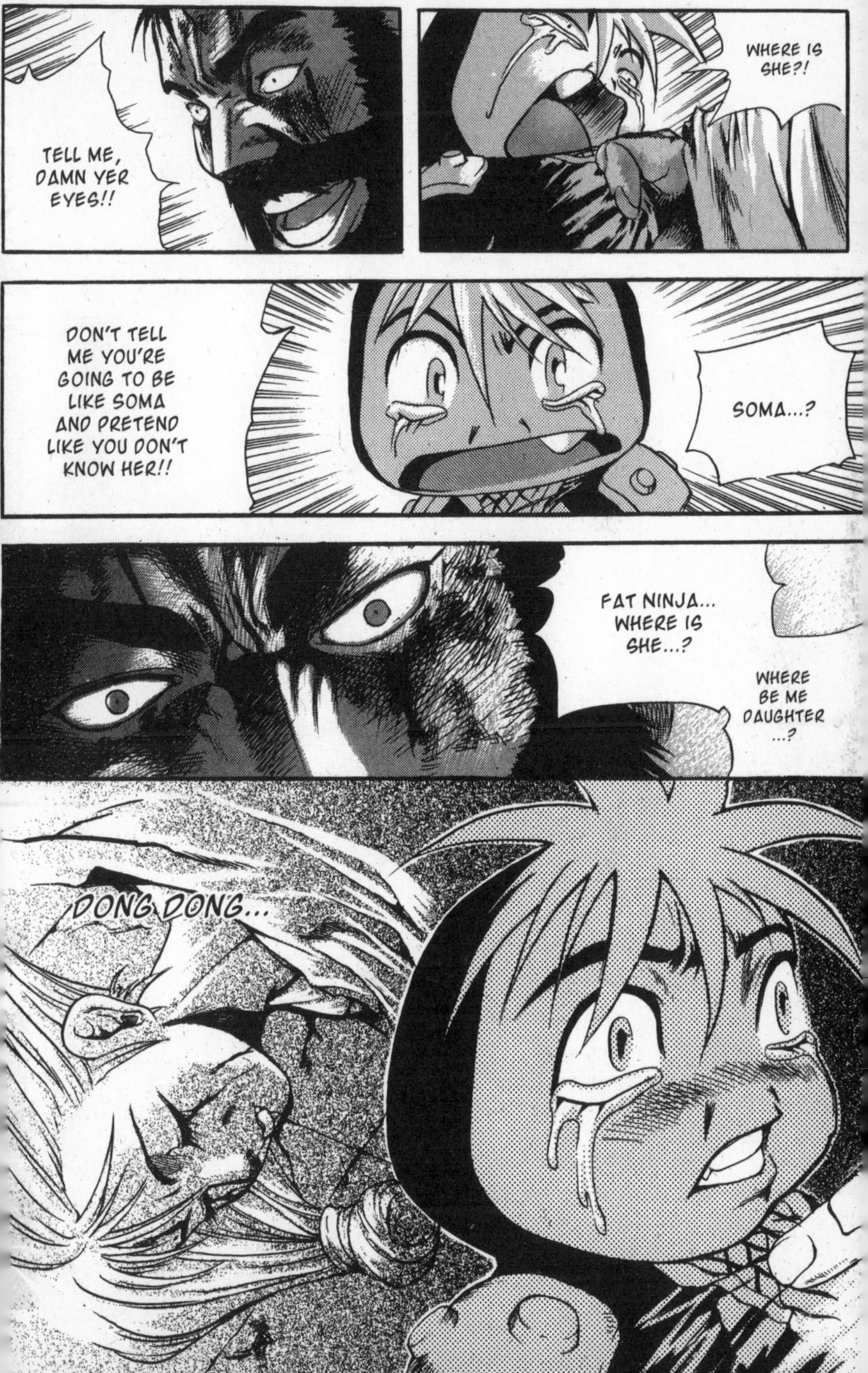
WHERE IS SHE?!
TELL ME, DAMN YER EYES!!
SOMA...?
DON'T TELL ME YOU'RE GOING TO BE LIKE SOMA AND PRETEND LIKE YOU DON'T KNOW HER!!
FAT NINJA... WHERE IS SHE...?
WHERE BE ME DAUGHTER ...?
DONG DONG...

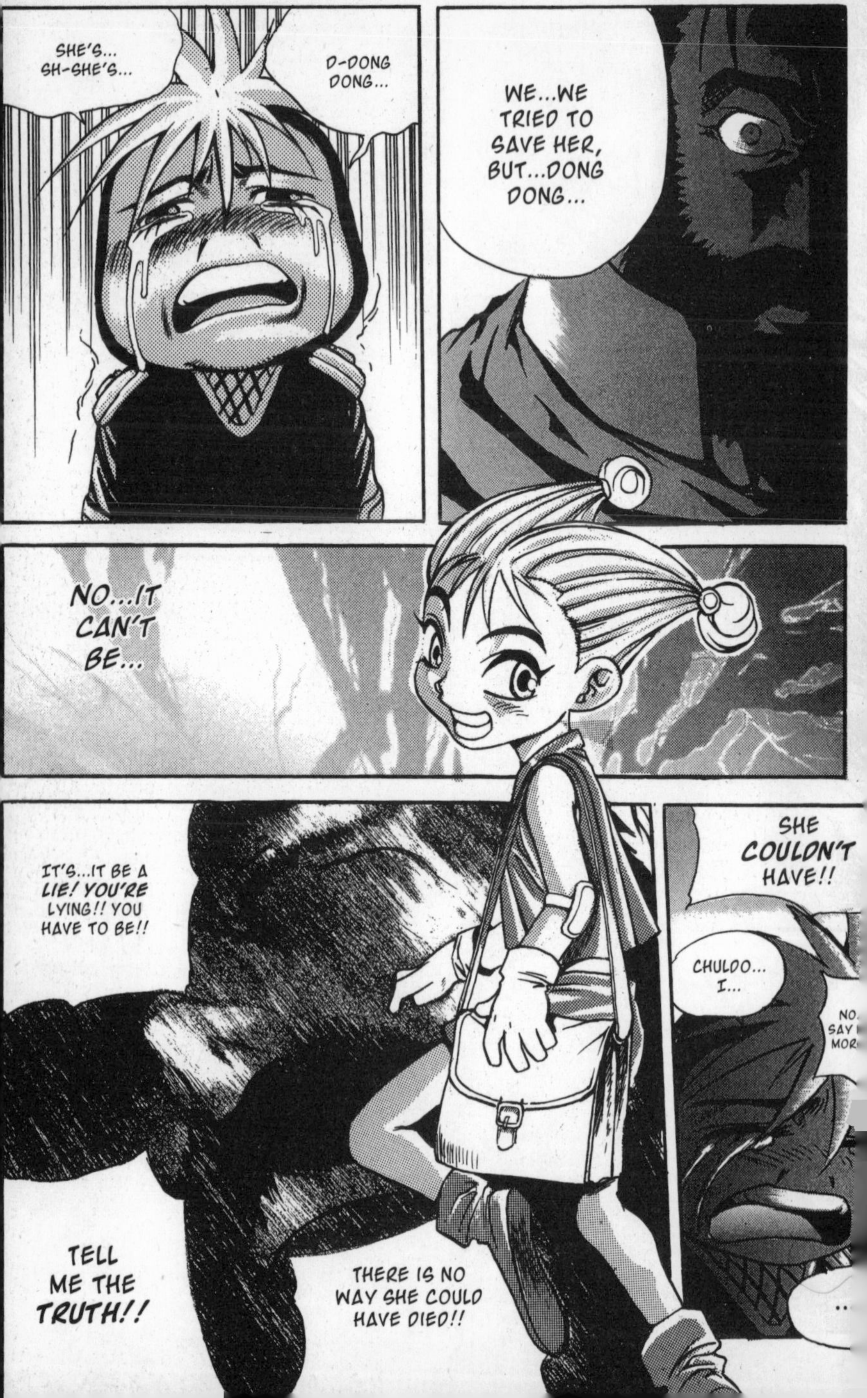

SHE'S... SH-SHE'S...
D-DONG DONG...
WE...WE TRIED TO SAVE HER, BUT...DONG DONG...
NO...IT CAN'T BE...
IT'S...IT BE A LIE! YOU'RE LYING!! YOU HAVE TO BE!!
SHE COULDN'T HAVE!!
CHULDO... I...
TELL ME THE TRUTH!!
THERE IS NO WAY SHE COULD HAVE DIED!!

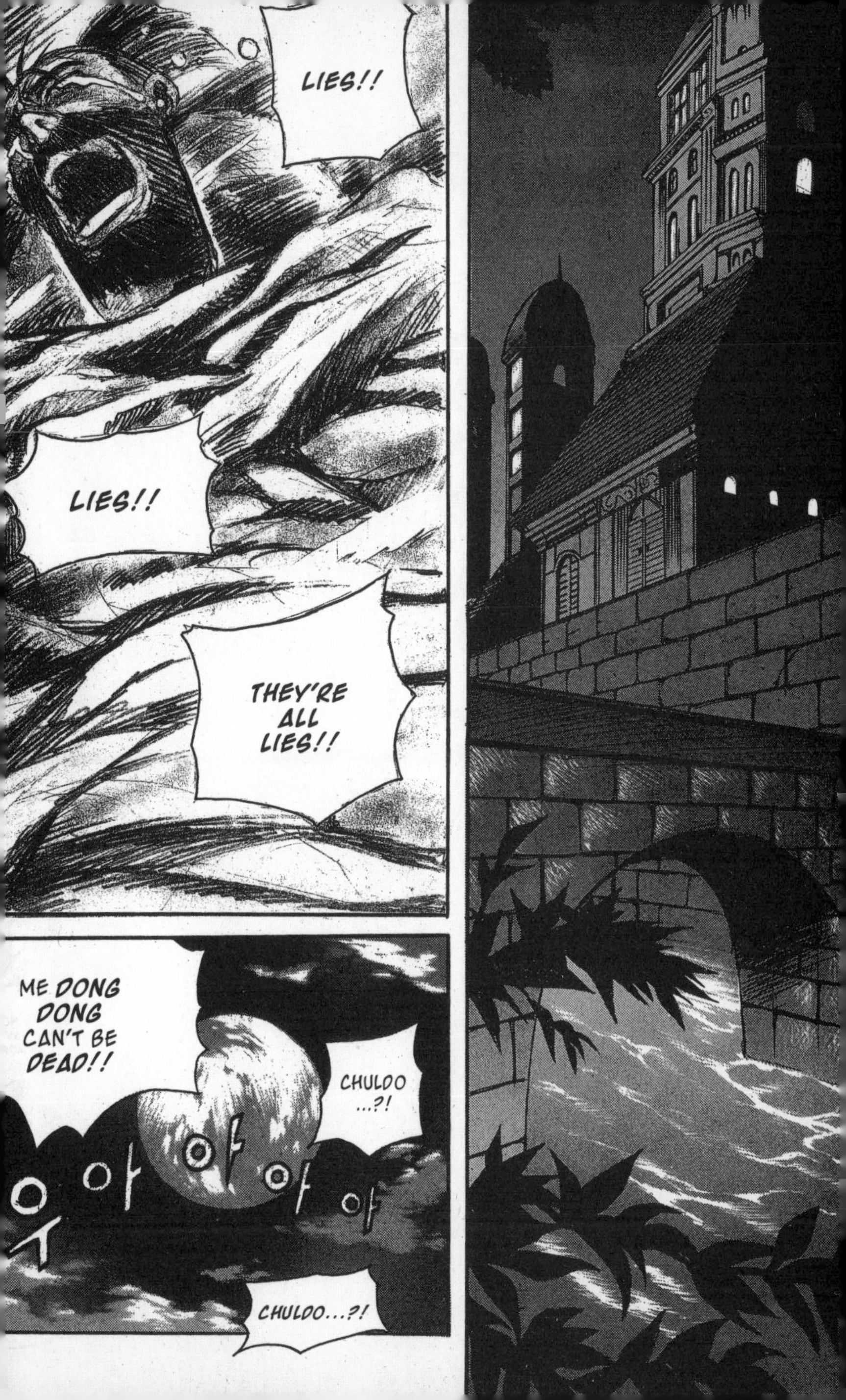
LIES!!
LIES!!
THEY'RE ALL LIES!!
ME DONG DONG CAN'T BE DEAD!!
CHULDO ...?!
CHULDO...?!

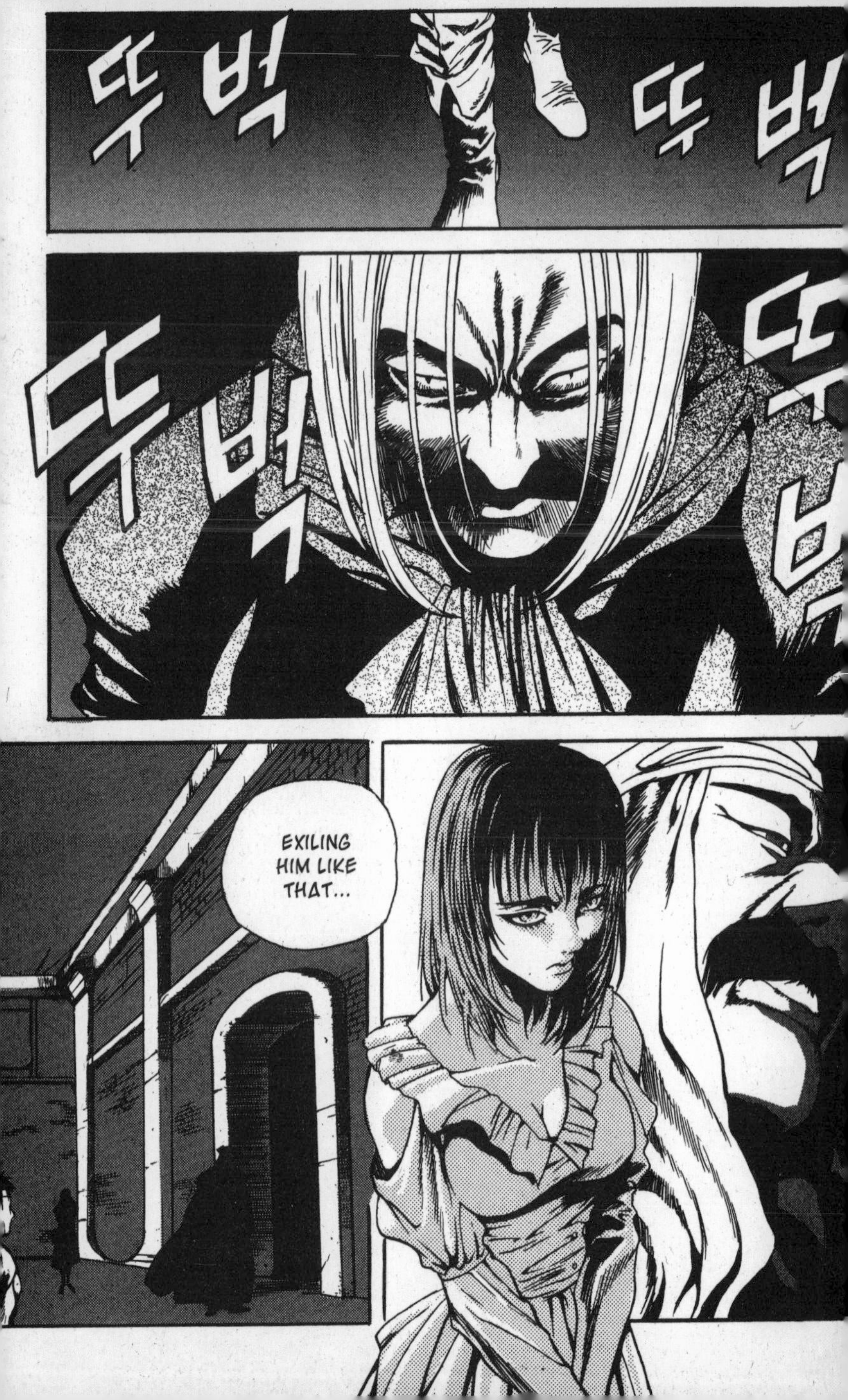

뚜벅
뚜벅
뚜벅
뚜벅
EXILING HIM LIKE THAT...

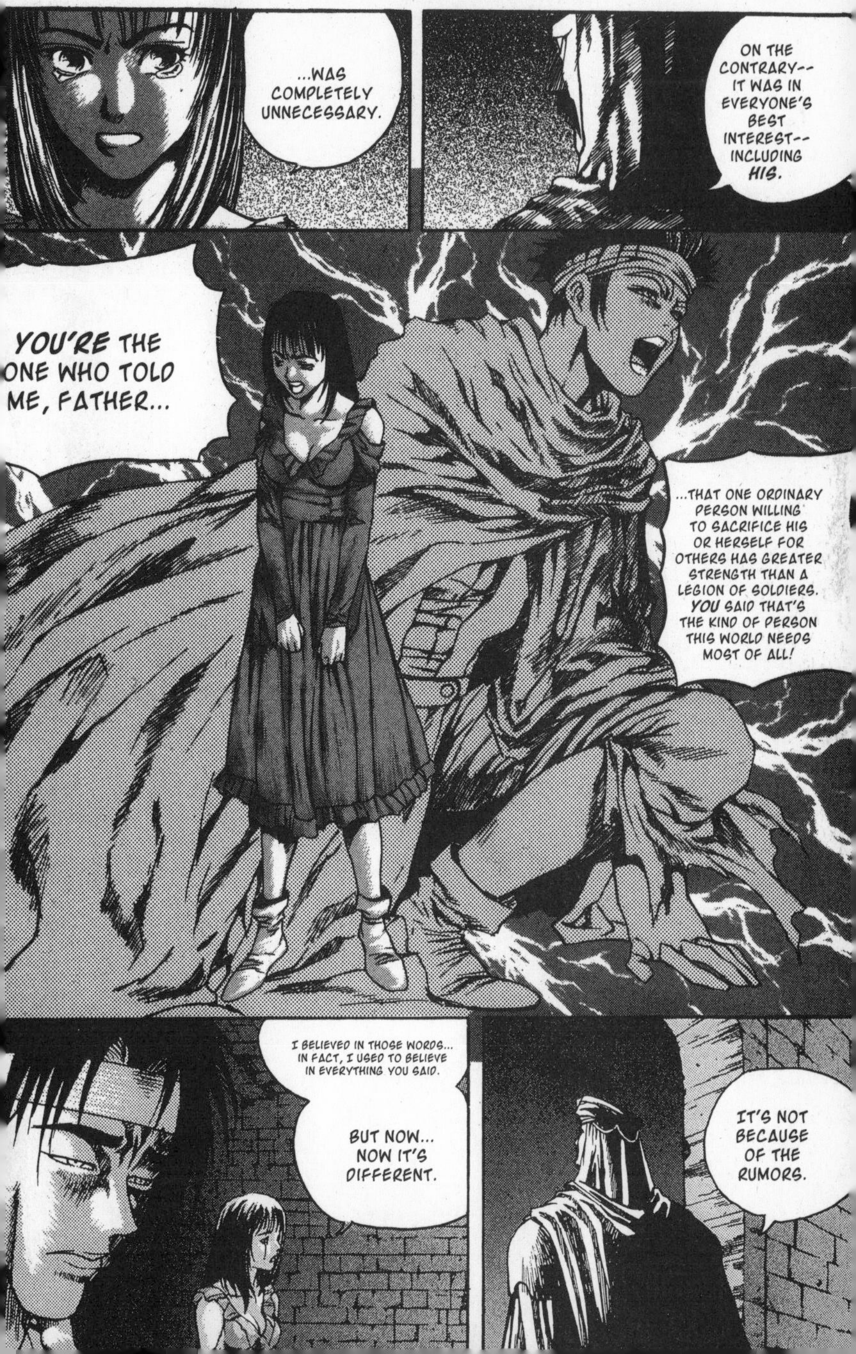
...WAS COMPLETELY UNNECESSARY.
ON THE CONTRARY-- IT WAS IN EVERYONE'S BEST INTEREST-- INCLUDING HIS.
YOU'RE THE ONE WHO TOLD ME, FATHER...
...THAT ONE ORDINARY PERSON WILLING TO SACRIFICE HIS OR HERSELF FOR OTHERS HAS GREATER STRENGTH THAN A LEGION OF SOLDIERS. YOU SAID THAT'S THE KIND OF PERSON THIS WORLD NEEDS MOST OF ALL!
I BELIEVED IN THOSE WORDS... IN FACT, I USED TO BELIEVE IN EVERYTHING YOU SAID.
BUT NOW... NOW IT'S DIFFERENT.
IT'S NOT BECAUSE OF THE RUMORS.

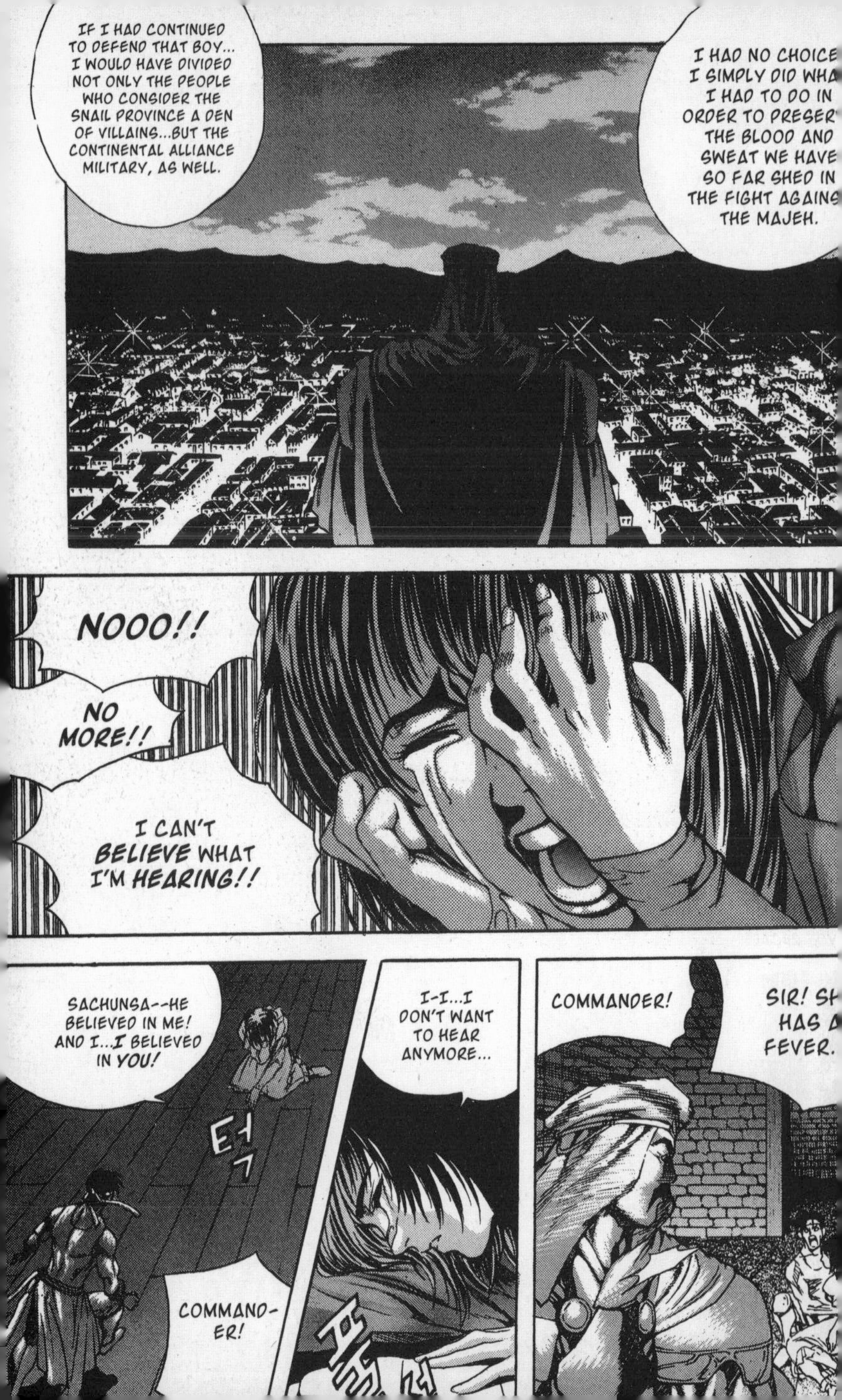
IF I HAD CONTINUED TO DEFEND THAT BOY... I WOULD HAVE DIVIDED NOT ONLY THE PEOPLE WHO CONSIDER THE SNAIL PROVINCE A DEN OF VILLAINS...BUT THE CONTINENTAL ALLIANCE MILITARY, AS WELL.
I HAD NO CHOICE I SIMPLY DID WHA I HAD TO DO IN ORDER TO PRESER THE BLOOD AND SWEAT WE HAVE SO FAR SHED IN THE FIGHT AGAINS THE MAJEH.
NOOO!!
NO MORE!!
I CAN'T BELIEVE WHAT I'M HEARING!!
SACHUNSA--HE BELIEVED IN ME! AND I...I BELIEVED IN YOU!
COMMAND-ER!
I-I...I DON'T WANT TO HEAR ANYMORE...
COMMANDER!
SIR! SH HAS A FEVER.

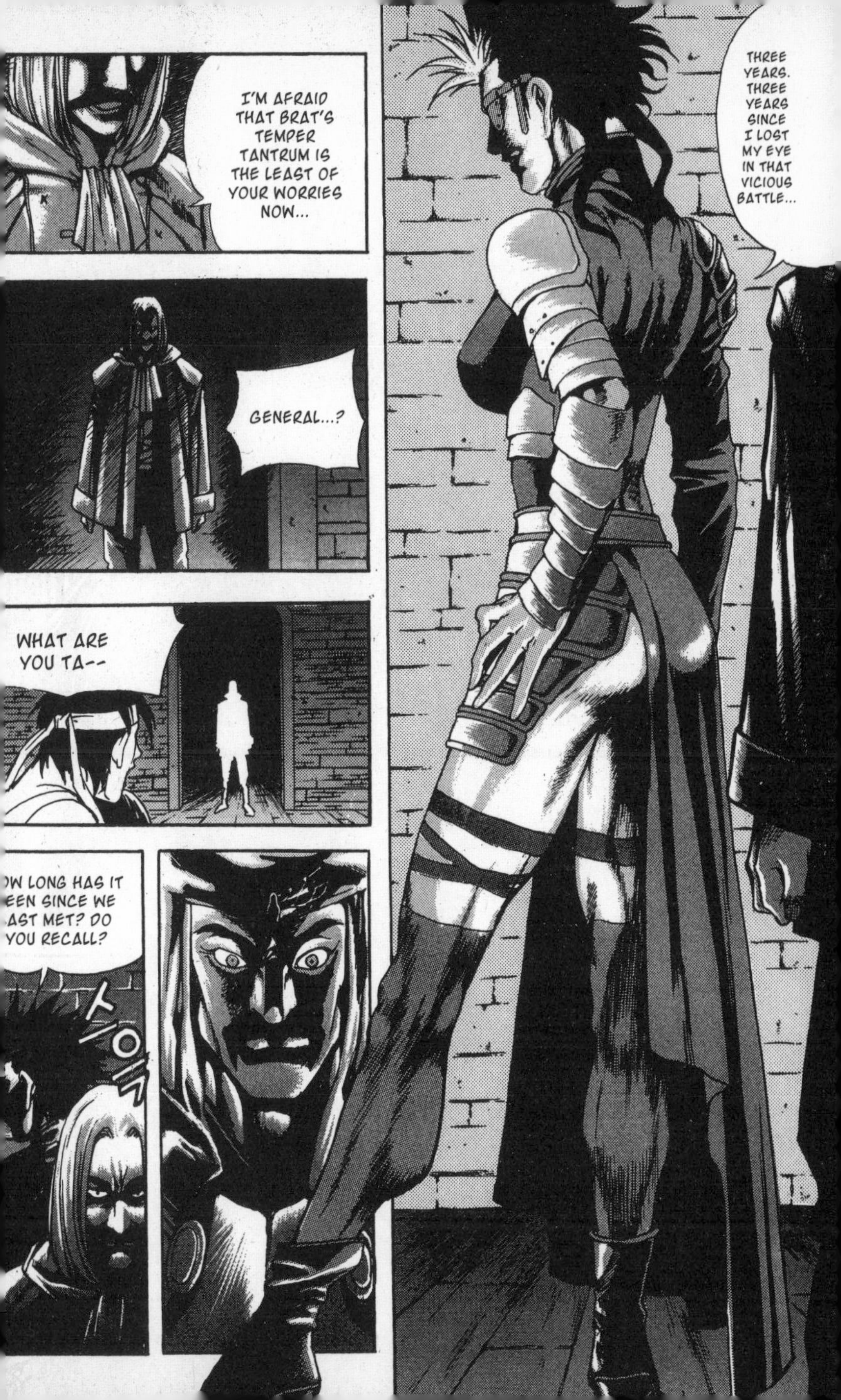
I'M AFRAID THAT BRAT'S TEMPER TANTRUM IS THE LEAST OF YOUR WORRIES NOW...
GENERAL...?
WHAT ARE YOU TA--
OW LONG HAS IT EEN SINCE WE AST MET? DO YOU RECALL?
THREE YEARS. THREE YEARS SINCE I LOST MY EYE IN THAT VICIOUS BATTLE...

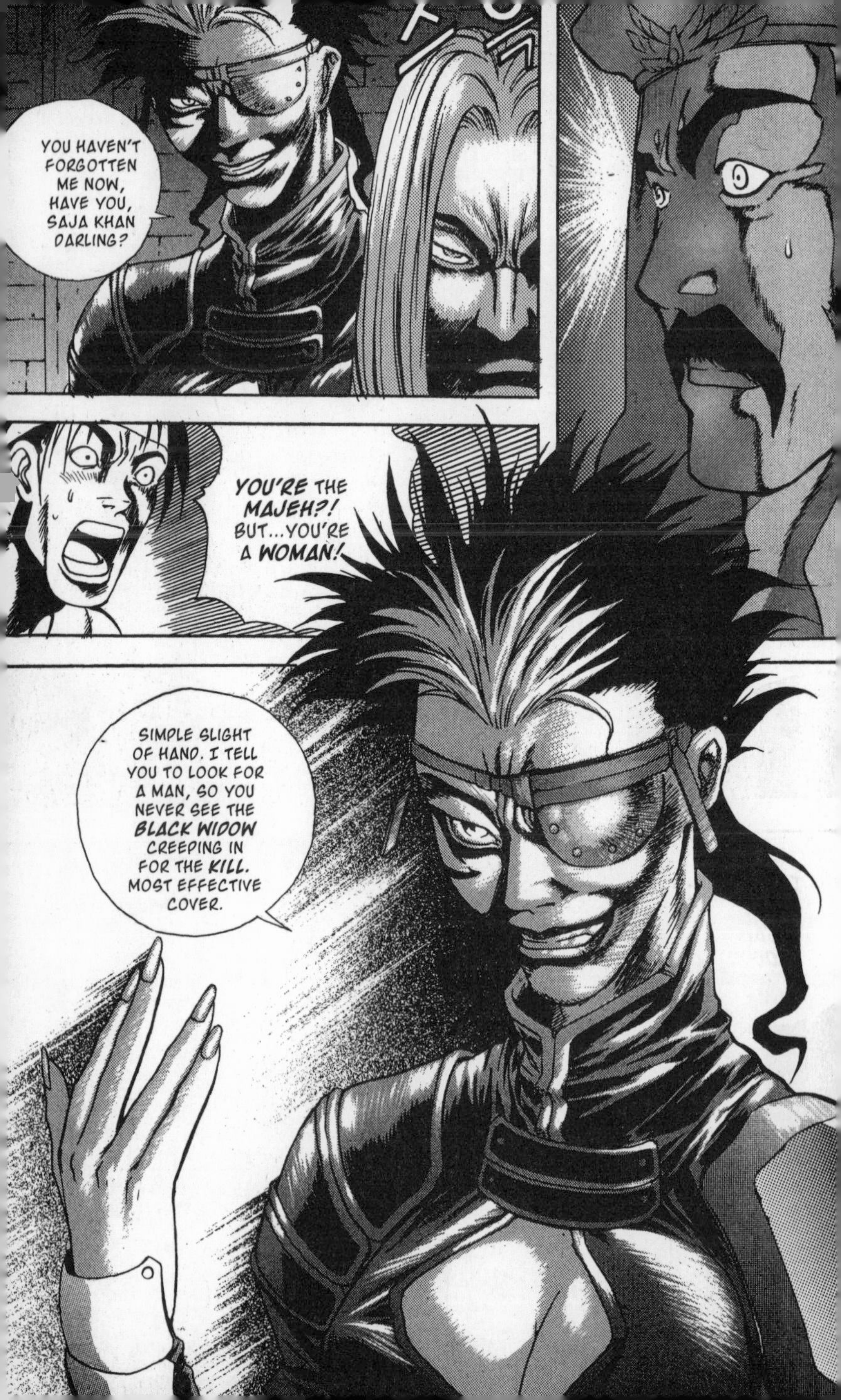
YOU HAVEN'T FORGOTTEN ME NOW, HAVE YOU, SAJA KHAN DARLING?
YOU'RE THE MAJEH?! BUT...YOU'RE A WOMAN!
SIMPLE SLIGHT OF HAND. I TELL YOU TO LOOK FOR A MAN, SO YOU NEVER SEE THE BLACK WIDOW CREEPING IN FOR THE KILL. MOST EFFECTIVE COVER.

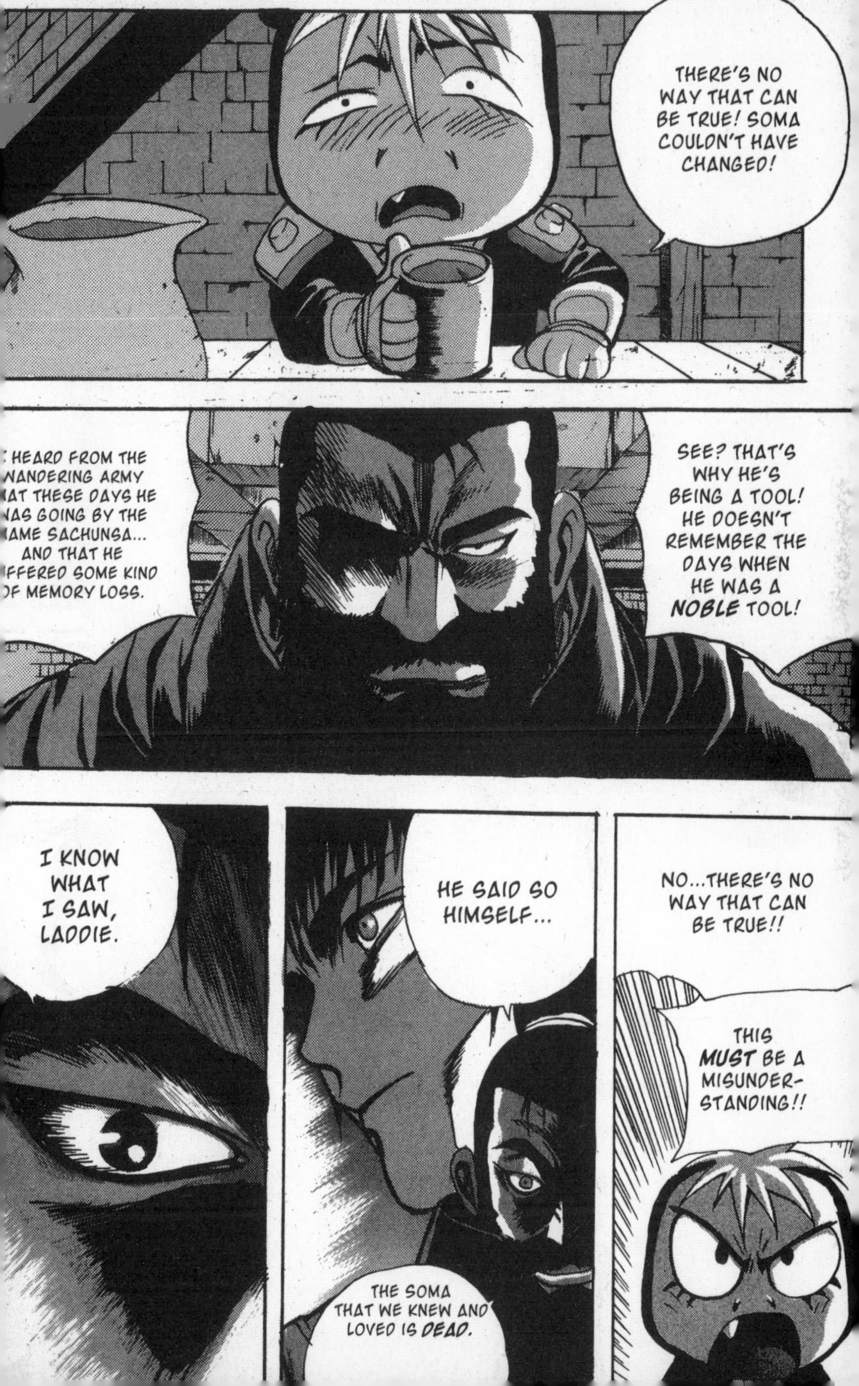

THERE'S NO WAY THAT CAN BE TRUE! SOMA COULDN'T HAVE CHANGED!
HEARD FROM THE WANDERING ARMY AT THESE DAYS HE AS GOING BY THE AME SACHUNSA... AND THAT HE FFERED SOME KIND OF MEMORY LOSS.
SEE? THAT'S WHY HE'S BEING A TOOL! HE DOESN'T REMEMBER THE DAYS WHEN HE WAS A ***NOBLE*** TOOL!
I KNOW WHAT I SAW, LADDIE.
HE SAID SO HIMSELF...
THE SOMA THAT WE KNEW AND LOVED IS ***DEAD***.
NO...THERE'S NO WAY THAT CAN BE TRUE!!
THIS ***MUST*** BE A MISUNDER-STANDING!!

AW, SHUT UP, YEH GIT! SOMA *THIS*, SOMA *THAT!!* I SAY TO *HELL* WITH *HIM!!*

IF YOU LOVE 'IM SO MUCH, THEN GO MARRY 'IM!

I C
AVE
ME D
DON
DEA
WITH
YE!

I DON'T NEED HIM, AND I DON'T NEED Y--

TH-TH
MAJEH.

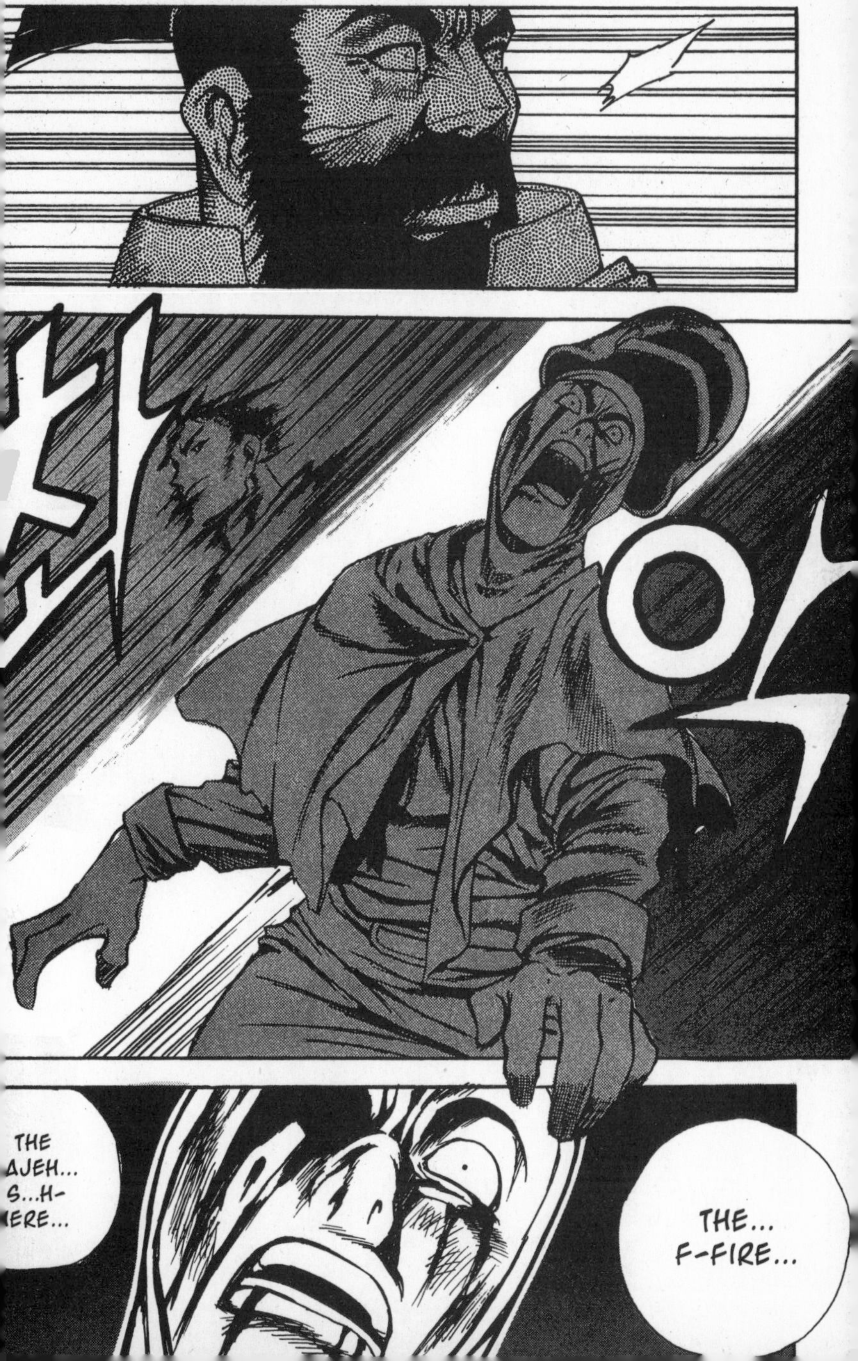
THE
AJEH...
S...H-
ERE...
THE...
F-FIRE...

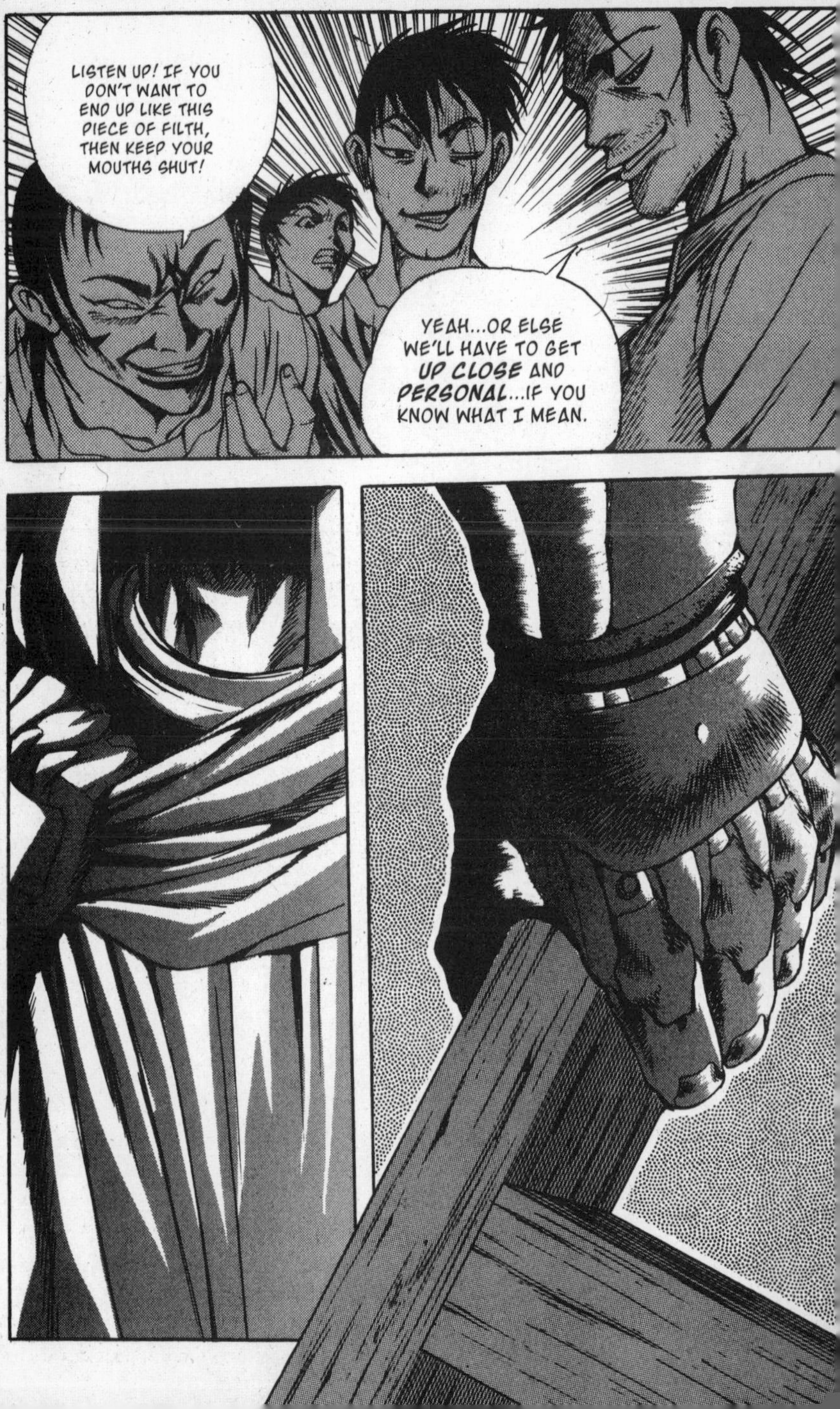
LISTEN UP! IF YOU DON'T WANT TO END UP LIKE THIS PIECE OF FILTH, THEN KEEP YOUR MOUTHS SHUT!
YEAH...OR ELSE WE'LL HAVE TO GET *UP CLOSE* AND *PERSONAL*...IF YOU KNOW WHAT I MEAN.

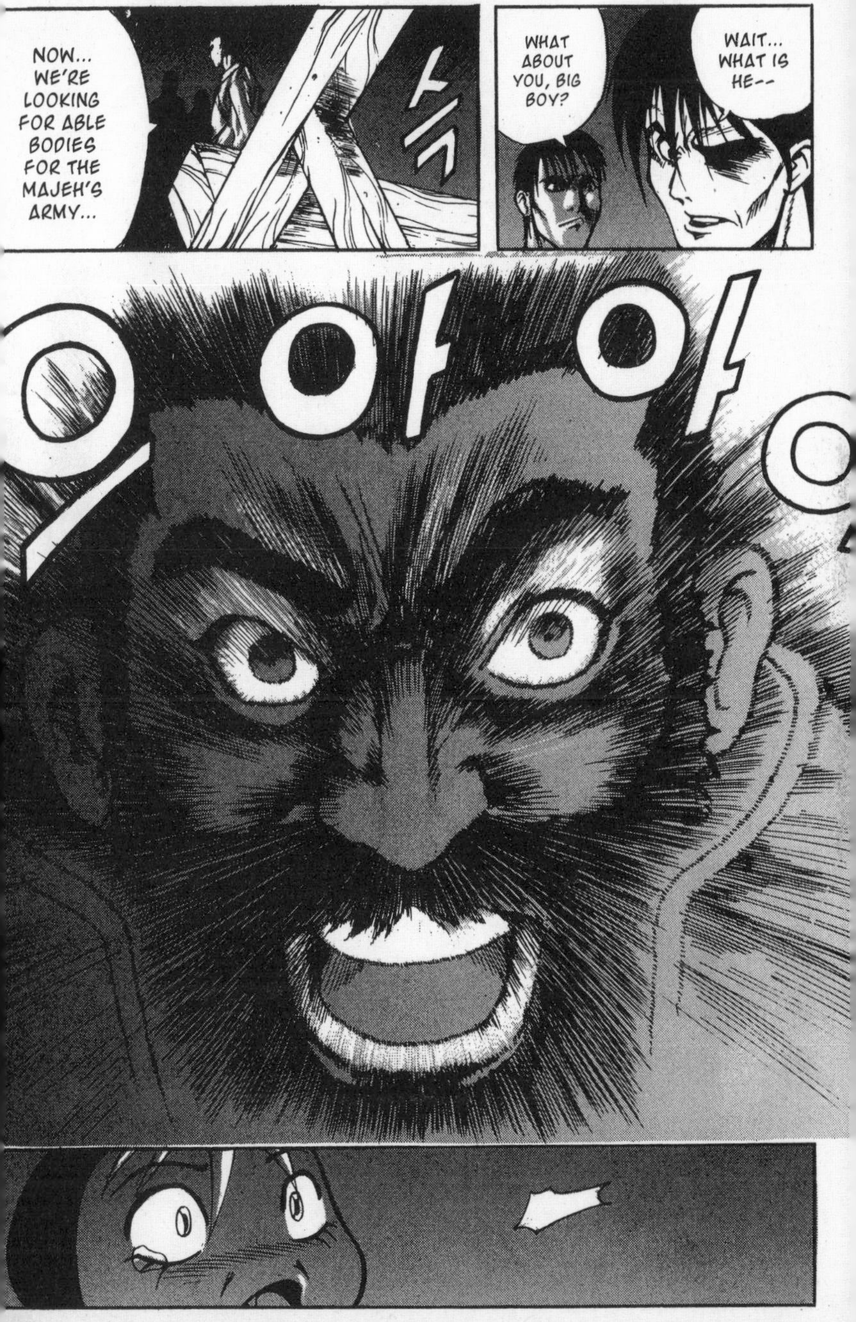
NOW... WE'RE LOOKING FOR ABLE BODIES FOR THE MAJEH'S ARMY...
WAIT... WHAT IS HE--
WHAT ABOUT YOU, BIG BOY?
OOF OOF O

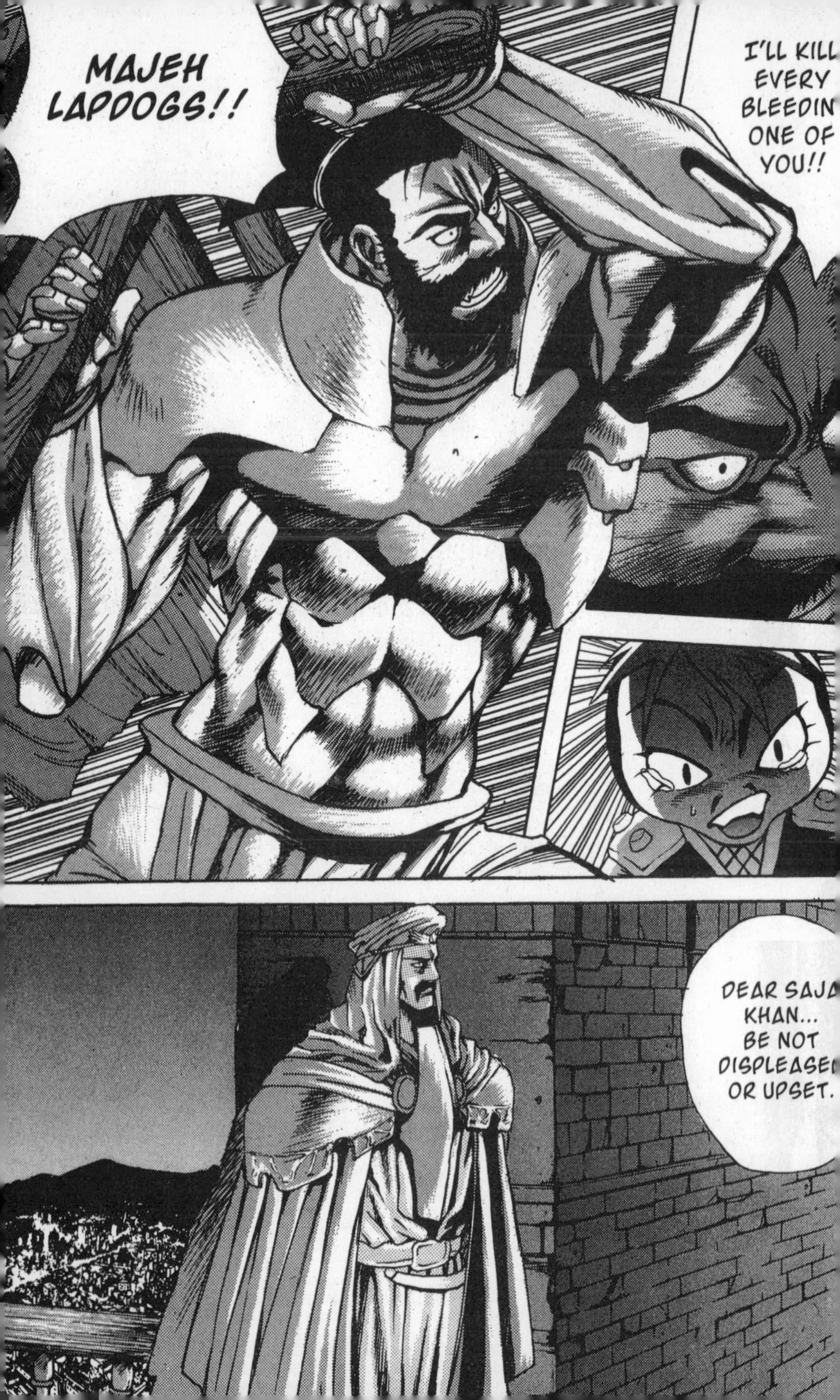
MAJEH LAPDOGS!!
I'LL KILL EVERY BLEEDIN ONE OF YOU!!
DEAR SAJA KHAN... BE NOT DISPLEASE OR UPSET.

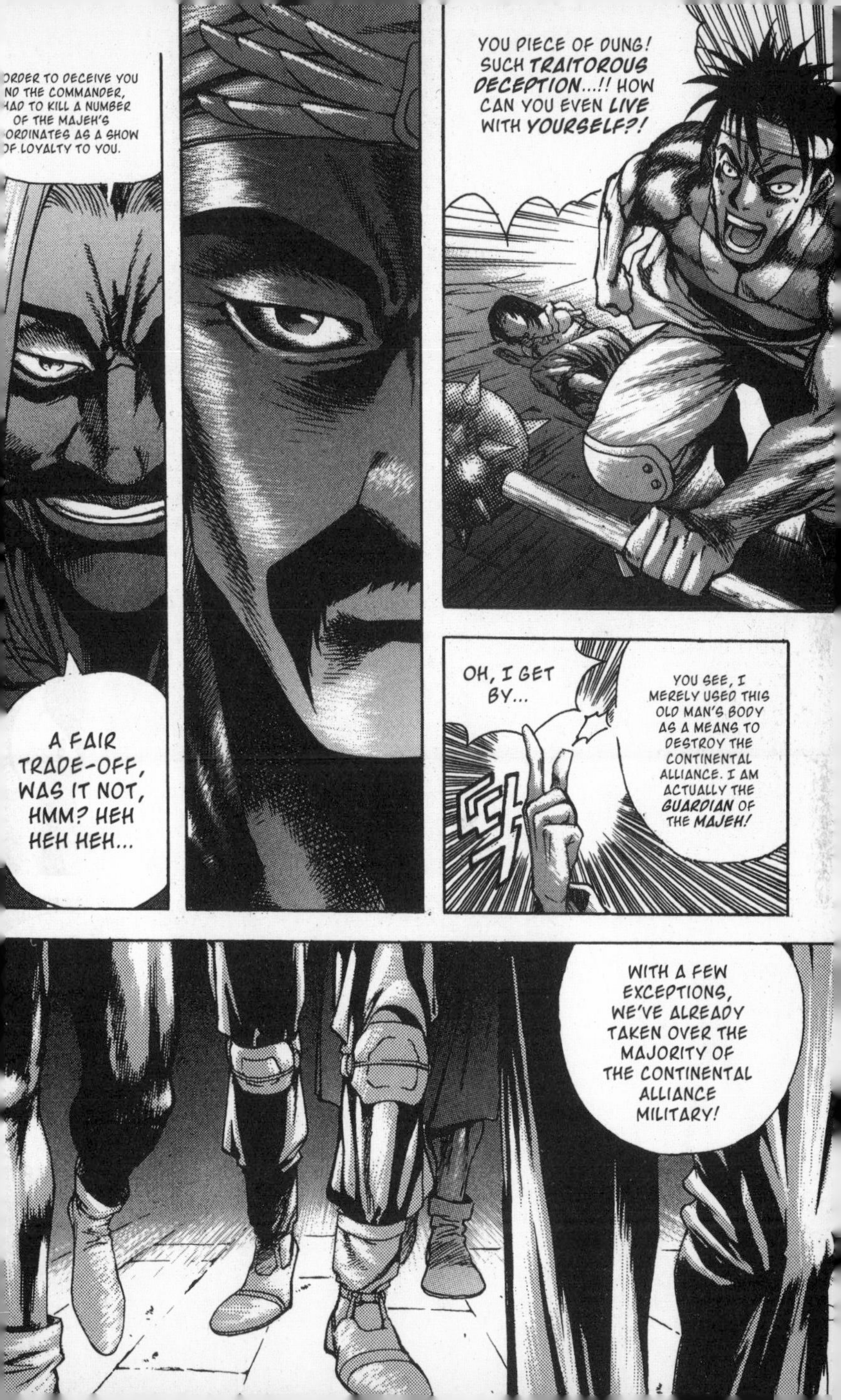
ORDER TO DECEIVE YOU NO THE COMMANDER, HAD TO KILL A NUMBER OF THE MAJEH'S ORDINATES AS A SHOW OF LOYALTY TO YOU.
YOU PIECE OF DUNG! SUCH TRAITOROUS DECEPTION...!! HOW CAN YOU EVEN LIVE WITH YOURSELF?!
A FAIR TRADE-OFF, WAS IT NOT, HMM? HEH HEH HEH...
OH, I GET BY...
YOU SEE, I MERELY USED THIS OLD MAN'S BODY AS A MEANS TO DESTROY THE CONTINENTAL ALLIANCE. I AM ACTUALLY THE GUARDIAN OF THE MAJEH!
WITH A FEW EXCEPTIONS, WE'VE ALREADY TAKEN OVER THE MAJORITY OF THE CONTINENTAL ALLIANCE MILITARY!

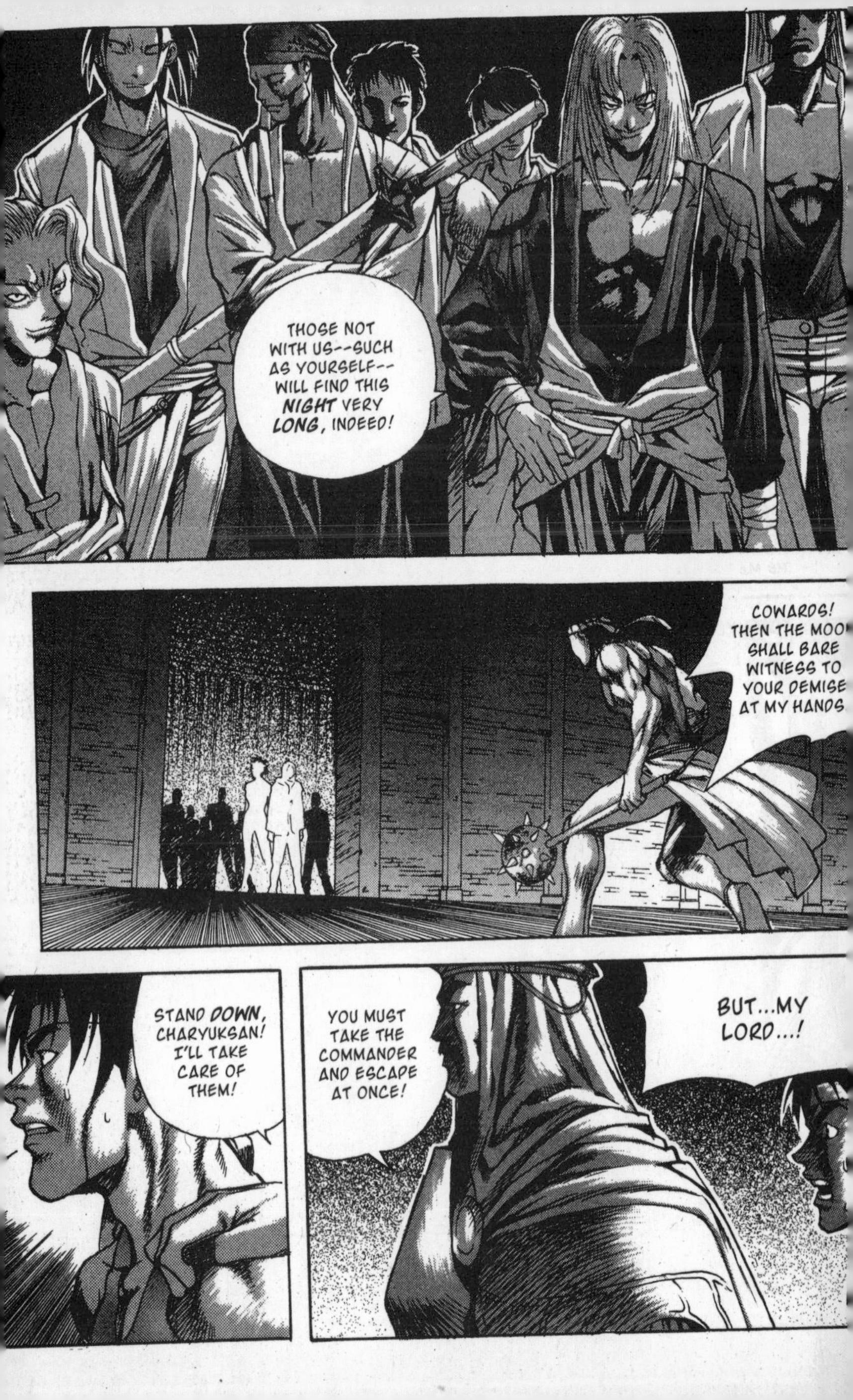
THOSE NOT WITH US--SUCH AS YOURSELF--WILL FIND THIS NIGHT VERY LONG, INDEED!
COWARDS! THEN THE MOO SHALL BARE WITNESS TO YOUR DEMISE AT MY HANDS
BUT...MY LORD...!
YOU MUST TAKE THE COMMANDER AND ESCAPE AT ONCE!
STAND DOWN, CHARYUKSAN! I'LL TAKE CARE OF THEM!

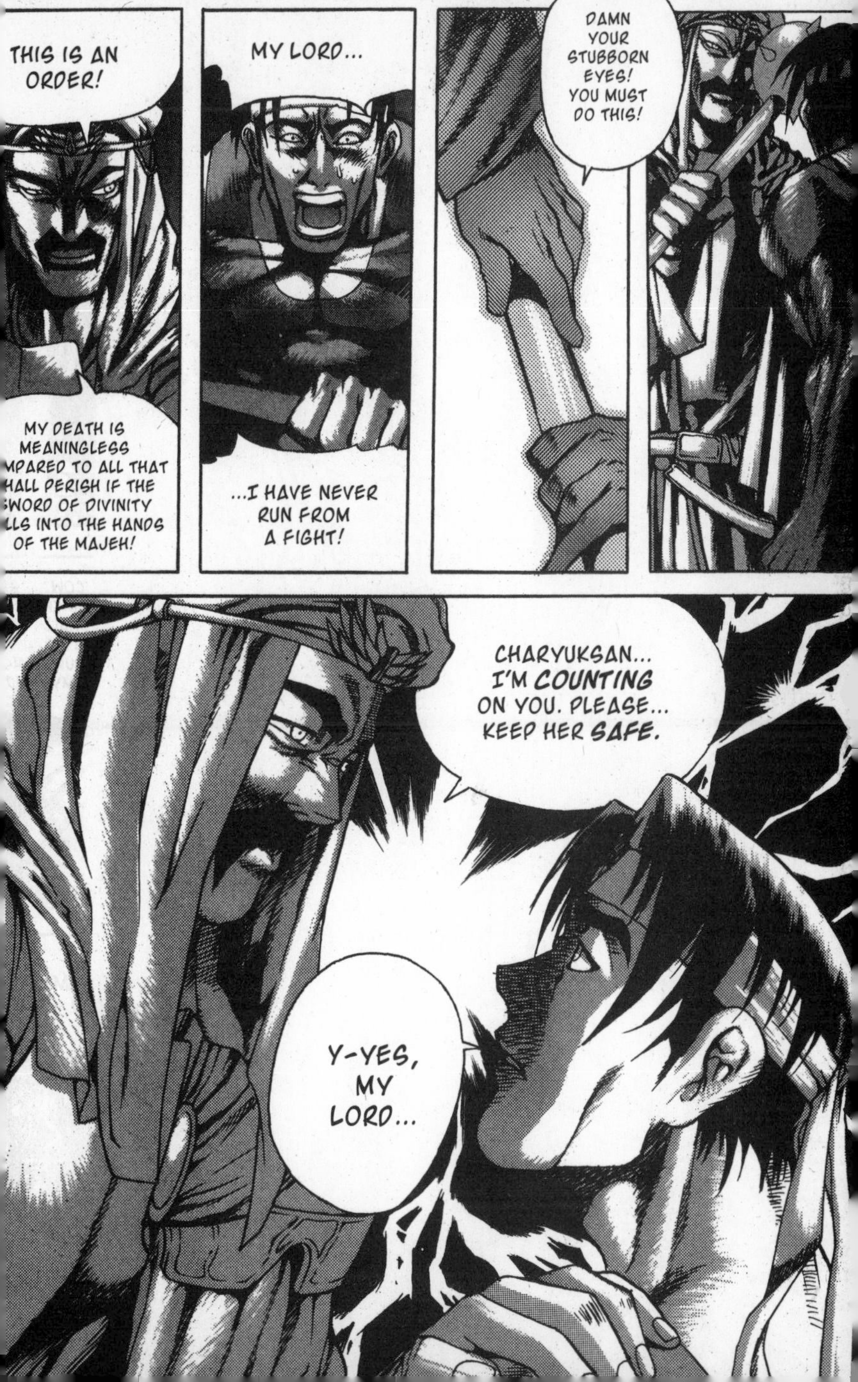
THIS IS AN ORDER!
MY DEATH IS MEANINGLESS
MPARED TO ALL THAT
HALL PERISH IF THE
SWORD OF DIVINITY
LLS INTO THE HANDS
OF THE MAJEH!
MY LORD...
...I HAVE NEVER RUN FROM A FIGHT!
DAMN YOUR STUBBORN EYES! YOU MUST DO THIS!
CHARYUKSAN... I'M COUNTING ON YOU. PLEASE... KEEP HER SAFE.
Y-YES, MY LORD...

HOW TOUCHING. AND HERE I AM, MINUS AN EYE AND A HANKY.

FOOLS... THERE IS NO ESCAPE. THE SWORD WILL BE MINE...AND YOU WILL ALL PERISH BEFORE THE COCK'S CROW.

I'LL ADMIT THAT I'VE PLAYED RIGHT INTO YOUR TRAP...

...BUT YOU WILL FIND SNAPPING IT SHUT A FAR BLOODIER AFFAIR!!

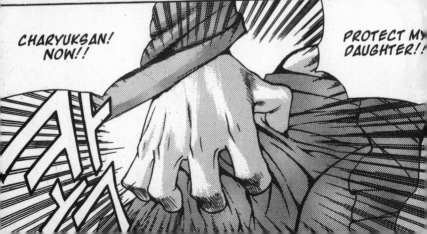

CHARYUKSAN! NOW!!

PROTECT MY DAUGHTER!!

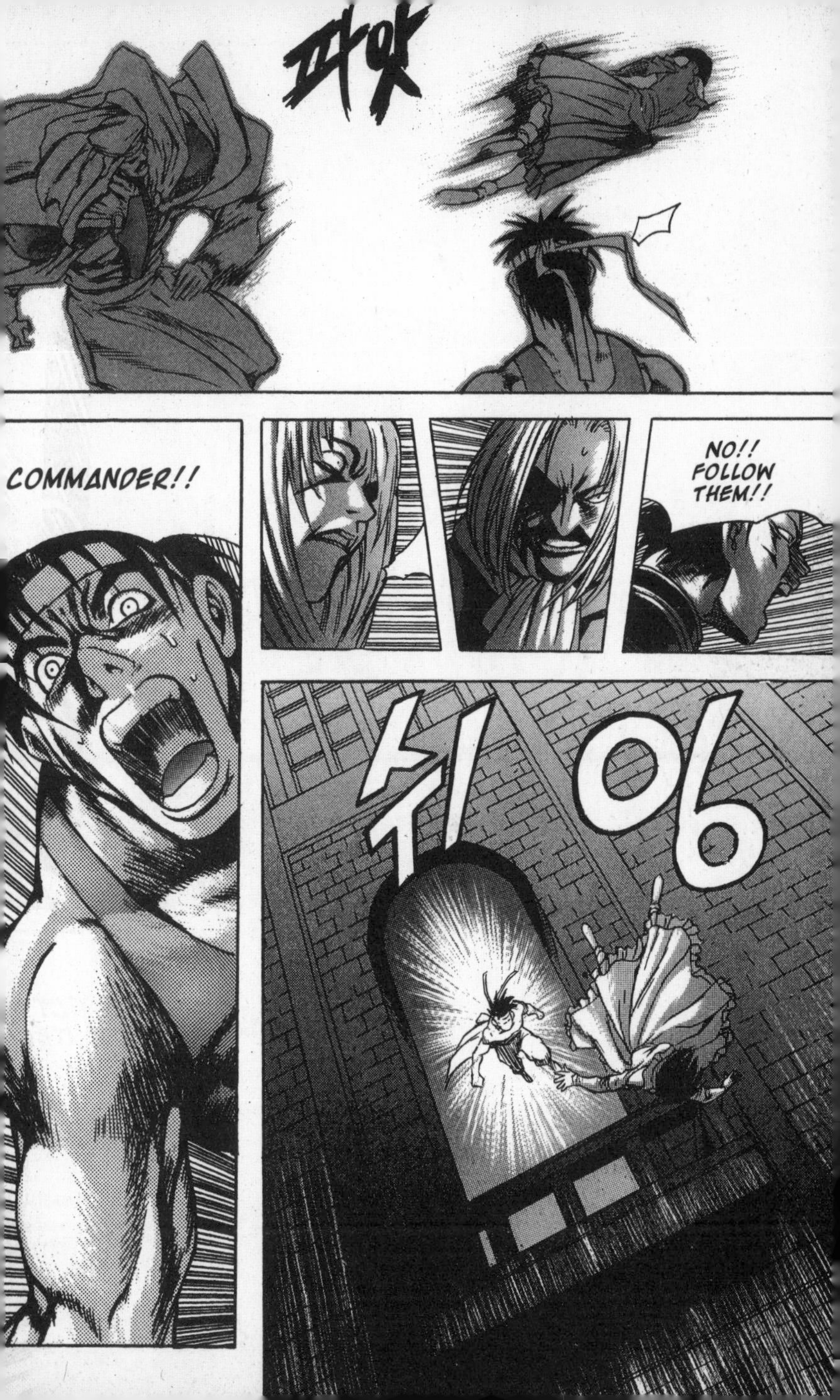

파앗
COMMANDER!!
NO!! FOLLOW THEM!!
쉬이

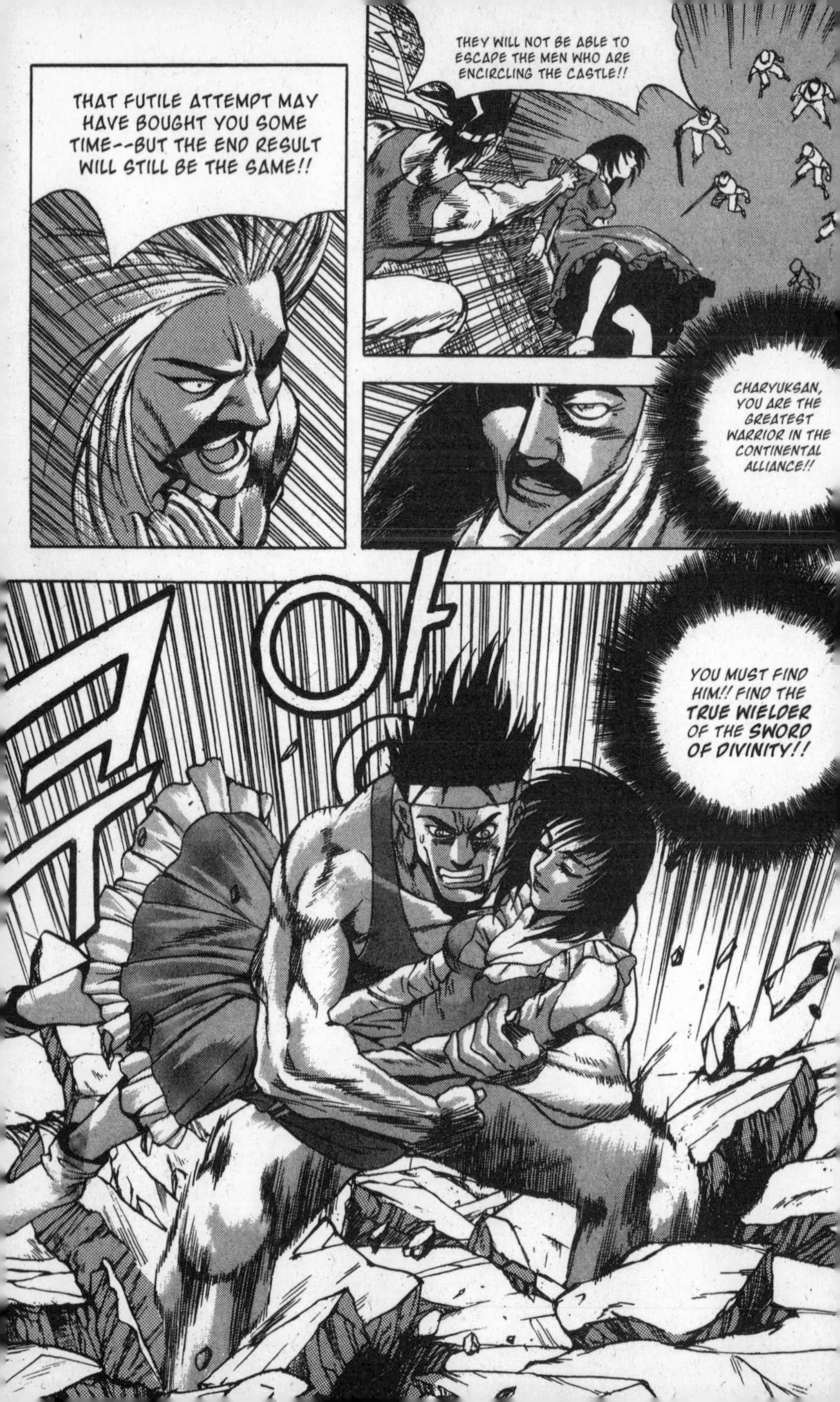
THAT FUTILE ATTEMPT MAY HAVE BOUGHT YOU SOME TIME--BUT THE END RESULT WILL STILL BE THE SAME!!
THEY WILL NOT BE ABLE TO ESCAPE THE MEN WHO ARE ENCIRCLING THE CASTLE!!
CHARYUKSAN, YOU ARE THE GREATEST WARRIOR IN THE CONTINENTAL ALLIANCE!!
YOU MUST FIND HIM!! FIND THE TRUE WIELDER OF THE SWORD OF DIVINITY!!

BLADE OF HEAVEN

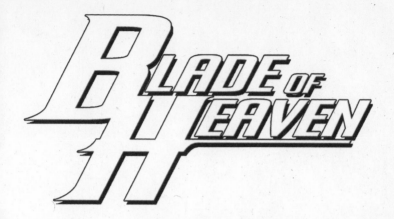

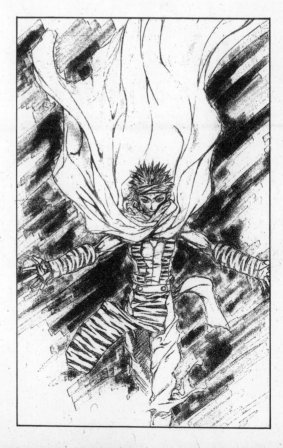

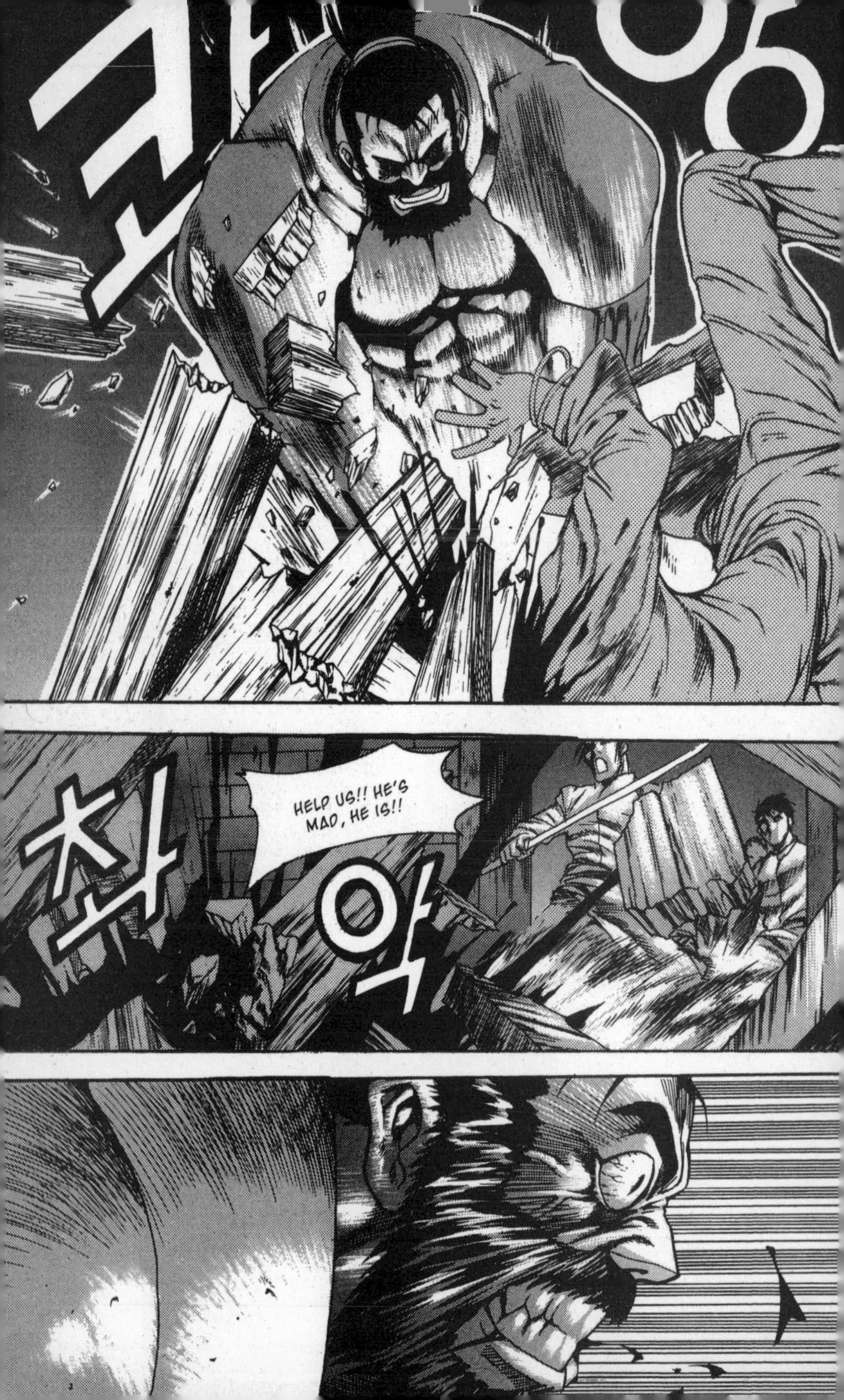
HELP US!! HE'S MAD, HE IS!!

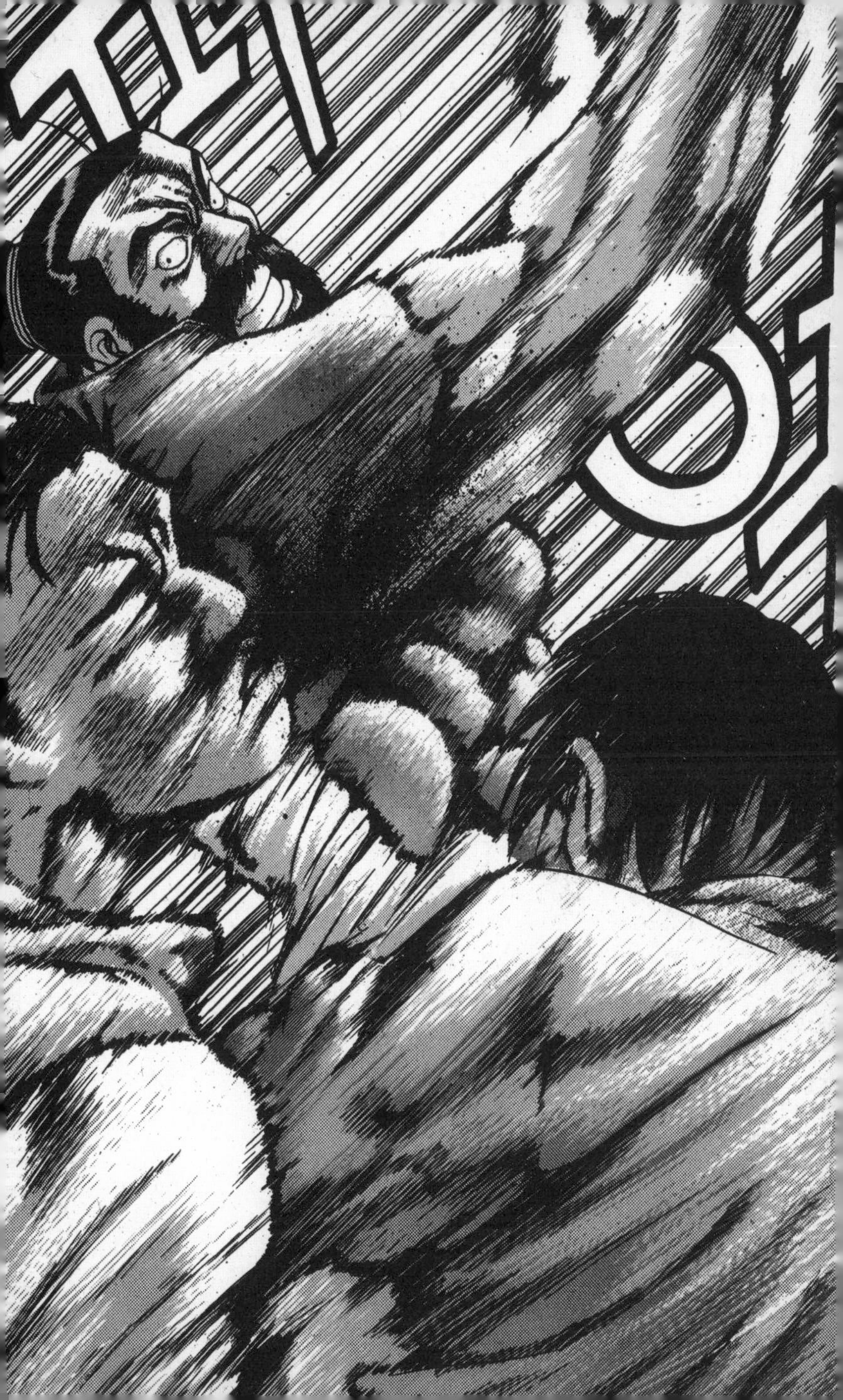

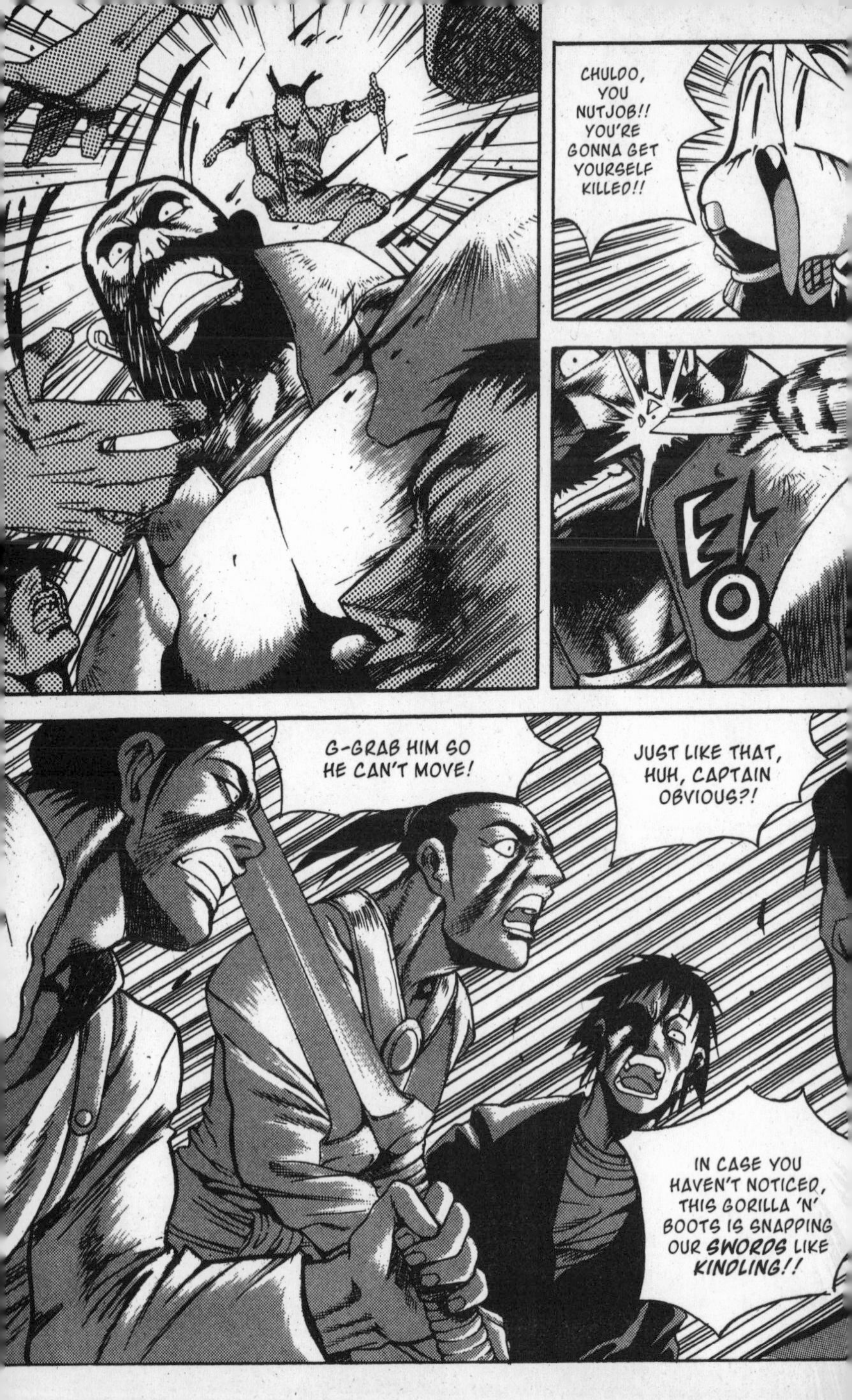
CHULDO, YOU NUTJOB!! YOU'RE GONNA GET YOURSELF KILLED!!
G-GRAB HIM SO HE CAN'T MOVE!
JUST LIKE THAT, HUH, CAPTAIN OBVIOUS?!
IN CASE YOU HAVEN'T NOTICED, THIS GORILLA 'N' BOOTS IS SNAPPING OUR SWORDS LIKE KINDLING!!

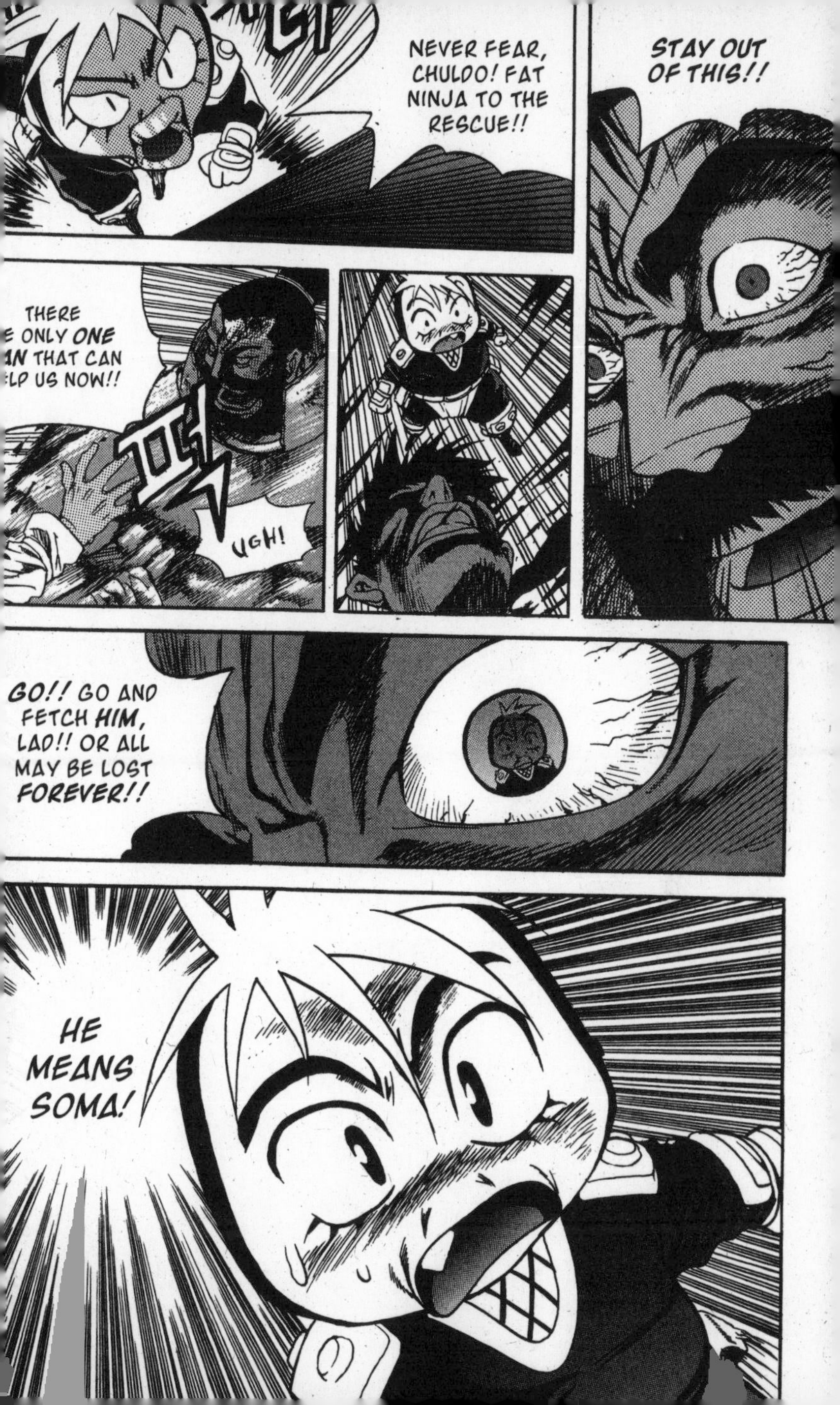
NEVER FEAR, CHULDO! FAT NINJA TO THE RESCUE!!
STAY OUT OF THIS!!
THERE E ONLY ONE AN THAT CAN ELP US NOW!!
UGH!
GO!! GO AND FETCH HIM, LAD!! OR ALL MAY BE LOST FOREVER!!
HE MEANS SOMA!

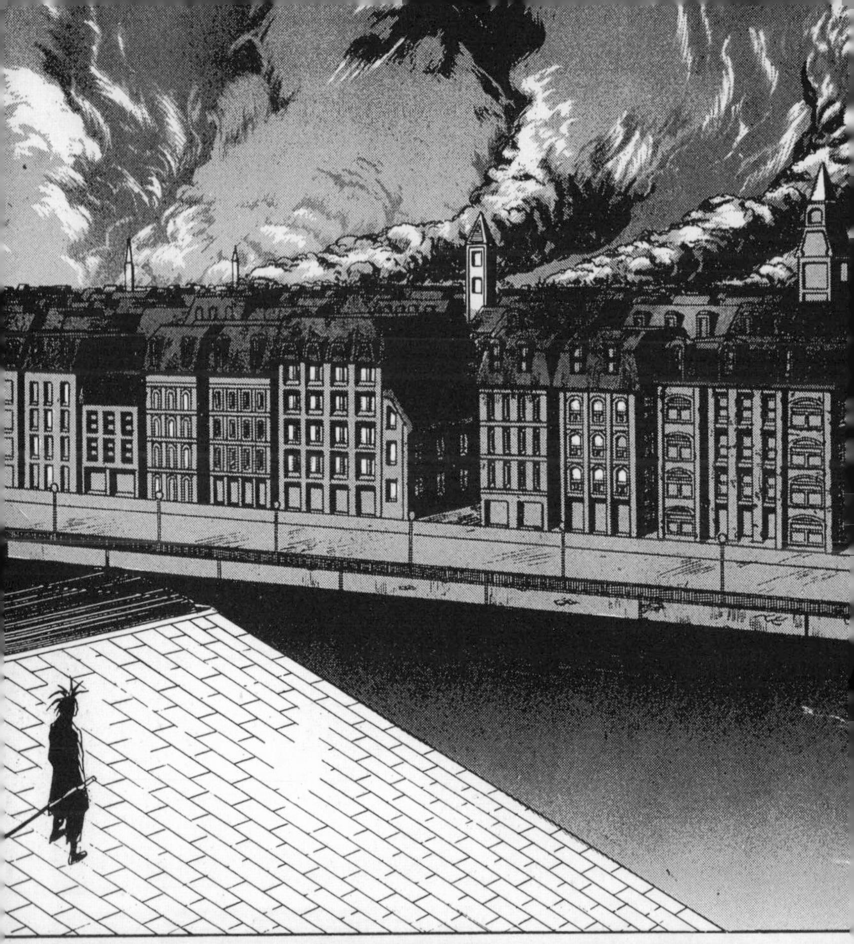

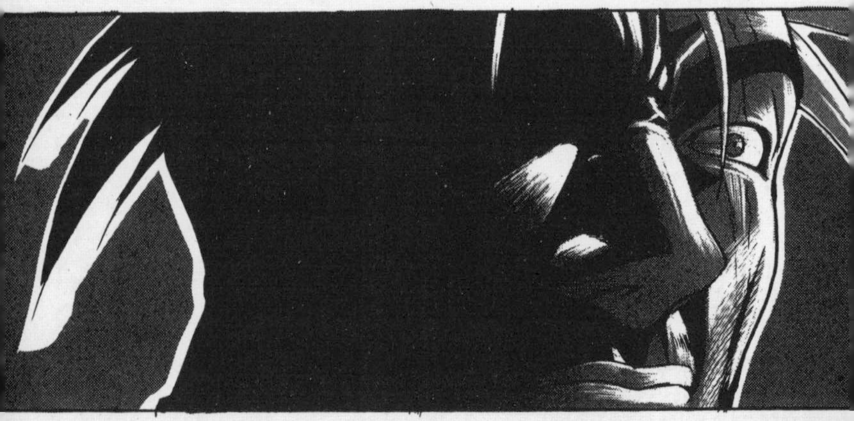

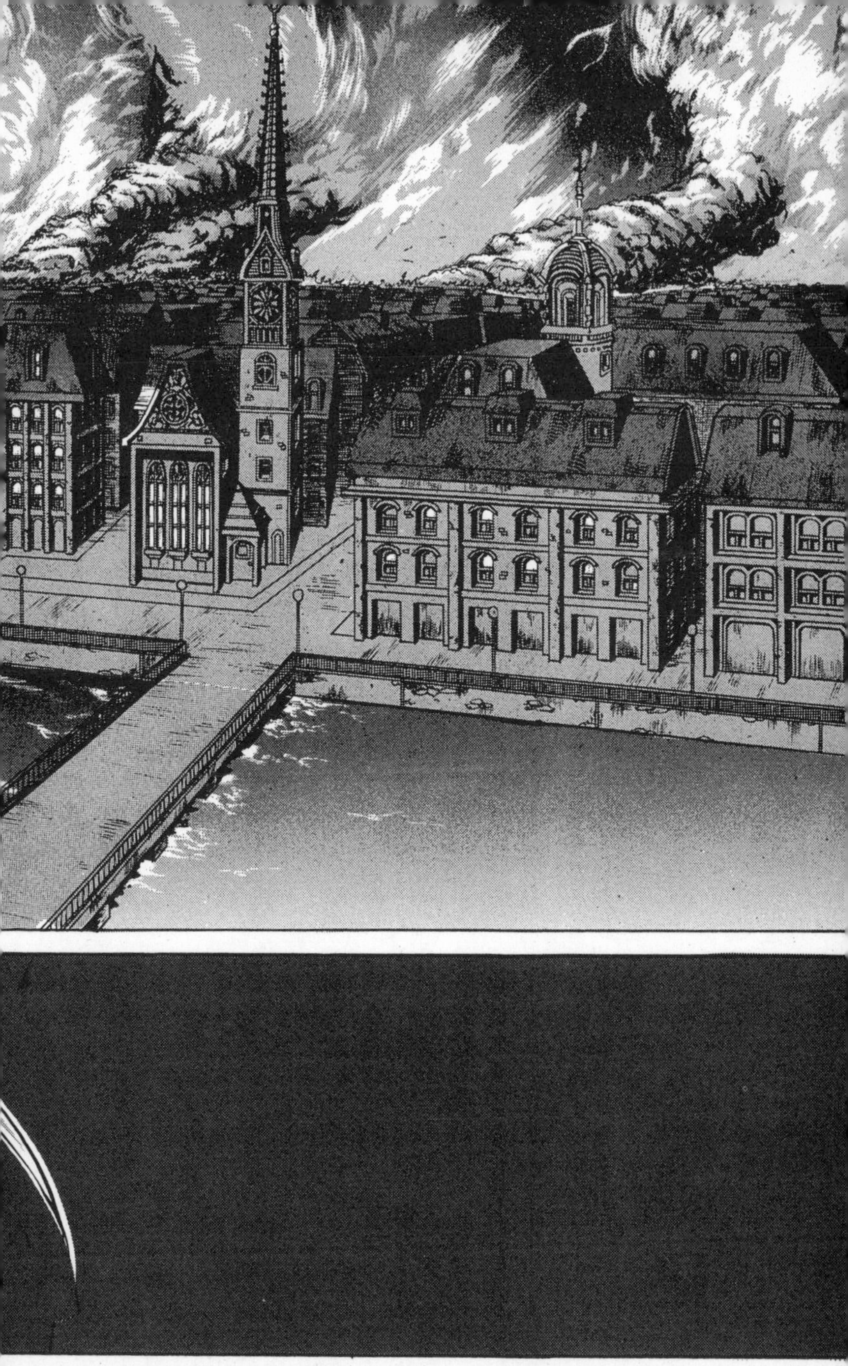

JUST LOOK AT THAT FIRE BURN...

I SEE I'M NOT THE ONLY ONE OUT FOR A WALK.

IT'S RARE SOMETHING SO BEAUTIFUL IS EQUALLY AS DEADLY.

NATURE'S FIREWORKS, THEY ARE! HEH HEH...!

WATTAYA SAY, BROTHER? CARE FOR A DRINK TO TAKE THE NIP OUT OF THE NIGHT?

SUIT YOURSELF. NEED TO G ALL SOUR IN FACE ABC IT.

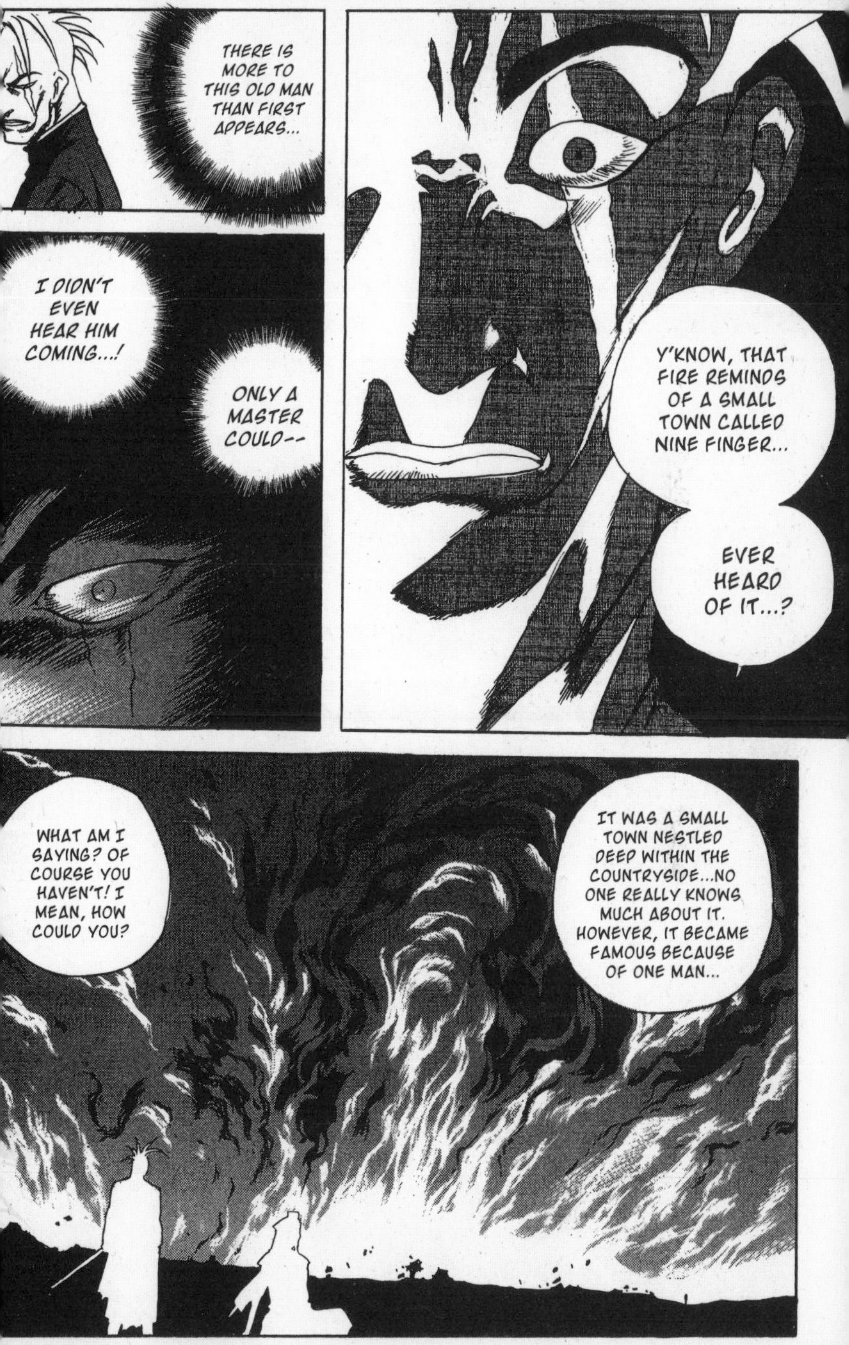

THERE IS MORE TO THIS OLD MAN THAN FIRST APPEARS...
I DIDN'T EVEN HEAR HIM COMING...!
ONLY A MASTER COULD--
Y'KNOW, THAT FIRE REMINDS OF A SMALL TOWN CALLED NINE FINGER...
EVER HEARD OF IT...?
WHAT AM I SAYING? OF COURSE YOU HAVEN'T! I MEAN, HOW COULD YOU?
IT WAS A SMALL TOWN NESTLED DEEP WITHIN THE COUNTRYSIDE...NO ONE REALLY KNOWS MUCH ABOUT IT. HOWEVER, IT BECAME FAMOUS BECAUSE OF ONE MAN...

THIS MAN GOUGED OUT ONE EYE FROM EACH MAN, WOMAN AND CHILD IN THAT TOWN. IF THAT WASN'T ENOUGH, ONCE HE SEVERED THEIR LEFT PINKIES, HE SET THE ENTIRE TOWN ON FIRE!

I HEARD HE DID IT TO AVENGE THE DEATH OF HIS WIFE AND CHILD...OR SOMETHING LIKE THAT. FROM THAT DAY FORWARD, HE WAS KNOWN AS THE *NINE FINGER DEMON.*

...HENCE THE NAME OF THE TOWN WAS CHANGED TO NINE FINGER.

ALAS, T... TOWN N... LONGE... EXISTS... WATCHIN... THIS TOW... BURN... REMINDE... ME OF... THEY S... THE DEM... COULD OUT... LIGHTNIN... HE WAS... FAST...

THOUGH HE WASN'T WITHOUT A FLAW OR TWO OF HIS OWN. Y'SEE, AS HIS NICKNAME SUGGESTS, HE HAD ONLY *ONE EYE* AND *NINE FINGERS.*

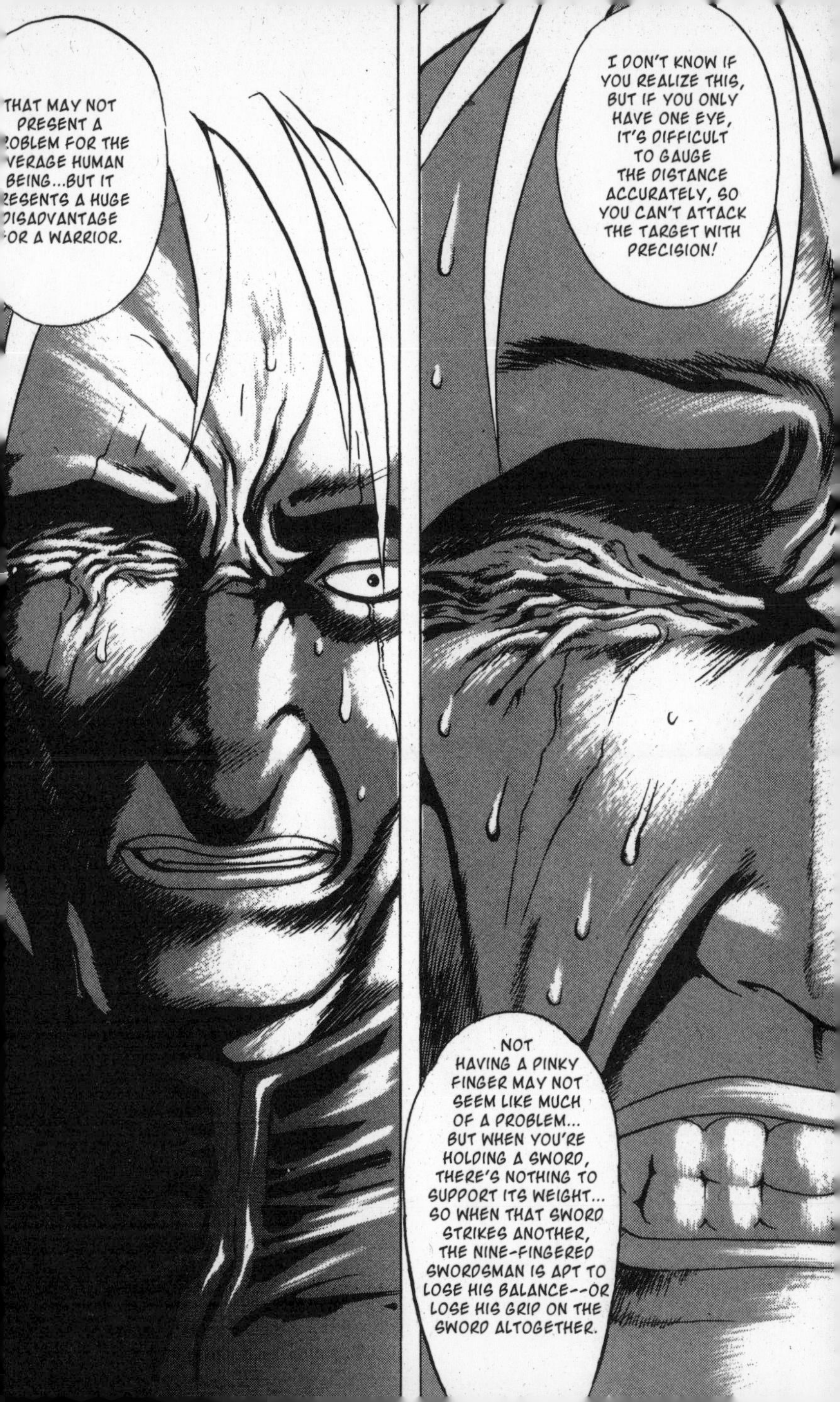
I DON'T KNOW IF YOU REALIZE THIS, BUT IF YOU ONLY HAVE ONE EYE, IT'S DIFFICULT TO GAUGE THE DISTANCE ACCURATELY, SO YOU CAN'T ATTACK THE TARGET WITH PRECISION!
THAT MAY NOT PRESENT A ROBLEM FOR THE VERAGE HUMAN BEING...BUT IT RESENTS A HUGE DISADVANTAGE FOR A WARRIOR.
NOT HAVING A PINKY FINGER MAY NOT SEEM LIKE MUCH OF A PROBLEM... BUT WHEN YOU'RE HOLDING A SWORD, THERE'S NOTHING TO SUPPORT ITS WEIGHT... SO WHEN THAT SWORD STRIKES ANOTHER, THE NINE-FINGERED SWORDSMAN IS APT TO LOSE HIS BALANCE--OR LOSE HIS GRIP ON THE SWORD ALTOGETHER.

HMM...STRANGE I'M REMINDED OF HIM WHEN I LOOK AT YOU, BEING AS YOU HAVE NOTHING WRONG WITH YOUR BODY...

QUICK-TEMPERED, THAT ONE.

HMPH. LI IS THE SA NO MATT HOW YC LOOK AT

HUH...? HE LEFT ALREADY?

WAS IT SOMETHING I SAID...?

IT'S ALL JUST A DOG'S DREAM...

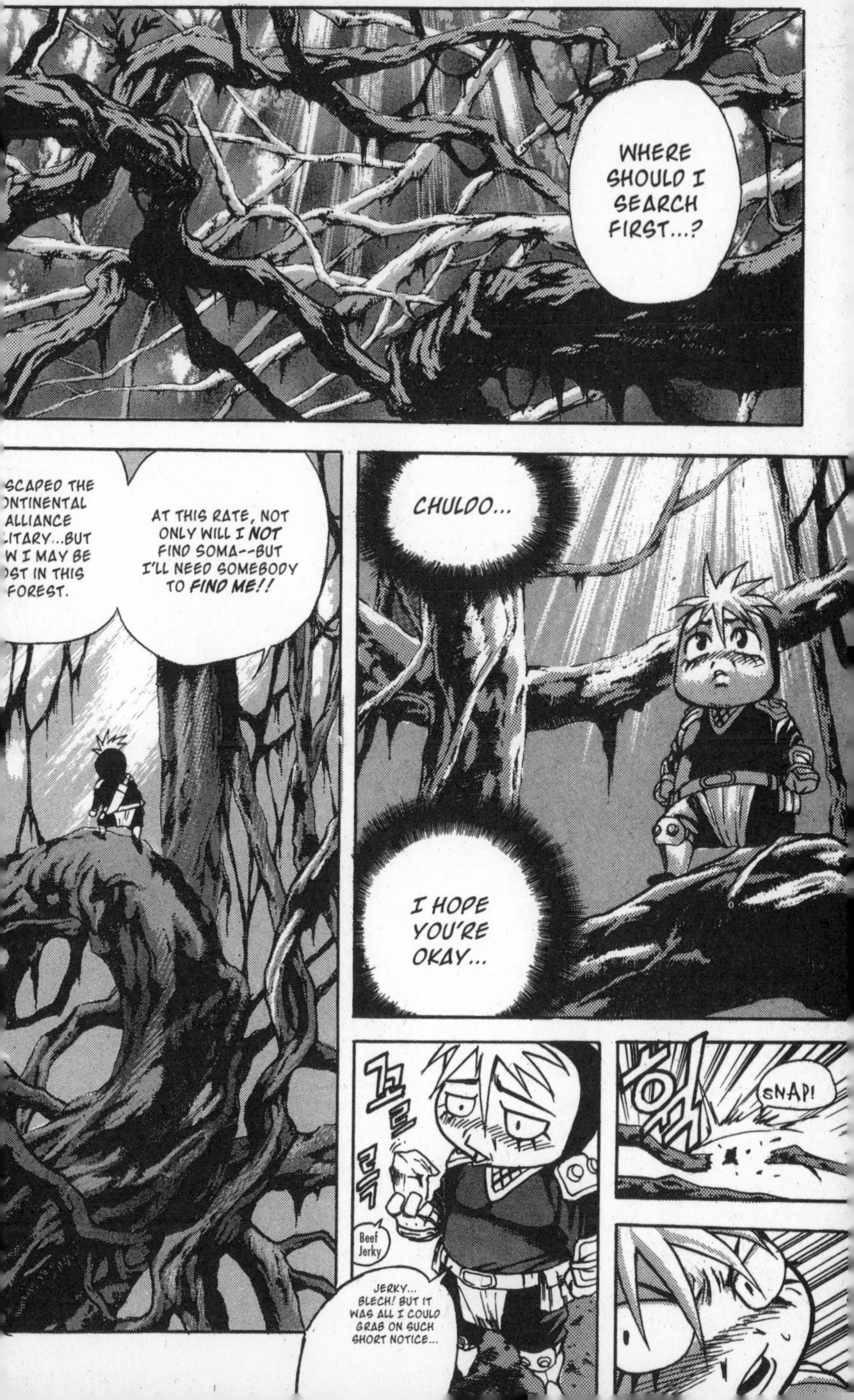
WHERE SHOULD I SEARCH FIRST...?
SCAPED THE ONTINENTAL ALLIANCE LITARY...BUT W I MAY BE OST IN THIS FOREST.
AT THIS RATE, NOT ONLY WILL I NOT FIND SOMA--BUT I'LL NEED SOMEBODY TO FIND ME!!
CHULDO...
I HOPE YOU'RE OKAY...
Beef Jerky
JERKY... BLECH! BUT IT WAS ALL I COULD GRAB ON SUCH SHORT NOTICE...
SNAP!

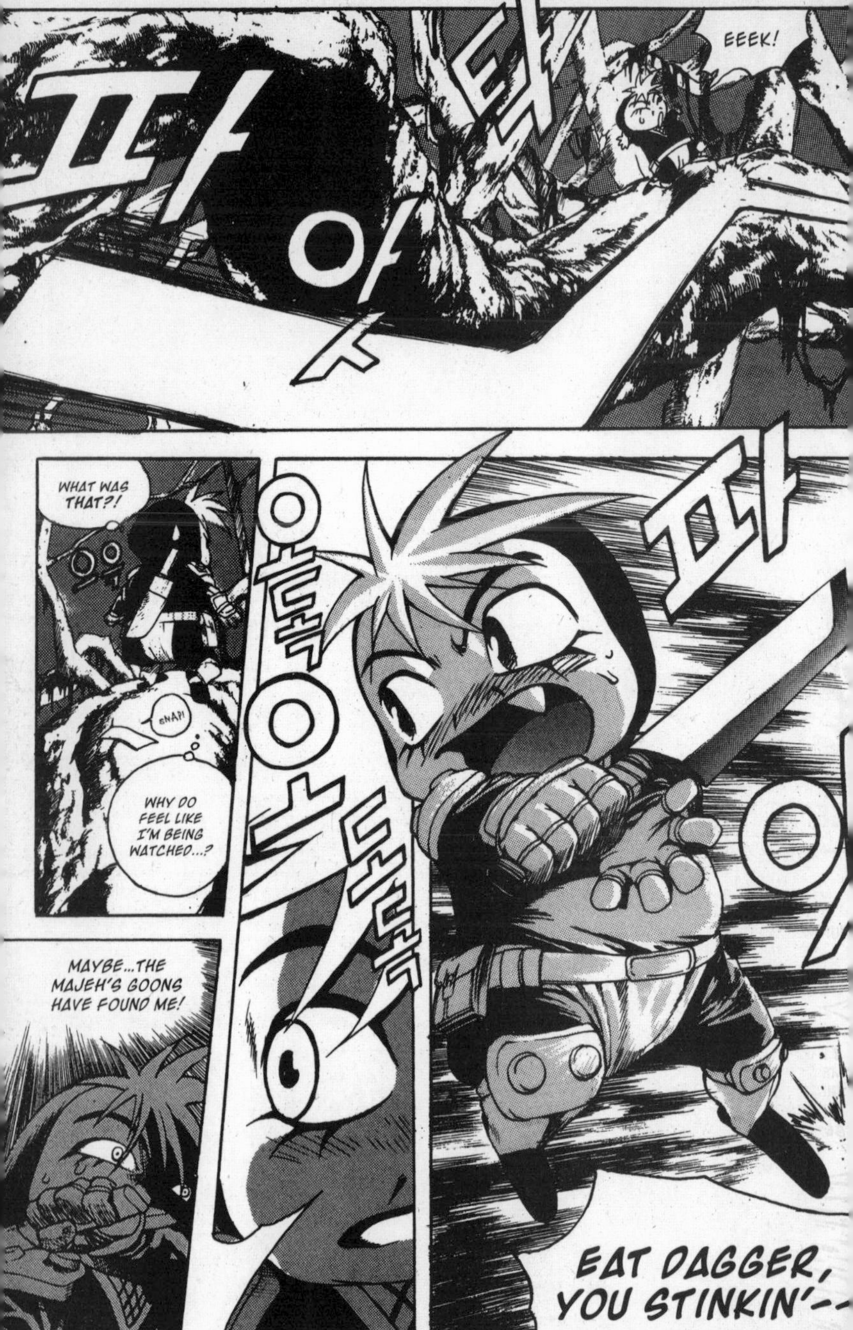
EEEK!
WHAT WAS THAT?!
SNAP!
WHY DO FEEL LIKE I'M BEING WATCHED...?
MAYBE...THE MAJEH'S GOONS HAVE FOUND ME!
EAT DAGGER, YOU STINKIN'--

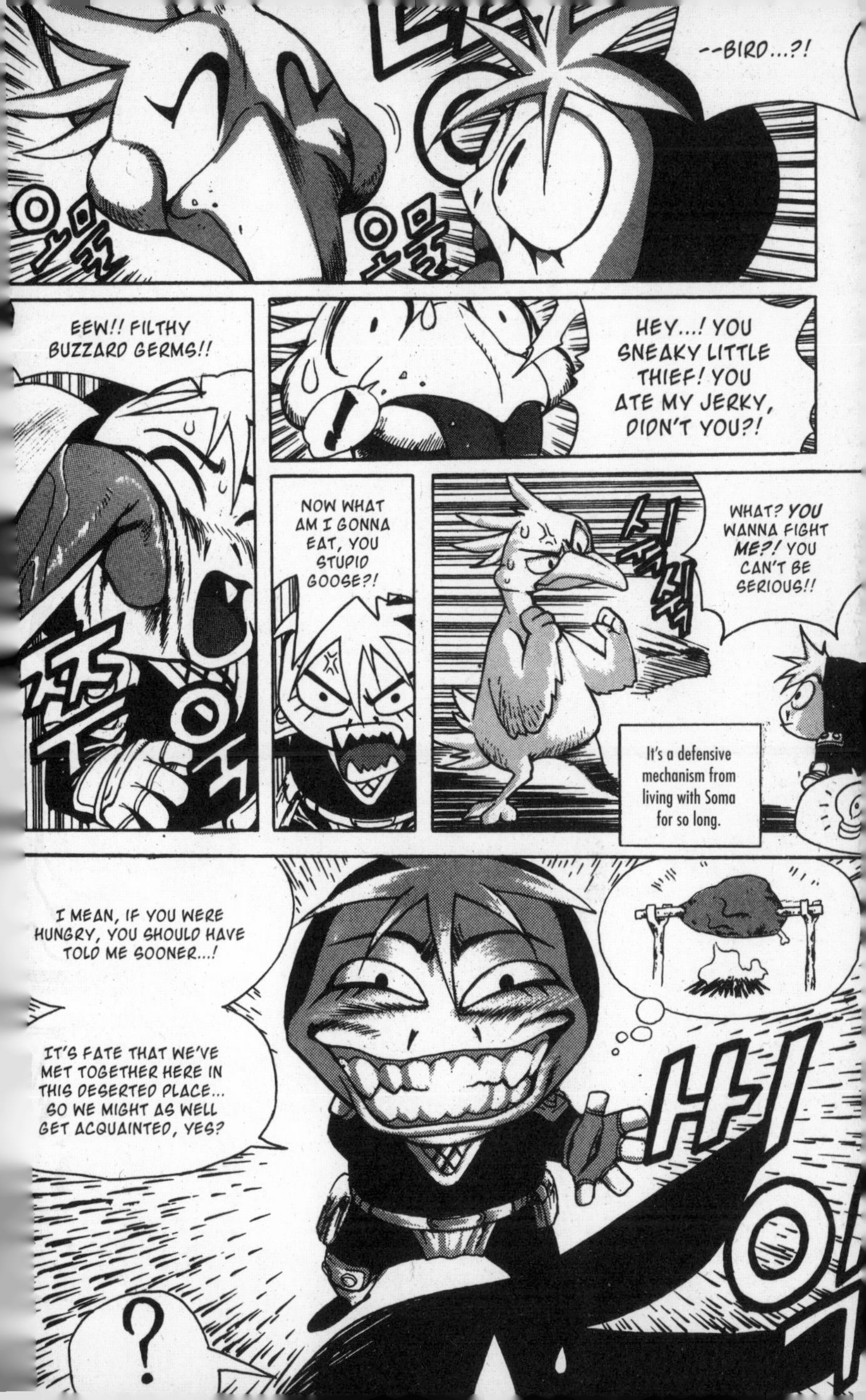

--BIRD...?!
EEW!! FILTHY BUZZARD GERMS!!
HEY...! YOU SNEAKY LITTLE THIEF! YOU ATE MY JERKY, DIDN'T YOU?!
NOW WHAT AM I GONNA EAT, YOU STUPID GOOSE?!
WHAT? YOU WANNA FIGHT ME?! YOU CAN'T BE SERIOUS!!
It's a defensive mechanism from living with Soma for so long.
I MEAN, IF YOU WERE HUNGRY, YOU SHOULD HAVE TOLD ME SOONER...!
IT'S FATE THAT WE'VE MET TOGETHER HERE IN THIS DESERTED PLACE... SO WE MIGHT AS WELL GET ACQUAINTED, YES?
?

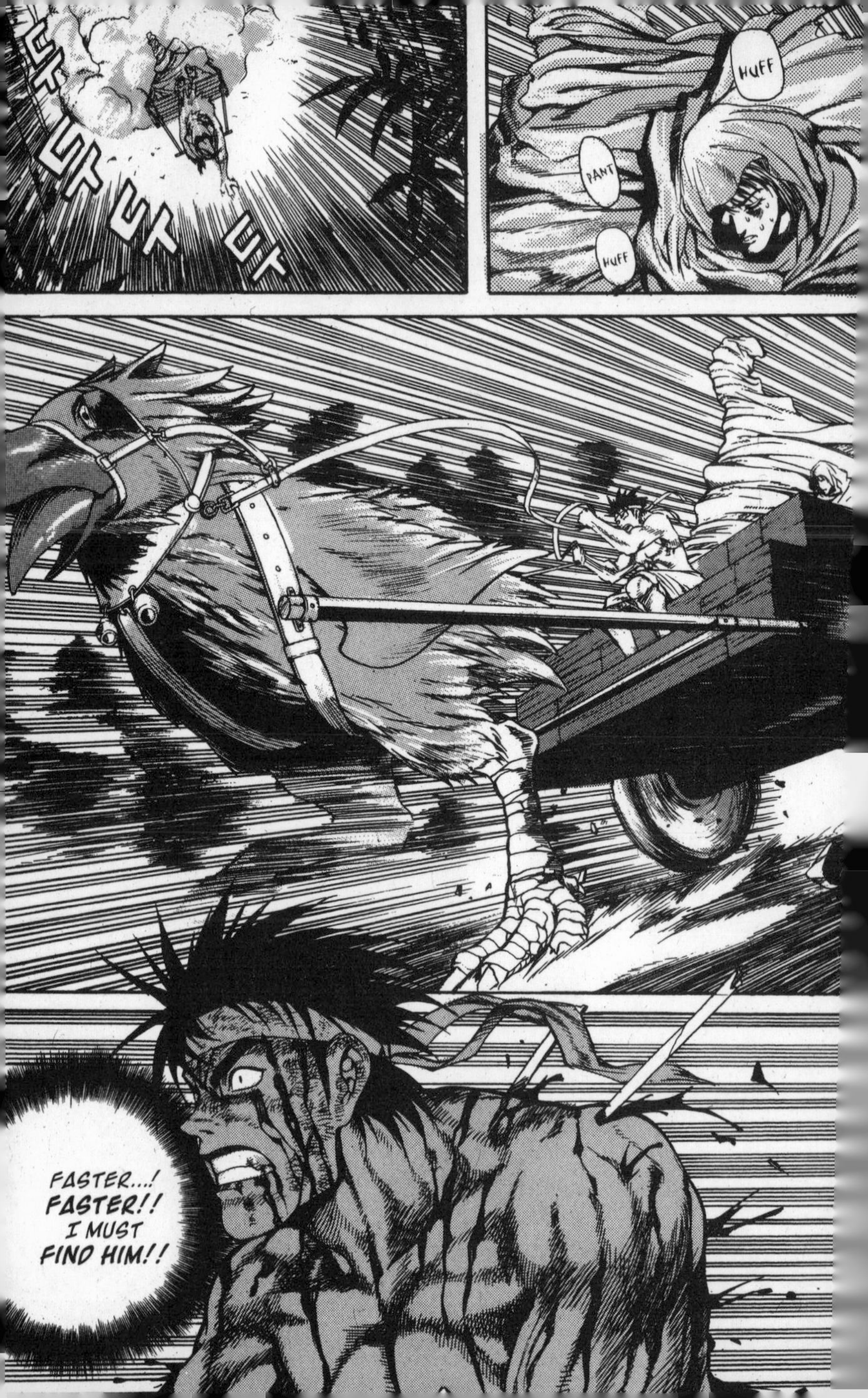

HUFF
PANT
HUFF
FASTER...! FASTER!! I MUST FIND HIM!!

BLADE OF HEAVEN

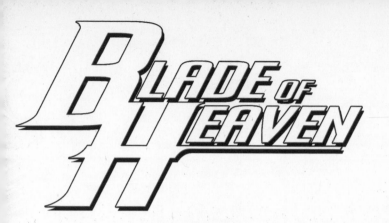

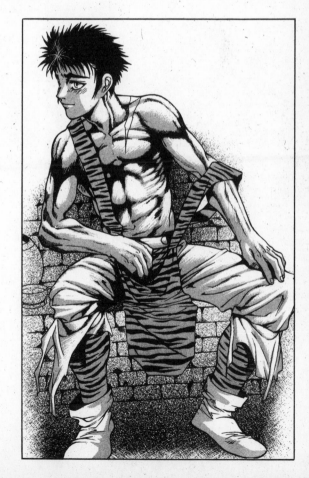

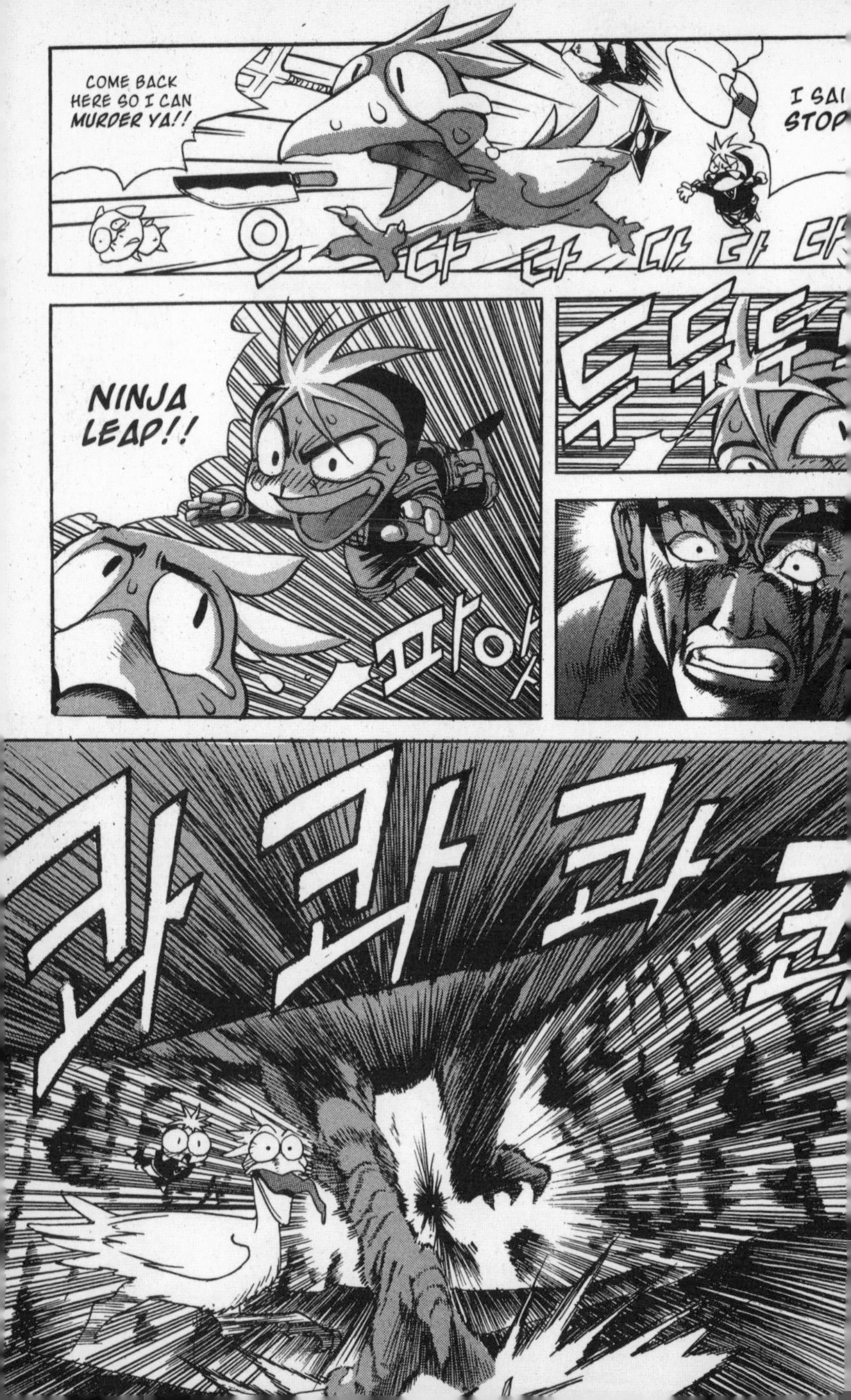
COME BACK HERE SO I CAN MURDER YA!!
I SAI STOP
NINJA LEAP!!

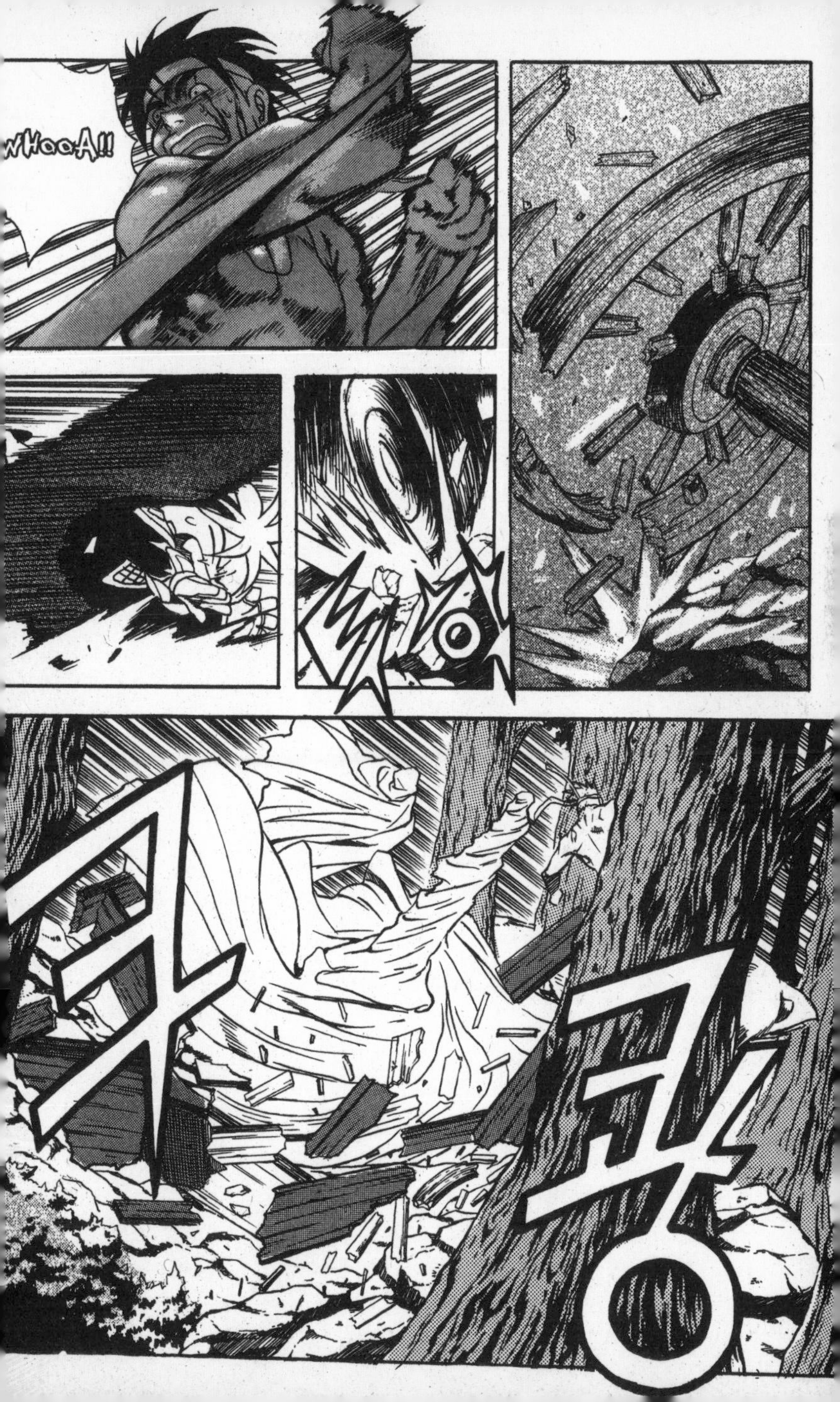
wHaaA!!

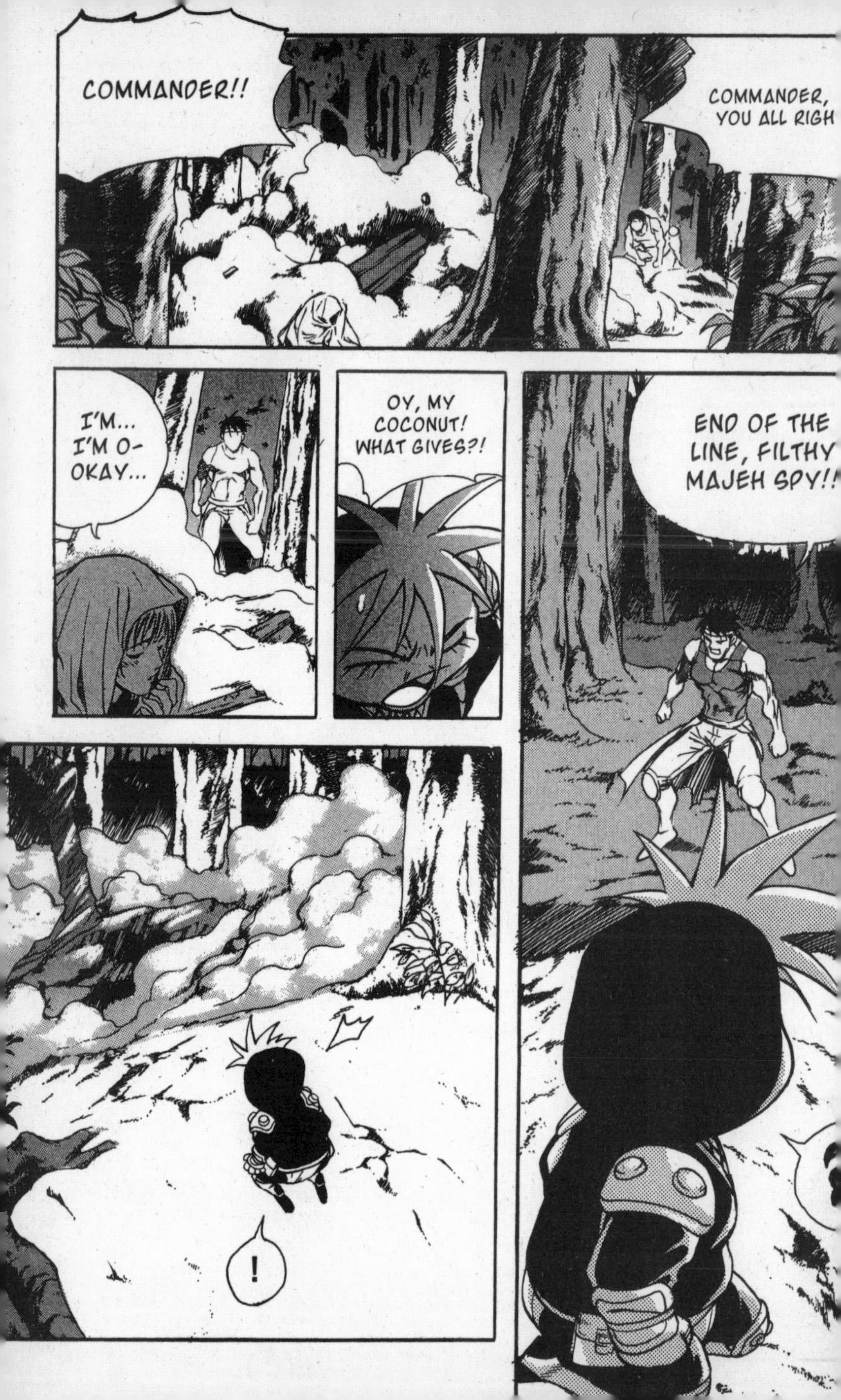

COMMANDER!!
COMMANDER, YOU ALL RIGH
I'M... I'M O-OKAY...
OY, MY COCONUT! WHAT GIVES?!
END OF THE LINE, FILTHY MAJEH SPY!!
!

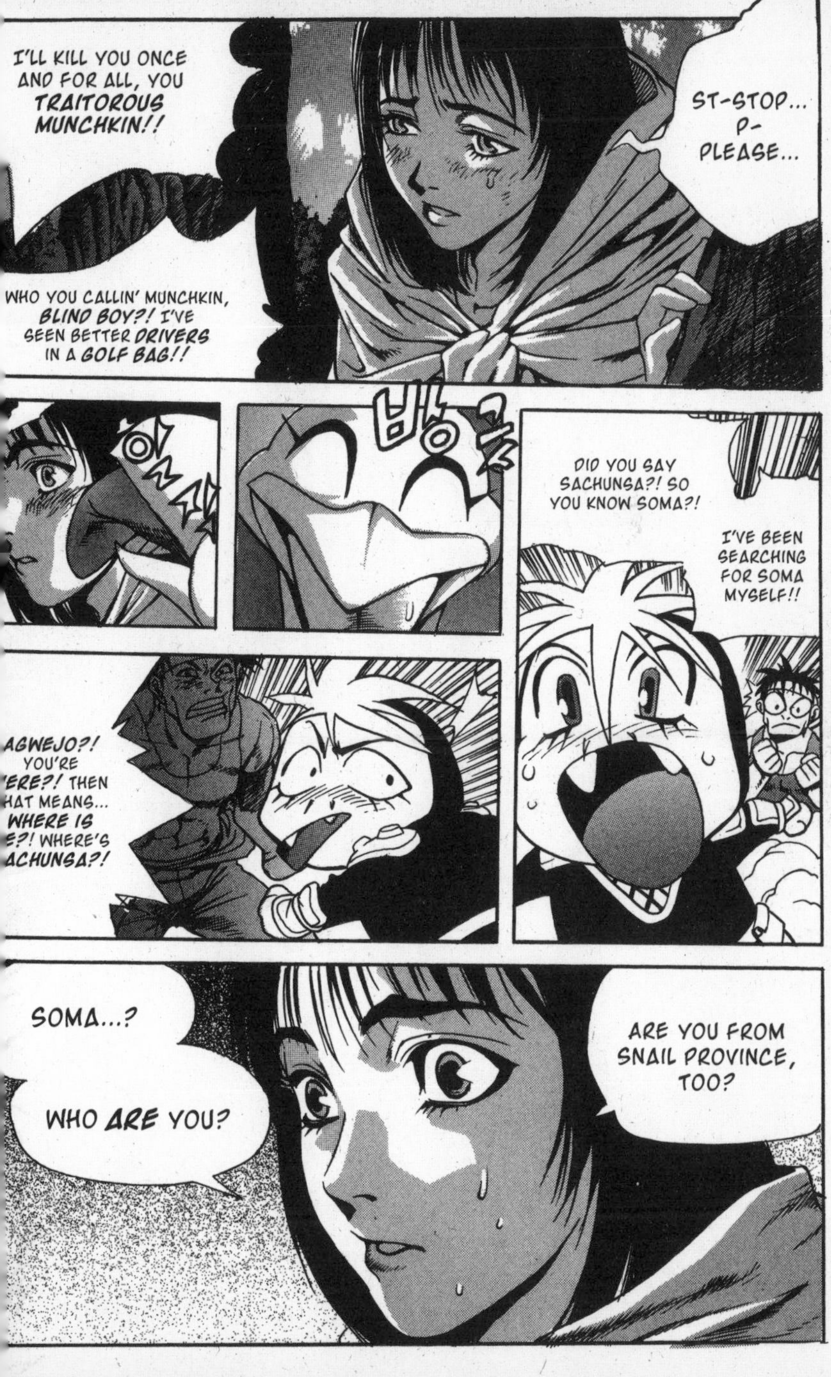
I'LL KILL YOU ONCE AND FOR ALL, YOU TRAITOROUS MUNCHKIN!!
ST-STOP... P-PLEASE...
WHO YOU CALLIN' MUNCHKIN, BLIND BOY?! I'VE SEEN BETTER DRIVERS IN A GOLF BAG!!
DID YOU SAY SACHUNSA?! SO YOU KNOW SOMA?!
I'VE BEEN SEARCHING FOR SOMA MYSELF!!
AGWEJO?! YOU'RE ERE?! THEN HAT MEANS... WHERE IS E?! WHERE'S ACHUNSA?!
SOMA...?
WHO ARE YOU?
ARE YOU FROM SNAIL PROVINCE, TOO?

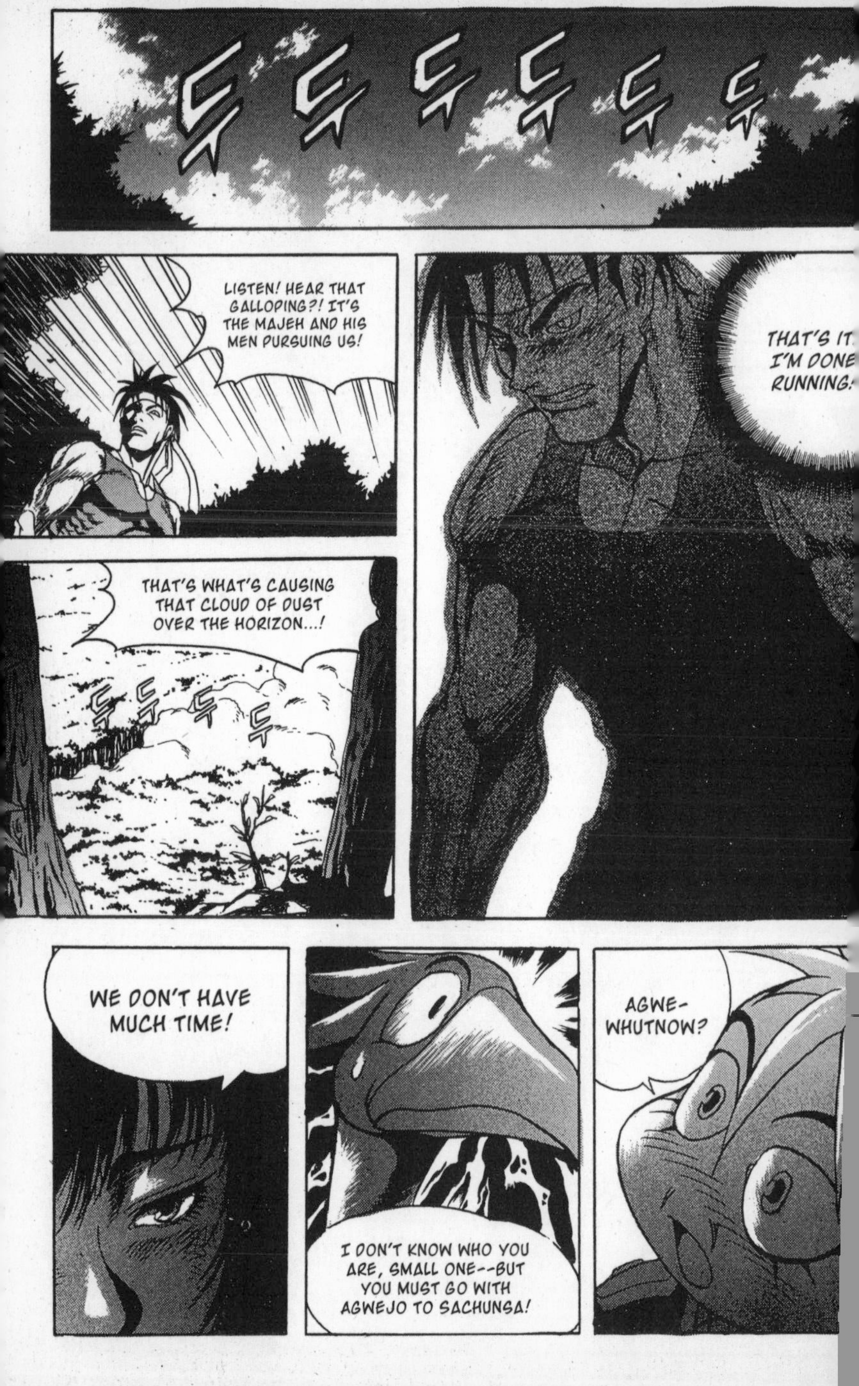
두 두 두 두 두 두
LISTEN! HEAR THAT GALLOPING?! IT'S THE MAJEH AND HIS MEN PURSUING US!
THAT'S WHAT'S CAUSING THAT CLOUD OF DUST OVER THE HORIZON...!
두 두 두 두
THAT'S IT. I'M DONE RUNNING!
WE DON'T HAVE MUCH TIME!
I DON'T KNOW WHO YOU ARE, SMALL ONE--BUT YOU MUST GO WITH AGWEJO TO SACHUNSA!
AGWE-WHUTNOW?

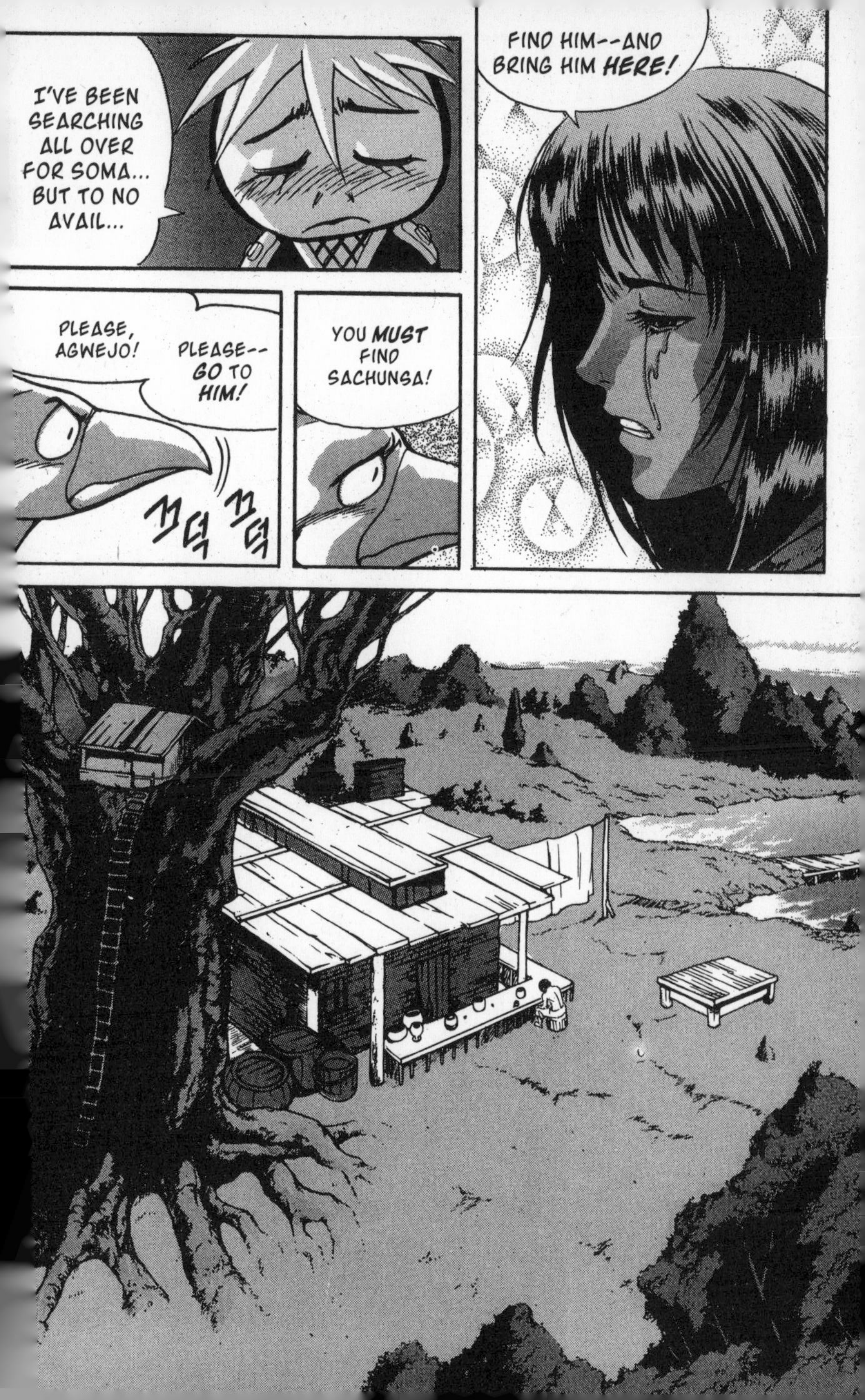
I'VE BEEN SEARCHING ALL OVER FOR SOMA... BUT TO NO AVAIL...
FIND HIM--AND BRING HIM HERE!
PLEASE, AGWEJO!
PLEASE--GO TO HIM!
YOU MUST FIND SACHUNSA!
끄덕 끄덕

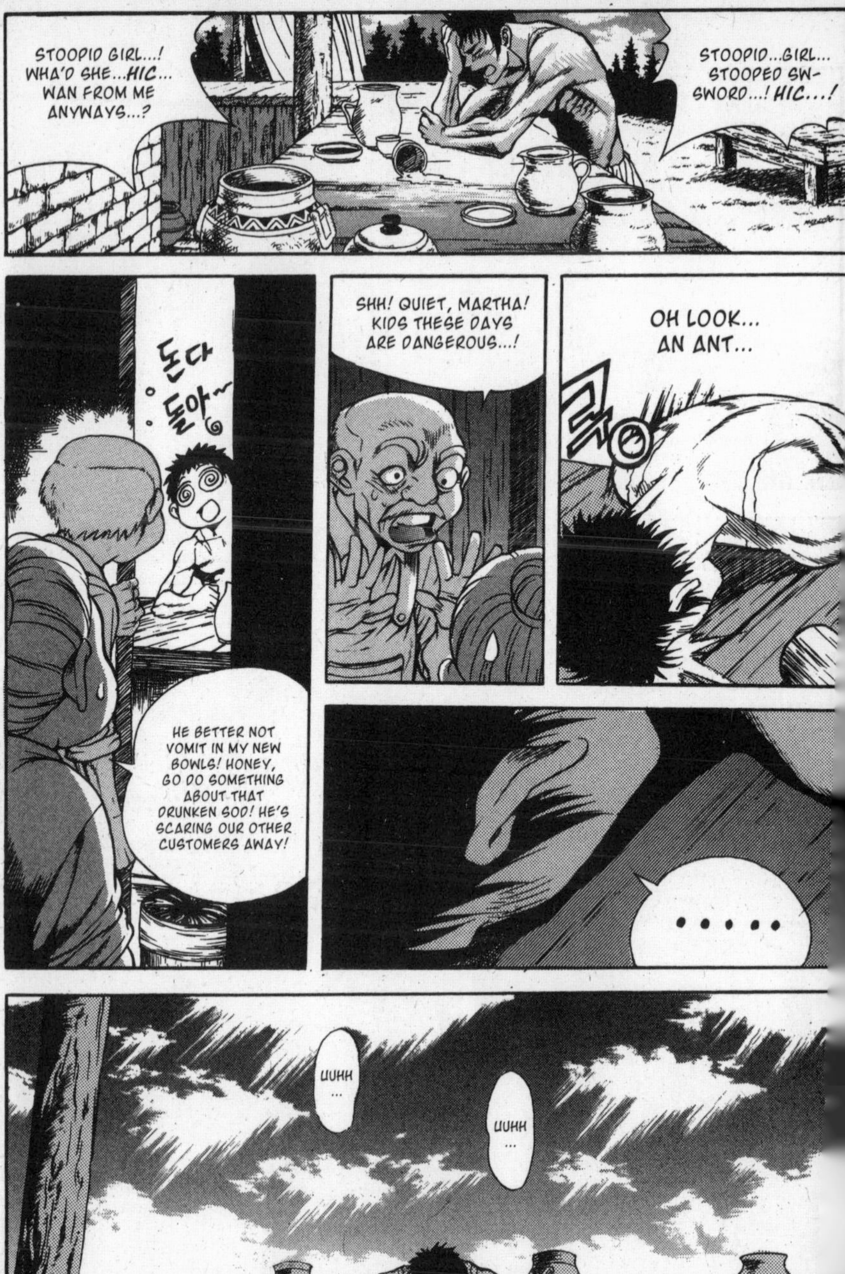
STOOPID GIRL...! WHA'D SHE...HIC... WAN FROM ME ANYWAYS...?
STOOPID...GIRL... STOOPED SW-SWORD...! HIC...!
돈다 돌아~
SHH! QUIET, MARTHA! KIDS THESE DAYS ARE DANGEROUS...!
OH LOOK... AN ANT...
HE BETTER NOT VOMIT IN MY NEW BOWLS! HONEY, GO DO SOMETHING ABOUT THAT DRUNKEN SOD! HE'S SCARING OUR OTHER CUSTOMERS AWAY!
.....
UUHH ...
UUHH ...

HEEEY...NOW I SEE WHY THA' OLD PERV... HIC...KEPT DRINKIN' THAT MONKEY PEE OF HIS...! BEIN' DRUNK MAKES THE OWIES GO 'WAY!

YEP. I'M GONNA VOM.

POOR BOY! HE'S GONE COMPLETELY DAFT!

ANOTHER...? WELL, MISTAH RABBIT, DON' MIND IF I DO...

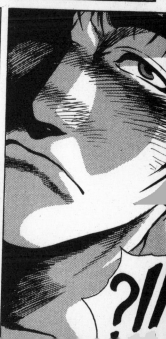

BURP! HUH...? ALL GONE...?

?!//

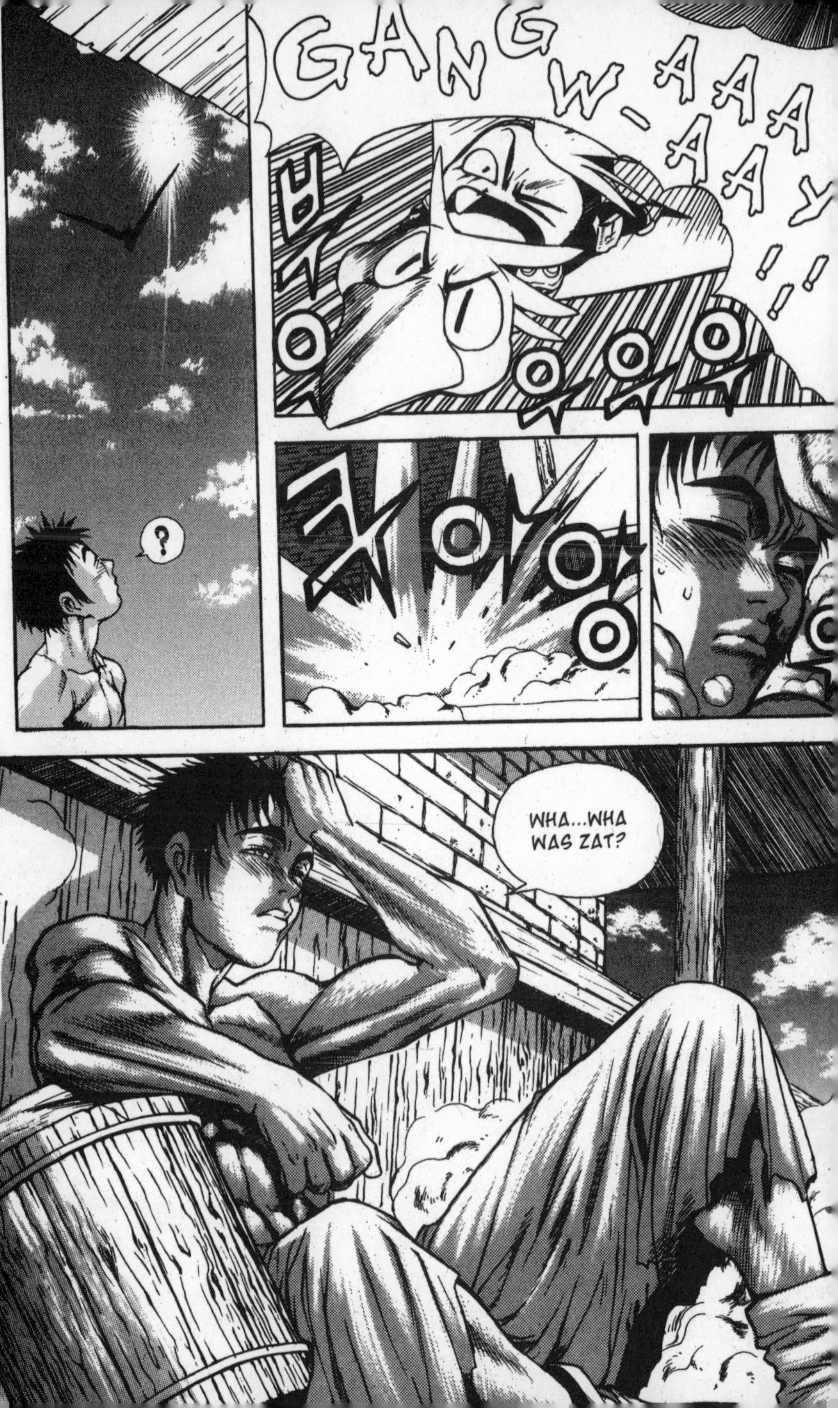
GANG
W-AAAA-AAAY!!!
HOOOOO
?
ZOOOOO
OO
WHA...WHA WAS ZAT?

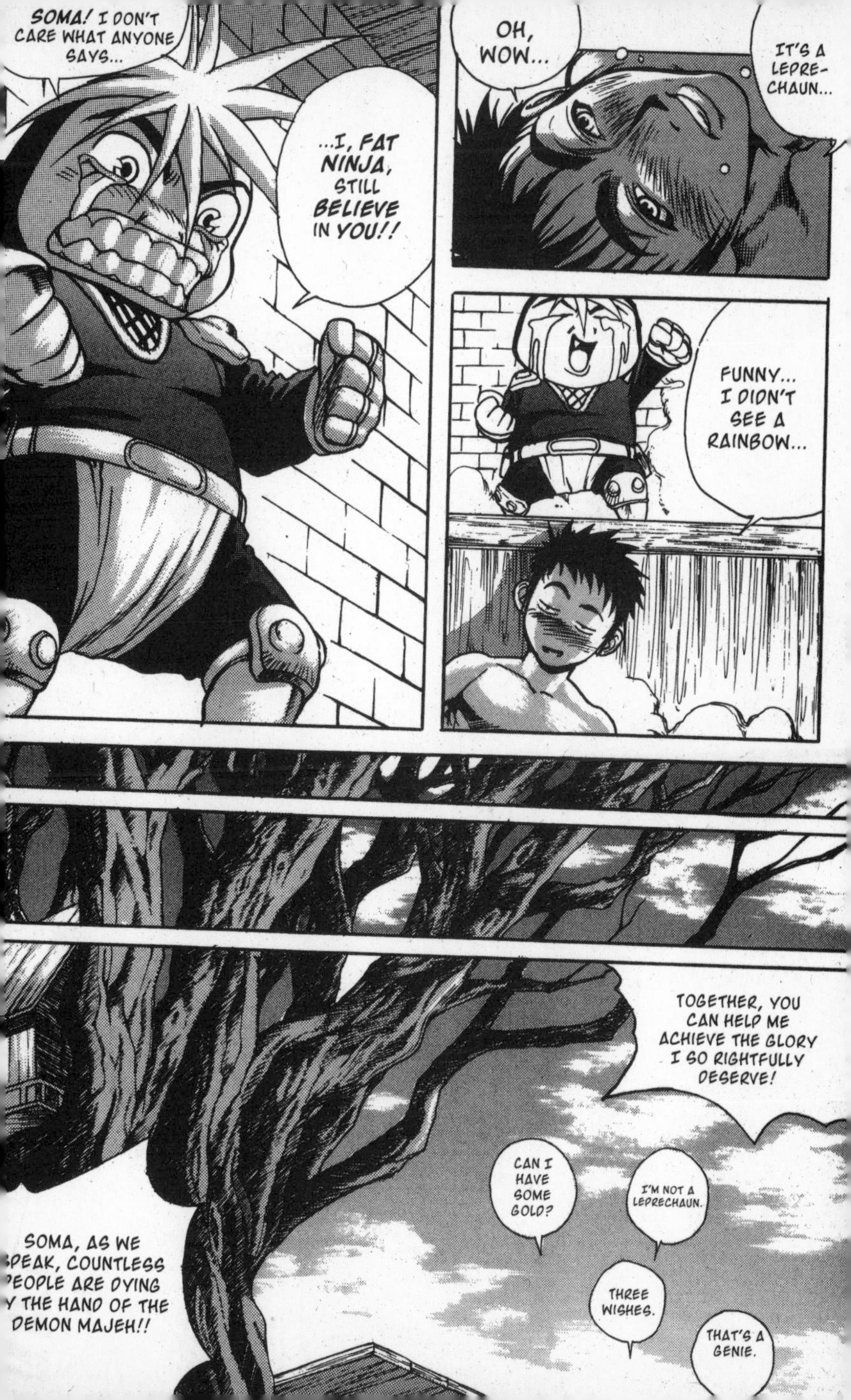
SOMA! I DON'T CARE WHAT ANYONE SAYS...
...I, FAT NINJA, STILL BELIEVE IN YOU!!
OH, WOW...
IT'S A LEPRE-CHAUN...
FUNNY... I DIDN'T SEE A RAINBOW...
TOGETHER, YOU CAN HELP ME ACHIEVE THE GLORY I SO RIGHTFULLY DESERVE!
SOMA, AS WE SPEAK, COUNTLESS PEOPLE ARE DYING BY THE HAND OF THE DEMON MAJEH!!
CAN I HAVE SOME GOLD?
I'M NOT A LEPRECHAUN.
THREE WISHES.
THAT'S A GENIE.

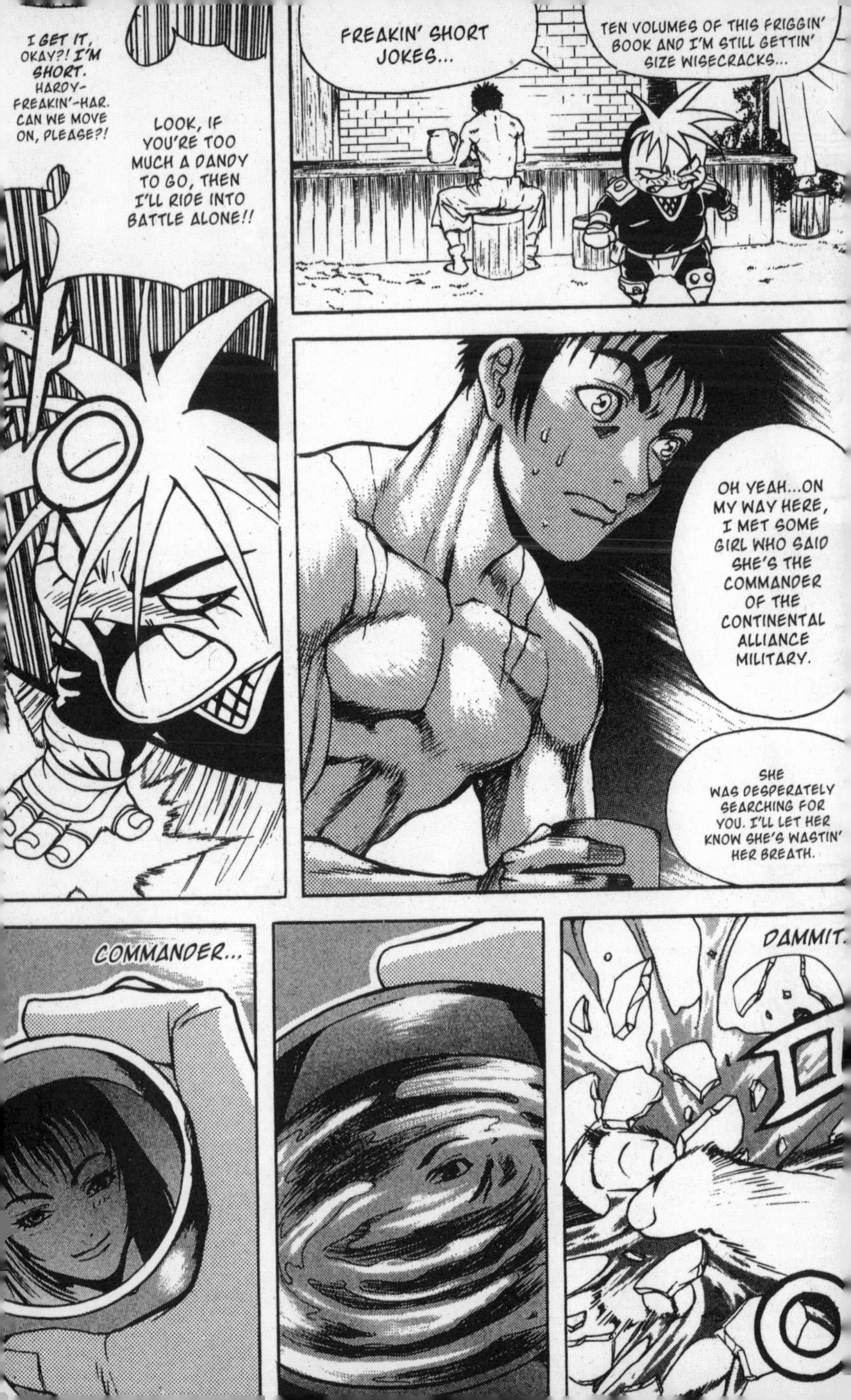
FREAKIN' SHORT JOKES...
TEN VOLUMES OF THIS FRIGGIN' BOOK AND I'M STILL GETTIN' SIZE WISECRACKS...
I GET IT, OKAY?! I'M SHORT. HARDY-FREAKIN'-HAR. CAN WE MOVE ON, PLEASE?!
LOOK, IF YOU'RE TOO MUCH A DANDY TO GO, THEN I'LL RIDE INTO BATTLE ALONE!!
OH YEAH...ON MY WAY HERE, I MET SOME GIRL WHO SAID SHE'S THE COMMANDER OF THE CONTINENTAL ALLIANCE MILITARY.
SHE WAS DESPERATELY SEARCHING FOR YOU. I'LL LET HER KNOW SHE'S WASTIN' HER BREATH.
COMMANDER...
DAMMIT.

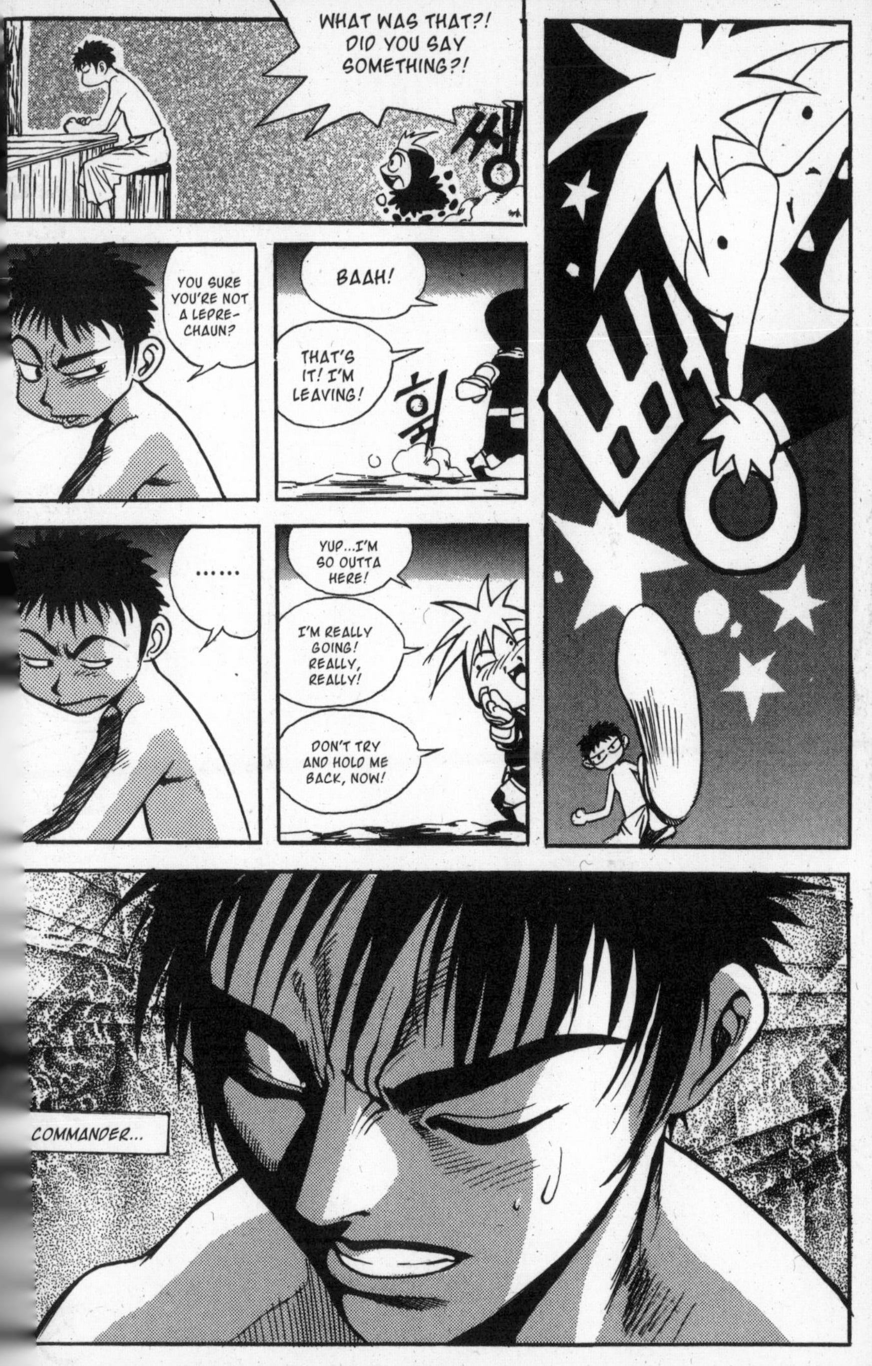
WHAT WAS THAT?! DID YOU SAY SOMETHING?!
YOU SURE YOU'RE NOT A LEPRE-CHAUN?
BAAH!
THAT'S IT! I'M LEAVING!
......
YUP...I'M SO OUTTA HERE!
I'M REALLY GOING! REALLY, REALLY!
DON'T TRY AND HOLD ME BACK, NOW!
COMMANDER...

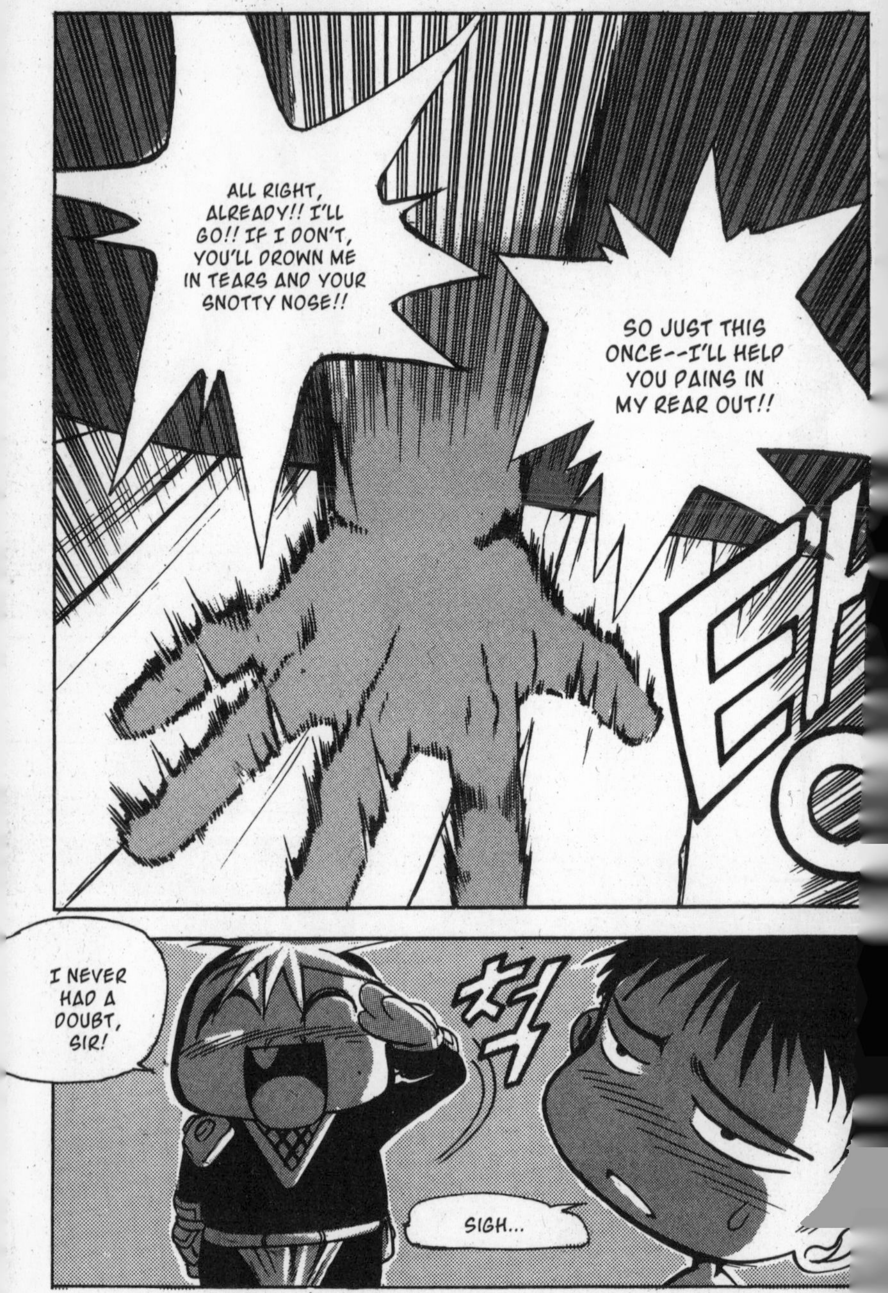
ALL RIGHT, ALREADY!! I'LL GO!! IF I DON'T, YOU'LL DROWN ME IN TEARS AND YOUR SNOTTY NOSE!!
SO JUST THIS ONCE--I'LL HELP YOU PAINS IN MY REAR OUT!!
I NEVER HAD A DOUBT, SIR!
SIGH...

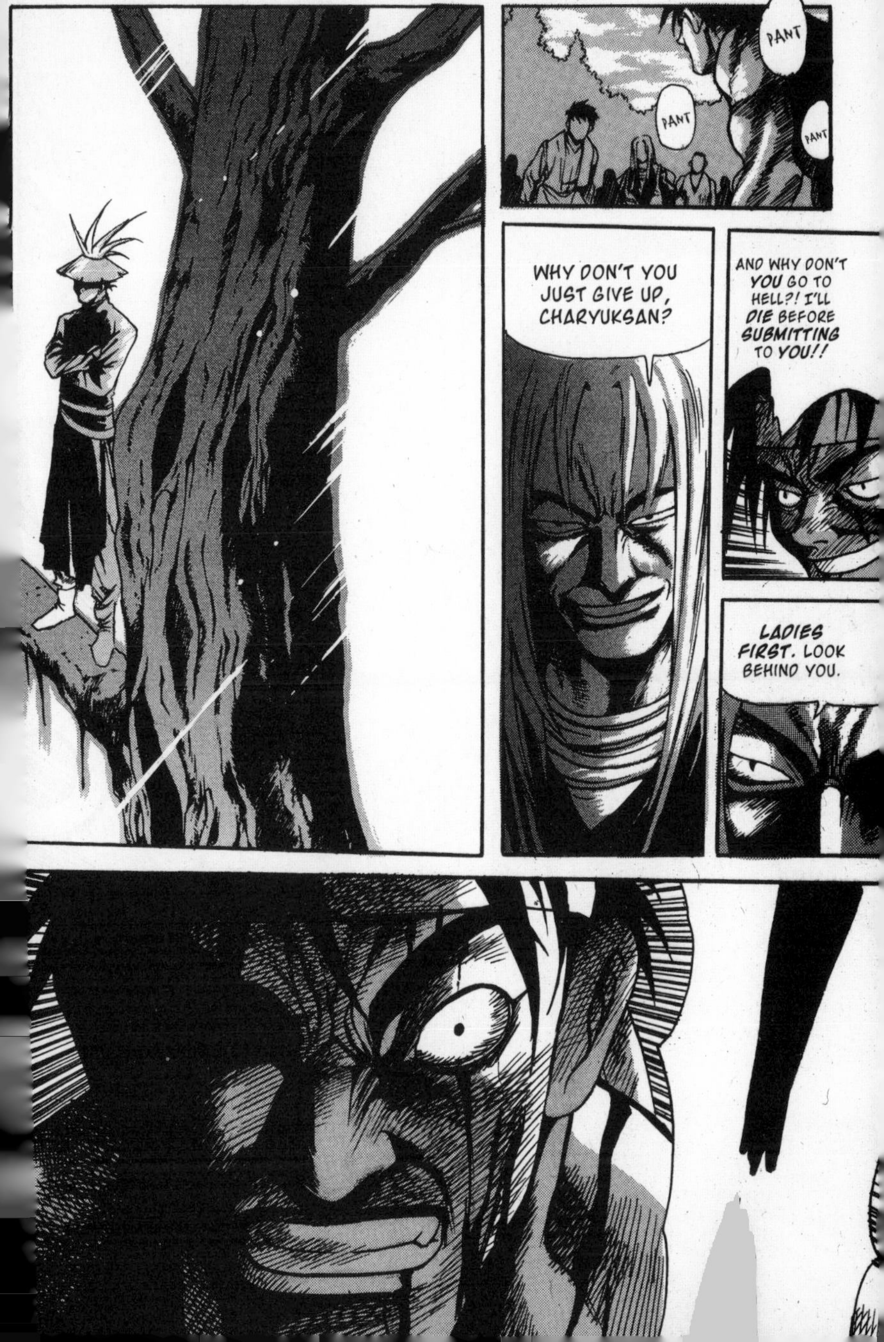
PANT
PANT
PANT
WHY DON'T YOU JUST GIVE UP, CHARYUKSAN?
AND WHY DON'T YOU GO TO HELL?! I'LL DIE BEFORE SUBMITTING TO YOU!!
LADIES FIRST. LOOK BEHIND YOU.

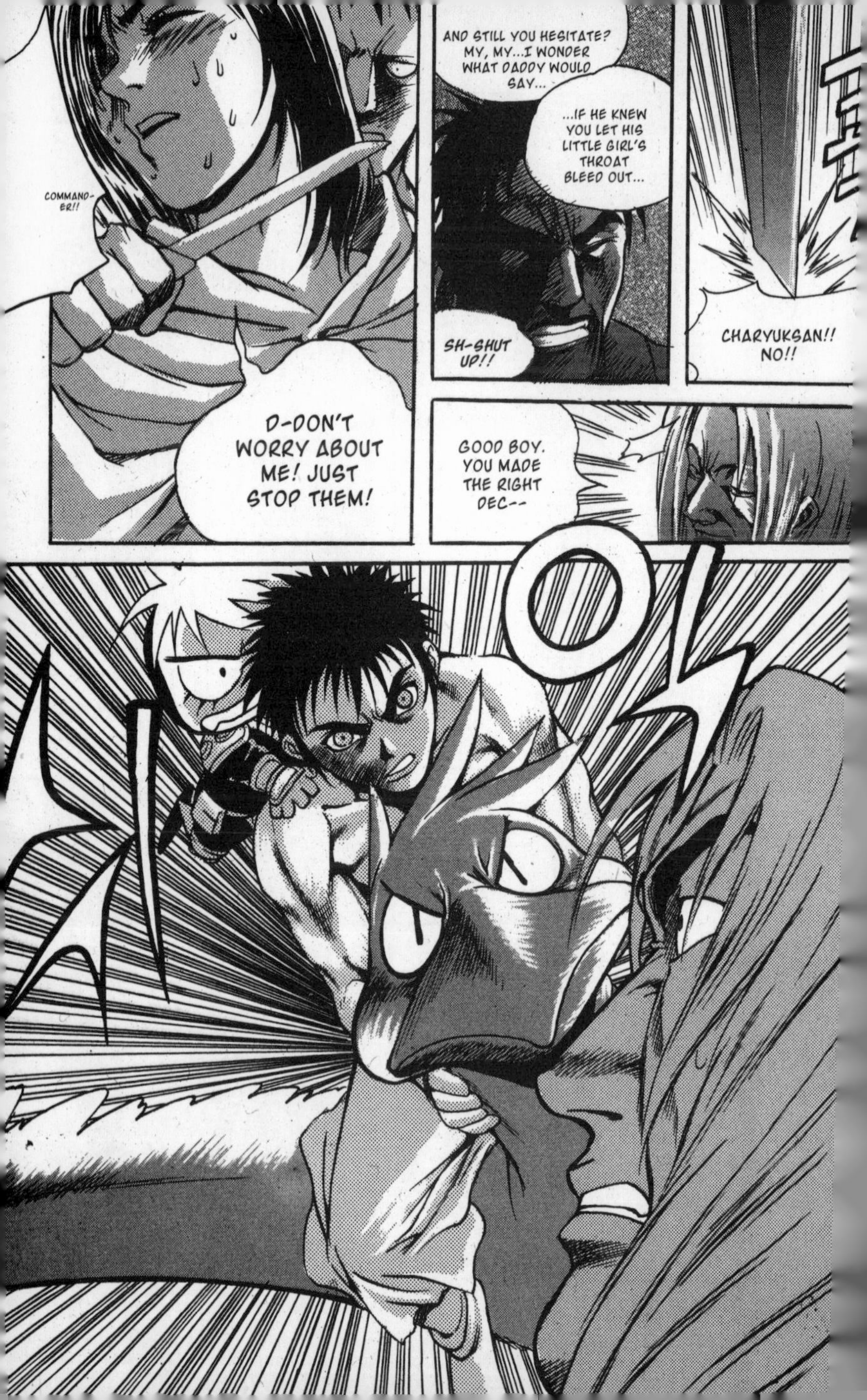

AND STILL YOU HESITATE? MY, MY...I WONDER WHAT DADDY WOULD SAY...
...IF HE KNEW YOU LET HIS LITTLE GIRL'S THROAT BLEED OUT...
CHARYUKSAN!! NO!!
SH-SHUT UP!!
COMMANDER!!
D-DON'T WORRY ABOUT ME! JUST STOP THEM!
GOOD BOY. YOU MADE THE RIGHT DEC--

BLADE OF HEAVEN

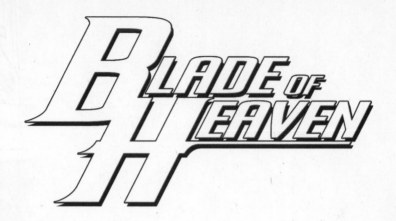

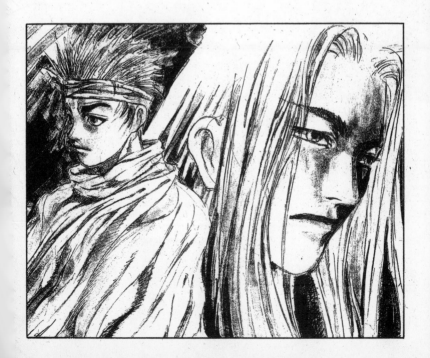

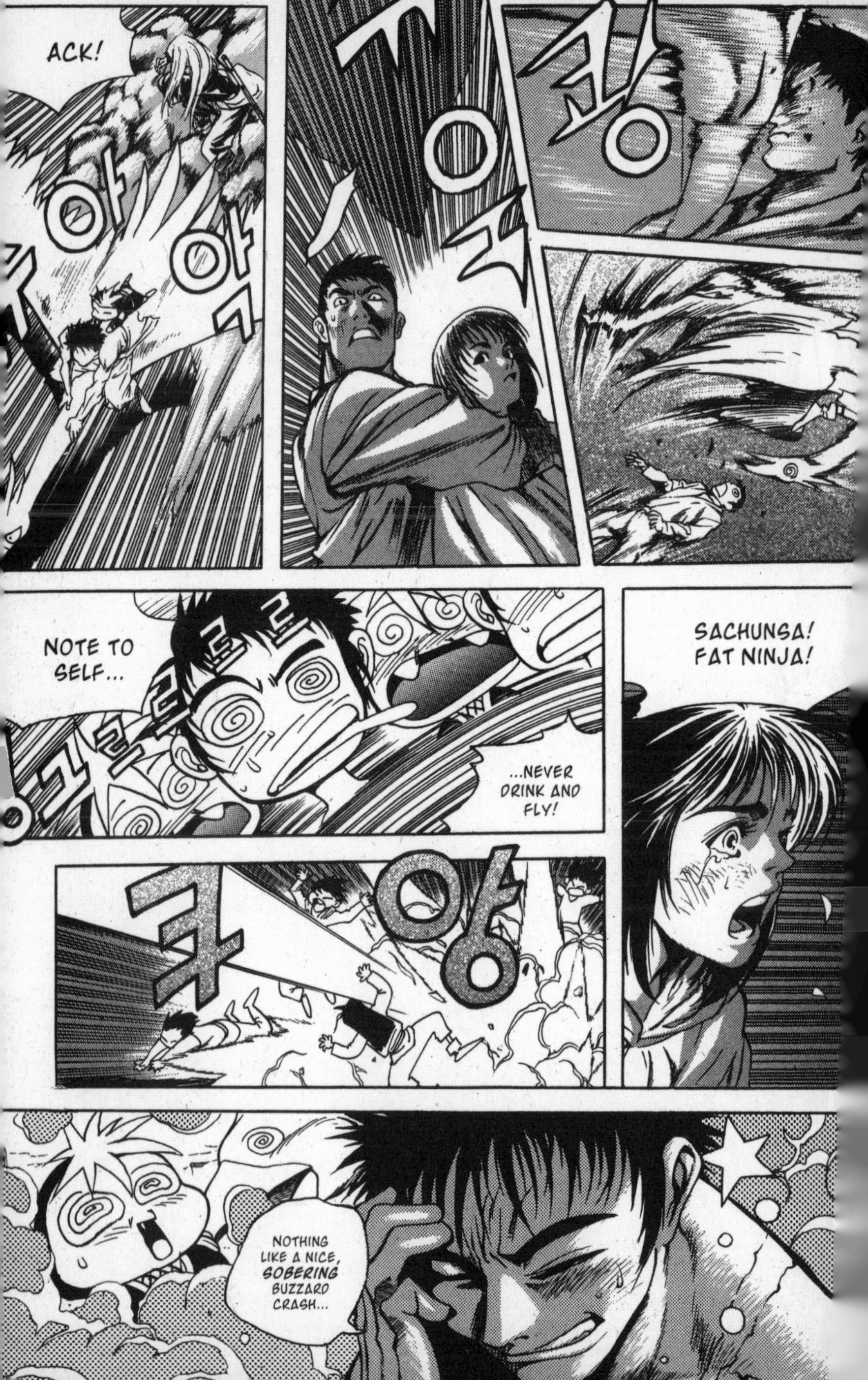
ACK!
NOTE TO SELF...
...NEVER DRINK AND FLY!
SACHUNSA! FAT NINJA!
NOTHING LIKE A NICE, SOBERING BUZZARD CRASH...

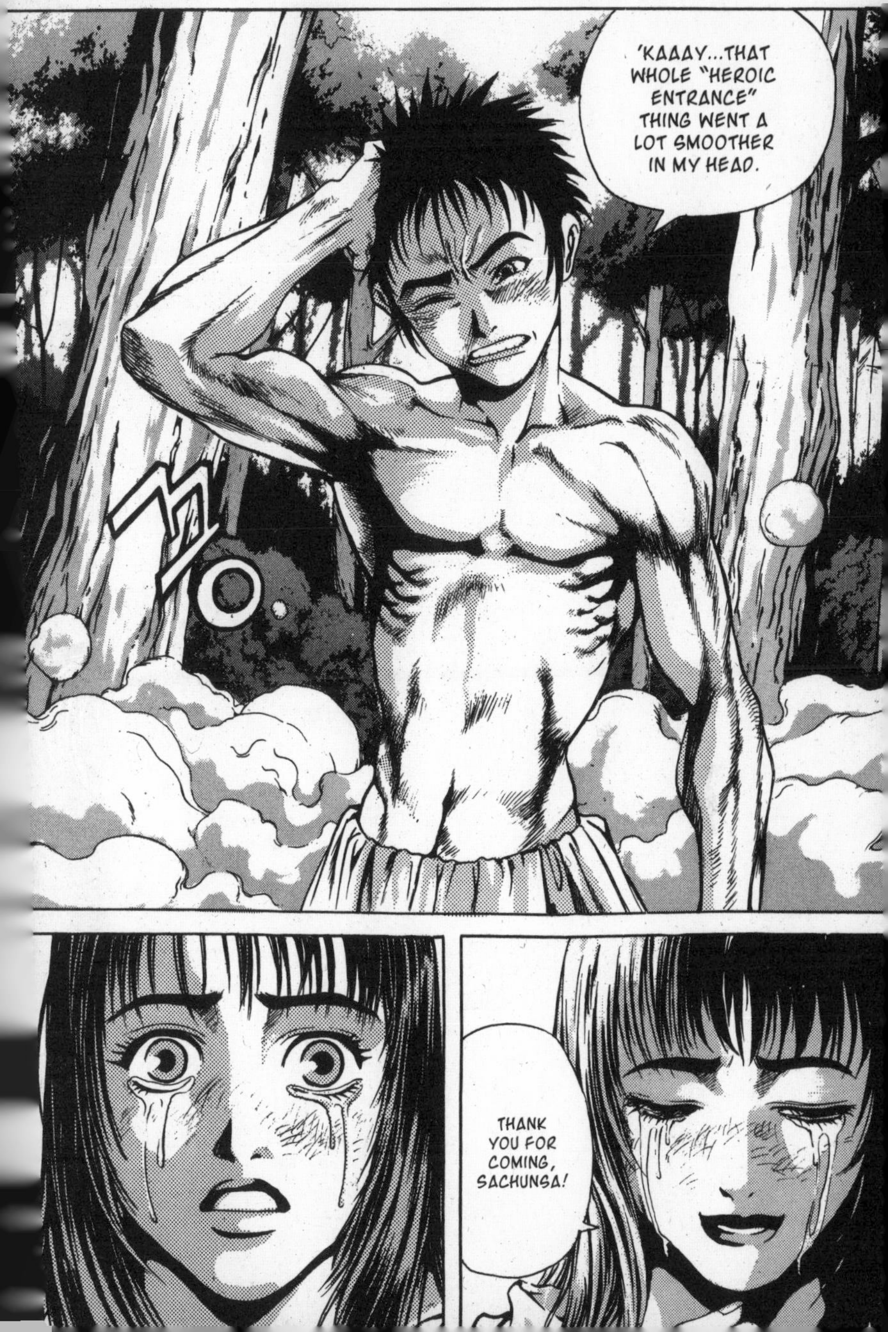
'KAAAY...THAT WHOLE "HEROIC ENTRANCE" THING WENT A LOT SMOOTHER IN MY HEAD.
THANK YOU FOR COMING, SACHUNSA!

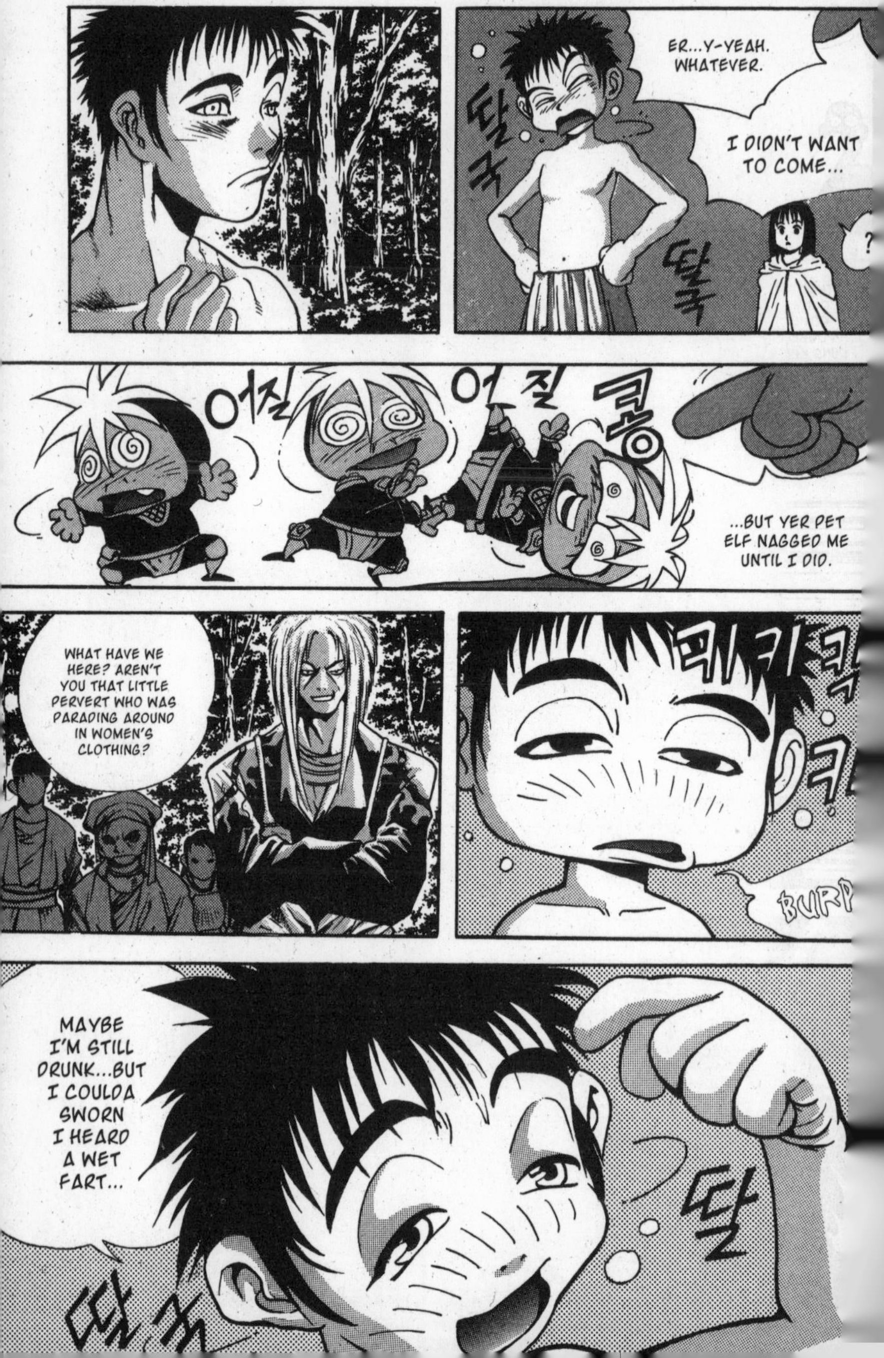
ER...Y-YEAH. WHATEVER.
딸꾹
I DIDN'T WANT TO COME...
딸꾹
?
어질
어질
쿵
...BUT YER PET ELF NAGGED ME UNTIL I DID.
WHAT HAVE WE HERE? AREN'T YOU THAT LITTLE PERVERT WHO WAS PARADING AROUND IN WOMEN'S CLOTHING?
BURP
MAYBE I'M STILL DRUNK...BUT I COULDA SWORN I HEARD A WET FART...

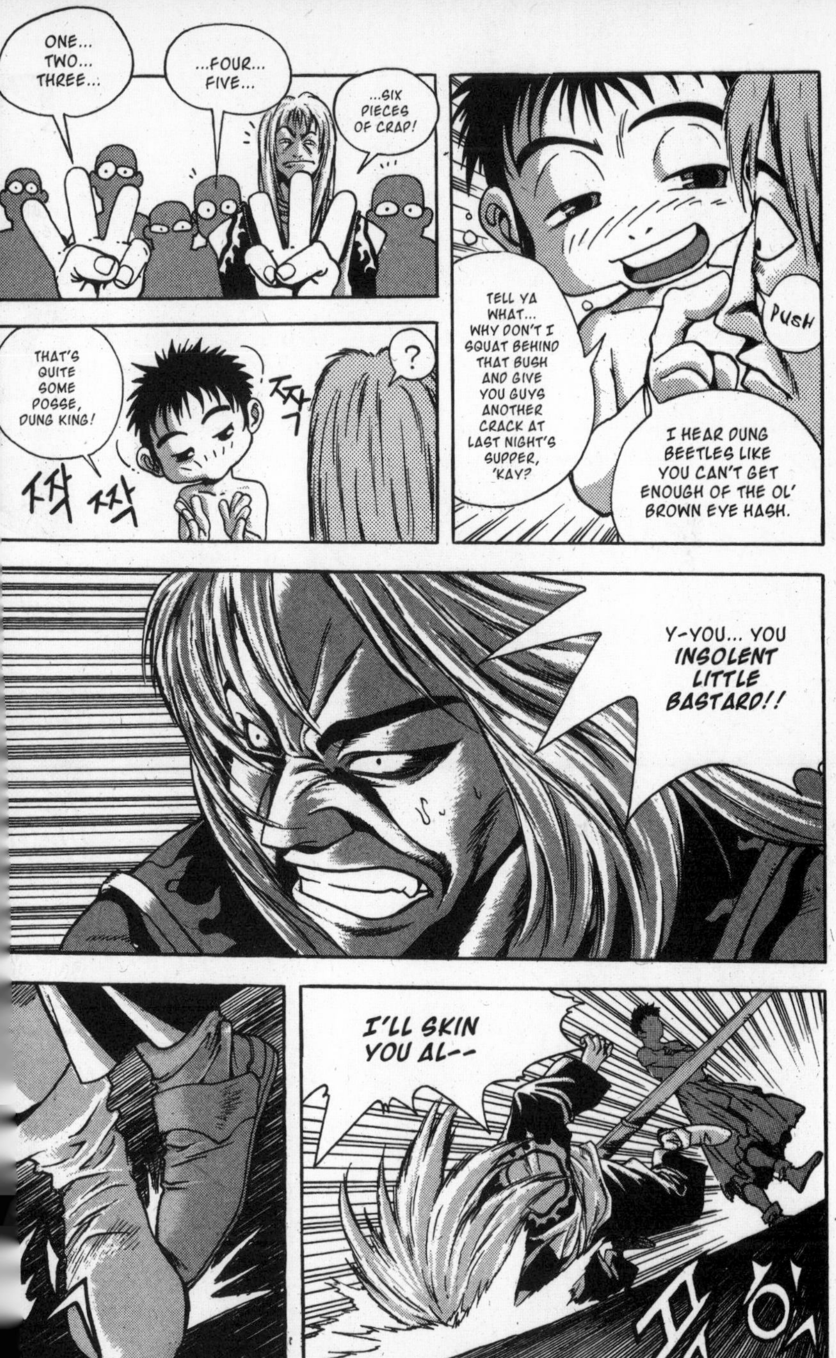
ONE... TWO... THREE...
...FOUR... FIVE...
...SIX PIECES OF CRAP!
TELL YA WHAT... WHY DON'T I SQUAT BEHIND THAT BUSH AND GIVE YOU GUYS ANOTHER CRACK AT LAST NIGHT'S SUPPER, 'KAY?
PUSH
I HEAR DUNG BEETLES LIKE YOU CAN'T GET ENOUGH OF THE OL' BROWN EYE HASH.
THAT'S QUITE SOME POSSE, DUNG KING!
?
짝
짝 짝
Y-YOU... YOU INSOLENT LITTLE BASTARD!!
I'LL SKIN YOU AL--

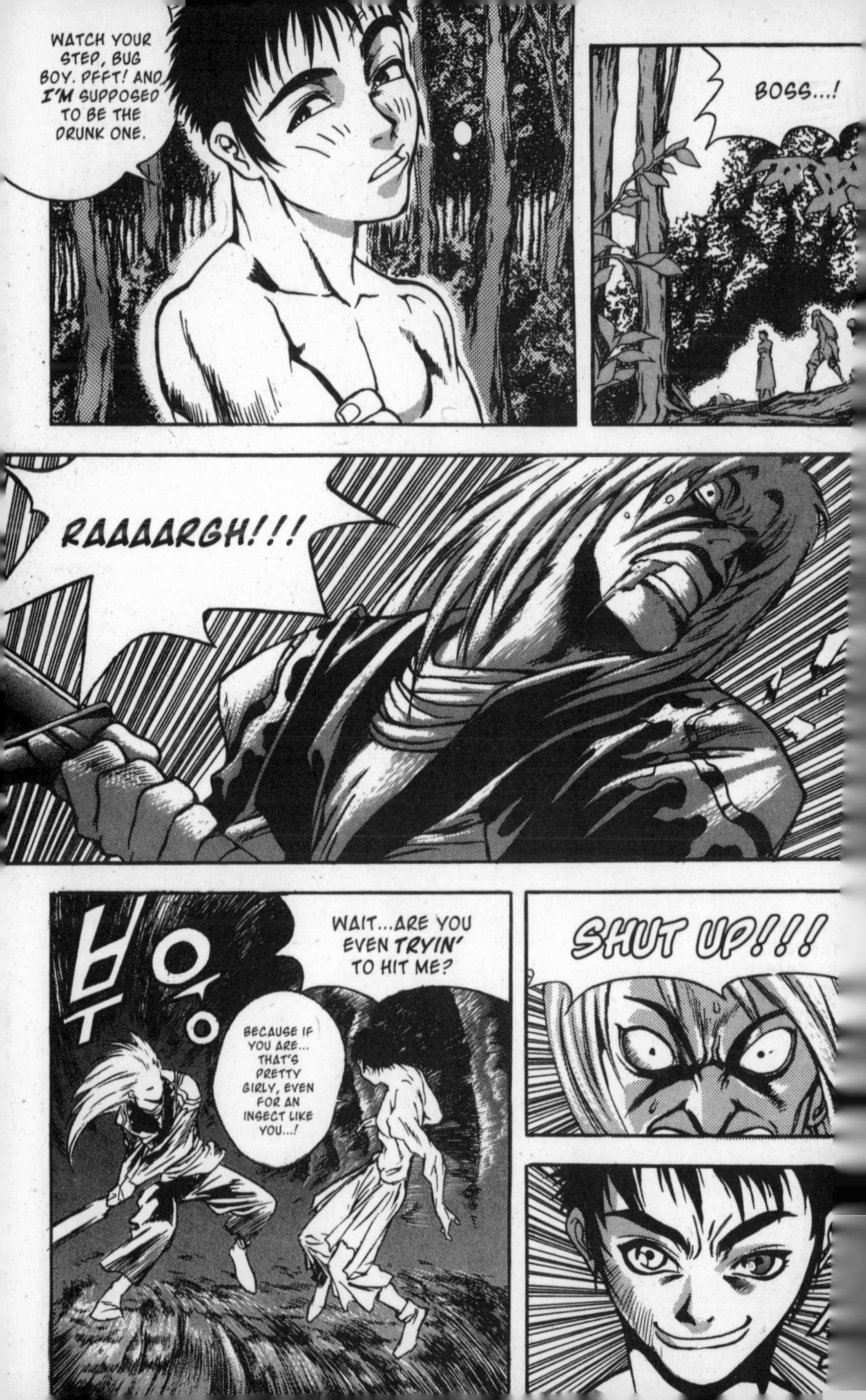
WATCH YOUR STEP, BUG BOY. PFFT! AND I'M SUPPOSED TO BE THE DRUNK ONE.
BOSS...!
RAAAARGH!!!
WAIT...ARE YOU EVEN TRYIN' TO HIT ME?
BECAUSE IF YOU ARE... THAT'S PRETTY GIRLY, EVEN FOR AN INSECT LIKE YOU...!
SHUT UP!!!

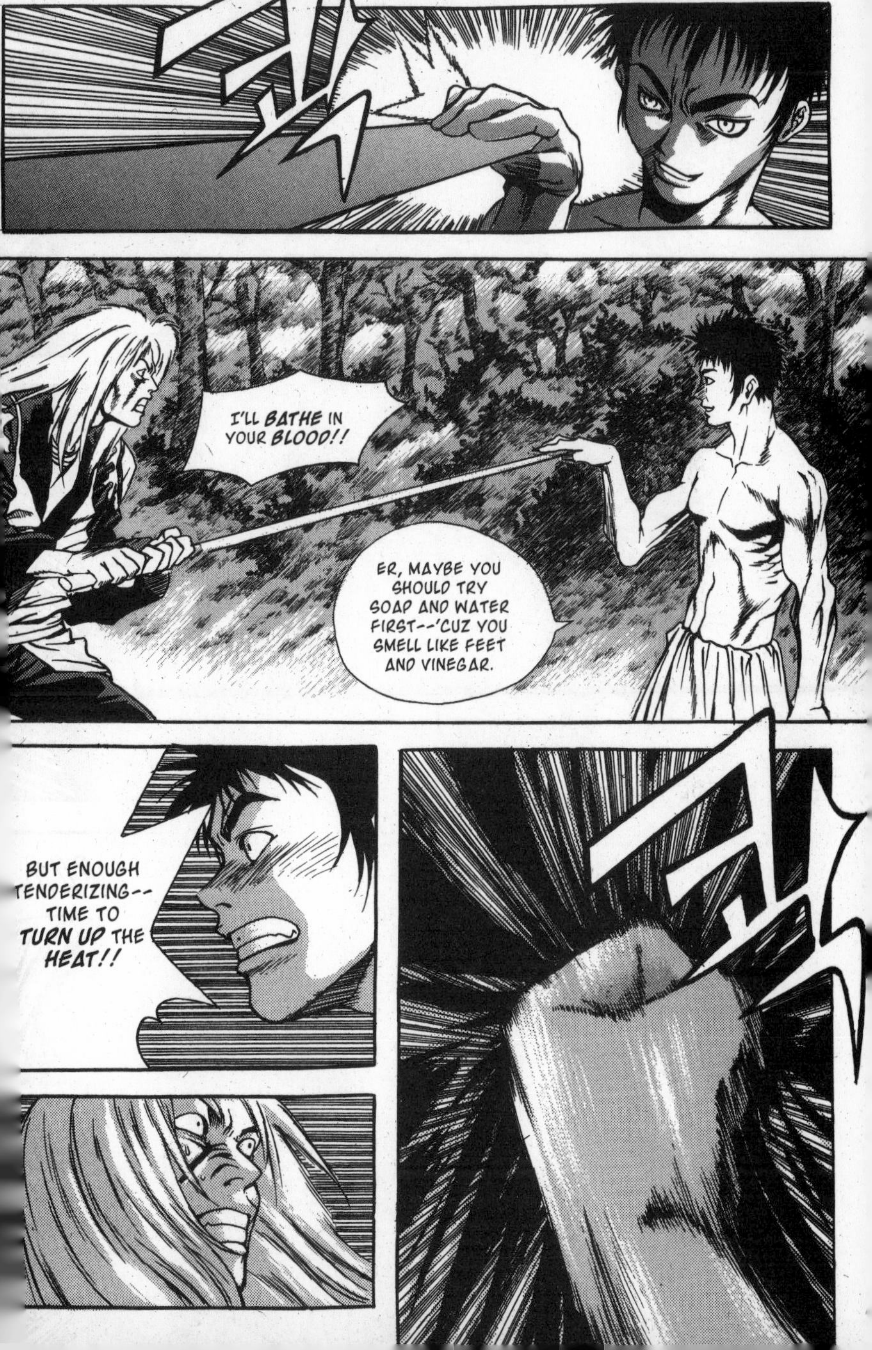
I'LL BATHE IN YOUR BLOOD!!
ER, MAYBE YOU SHOULD TRY SOAP AND WATER FIRST--'CUZ YOU SMELL LIKE FEET AND VINEGAR.
BUT ENOUGH TENDERIZING--TIME TO TURN UP THE HEAT!!

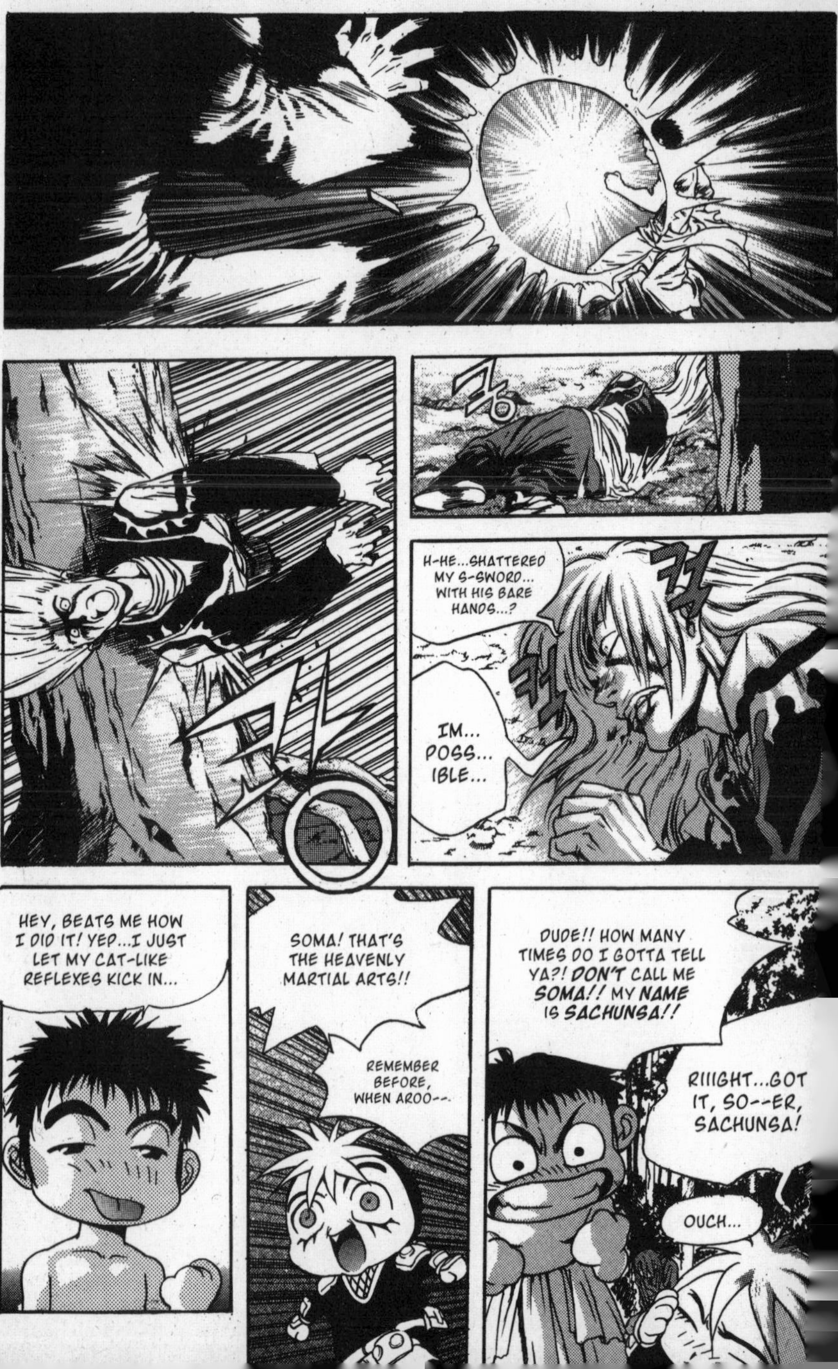
H-HE...SHATTERED MY S-SWORD... WITH HIS BARE HANDS...?
IM... POSS... IBLE...
HEY, BEATS ME HOW I DID IT! YEP...I JUST LET MY CAT-LIKE REFLEXES KICK IN...
SOMA! THAT'S THE HEAVENLY MARTIAL ARTS!!
REMEMBER BEFORE, WHEN AROO--.
DUDE!! HOW MANY TIMES DO I GOTTA TELL YA?! DON'T CALL ME SOMA!! MY NAME IS SACHUNSA!!
RIIIGHT...GOT IT, SO--ER, SACHUNSA!
OUCH...

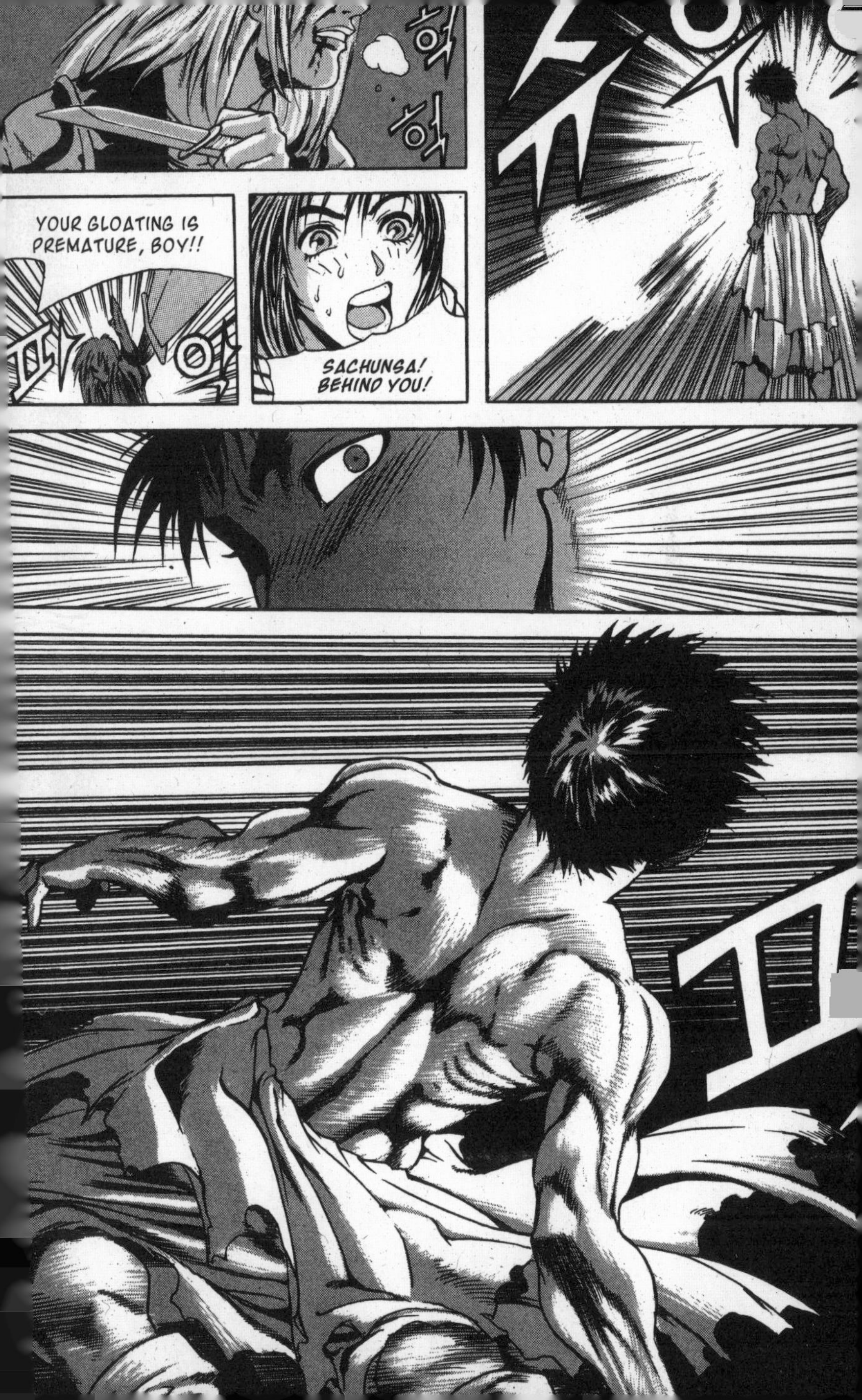
YOUR GLOATING IS PREMATURE, BOY!!
SACHUNSA! BEHIND YOU!

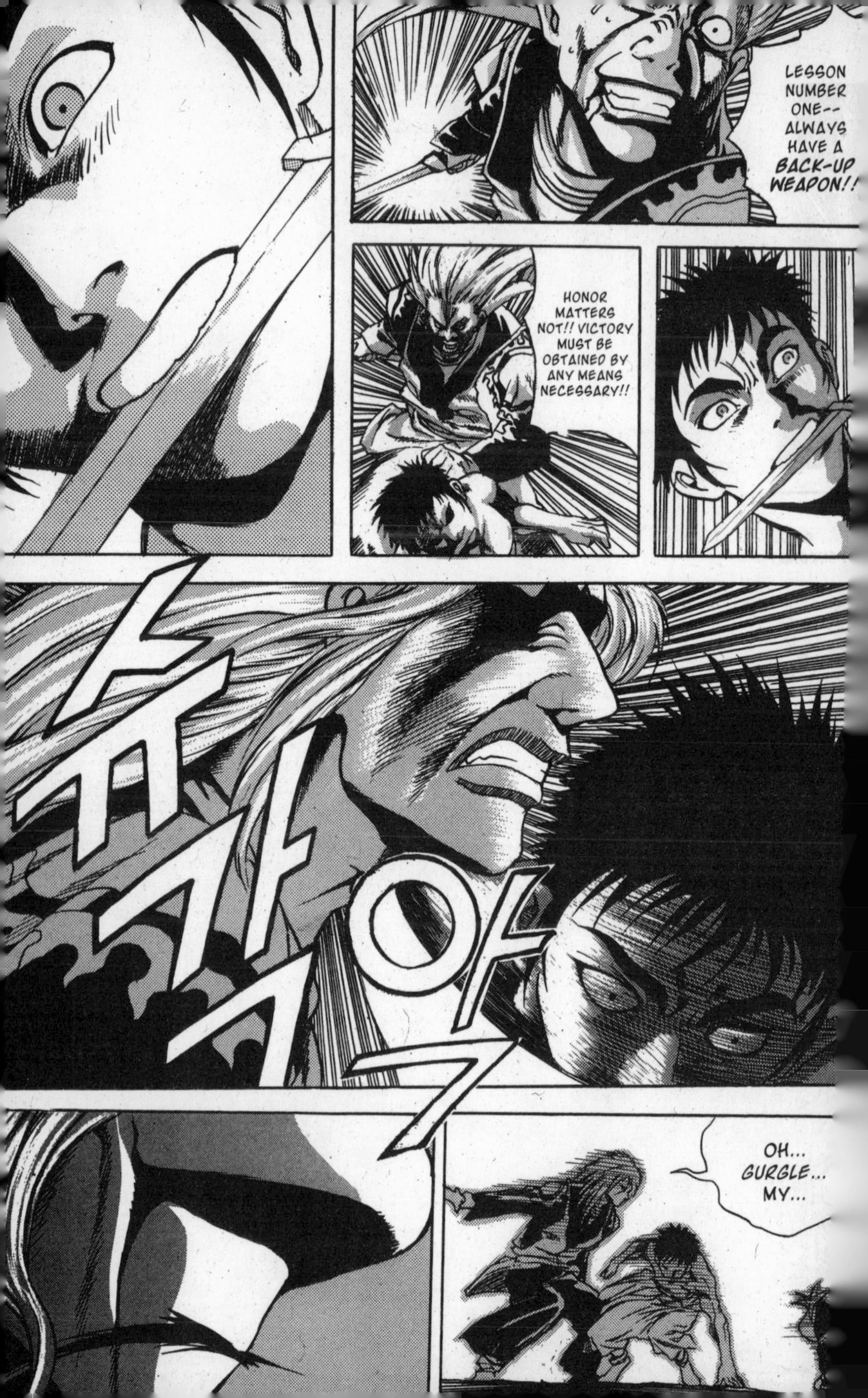
LESSON NUMBER ONE--ALWAYS HAVE A BACK-UP WEAPON!!
HONOR MATTERS NOT!! VICTORY MUST BE OBTAINED BY ANY MEANS NECESSARY!!
OH... GURGLE... MY...

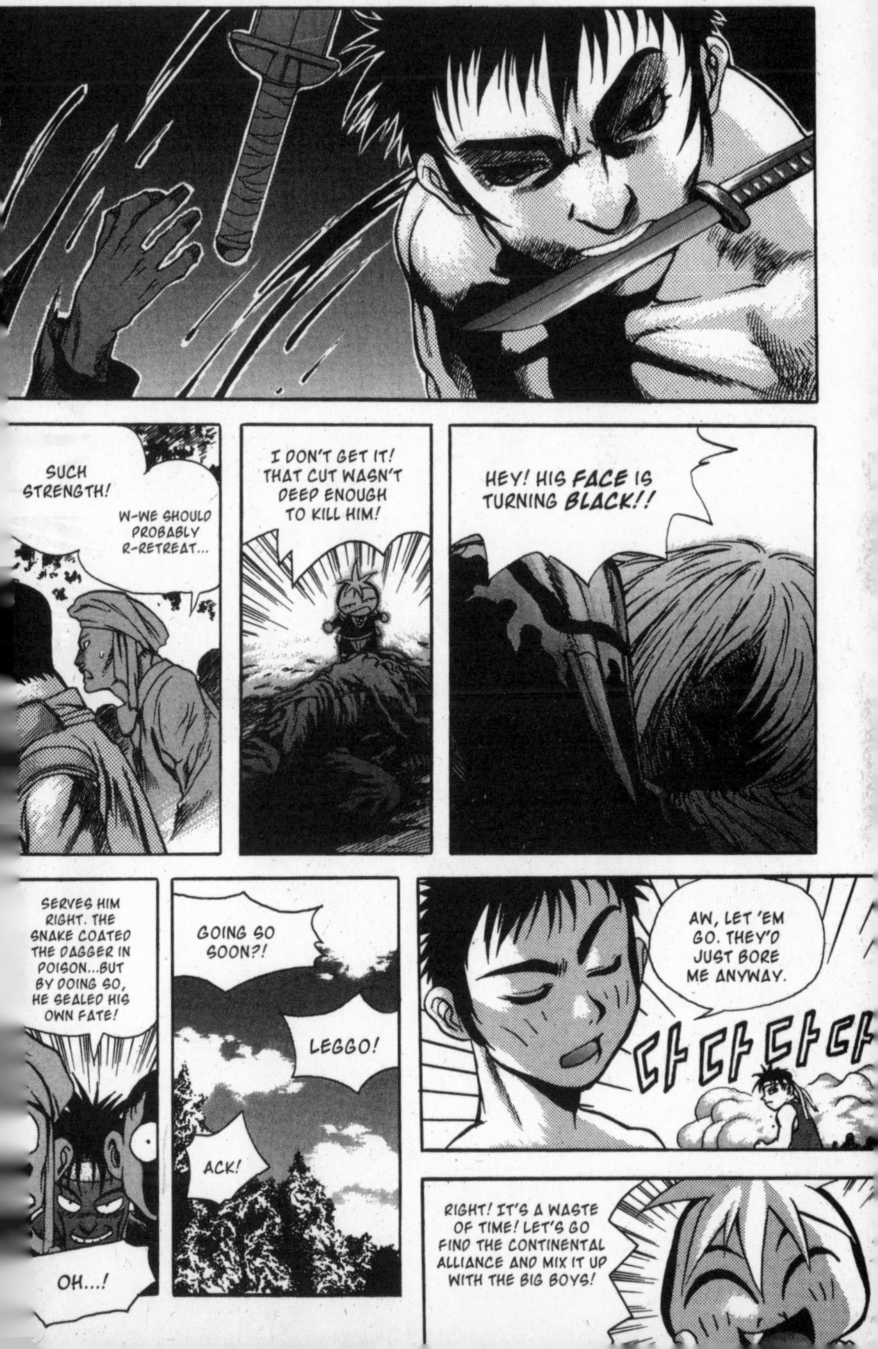
SUCH STRENGTH!
W-WE SHOULD PROBABLY R-RETREAT...
I DON'T GET IT! THAT CUT WASN'T DEEP ENOUGH TO KILL HIM!
HEY! HIS **FACE** IS TURNING **BLACK!!**
SERVES HIM RIGHT. THE SNAKE COATED THE DAGGER IN POISON...BUT BY DOING SO, HE SEALED HIS OWN FATE!
OH...!
GOING SO SOON?!
LEGGO!
ACK!
AW, LET 'EM GO. THEY'D JUST BORE ME ANYWAY.
RIGHT! IT'S A WASTE OF TIME! LET'S GO FIND THE CONTINENTAL ALLIANCE AND MIX IT UP WITH THE BIG BOYS!

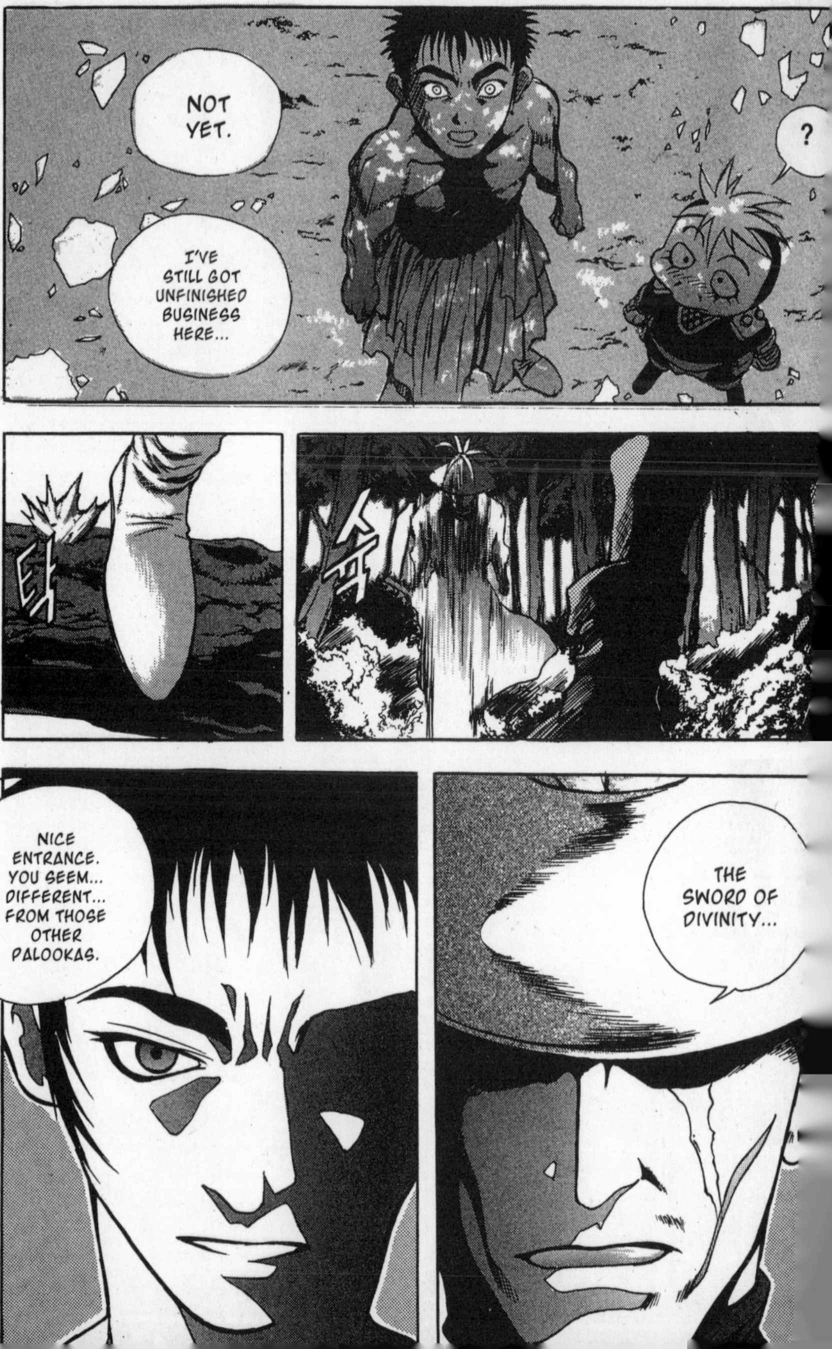
NOT YET.
I'VE STILL GOT UNFINISHED BUSINESS HERE...
?
탁
NICE ENTRANCE. YOU SEEM... DIFFERENT... FROM THOSE OTHER PALOOKAS.
THE SWORD OF DIVINITY...

THE ONE WHO WIELDS IT WILL BE UNSTOPPABLE.

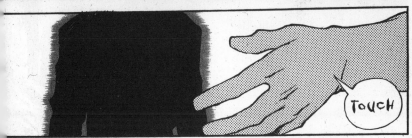

TOUCH

YOU MUST DECIDE... EITHER STAND ASIDE, OR DIE WHERE YOU STAND!

WHOA, WHOA! EASY, SHEILA! COMING ON A WEE BIT STRONG, ARE WE?

THE RULES SAY WE GOTTA BERATE EACH OTHER WITH SNIDE INSULTS FIRST *BEFORE* I KICK YOUR BUTT!

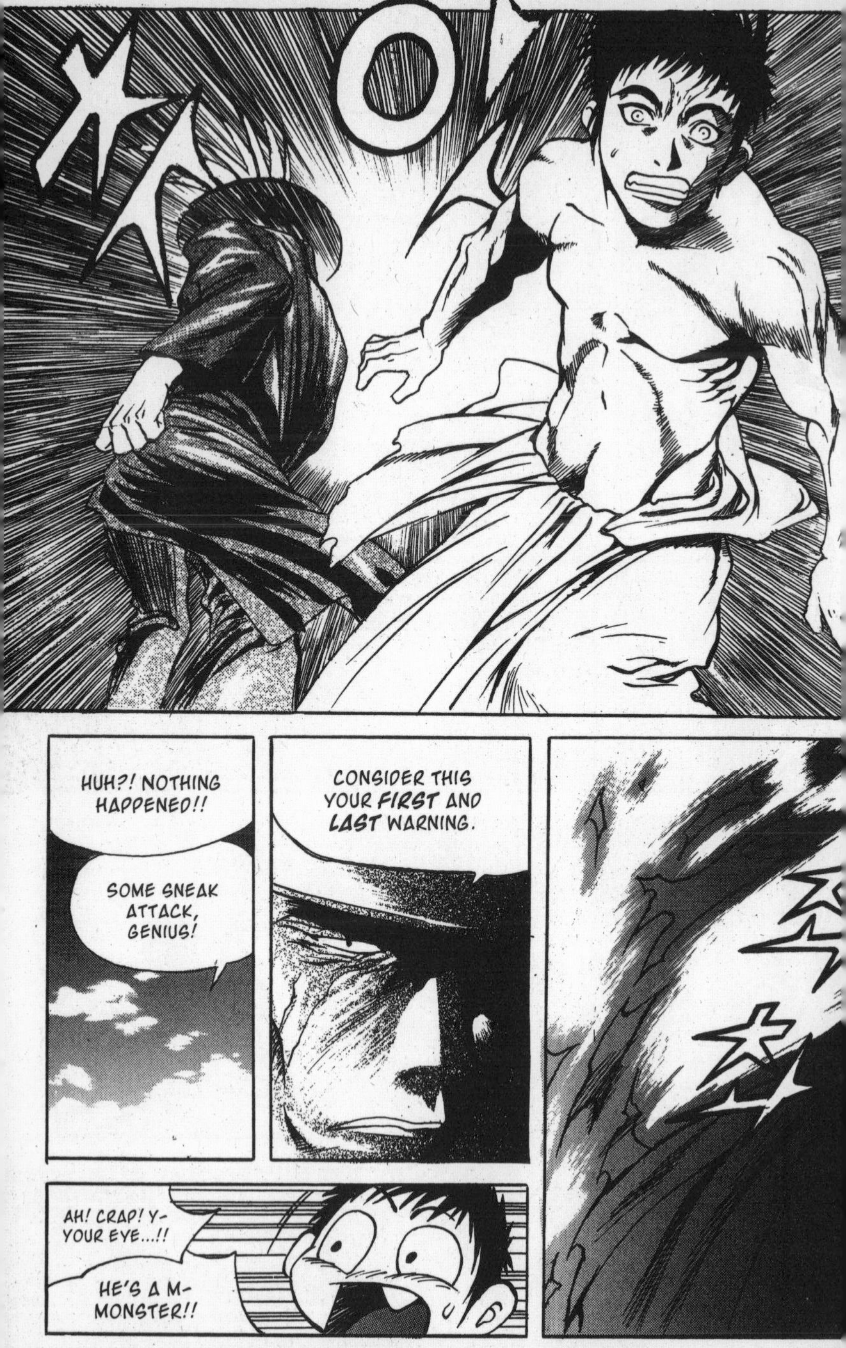
HUH?! NOTHING HAPPENED!!
SOME SNEAK ATTACK, GENIUS!
CONSIDER THIS YOUR FIRST AND LAST WARNING.
AH! CRAP! Y-YOUR EYE...!!
HE'S A M-MONSTER!!

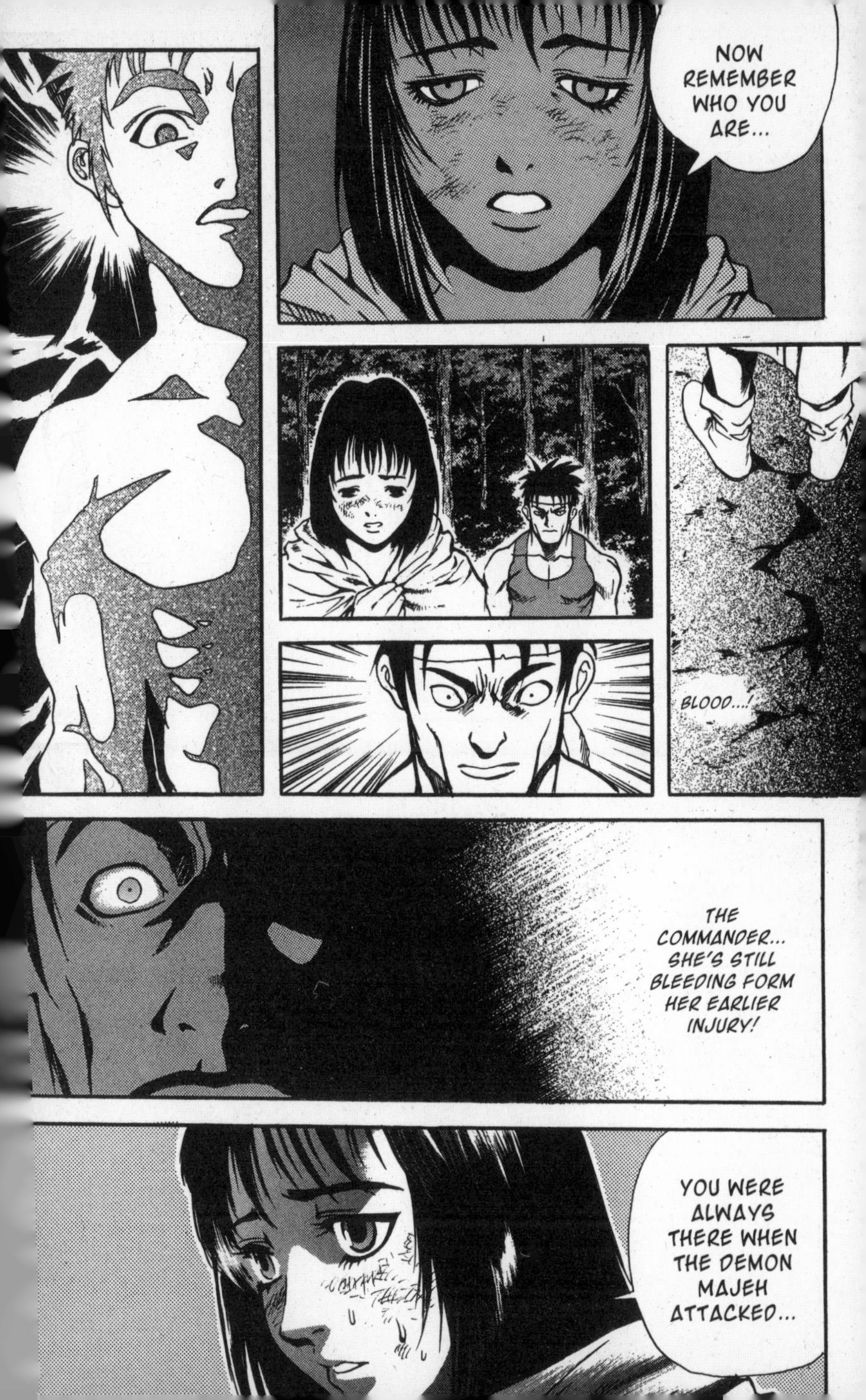
NOW REMEMBER WHO YOU ARE...
BLOOD...!
THE COMMANDER... SHE'S STILL BLEEDING FORM HER EARLIER INJURY!
YOU WERE ALWAYS THERE WHEN THE DEMON MAJEH ATTACKED...

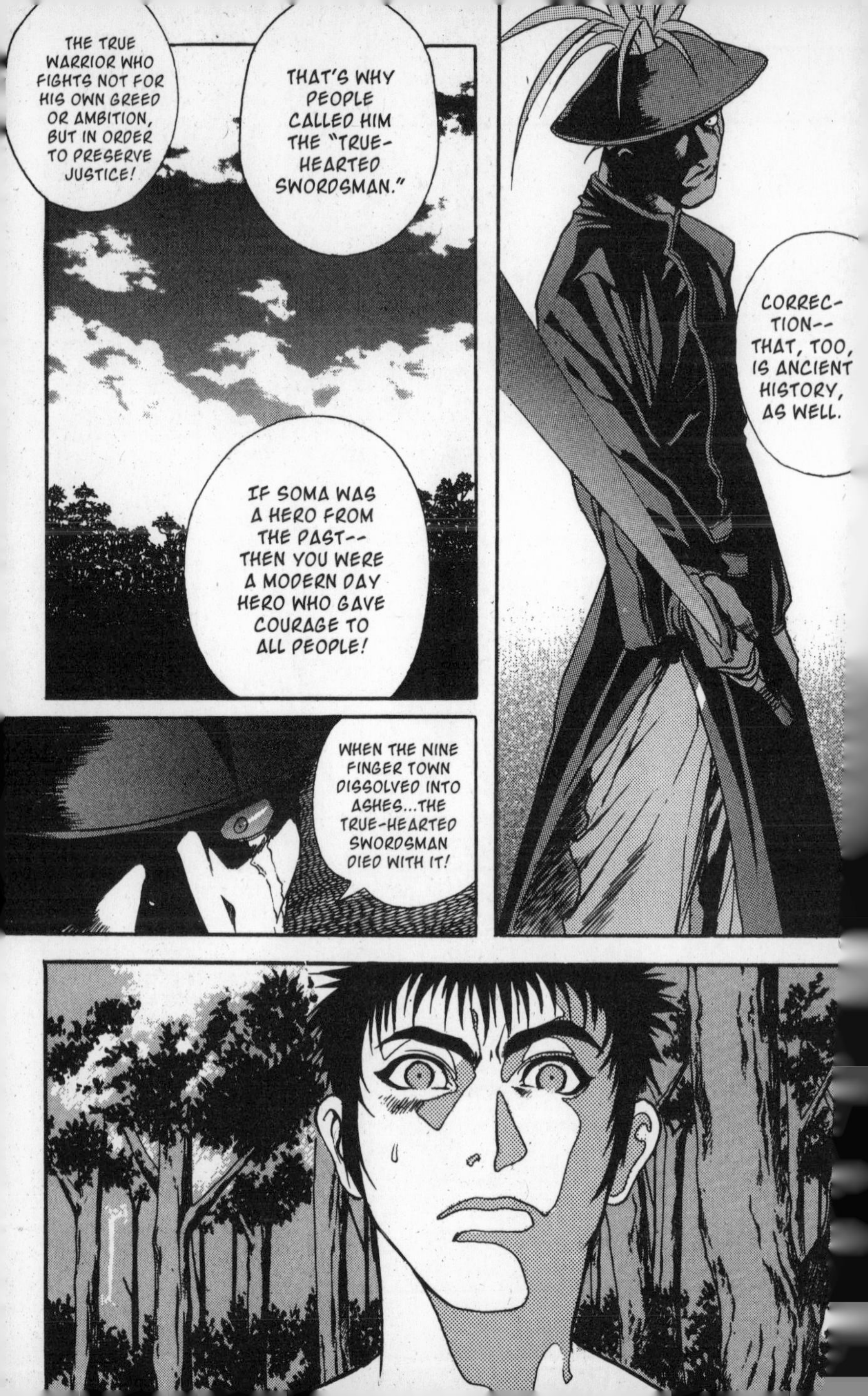
THAT'S WHY PEOPLE CALLED HIM THE "TRUE-HEARTED SWORDSMAN."
THE TRUE WARRIOR WHO FIGHTS NOT FOR HIS OWN GREED OR AMBITION, BUT IN ORDER TO PRESERVE JUSTICE!
IF SOMA WAS A HERO FROM THE PAST-- THEN YOU WERE A MODERN DAY HERO WHO GAVE COURAGE TO ALL PEOPLE!
CORREC-TION-- THAT, TOO, IS ANCIENT HISTORY, AS WELL.
WHEN THE NINE FINGER TOWN DISSOLVED INTO ASHES...THE TRUE-HEARTED SWORDSMAN DIED WITH IT!

BLADE OF HEAVEN

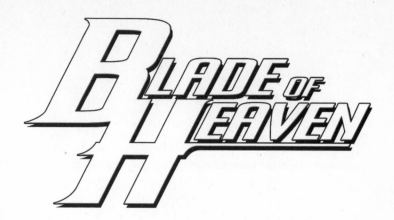

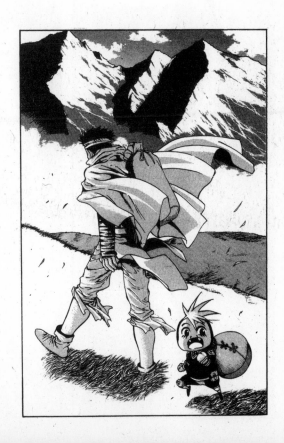

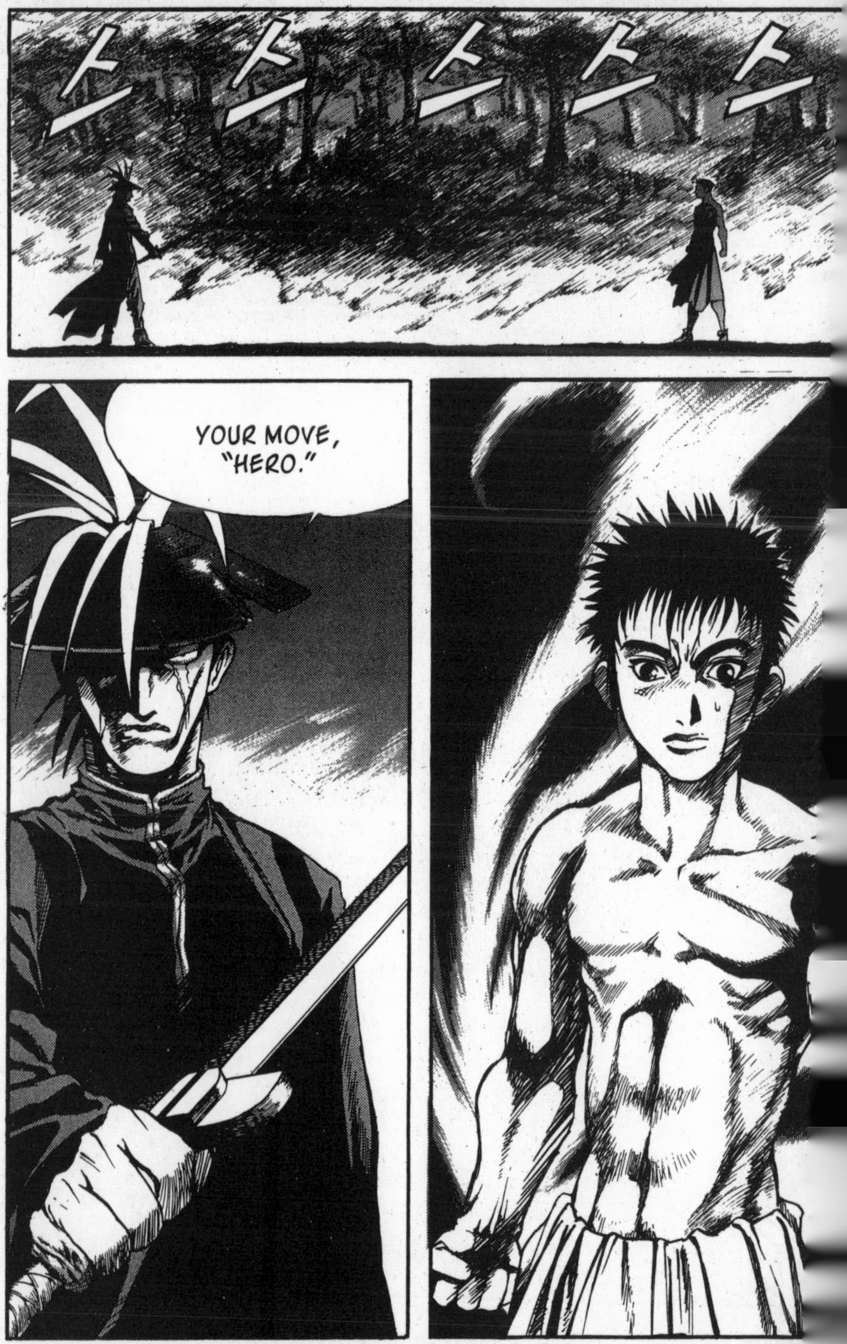
ト
ト
ト
ト
ト
YOUR MOVE, "HERO."

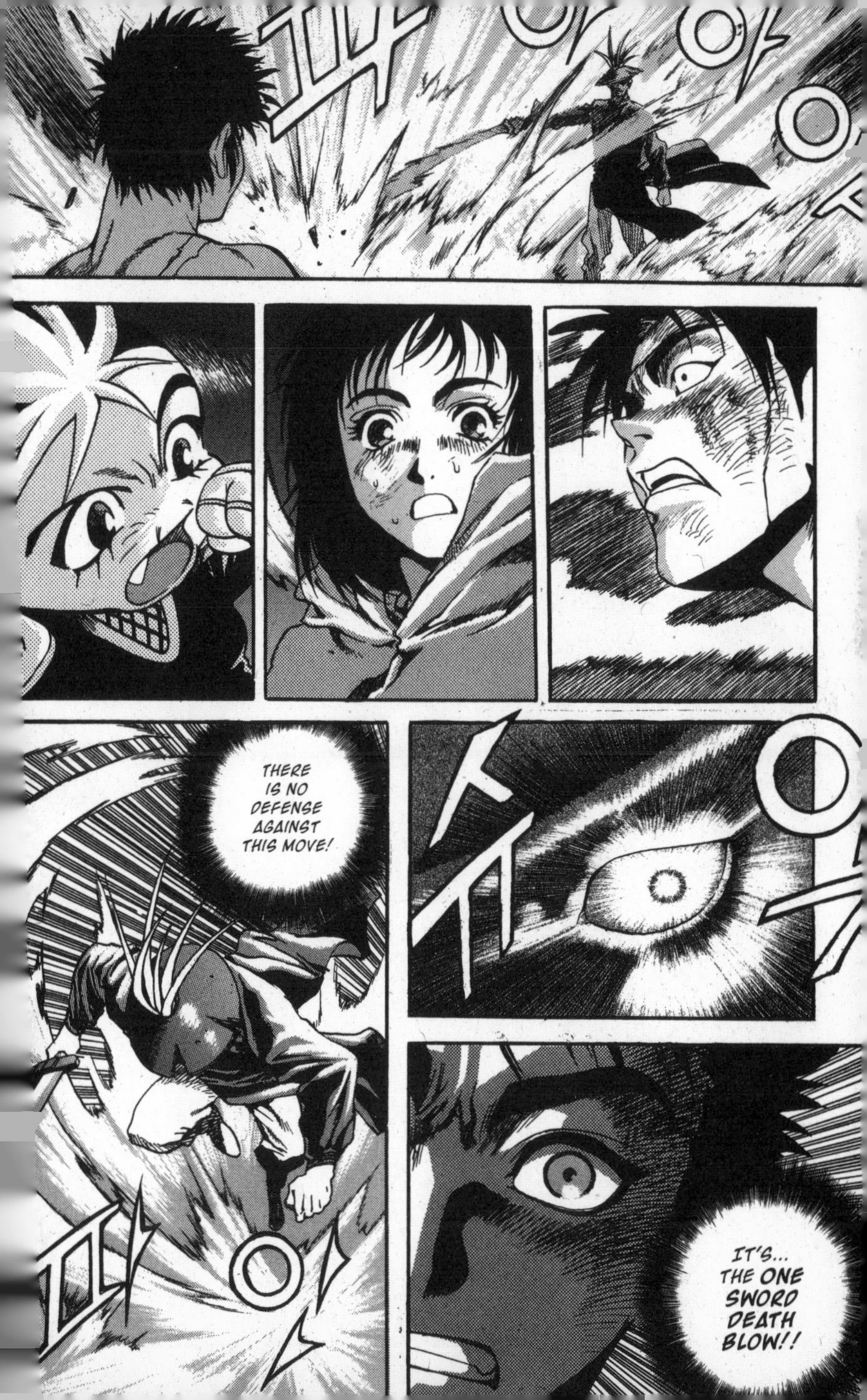
THERE IS NO DEFENSE AGAINST THIS MOVE!
IT'S... THE ONE SWORD DEATH BLOW!!

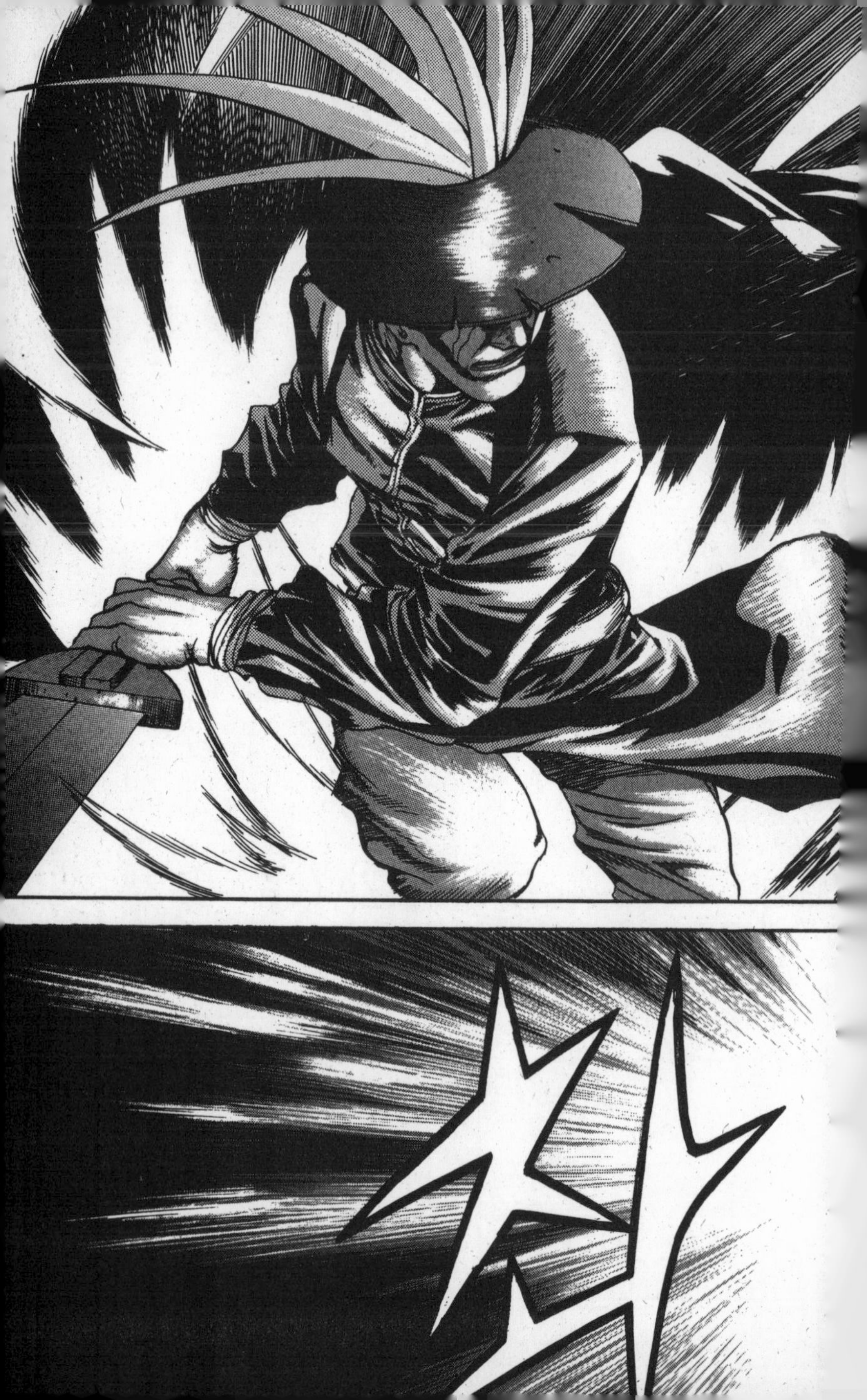

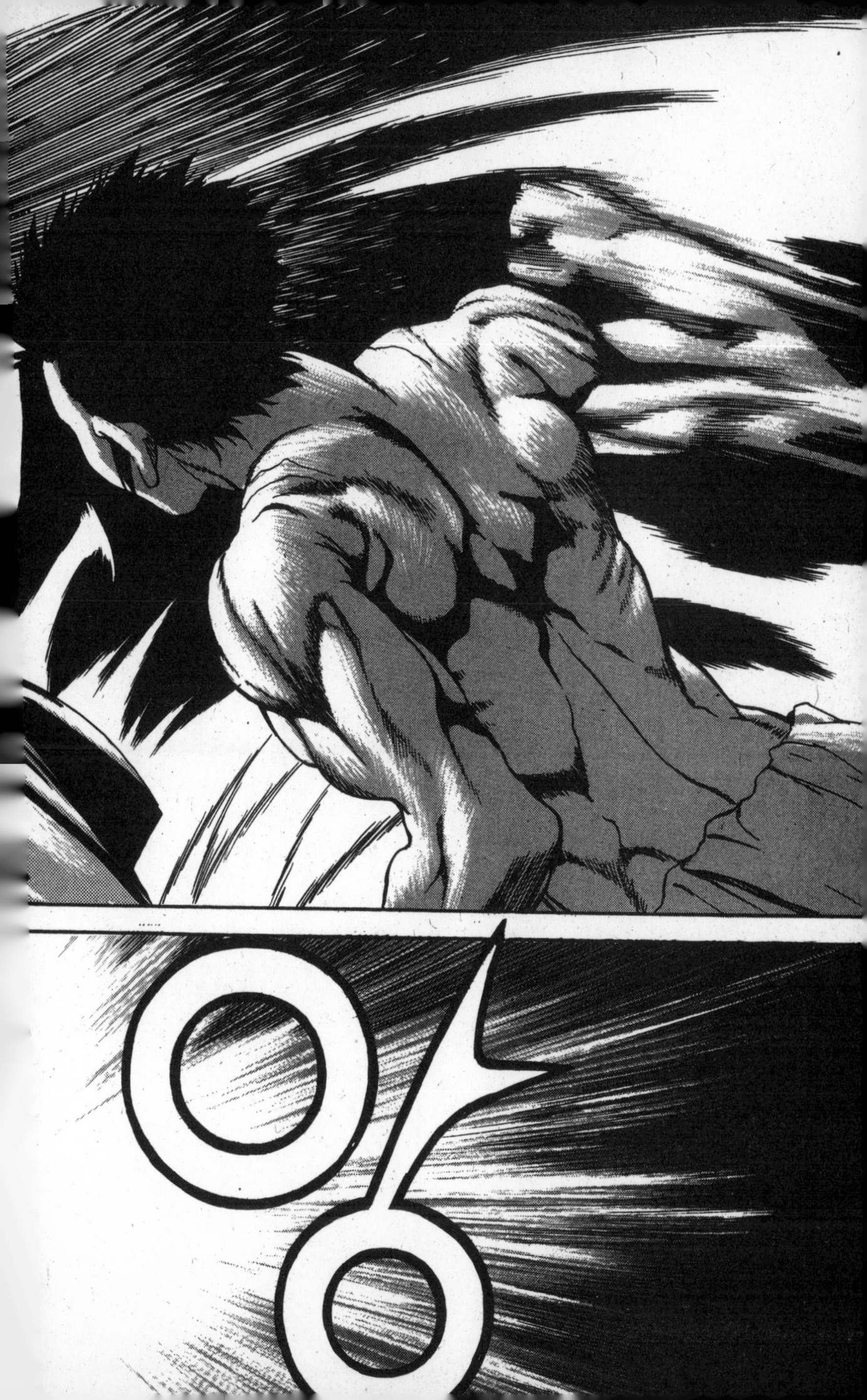

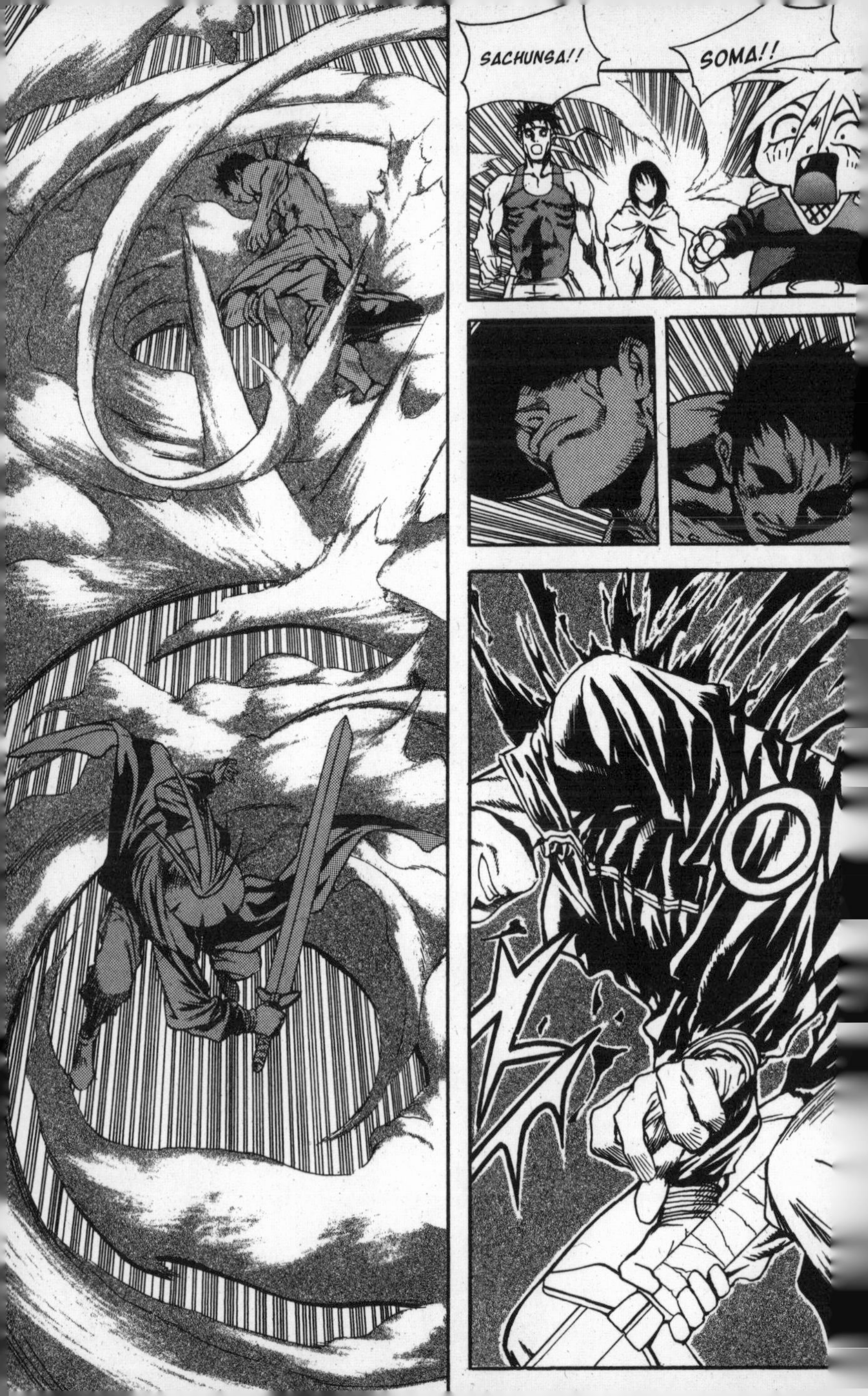
SOMA!!
SACHUNSA!!

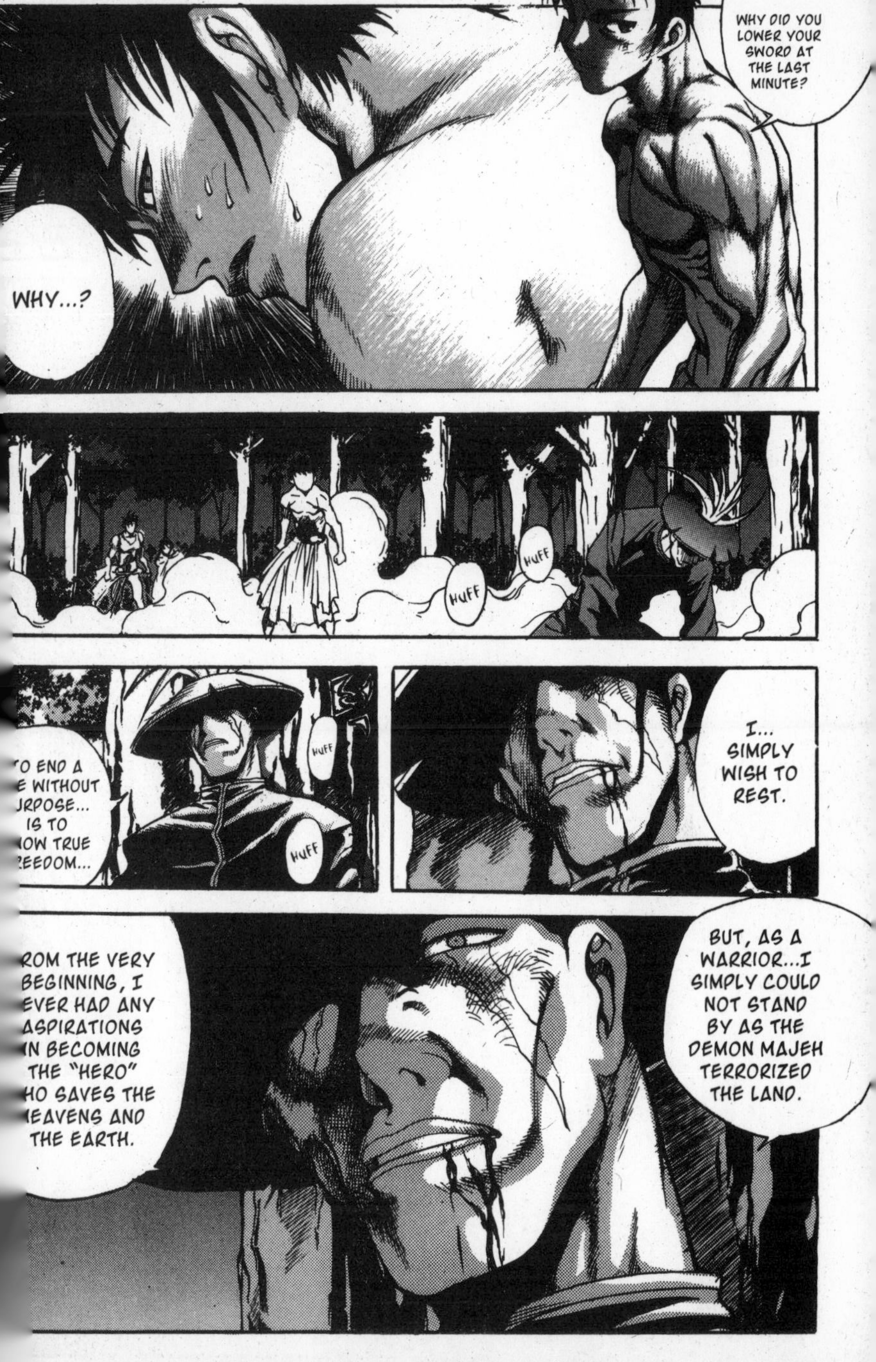
WHY...?
WHY DID YOU LOWER YOUR SWORD AT THE LAST MINUTE?
HUFF
HUFF
O END A E WITHOUT URPOSE... IS TO IOW TRUE REEDOM...
HUFF
HUFF
I... SIMPLY WISH TO REST.
ROM THE VERY BEGINNING, I EVER HAD ANY ASPIRATIONS IN BECOMING THE "HERO" HO SAVES THE EAVENS AND THE EARTH.
BUT, AS A WARRIOR...I SIMPLY COULD NOT STAND BY AS THE DEMON MAJEH TERRORIZED THE LAND.

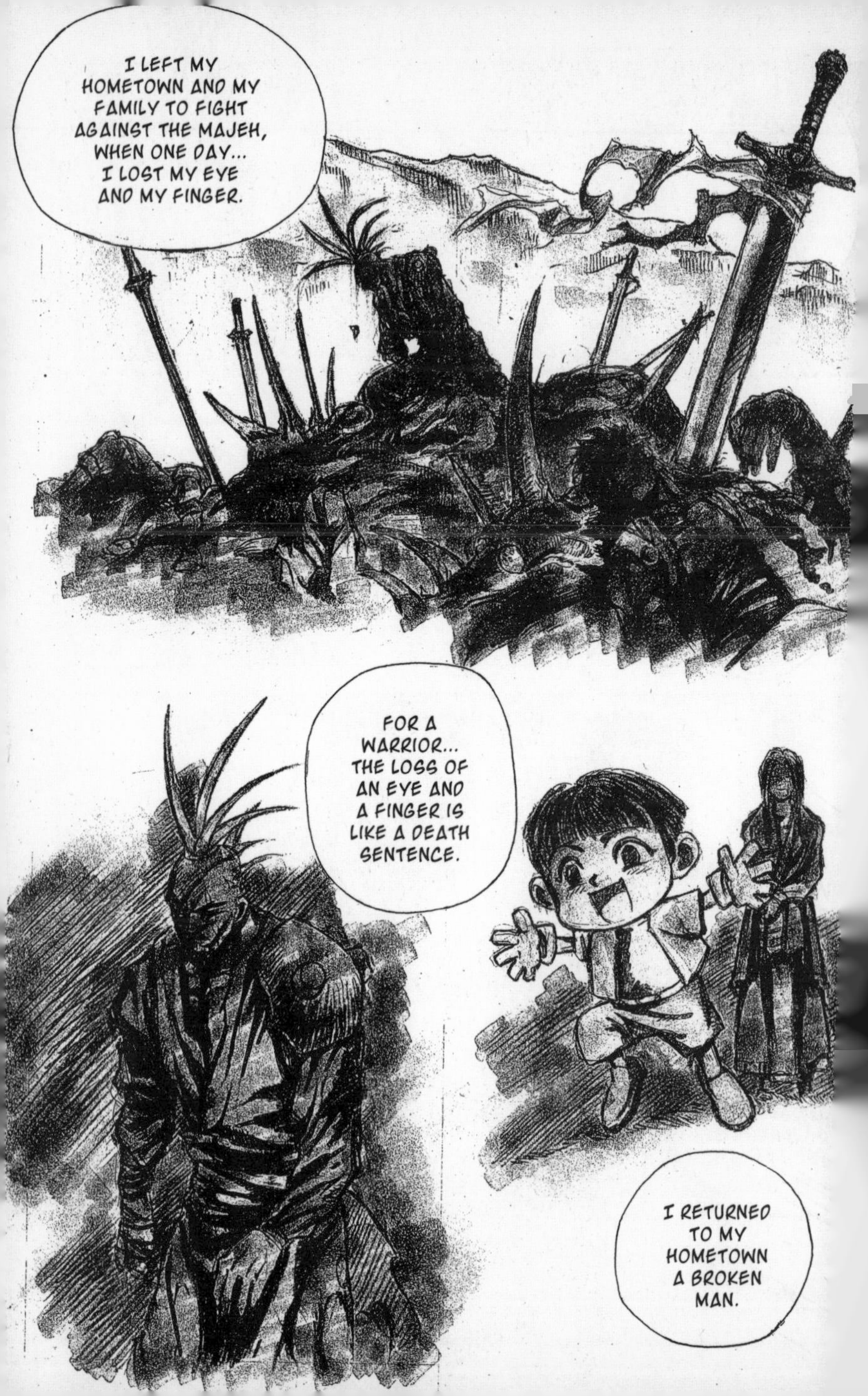
I LEFT MY HOMETOWN AND MY FAMILY TO FIGHT AGAINST THE MAJEH, WHEN ONE DAY... I LOST MY EYE AND MY FINGER.
FOR A WARRIOR... THE LOSS OF AN EYE AND A FINGER IS LIKE A DEATH SENTENCE.
I RETURNED TO MY HOMETOWN A BROKEN MAN.

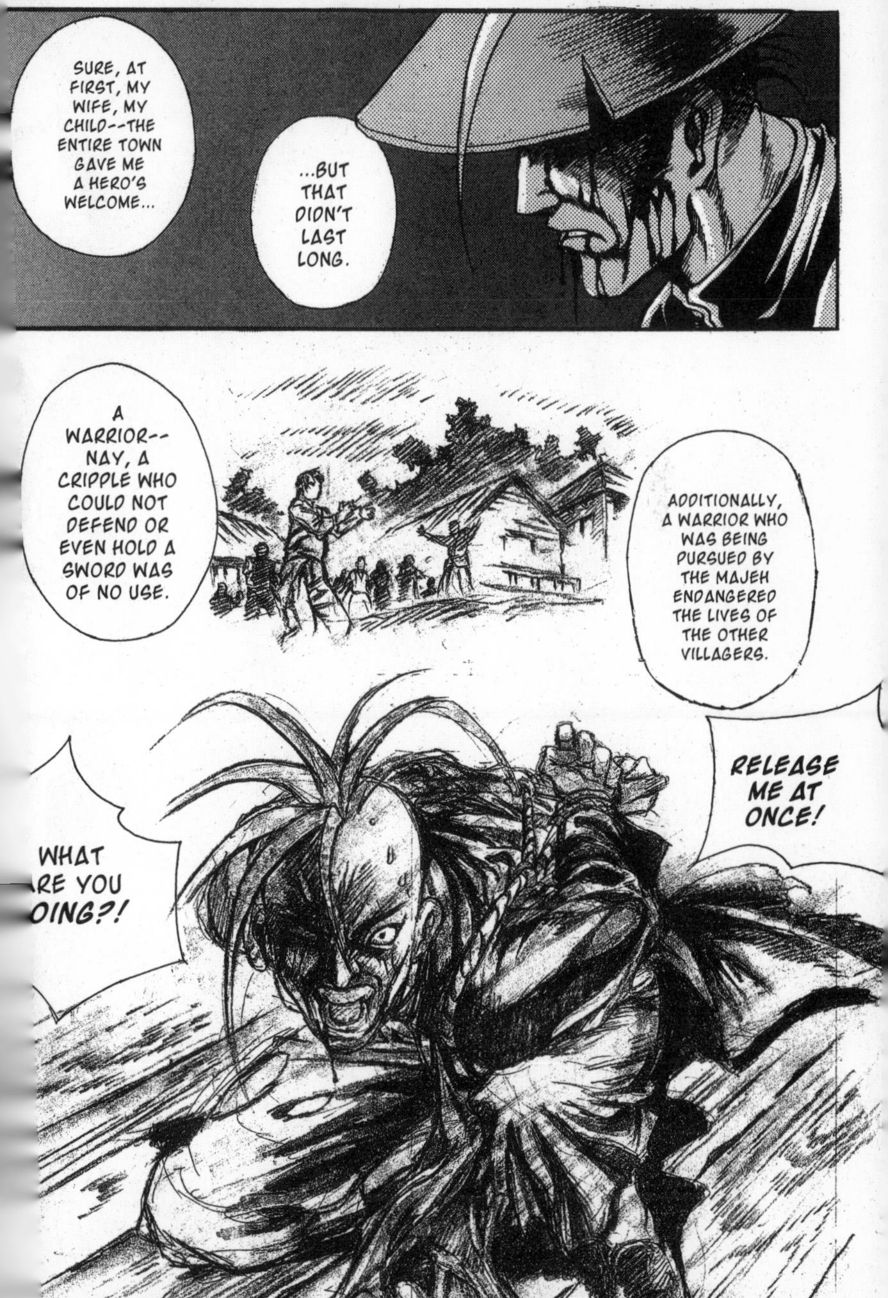
SURE, AT FIRST, MY WIFE, MY CHILD--THE ENTIRE TOWN GAVE ME A HERO'S WELCOME...
...BUT THAT DIDN'T LAST LONG.
A WARRIOR--NAY, A CRIPPLE WHO COULD NOT DEFEND OR EVEN HOLD A SWORD WAS OF NO USE.
ADDITIONALLY, A WARRIOR WHO WAS BEING PURSUED BY THE MAJEH ENDANGERED THE LIVES OF THE OTHER VILLAGERS.
RELEASE ME AT ONCE!

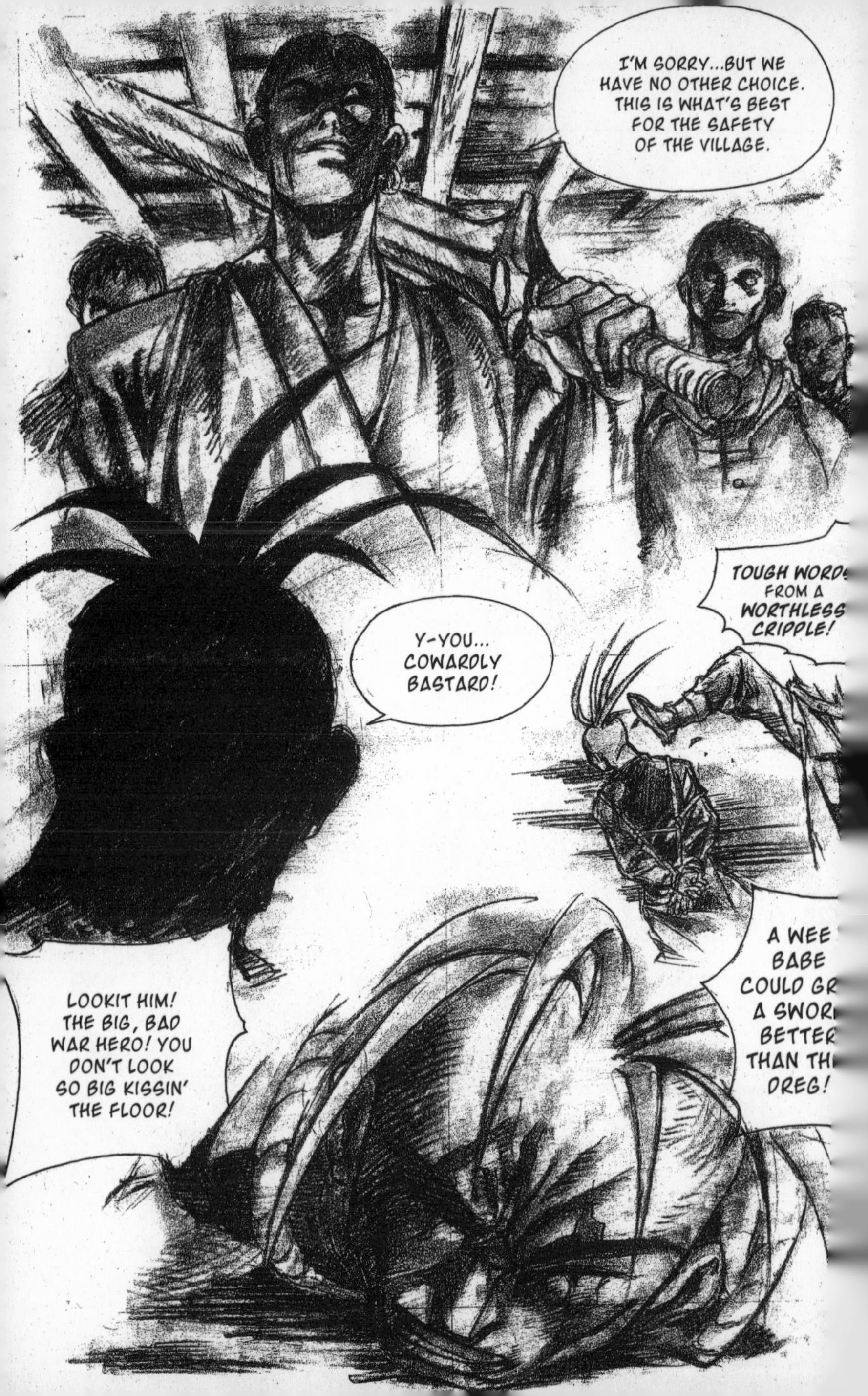
I'M SORRY...BUT WE HAVE NO OTHER CHOICE. THIS IS WHAT'S BEST FOR THE SAFETY OF THE VILLAGE.
TOUGH WORD FROM A WORTHLESS CRIPPLE!
Y-YOU... COWARDLY BASTARD!
A WEE BABE COULD GR A SWOR BETTER THAN TH DREG!
LOOKIT HIM! THE BIG, BAD WAR HERO! YOU DON'T LOOK SO BIG KISSIN' THE FLOOR!

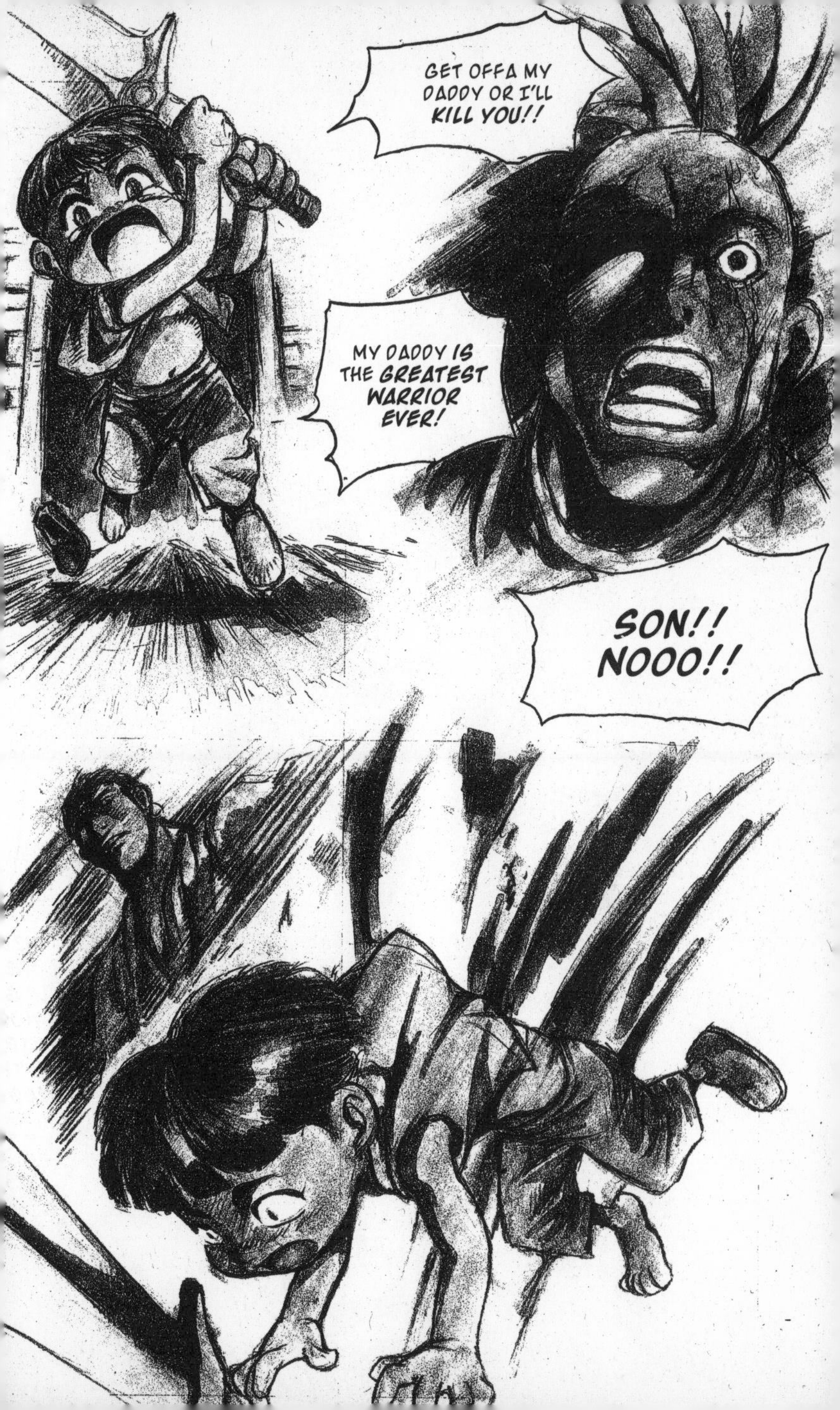
GET OFFA MY DADDY OR I'LL KILL YOU!!
MY DADDY IS THE GREATEST WARRIOR EVER!
SON!! NOOO!!

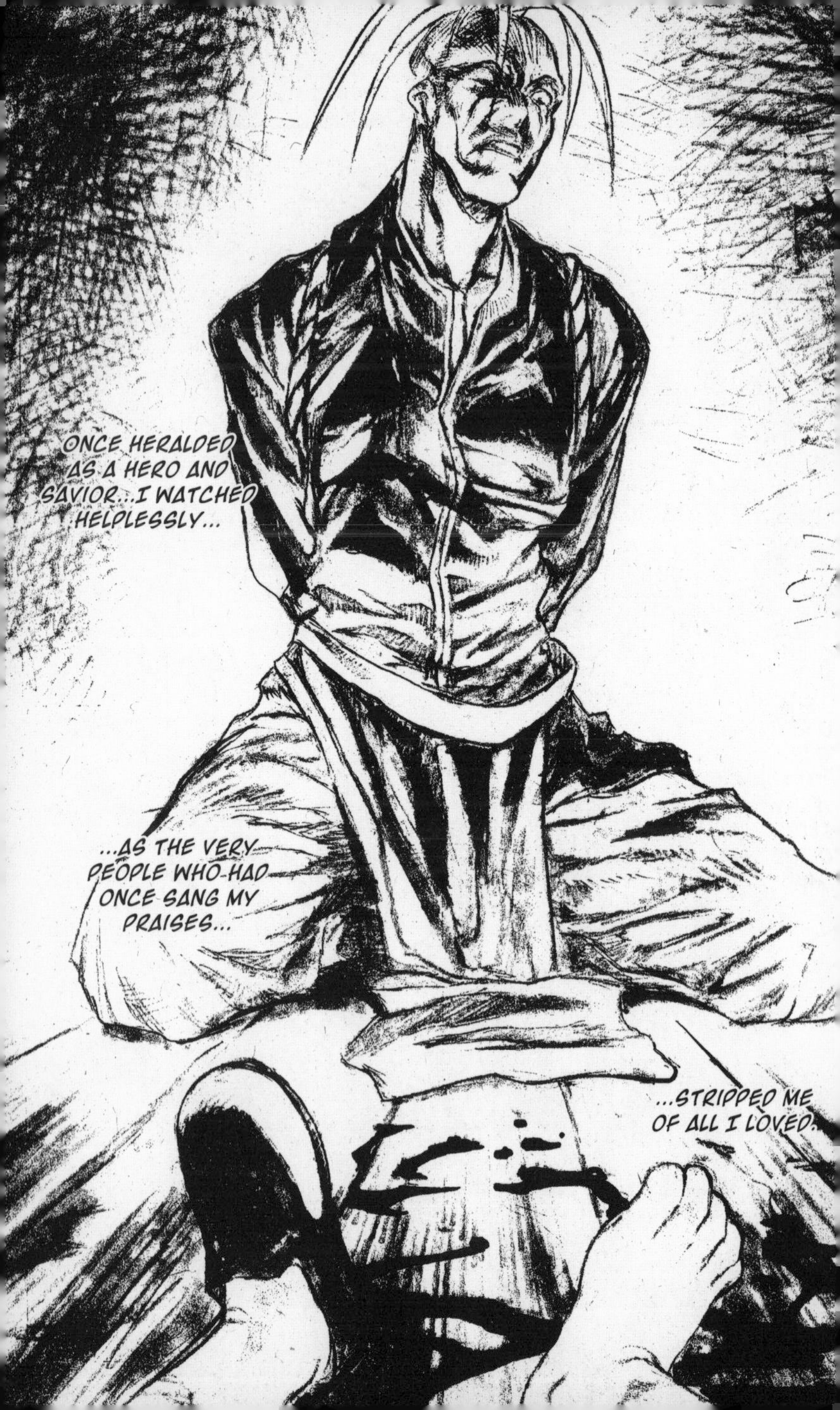
ONCE HERALDED AS A HERO AND SAVIOR...I WATCHED HELPLESSLY...
...AS THE VERY PEOPLE WHO HAD ONCE SANG MY PRAISES...
...STRIPPED ME OF ALL I LOVED.

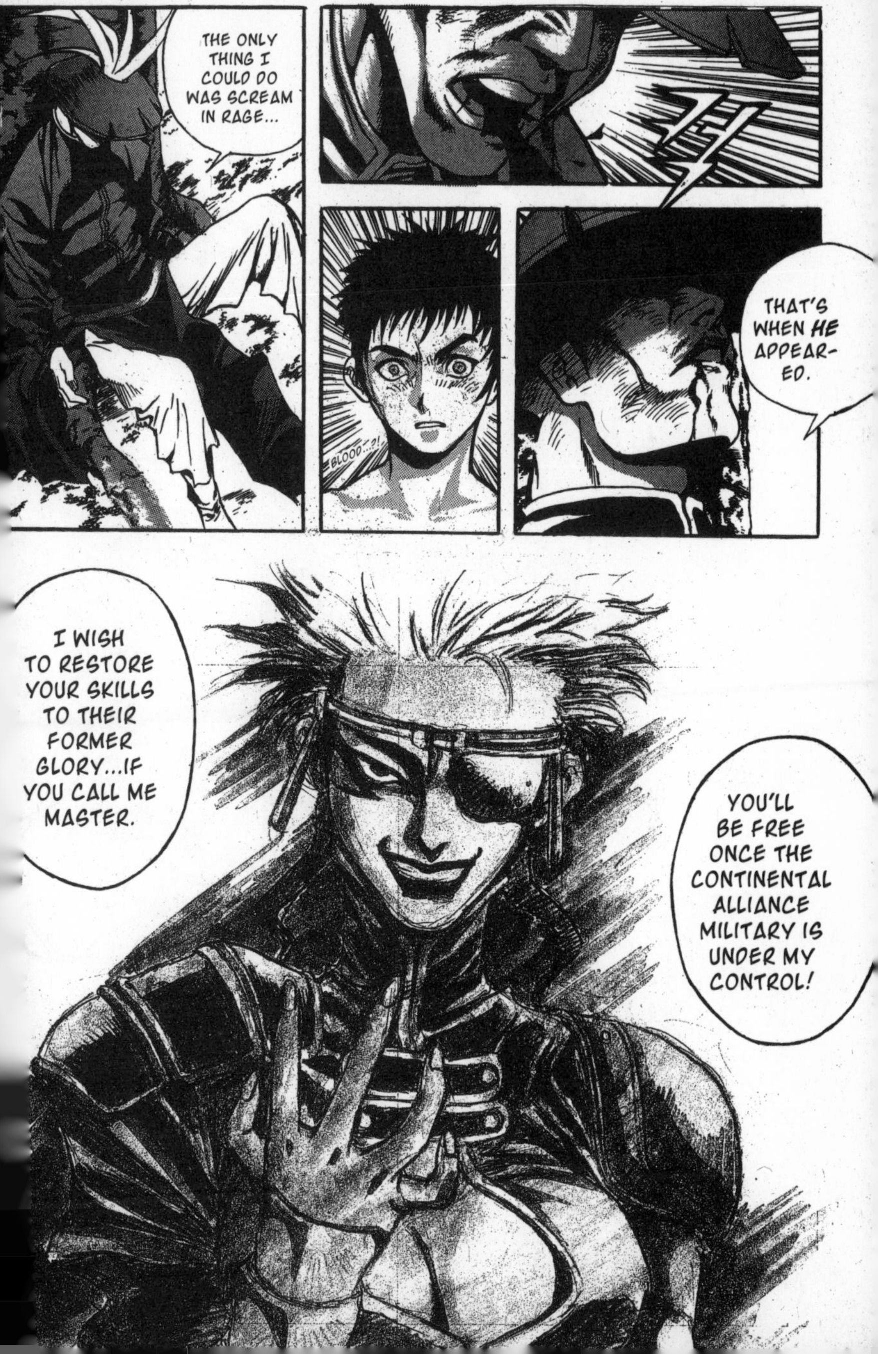

THE ONLY THING I COULD DO WAS SCREAM IN RAGE...
BLOOD...?!
THAT'S WHEN HE APPEARED.
I WISH TO RESTORE YOUR SKILLS TO THEIR FORMER GLORY...IF YOU CALL ME MASTER.
YOU'LL BE FREE ONCE THE CONTINENTAL ALLIANCE MILITARY IS UNDER MY CONTROL!

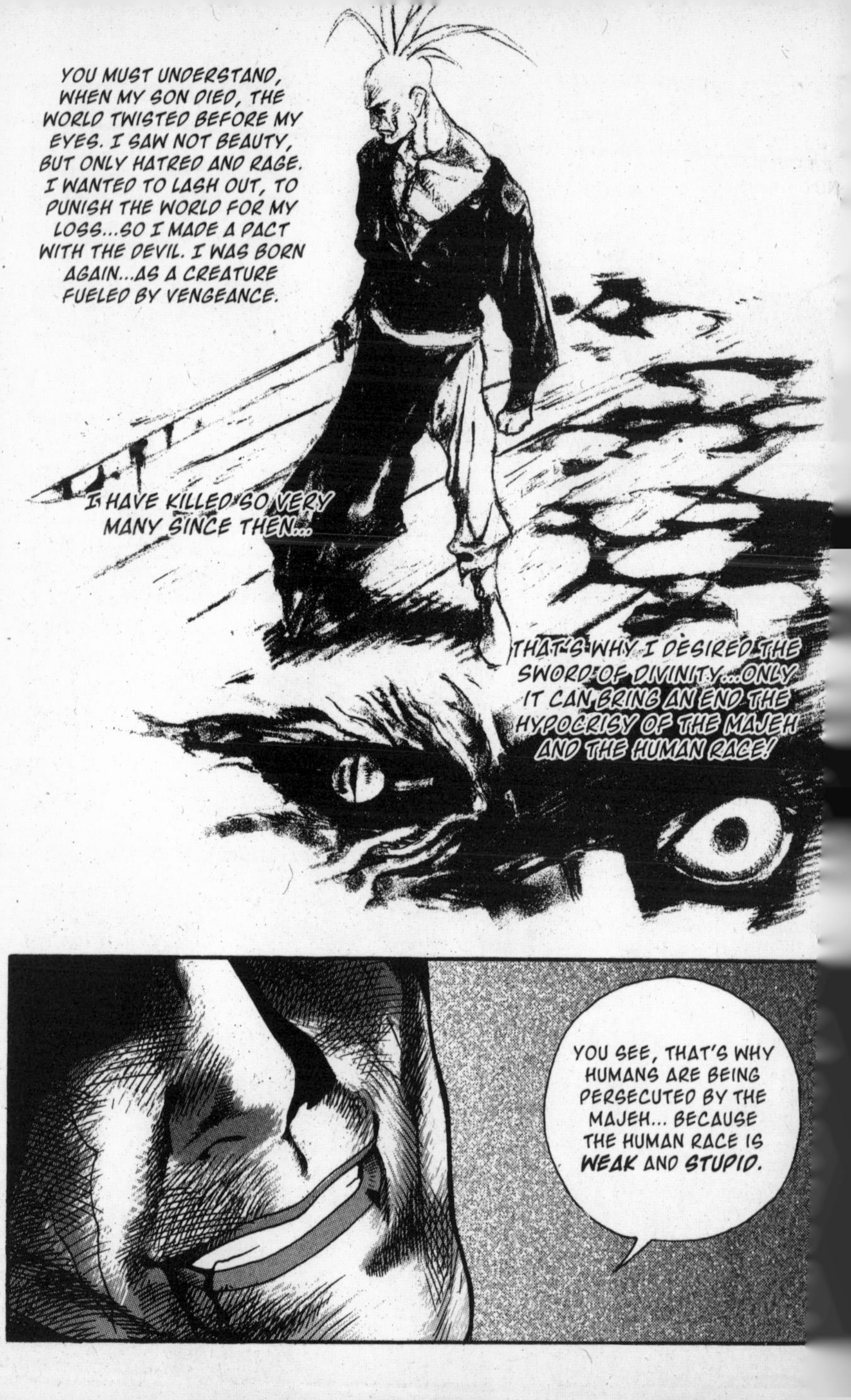
YOU MUST UNDERSTAND, WHEN MY SON DIED, THE WORLD TWISTED BEFORE MY EYES. I SAW NOT BEAUTY, BUT ONLY HATRED AND RAGE. I WANTED TO LASH OUT, TO PUNISH THE WORLD FOR MY LOSS...SO I MADE A PACT WITH THE DEVIL. I WAS BORN AGAIN...AS A CREATURE FUELED BY VENGEANCE.
I HAVE KILLED SO VERY MANY SINCE THEN...
THAT'S WHY I DESIRED THE SWORD OF DIVINITY...ONLY IT CAN BRING AN END THE HYPOCRISY OF THE MAJEH AND THE HUMAN RACE!
YOU SEE, THAT'S WHY HUMANS ARE BEING PERSECUTED BY THE MAJEH... BECAUSE THE HUMAN RACE IS **WEAK** AND **STUPID**.

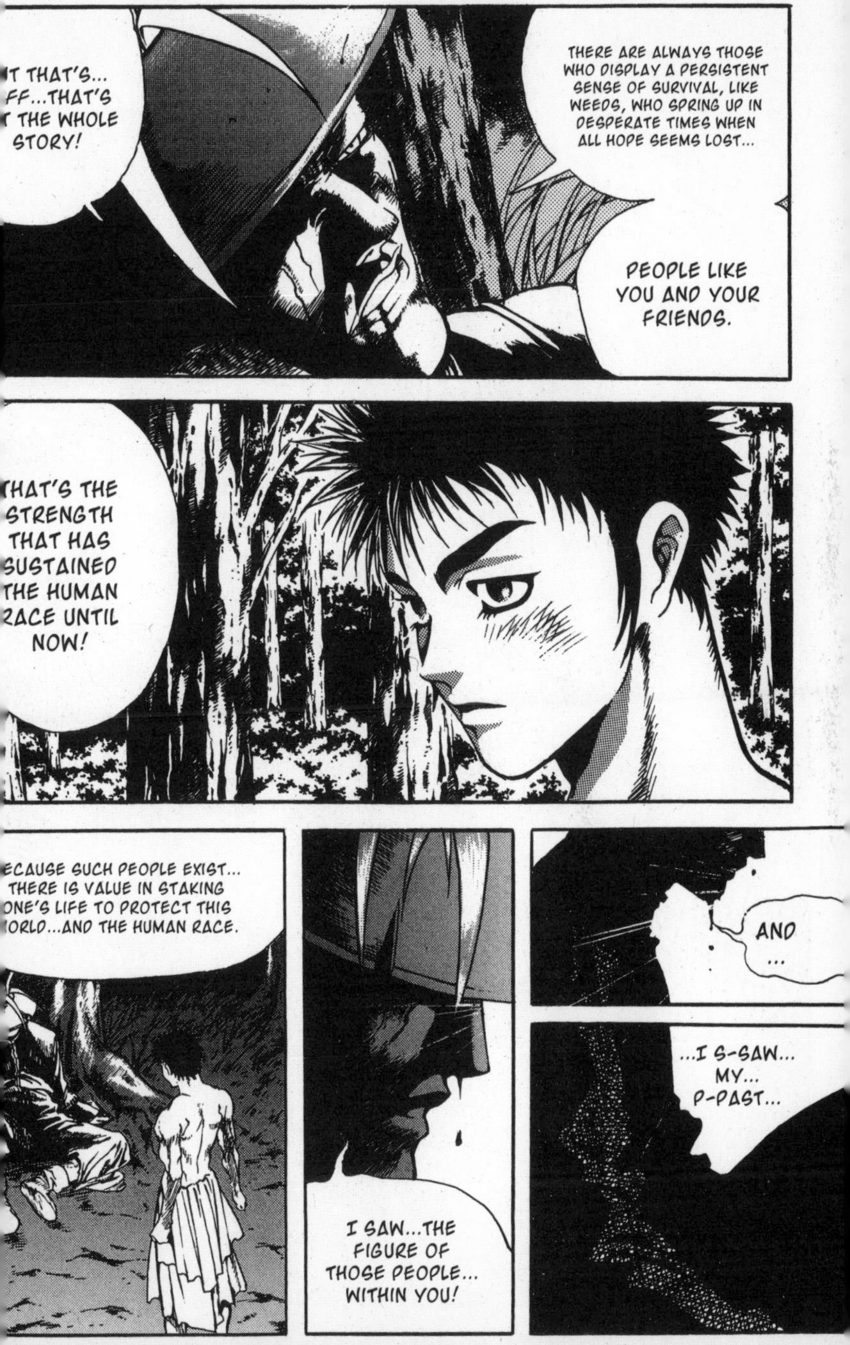
T THAT'S... FF...THAT'S T THE WHOLE STORY!
THERE ARE ALWAYS THOSE WHO DISPLAY A PERSISTENT SENSE OF SURVIVAL, LIKE WEEDS, WHO SPRING UP IN DESPERATE TIMES WHEN ALL HOPE SEEMS LOST...
PEOPLE LIKE YOU AND YOUR FRIENDS.
HAT'S THE STRENGTH THAT HAS SUSTAINED THE HUMAN ACE UNTIL NOW!
ECAUSE SUCH PEOPLE EXIST... THERE IS VALUE IN STAKING ONE'S LIFE TO PROTECT THIS ORLD...AND THE HUMAN RACE.
I SAW...THE FIGURE OF THOSE PEOPLE... WITHIN YOU!
AND ...
...I S-SAW... MY... P-PAST...

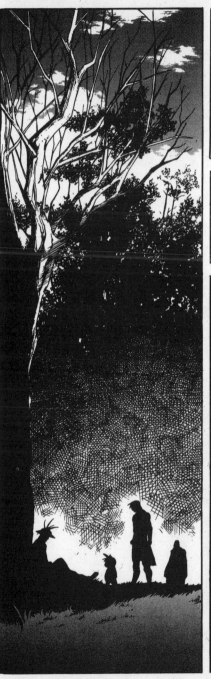

HE'S DEAD.

IT SEEMS... LIKE HE LIVED A VERY UNHAPPY LIFE.

PERHAPS...BU IN DEATH...

...HE FINALLY HAS THE PEACE THAT HAD SO ELUDED HIM IN LIFE.

SACHUNSA WHAT WILL YOU DO NOW...?

BLADE OF HEAVEN

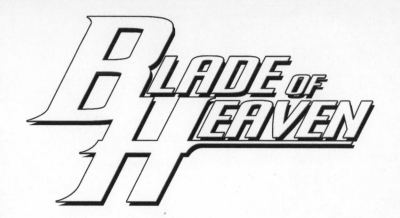

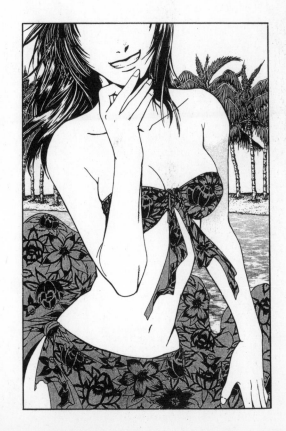

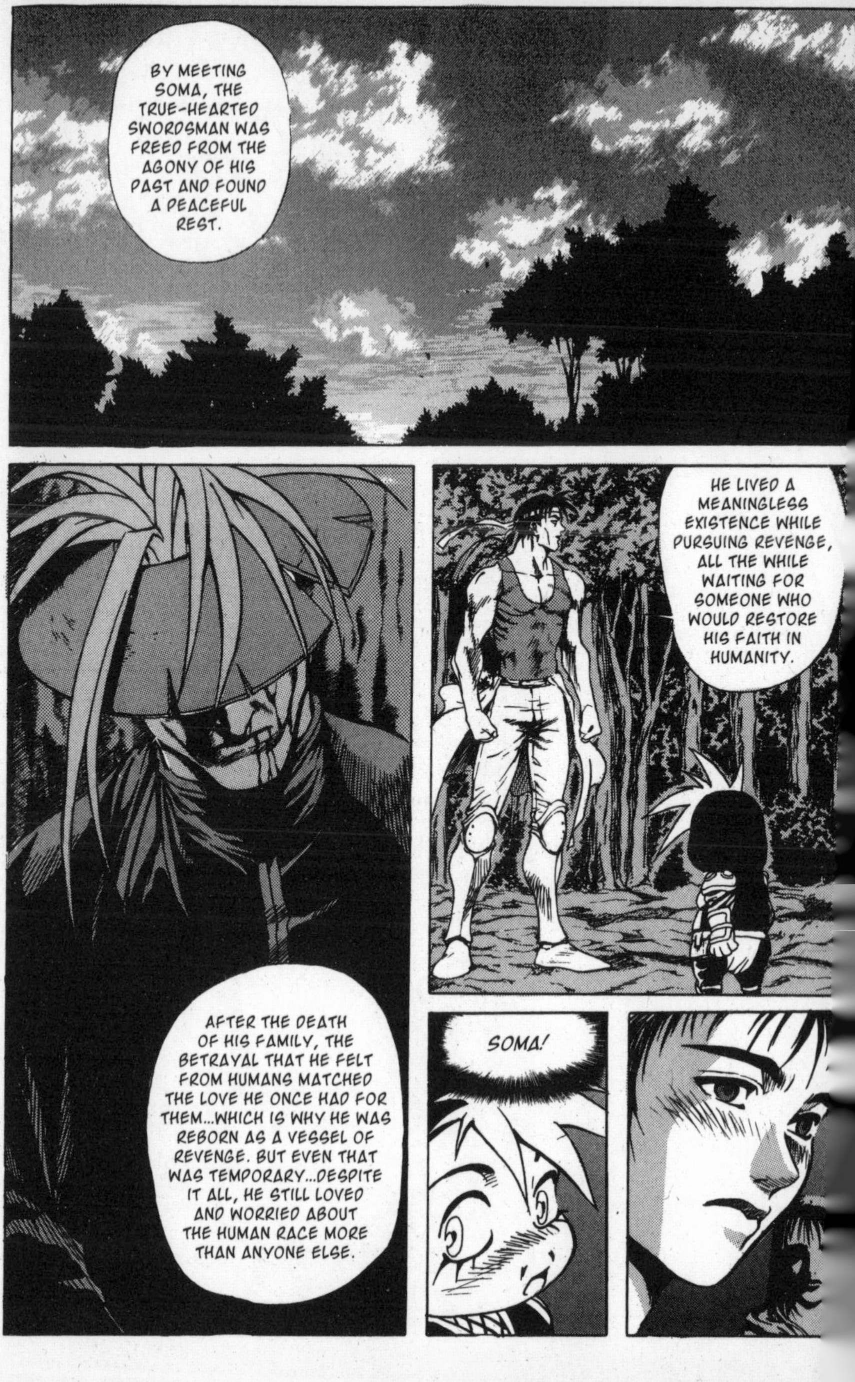
BY MEETING SOMA, THE TRUE-HEARTED SWORDSMAN WAS FREED FROM THE AGONY OF HIS PAST AND FOUND A PEACEFUL REST.
HE LIVED A MEANINGLESS EXISTENCE WHILE PURSUING REVENGE, ALL THE WHILE WAITING FOR SOMEONE WHO WOULD RESTORE HIS FAITH IN HUMANITY.
AFTER THE DEATH OF HIS FAMILY, THE BETRAYAL THAT HE FELT FROM HUMANS MATCHED THE LOVE HE ONCE HAD FOR THEM...WHICH IS WHY HE WAS REBORN AS A VESSEL OF REVENGE. BUT EVEN THAT WAS TEMPORARY...DESPITE IT ALL, HE STILL LOVED AND WORRIED ABOUT THE HUMAN RACE MORE THAN ANYONE ELSE.
SOMA!

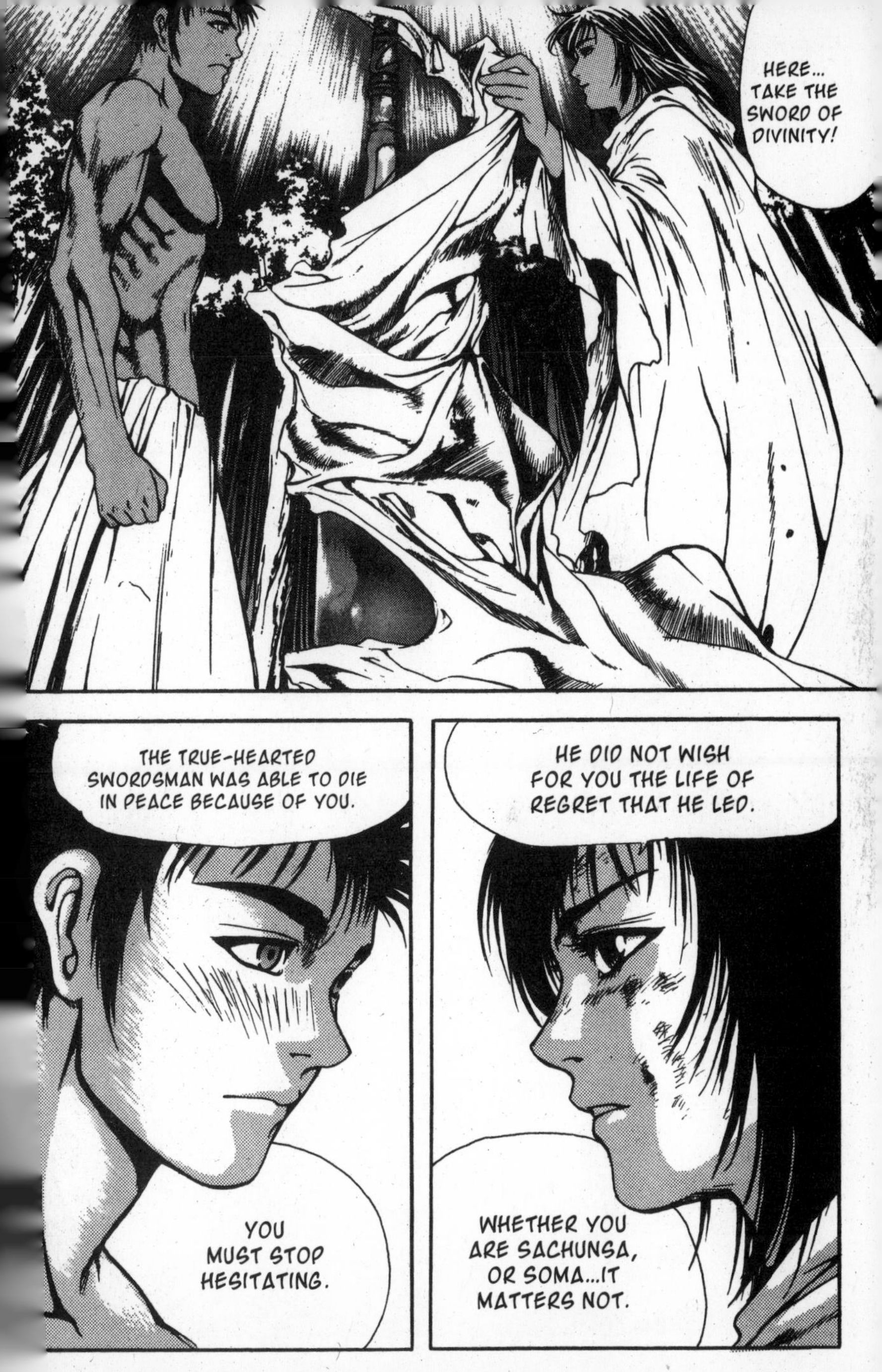
HERE... TAKE THE SWORD OF DIVINITY!
THE TRUE-HEARTED SWORDSMAN WAS ABLE TO DIE IN PEACE BECAUSE OF YOU.
YOU MUST STOP HESITATING.
HE DID NOT WISH FOR YOU THE LIFE OF REGRET THAT HE LED.
WHETHER YOU ARE SACHUNSA, OR SOMA...IT MATTERS NOT.

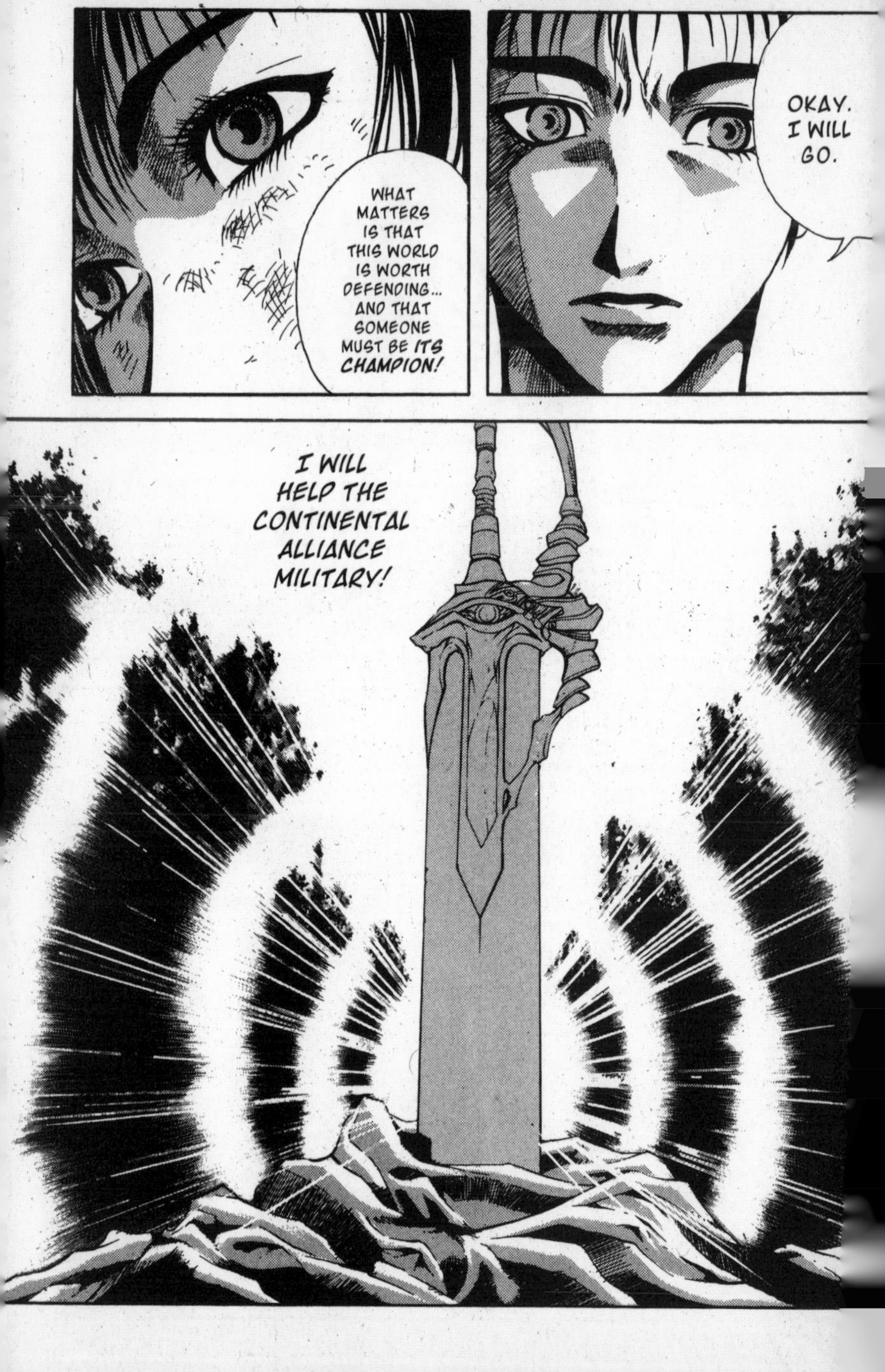
WHAT MATTERS IS THAT THIS WORLD IS WORTH DEFENDING... AND THAT SOMEONE MUST BE ITS CHAMPION!
OKAY. I WILL GO.
I WILL HELP THE CONTINENTAL ALLIANCE MILITARY!

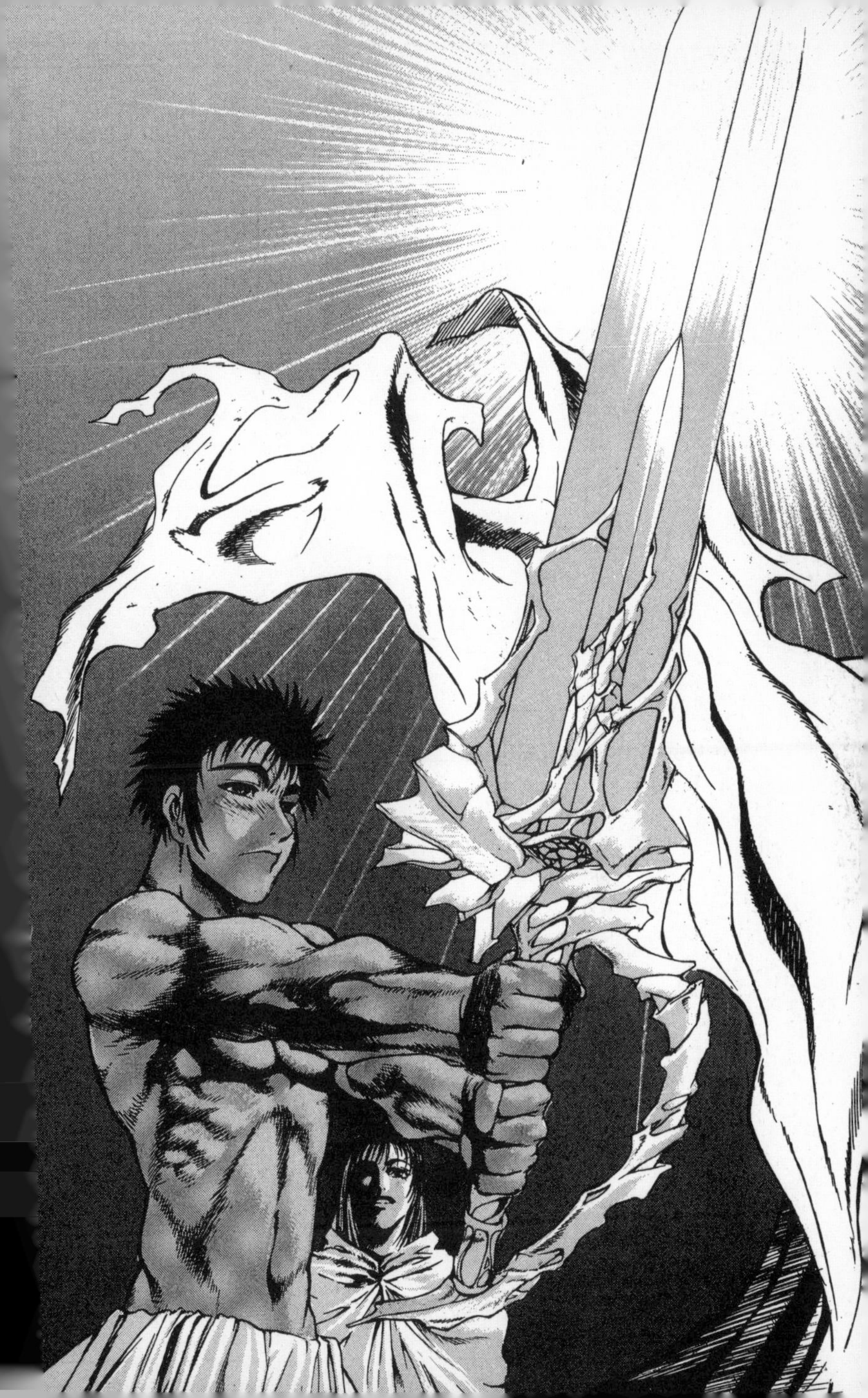

MY BELO
COMMAND

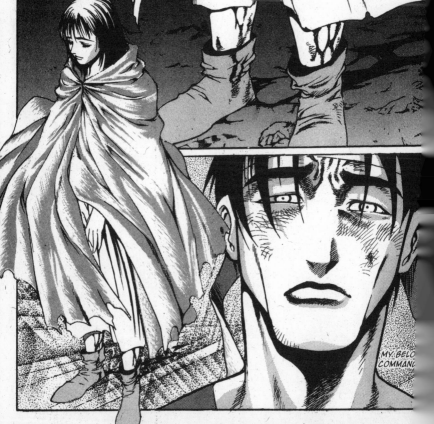

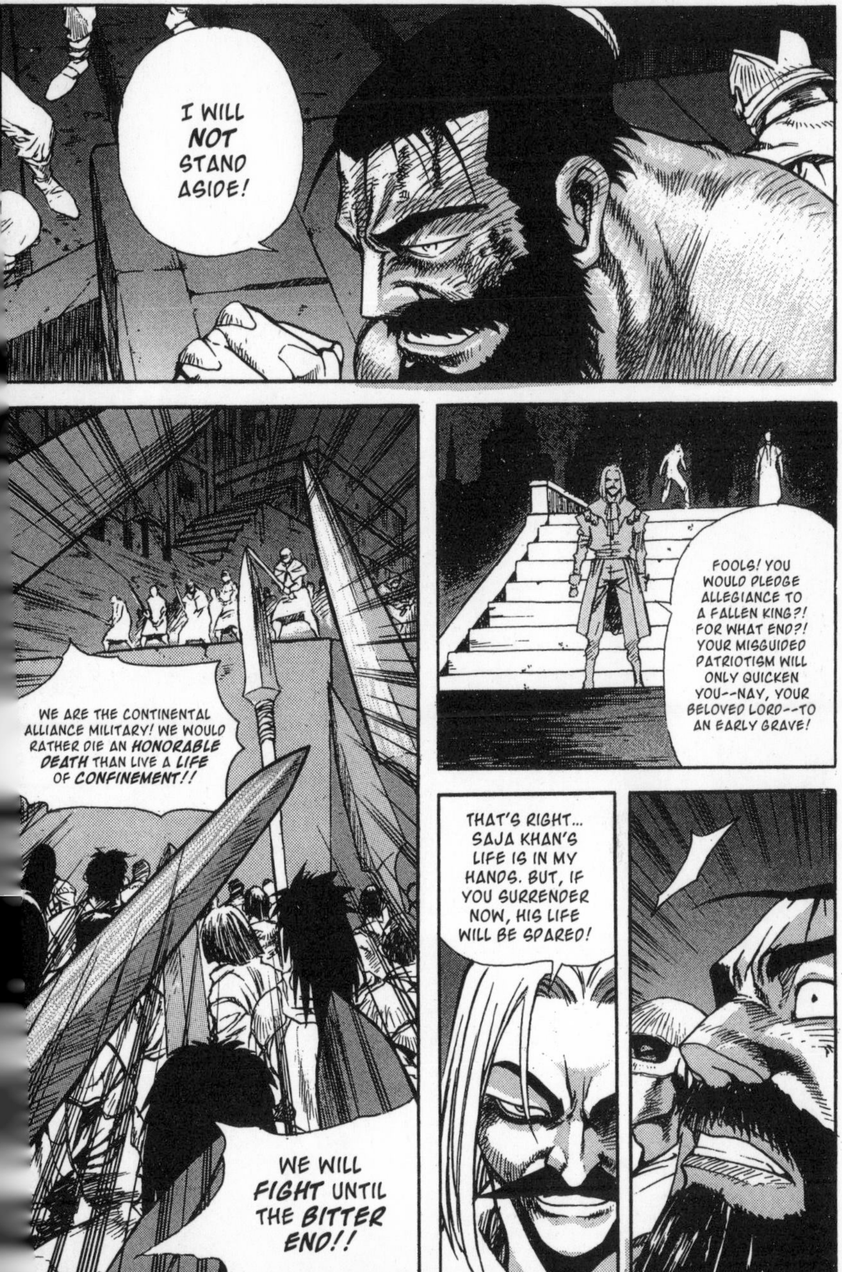
I WILL NOT STAND ASIDE!
WE ARE THE CONTINENTAL ALLIANCE MILITARY! WE WOULD RATHER DIE AN HONORABLE DEATH THAN LIVE A LIFE OF CONFINEMENT!!
WE WILL FIGHT UNTIL THE BITTER END!!
FOOLS! YOU WOULD PLEDGE ALLEGIANCE TO A FALLEN KING?! FOR WHAT END?! YOUR MISGUIDED PATRIOTISM WILL ONLY QUICKEN YOU--NAY, YOUR BELOVED LORD--TO AN EARLY GRAVE!
THAT'S RIGHT... SAJA KHAN'S LIFE IS IN MY HANDS. BUT, IF YOU SURRENDER NOW, HIS LIFE WILL BE SPARED!

LOOK! IT'S SAJA KHAN...!

LORD KHAN!

YEAH...YOU DON'
WANT US TO COM
DOWN THERE!

WHAT A SMASHING IDEA...

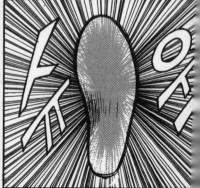

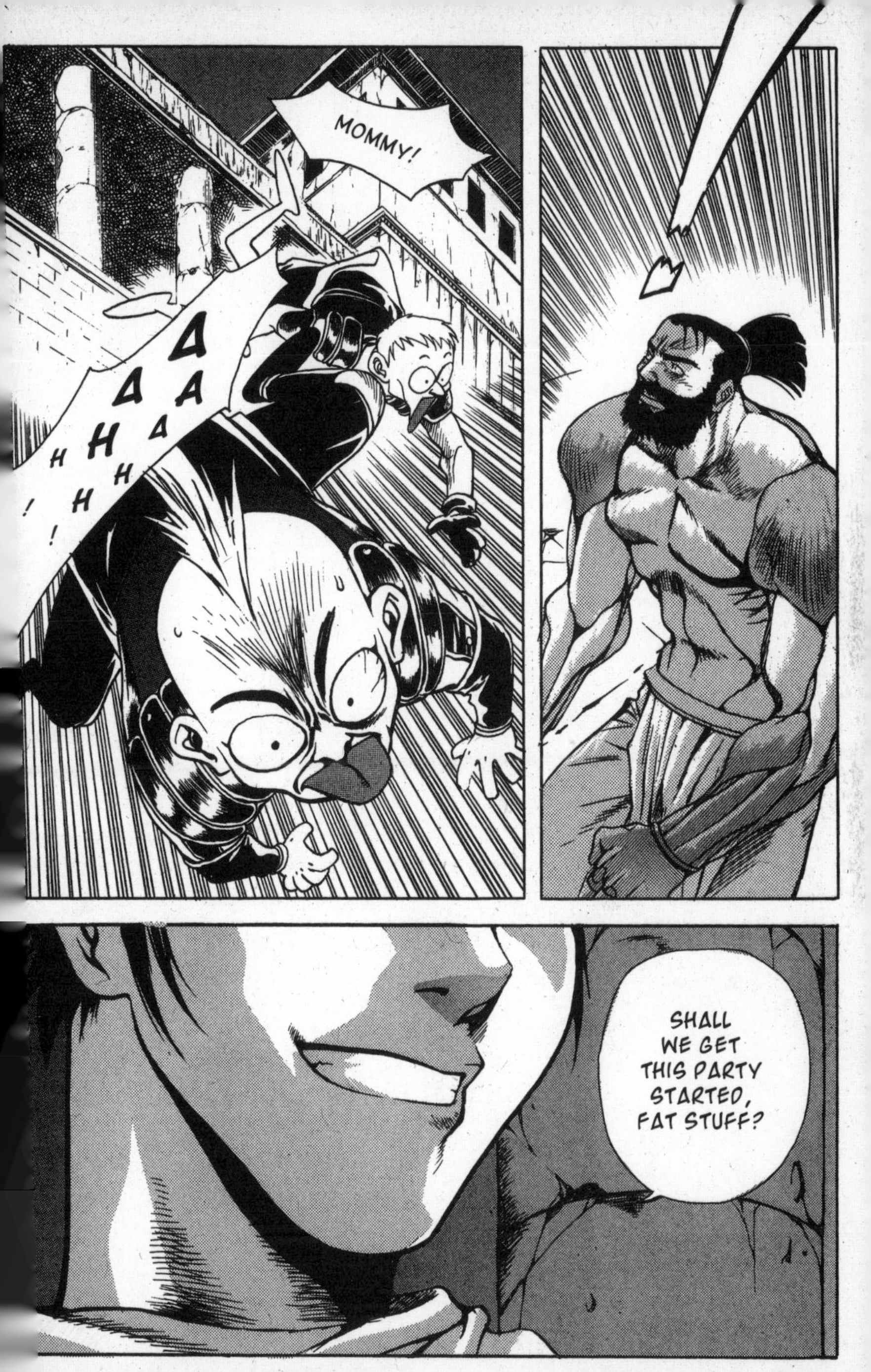
MOMMY!
AAAAAAHHHHH!!
SHALL WE GET THIS PARTY STARTED, FAT STUFF?

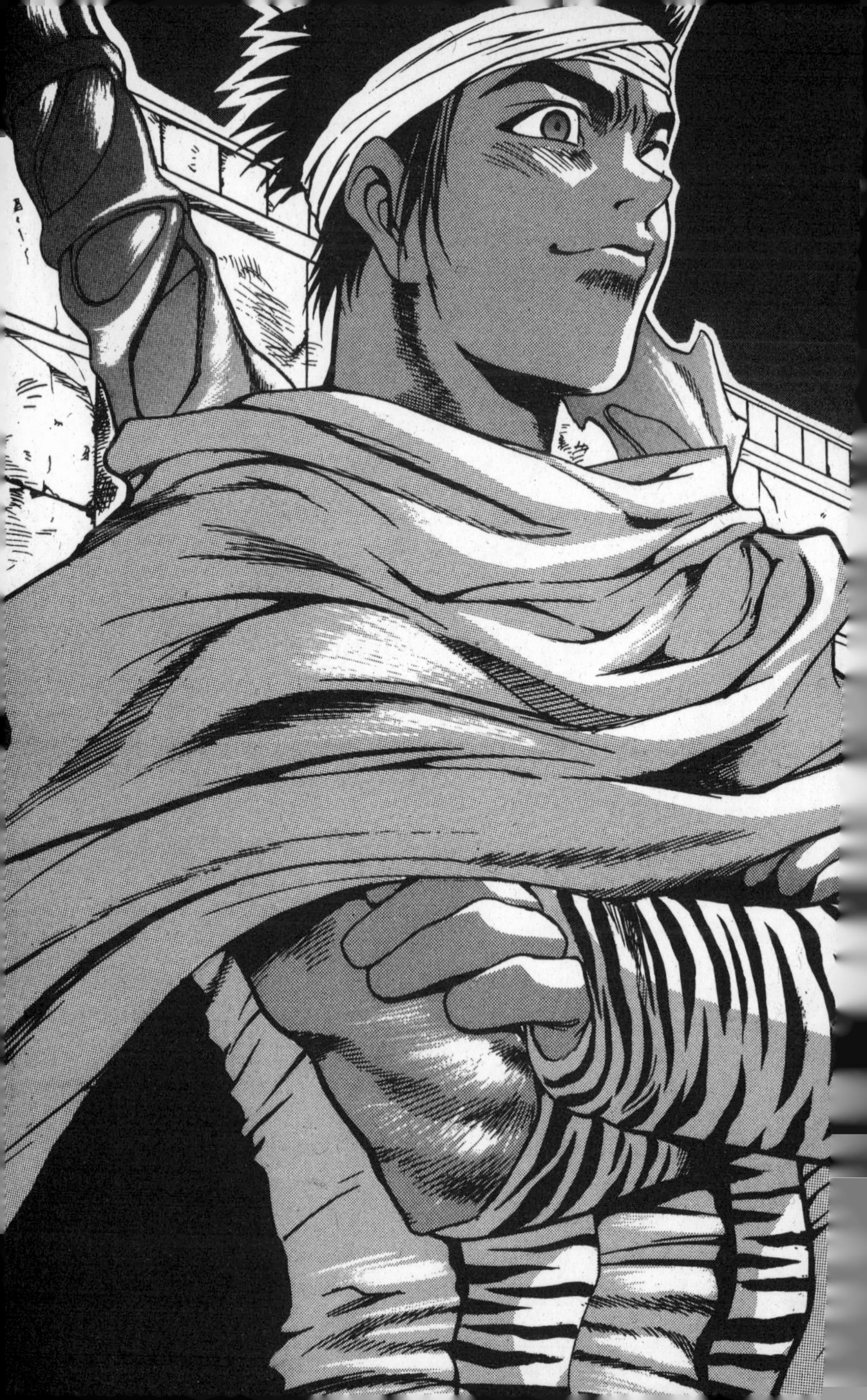

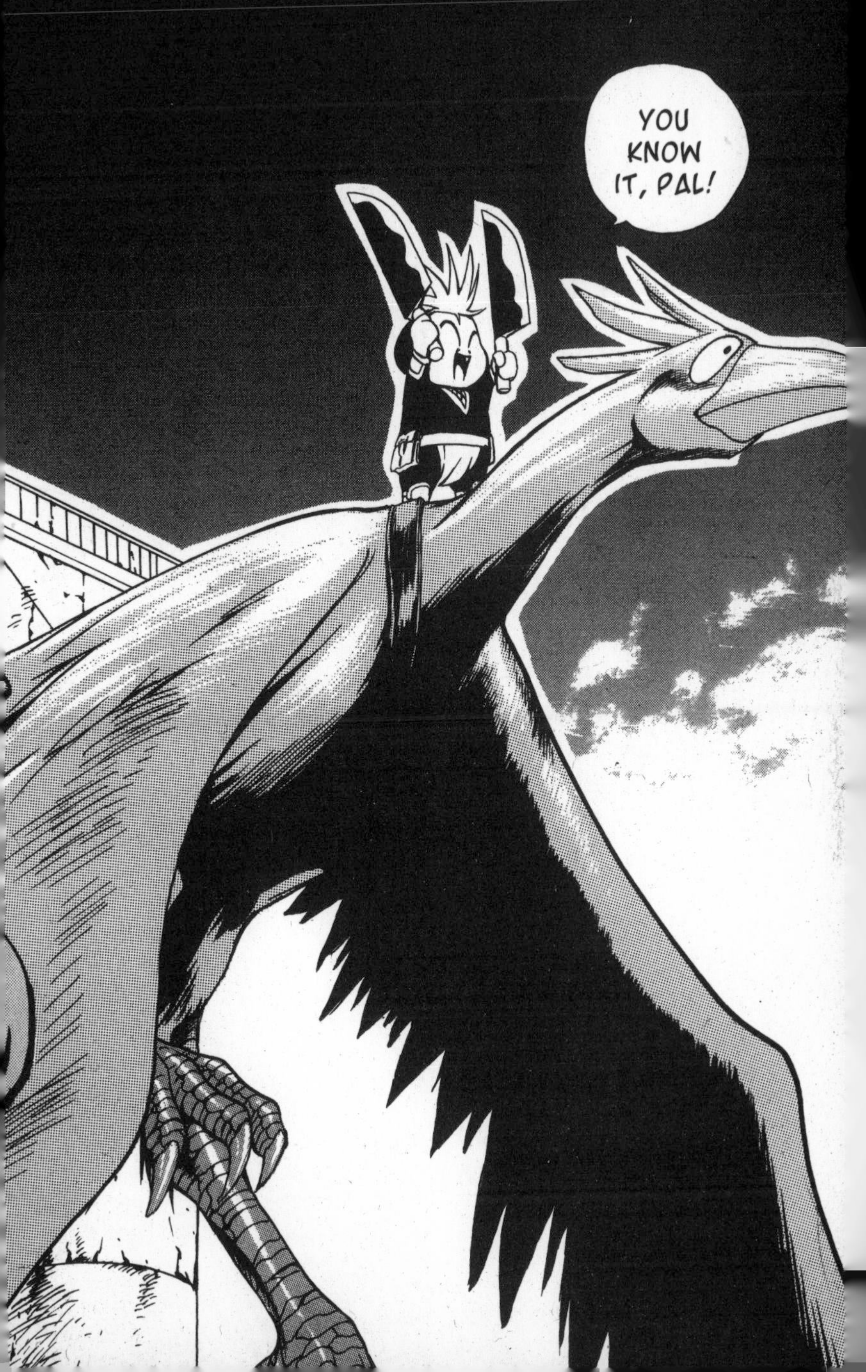
YOU KNOW IT, PAL!

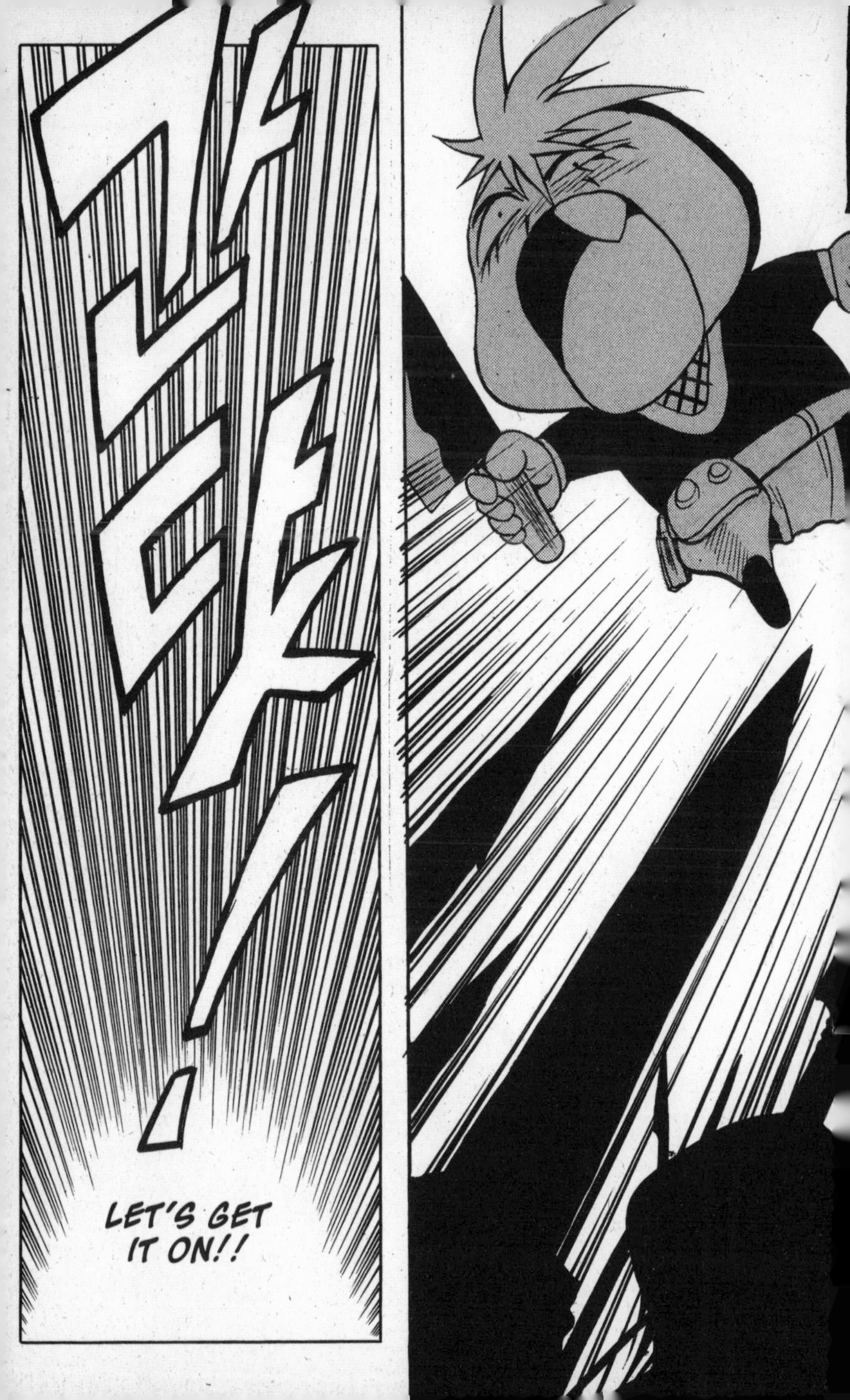
LET'S GET IT ON!!

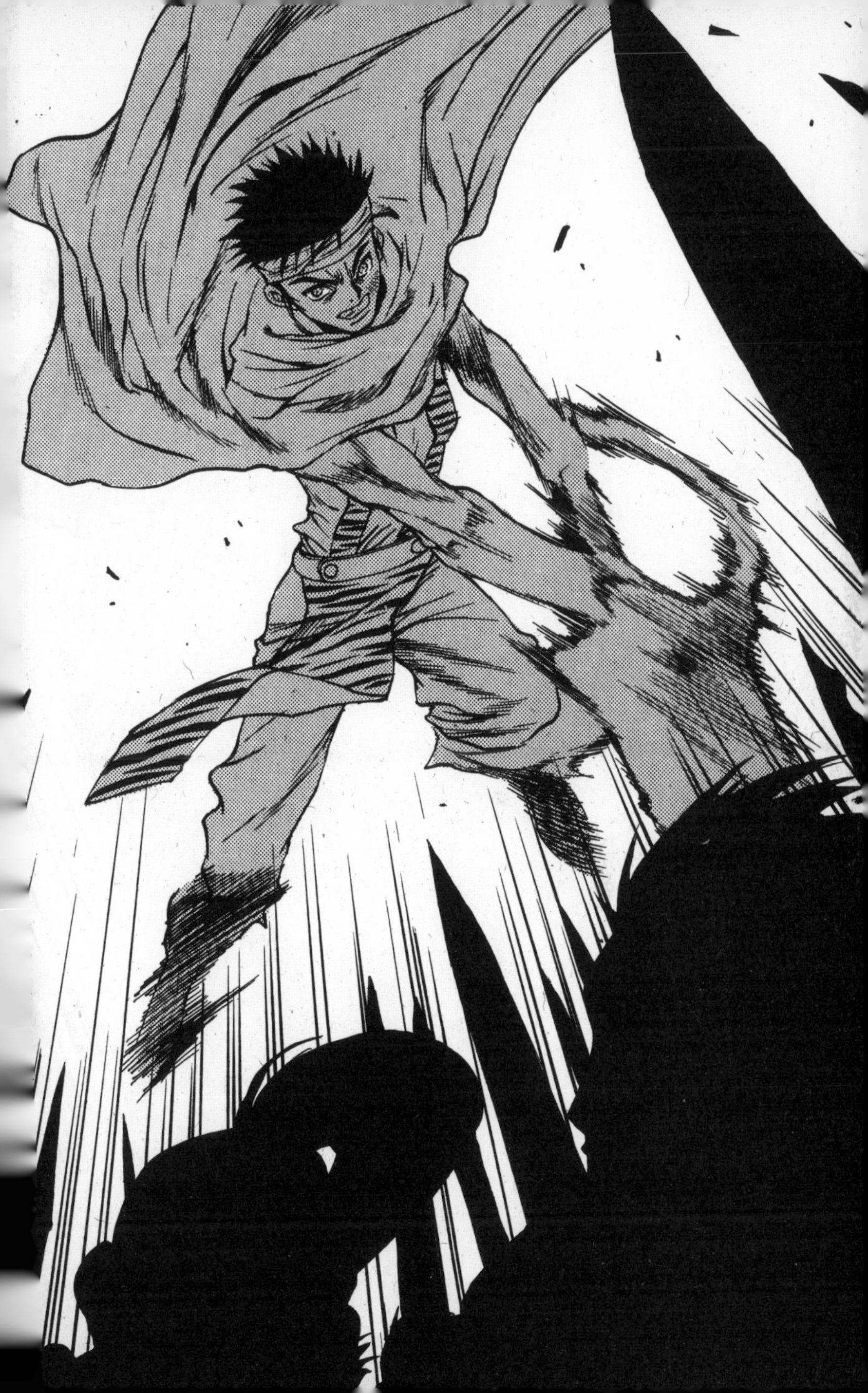

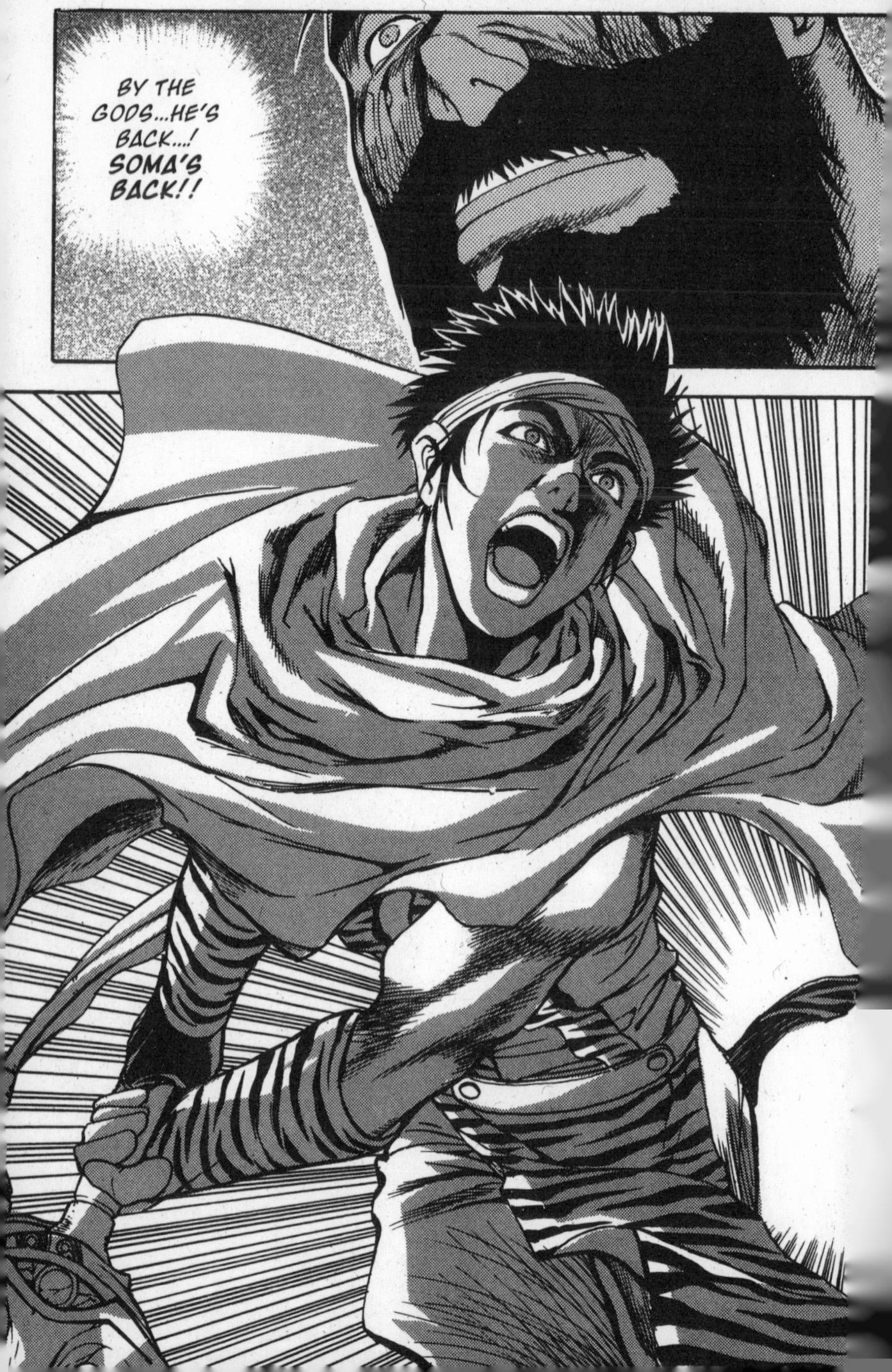
BY THE GODS...HE'S BACK...! SOMA'S BACK!!

BLADE OF HEAVEN

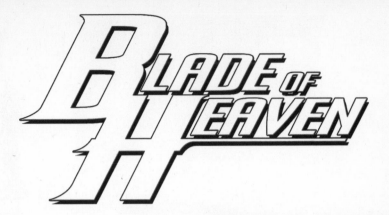

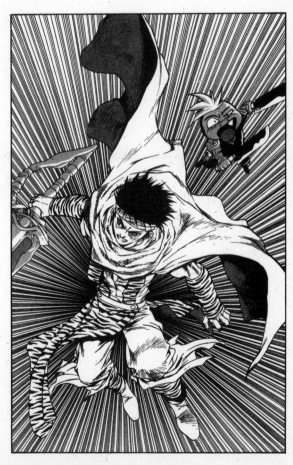

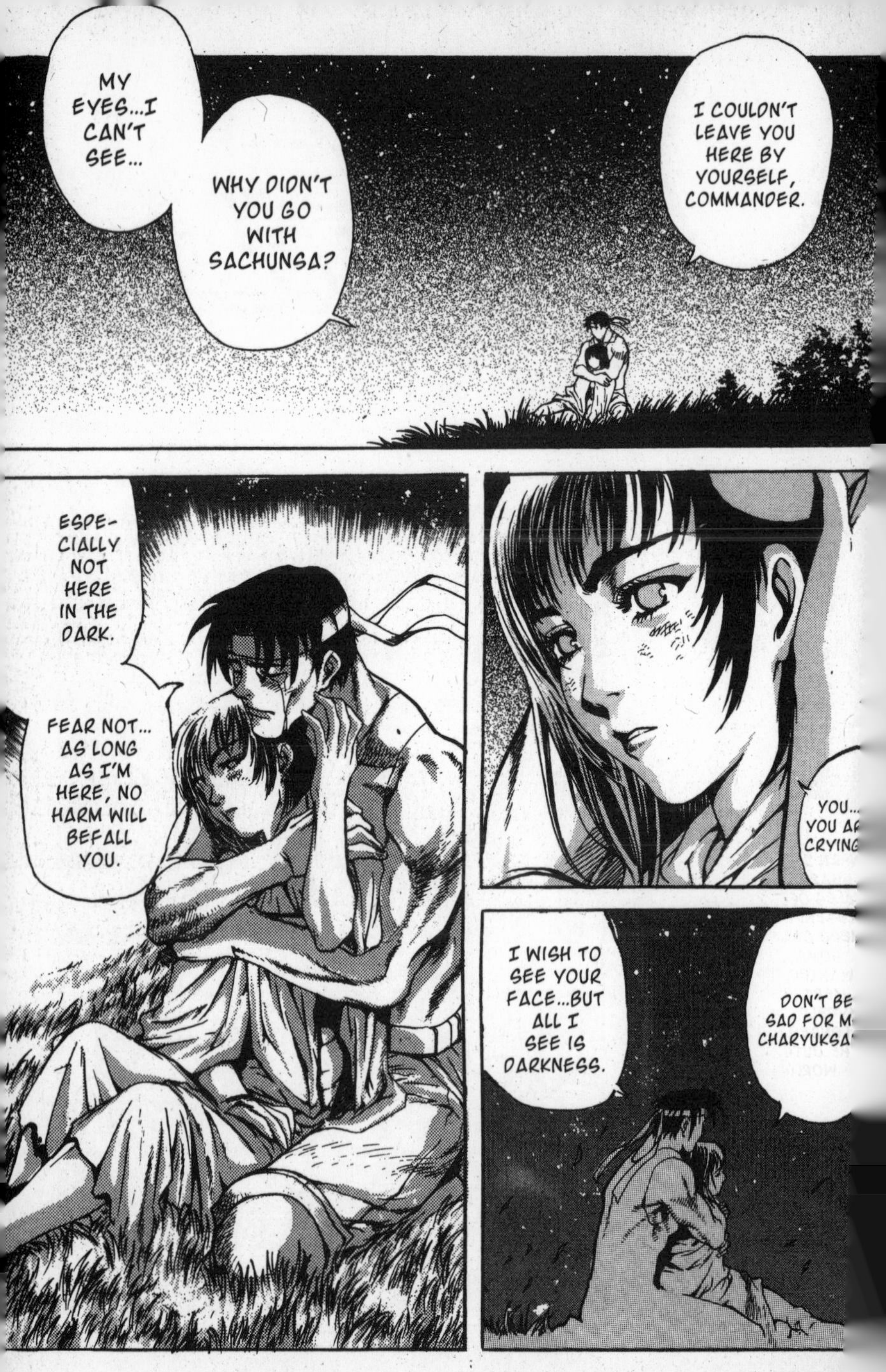
MY EYES...I CAN'T SEE...
WHY DIDN'T YOU GO WITH SACHUNSA?
I COULDN'T LEAVE YOU HERE BY YOURSELF, COMMANDER.
ESPE-CIALLY NOT HERE IN THE DARK.
FEAR NOT... AS LONG AS I'M HERE, NO HARM WILL BEFALL YOU.
YOU... YOU AR CRYING
I WISH TO SEE YOUR FACE...BUT ALL I SEE IS DARKNESS.
DON'T BE SAD FOR M CHARYUKSA

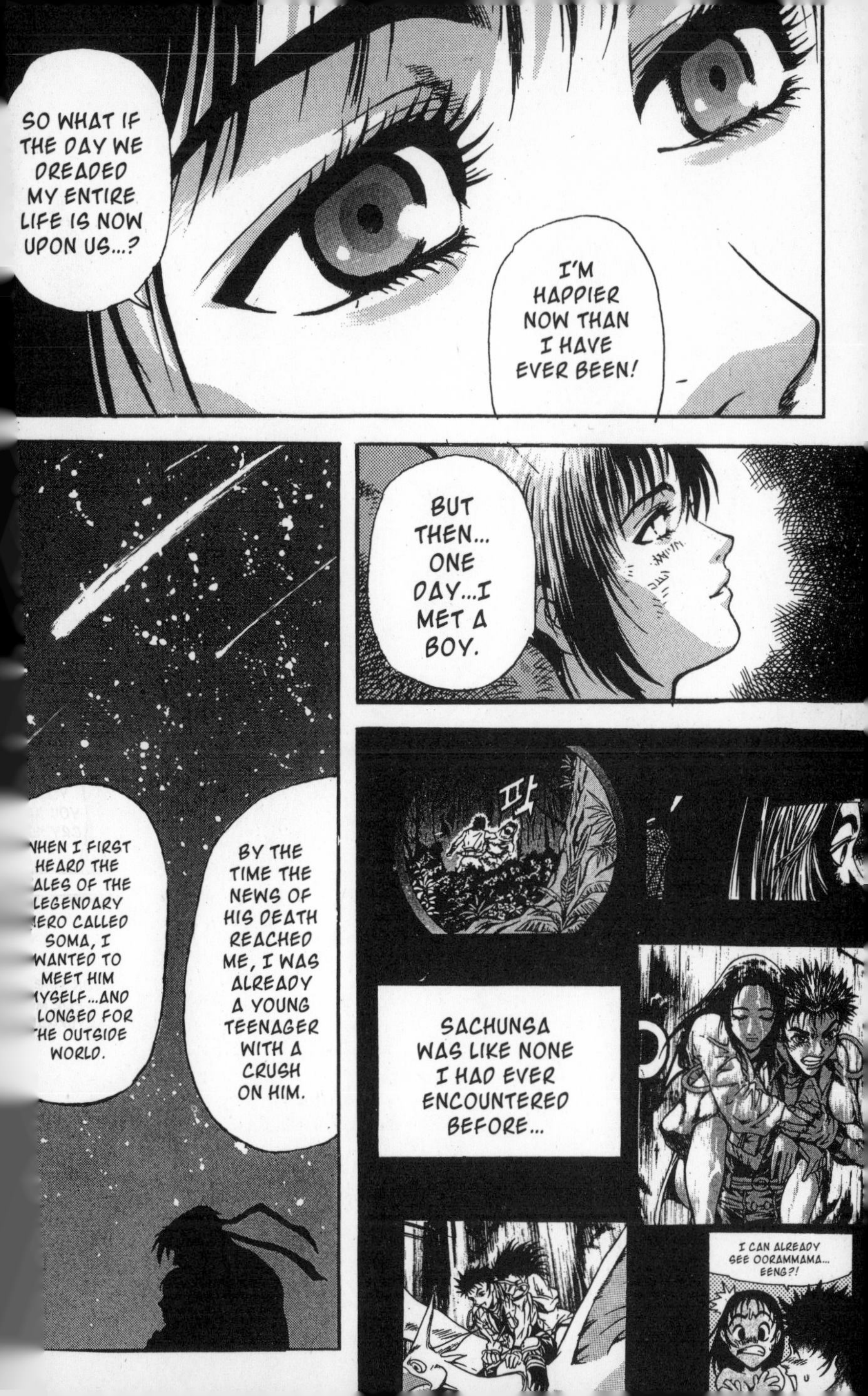
SO WHAT IF THE DAY WE DREADED MY ENTIRE LIFE IS NOW UPON US...?
I'M HAPPIER NOW THAN I HAVE EVER BEEN!
HEN I FIRST EARD THE ALES OF THE EGENDARY ERO CALLED SOMA, I WANTED TO MEET HIM YSELF...AND LONGED FOR HE OUTSIDE WORLD.
BY THE TIME THE NEWS OF HIS DEATH REACHED ME, I WAS ALREADY A YOUNG TEENAGER WITH A CRUSH ON HIM.
BUT THEN... ONE DAY...I MET A BOY.
팍
SACHUNSA WAS LIKE NONE I HAD EVER ENCOUNTERED BEFORE...
I CAN ALREADY SEE OORAMMAMA... EENG?!

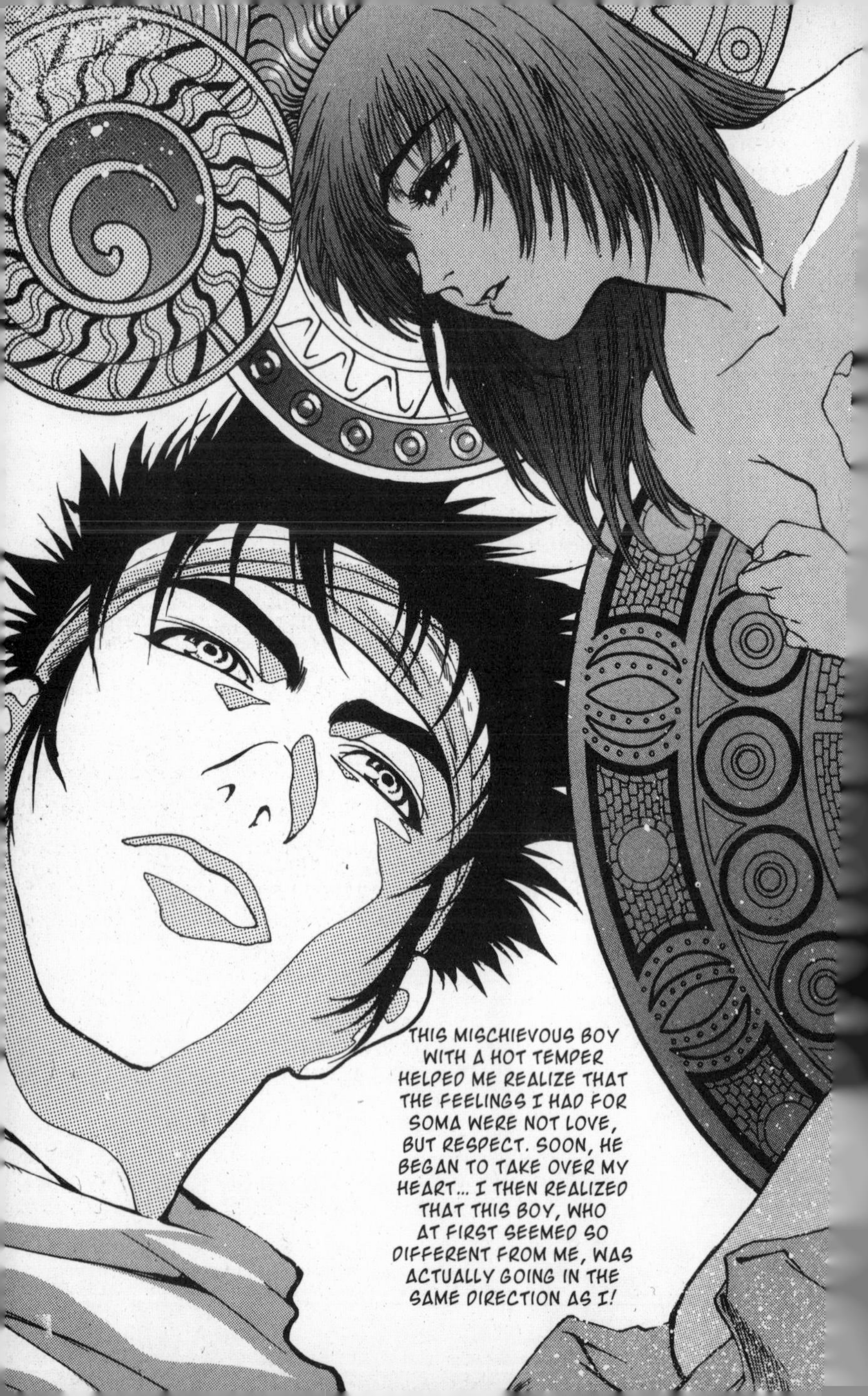
THIS MISCHIEVOUS BOY WITH A HOT TEMPER HELPED ME REALIZE THAT THE FEELINGS I HAD FOR SOMA WERE NOT LOVE, BUT RESPECT. SOON, HE BEGAN TO TAKE OVER MY HEART... I THEN REALIZED THAT THIS BOY, WHO AT FIRST SEEMED SO DIFFERENT FROM ME, WAS ACTUALLY GOING IN THE SAME DIRECTION AS I!

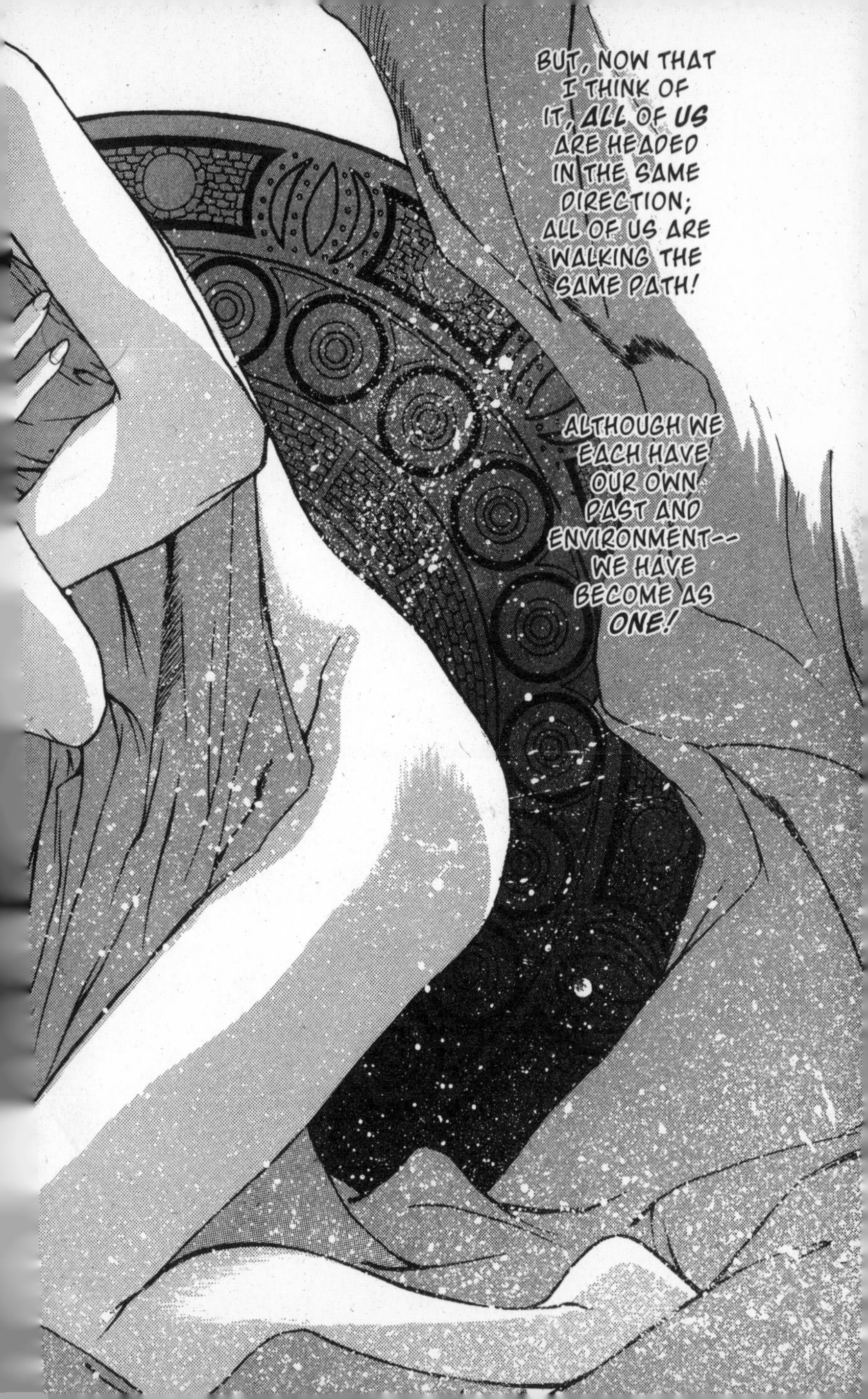
BUT, NOW THAT I THINK OF IT, ALL OF US ARE HEADED IN THE SAME DIRECTION; ALL OF US ARE WALKING THE SAME PATH!
ALTHOUGH WE EACH HAVE OUR OWN PAST AND ENVIRONMENT-- WE HAVE BECOME AS ONE!

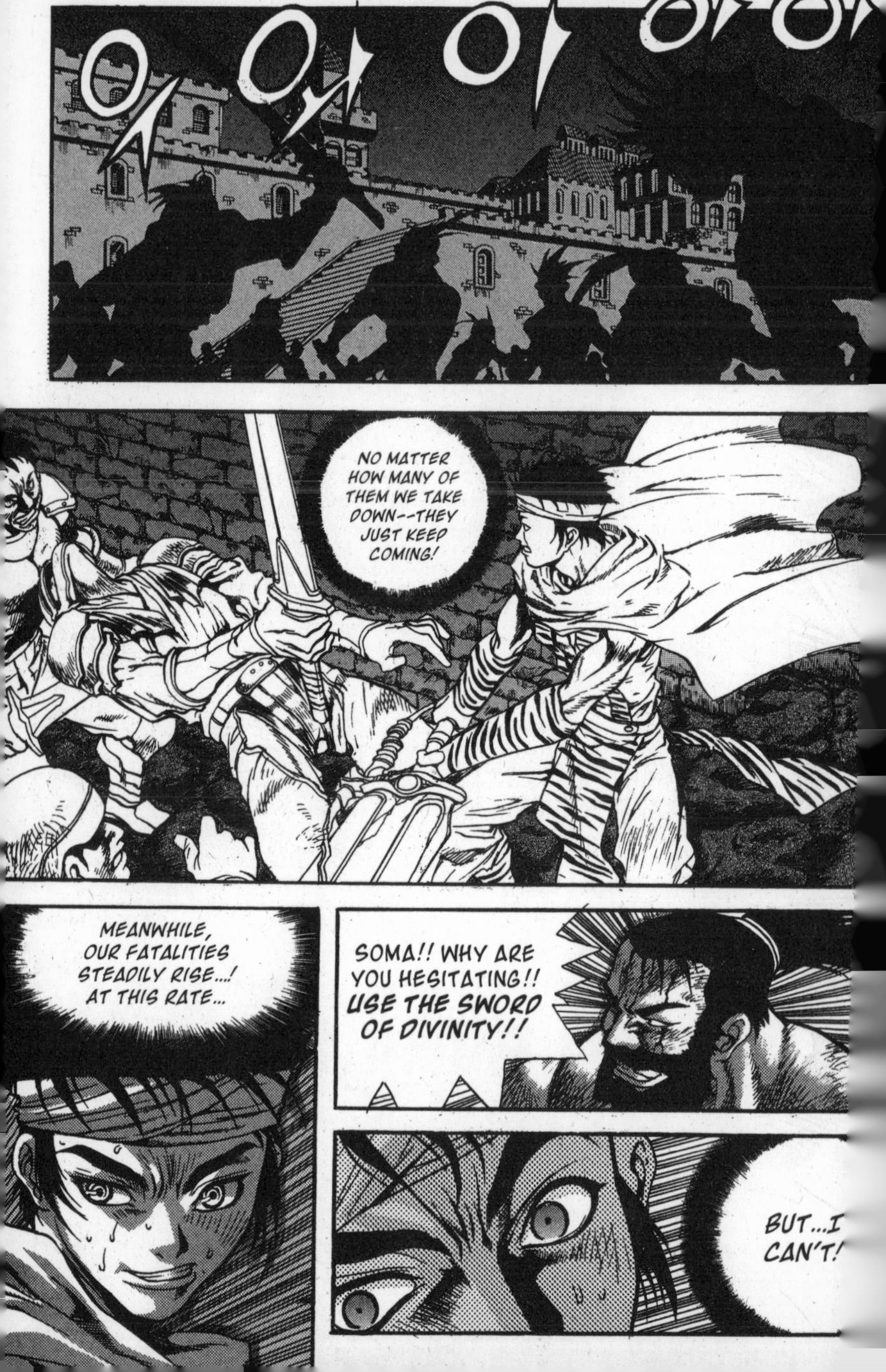
NO MATTER HOW MANY OF THEM WE TAKE DOWN--THEY JUST KEEP COMING!
MEANWHILE, OUR FATALITIES STEADILY RISE...! AT THIS RATE...
SOMA!! WHY ARE YOU HESITATING!! **USE THE SWORD OF DIVINITY!!**
BUT...I CAN'T!

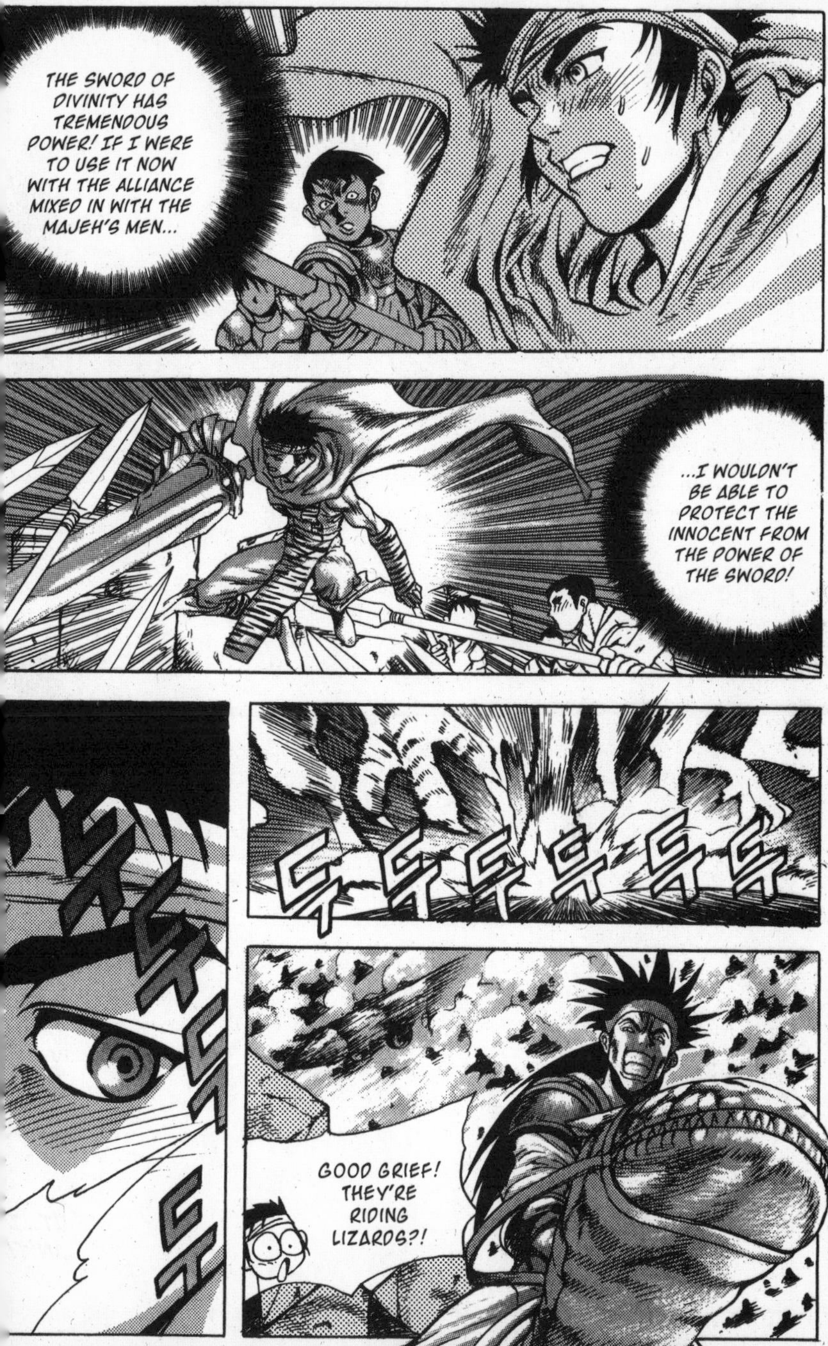
THE SWORD OF DIVINITY HAS TREMENDOUS POWER! IF I WERE TO USE IT NOW WITH THE ALLIANCE MIXED IN WITH THE MAJEH'S MEN...
...I WOULDN'T BE ABLE TO PROTECT THE INNOCENT FROM THE POWER OF THE SWORD!
GOOD GRIEF! THEY'RE RIDING LIZARDS?!

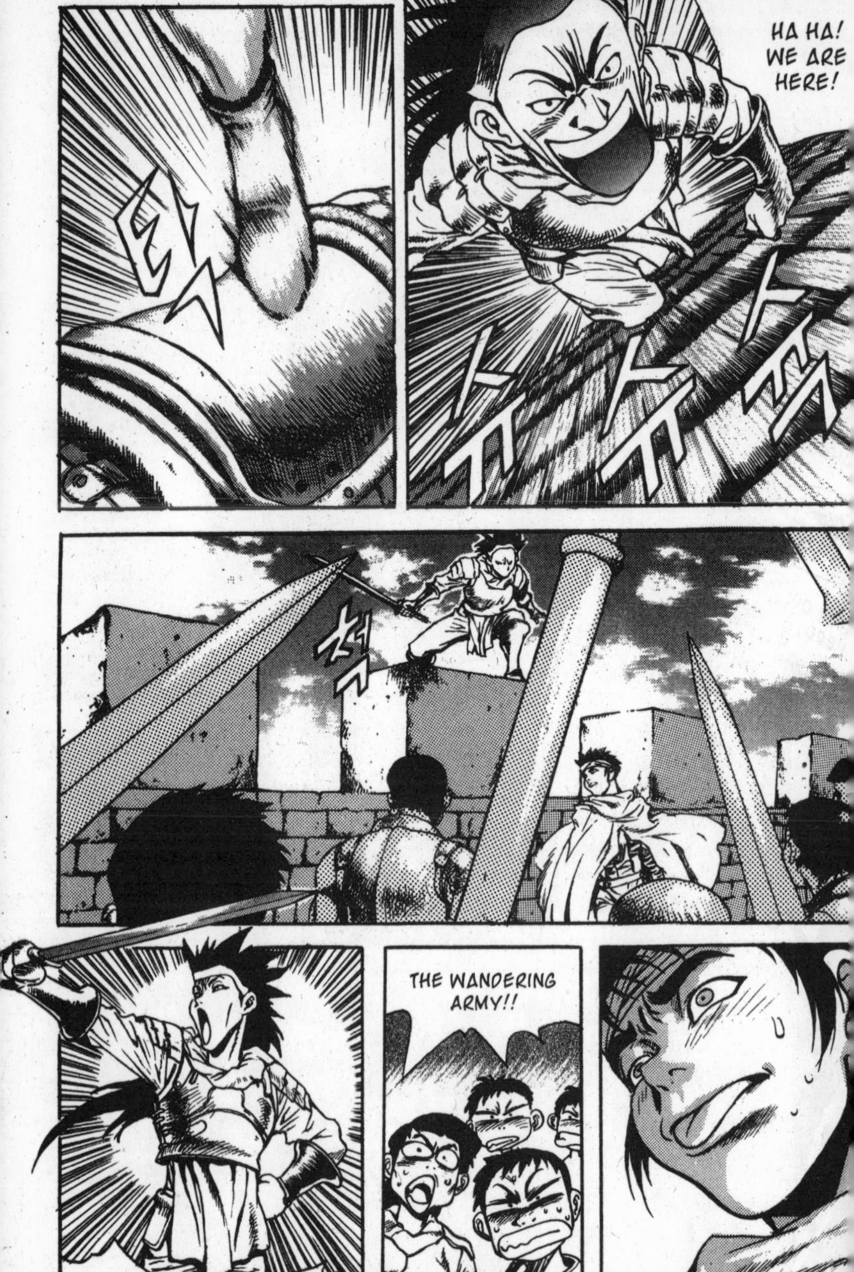
HA HA! WE ARE HERE!
FEEL THE WRATH OF THE FAKE SOMA!
THE WANDERING ARMY!!

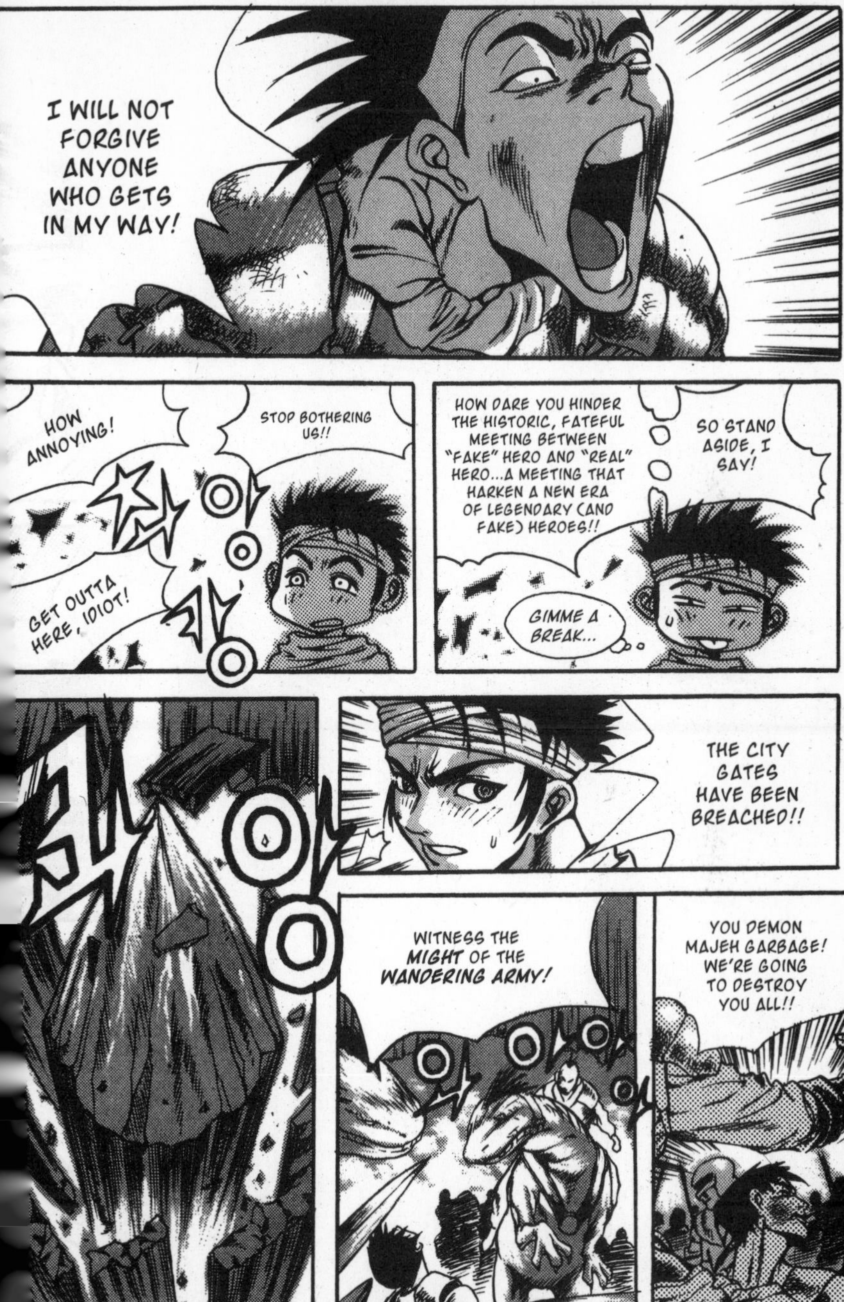
I WILL NOT FORGIVE ANYONE WHO GETS IN MY WAY!
HOW ANNOYING!
STOP BOTHERING US!!
GET OUTTA HERE, IDIOT!
HOW DARE YOU HINDER THE HISTORIC, FATEFUL MEETING BETWEEN "FAKE" HERO AND "REAL" HERO...A MEETING THAT HARKEN A NEW ERA OF LEGENDARY (AND FAKE) HEROES!!
SO STAND ASIDE, I SAY!
GIMME A BREAK...
THE CITY GATES HAVE BEEN BREACHED!!
WITNESS THE MIGHT OF THE WANDERING ARMY!
YOU DEMON MAJEH GARBAGE! WE'RE GOING TO DESTROY YOU ALL!!

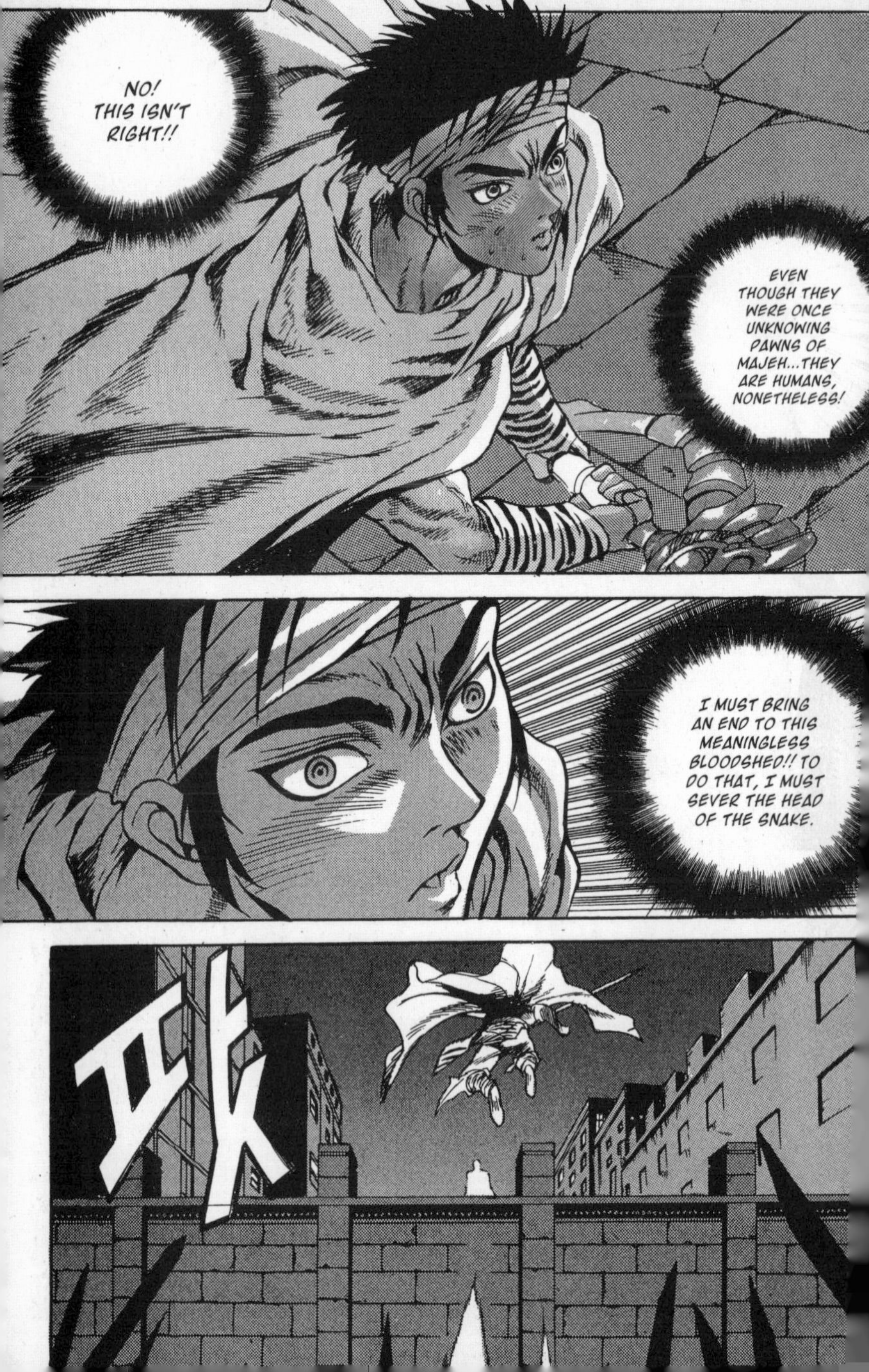
NO! THIS ISN'T RIGHT!!
EVEN THOUGH THEY WERE ONCE UNKNOWING PAWNS OF MAJEH...THEY ARE HUMANS, NONETHELESS!
I MUST BRING AN END TO THIS MEANINGLESS BLOODSHED!! TO DO THAT, I MUST SEVER THE HEAD OF THE SNAKE.

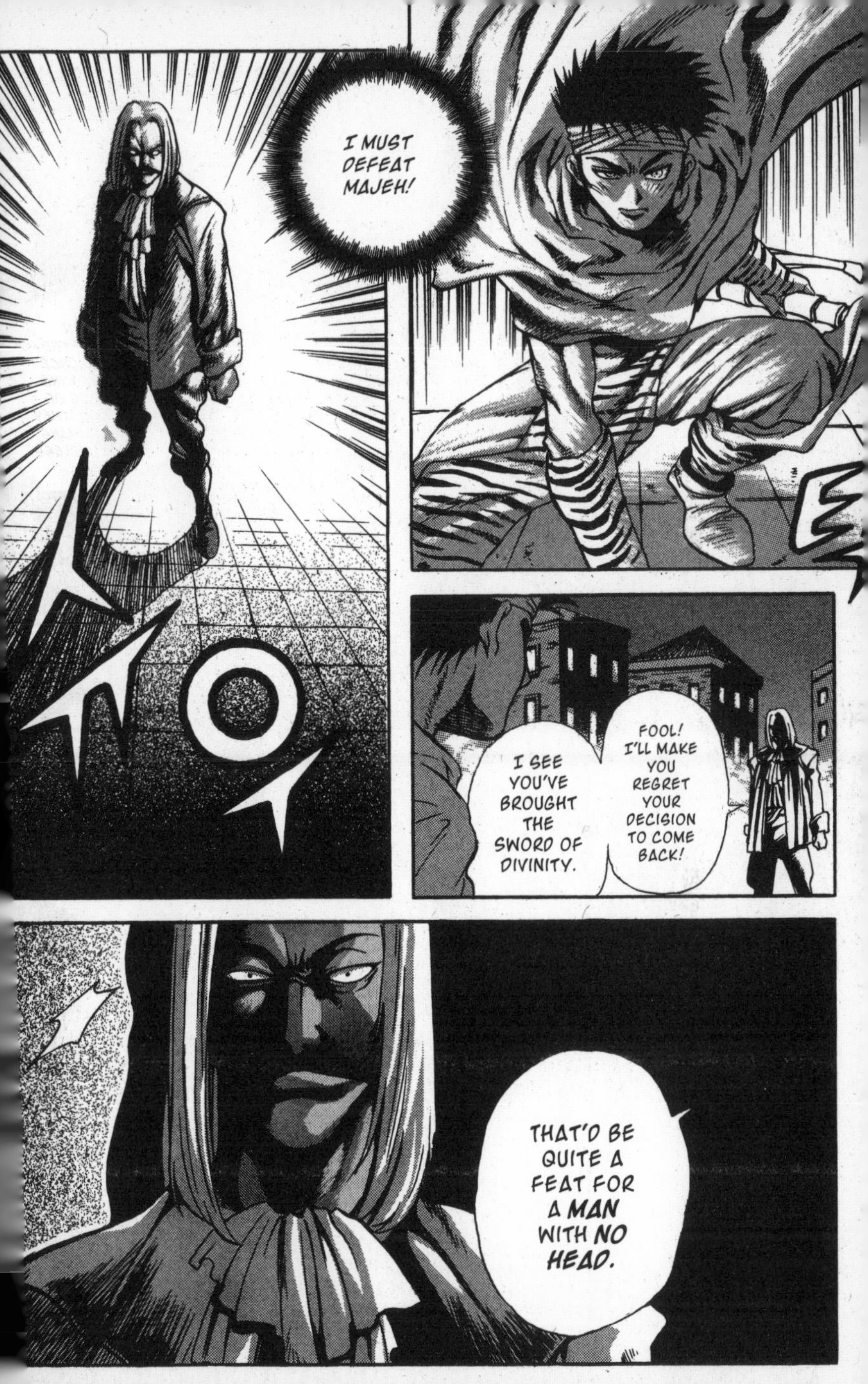
I MUST DEFEAT MAJEH!
I SEE YOU'VE BROUGHT THE SWORD OF DIVINITY.
FOOL! I'LL MAKE YOU REGRET YOUR DECISION TO COME BACK!
THAT'D BE QUITE A FEAT FOR A MAN WITH NO HEAD.

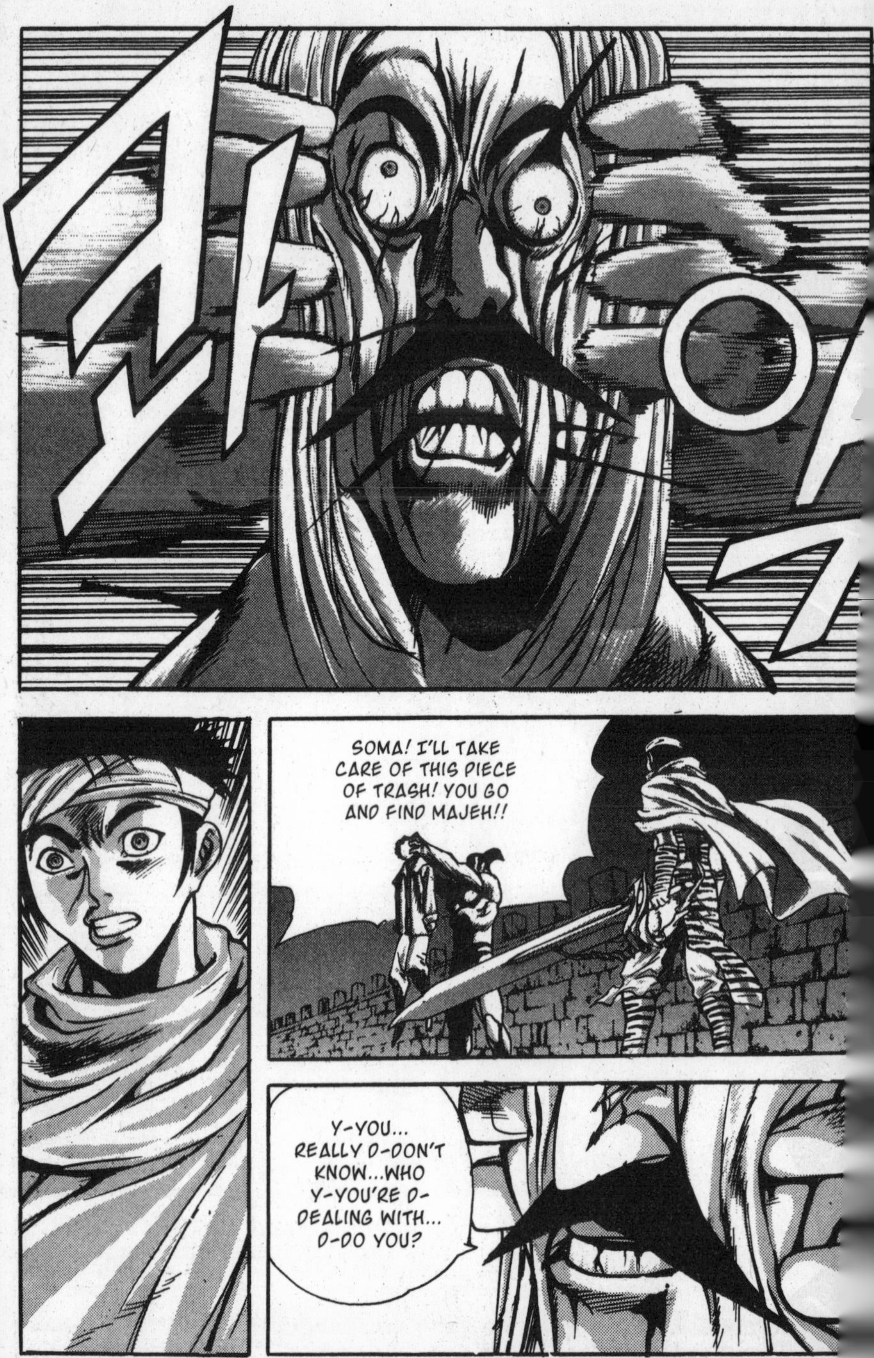
SOMA! I'LL TAKE CARE OF THIS PIECE OF TRASH! YOU GO AND FIND MAJEH!!
Y-YOU... REALLY D-DON'T KNOW...WHO Y-YOU'RE D-DEALING WITH... D-DO YOU?

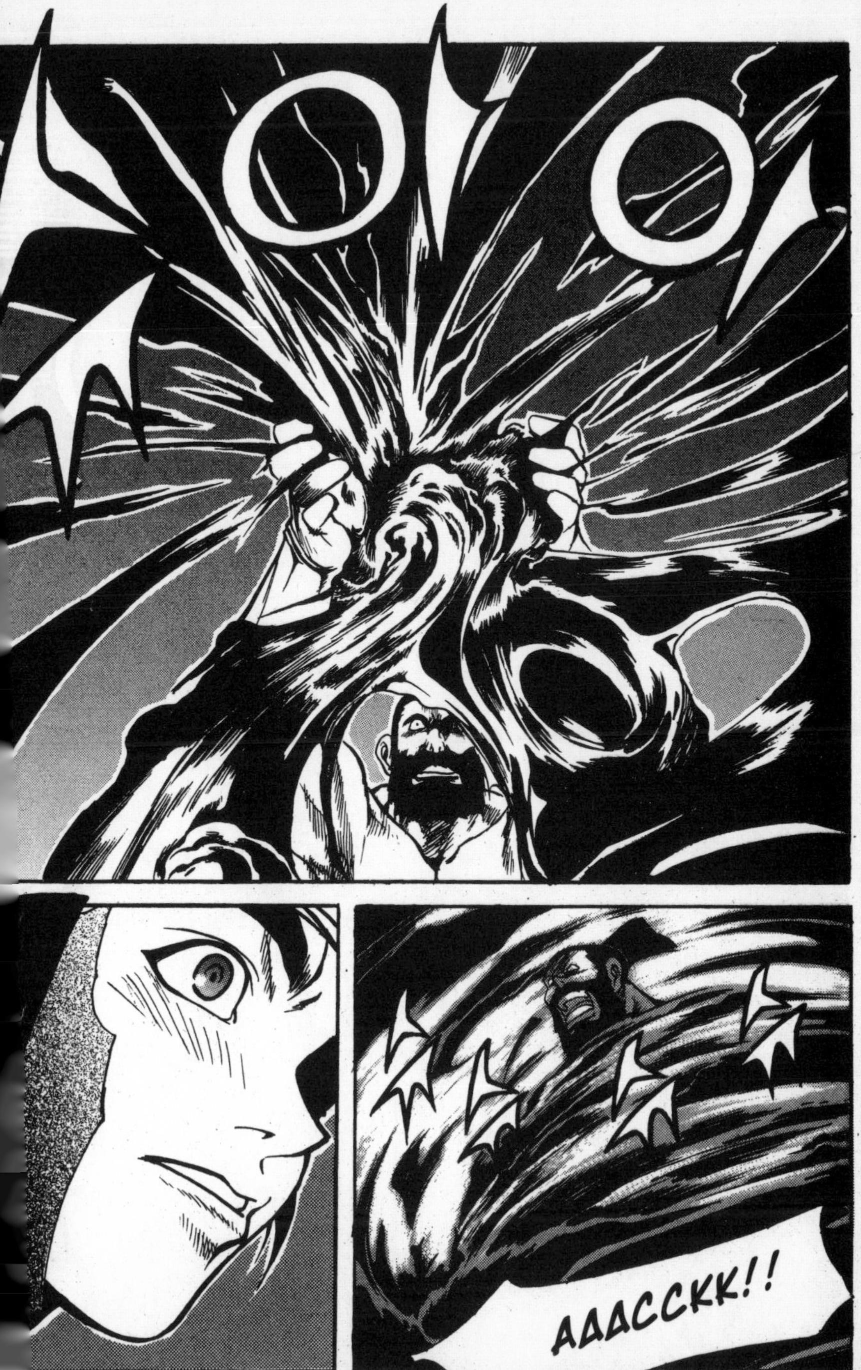
AAACCKK!!

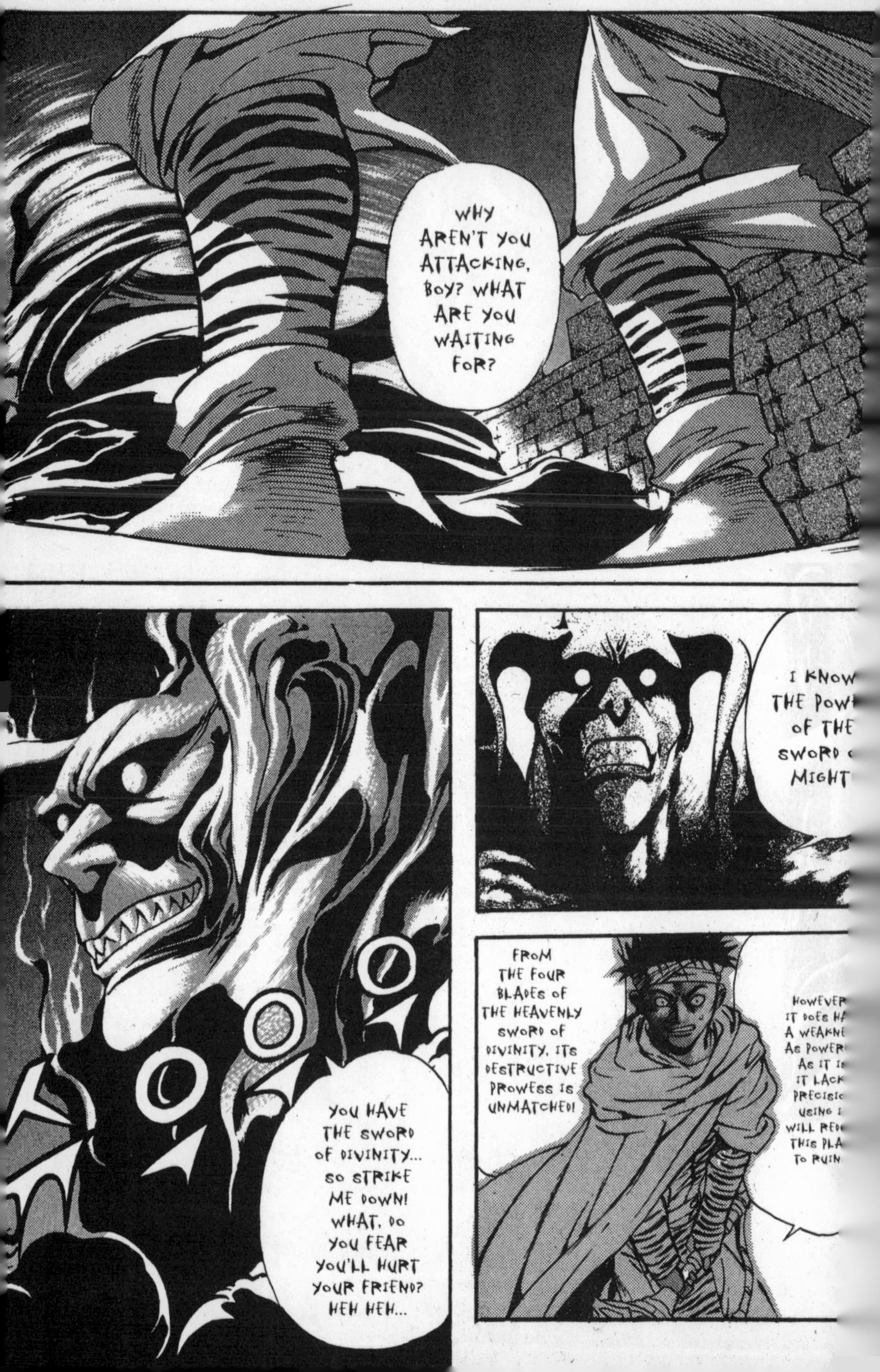

WHY AREN'T YOU ATTACKING, BOY? WHAT ARE YOU WAITING FOR?
YOU HAVE THE SWORD OF DIVINITY... SO STRIKE ME DOWN! WHAT, DO YOU FEAR YOU'LL HURT YOUR FRIEND? HEH HEH...
I KNOW THE POW OF THE SWORD MIGHT
FROM THE FOUR BLADES OF THE HEAVENLY SWORD OF DIVINITY, ITS DESTRUCTIVE PROWESS IS UNMATCHED!
HOWEVER IT DOES HA A WEAKNE AS POWER AS IT IS IT LACK PRECISIO USING I WILL RED THIS PLA TO RUIN

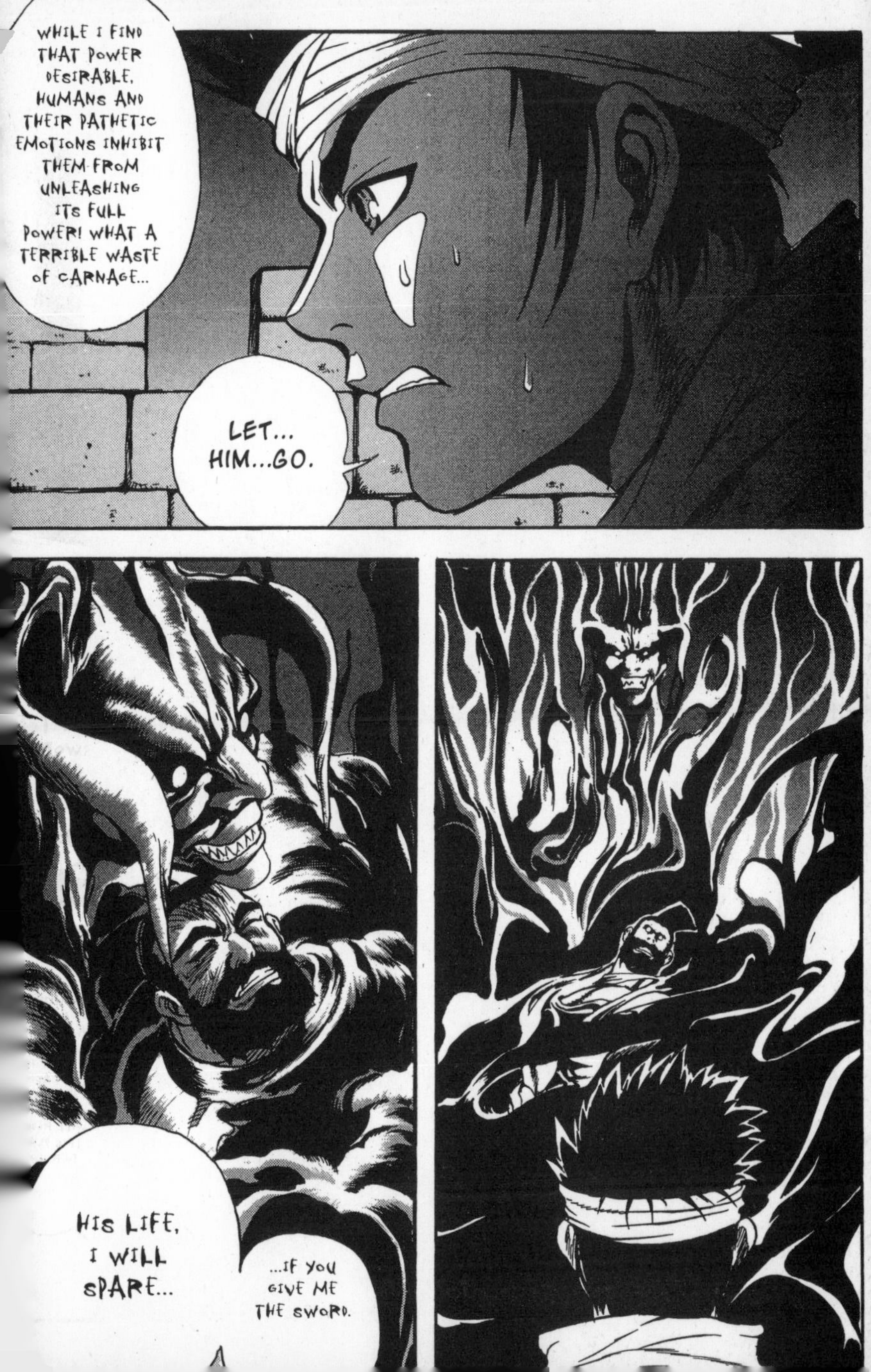
WHILE I FIND THAT POWER DESIRABLE, HUMANS AND THEIR PATHETIC EMOTIONS INHIBIT THEM FROM UNLEASHING ITS FULL POWER! WHAT A TERRIBLE WASTE OF CARNAGE...
LET... HIM...GO.
HIS LIFE, I WILL SPARE...
...IF YOU GIVE ME THE SWORD.

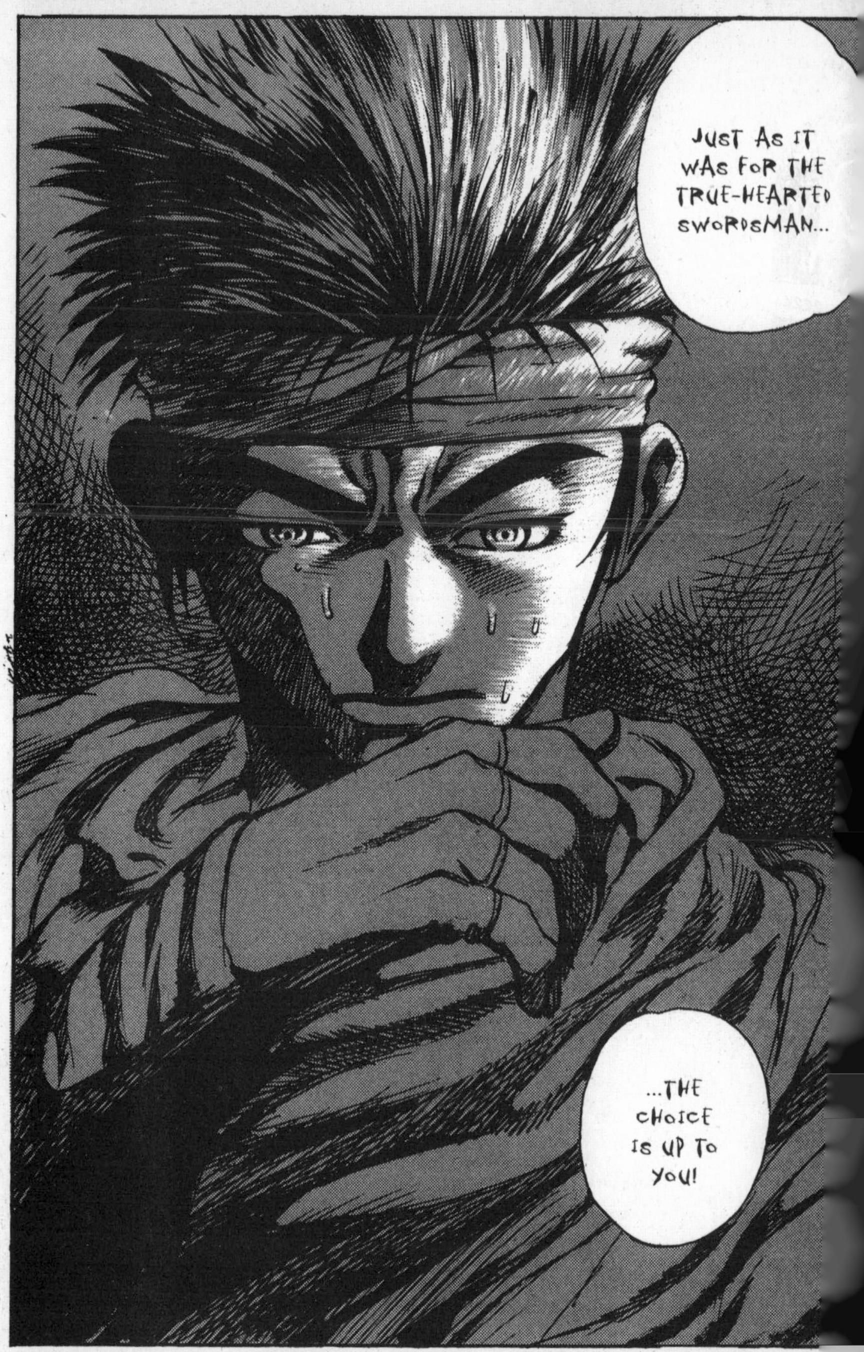
JUST AS IT WAS FOR THE TRUE-HEARTED SWORDSMAN...
...THE CHOICE IS UP TO YOU!

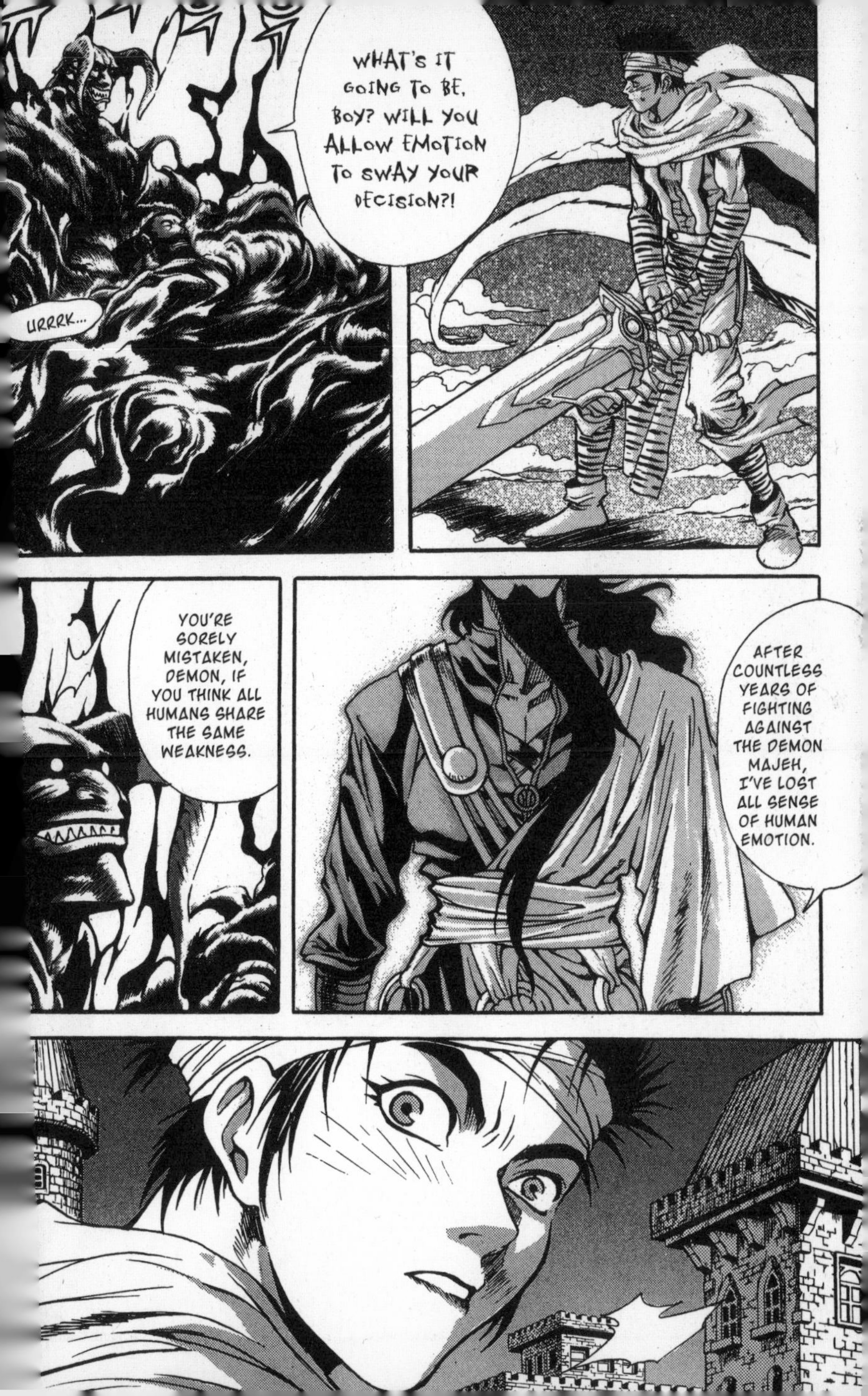
URRRK...
WHAT'S IT GOING TO BE, BOY? WILL YOU ALLOW EMOTION TO SWAY YOUR DECISION?!
AFTER COUNTLESS YEARS OF FIGHTING AGAINST THE DEMON MAJEH, I'VE LOST ALL SENSE OF HUMAN EMOTION.
YOU'RE SORELY MISTAKEN, DEMON, IF YOU THINK ALL HUMANS SHARE THE SAME WEAKNESS.

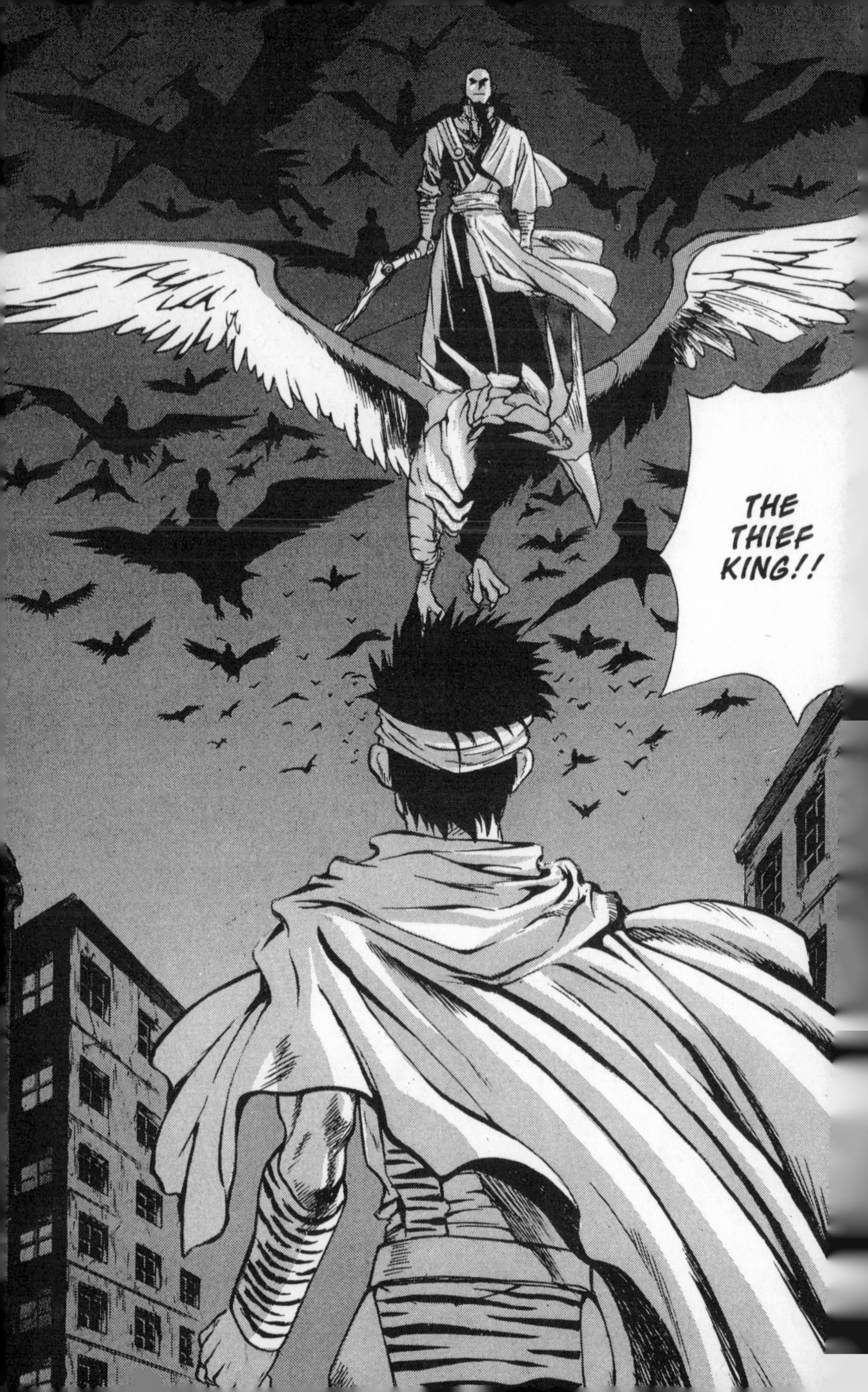
THE THIEF KING!!

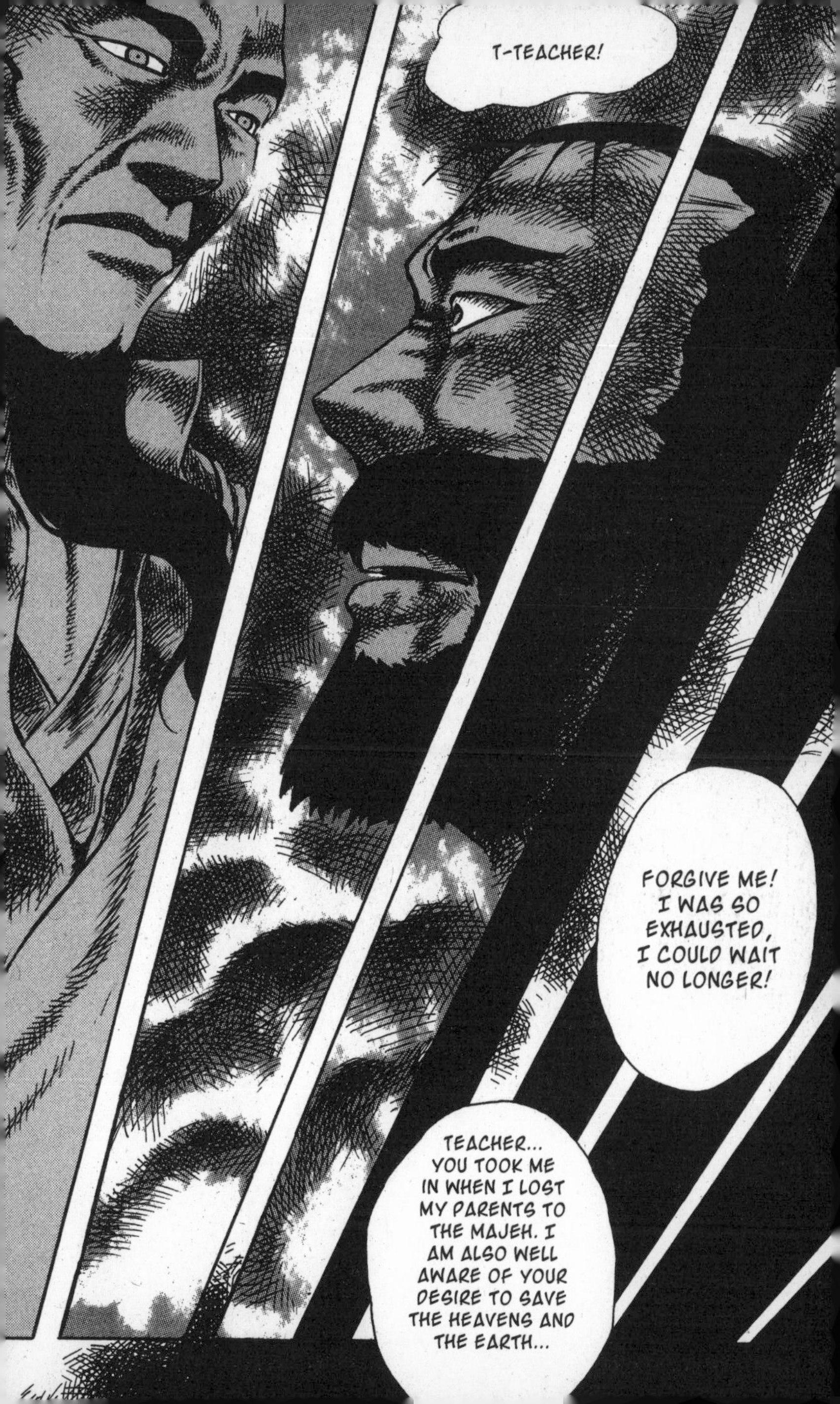
T-TEACHER!
FORGIVE ME! I WAS SO EXHAUSTED, I COULD WAIT NO LONGER!
TEACHER... YOU TOOK ME IN WHEN I LOST MY PARENTS TO THE MAJEH. I AM ALSO WELL AWARE OF YOUR DESIRE TO SAVE THE HEAVENS AND THE EARTH...

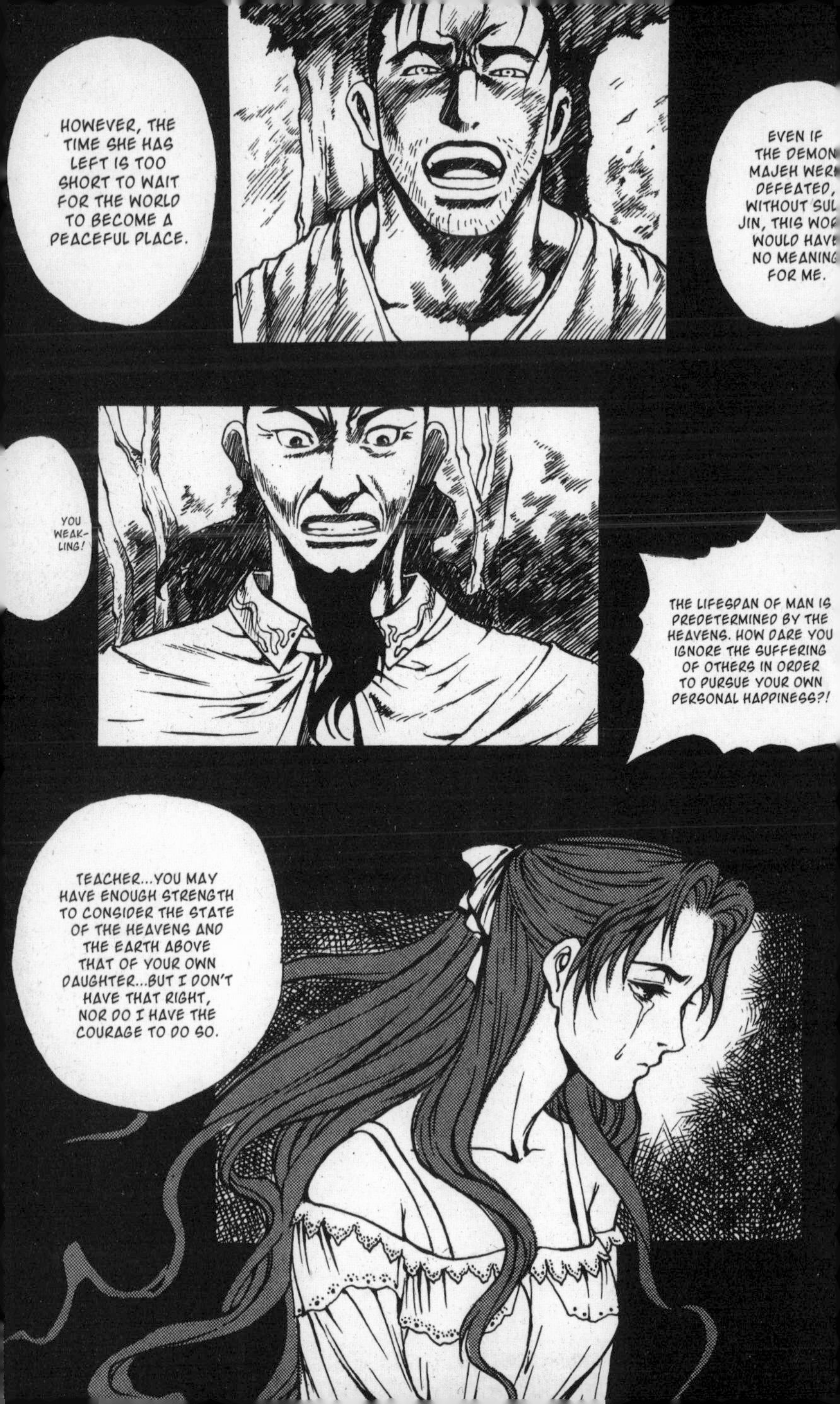
EVEN IF THE DEMON MAJEH WER DEFEATED, WITHOUT SUL JIN, THIS WOR WOULD HAVE NO MEANING FOR ME.
HOWEVER, THE TIME SHE HAS LEFT IS TOO SHORT TO WAIT FOR THE WORLD TO BECOME A PEACEFUL PLACE.
YOU WEAK-LING!
THE LIFESPAN OF MAN IS PREDETERMINED BY THE HEAVENS. HOW DARE YOU IGNORE THE SUFFERING OF OTHERS IN ORDER TO PURSUE YOUR OWN PERSONAL HAPPINESS?!
TEACHER...YOU MAY HAVE ENOUGH STRENGTH TO CONSIDER THE STATE OF THE HEAVENS AND THE EARTH ABOVE THAT OF YOUR OWN DAUGHTER...BUT I DON'T HAVE THAT RIGHT, NOR DO I HAVE THE COURAGE TO DO SO.

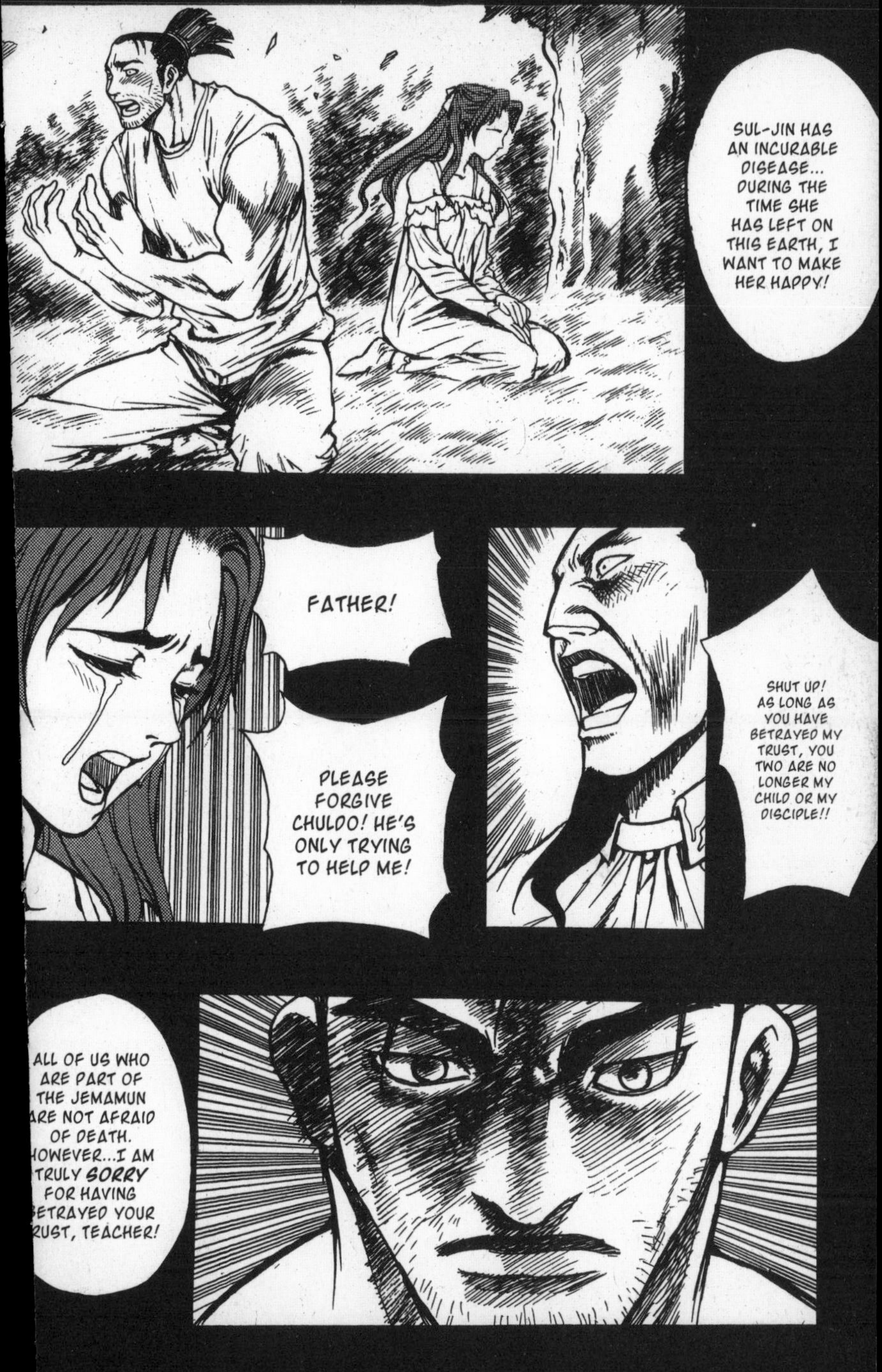
SUL-JIN HAS AN INCURABLE DISEASE... DURING THE TIME SHE HAS LEFT ON THIS EARTH, I WANT TO MAKE HER HAPPY!
FATHER!
PLEASE FORGIVE CHULDO! HE'S ONLY TRYING TO HELP ME!
SHUT UP! AS LONG AS YOU HAVE BETRAYED MY TRUST, YOU TWO ARE NO LONGER MY CHILD OR MY DISCIPLE!!
ALL OF US WHO ARE PART OF THE JEMAMUN ARE NOT AFRAID OF DEATH. HOWEVER...I AM TRULY SORRY FOR HAVING BETRAYED YOUR TRUST, TEACHER!

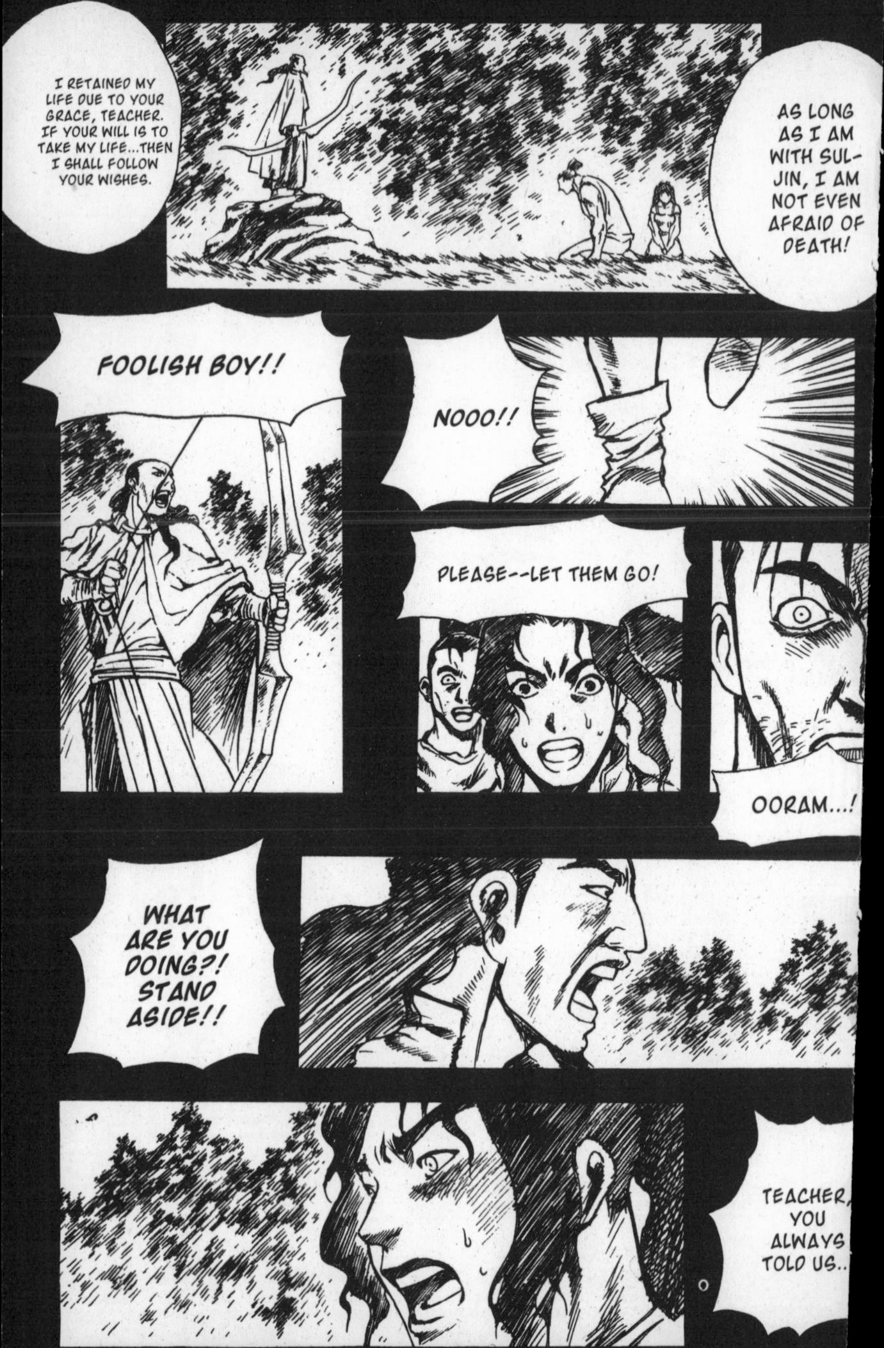
I RETAINED MY LIFE DUE TO YOUR GRACE, TEACHER. IF YOUR WILL IS TO TAKE MY LIFE...THEN I SHALL FOLLOW YOUR WISHES.
AS LONG AS I AM WITH SUL-JIN, I AM NOT EVEN AFRAID OF DEATH!
FOOLISH BOY!!
NOOO!!
PLEASE--LET THEM GO!
OORAM...!
WHAT ARE YOU DOING?! STAND ASIDE!!
TEACHER, YOU ALWAYS TOLD US..

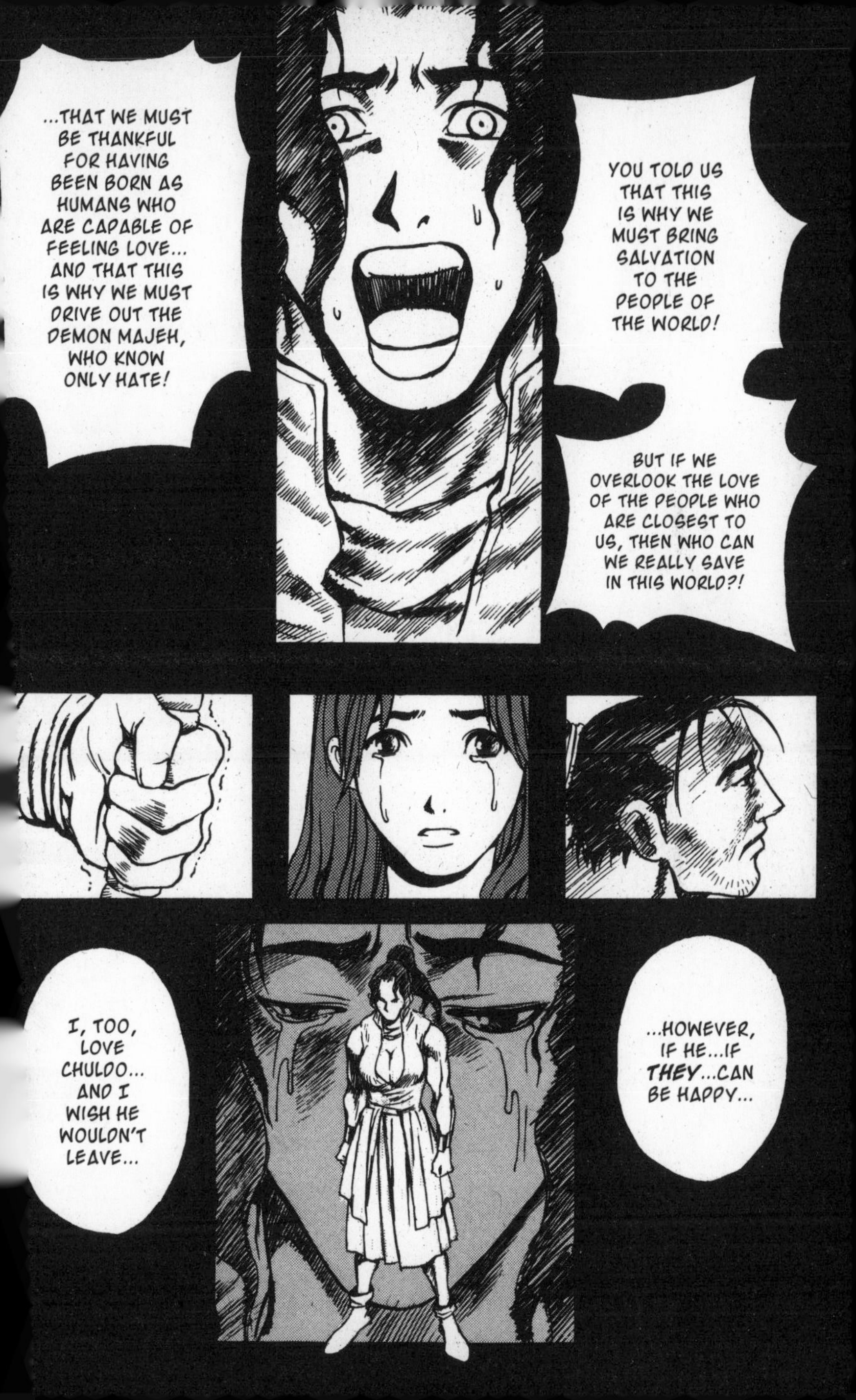
...THAT WE MUST BE THANKFUL FOR HAVING BEEN BORN AS HUMANS WHO ARE CAPABLE OF FEELING LOVE... AND THAT THIS IS WHY WE MUST DRIVE OUT THE DEMON MAJEH, WHO KNOW ONLY HATE!
YOU TOLD US THAT THIS IS WHY WE MUST BRING SALVATION TO THE PEOPLE OF THE WORLD!
BUT IF WE OVERLOOK THE LOVE OF THE PEOPLE WHO ARE CLOSEST TO US, THEN WHO CAN WE REALLY SAVE IN THIS WORLD?!
I, TOO, LOVE CHULDO... AND I WISH HE WOULDN'T LEAVE...
...HOWEVER, IF HE...IF THEY...CAN BE HAPPY...

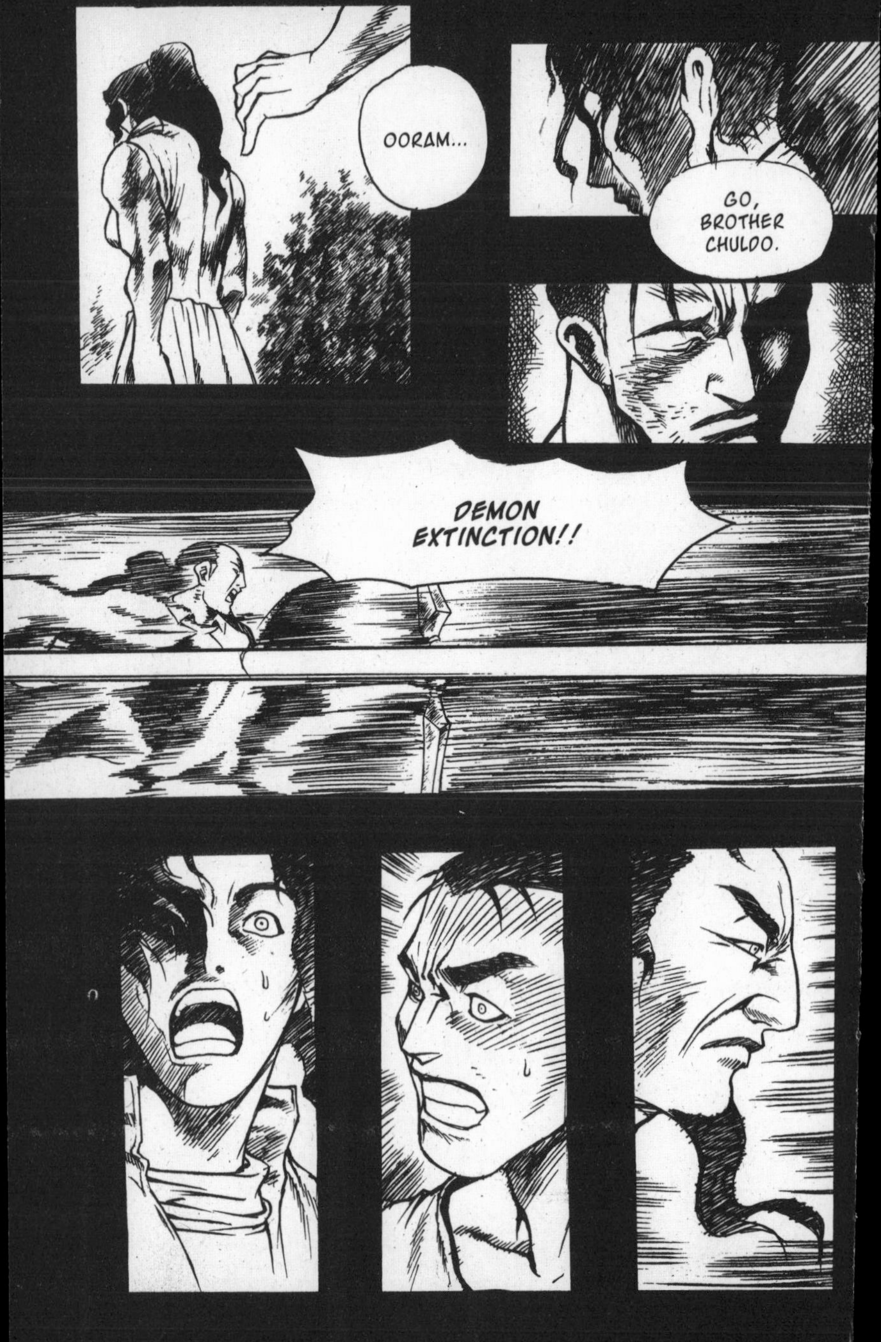
OORAM...
GO, BROTHER CHULDO.
DEMON EXTINCTION!!

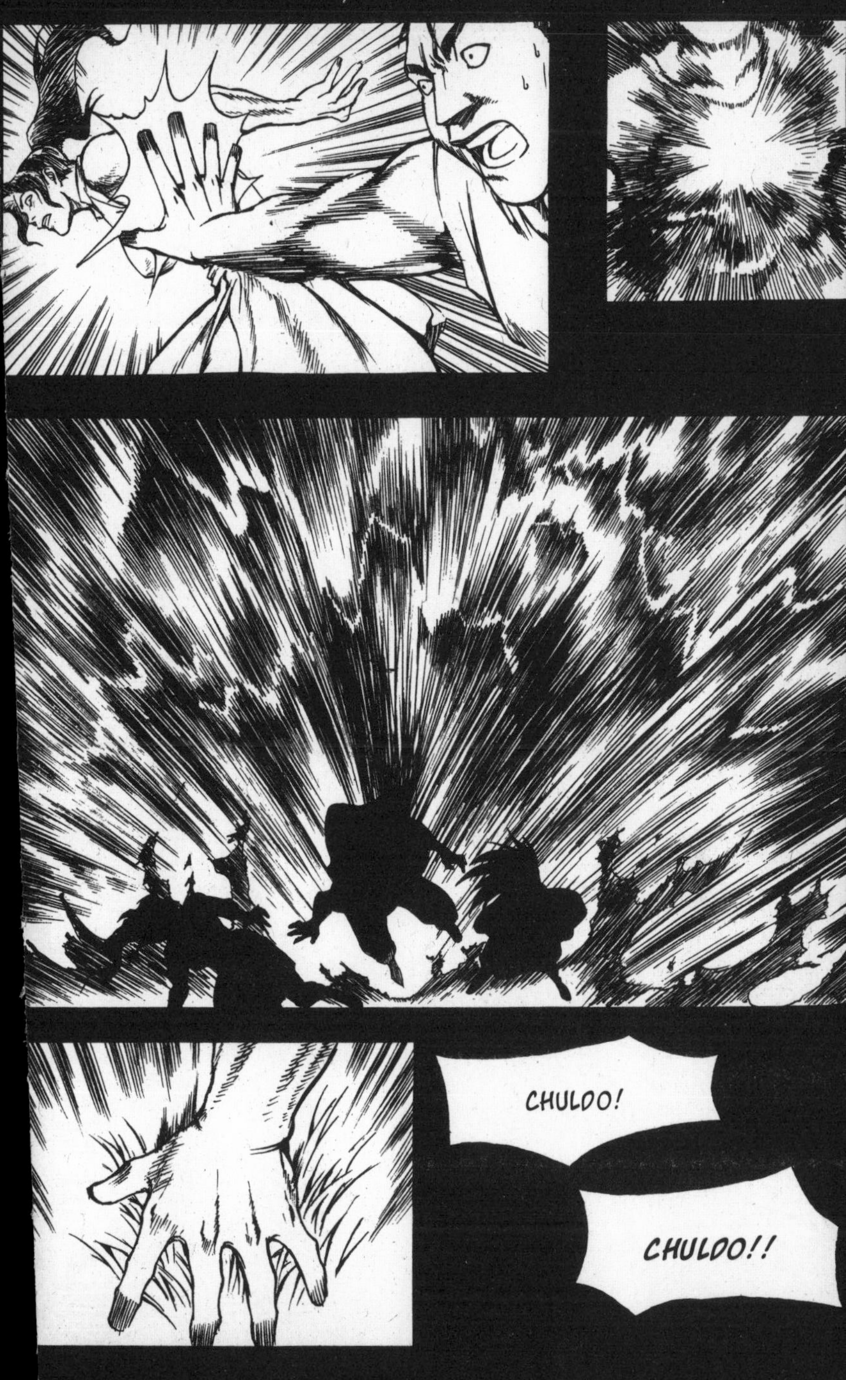
CHULDO!
CHULDO!!

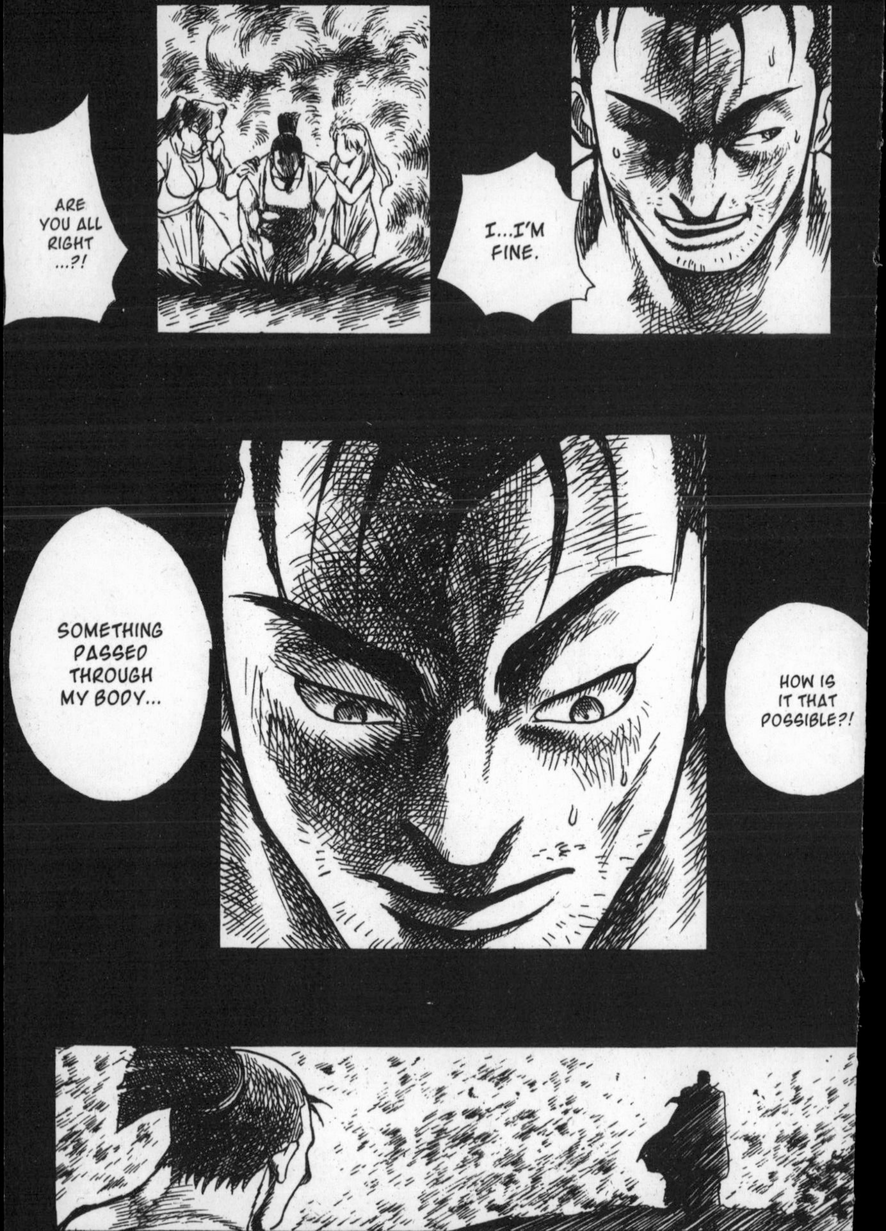
ARE YOU ALL RIGHT ...?!
I...I'M FINE.
SOMETHING PASSED THROUGH MY BODY...
HOW IS IT THAT POSSIBLE?!

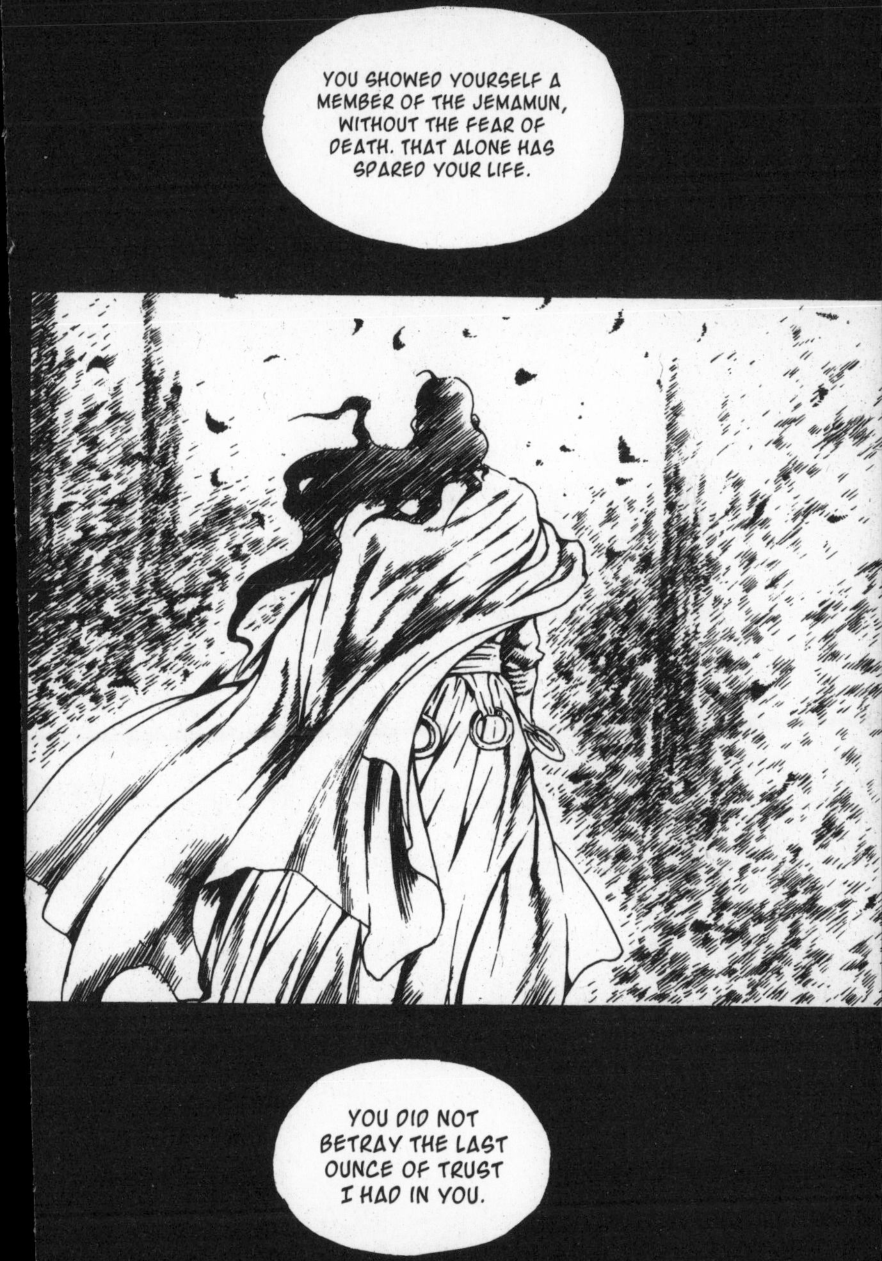
YOU SHOWED YOURSELF A MEMBER OF THE JEMAMUN, WITHOUT THE FEAR OF DEATH. THAT ALONE HAS SPARED YOUR LIFE.
YOU DID NOT BETRAY THE LAST OUNCE OF TRUST I HAD IN YOU.

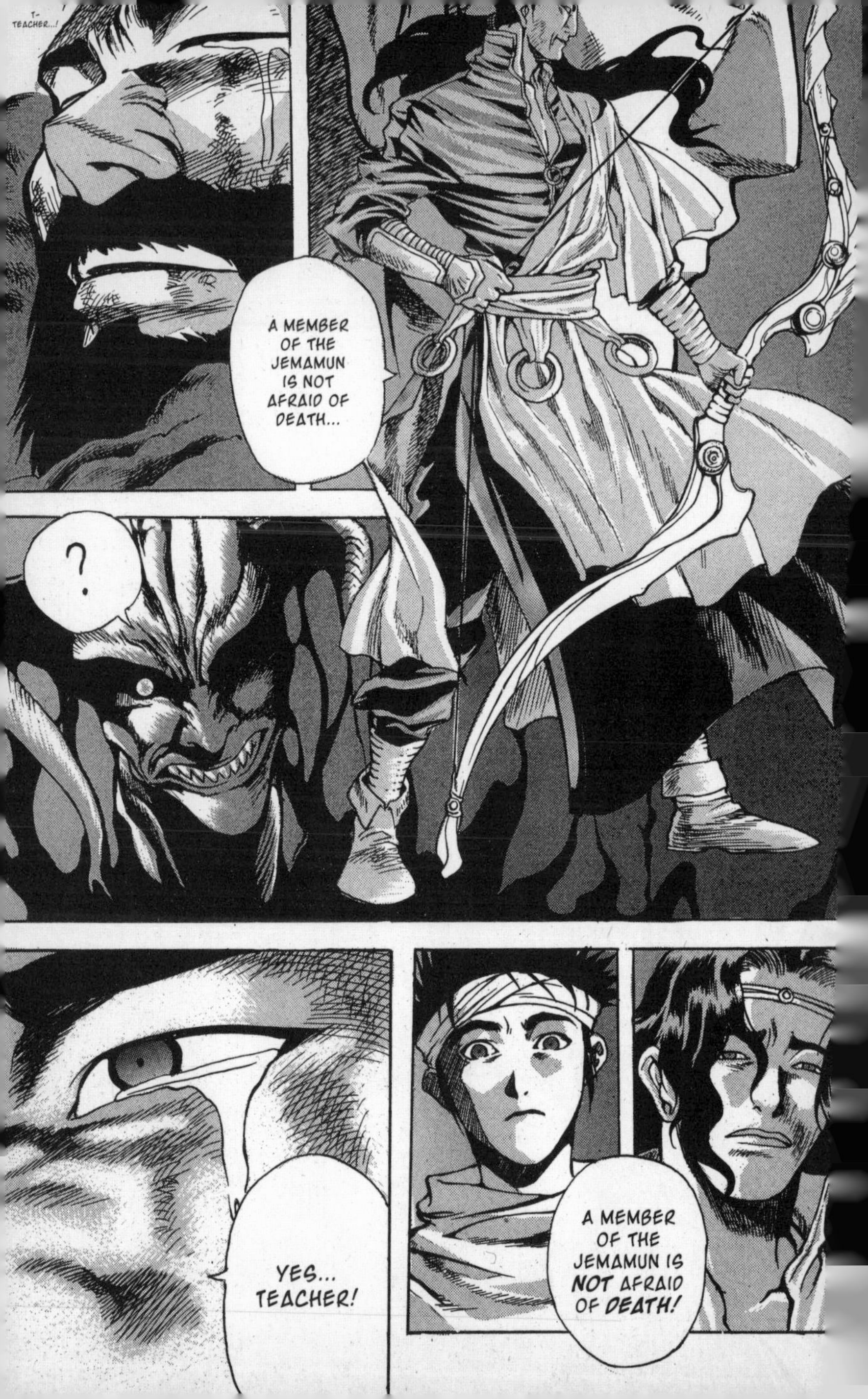
T-TEACHER...!
A MEMBER OF THE JEMAMUN IS NOT AFRAID OF DEATH...
?
YES... TEACHER!
A MEMBER OF THE JEMAMUN IS NOT AFRAID OF DEATH!

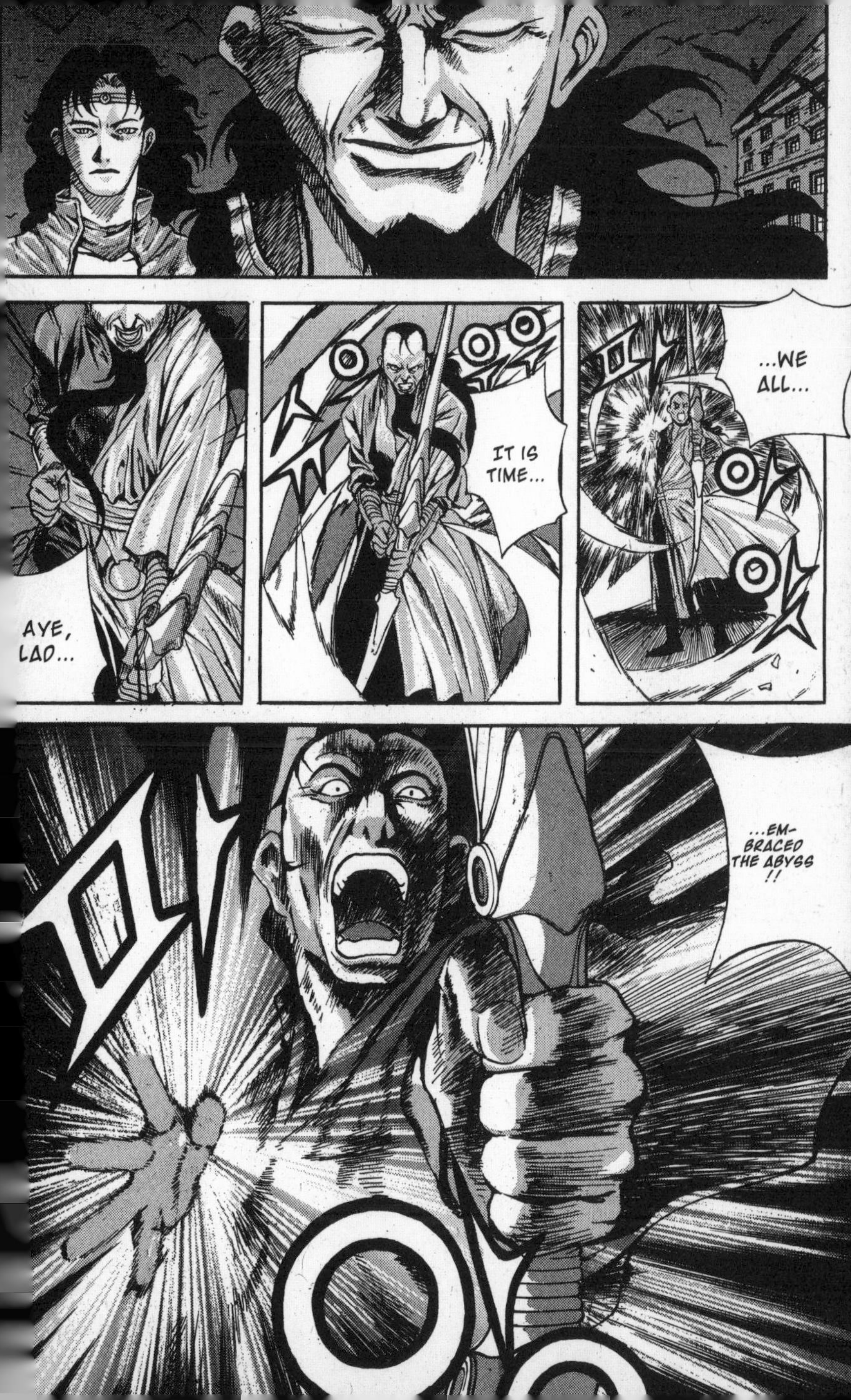
AYE, LAD...
IT IS TIME...
...WE ALL...
...EM-BRACED THE ABYSS !!

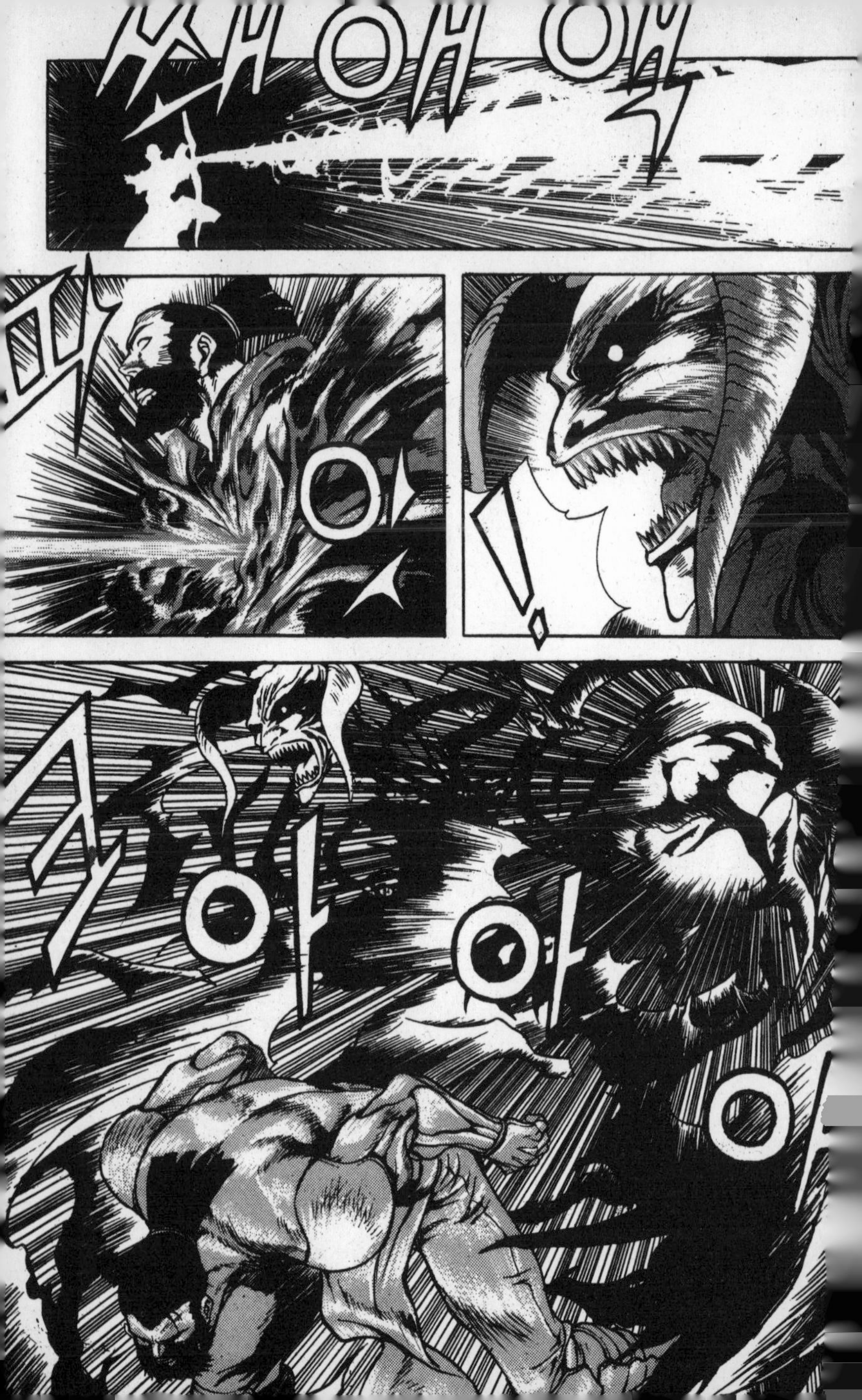
싸아아아악
크아아아

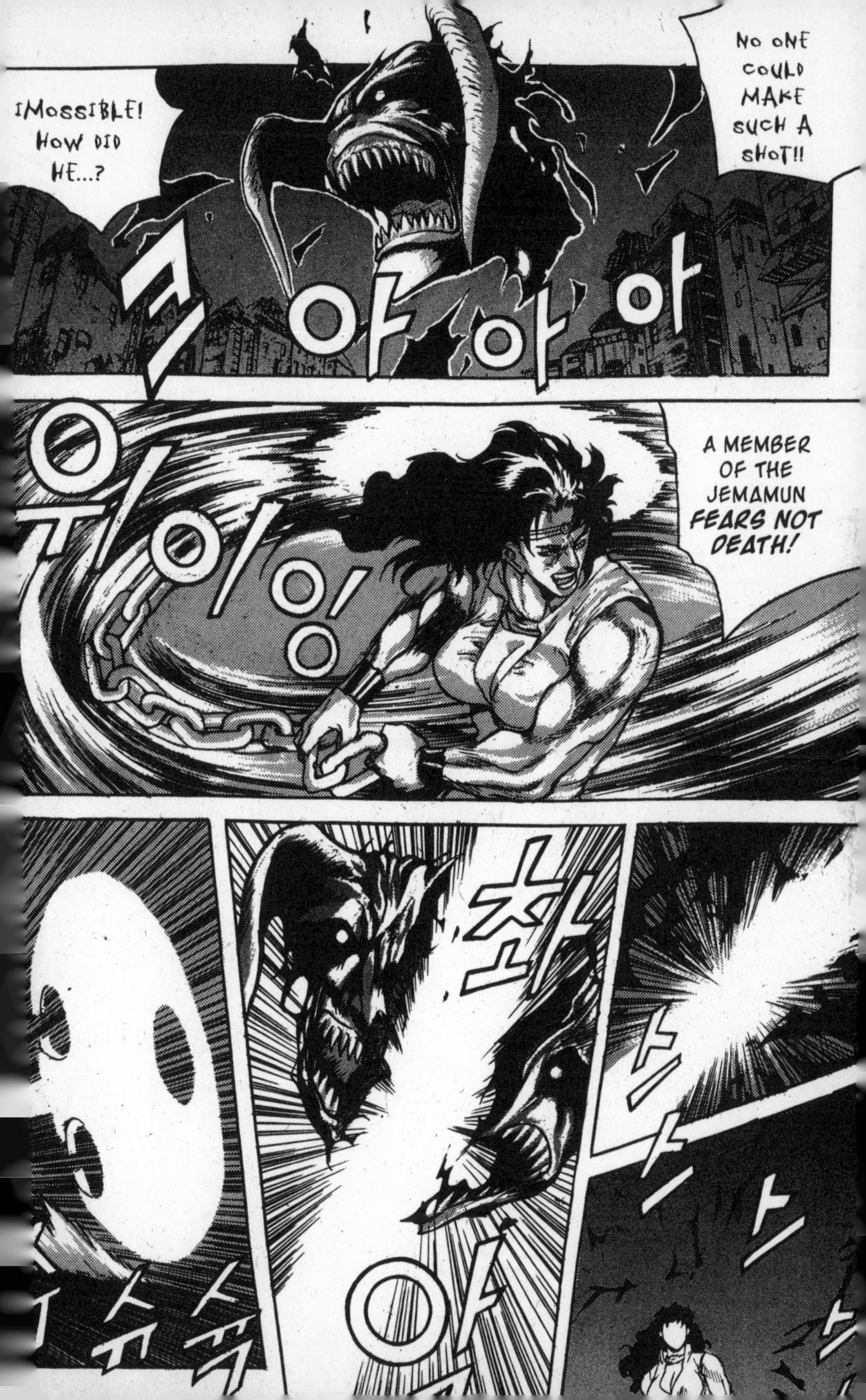
IMOSSIBLE! HOW DID HE...?
NO ONE COULD MAKE SUCH A SHOT!!
A MEMBER OF THE JEMAMUN FEARS NOT DEATH!

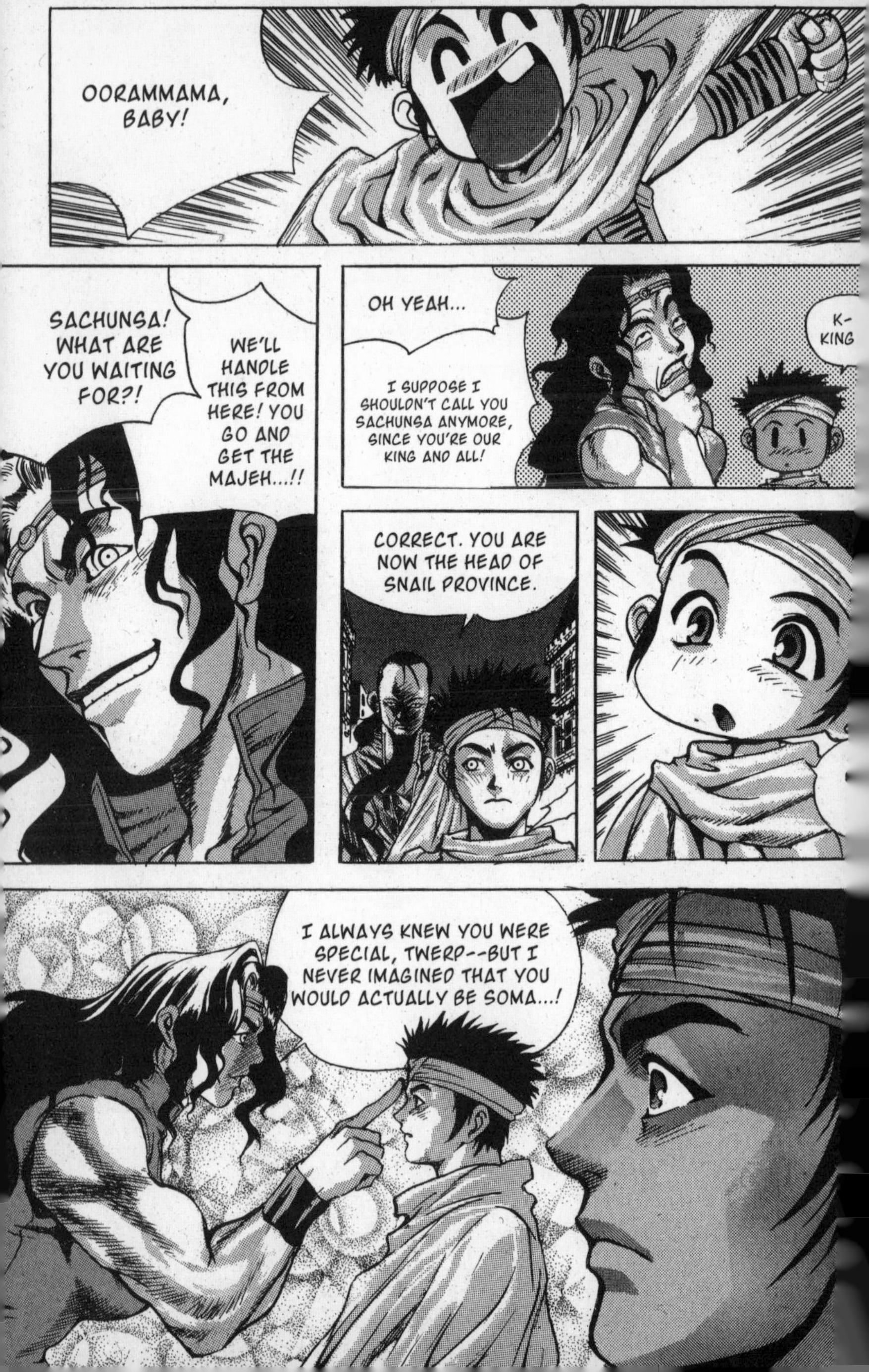
OORAMMAMA, BABY!
SACHUNSA! WHAT ARE YOU WAITING FOR?!
WE'LL HANDLE THIS FROM HERE! YOU GO AND GET THE MAJEH...!!
OH YEAH...
I SUPPOSE I SHOULDN'T CALL YOU SACHUNSA ANYMORE, SINCE YOU'RE OUR KING AND ALL!
K-KING
CORRECT. YOU ARE NOW THE HEAD OF SNAIL PROVINCE.
I ALWAYS KNEW YOU WERE SPECIAL, TWERP--BUT I NEVER IMAGINED THAT YOU WOULD ACTUALLY BE SOMA...!

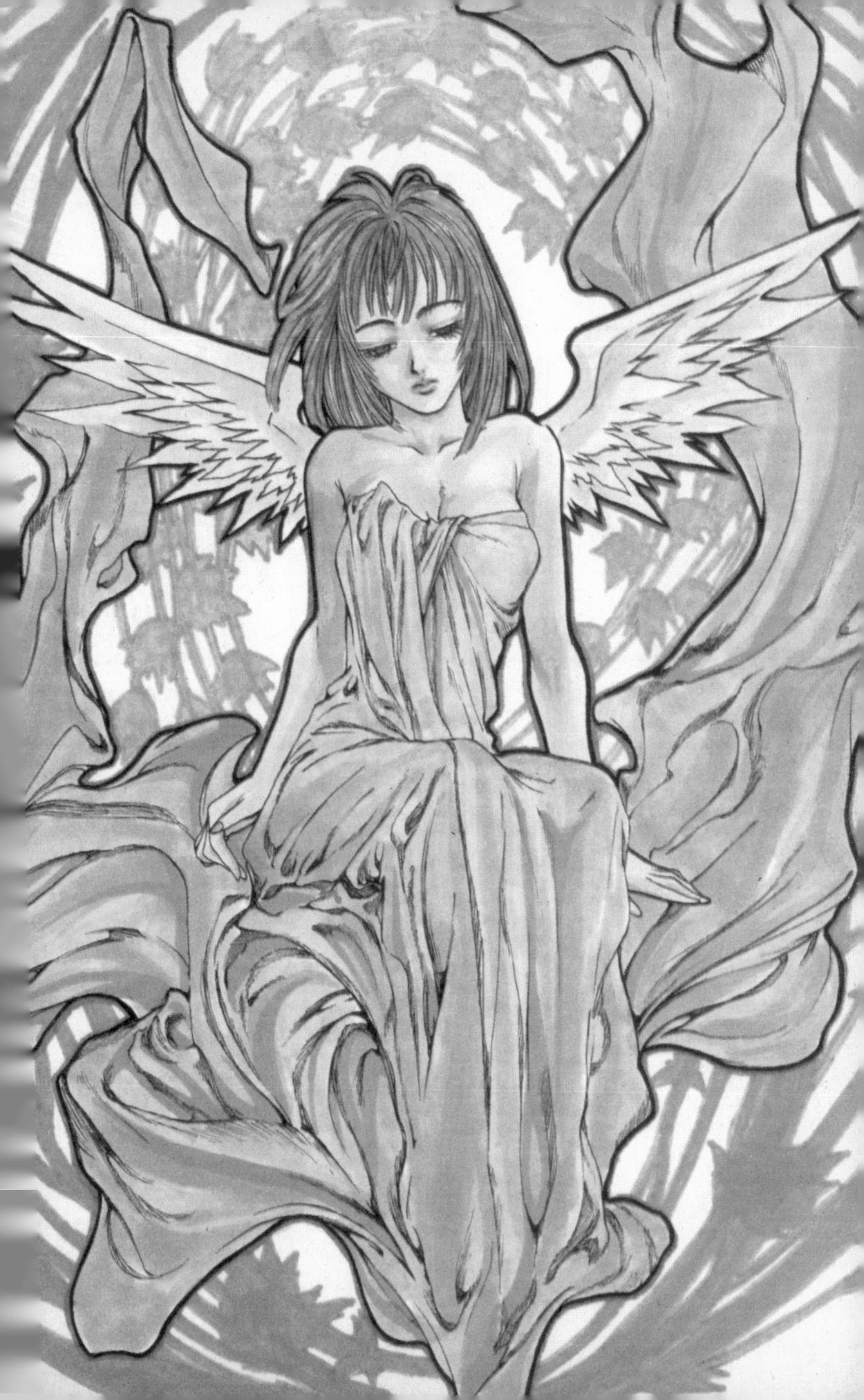

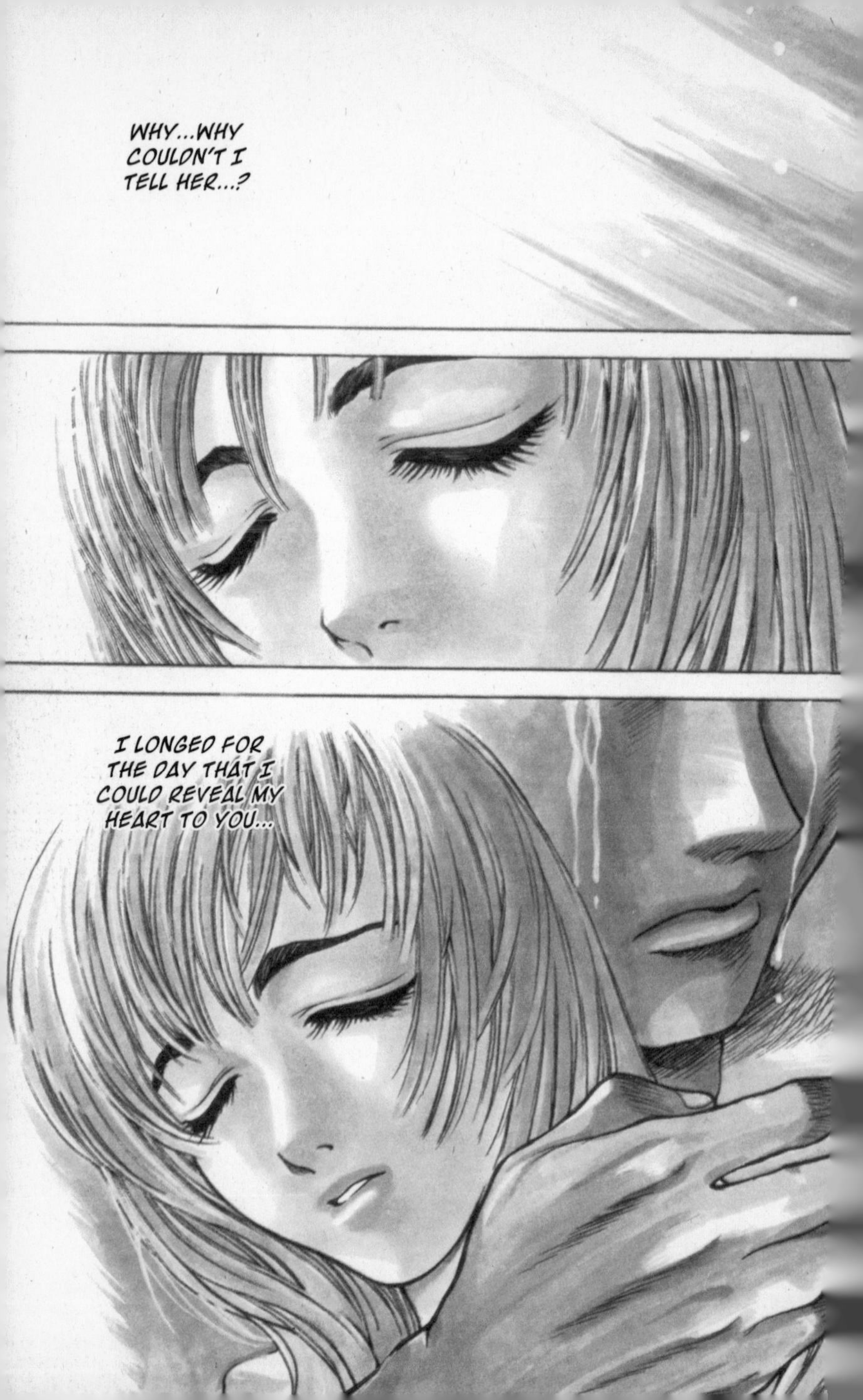
WHY...WHY COULDN'T I TELL HER...?
I LONGED FOR THE DAY THAT I COULD REVEAL MY HEART TO YOU...

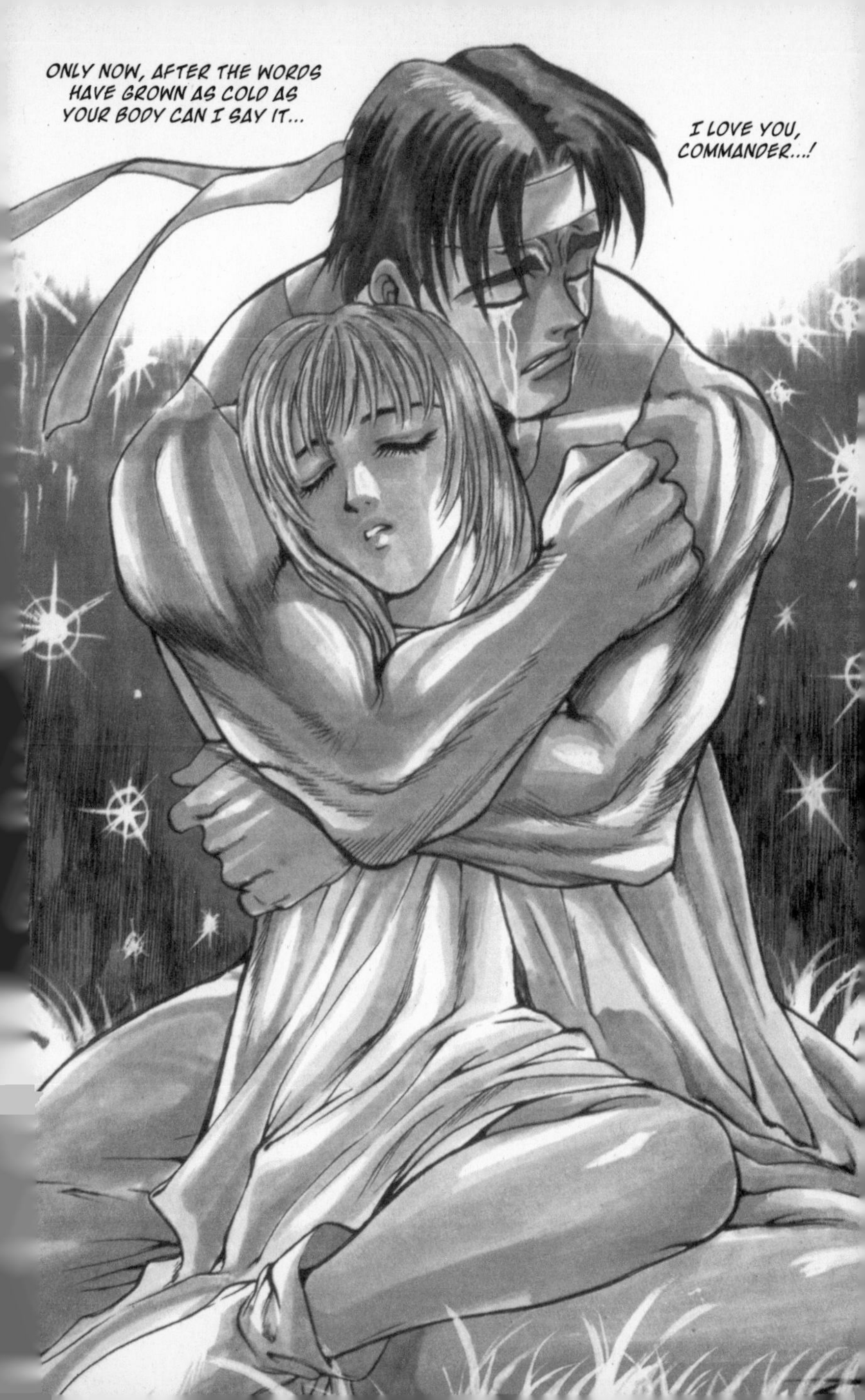
ONLY NOW, AFTER THE WORDS HAVE GROWN AS COLD AS YOUR BODY CAN I SAY IT...
I LOVE YOU, COMMANDER...!

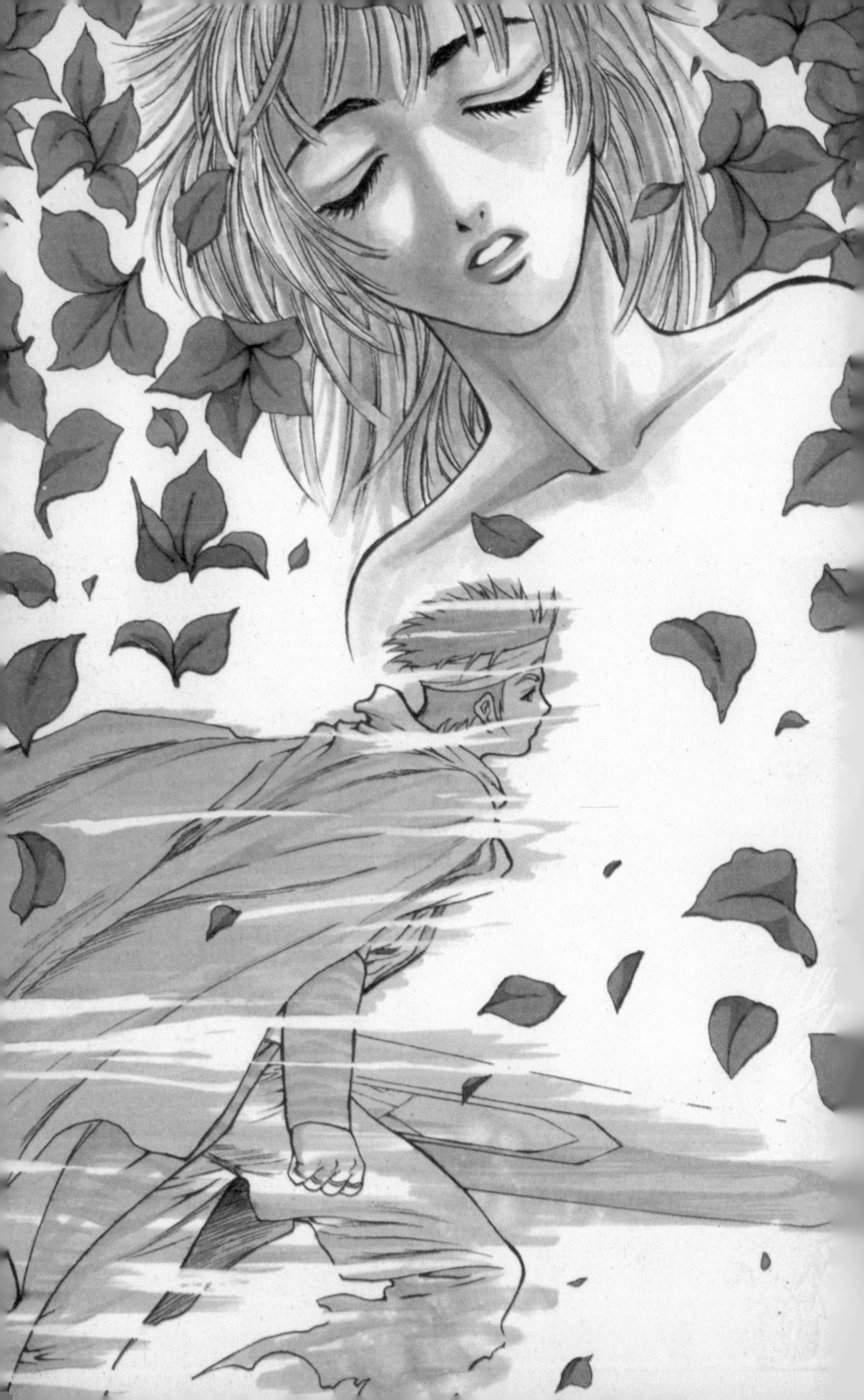

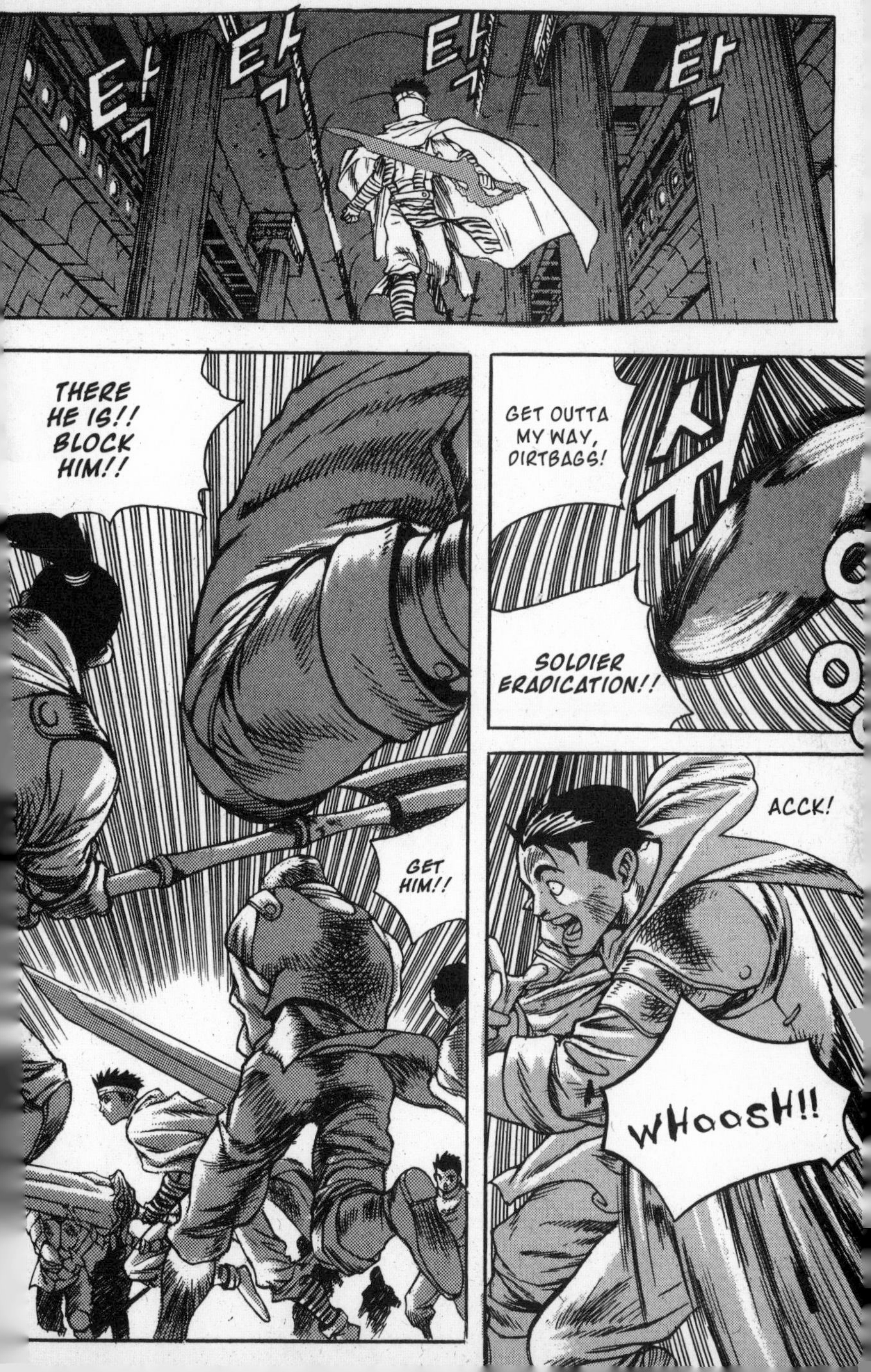

탁
탁
탁
탁
THERE HE IS!! BLOCK HIM!!
GET HIM!!
GET OUTTA MY WAY, DIRTBAGS!
SOLDIER ERADICATION!!
ACCK!
WHOOSH!!

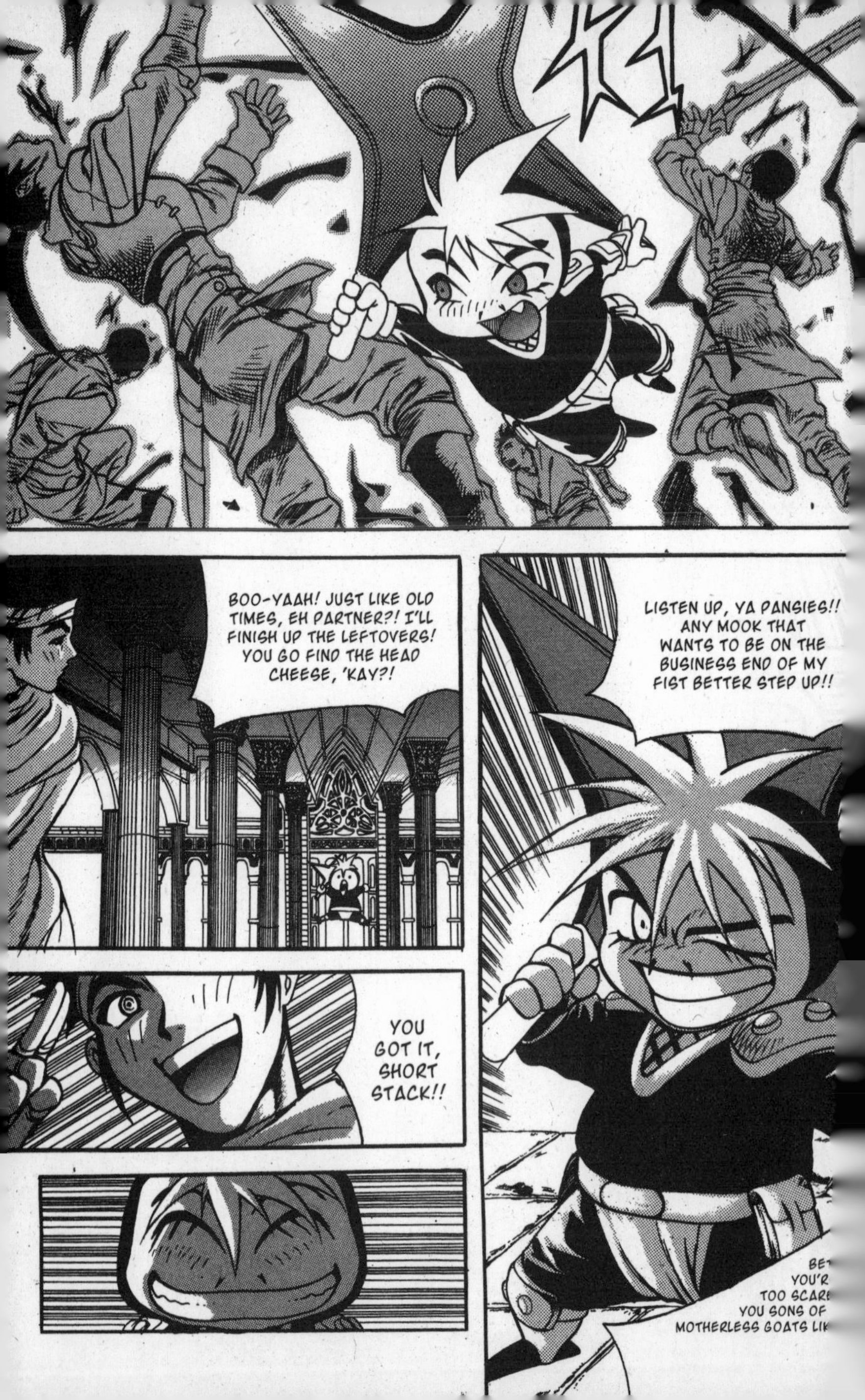
BOO-YAAH! JUST LIKE OLD TIMES, EH PARTNER?! I'LL FINISH UP THE LEFTOVERS! YOU GO FIND THE HEAD CHEESE, 'KAY?!
YOU GOT IT, SHORT STACK!!
LISTEN UP, YA PANSIES!! ANY MOOK THAT WANTS TO BE ON THE BUSINESS END OF MY FIST BETTER STEP UP!!
BE
YOU'R
TOO SCARE
YOU SONS OF
MOTHERLESS GOATS LIK

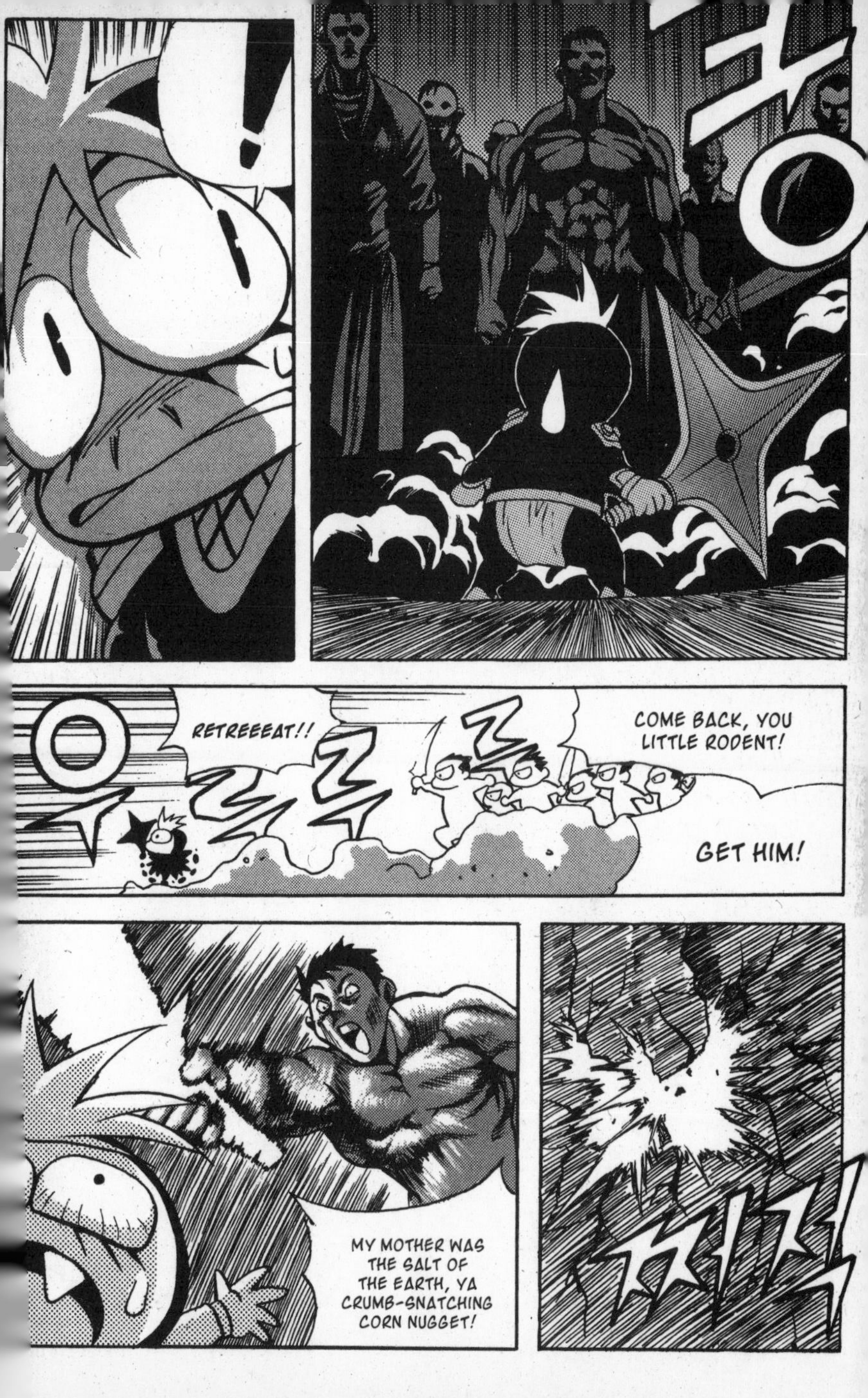

RETREEEAT!!
COME BACK, YOU LITTLE RODENT!
GET HIM!
MY MOTHER WAS THE SALT OF THE EARTH, YA CRUMB-SNATCHING CORN NUGGET!

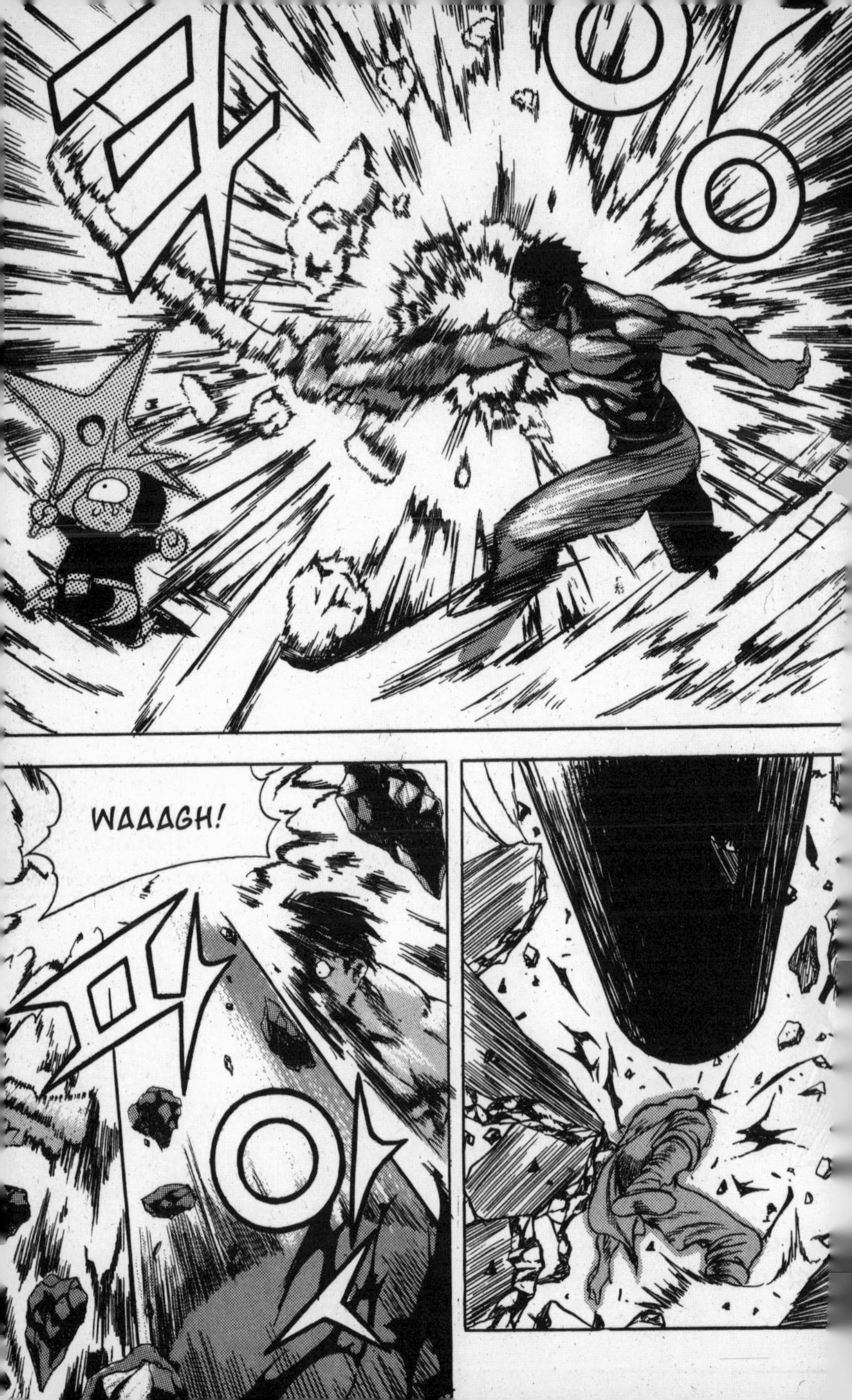
WAAAGH!

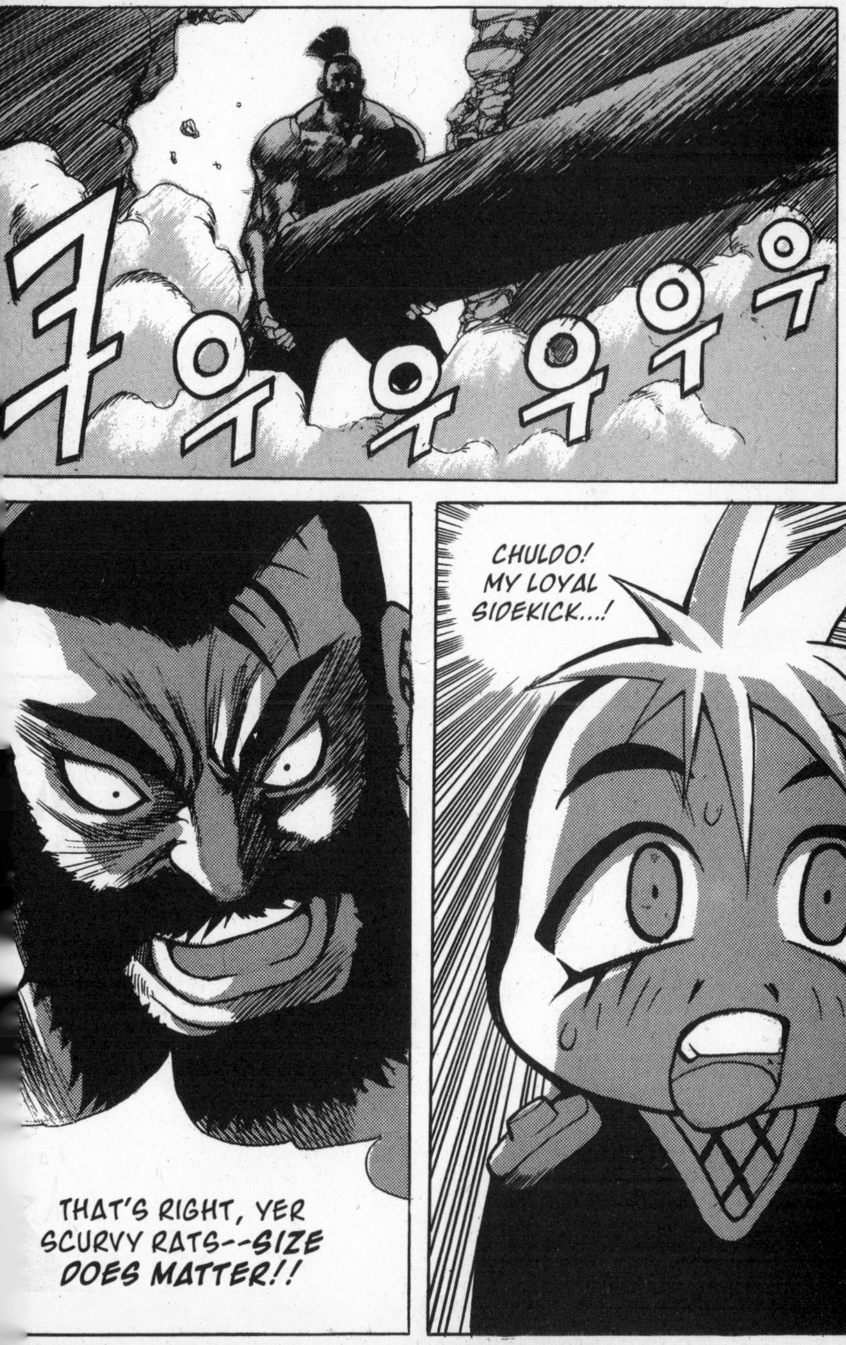
THAT'S RIGHT, YER SCURVY RATS--SIZE DOES MATTER!!
CHULDO! MY LOYAL SIDEKICK...!

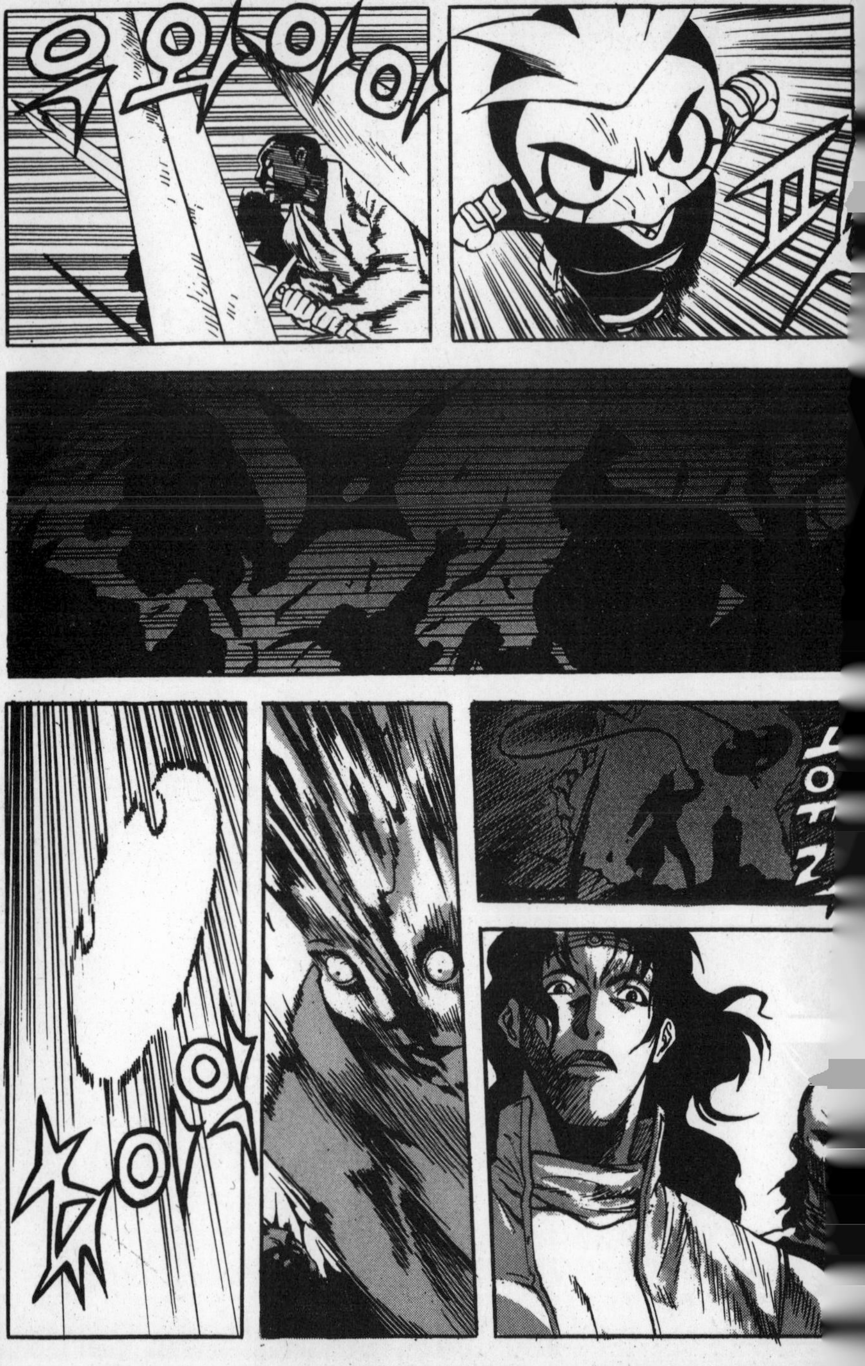

으와아아

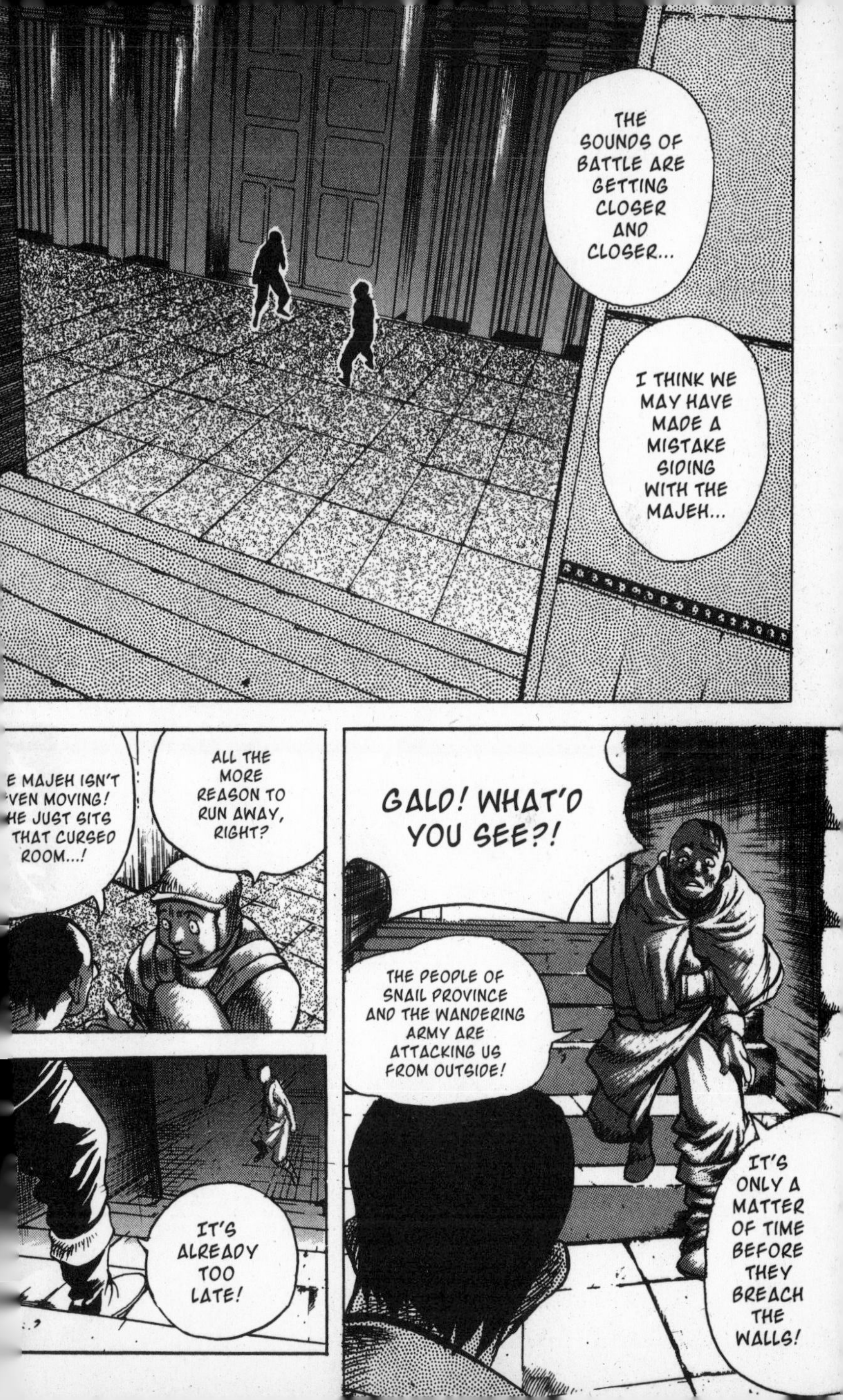
THE SOUNDS OF BATTLE ARE GETTING CLOSER AND CLOSER...
I THINK WE MAY HAVE MADE A MISTAKE SIDING WITH THE MAJEH...
E MAJEH ISN'T VEN MOVING! HE JUST SITS THAT CURSED ROOM...!
ALL THE MORE REASON TO RUN AWAY, RIGHT?
GALD! WHAT'D YOU SEE?!
THE PEOPLE OF SNAIL PROVINCE AND THE WANDERING ARMY ARE ATTACKING US FROM OUTSIDE!
IT'S ONLY A MATTER OF TIME BEFORE THEY BREACH THE WALLS!
IT'S ALREADY TOO LATE!

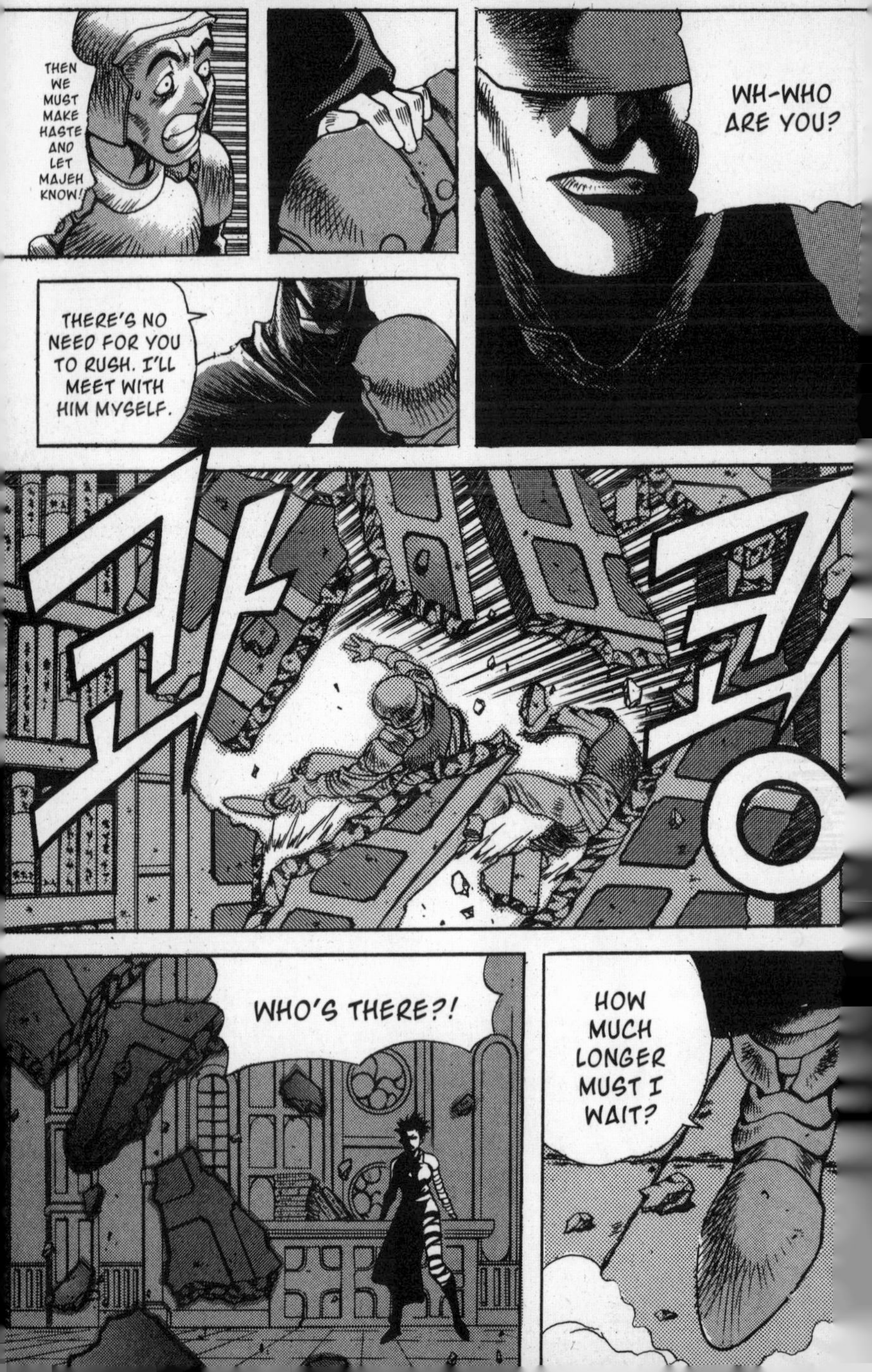
THEN WE MUST MAKE HASTE AND LET MAJEH KNOW!
WH-WHO ARE YOU?
THERE'S NO NEED FOR YOU TO RUSH. I'LL MEET WITH HIM MYSELF.
WHO'S THERE?!
HOW MUCH LONGER MUST I WAIT?

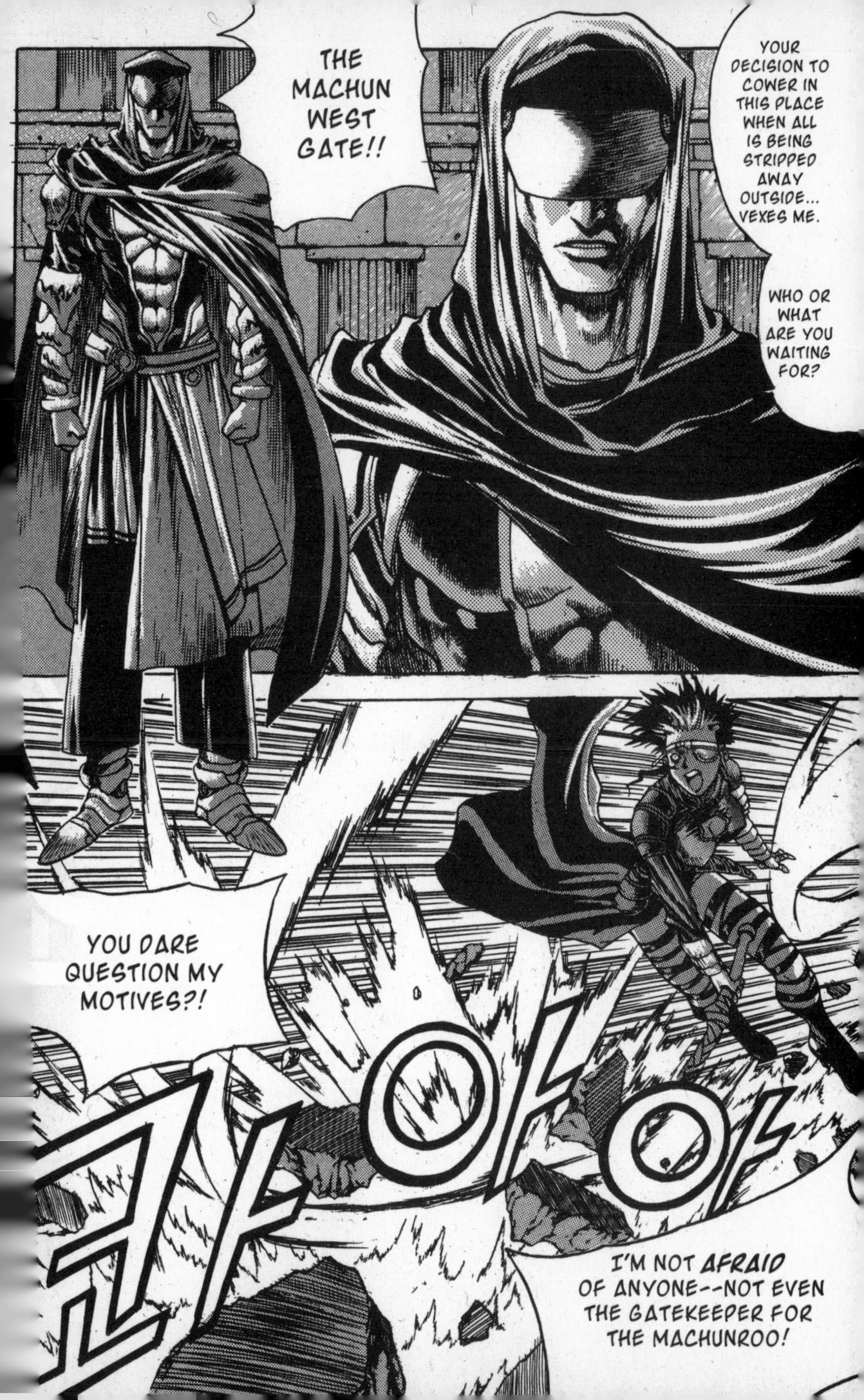
THE MACHUN WEST GATE!!
YOUR DECISION TO COWER IN THIS PLACE WHEN ALL IS BEING STRIPPED AWAY OUTSIDE... VEXES ME.
WHO OR WHAT ARE YOU WAITING FOR?
YOU DARE QUESTION MY MOTIVES?!
I'M NOT AFRAID OF ANYONE--NOT EVEN THE GATEKEEPER FOR THE MACHUNROO!

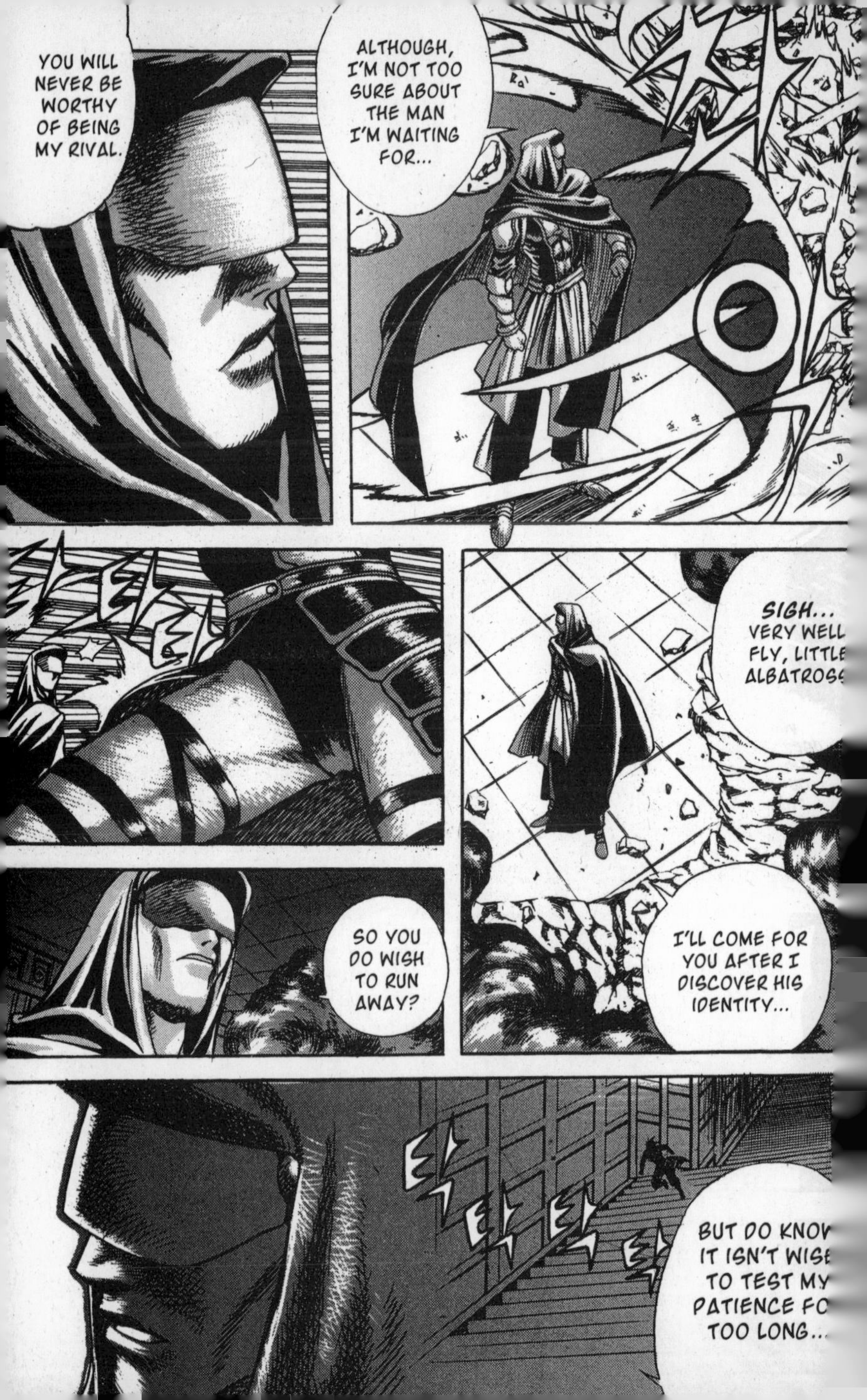
YOU WILL NEVER BE WORTHY OF BEING MY RIVAL.
ALTHOUGH, I'M NOT TOO SURE ABOUT THE MAN I'M WAITING FOR...
SO YOU DO WISH TO RUN AWAY?
SIGH... VERY WELL FLY, LITTLE ALBATROSS
I'LL COME FOR YOU AFTER I DISCOVER HIS IDENTITY...
BUT DO KNOW IT ISN'T WISE TO TEST MY PATIENCE FO TOO LONG...

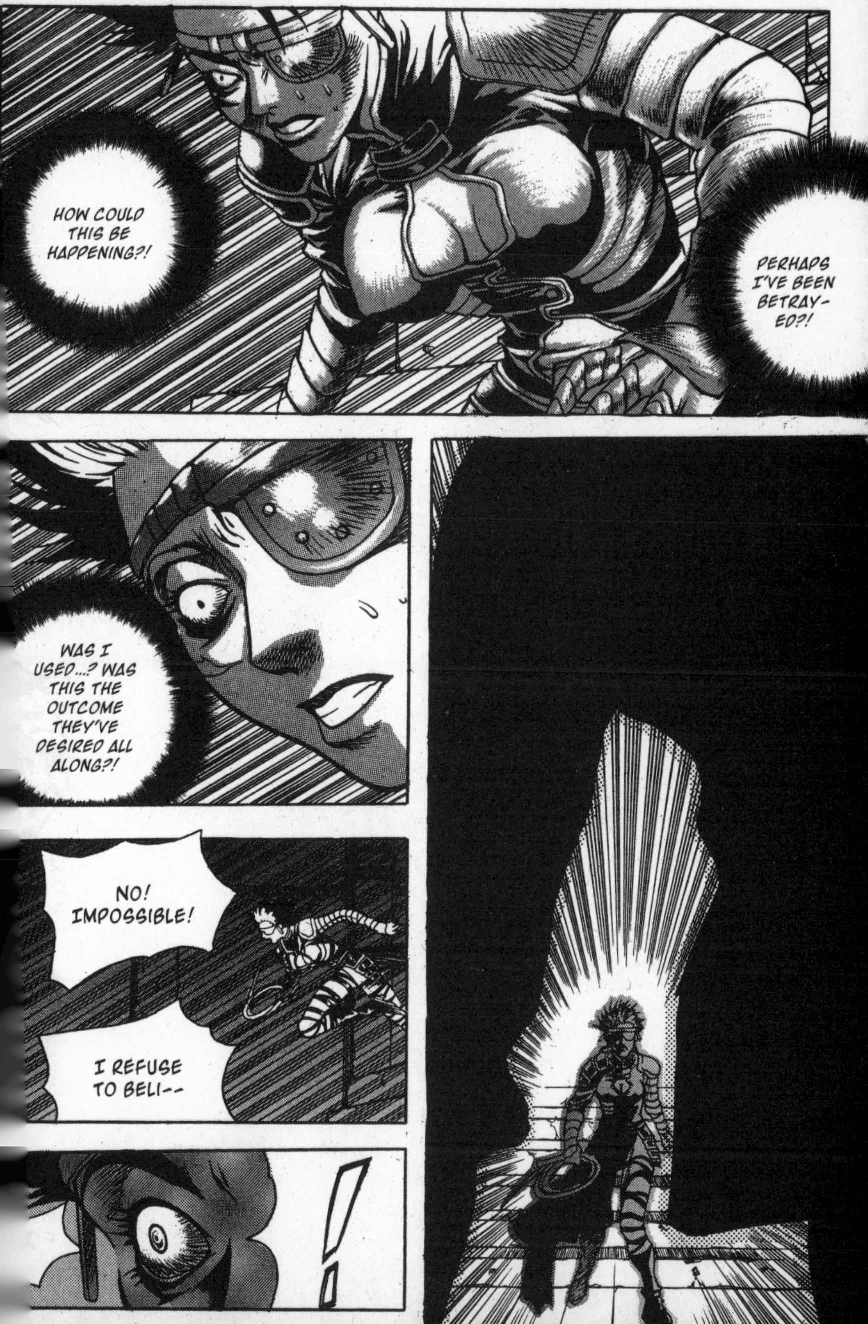
HOW COULD THIS BE HAPPENING?!
PERHAPS I'VE BEEN BETRAY-ED?!
WAS I USED...? WAS THIS THE OUTCOME THEY'VE DESIRED ALL ALONG?!
NO! IMPOSSIBLE!
I REFUSE TO BELI--

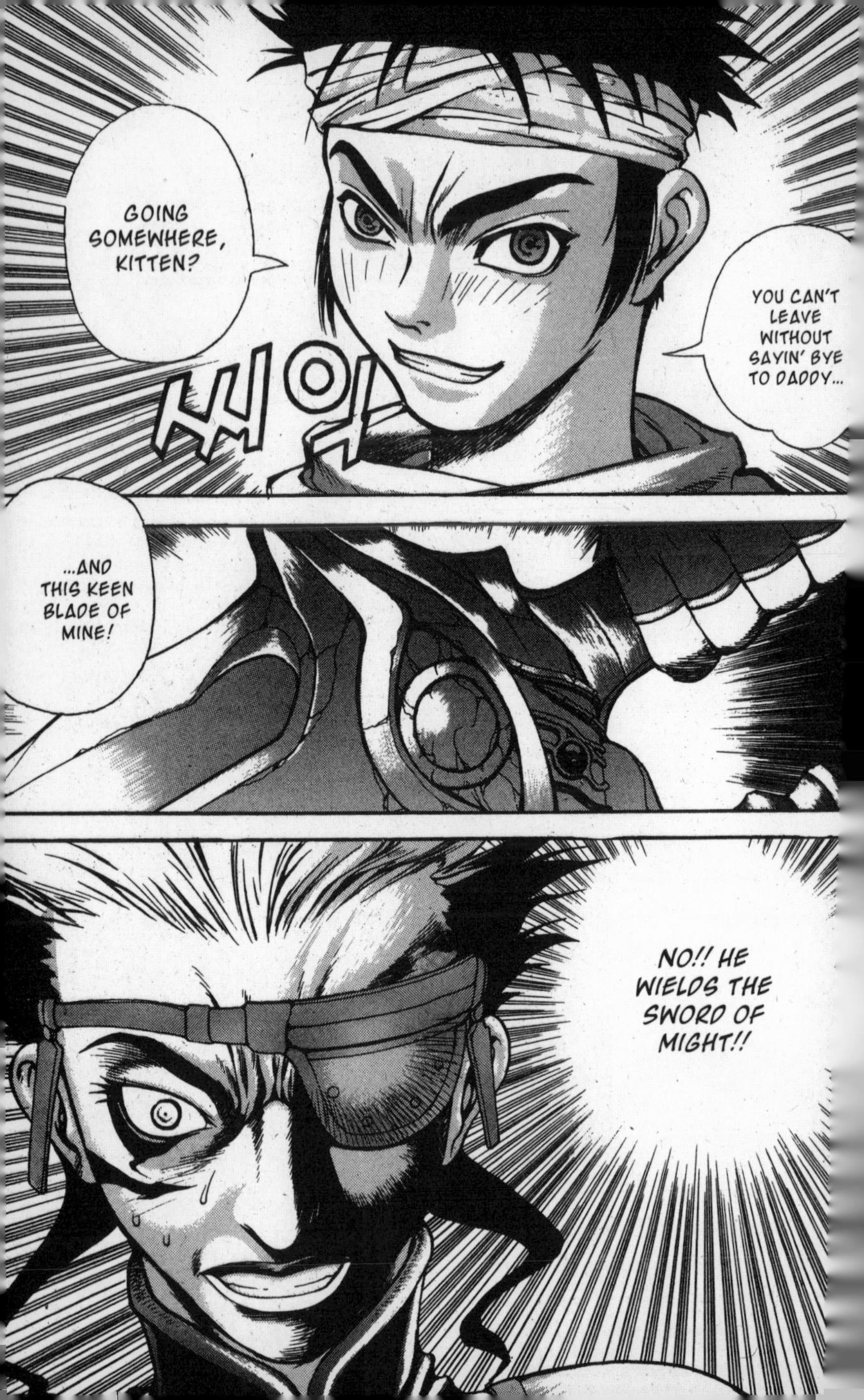
GOING SOMEWHERE, KITTEN?
씨익
YOU CAN'T LEAVE WITHOUT SAYIN' BYE TO DADDY...
...AND THIS KEEN BLADE OF MINE!
NO!! HE WIELDS THE SWORD OF MIGHT!!

BLADE OF HEAVEN

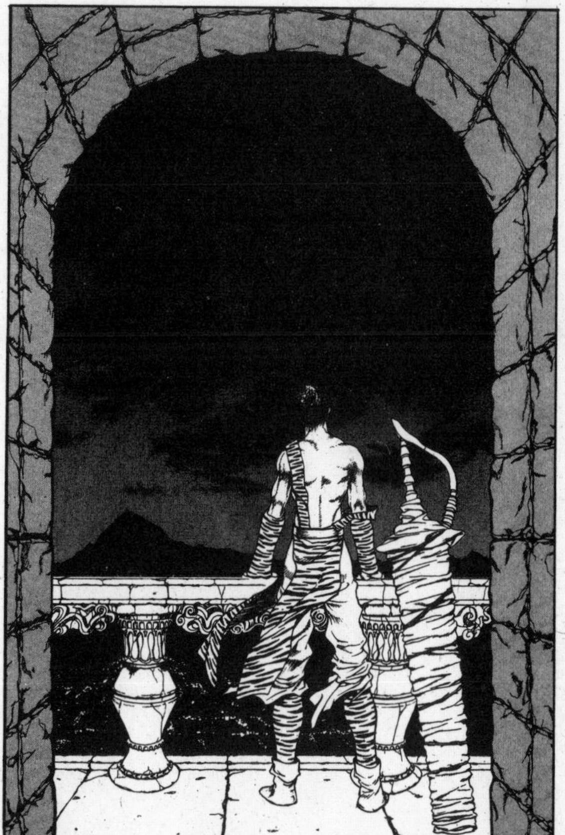

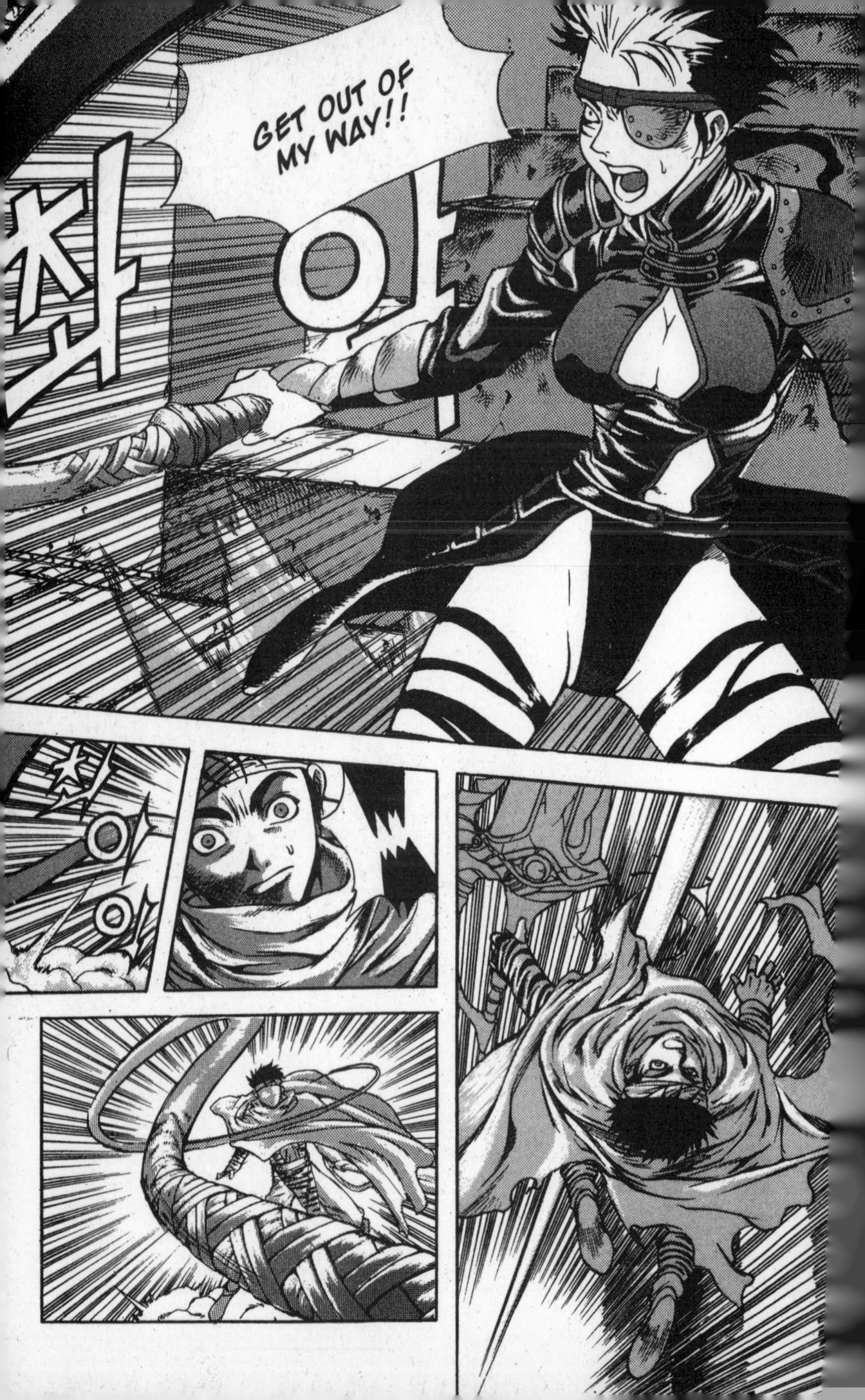
GET OUT OF MY WAY!!

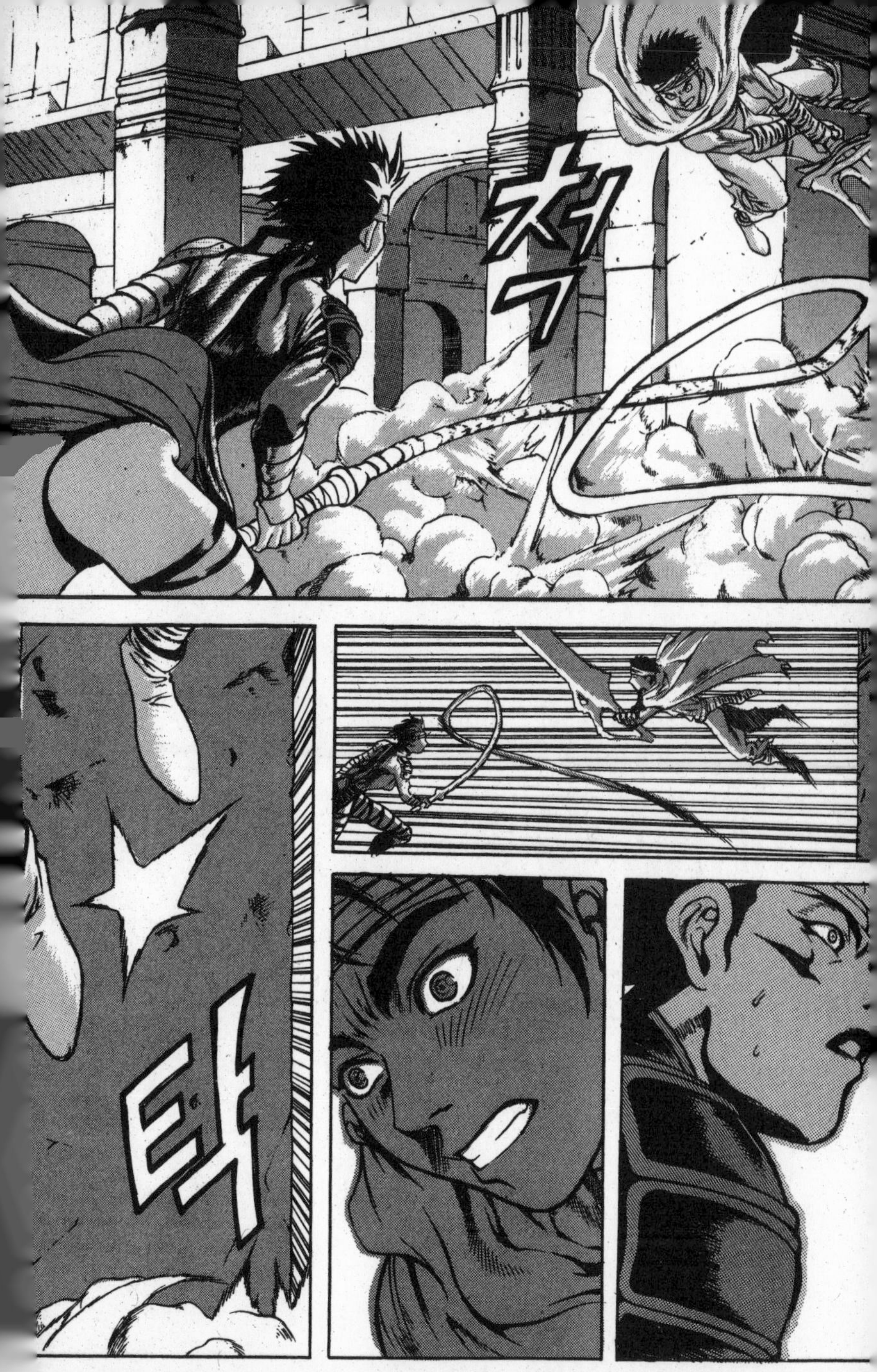

착
탁

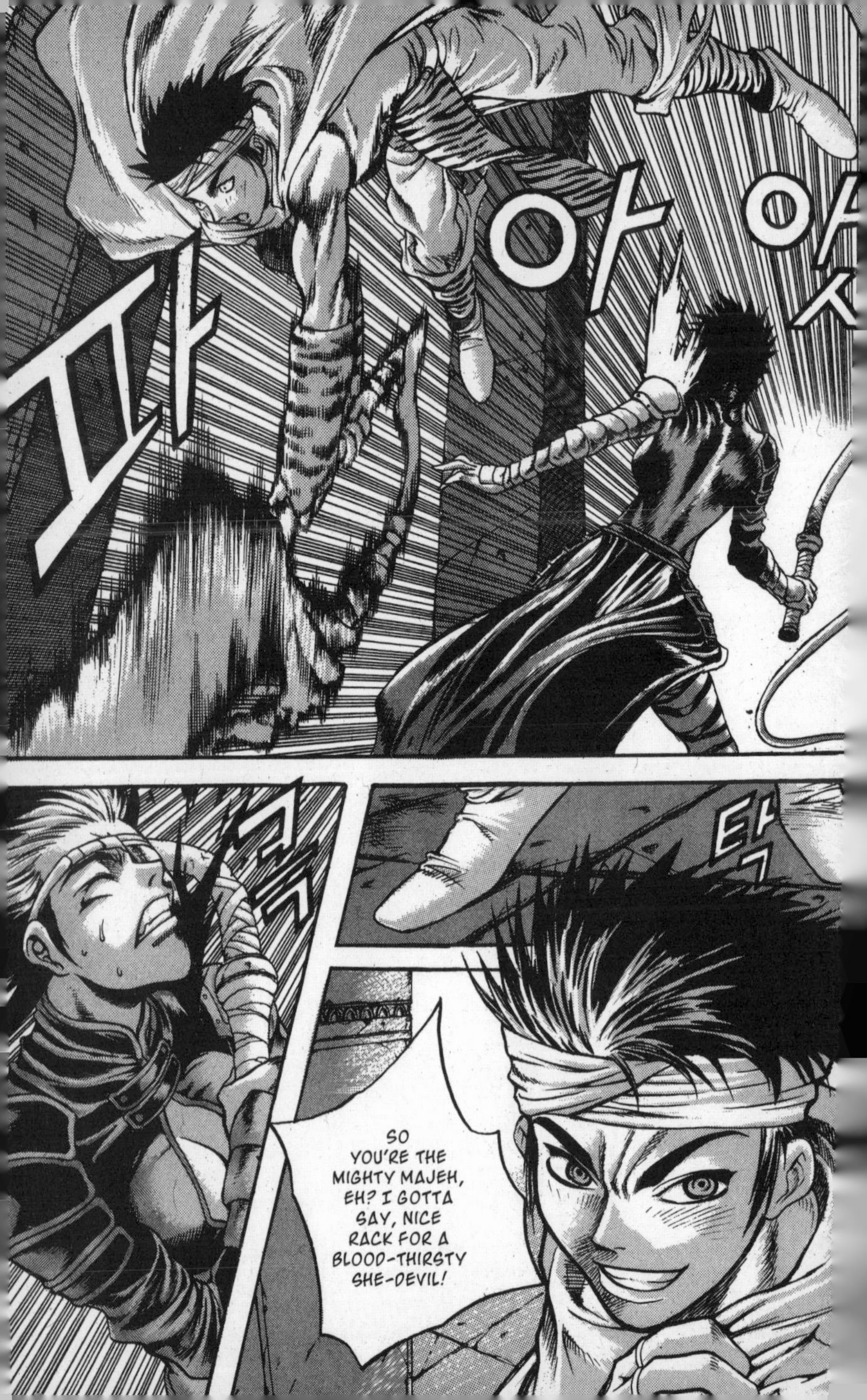
SO YOU'RE THE MIGHTY MAJEH, EH? I GOTTA SAY, NICE RACK FOR A BLOOD-THIRSTY SHE-DEVIL!

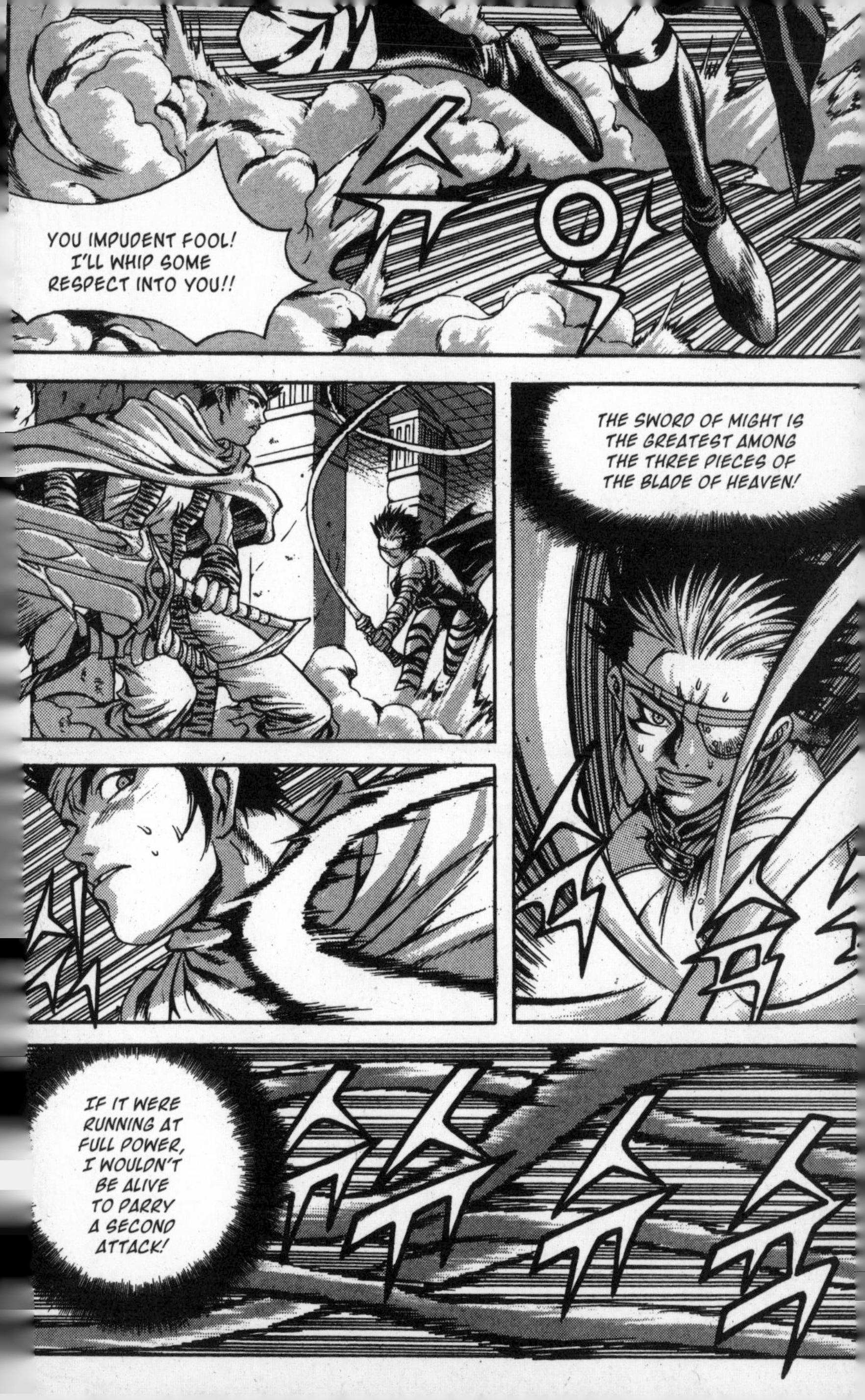
YOU IMPUDENT FOOL! I'LL WHIP SOME RESPECT INTO YOU!!
THE SWORD OF MIGHT IS THE GREATEST AMONG THE THREE PIECES OF THE BLADE OF HEAVEN!
IF IT WERE RUNNING AT FULL POWER, I WOULDN'T BE ALIVE TO PARRY A SECOND ATTACK!

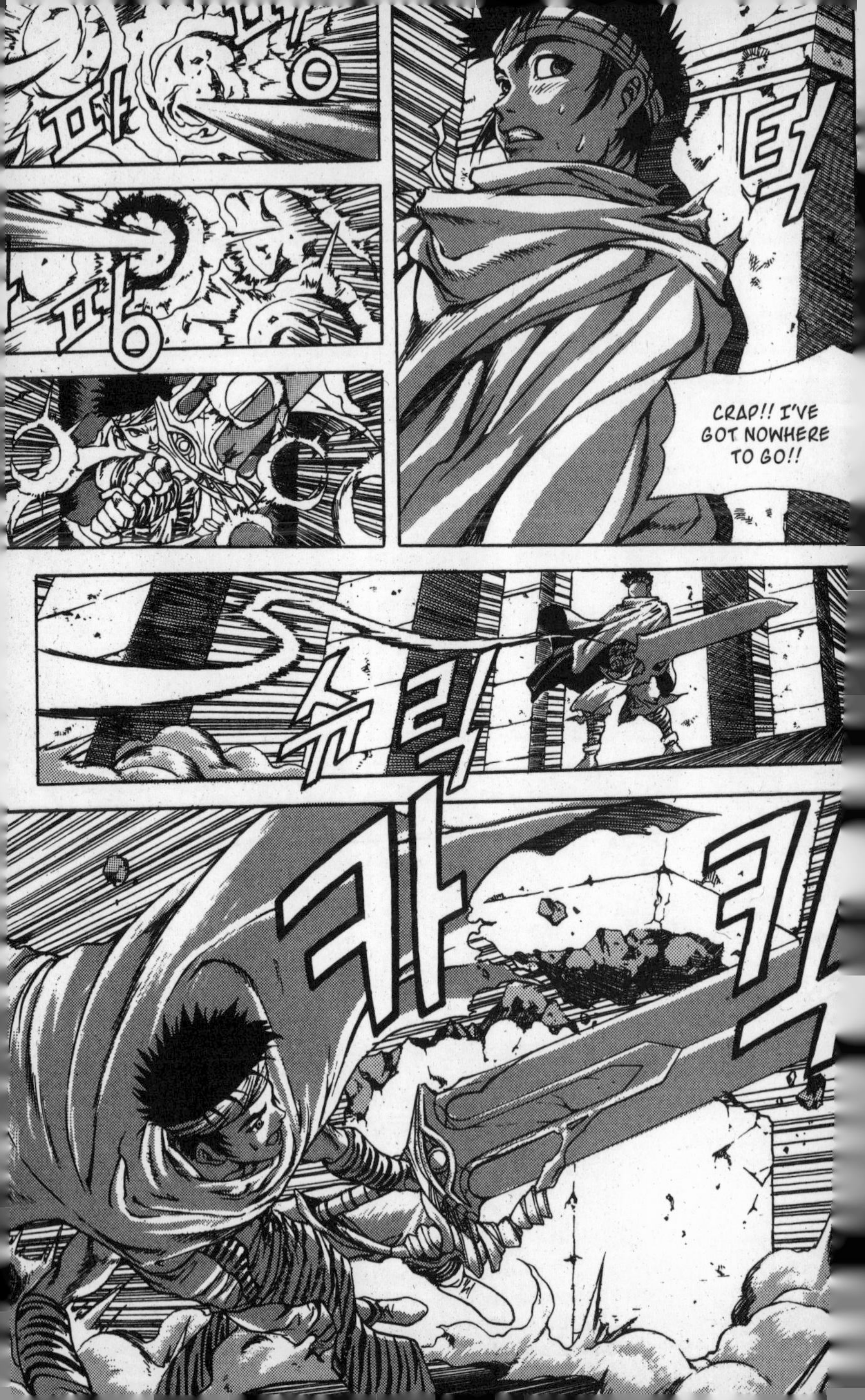
턱
CRAP!! I'VE GOT NOWHERE TO GO!!

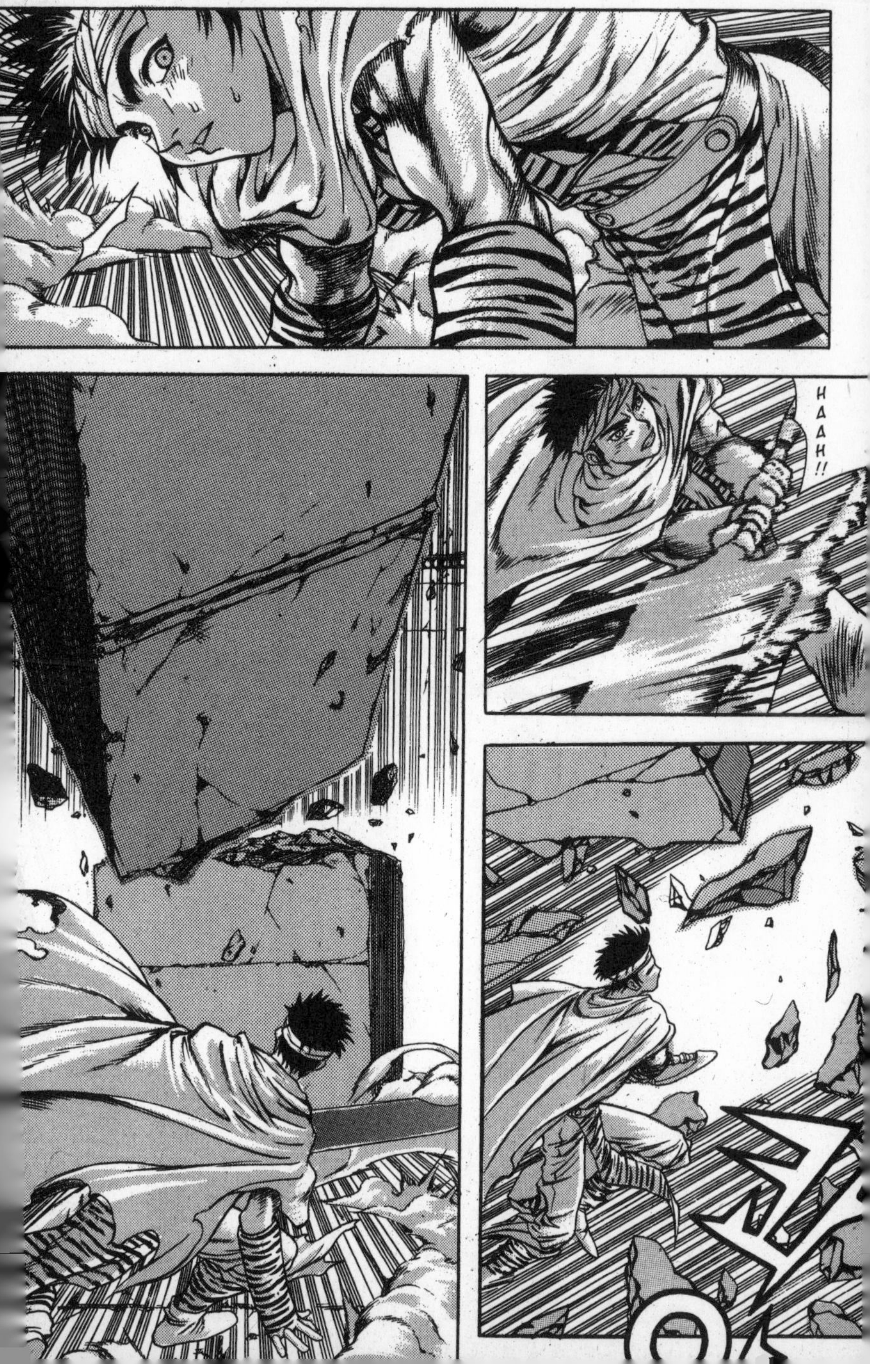
HAAH!!

I NEED TO SEIZE THE MOMENT AND LOOK FOR AN OPPORTUNITY...

...WHILE THE BOY IS STILL BECOMING ACCUSTOMED TO THE SWORD OF MIGHT!!

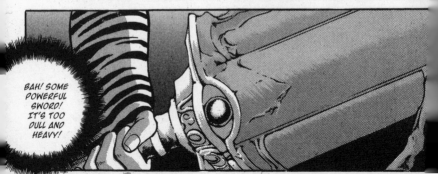

BAH! SOME POWERFUL SWORD! IT'S TOO DULL AND HEAVY!

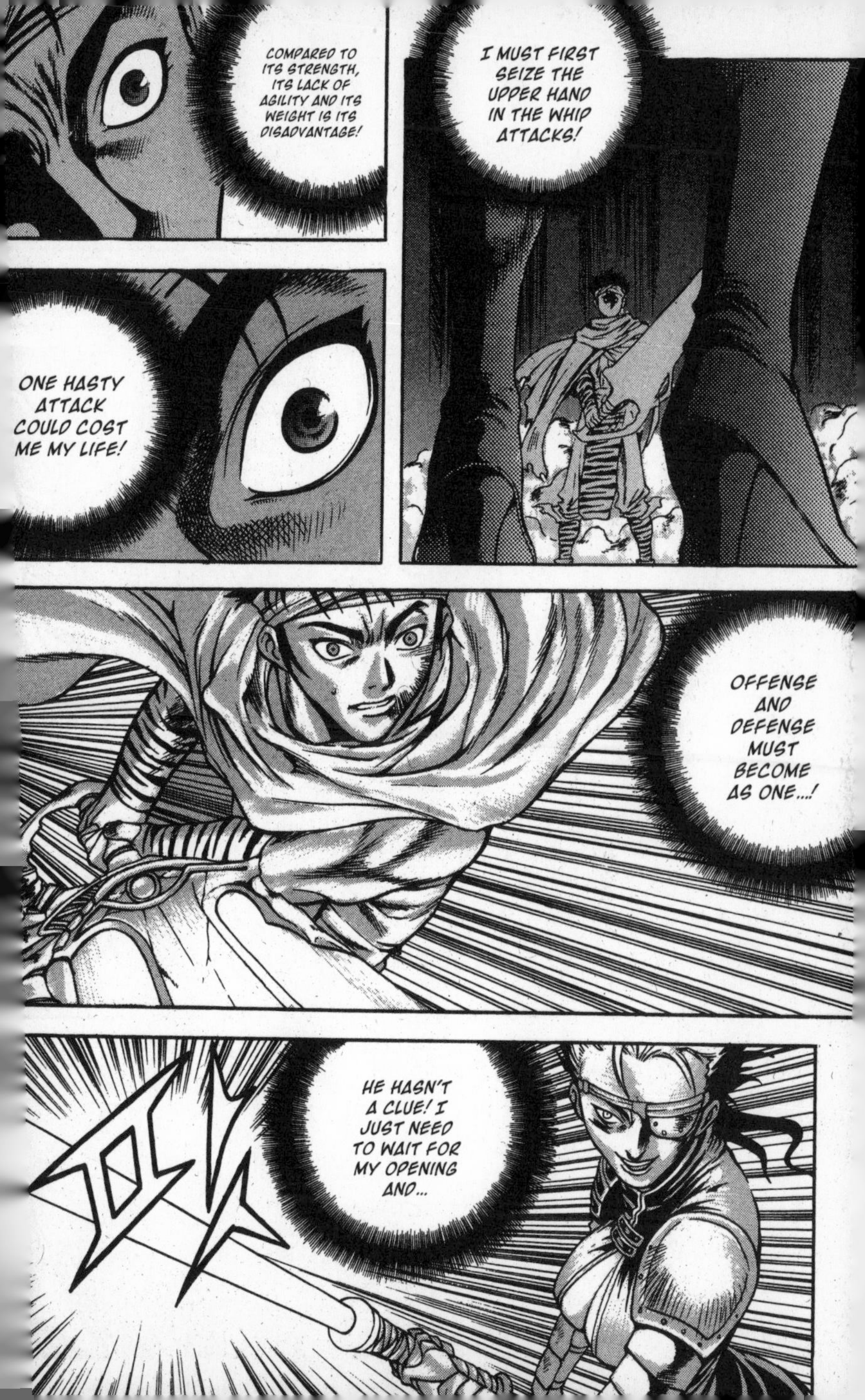
COMPARED TO ITS STRENGTH, ITS LACK OF AGILITY AND ITS WEIGHT IS ITS DISADVANTAGE!
I MUST FIRST SEIZE THE UPPER HAND IN THE WHIP ATTACKS!
ONE HASTY ATTACK COULD COST ME MY LIFE!
OFFENSE AND DEFENSE MUST BECOME AS ONE...!
HE HASN'T A CLUE! I JUST NEED TO WAIT FOR MY OPENING AND...

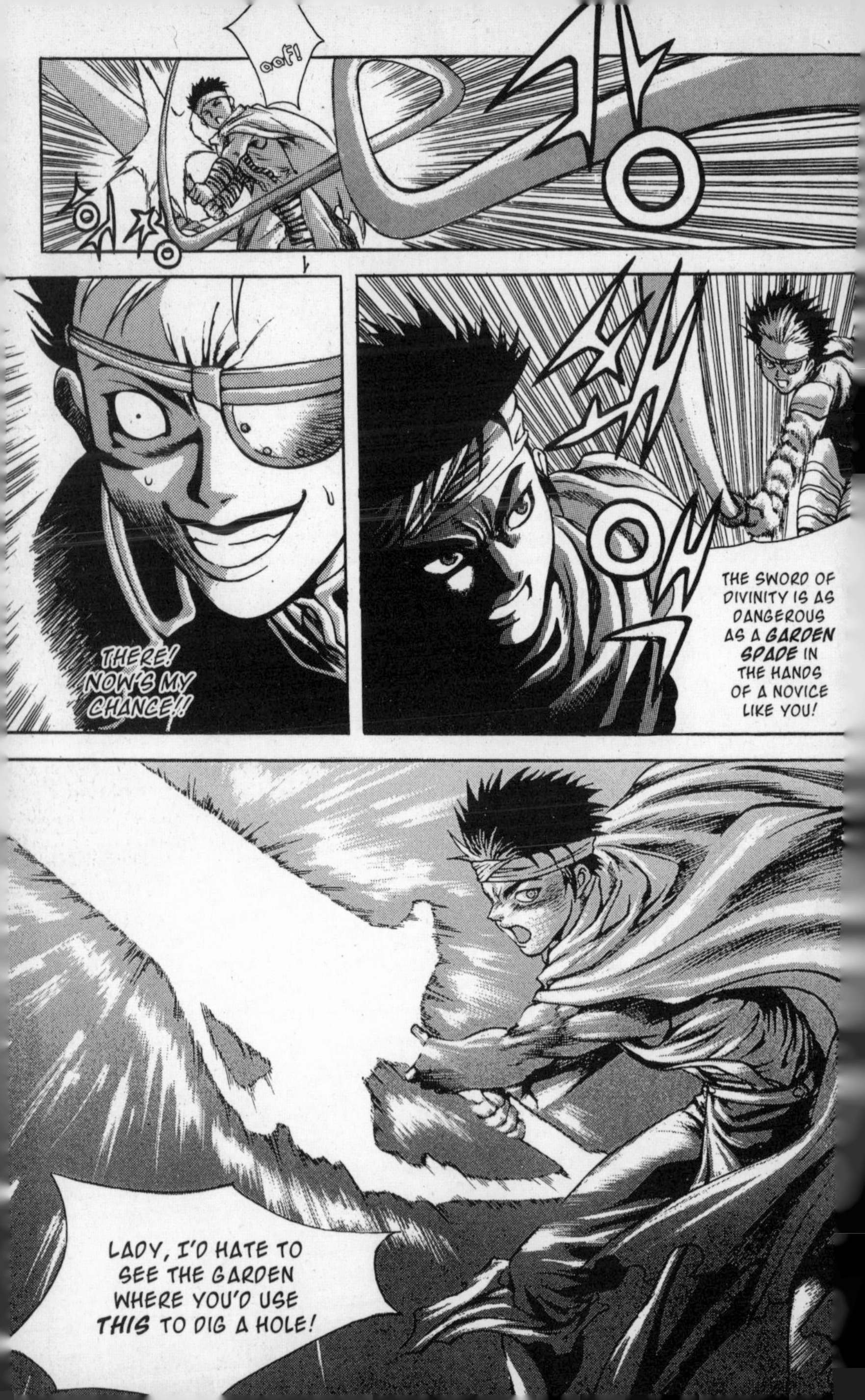
OOF!
THERE! NOW'S MY CHANCE!!
THE SWORD OF DIVINITY IS AS DANGEROUS AS A GARDEN SPADE IN THE HANDS OF A NOVICE LIKE YOU!
LADY, I'D HATE TO SEE THE GARDEN WHERE YOU'D USE THIS TO DIG A HOLE!

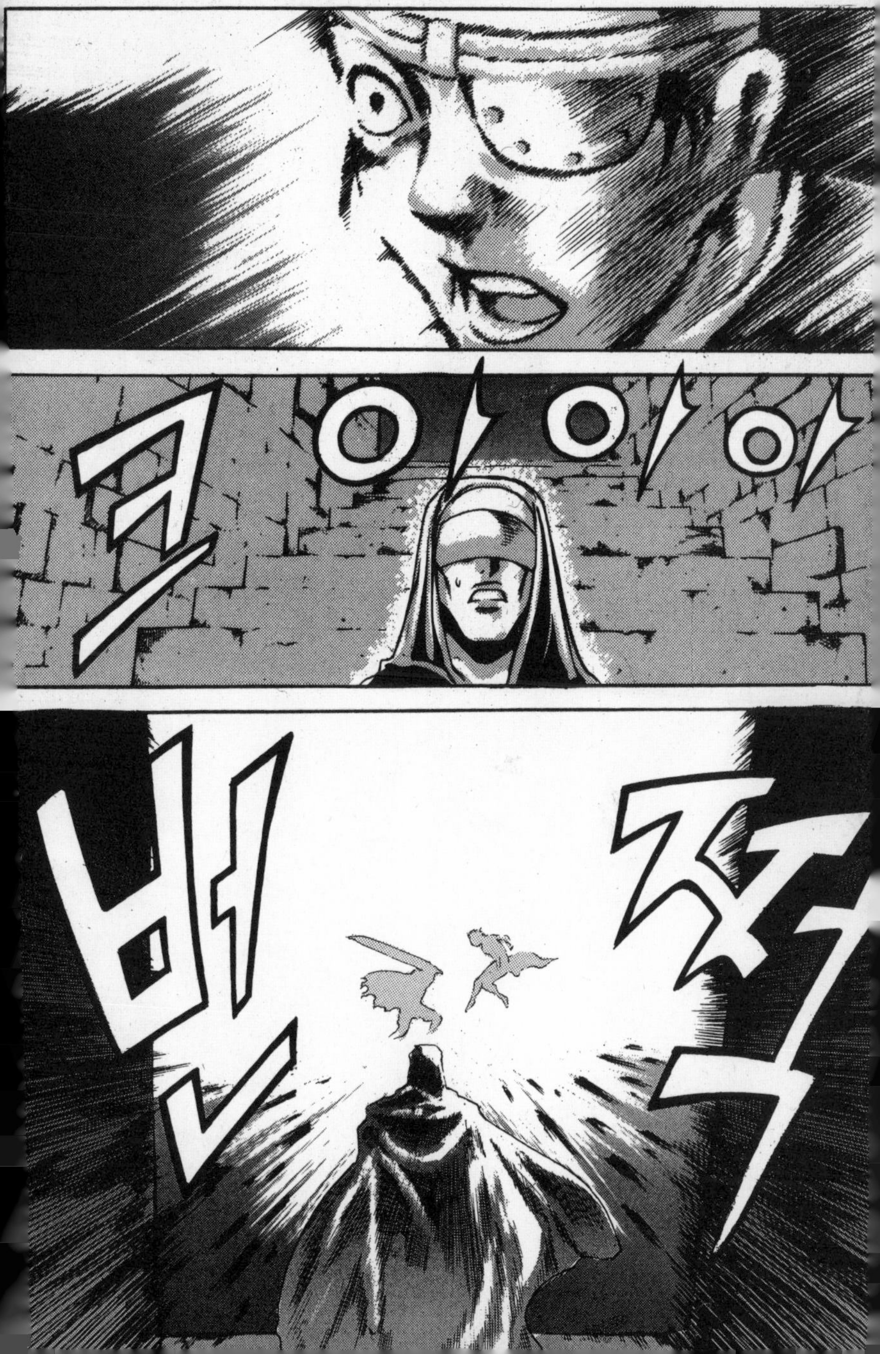

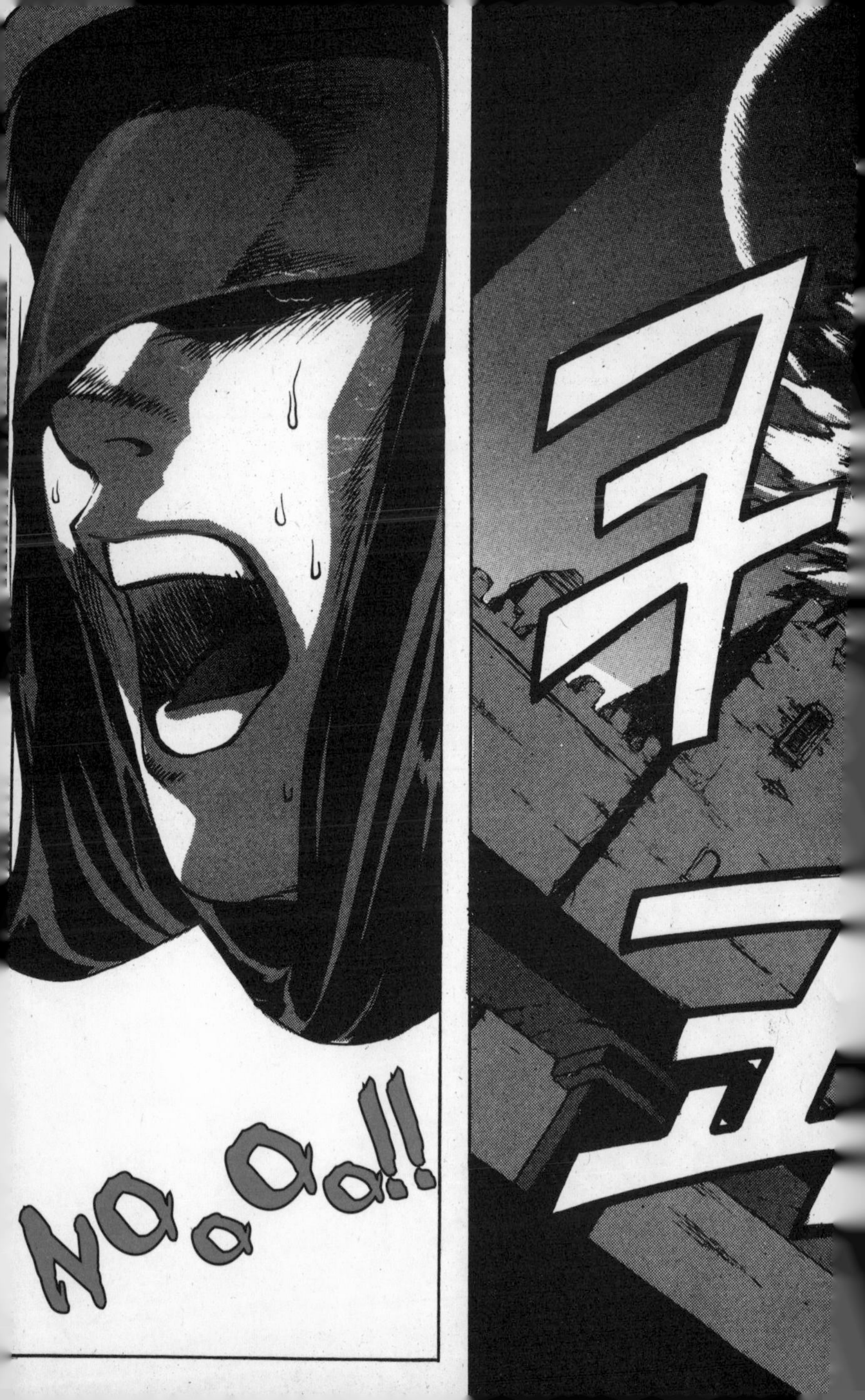
Naaaa!!

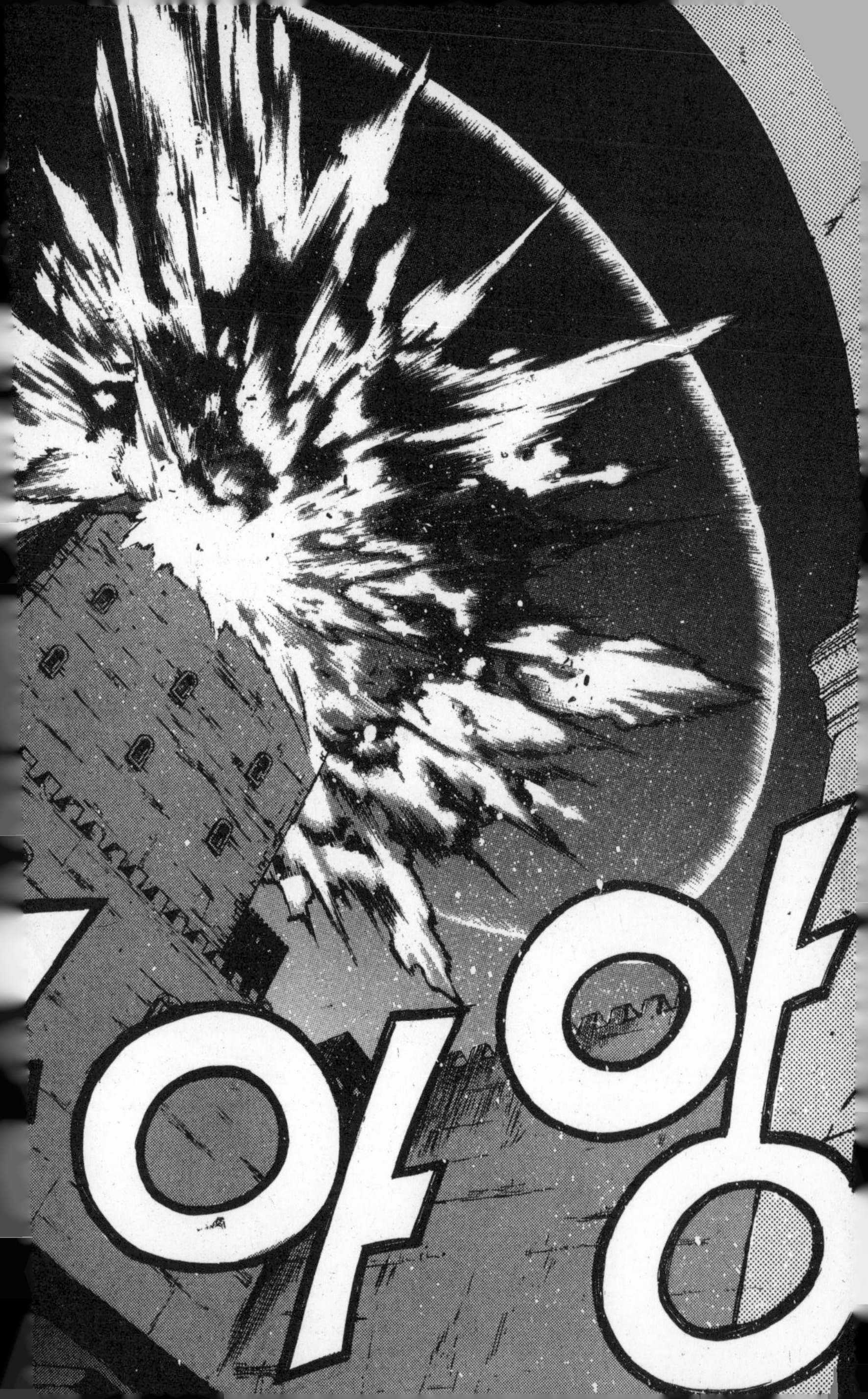

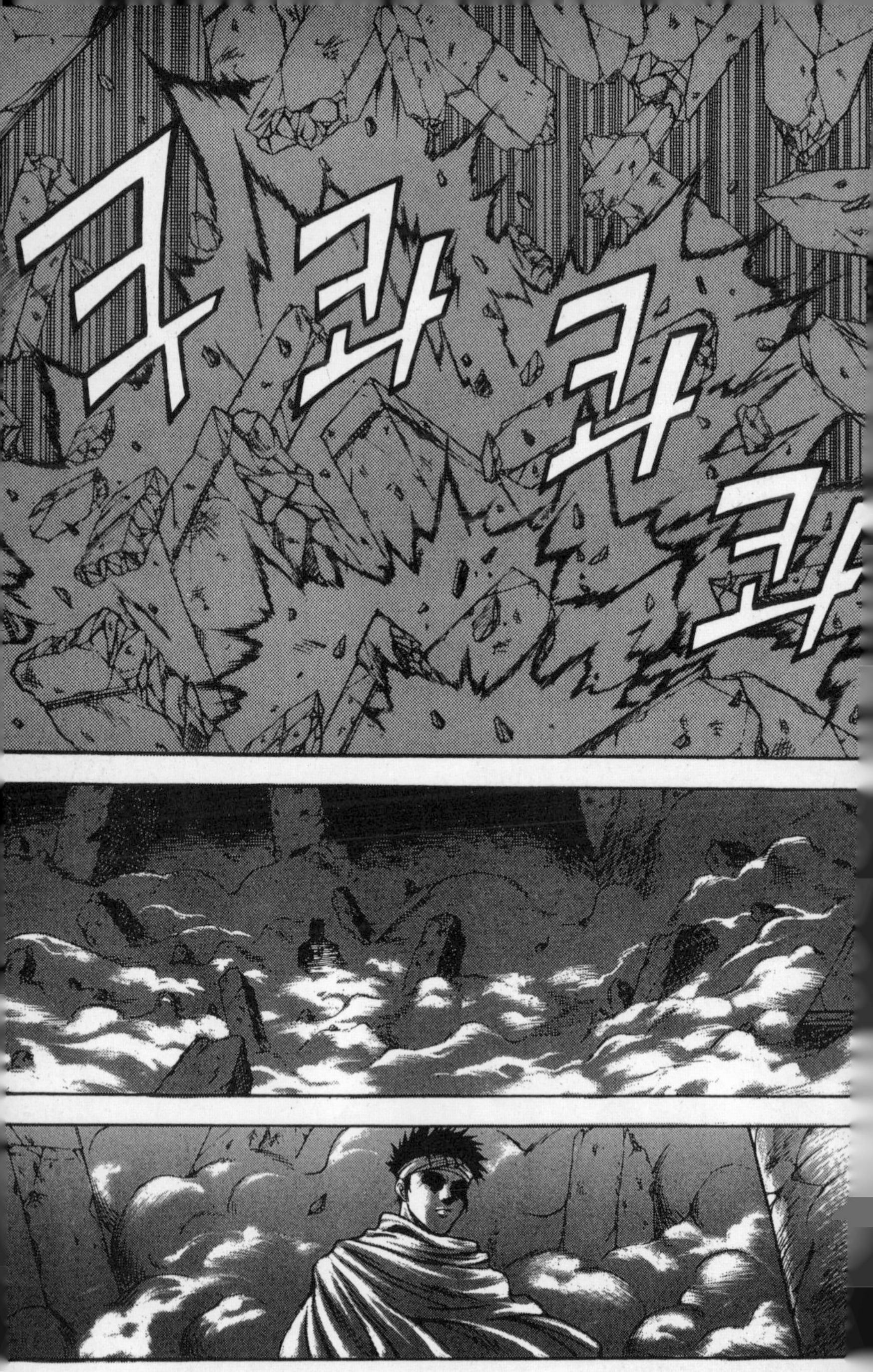
쿠콰콰콰

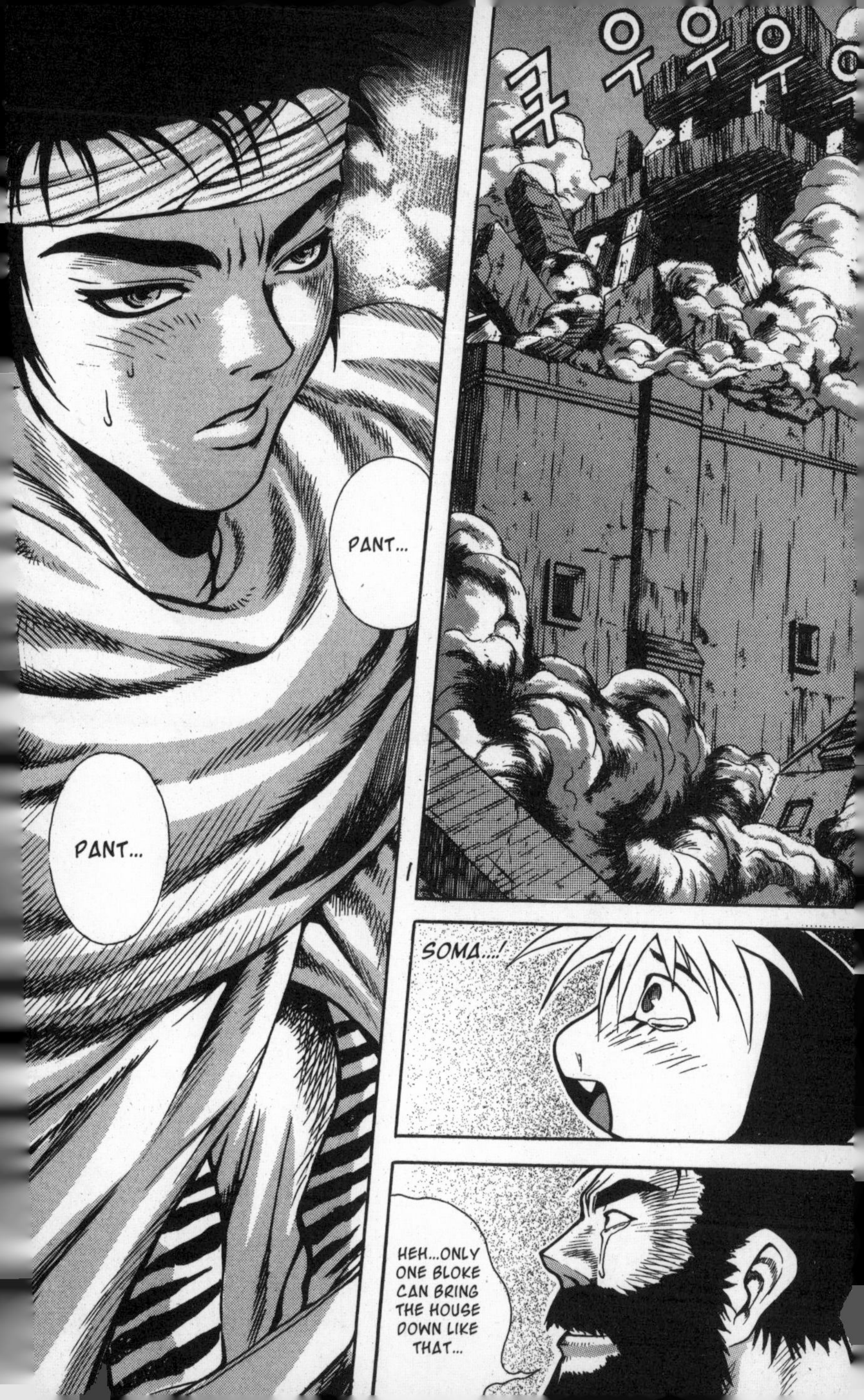
PANT...
PANT...
SOMA...!
HEH...ONLY ONE BLOKE CAN BRING THE HOUSE DOWN LIKE THAT...

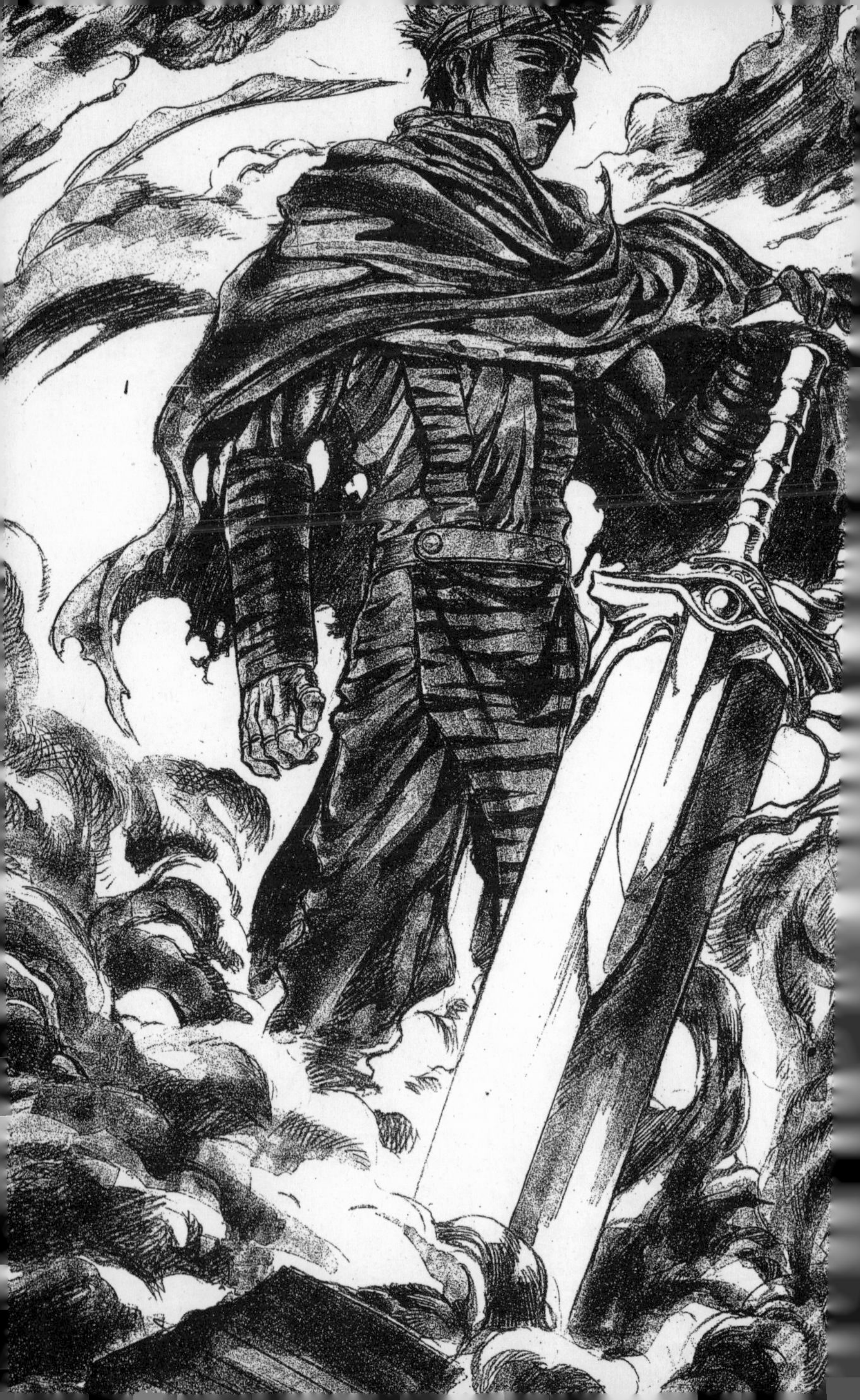

BLADE OF HEAVEN

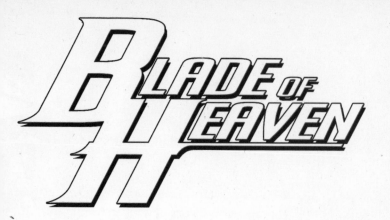

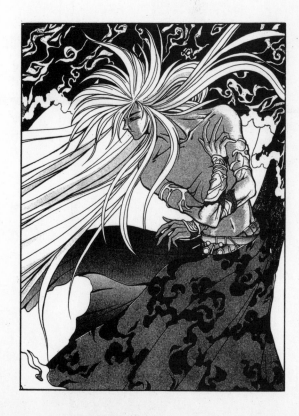

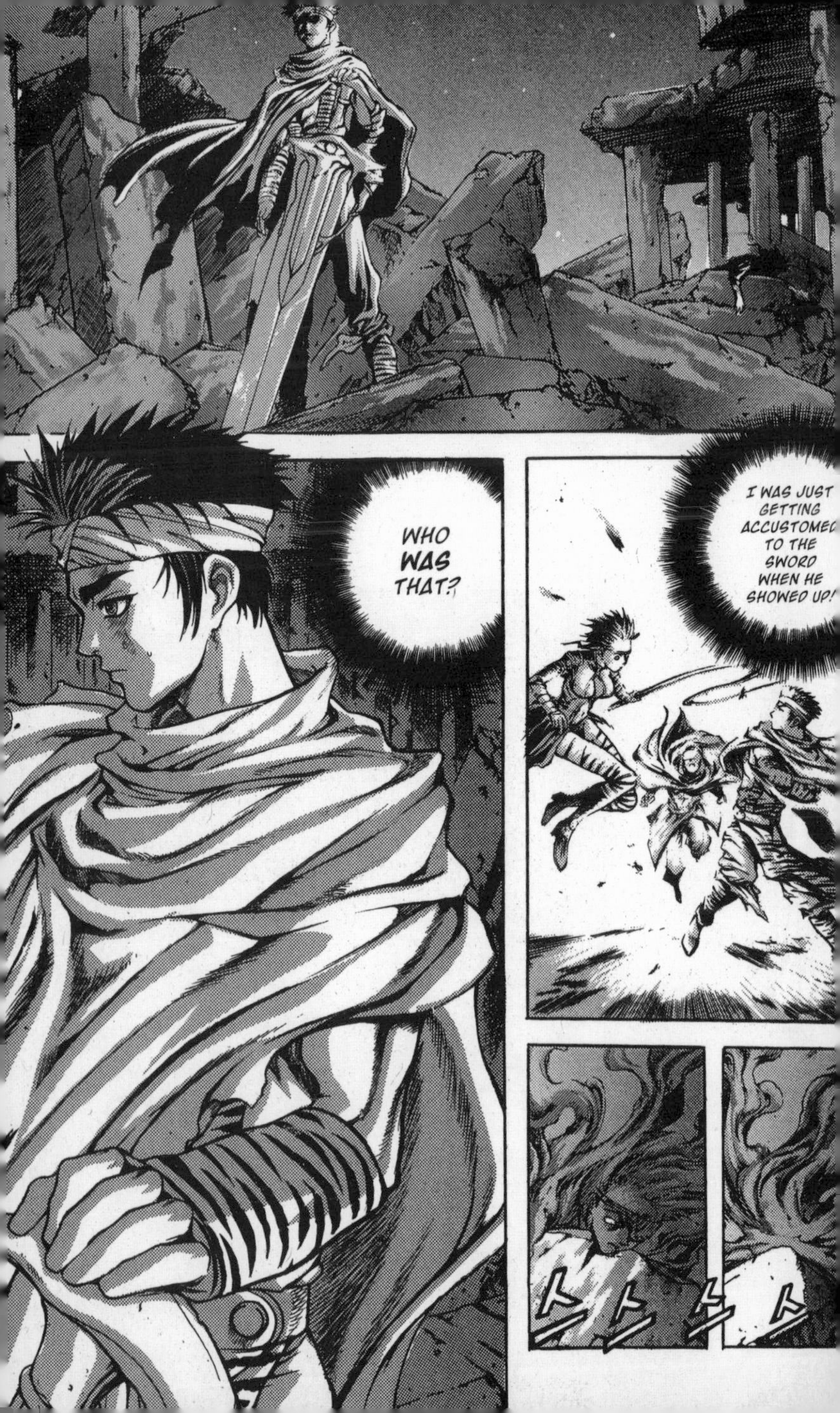
I WAS JUST GETTING ACCUSTOMED TO THE SWORD WHEN HE SHOWED UP!
WHO WAS THAT?

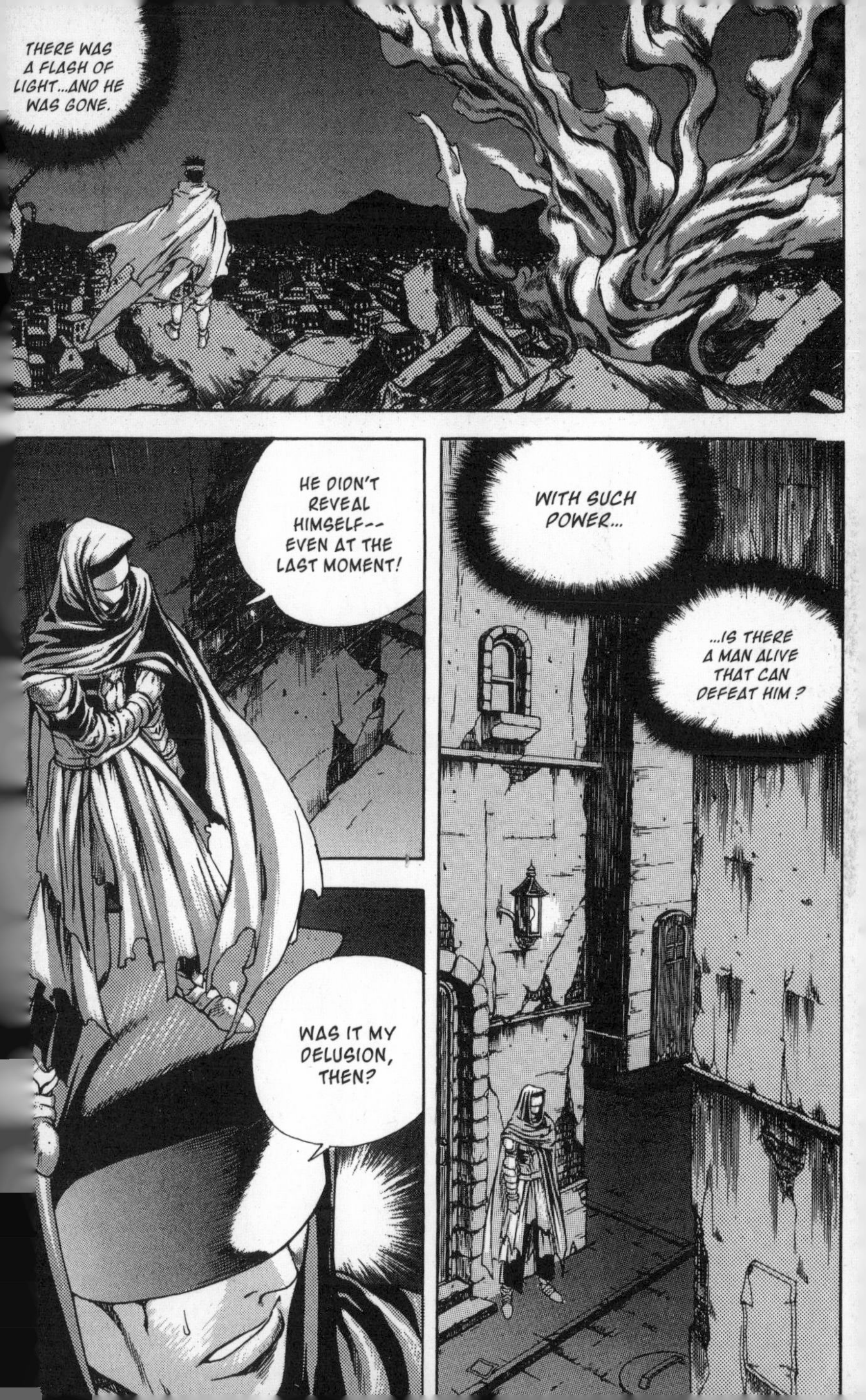
THERE WAS A FLASH OF LIGHT...AND HE WAS GONE.
WITH SUCH POWER...
...IS THERE A MAN ALIVE THAT CAN DEFEAT HIM ?
HE DIDN'T REVEAL HIMSELF--EVEN AT THE LAST MOMENT!
WAS IT MY DELUSION, THEN?

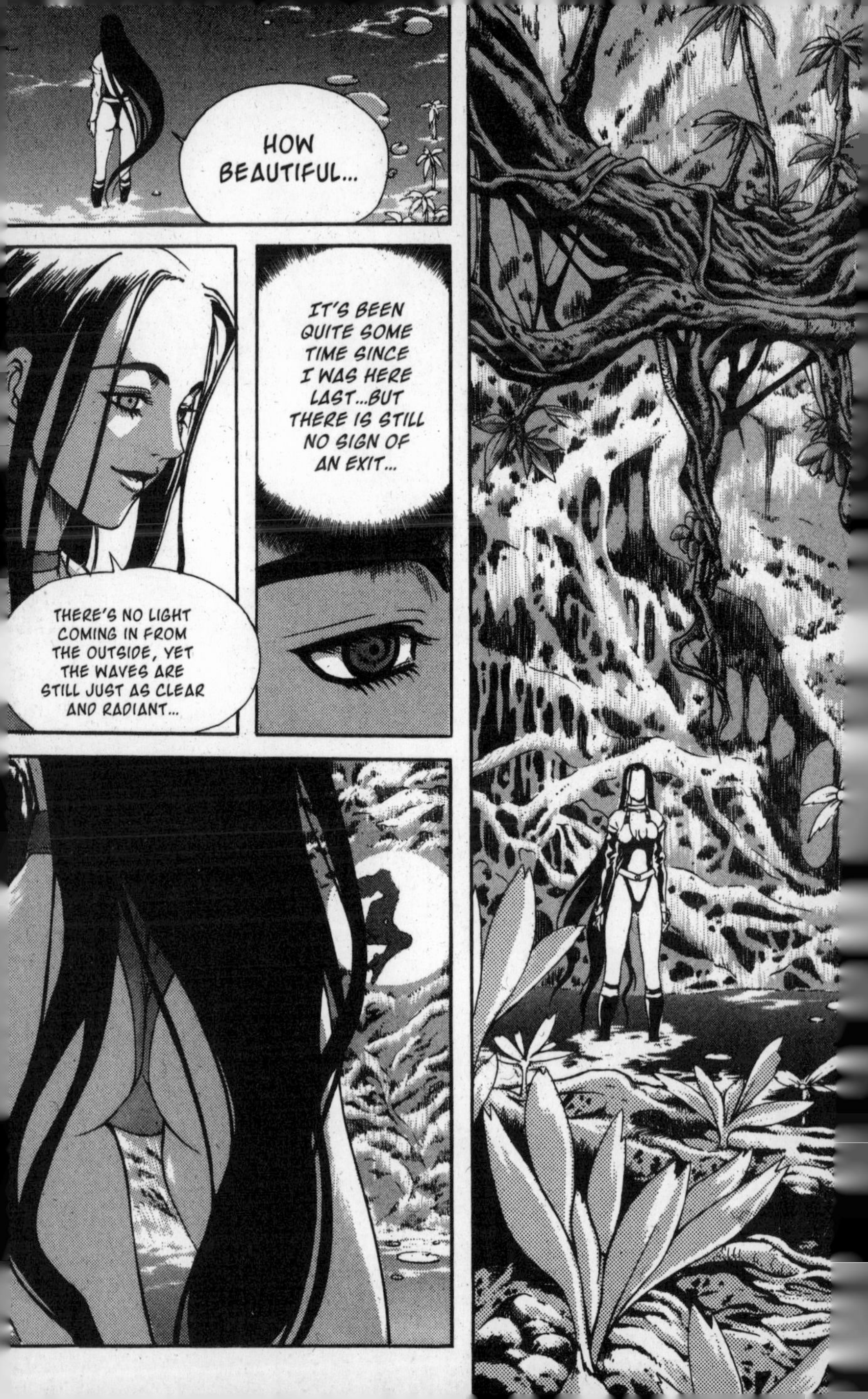
HOW BEAUTIFUL...
IT'S BEEN QUITE SOME TIME SINCE I WAS HERE LAST...BUT THERE IS STILL NO SIGN OF AN EXIT...
THERE'S NO LIGHT COMING IN FROM THE OUTSIDE, YET THE WAVES ARE STILL JUST AS CLEAR AND RADIANT...

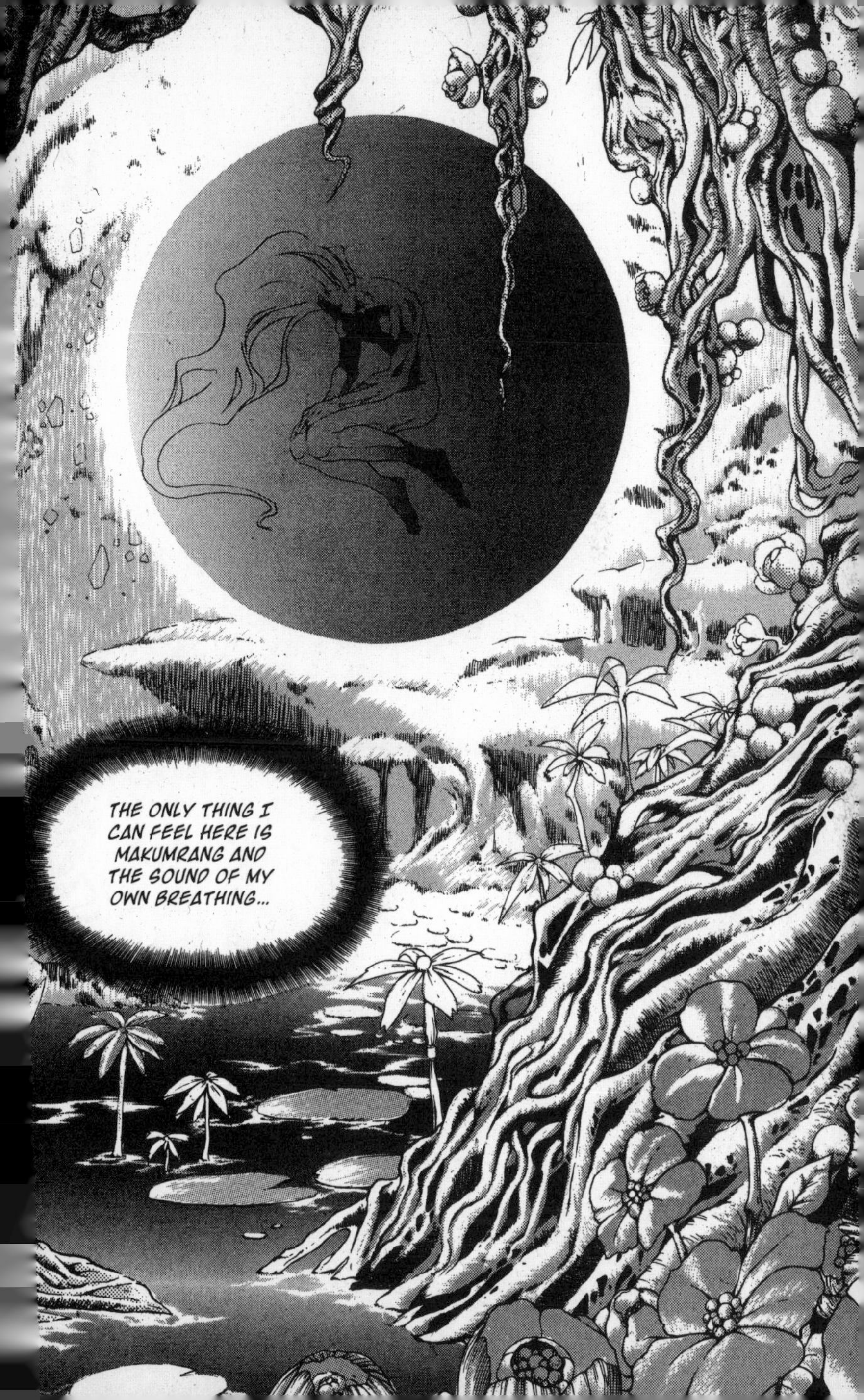
THE ONLY THING I CAN FEEL HERE IS MAKUMRANG AND THE SOUND OF MY OWN BREATHING...

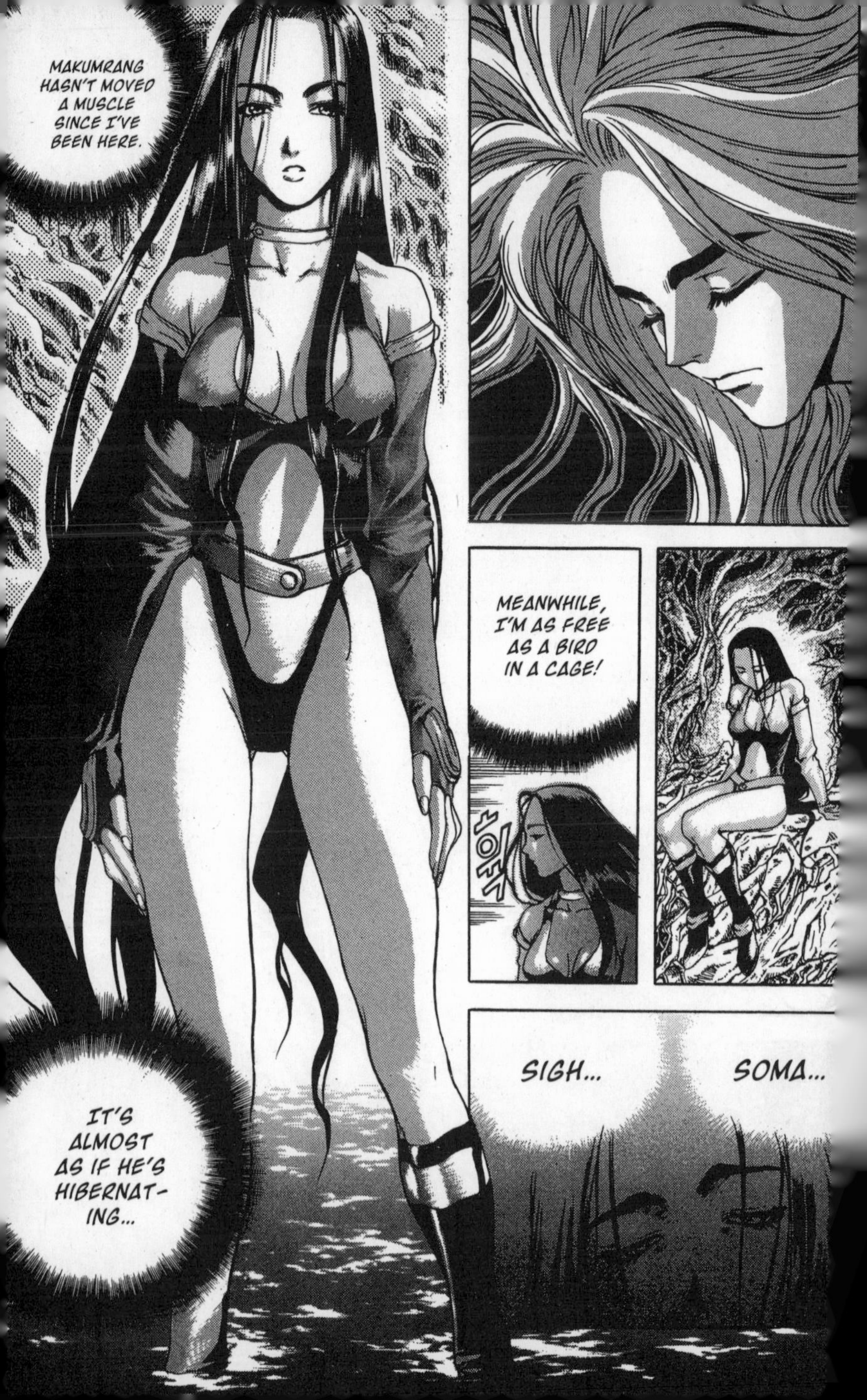
MAKUMRANG HASN'T MOVED A MUSCLE SINCE I'VE BEEN HERE.
IT'S ALMOST AS IF HE'S HIBERNAT-ING...
MEANWHILE, I'M AS FREE AS A BIRD IN A CAGE!
SIGH...
SOMA...

HOW I MISS YOU SO!

SQUAWK!

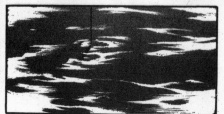

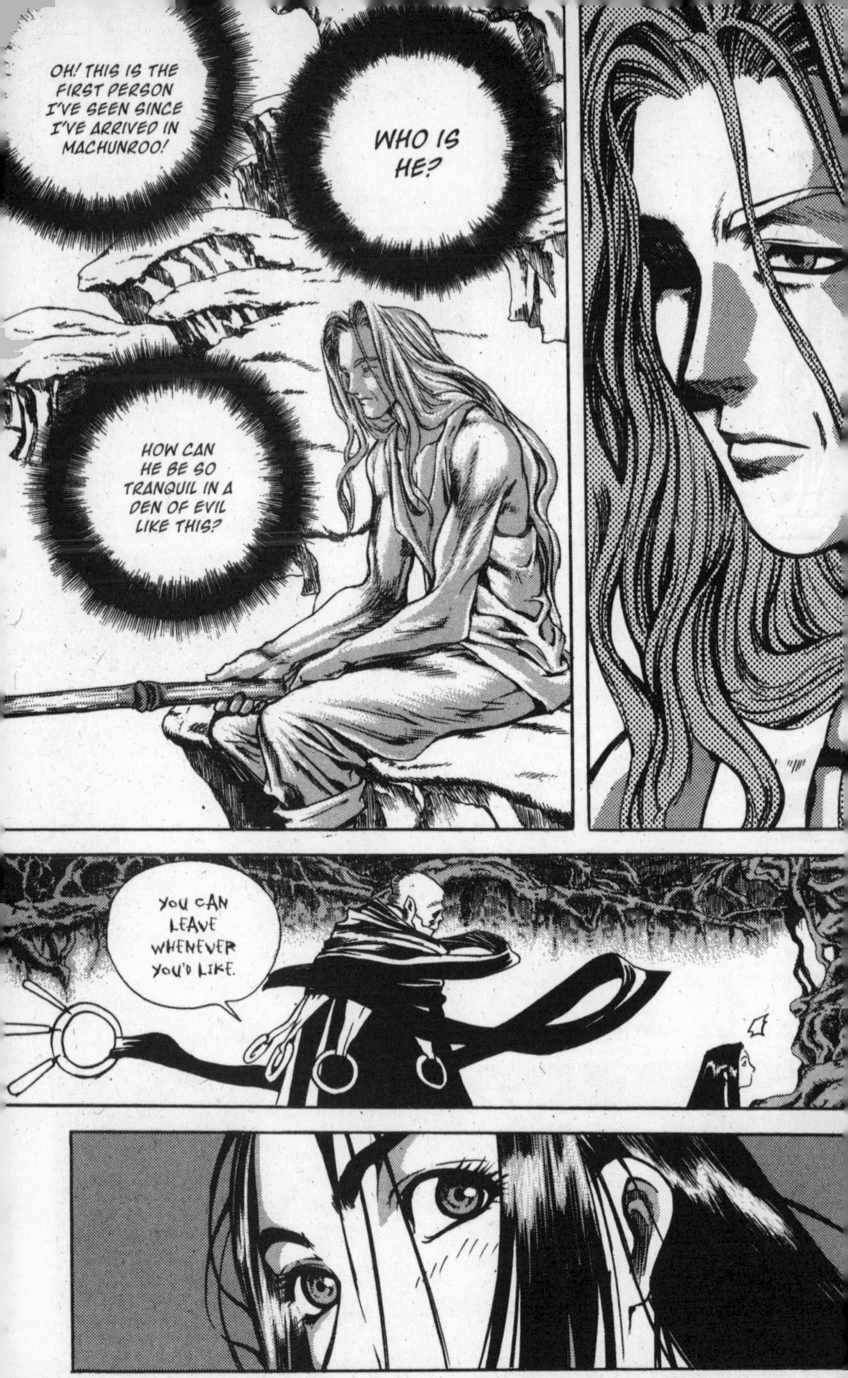
OH! THIS IS THE FIRST PERSON I'VE SEEN SINCE I'VE ARRIVED IN MACHUNROO!
WHO IS HE?
HOW CAN HE BE SO TRANQUIL IN A DEN OF EVIL LIKE THIS?
YOU CAN LEAVE WHENEVER YOU'D LIKE.

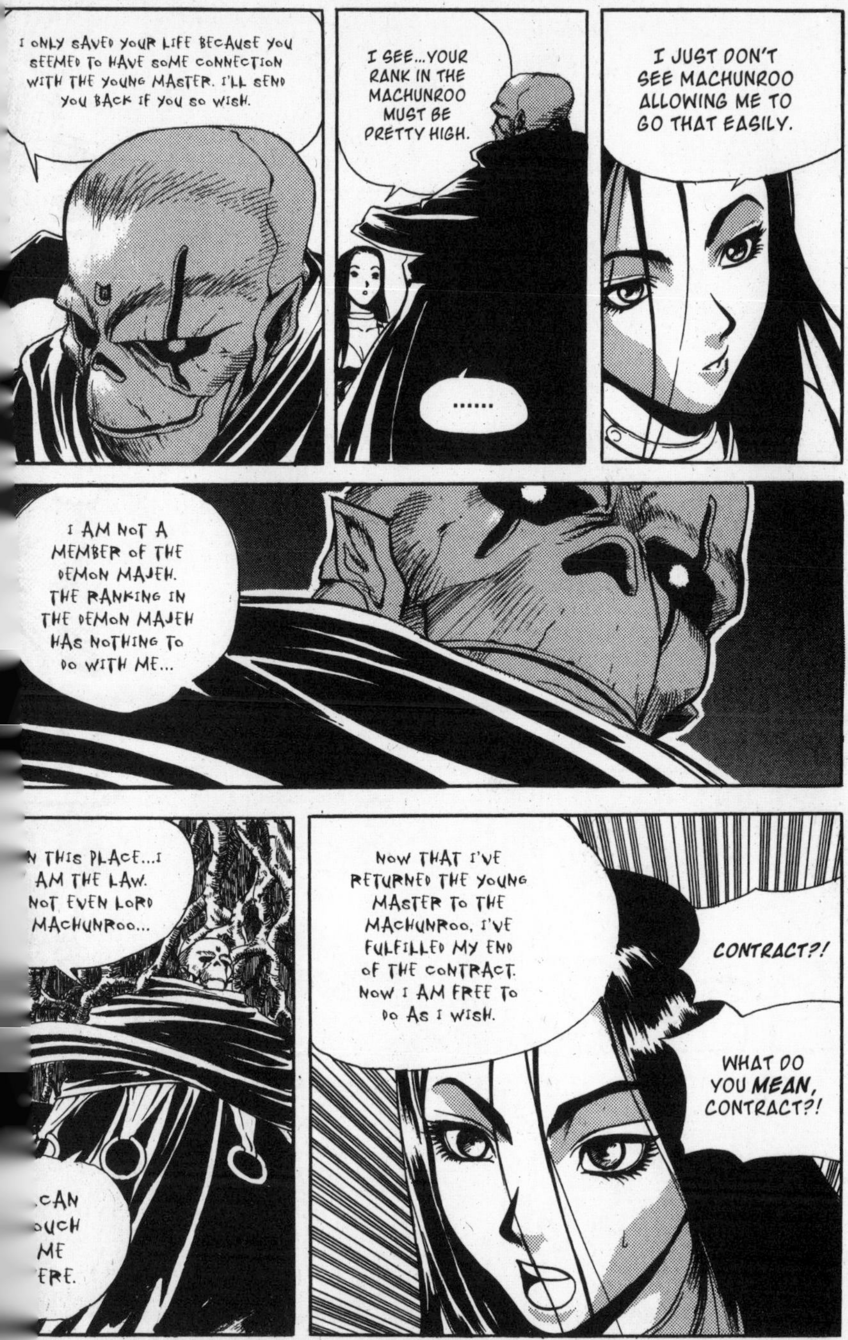
I ONLY SAVED YOUR LIFE BECAUSE YOU SEEMED TO HAVE SOME CONNECTION WITH THE YOUNG MASTER. I'LL SEND YOU BACK IF YOU SO WISH.
I SEE...YOUR RANK IN THE MACHUNROO MUST BE PRETTY HIGH.
......
I JUST DON'T SEE MACHUNROO ALLOWING ME TO GO THAT EASILY.
I AM NOT A MEMBER OF THE DEMON MAJEH. THE RANKING IN THE DEMON MAJEH HAS NOTHING TO DO WITH ME...
N THIS PLACE...I AM THE LAW. NOT EVEN LORD MACHUNROO...
.CAN OUCH ME ERE.
NOW THAT I'VE RETURNED THE YOUNG MASTER TO THE MACHUNROO, I'VE FULFILLED MY END OF THE CONTRACT. NOW I AM FREE TO DO AS I WISH.
CONTRACT?!
WHAT DO YOU MEAN, CONTRACT?!

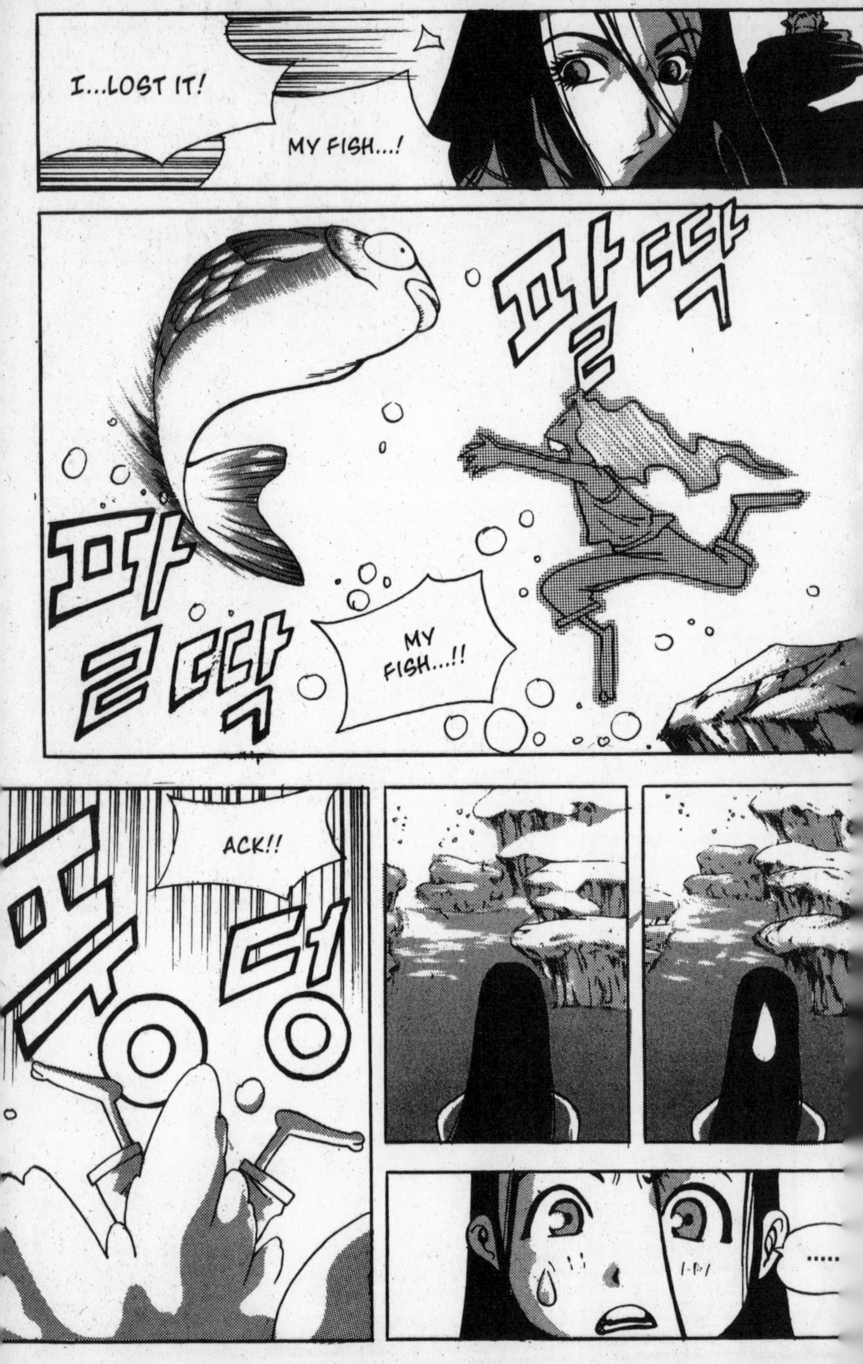
I...LOST IT!
MY FISH...!
팔딱
팔딱
MY FISH...!!
ACK!!
.....

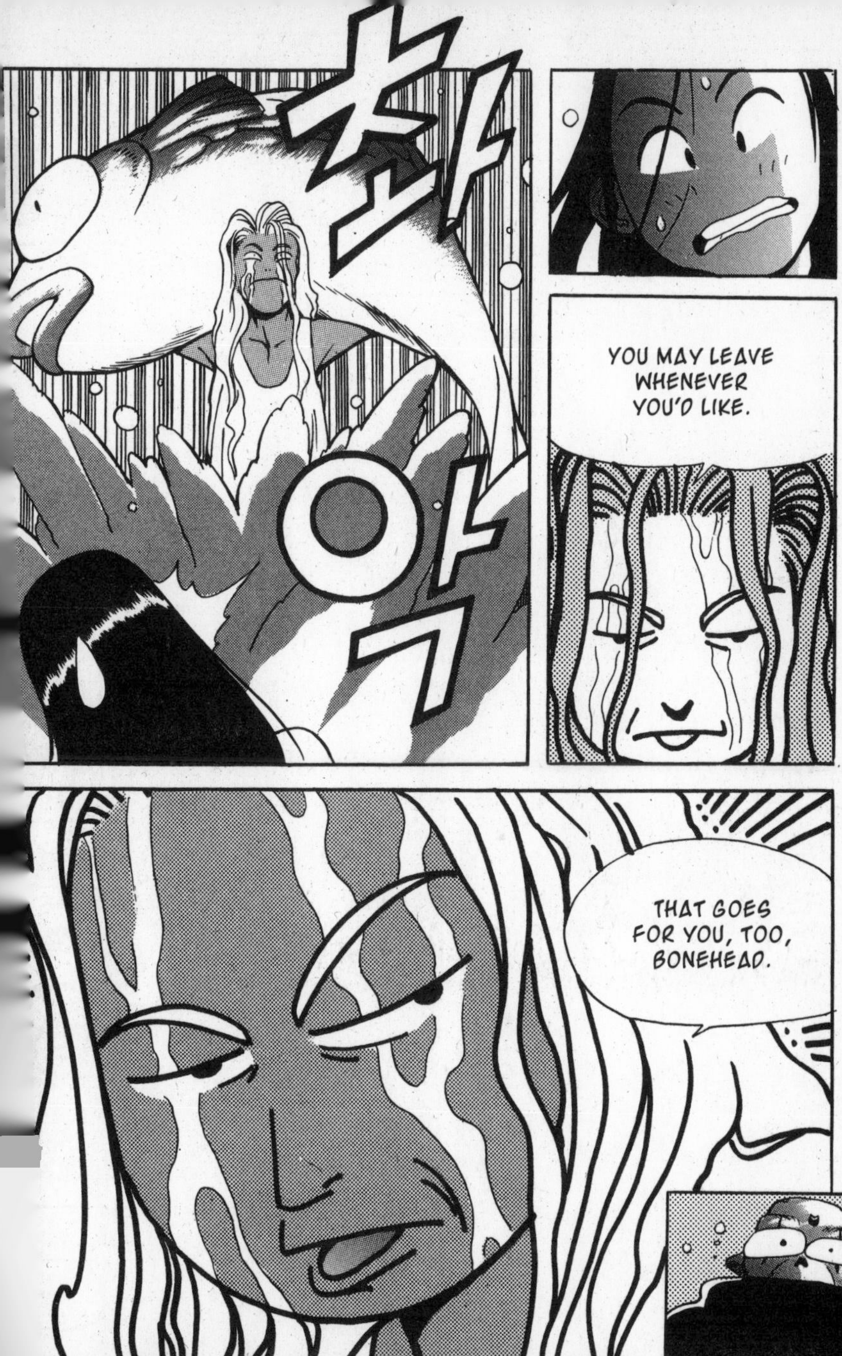
YOU MAY LEAVE WHENEVER YOU'D LIKE.
THAT GOES FOR YOU, TOO, BONEHEAD.

YOU'RE RIGHT... AS LONG AS YOU'VE KEPT YOUR PROMISE TO ME, YOUR CONTRACT IS COMPLETE.

HA HA HA... HIS SELF-CONFIDENCE IS THE SAME NOW AS IT WAS BEFORE!

WHO IS THAT WEIRDO...?

WHAT'S SO FUNNY?

HEH HEH...

THE QUEEREST FELLOW IN THE DEMON MAJEH...

HE IS THE LORD OF THE MACHUNRO

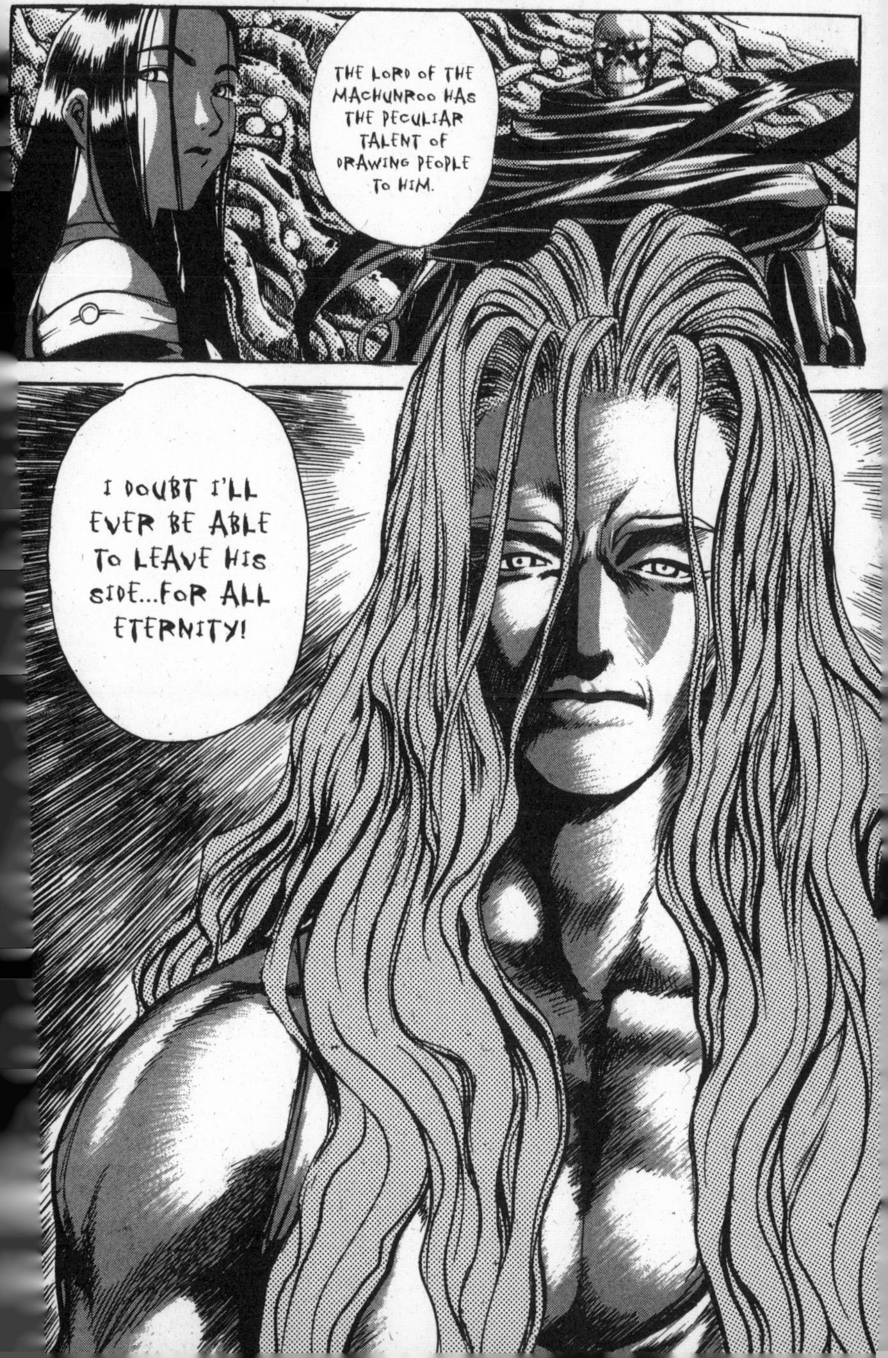
THE LORD OF THE MACHUNROO HAS THE PECULIAR TALENT OF DRAWING PEOPLE TO HIM.
I DOUBT I'LL EVER BE ABLE TO LEAVE HIS SIDE...FOR ALL ETERNITY!

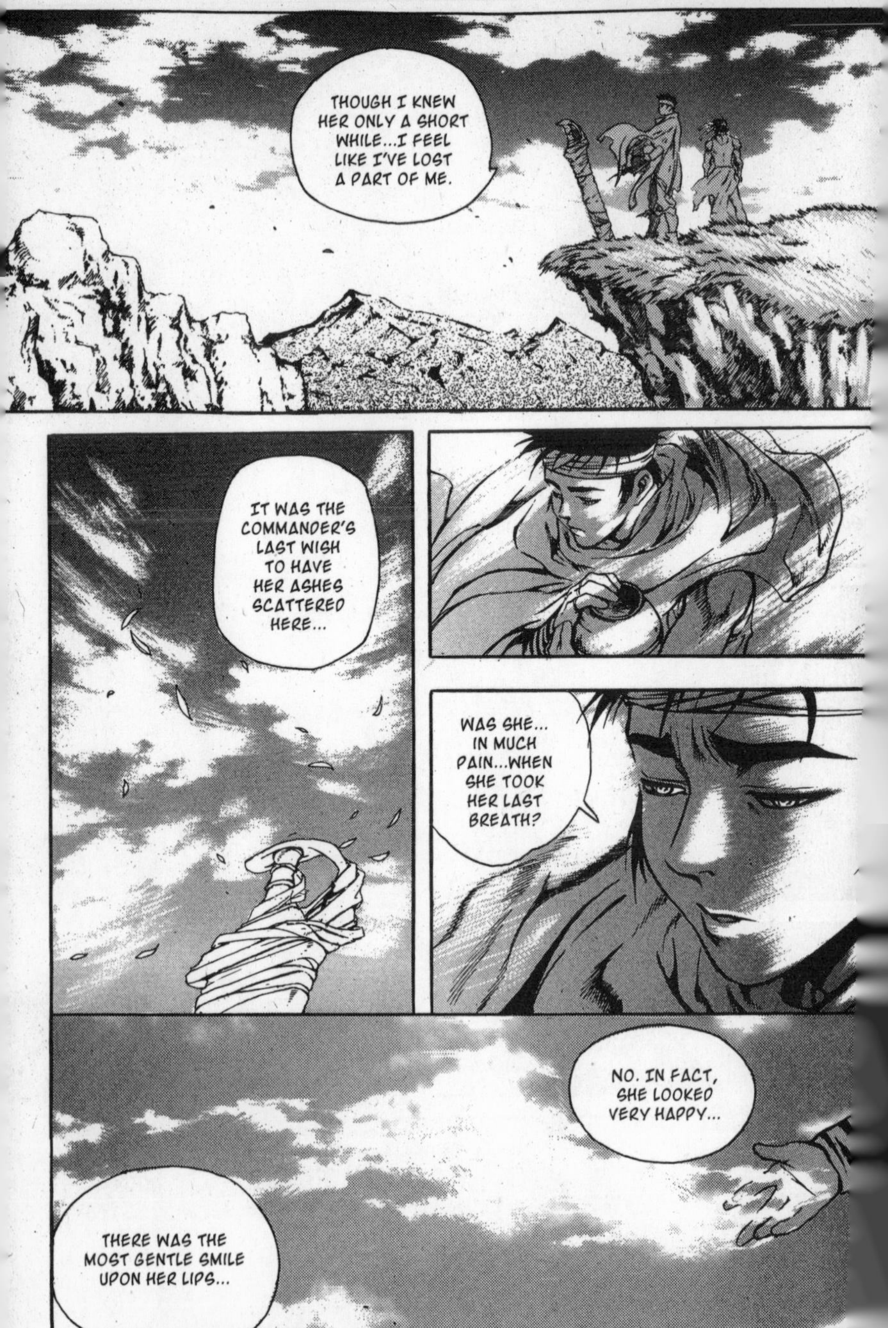
THOUGH I KNEW HER ONLY A SHORT WHILE...I FEEL LIKE I'VE LOST A PART OF ME.
IT WAS THE COMMANDER'S LAST WISH TO HAVE HER ASHES SCATTERED HERE...
WAS SHE... IN MUCH PAIN...WHEN SHE TOOK HER LAST BREATH?
NO. IN FACT, SHE LOOKED VERY HAPPY...
THERE WAS THE MOST GENTLE SMILE UPON HER LIPS...

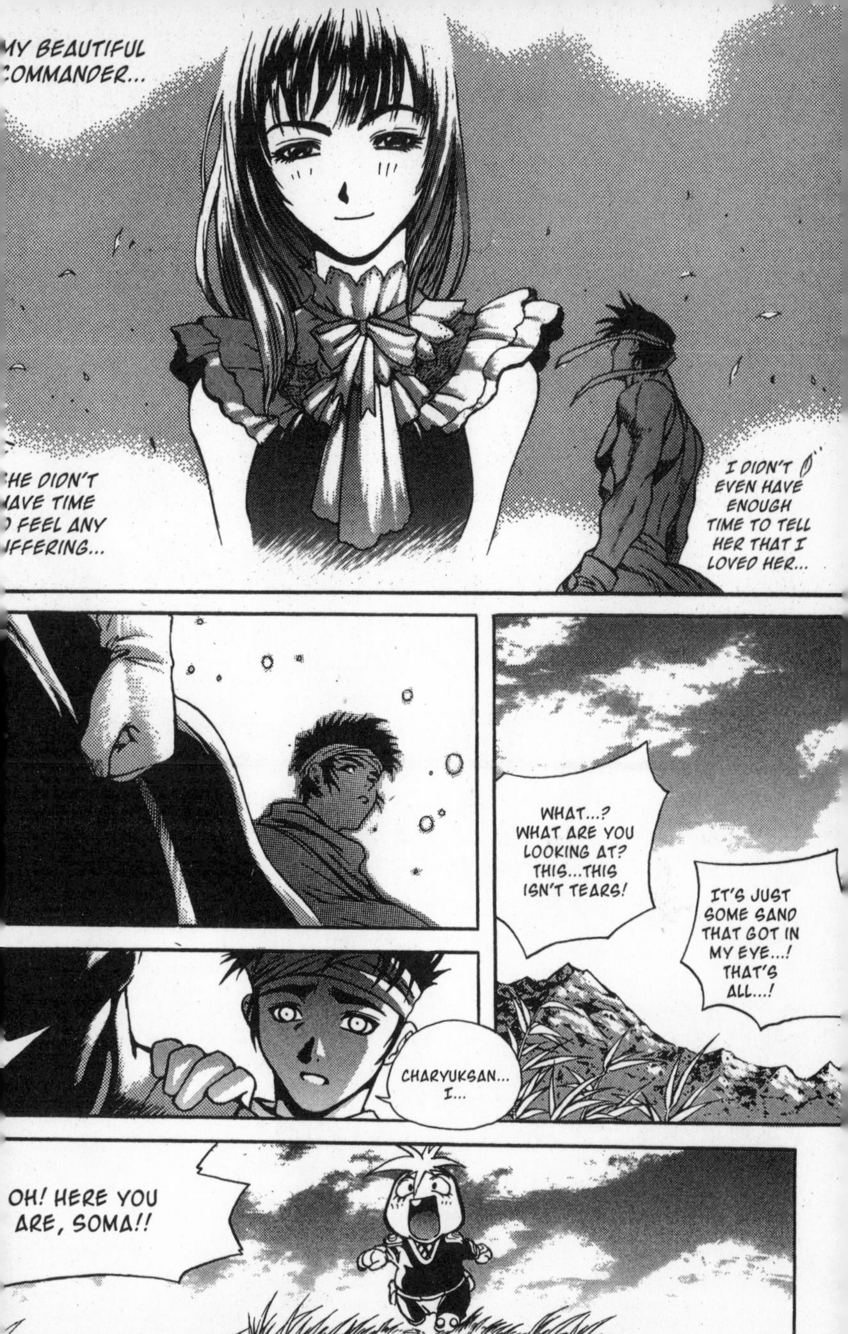
MY BEAUTIFUL
COMMANDER...
HE DIDN'T
HAVE TIME
O FEEL ANY
UFFERING...
I DIDN'T EVEN HAVE ENOUGH TIME TO TELL HER THAT I LOVED HER...
WHAT...? WHAT ARE YOU LOOKING AT? THIS...THIS ISN'T TEARS!
IT'S JUST SOME SAND THAT GOT IN MY EYE...! THAT'S ALL...!
CHARYUKSAN... I...
OH! HERE YOU ARE, SOMA!!

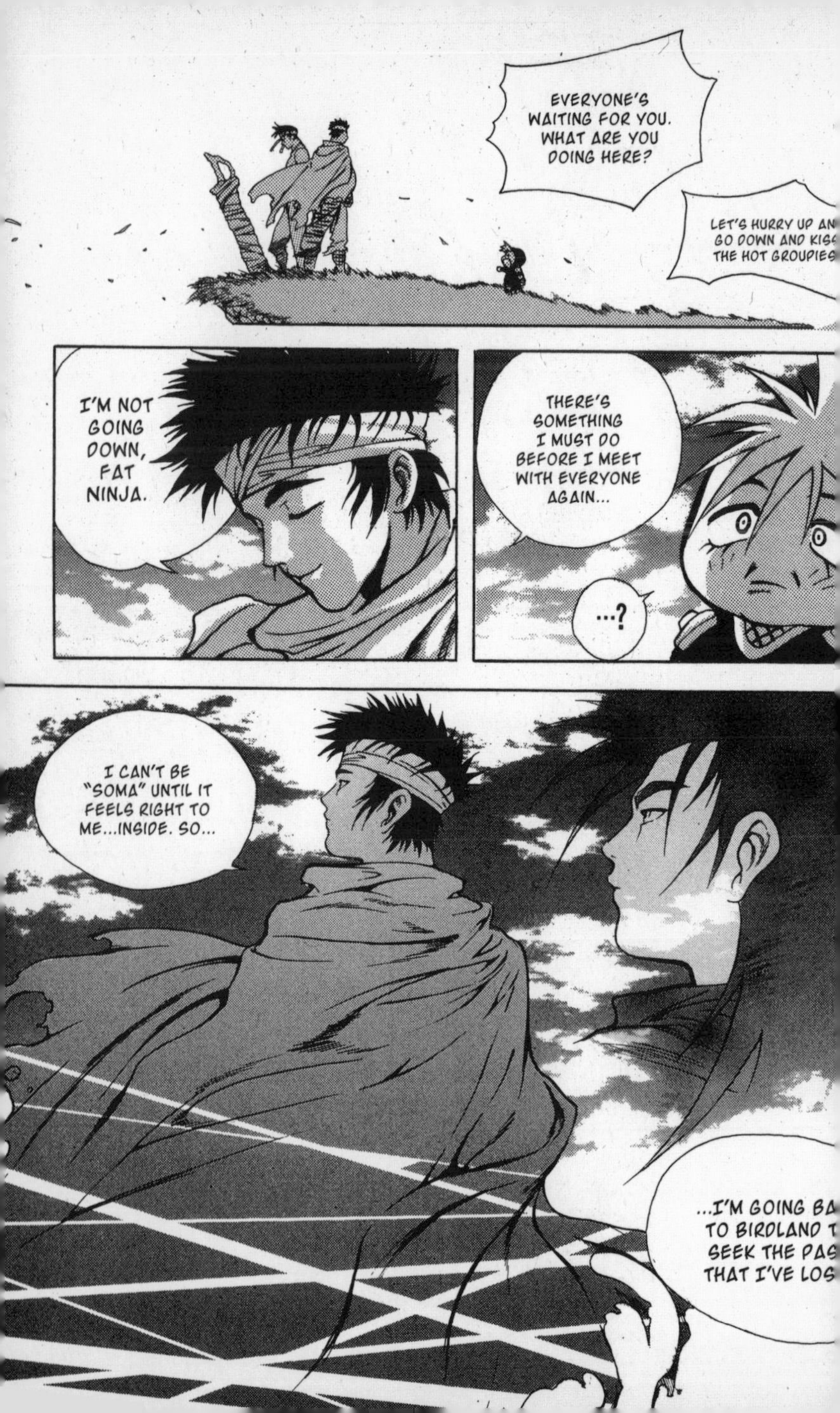
EVERYONE'S WAITING FOR YOU. WHAT ARE YOU DOING HERE?
LET'S HURRY UP AN GO DOWN AND KISS THE HOT GROUPIES
I'M NOT GOING DOWN, FAT NINJA.
THERE'S SOMETHING I MUST DO BEFORE I MEET WITH EVERYONE AGAIN...
...?
I CAN'T BE "SOMA" UNTIL IT FEELS RIGHT TO ME...INSIDE. SO...
...I'M GOING BA TO BIRDLAND T SEEK THE PAS THAT I'VE LOS

BLADE OF HEAVEN

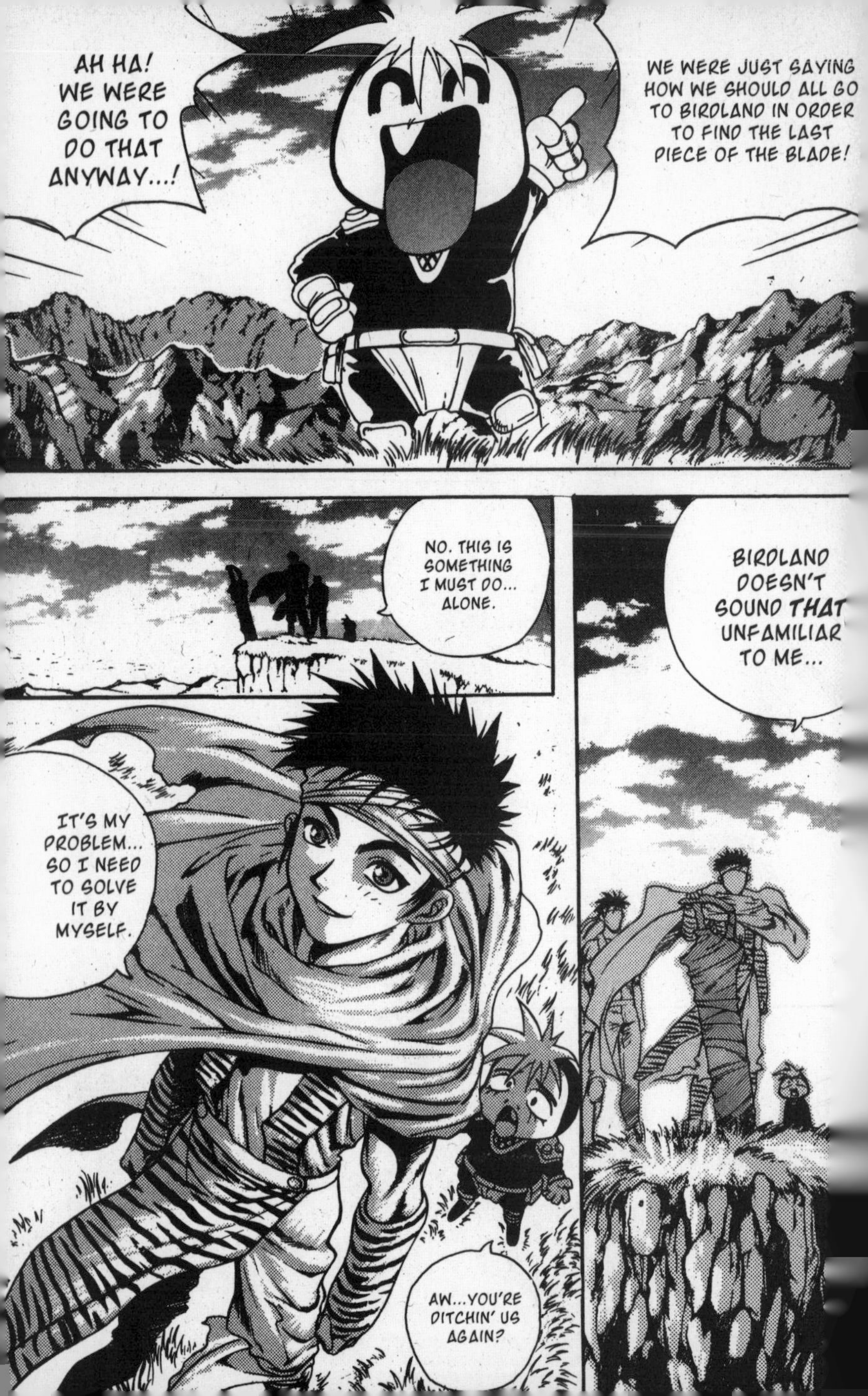
AH HA! WE WERE GOING TO DO THAT ANYWAY...!
WE WERE JUST SAYING HOW WE SHOULD ALL GO TO BIRDLAND IN ORDER TO FIND THE LAST PIECE OF THE BLADE!
NO. THIS IS SOMETHING I MUST DO... ALONE.
IT'S MY PROBLEM... SO I NEED TO SOLVE IT BY MYSELF.
AW...YOU'RE DITCHIN' US AGAIN?
BIRDLAND DOESN'T SOUND THAT UNFAMILIAR TO ME...

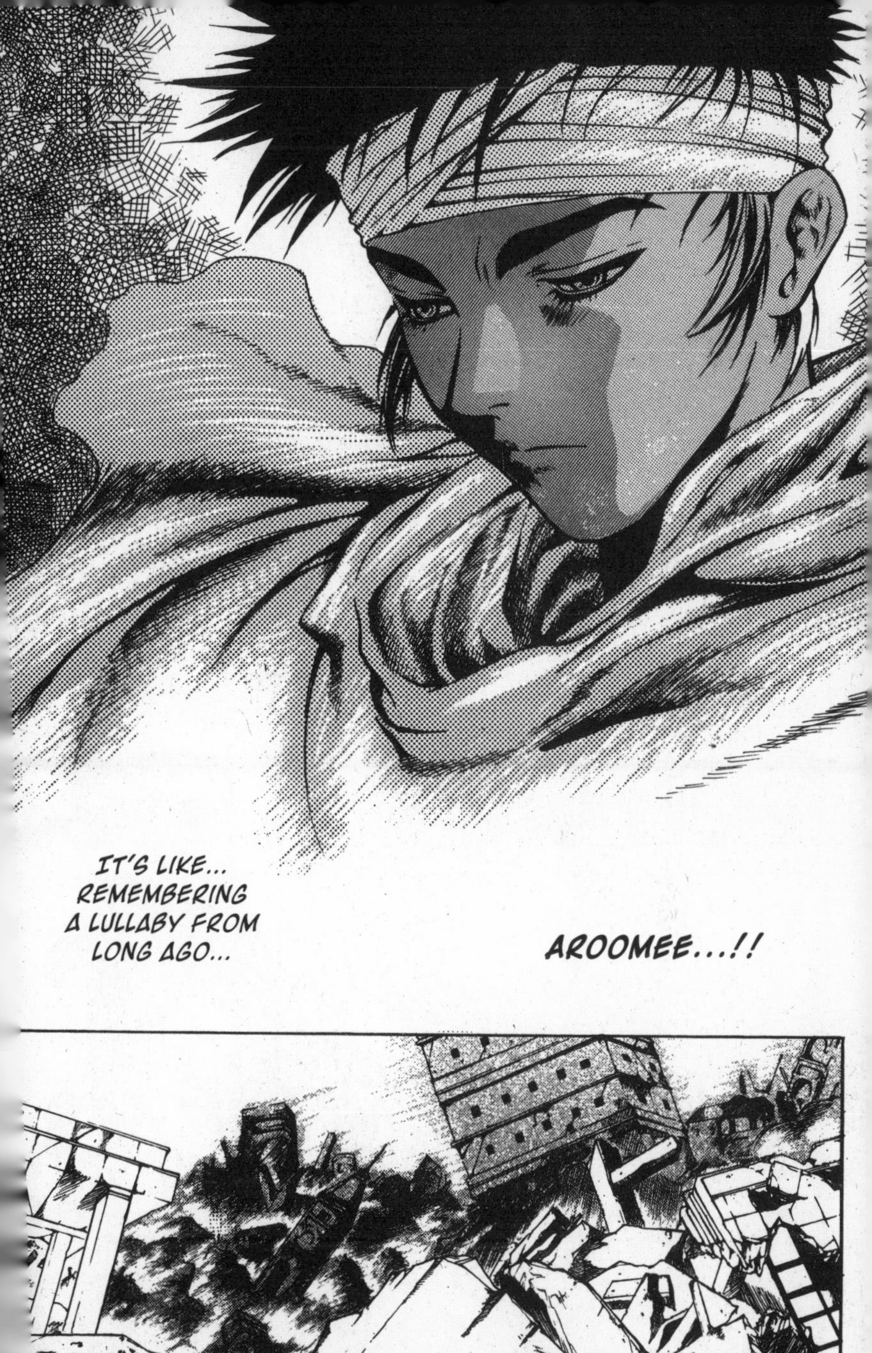

IT'S LIKE... REMEMBERING A LULLABY FROM LONG AGO...
AROOMEE...!!

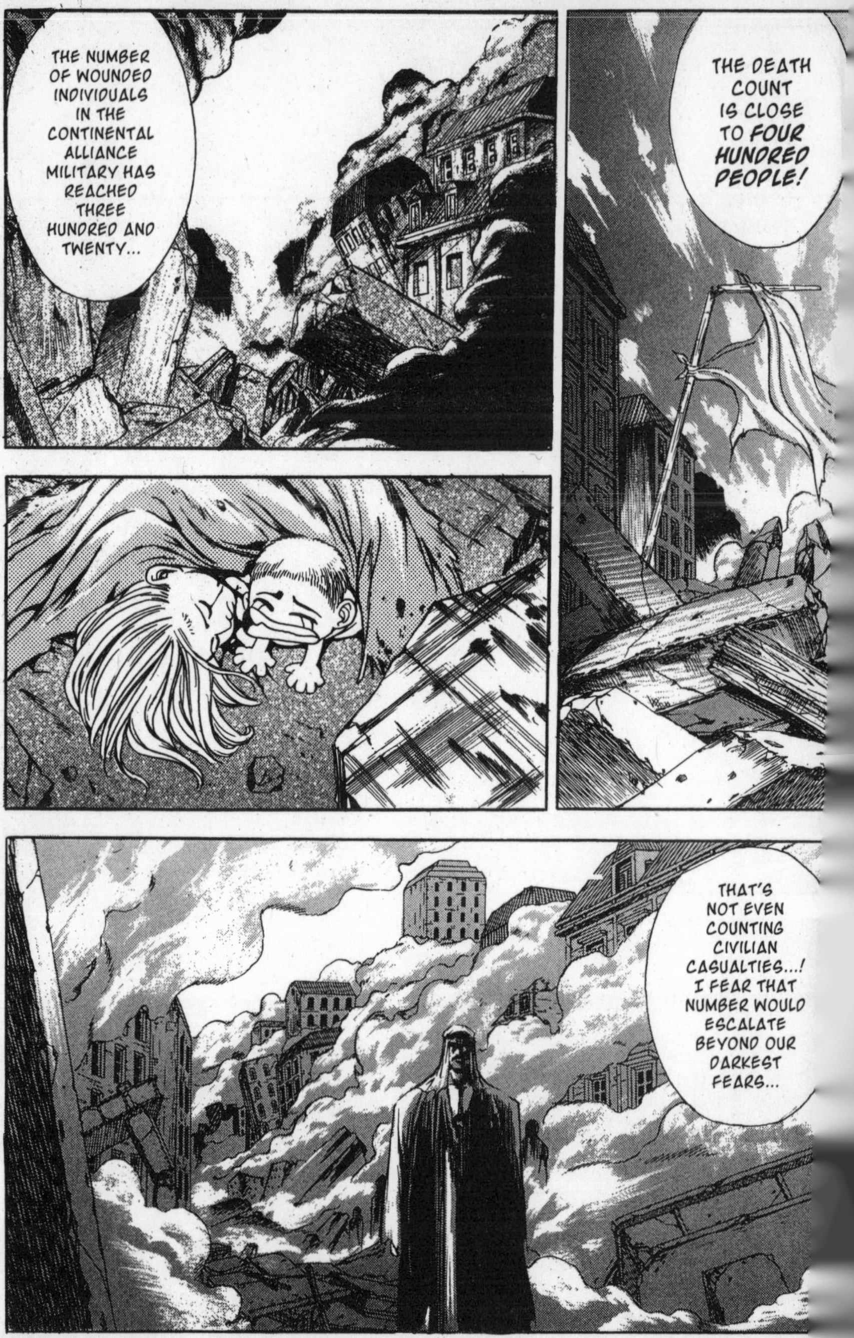
THE NUMBER OF WOUNDED INDIVIDUALS IN THE CONTINENTAL ALLIANCE MILITARY HAS REACHED THREE HUNDRED AND TWENTY...
THE DEATH COUNT IS CLOSE TO FOUR HUNDRED PEOPLE!
THAT'S NOT EVEN COUNTING CIVILIAN CASUALTIES...! I FEAR THAT NUMBER WOULD ESCALATE BEYOND OUR DARKEST FEARS...

MOST OF THE REMAINING ENEMIES HAVE BEEN PUT TO DEATH...THOUGH THE MAJORITY OF THEM WERE HUMANS...

PWAH HA HA HA!! IN ORDER TO ACHIEVE GREATNESS, A GREAT SACRIFICE IS OFTEN NECESSARY!

I'VE LOST ABOUT FORTY OF MY MEN-- BUT AS A LEADER I MUST TAKE THAT LOSS IN STRIDE!

I'M SORRY, MY CHILD...

I'M SORRY FOR NOT BEING ABLE TO PROTECT YOUR PARENTS...

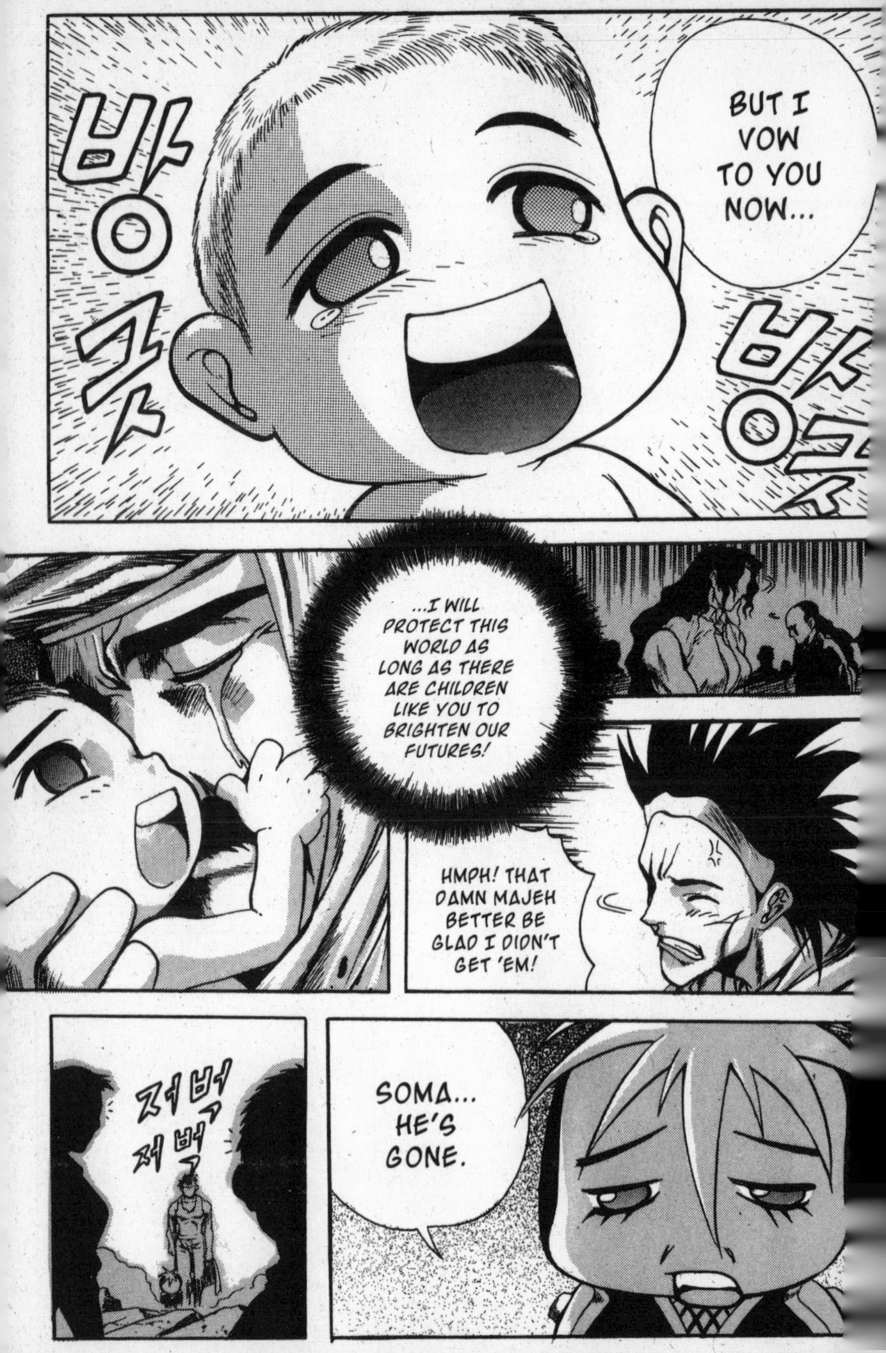
방긋
BUT I VOW TO YOU NOW...
방긋
...I WILL PROTECT THIS WORLD AS LONG AS THERE ARE CHILDREN LIKE YOU TO BRIGHTEN OUR FUTURES!
HMPH! THAT DAMN MAJEH BETTER BE GLAD I DIDN'T GET 'EM!
저벅
저벅
SOMA... HE'S GONE.

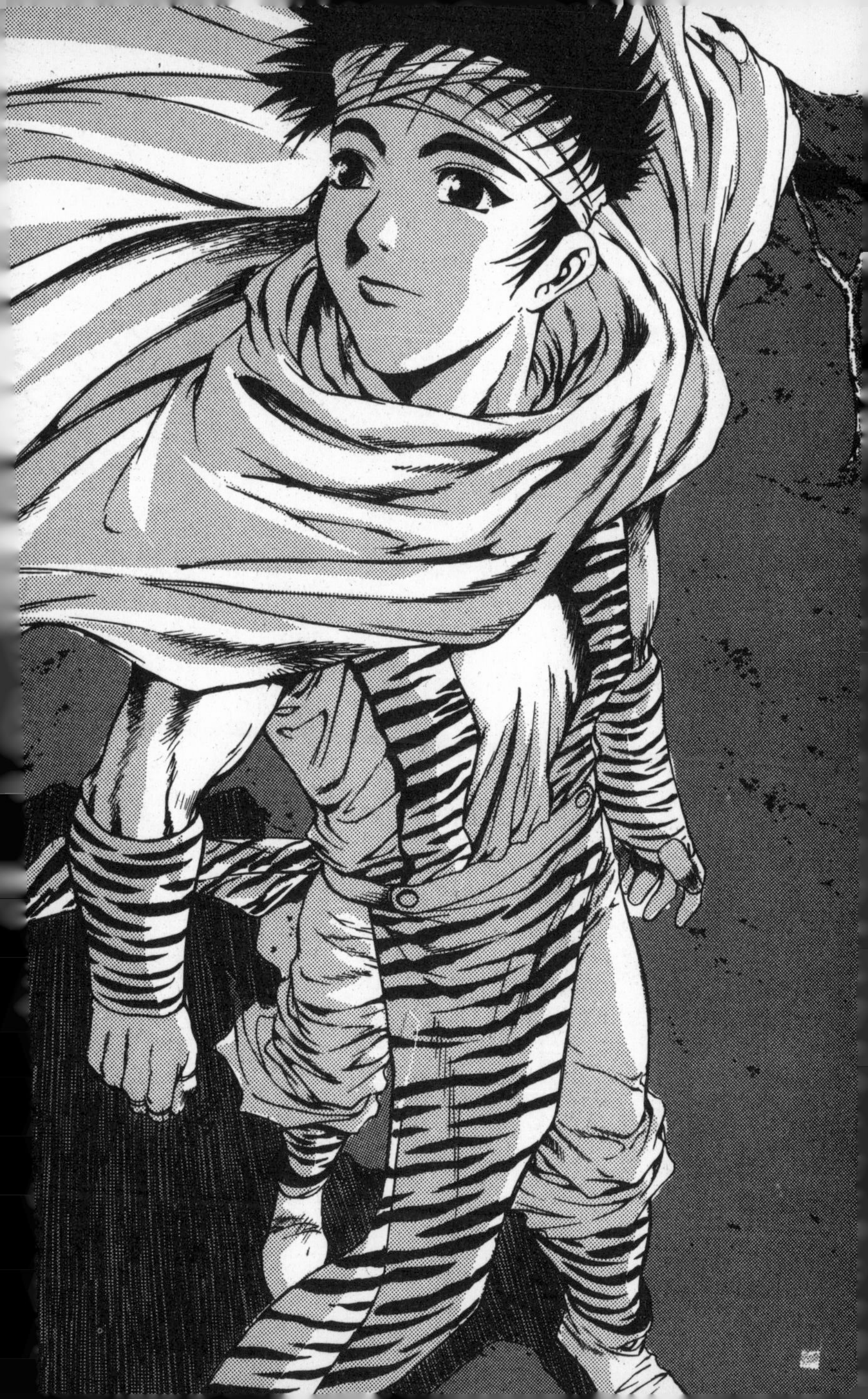

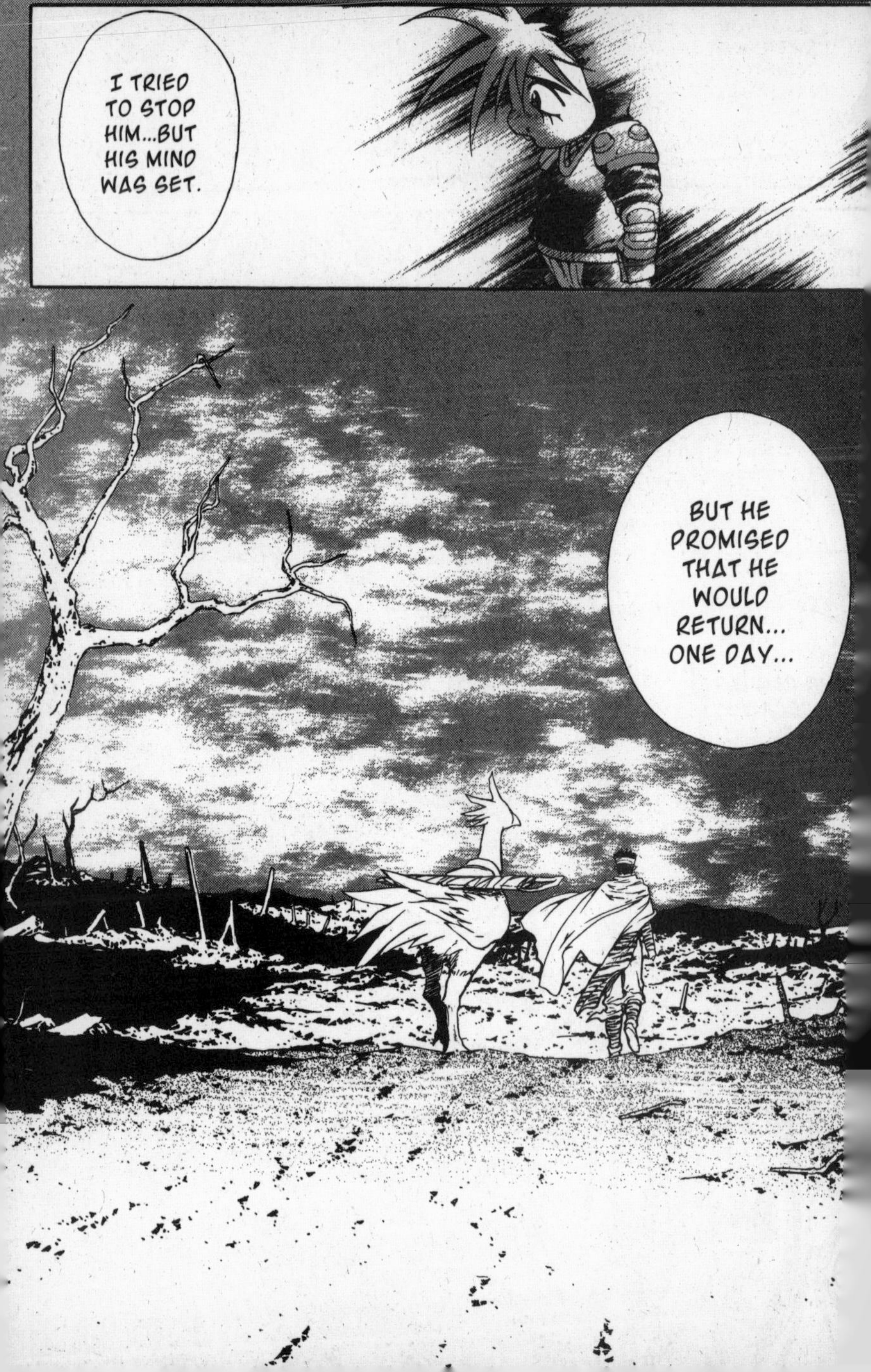
I TRIED TO STOP HIM...BUT HIS MIND WAS SET.
BUT HE PROMISED THAT HE WOULD RETURN... ONE DAY...

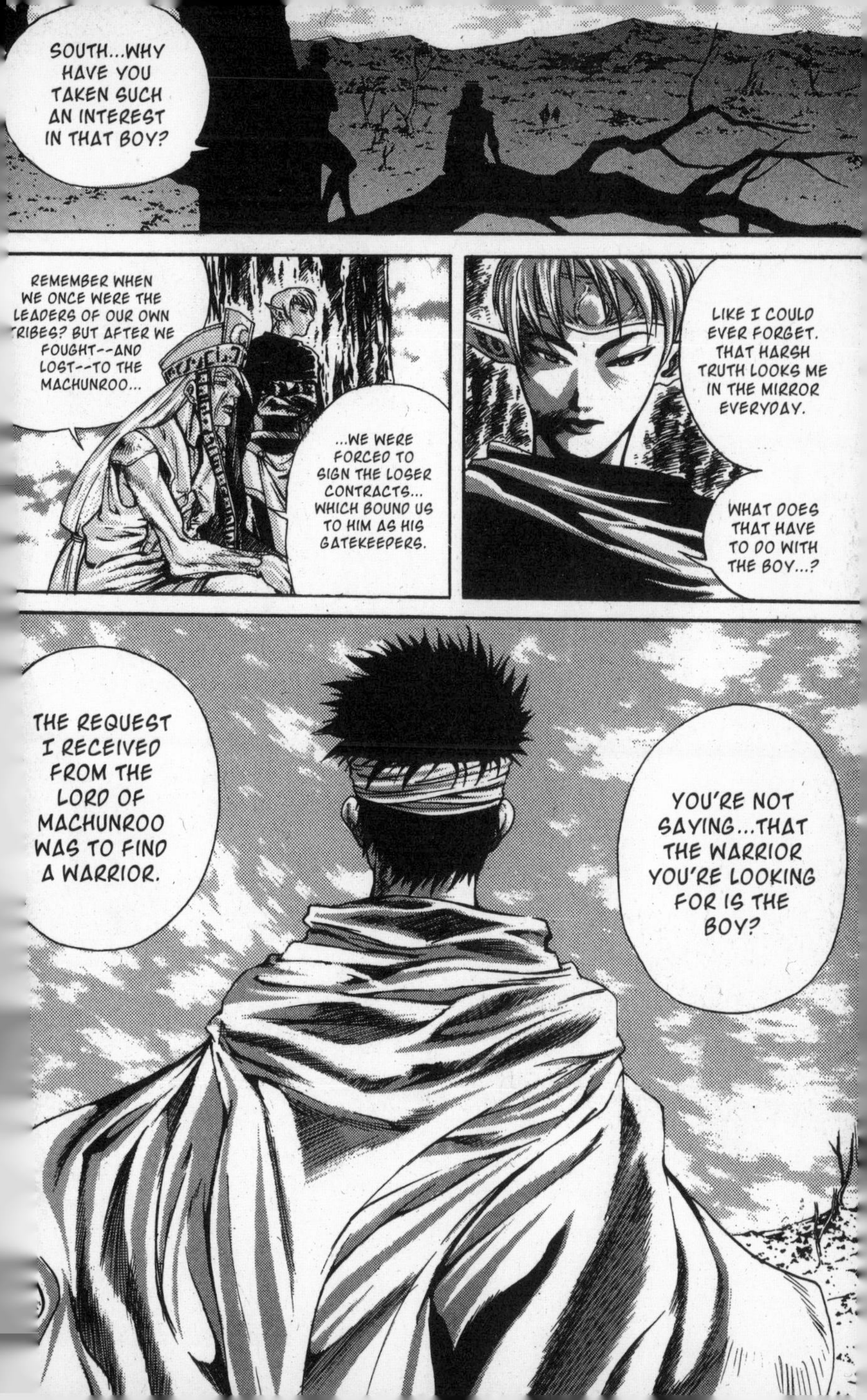
SOUTH...WHY HAVE YOU TAKEN SUCH AN INTEREST IN THAT BOY?
REMEMBER WHEN WE ONCE WERE THE LEADERS OF OUR OWN TRIBES? BUT AFTER WE FOUGHT--AND LOST--TO THE MACHUNROO...
...WE WERE FORCED TO SIGN THE LOSER CONTRACTS... WHICH BOUND US TO HIM AS HIS GATEKEEPERS.
LIKE I COULD EVER FORGET. THAT HARSH TRUTH LOOKS ME IN THE MIRROR EVERYDAY.
WHAT DOES THAT HAVE TO DO WITH THE BOY...?
THE REQUEST I RECEIVED FROM THE LORD OF MACHUNROO WAS TO FIND A WARRIOR.
YOU'RE NOT SAYING...THAT THE WARRIOR YOU'RE LOOKING FOR IS THE BOY?

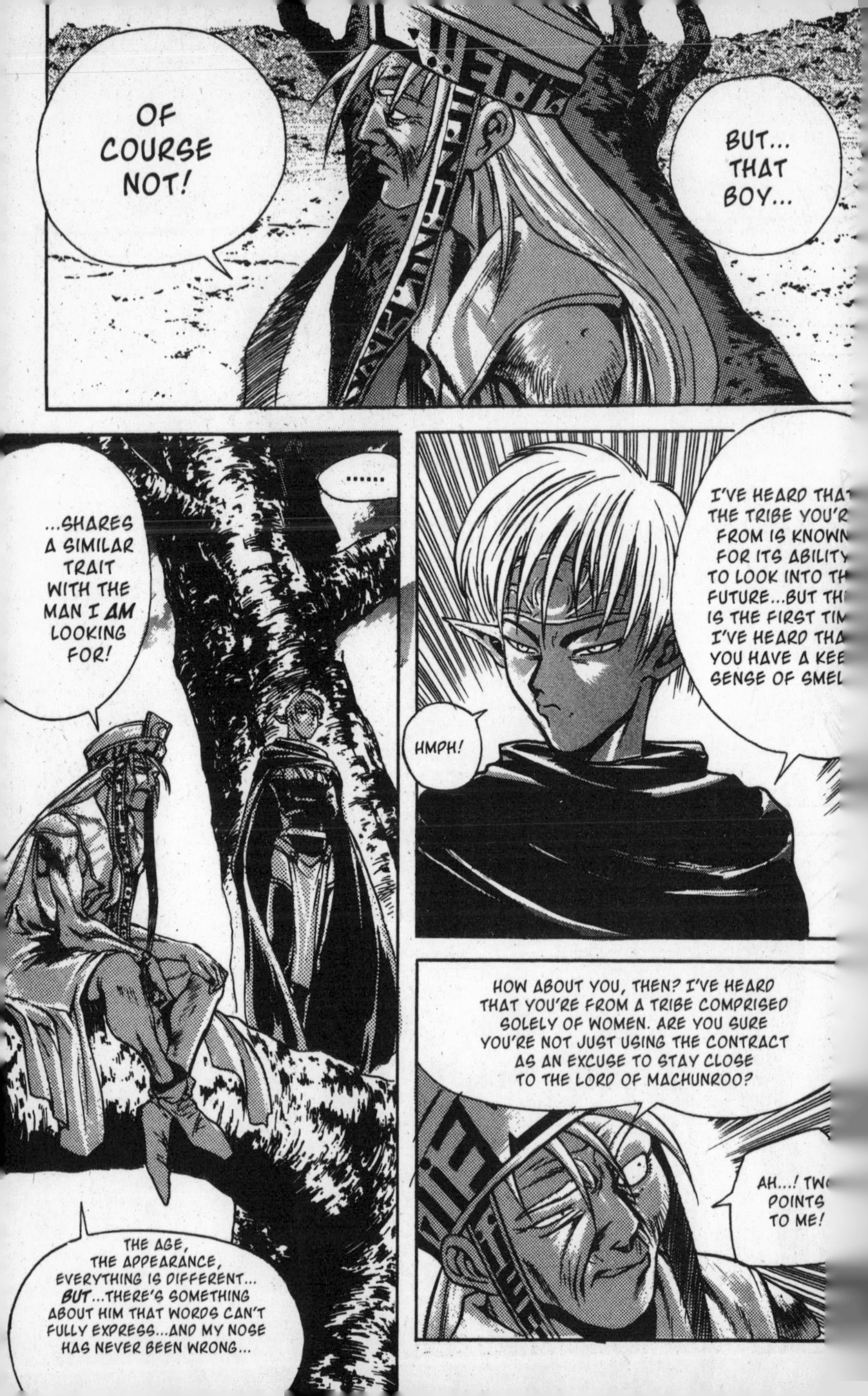

OF COURSE NOT!
BUT... THAT BOY...
...SHARES A SIMILAR TRAIT WITH THE MAN I **AM** LOOKING FOR!
......
I'VE HEARD THAT THE TRIBE YOU'R FROM IS KNOWN FOR ITS ABILITY TO LOOK INTO TH FUTURE...BUT TH IS THE FIRST TIM I'VE HEARD THA YOU HAVE A KEE SENSE OF SMEL
HMPH!
THE AGE, THE APPEARANCE, EVERYTHING IS DIFFERENT... **BUT**...THERE'S SOMETHING ABOUT HIM THAT WORDS CAN'T FULLY EXPRESS...AND MY NOSE HAS NEVER BEEN WRONG...
HOW ABOUT YOU, THEN? I'VE HEARD THAT YOU'RE FROM A TRIBE COMPRISED SOLELY OF WOMEN. ARE YOU SURE YOU'RE NOT JUST USING THE CONTRACT AS AN EXCUSE TO STAY CLOSE TO THE LORD OF MACHUNROO?
AH...! TW POINTS TO ME!

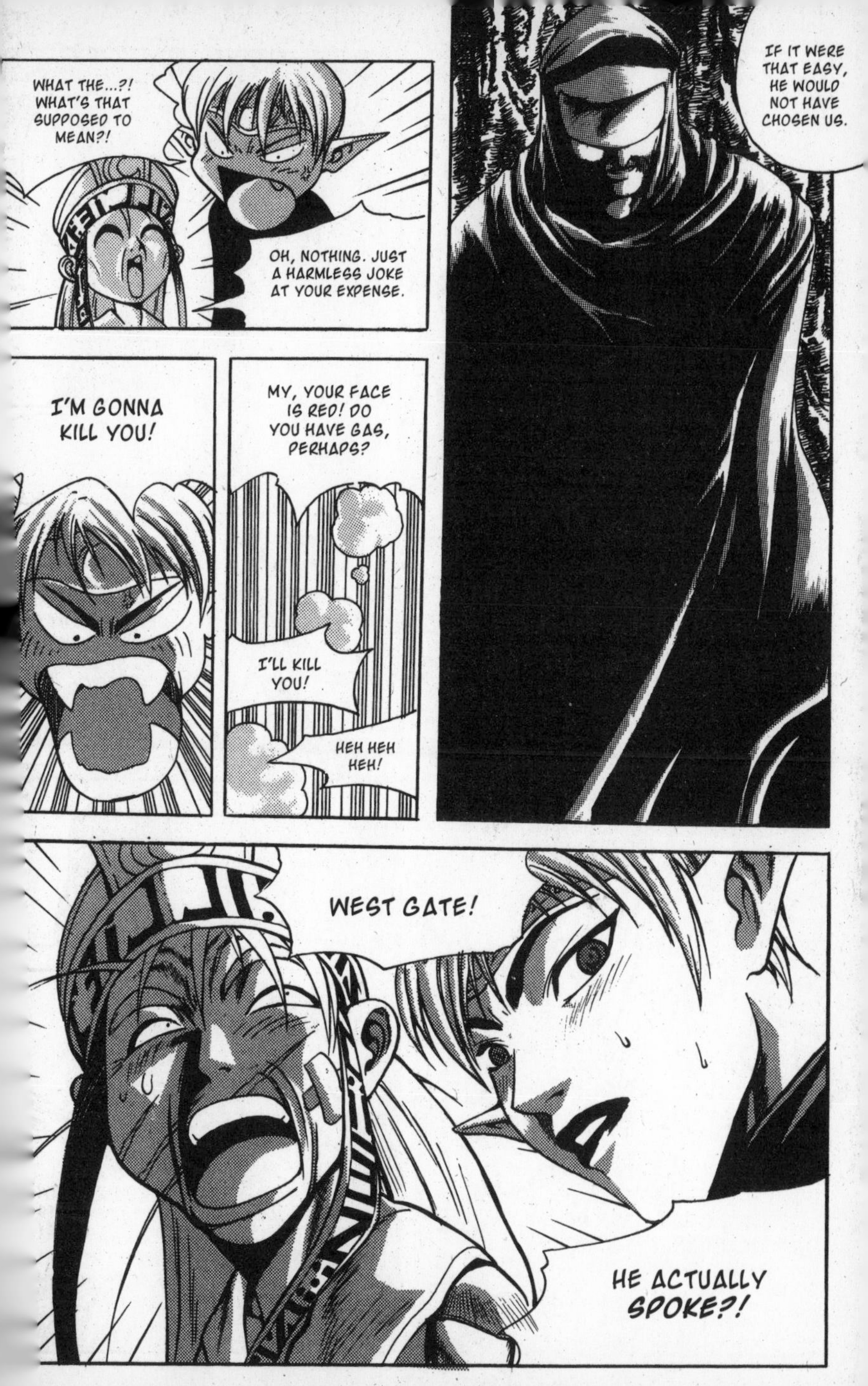
WHAT THE...?! WHAT'S THAT SUPPOSED TO MEAN?!
OH, NOTHING. JUST A HARMLESS JOKE AT YOUR EXPENSE.
I'M GONNA KILL YOU!
MY, YOUR FACE IS RED! DO YOU HAVE GAS, PERHAPS?
I'LL KILL YOU!
HEH HEH HEH!
IF IT WERE THAT EASY, HE WOULD NOT HAVE CHOSEN US.
WEST GATE!
HE ACTUALLY SPOKE?!

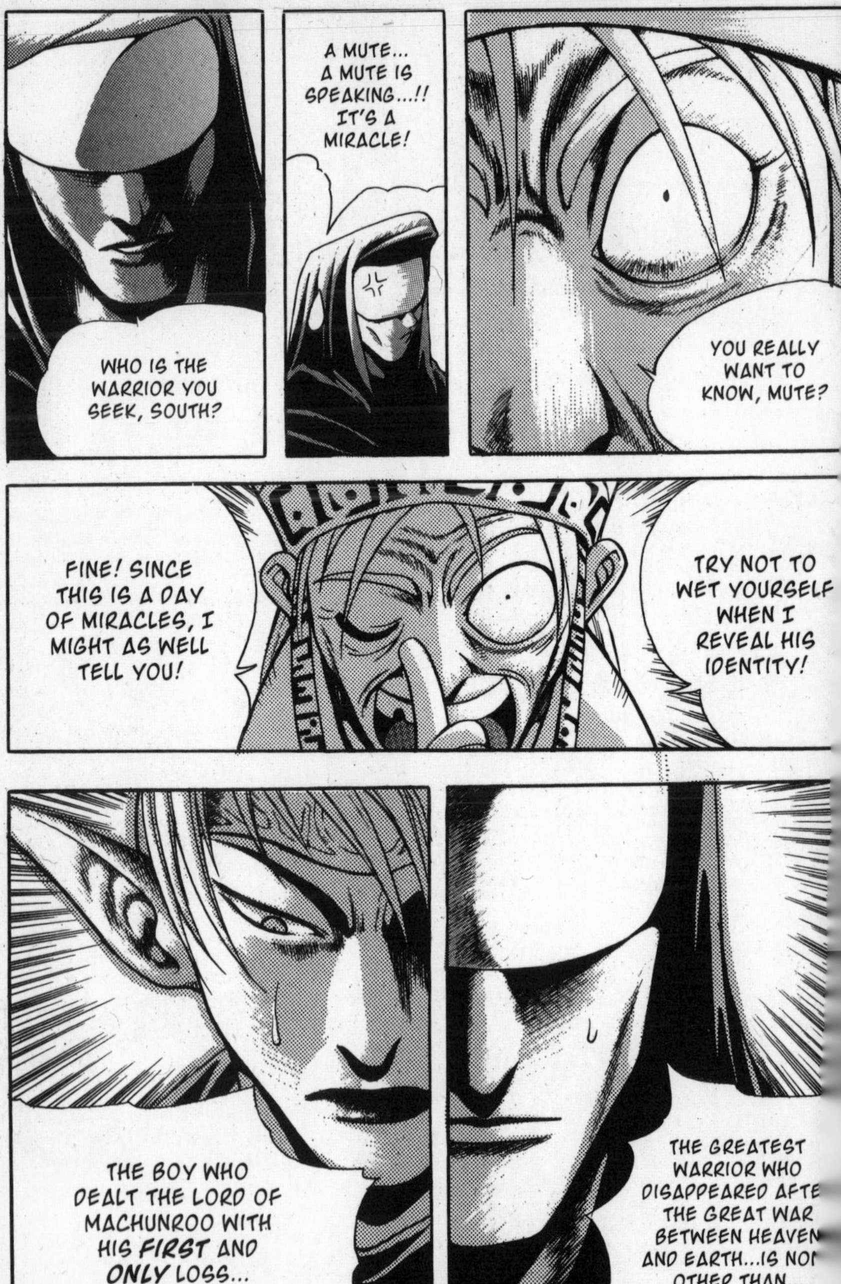

A MUTE... A MUTE IS SPEAKING...!! IT'S A MIRACLE!
WHO IS THE WARRIOR YOU SEEK, SOUTH?
YOU REALLY WANT TO KNOW, MUTE?
FINE! SINCE THIS IS A DAY OF MIRACLES, I MIGHT AS WELL TELL YOU!
TRY NOT TO WET YOURSELF WHEN I REVEAL HIS IDENTITY!
THE BOY WHO DEALT THE LORD OF MACHUNROO WITH HIS FIRST AND ONLY LOSS...
THE GREATEST WARRIOR WHO DISAPPEARED AFTE THE GREAT WAR BETWEEN HEAVEN AND EARTH...IS NO OTHER THAN...

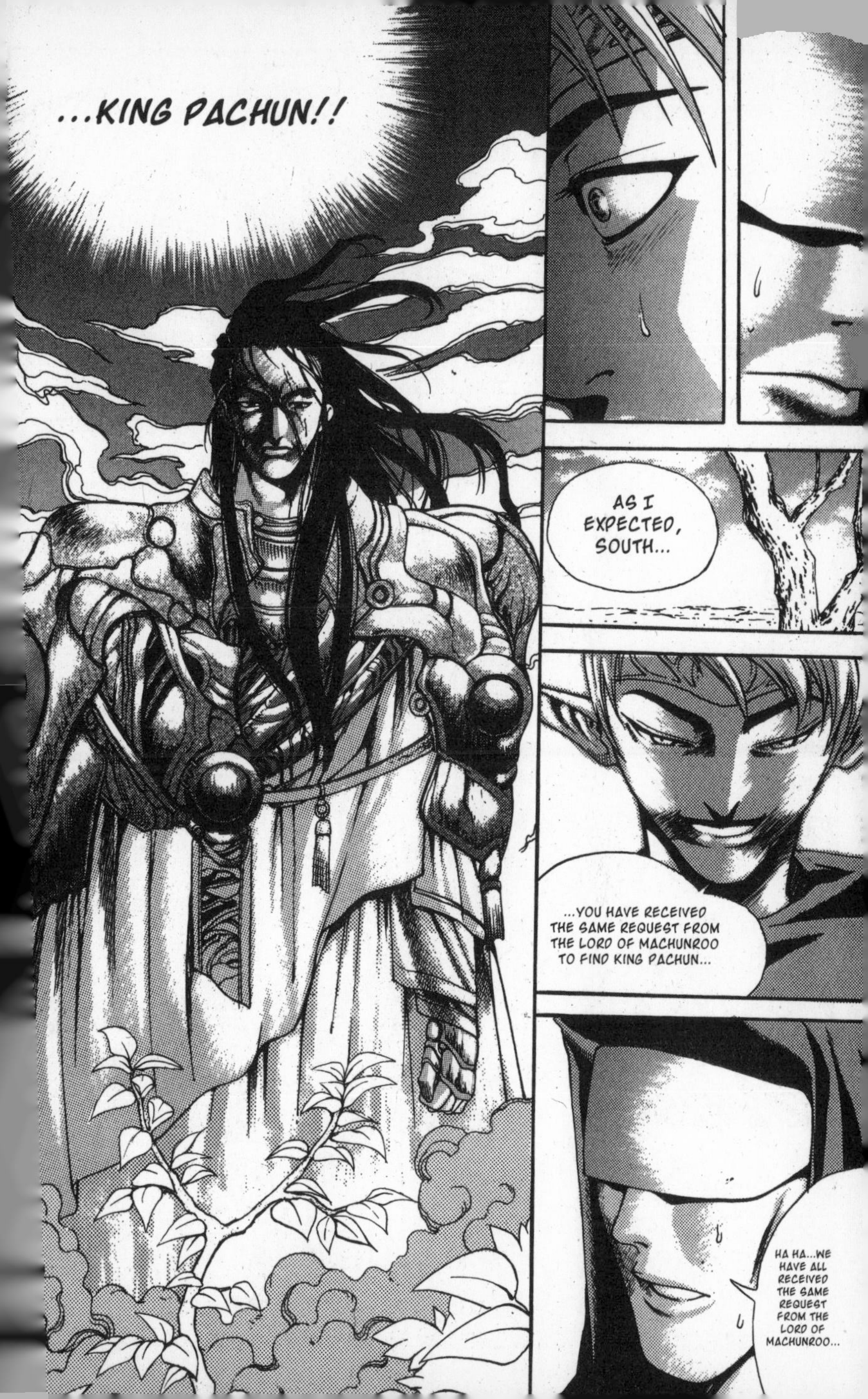
...KING PACHUN!!
AS I EXPECTED, SOUTH...
...YOU HAVE RECEIVED THE SAME REQUEST FROM THE LORD OF MACHUNROO TO FIND KING PACHUN...
HA HA...WE HAVE ALL RECEIVED THE SAME REQUEST FROM THE LORD OF MACHUNROO...

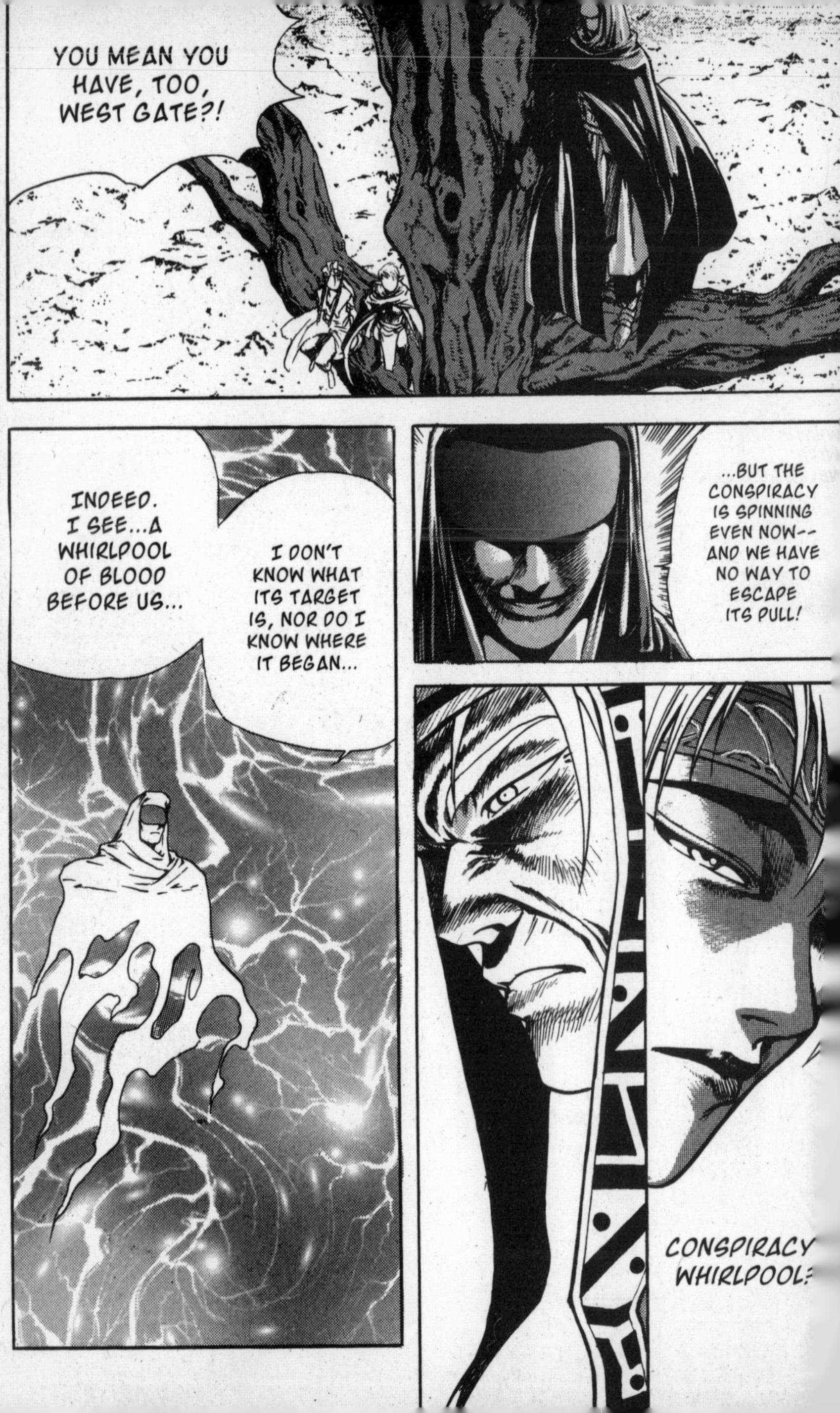
YOU MEAN YOU HAVE, TOO, WEST GATE?!
...BUT THE CONSPIRACY IS SPINNING EVEN NOW-- AND WE HAVE NO WAY TO ESCAPE ITS PULL!
I DON'T KNOW WHAT ITS TARGET IS, NOR DO I KNOW WHERE IT BEGAN...
INDEED. I SEE...A WHIRLPOOL OF BLOOD BEFORE US...
CONSPIRACY WHIRLPOOL?

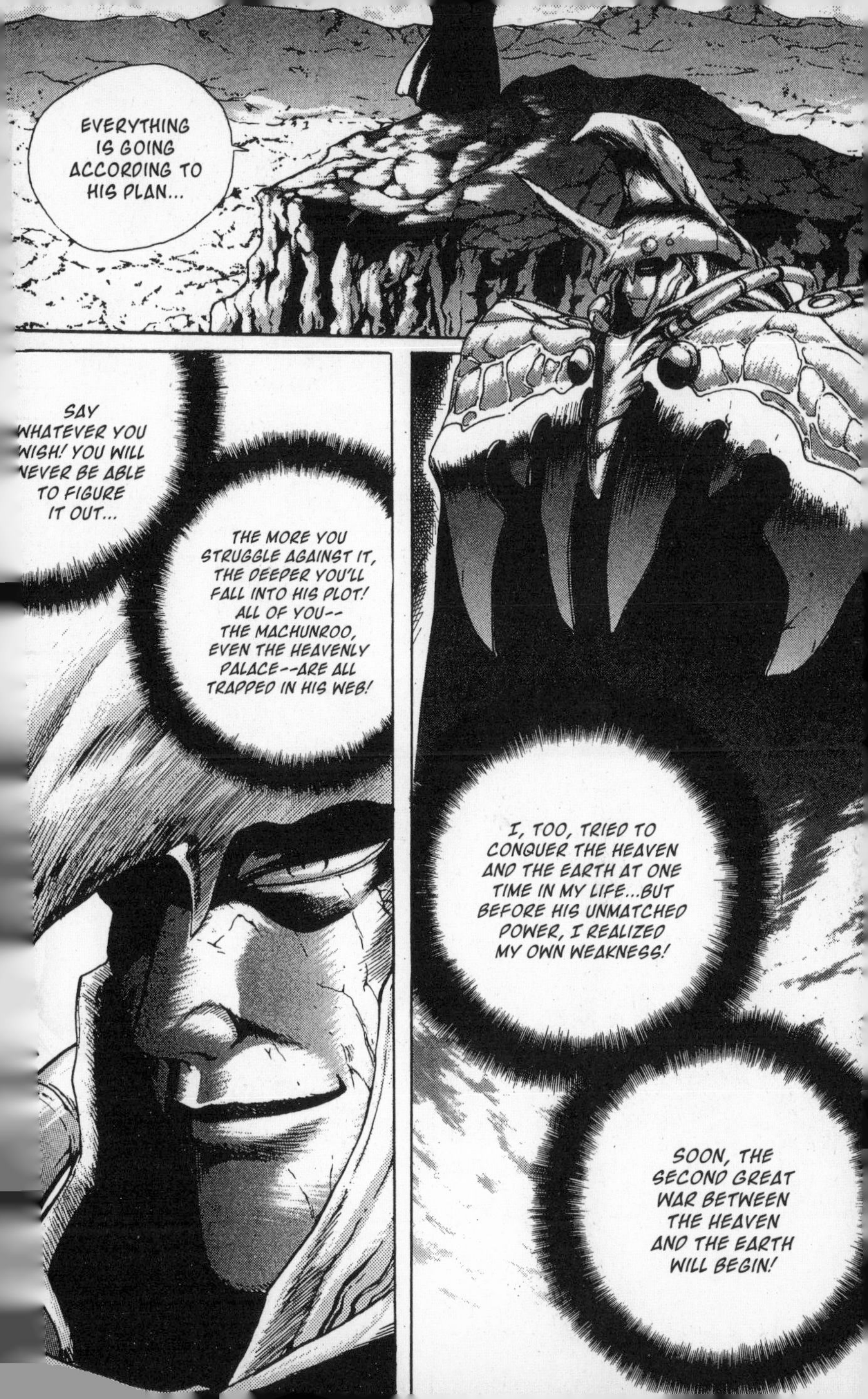
EVERYTHING IS GOING ACCORDING TO HIS PLAN...
SAY WHATEVER YOU WISH! YOU WILL NEVER BE ABLE TO FIGURE IT OUT...
THE MORE YOU STRUGGLE AGAINST IT, THE DEEPER YOU'LL FALL INTO HIS PLOT! ALL OF YOU-- THE MACHUNROO, EVEN THE HEAVENLY PALACE--ARE ALL TRAPPED IN HIS WEB!
I, TOO, TRIED TO CONQUER THE HEAVEN AND THE EARTH AT ONE TIME IN MY LIFE...BUT BEFORE HIS UNMATCHED POWER, I REALIZED MY OWN WEAKNESS!
SOON, THE SECOND GREAT WAR BETWEEN THE HEAVEN AND THE EARTH WILL BEGIN!

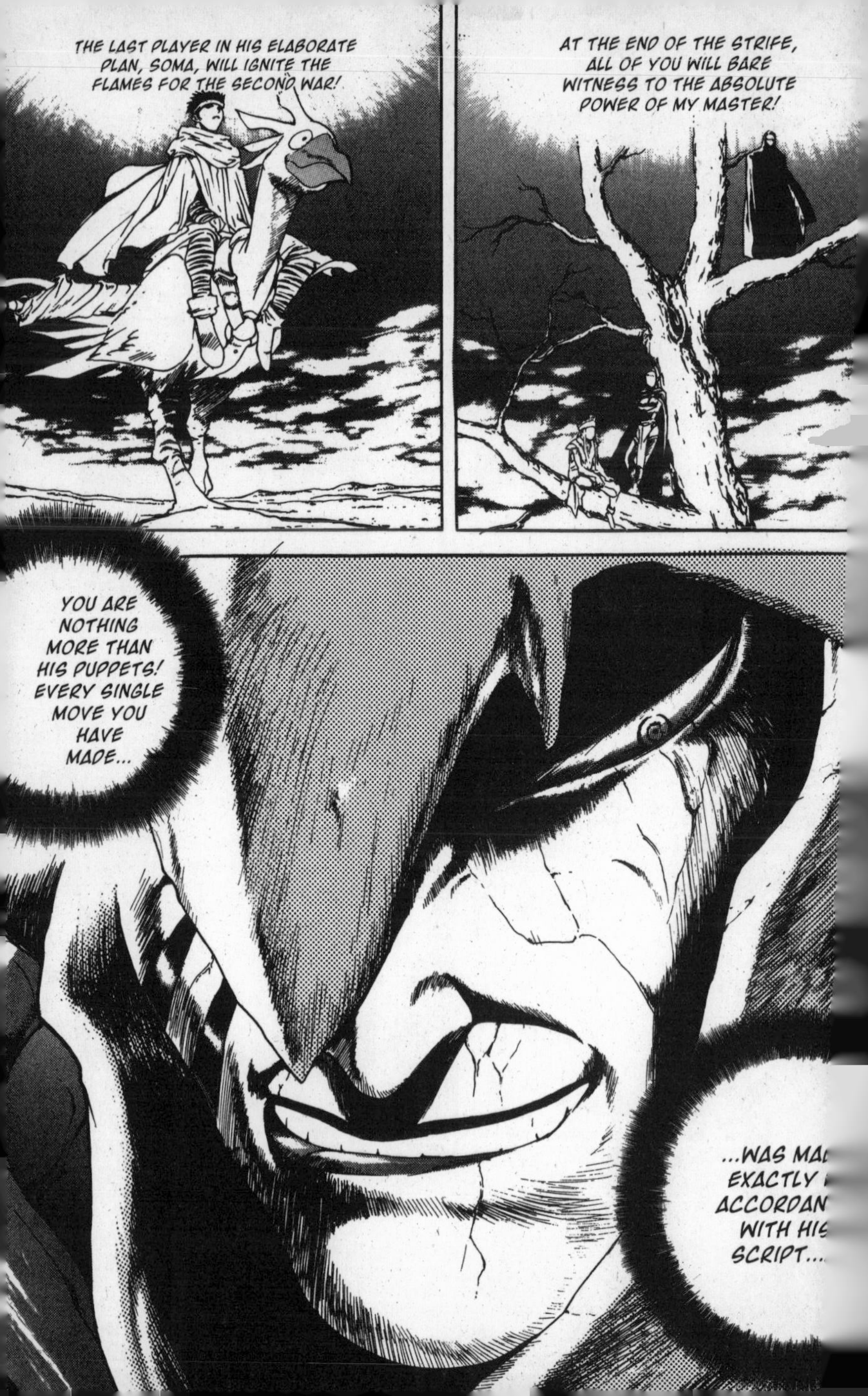
THE LAST PLAYER IN HIS ELABORATE PLAN, SOMA, WILL IGNITE THE FLAMES FOR THE SECOND WAR!
AT THE END OF THE STRIFE, ALL OF YOU WILL BARE WITNESS TO THE ABSOLUTE POWER OF MY MASTER!
YOU ARE NOTHING MORE THAN HIS PUPPETS! EVERY SINGLE MOVE YOU HAVE MADE...
...WAS MA EXACTLY ACCORDAN WITH HIS SCRIPT...

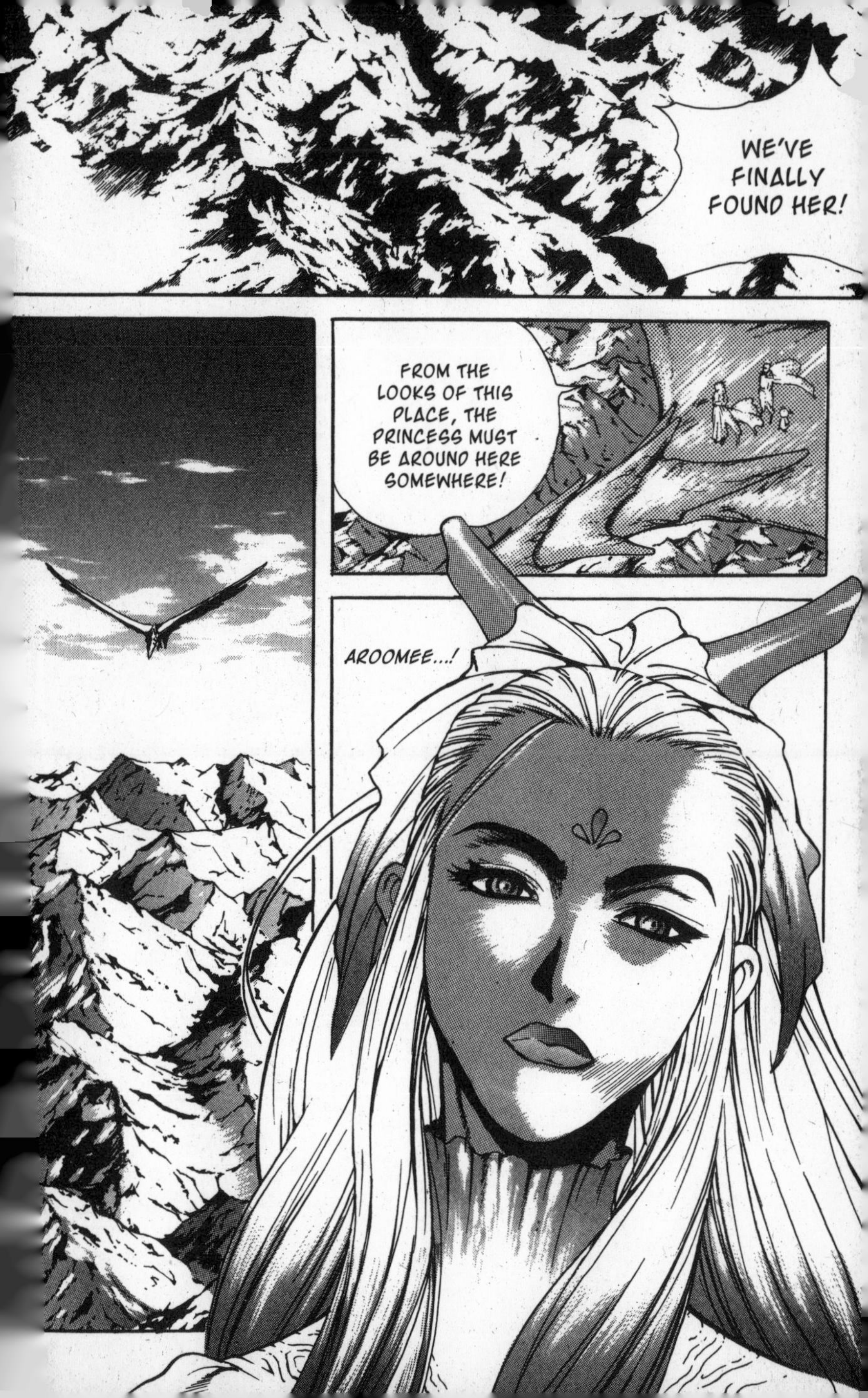
WE'VE FINALLY FOUND HER!
FROM THE LOOKS OF THIS PLACE, THE PRINCESS MUST BE AROUND HERE SOMEWHERE!
AROOMEE...!

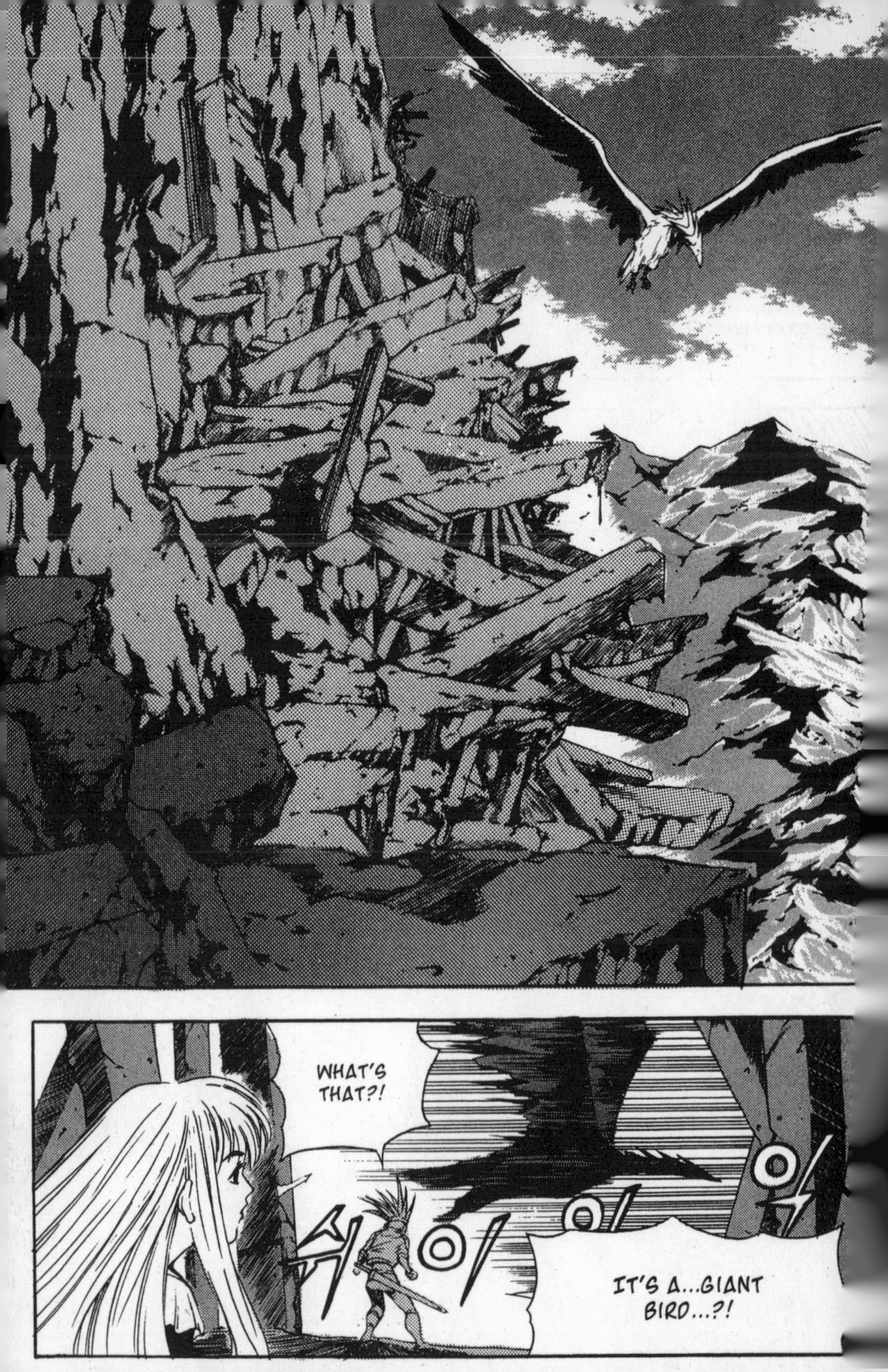
WHAT'S THAT?!
IT'S A...GIANT BIRD...?!

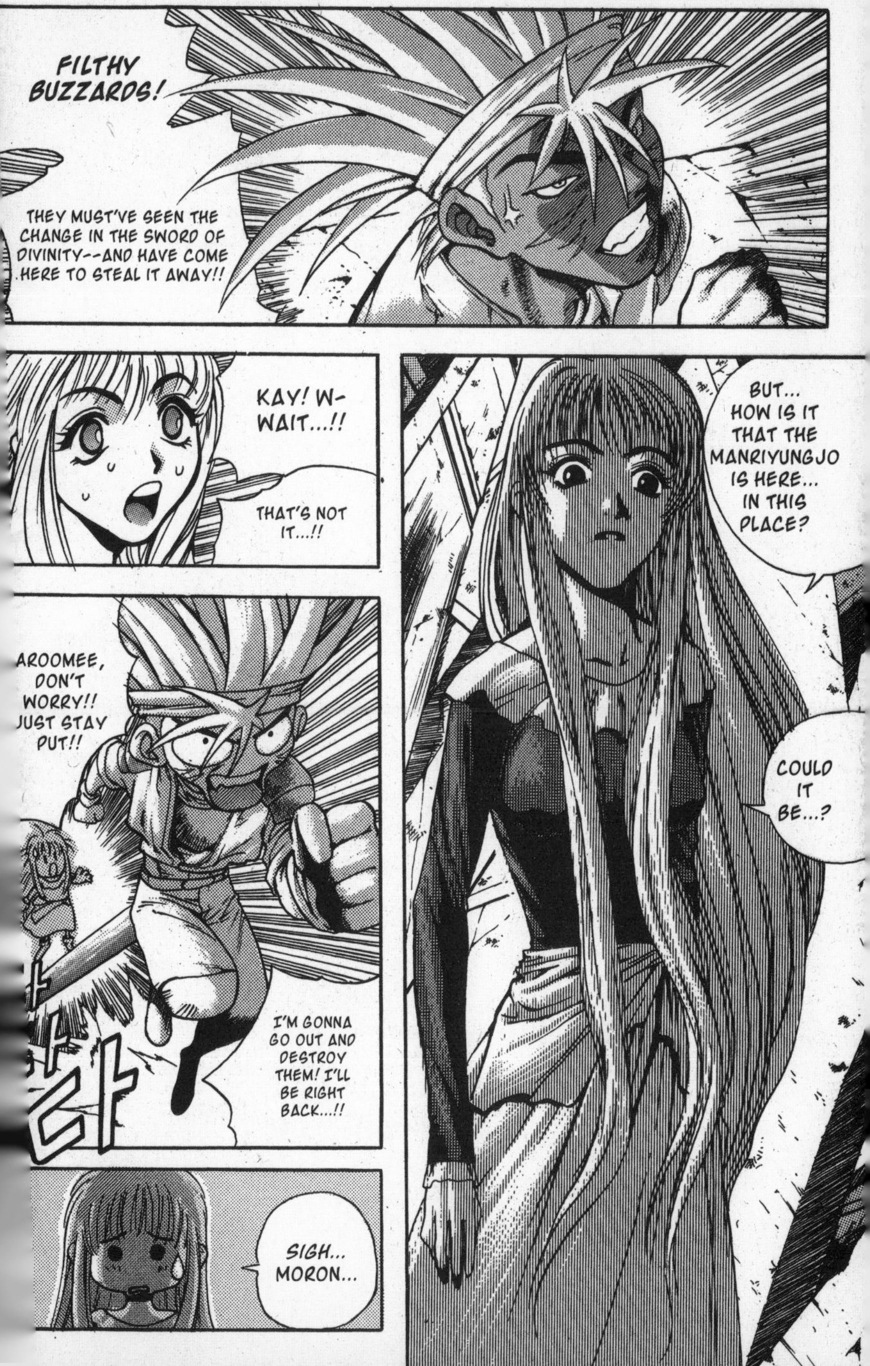
FILTHY BUZZARDS!
THEY MUST'VE SEEN THE CHANGE IN THE SWORD OF DIVINITY--AND HAVE COME HERE TO STEAL IT AWAY!!
KAY! W-WAIT...!!
THAT'S NOT IT...!!
AROOMEE, DON'T WORRY!! JUST STAY PUT!!
I'M GONNA GO OUT AND DESTROY THEM! I'LL BE RIGHT BACK...!!
SIGH... MORON...
BUT... HOW IS IT THAT THE MANRIYUNGJO IS HERE... IN THIS PLACE?
COULD IT BE...?

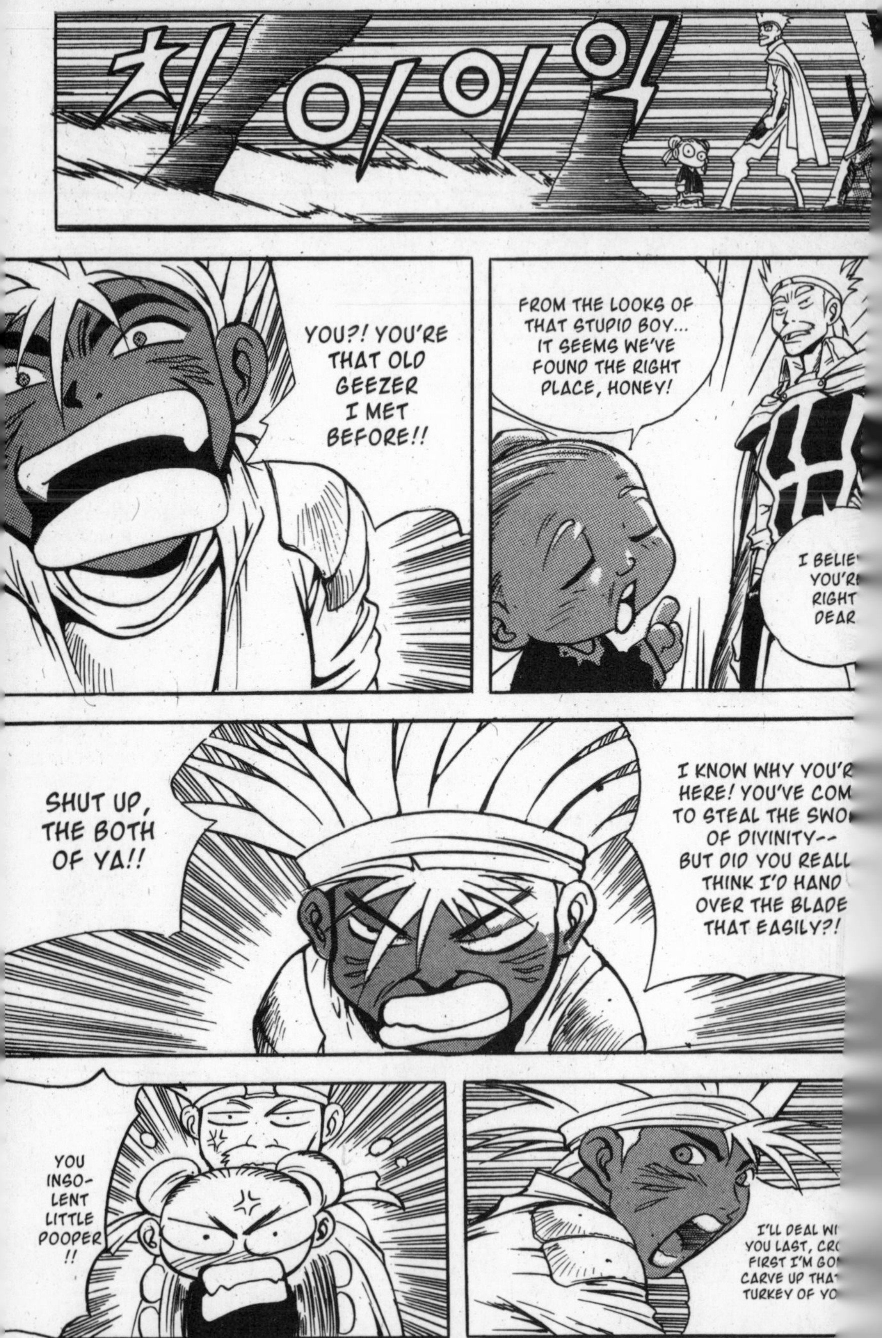
치이이이잉
YOU?! YOU'RE THAT OLD GEEZER I MET BEFORE!!
FROM THE LOOKS OF THAT STUPID BOY... IT SEEMS WE'VE FOUND THE RIGHT PLACE, HONEY!
I BELIE YOU'R RIGHT DEAR
SHUT UP, THE BOTH OF YA!!
I KNOW WHY YOU'R HERE! YOU'VE COM TO STEAL THE SWO OF DIVINITY-- BUT DID YOU REALL THINK I'D HAND OVER THE BLADE THAT EASILY?!
YOU INSO-LENT LITTLE POOPER !!
I'LL DEAL WI YOU LAST, CRO FIRST I'M GO CARVE UP THA TURKEY OF YO

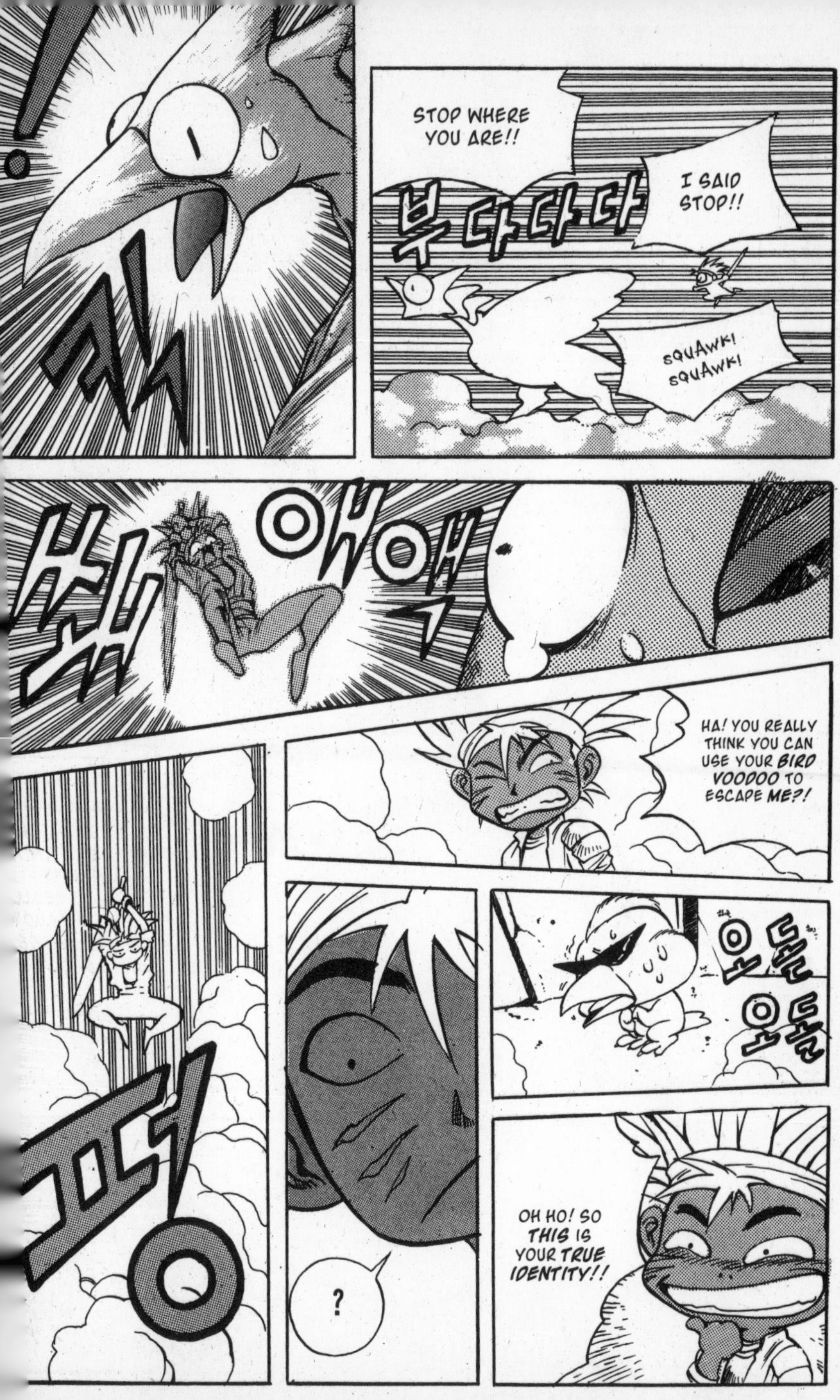
STOP WHERE YOU ARE!!
부다다다
I SAID STOP!!
SQUAWK! SQUAWK!
HA! YOU REALLY THINK YOU CAN USE YOUR BIRD VOODOO TO ESCAPE ME?!
?
OH HO! SO THIS IS YOUR TRUE IDENTITY!!

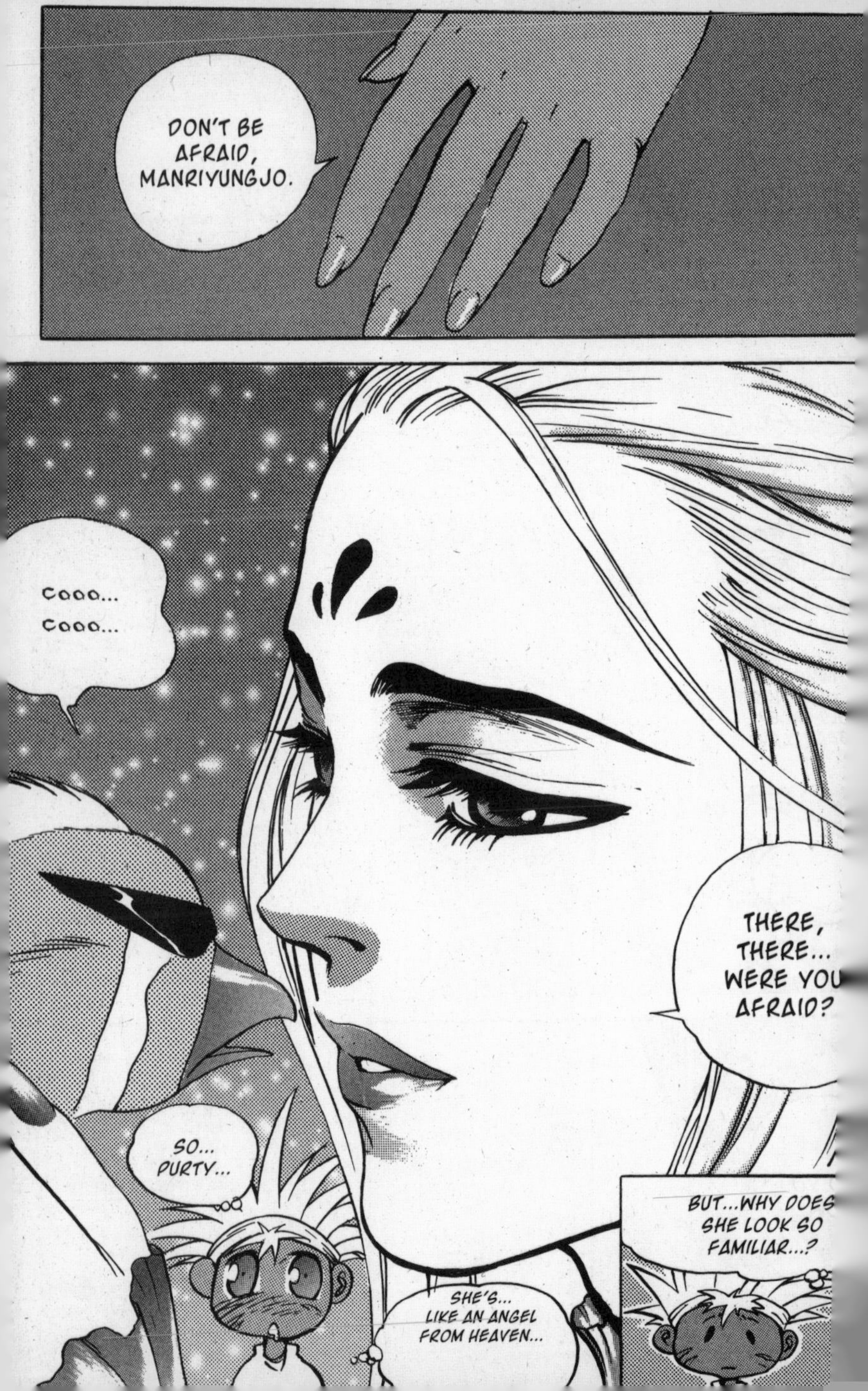
DON'T BE AFRAID, MANRIYUNGJO.
COOO... COOO...
THERE, THERE... WERE YOU AFRAID?
SO... PURTY...
SHE'S... LIKE AN ANGEL FROM HEAVEN...
BUT...WHY DOES SHE LOOK SO FAMILIAR...?

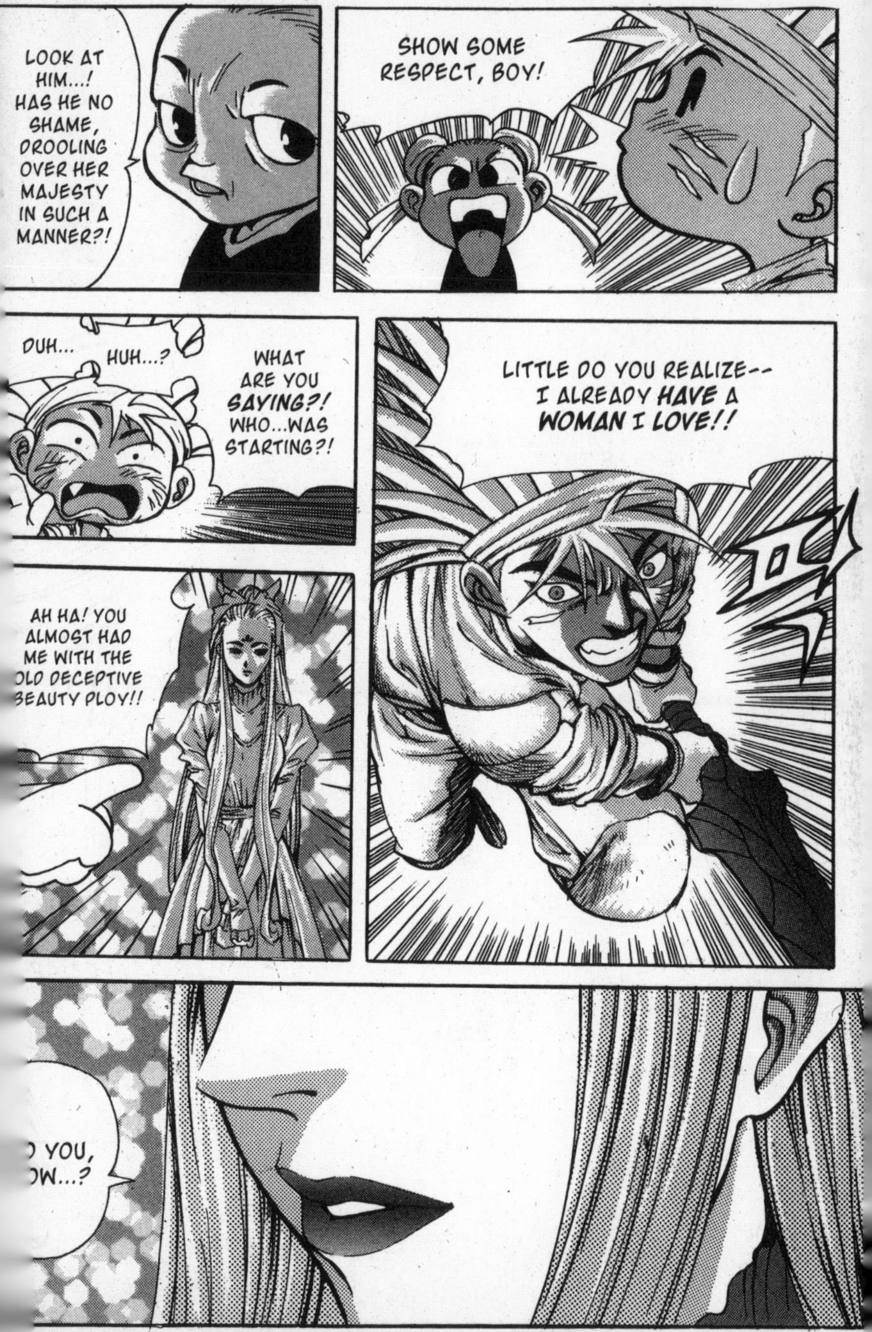
LOOK AT HIM...! HAS HE NO SHAME, DROOLING OVER HER MAJESTY IN SUCH A MANNER?!
SHOW SOME RESPECT, BOY!
DUH...
HUH...?
WHAT ARE YOU SAYING?! WHO...WAS STARTING?!
LITTLE DO YOU REALIZE-- I ALREADY HAVE A WOMAN I LOVE!!
AH HA! YOU ALMOST HAD ME WITH THE OLD DECEPTIVE BEAUTY PLOY!!
O YOU, OW...?

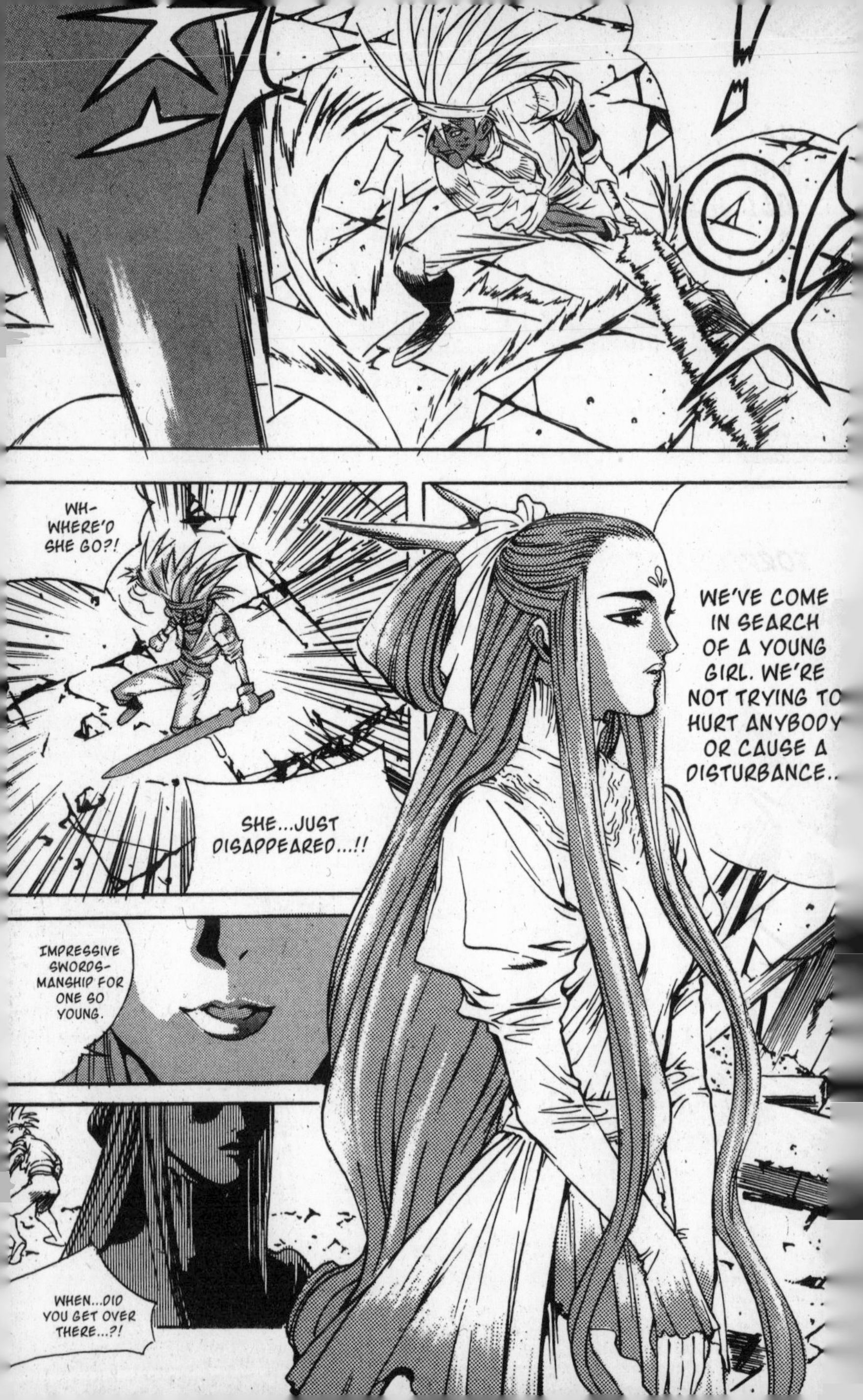
WH- WHERE'D SHE GO?!
WE'VE COME IN SEARCH OF A YOUNG GIRL. WE'RE NOT TRYING TO HURT ANYBODY OR CAUSE A DISTURBANCE...
SHE...JUST DISAPPEARED...!!
IMPRESSIVE SWORDS-MANSHIP FOR ONE SO YOUNG.
WHEN...DID YOU GET OVER THERE...?!

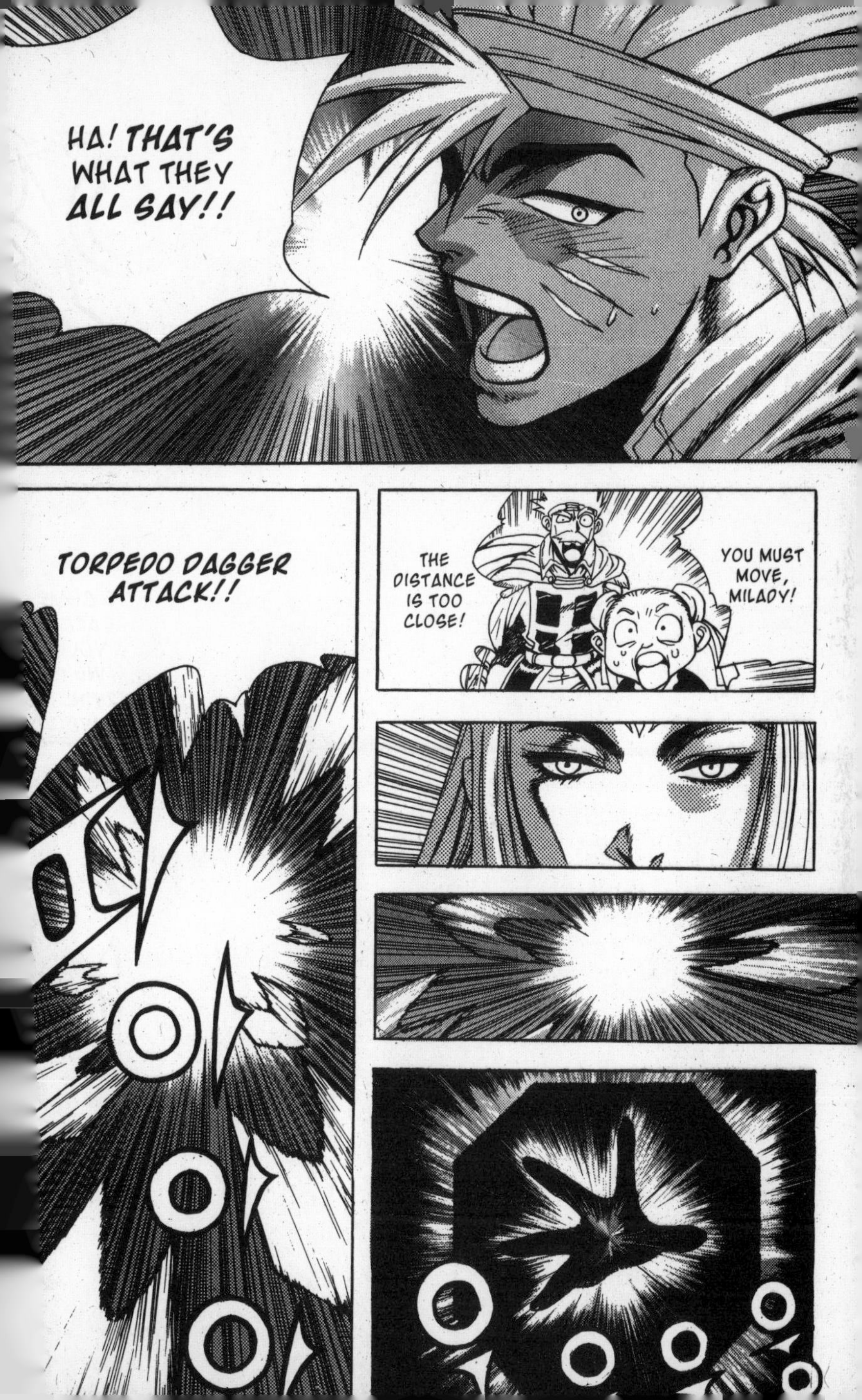
HA! THAT'S WHAT THEY ALL SAY!!
YOU MUST MOVE, MILADY!
THE DISTANCE IS TOO CLOSE!
TORPEDO DAGGER ATTACK!!

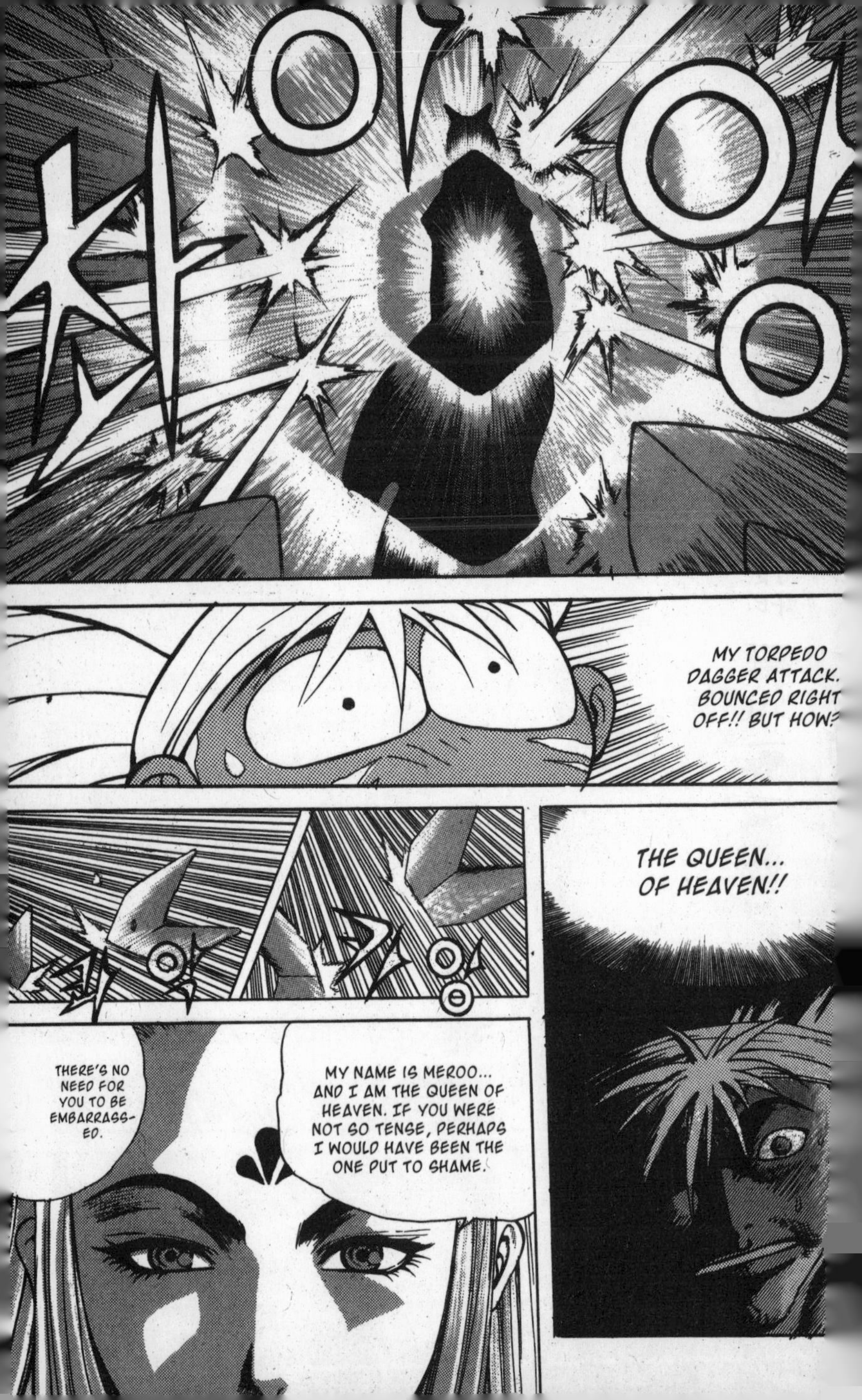

MY TORPEDO DAGGER ATTACK. BOUNCED RIGHT OFF!! BUT HOW?
THE QUEEN... OF HEAVEN!!
MY NAME IS MEROO... AND I AM THE QUEEN OF HEAVEN. IF YOU WERE NOT SO TENSE, PERHAPS I WOULD HAVE BEEN THE ONE PUT TO SHAME.
THERE'S NO NEED FOR YOU TO BE EMBARRASS-ED.

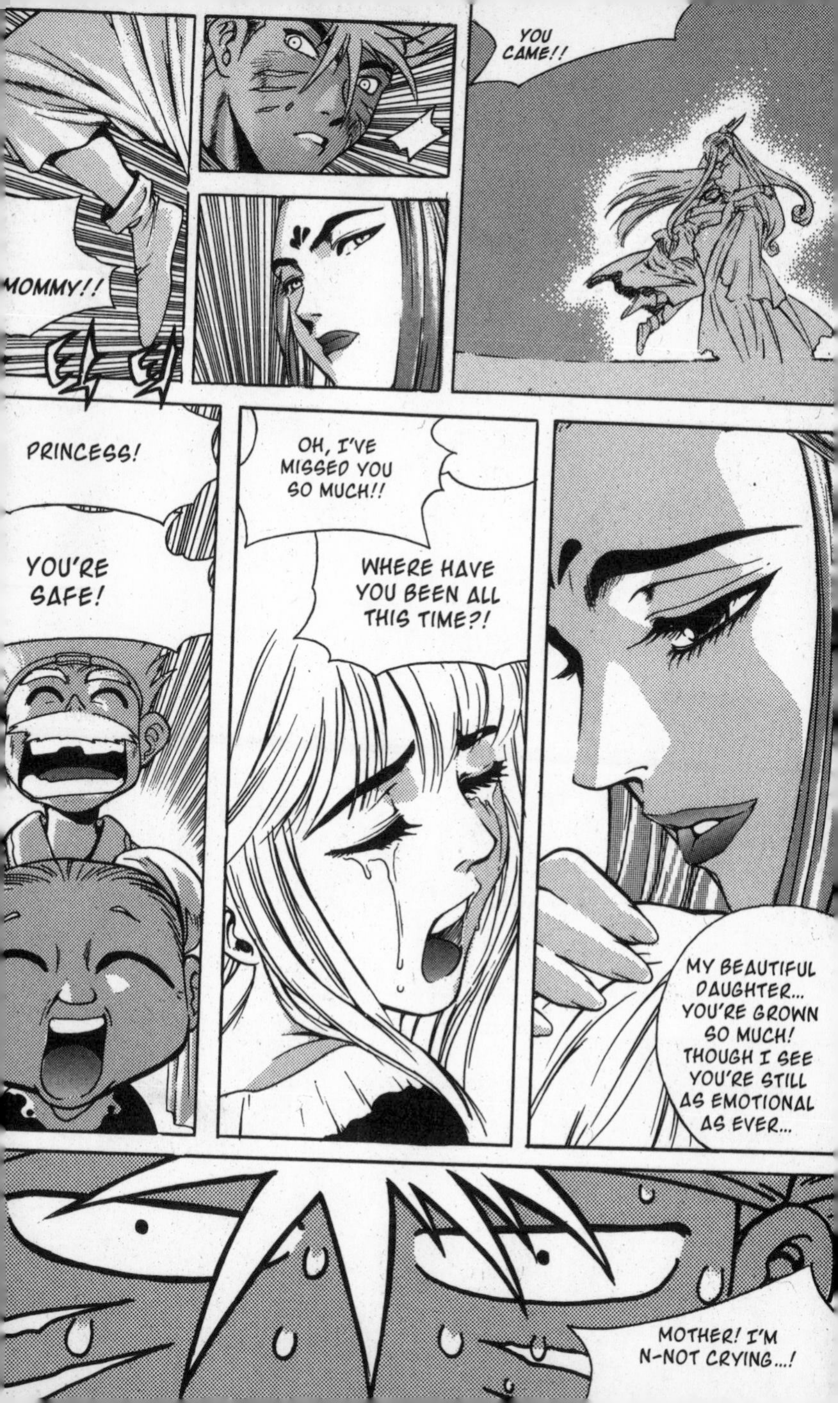
MOMMY!!
YOU CAME!!
PRINCESS!
YOU'RE SAFE!
OH, I'VE MISSED YOU SO MUCH!!
WHERE HAVE YOU BEEN ALL THIS TIME?!
MY BEAUTIFUL DAUGHTER... YOU'RE GROWN SO MUCH! THOUGH I SEE YOU'RE STILL AS EMOTIONAL AS EVER...
MOTHER! I'M N-NOT CRYING...!

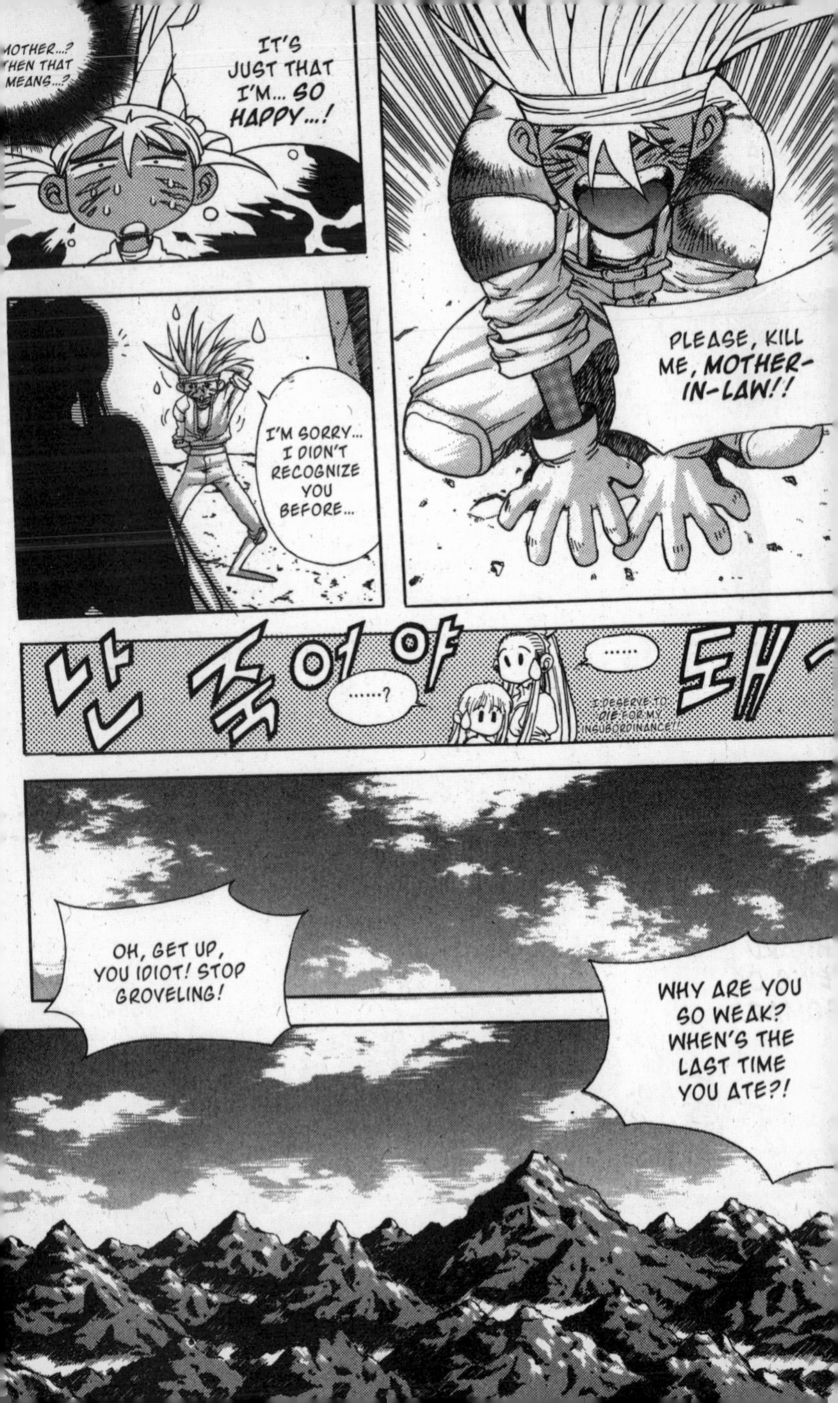
MOTHER...? THEN THAT MEANS...?
IT'S JUST THAT I'M... SO HAPPY...!
PLEASE, KILL ME, MOTHER-IN-LAW!!
I'M SORRY... I DIDN'T RECOGNIZE YOU BEFORE...
난 죽어야 돼-
......?
......
I DESERVE TO DIE FOR MY INSUBORDINANCE!!
OH, GET UP, YOU IDIOT! STOP GROVELING!
WHY ARE YOU SO WEAK? WHEN'S THE LAST TIME YOU ATE?!

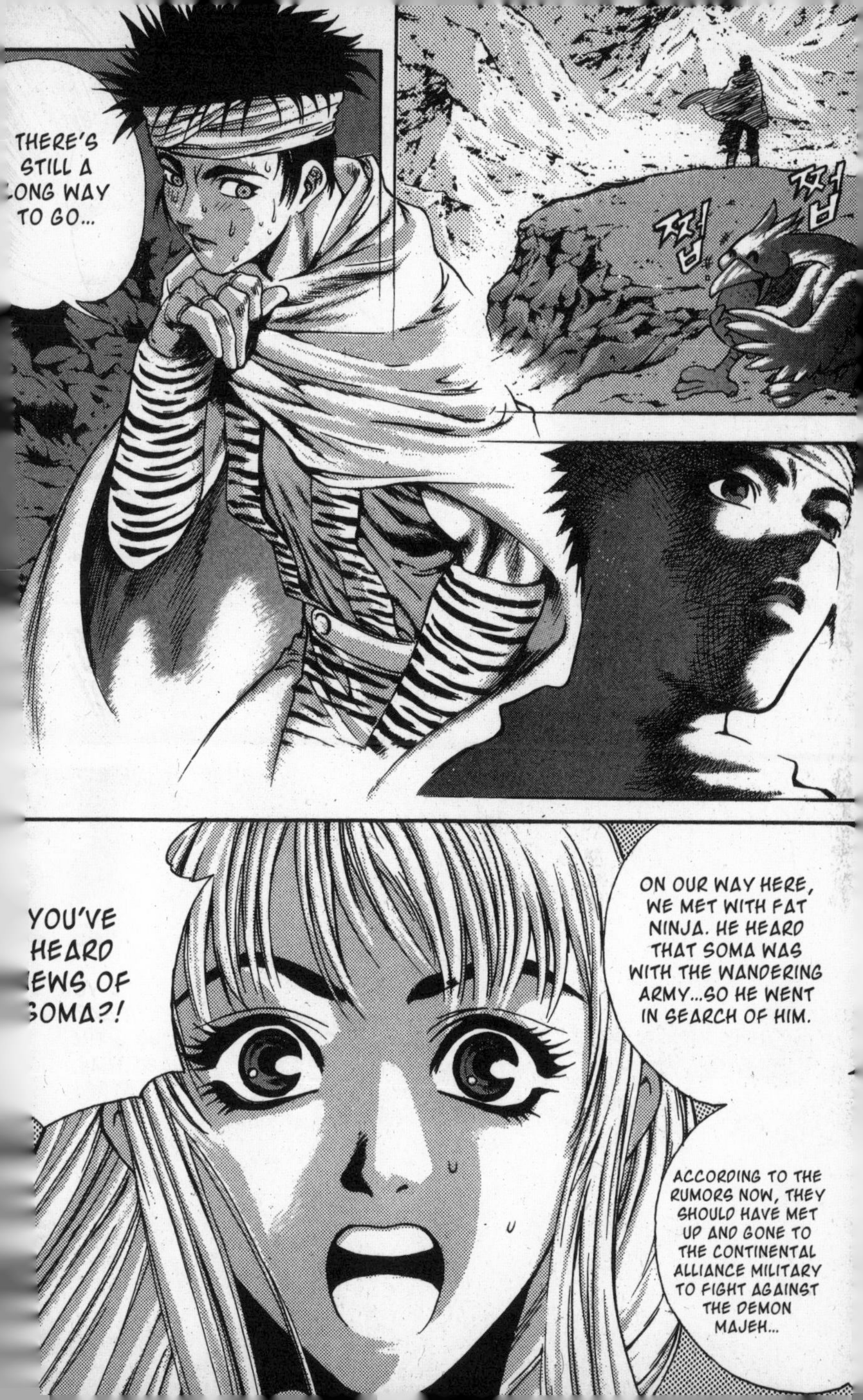
THERE'S STILL A ONG WAY TO GO...
YOU'VE HEARD EWS OF OMA?!
ON OUR WAY HERE, WE MET WITH FAT NINJA. HE HEARD THAT SOMA WAS WITH THE WANDERING ARMY...SO HE WENT IN SEARCH OF HIM.
ACCORDING TO THE RUMORS NOW, THEY SHOULD HAVE MET UP AND GONE TO THE CONTINENTAL ALLIANCE MILITARY TO FIGHT AGAINST THE DEMON MAJEH...

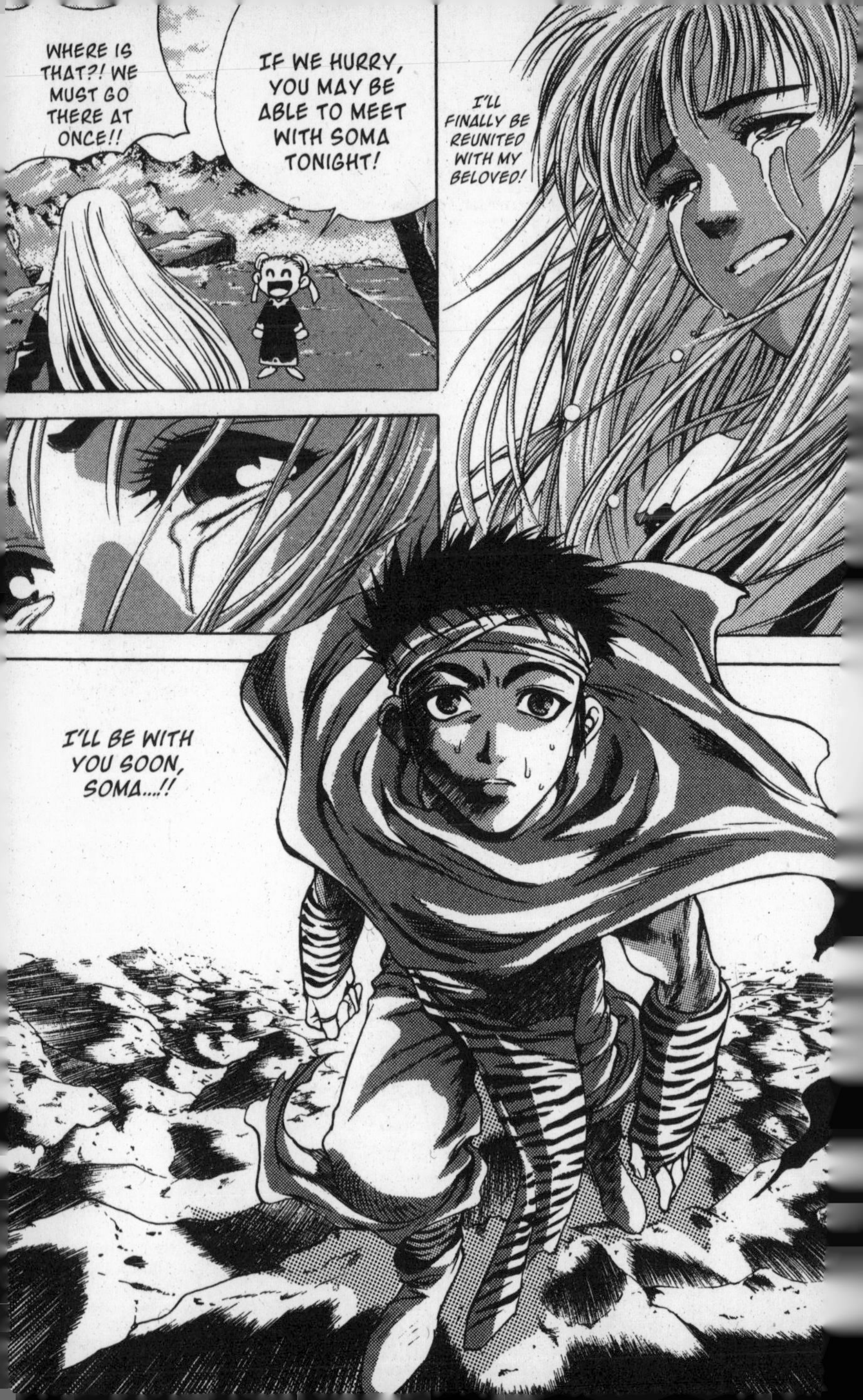
IF WE HURRY, YOU MAY BE ABLE TO MEET WITH SOMA TONIGHT!
WHERE IS THAT?! WE MUST GO THERE AT ONCE!!
I'LL FINALLY BE REUNITED WITH MY BELOVED!
I'LL BE WITH YOU SOON, SOMA...!!

BLADE OF HEAVEN

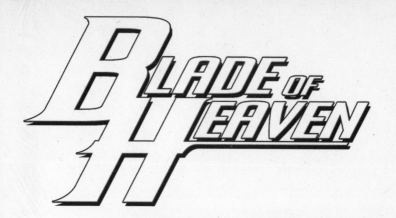

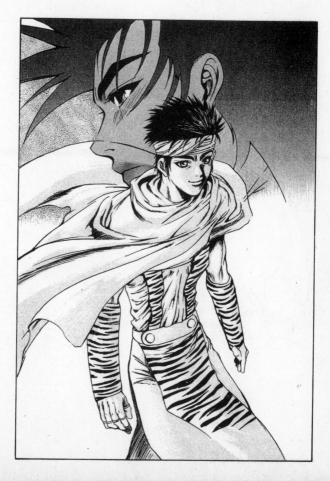

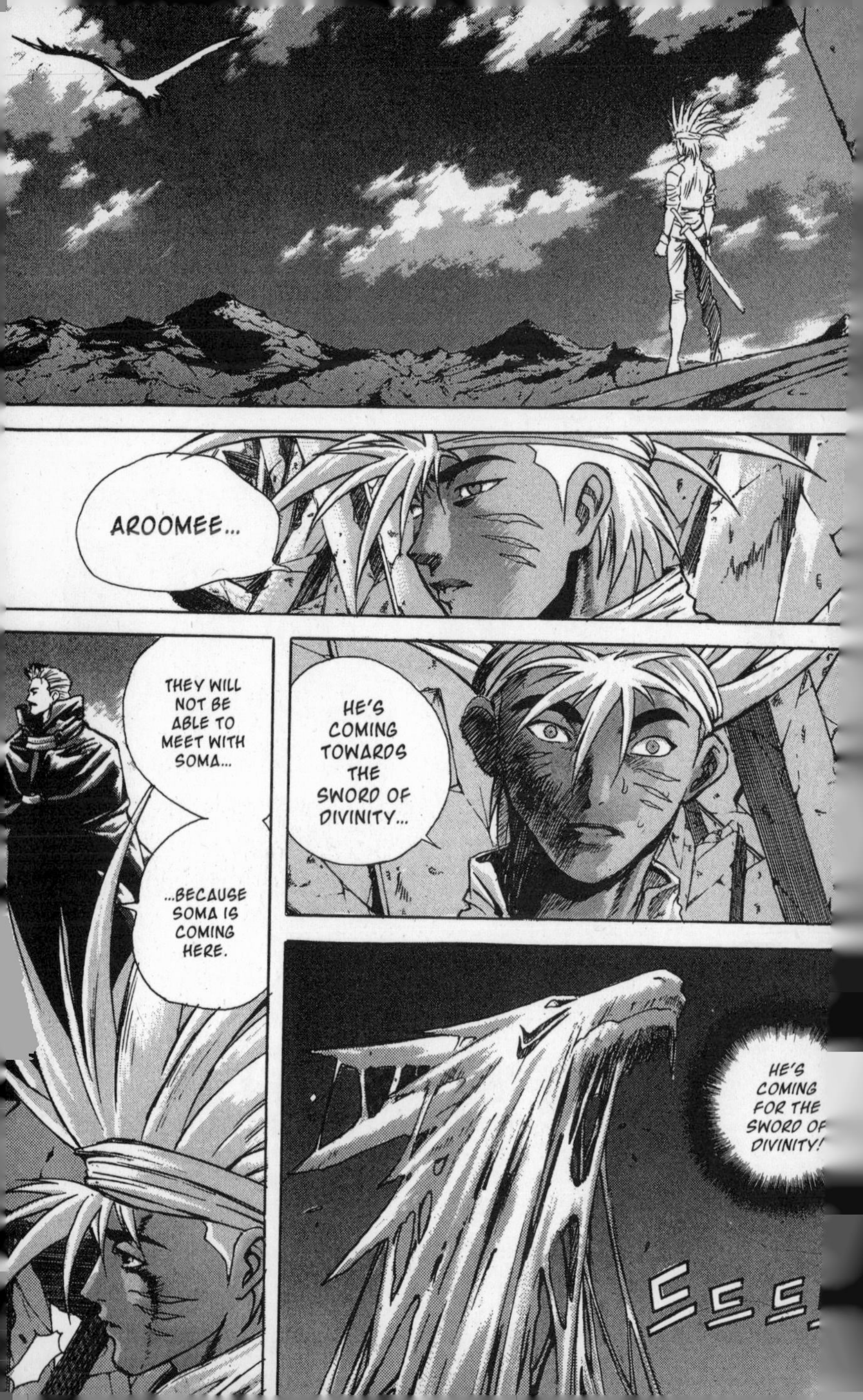
AROOMEE...
THEY WILL NOT BE ABLE TO MEET WITH SOMA...
...BECAUSE SOMA IS COMING HERE.
HE'S COMING TOWARDS THE SWORD OF DIVINITY...
HE'S COMING FOR THE SWORD OF DIVINITY!

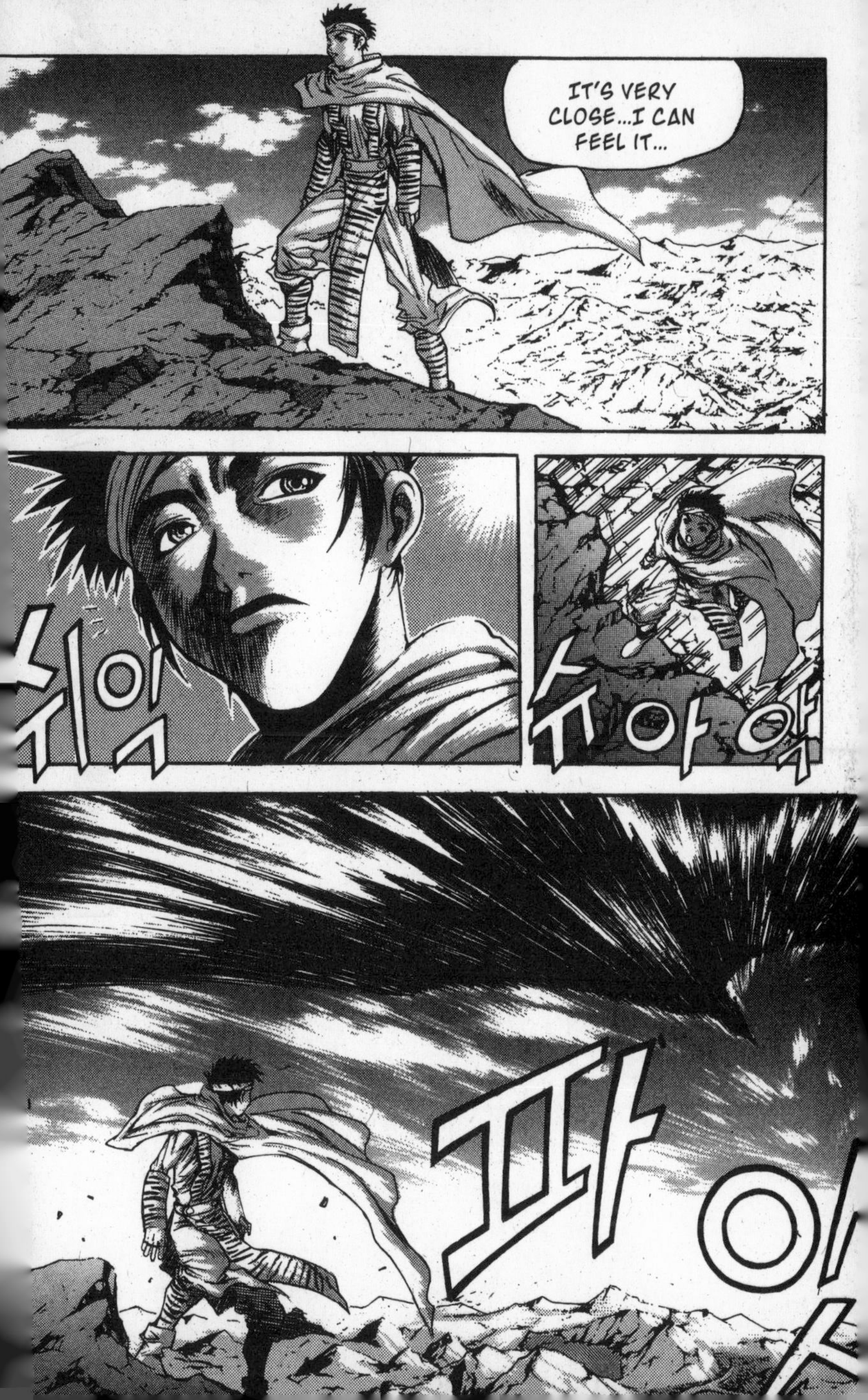
IT'S VERY CLOSE...I CAN FEEL IT...

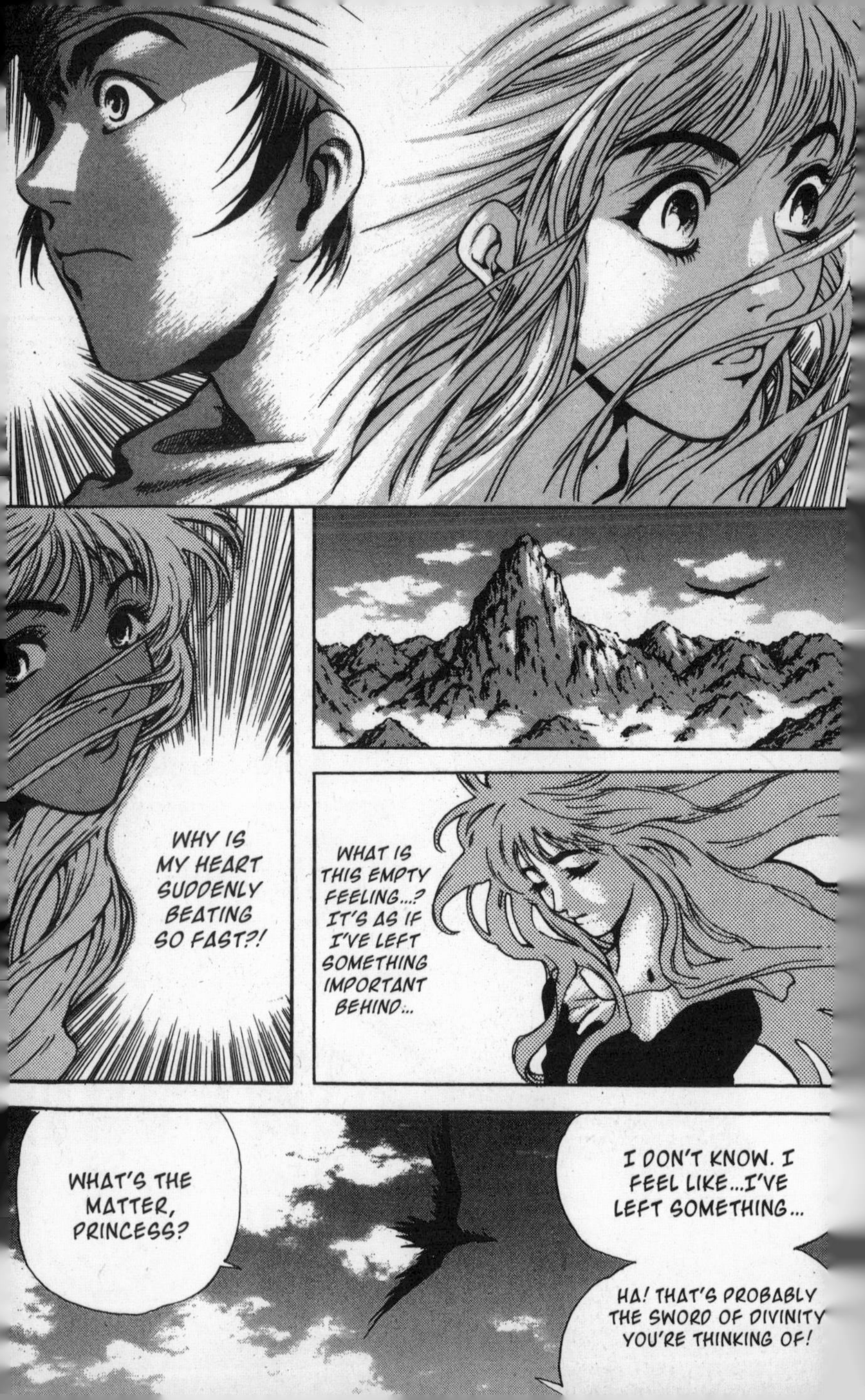
WHY IS MY HEART SUDDENLY BEATING SO FAST?!
WHAT IS THIS EMPTY FEELING...? IT'S AS IF I'VE LEFT SOMETHING IMPORTANT BEHIND...
WHAT'S THE MATTER, PRINCESS?
I DON'T KNOW. I FEEL LIKE...I'VE LEFT SOMETHING...
HA! THAT'S PROBABLY THE SWORD OF DIVINITY YOU'RE THINKING OF!

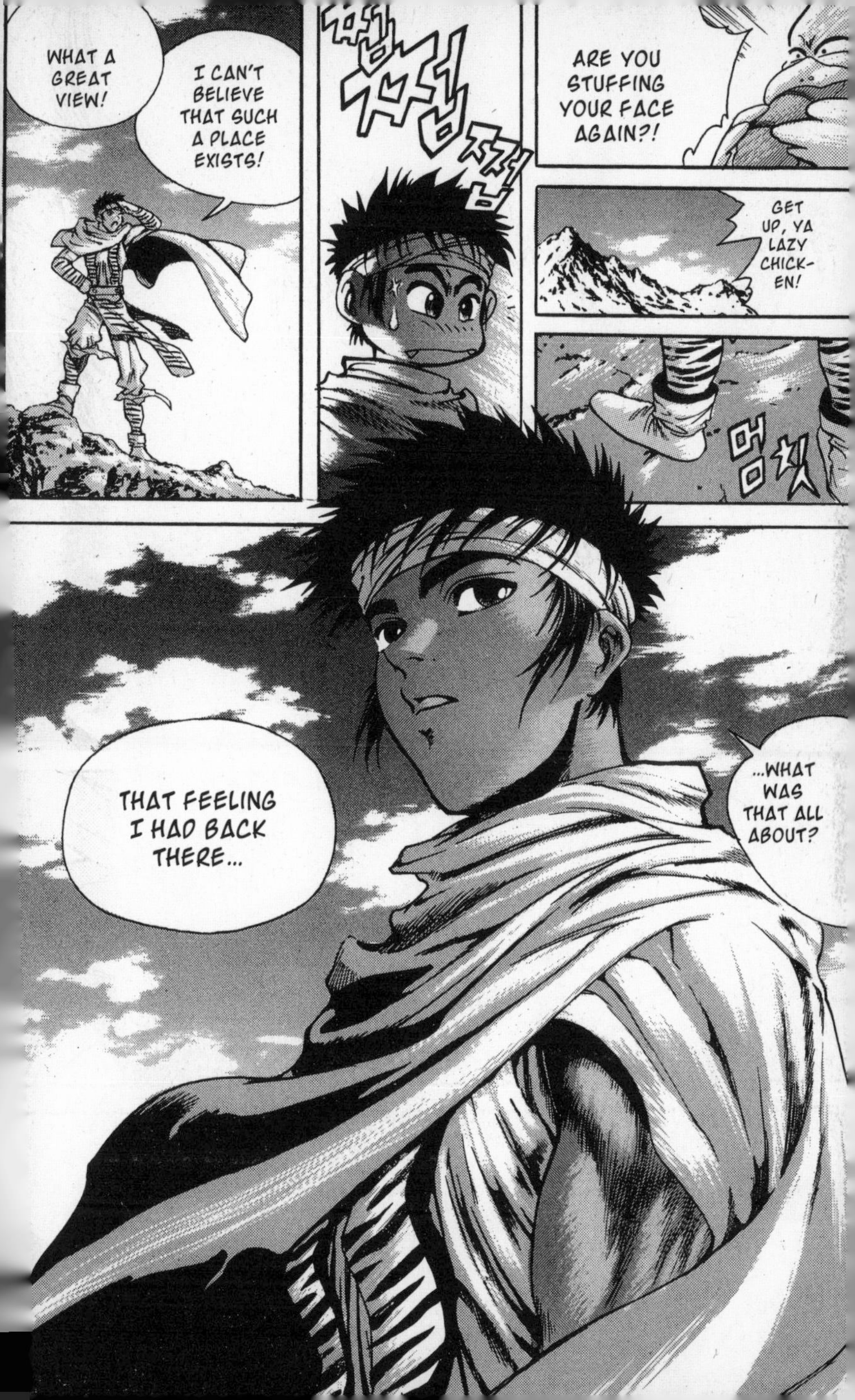
WHAT A GREAT VIEW!
I CAN'T BELIEVE THAT SUCH A PLACE EXISTS!
ARE YOU STUFFING YOUR FACE AGAIN?!
GET UP, YA LAZY CHICK-EN!
THAT FEELING I HAD BACK THERE...
...WHAT WAS THAT ALL ABOUT?

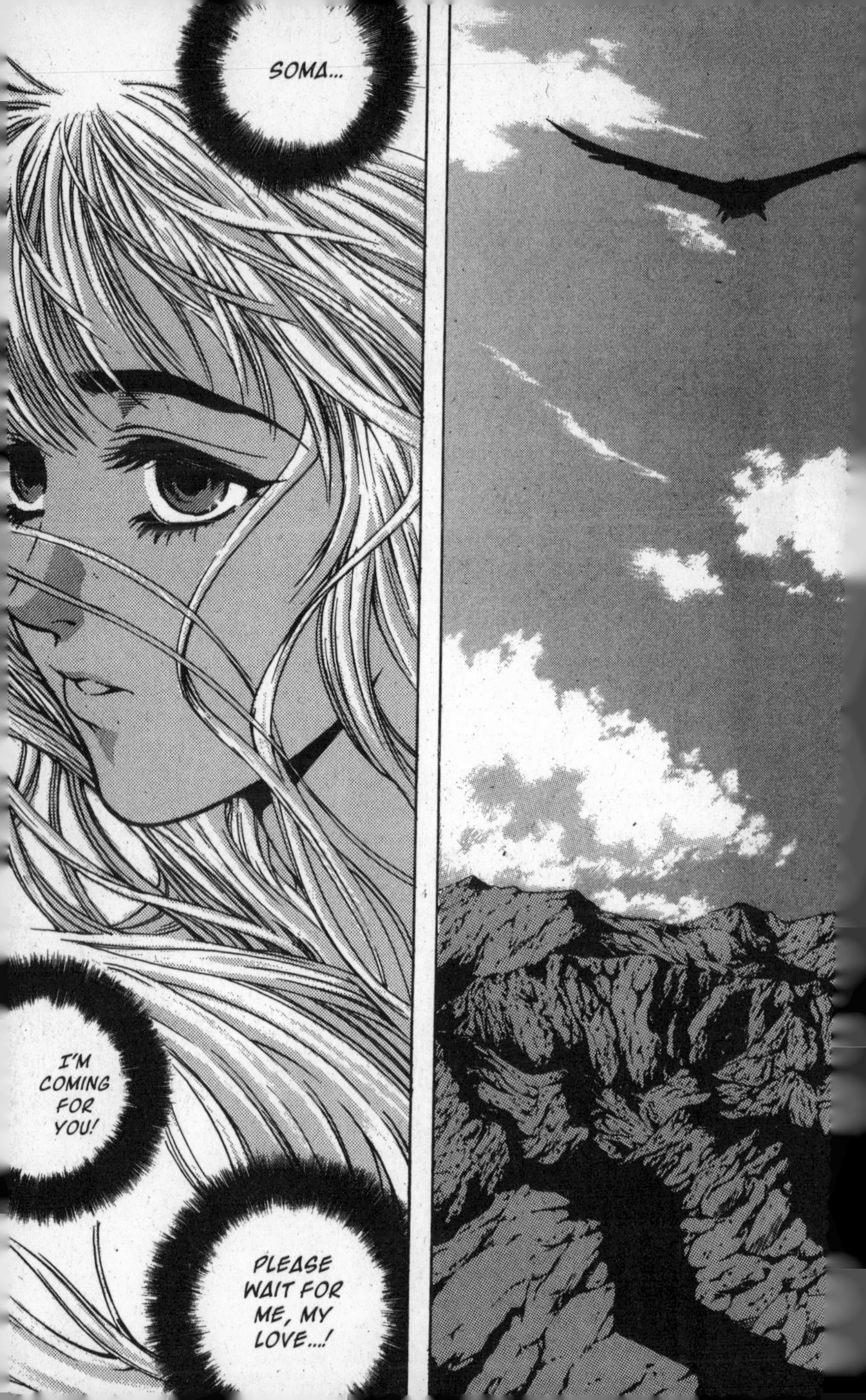
SOMA...
I'M COMING FOR YOU!
PLEASE WAIT FOR ME, MY LOVE...!

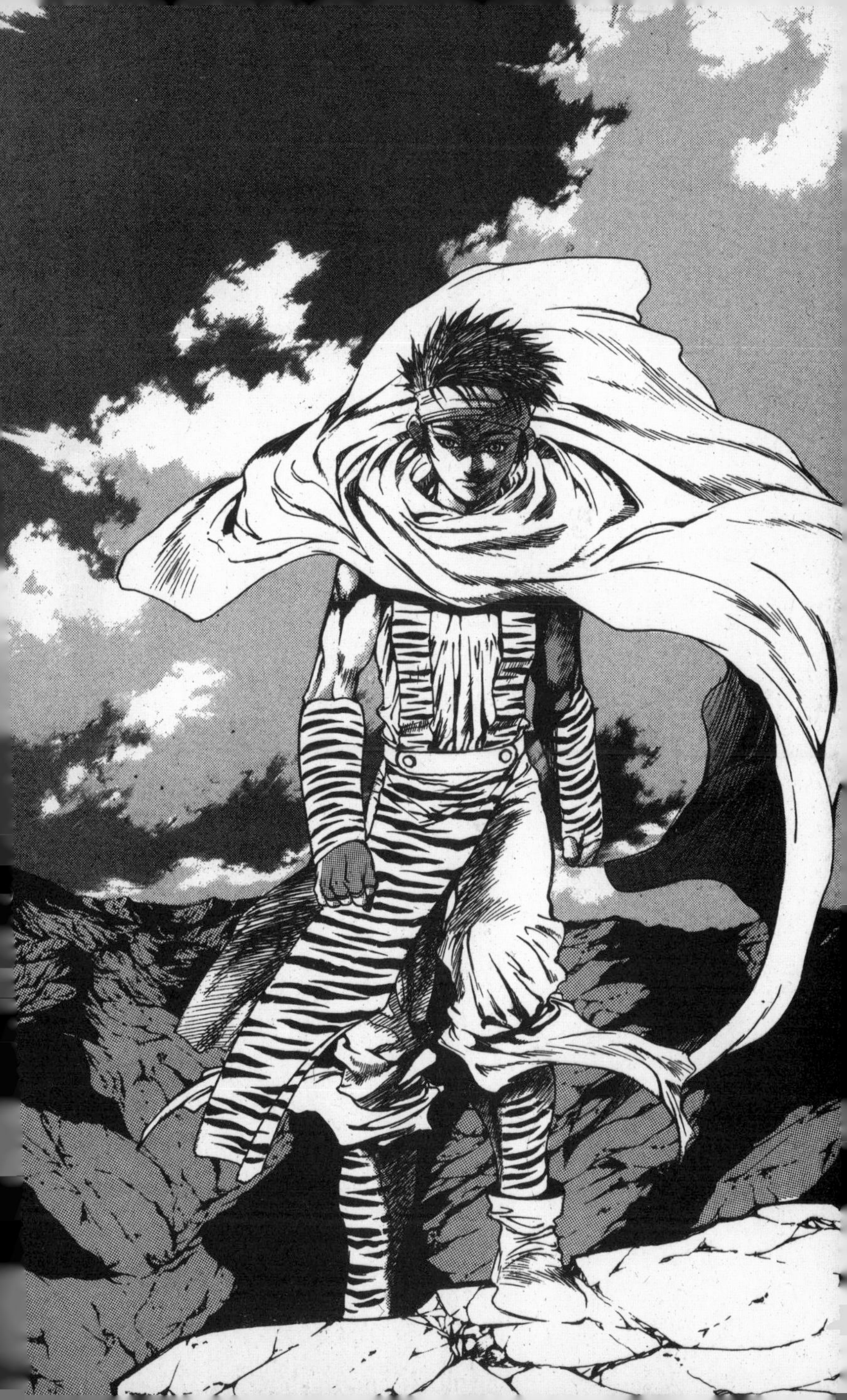

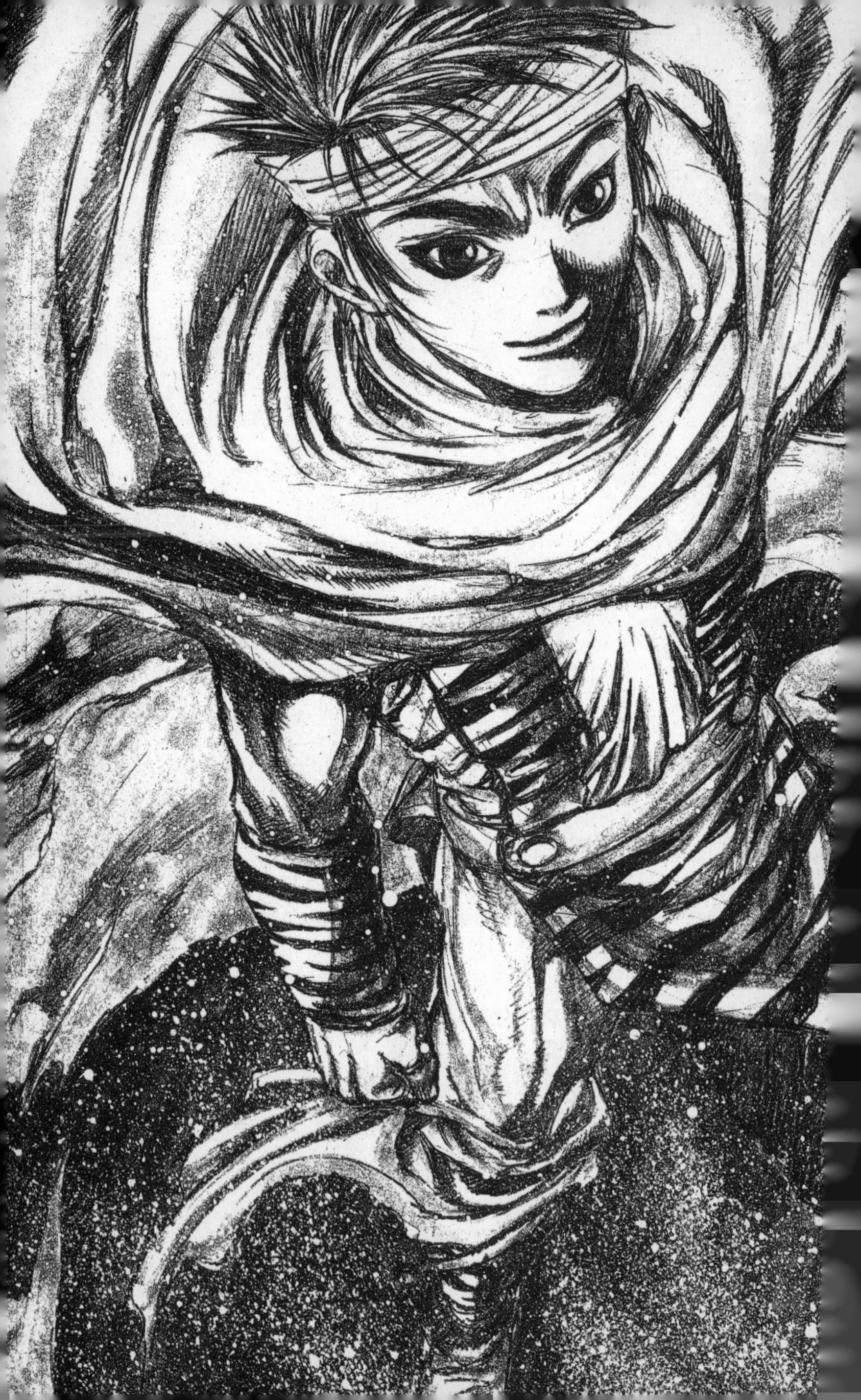

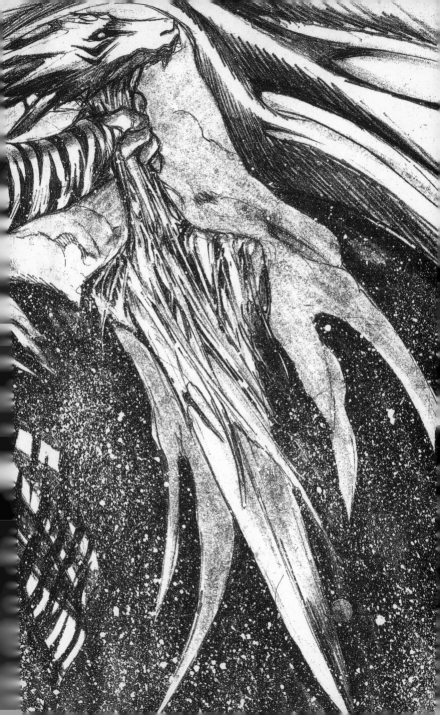

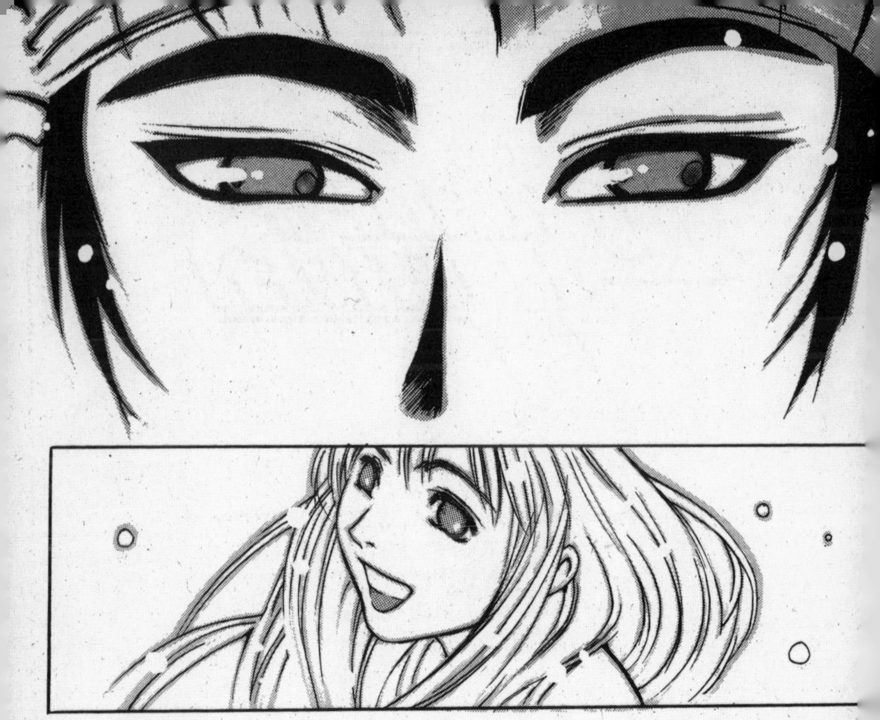

AROOMEE...

JUST THE NAME ALONE MAKES
MY HEART SKIP A BEAT!

I VOW I WILL FIND YOU...ALONG WITH
THE MEMORIES THAT I'VE LOST!

BLADE OF HEAVEN

WILL SOMA EVER RECOVER
HIS LOST MEMORIES?
WILL HE AND PRINCESS AROOMEE
EVER BE REUNITED?
AND WILL OUR LEGENDARY
WARRIOR EVER TRULY POSSESS
THE BLADE OF HEAVEN?

THE WORLD MAY NEVER KNOW...

BLADE OF HEAVEN

END

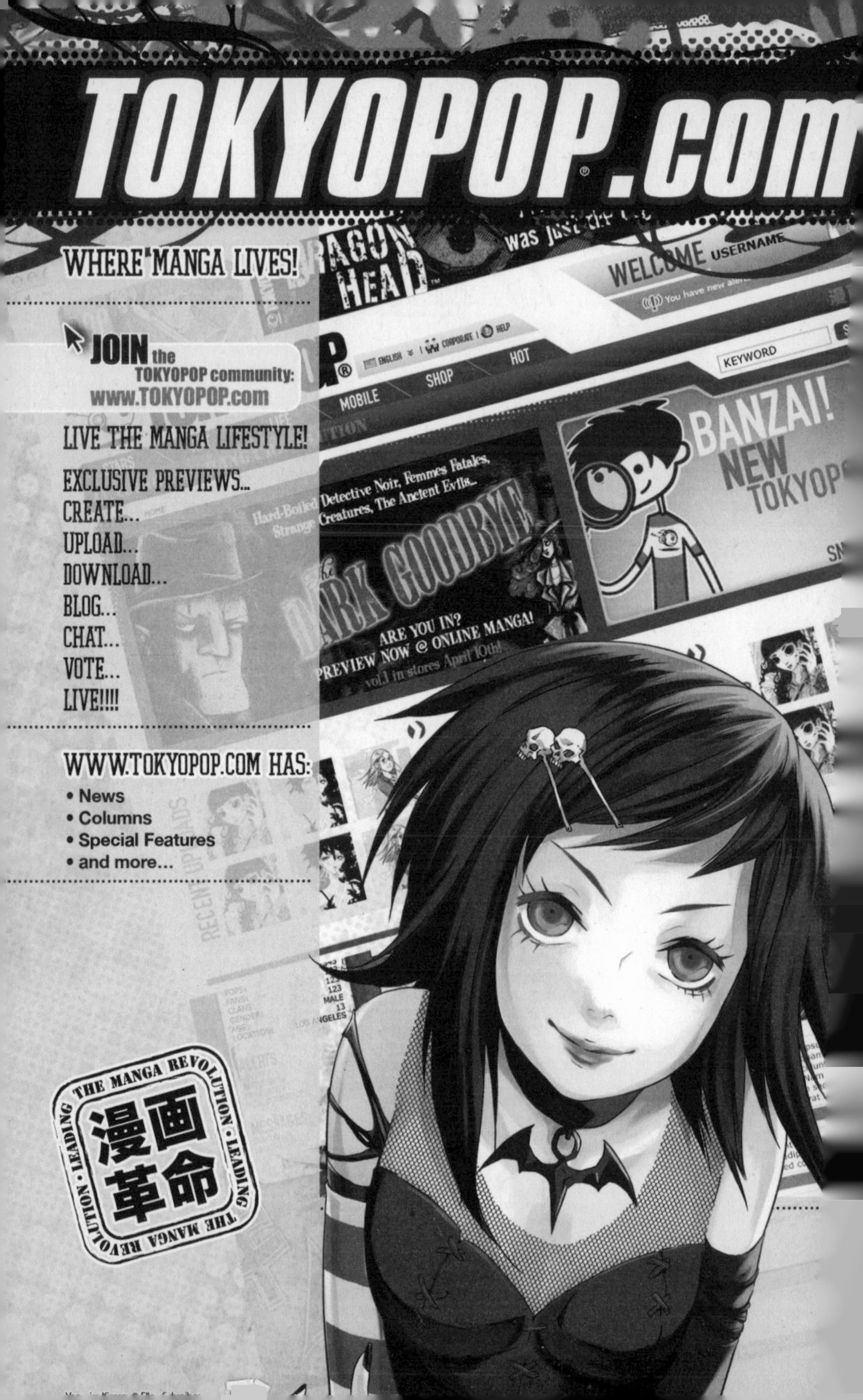
TOKYOPOP.com
WHERE MANGA LIVES!
JOIN the TOKYOPOP community: www.TOKYOPOP.com
LIVE THE MANGA LIFESTYLE!
EXCLUSIVE PREVIEWS...
CREATE...
UPLOAD...
DOWNLOAD...
BLOG...
CHAT...
VOTE...
LIVE!!!!
WWW.TOKYOPOP.COM HAS:
• News
• Columns
• Special Features
• and more...
WELCOME USERNAME
KEYWORD
MOBILE
SHOP
HOT
BANZAI! NEW TOKYOPOP
Hard-Boiled Detective Noir, Femmes Fatales, Strange Creatures, The Ancient Evils...
THE DARK GOODBYE
ARE YOU IN? PREVIEW NOW @ ONLINE MANGA!
vol.1 in stores April 10th!
THE MANGA REVOLUTION · LEADING · THE MANGA REVOLUTION · LEADING
漫画革命